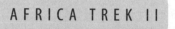

AFRICA TREK II

FROM MOUNT KILIMANJARO TO THE SEA OF GALILEE

AFRICA Trek II

14,000 KILOMETERS IN THE FOOTSTEPS OF MANKIND

From Mount Kilimanjaro to the Sea of Galilee

ALEXANDRE & SONIA POUSSIN

English translation by Philip Stewart

INKWATER PRESS

PORTLAND • OREGON
INKWATERPRESS.COM

www.inkwaterpress.com

ISBN-13 978-1-59299-358-1
ISBN-10 1-59299-358-3

Publisher: Inkwater Press

Originally published in France
© Editions Robert Laffont, S.A., Paris, 2005

1

To Philaé, to whom life is offered.

To Nelly Nthsalinthsali
and Wonderboy Nxumalo,
taken by AIDS

"Take this shell with you this in memory of me, and leave it at the most beautiful place you see, that way I will have traveled with you."

Jenny, the young paraplegic of Bogoria, Kenya

"The extraordinary is found in the path of ordinary people."

Paulo Coelho, *The Pilgrimage*

"Oh mysterious grace of life, I bless thee! I am, I breathe deeply all this soil of Africa! I love my place in the sun! O miracle! I have the amazing permission to be a man!"

Ernest Psichari, *Le Voyage du centurion*

"The confrontation with suffering and death, seen as mirrors of one's own suffering and one's own death, forced man to an altruistic overcoming which had become a metaphysical, artistic and poetic surpassing."

Xavier le Pichon, *Aux racines de l'homme*

"Man? He is the axis and the arrow of the Universe."

Pierre Teilhard de Chardin

The old man: "Where do you come from?"
Us: "From the Cape of Good Hope."
The old man: "Where is that?"
Us: "Where dreams begin."

Table of Contents

Table of Maps

A note on the metric system

Metric measures have been maintained throughout. Thank you for your patience and occasional frustration to translate them in your mind. We kept them because they're used all over Africa, even in former British colonies where people drive on the wrong side (oops, sorry, the left side)! Here are a few guides to understanding them.

One liter is a trifle more than a quart (U.S.) – 1.0567 qt. to be exact.

One kilo(gram) is almost exactly 2.2 pounds.
A metric ton (1000 kilos, or 2200 pounds) is thus similar to an avoirdupois ton (2000 pounds).

One kilometer = almost exactly 5/8 mile (.62137 mile).
Thus, each 1000 km recorded = 621 miles, and the whole trip of 14,000 km = 8,700 mi.

As for surface measure:
One hectare = 2.471 acres
One square kilometer = .3861 square mile

The Celsius (or centigrade) scale relates to Fahrenheit according to a tricky formula: temperature $C \times 9/5 + 32$ = temperature F.
It is easier just to keep in mind that 0° C is the freezing point of water (=32° F) and 100° C is its boiling point (=212° F). So below 0° C is getting pretty cold for humans and 40° C is very hot (=104° F).

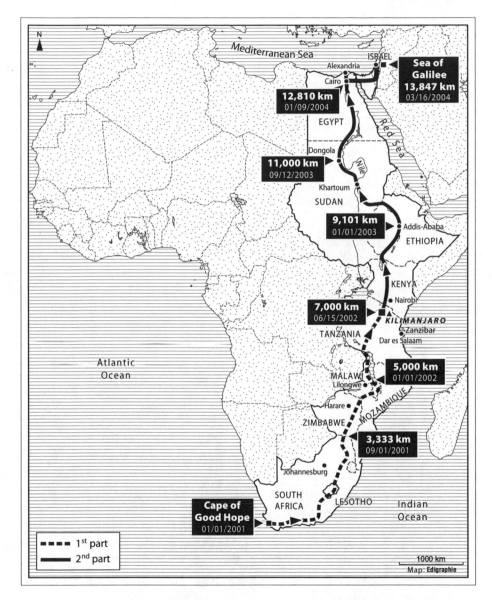

From the Cape of Good Hope to the Sea of Galilee

NORTH TANZANIA

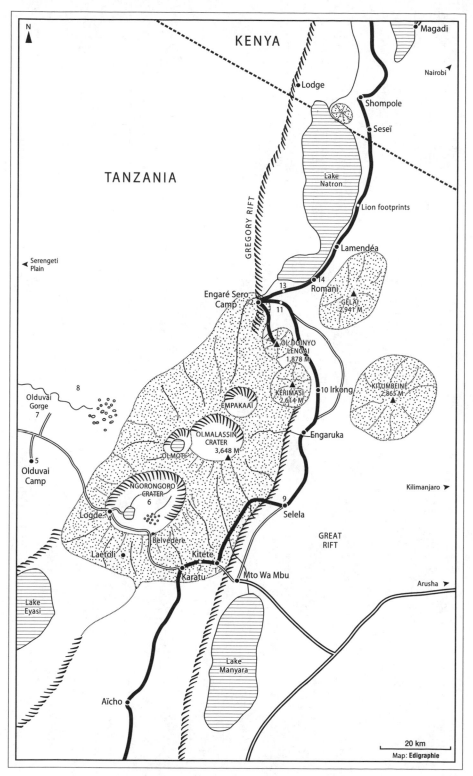

North Tanzania

CHAPTER 1

The World's Treasure

TANZANIA

V ery small, very tan, at the foot with happy feet.

From the foot of the mountain, we have returned to the crossroads at Kitete, where we left off our trek more than a month ago, in order to mark our mid-course point with a white stone: the eternal snows of Kilimanjaro. The summit is called the Uhuru peak, which means freedom in Swahili. A symbol that suits us well, after eighteen months of adventures and free encounters, from one village to another, from men to men, from the Cape of Good Hope which we left on 1 January 2001 at dawn. At the foot of Kili, we passed our seven thousandth kilometer. The figure is round. We did not make it on purpose. That's the way it is. At the moment of resuming the course of our steps, the moment of counting out anew our rosary of encounters, it pleases us to see in that a good augur, a second, recharged departure.

The crossroads has not changed. It is still a strip of earth that meets a strip of asphalt, symbol of a cultural shock. The dirt road that comes from the south is where we arrived from the end of the world, from the southernmost tip of the continent, patiently,

Africally. It's like the thread from a spool. It only has to be unwound. A roll of film. Let it turn. A whirlwind of images and memories, a relay of the heart in which we have not skipped a single stage, a chain of encounters of which we have forgotten no link. Five hundred one names. Almost as many families. That way. Within reach of soles.

It is ten in the morning, rush hour. Capharnaum in Kitete. Drained by this road, it's all the inside of Africa, people from the bush and lost villages who end up here: lean harvest sacks, dried corn and beans, lean men afflicted by poor nights, poor hopes and poor transportation, eyes staring into the void, stomachs empty and future uncertain. For them, this bit of road, this crossroads, is a shore. They wait to be carried off by a wave of metal and noise, in a bus for Arusha, the big city. They are intimidated. They do not know in what sauce they are going to be eaten, what the price of grain is, always lower when you are selling, always higher when you are buying. There is always a truck about to leave. Blue smoke, clamorous motors and horns concert. Kids running around, bearers of messages, clusters of idle, clumsy youths. Women in transit on stacks of sacks; piles of metal drums and the stomping of livestock in front of the stores. The last are lined up on both sides of the road, for more than a kilometer. In series. Simple metal sheet roofs on four pikes separated by plastic tarps. The positions are all the more precious the closer they are to the asphalt. There you find what modernity calls "curio shops," which pile up helter-skelter Zanzibar caps and "ebony" statuettes blackened with used motor oil, twisted and awkwardly carved, masks imported from the Congo, *made in China* African dolls and Maasai spears forged in his spare time by the next-door welder. These shops are a stop for the Land Cruisers – and the first contact of the New Zealander, American or Japanese tourist with Africa. The first shock since the airport: dust and filth, chaos and noise, bric-a-brac and racket; to the benefit of pins and needles in the legs, excess pressure in the bladder or itching in the purse. The pause is even indicated in the brochure.

The band of asphalt goes from east to west. It comes from Arusha and beyond, from the Swahili coast; it goes toward the center of the world, the crater of Ngorongoro, the gate to the vast plains of the Serengeti, the country's principal currency resource. The entire planet dreams of passing over this band of asphalt, on its way to the earthly paradise. And many do. Norias of shiny Land Cruisers go by with their precious cargo of tourists. Many are sleeping. Jet lag. They are all tidy in their brand new khakis. All pale from an elsewhere without sun. This is not sarcasm. That's the way it is. It is true that they look fragile. Here, two worlds watch each other go past. Africa in rags, dreaming of material prosperity and complexity, and the prosperous North that dreams of original purity and simplicity. We are at the crossroads and are looking for a friend whom we met the last time: Habiba.

She's a little wisp of nothing at all who carries her corner of Africa at arm's length. We had landed in her greasy spoon by chance, famished and fainting with heat, knowing we would make a side-trip to Arusha. We had worthily celebrated under her corrugated iron the end of our crossing of the heart of Tanzania, of its jungles infested with lions and tsetse flies, awkwardly seated elbow to elbow with poor wretches on tottering benches before a greasy dish. And our love for her had come with small steps, silently, stealthily. It had begun, once she was over her surprise at seeing two Whites sit down in her dark, crowded hut, with our usual spiel. Second surprise: the *muzungus*[1] spoke Swahili! Peals of laughter were echoed back. On Habiba's back, a severely handicapped little girl was tied up in a dirty loincloth. Habiba was cooking right on the ground scattered with rubble, crouched before a fire which another girl was energetically fanning. Each time she took hold of a plate, an egg or her can of rancid oil ill-stoppered by a ball of

---

[1] Whites, in Swahili.

plastic bag, she pivoted on her heels, threatening to trepan her little daughter on detached pieces of metal sheet. She had laughed at our worries. But she had a blind knowledge of her cramped hovel. She has been living there for twenty years, night and day. Sonia had taken the little one. Habiba had been quite moved by this. Here, no one touches the handicapped. It's bad luck. Friendship had moved up a notch. She had served me tomatoes with lemon juice, our first tomatoes in a long time. In Arusha, we had counted our teeth and our money! Eight teeth spoiled by lack of tomatoes and other things....She had understood where we had come from, and knew what we had been through. I had swallowed down all the tomatoes like a boor, while Sonia was going goo-goo with the baby. Habiba had served her some more in a sort of collusion: "Ah, men! They're all the same!"

Point blank, between two skillets, Habiba had then said to us in broken English: "Normally, muzungus are weird people who act strange. They get out of their cars, make with large strides a tour of the market with their camera to take our picture, but there are some here who don't want that or who want some money for it, and the muzungus don't like that, so instead they buy something or other, at far too high a price. When you have everything, why do you do that? Why do you want to take a picture of our misery and buy our junk?"

Then as if to correct herself, or soften what she had just said: "It's easy to tell that the women are nice but they are ill at ease with us, they want to give us something, but they don't know how to go about it, our poverty makes them uncomfortable, they would like to have a seat but don't have the time; as soon as it gets here, the group has to get going....And everyone is frustrated! We have only strange relations with muzungus. In the twenty years I've been here, you are the first to eat my *chapatis*....[2] Thanks for coming on foot, I am glad you are here."

---

[2] A flour crêpe without eggs, fried in oil.

That's how she inverted the roles. How many times have our hosts thanked us...whereas we receive so much. Thank you for making the encounter possible. We started to sniffle and a tear pearled in a corner of the eye, just as quickly modestly swallowed. Then the feasts had continued, teas and chapatis, not counting the spoonfuls of sugar, under the amused eyes of the gawkers. Here, a chapati is a serious breakfast, and we were on our third or fourth. Indecent. So it was true that Whites were ogres, needing to eat more...

With a stone, I had driven in all the ill-set nails of her shelter and flattened the jagged edges. Habiba had rounded up everyone in the street with her boisterous laughter. As the time passed, the joy of being there was being reinforced, the joy of celebrating our victory over the kilometers, over adversity. A joy tainted by a vague shame, rather despite ourselves, for being powerless among the weak – the honor we paid to her greasy spoon and her cooking, and, as always, our little show with its anecdotes and lion footprints, its falls and exclamations. We have ourselves become the buffoons at the fair....Despite that and the awareness of an imminent separation, friendship was growing with the passing minutes. A friendship of replete consumers, not only replete with chapatis. I was preparing to pay the bill serenely, but Habiba, with a smile that was already a gift, did not accept my money, she asked for only half. Incredulous, I asked why.

"You will take my name to Jerusalem."

"Are you a Christian or a Muslim?"

"Both."

As days have gone by, as months have gone by, we have become the bearers of names, bearers of African prayers. That was not in the plan. It's a request from our hosts. Unrefusable. The lightest burden in our walk in the footsteps of Man. The heaviest responsibility. When doubt will come, when we'll sink into the absurd, when our lives will be threatened, when deserts will lie before us or storm walls stand before us, when hunger, disease, boredom will overwhelm us, when the boiling African sky will cook our brains, we'll have to stick to these promises made, these little sparks of transmitted faith. Were they the last reasons we had left to keep walking.

This is what was going through my mind as I tied my backpack. Sonia was sympathizing with the fate of that little girl who would never know structure and an environment in which she could flower, and with Habiba, who every day in her life would be burdened down with that fact, with that fate, with no hope of freedom. And we felt guilty for having stopped there, for having done our spiel, for having taken advantage of the kindness of this woman worked to death by life, to have perhaps too noisily subjected her to the tale of our kilometers, our adventures, our pseudo-exploits, when every day she accomplished a hundred times more true ones.

When we emerged from the greasy spoon, she was gone. We felt sorry to leave her like that.

"Maybe she was vexed by the money I forced her to accept..."

As soon as we got going we heard behind us, "Alex, Sonia!"

And there she was, radiant, running to us holding a bunch of bananas.

Sonia melted into tears. In her poverty, in her distress, Habiba still had found the means of giving. She had gone to buy these bananas behind our back with the money I gave her because she had picked up in our conversation that we liked them The grandeur of the poor. For her gift had to be complete. We had suddenly become very small, with an immense heart to love the whole world. Love is a nuclear reaction.

Habiba or the world's treasure.

And there she is again. Habiba. In her shack. Just as we left her a month ago. With her burden on her back. Permanence of things. The same kindness and the same grime. It's just a little hard to get used to it again. To pass again from one sphere to another. From the requirement of comfort to the carefree filth. Just a point to get past. But once it's done, you don't think any more about it. You are free again. Habiba embraces us with emotion. It is her turn to cry.

"The muzungus always say that they will come back and they never do, yet here you are! I am so happy…"

Sonia extends her hands closed on a little present: a little flask of Parisian perfume received in our supply packages of spools and tapes. Habiba utters a stifled squeal of joy and plunges back into her arms. Little hands tightened around this gesture, with an angelic smile. If that was all we could get out of traveling, it would be worth it. It would be a collection of little diamonds. And diamonds are found in mud. We tell her about our Kili, Zanzibar, the dolphins, and here we go again with laughter and chapatis.

"So you are heading north again? To Maasai country?"

"Not right away, we still have an appointment with the scientists of Olduvai Gorge."

?

"Yes, you know, one of the cradles of humanity. The origins of man, the path of Laetoli…"

And Habiba starts laughing again. She has never been outside of Kitete.

We know that we will see her a third time. We leave her to her pots and start off toward the Ngorongoro along the hot asphalt. Rockets shoot past us all afternoon. We had forgotten that cars went so fast. On this escarpment that rises toward the massif of the volcanoes, the rich and fertile soil sustains fields of corn and grain, and also the famous coffee plantations of Karatu; the population is dense, children everywhere frolicking in their school uniforms on the way to school, in one direction or the other. Those who go in the morning pass the ones going in the afternoon. That is the Tanzanian trick for increasing the number of children receiving an education without increasing the number of schools. But what will these half-schoolchildren do? What will their jobs and income source be? Above the agricultural zone extends the immense foliation of the jungle that girds the Ngorongoro crater. The contrast between the two worlds is sharp. It is all the same difficult, from this populous countryside, to imagine that up there, beyond the crest, the world's largest animal sanctuary opens up. Here, the demographic pressure seems so strong. How can prosperity keep pace with demographic growth?

As soon as we start walking, our reflections get going again. With no order, using whatever material is at hand. Adrenaline and endorphins must have something to do with it. It's like a mechanism, walking needs fuel, reflection, grain to grind. And reflection needs walking to be activated. Maybe one has to walk to realize that poverty multiplies faster than wealth. And that it is more difficult to realize this in a UNESCO or World Bank office building, where you patiently await the resurgence, the take-off, the growth, the way you wait for Godot. By walking: it's not a scientific demonstration, argued with statistical tools and indicators, it's just a blatant reality standing there before you, from a cornfield invaded by children returning from school, avidly and nervously shucking still-green ears. Africa is obviously making progress, but much less rapidly than it needs. That's what it's all about.

The resumption is hard. The climb from Karatu is hard. We are drenched. Hypoglycemic. The metabolism too has to get readapted. A month ago we were knocking down forty-eight kilometers with one noodle soup and two cookies. And here, with our kilo of chapatis and bananas on board, we stall at the thirteenth kilometer. We will not get to paradise tonight. A Coke pause. In the shop, a little girl comes straight up to Sonia and, with arms extended, indicates that she wants to sit on her lap. It is a strange enough occurrence to make her melt. Sonia has been adopted. Three-year- or three-year-old eyes dominate a face haloed in black curls.

"*Jina lako nani?*" (What's your name?)

"Rehema."

That's all we will get out of her. She is just happy to be there, babbling on my wife's lap. She asks for nothing. Is she the owner's daughter? No. Do you know her? Yes, we see her from time to time, she comes and begs us for cookies. But right now, Rehema is not asking for anything. She ensconces her heat on Sonia's breast and seems to want to sleep. And she goes to sleep. She has come the way a little cat would. Except that she's a little girl. A love of a fragile heart. In her semi-sleeping state, Rehema starts to search Sonia's shirt. Aha! we think. We see through her ploy: could she be a little thief? Except that little worm is not searching her pockets but playing with the buttons on her shirt. Fascinated, we keep watching her. And finally get it. She is looking for a breast. She goes straight to Sonia's chest with one thing in mind; in Africa, ample bosoms are for providing milk...

Sonia, perplexed, replies: *"Sina maziwa, sina hapana mama, sina watoto..."* (I have no milk, I am not a mama, I have no children...)

And the tyke, vexed, looks at herself in Sonia's glasses which are hanging from her neck. A new ploy, irresistible mimics, like a star before the mirror in her dressing room. She gets close, breaks out laughing to see herself distorted by the convex lenses, raises her arms, makes her fingers dance. The happiness of seeing this little girl happy with nothing. Abandoned? Life is truly what triumphs.

In the meantime, in the greasy spoon, a mob of idle loiterers troubles the serenity of the scene. They are not there for something to drink. They are there to look at us. A free show. This is the ransom of proximity: a dart fired at our intimacy. Fair enough. But there too we need some time to readapt.

We go out with Rehema. Since she has adopted us, we will sleep at her place: *"Iko wapi yako nyumba?"* (Where is your house?)

And her little bitty voice answers: *"Paka hapa!"* (Over there!)

We follow her cross-country for a long while in the setting sun. With this elevation the view over the Rift is stunning. We are not very far from the gateway to Ngorongoro Park. As far as we can see, the fertile slope is absorbed by the great fracture in the earth, far below. We have our back to the volcanoes. In the distance, very far to the east, above the Rift, above the red haze emerges Kili's hoary head where we were mere lice a few days ago. In the cornstalks, we come suddenly to a clearing with a thatched roof mud hut in the middle. An old woman is busy with her dishes. She stands up when she sees us – as much as her hunched back allows her. The weight of years. The weight of cares. She greets us however with a broad smile: *"Karibuni! Habari yako!"* (Welcome! How are you?)

"Chikamou Mama, mzuri sana, asante. Wazekani lala hapa? Sisi kuwa na tenti." (Our respects, madame, we are well, thank you. Is it possible we could sleep here? We have a tent.)

"Hakuna shida. Karibu!" (No problem. Make yourselves at home.)

"Iko wapi Mzee?" (Where is the father? – literally, the master.)

The old woman gives us to understand in a mixture of English and Swahili: "He is dead. My daughter is dead. My son is dead, everyone is dead. All I have left is Rehema and Augustino: there he is now!"

Behind us a well-dressed teenager comes up.

"Hello! What are you looking for?"

"We met Rehema, and thought she was lost..."

"She is looking for a mother. Hers died of AIDS last year. Her father was some unknown from the city. He must be dead too. I am her cousin and I too am an orphan, but I at least am not HIV-positive, I was born before my father did something stupid."

The blade has fallen. With a glance at Rehema, we understand the drama. The infernal chain reaction has fallen on this family. She is HIV-positive, like so many millions of African children whose parents were unable to adapt their practices in time to the epidemic: the ABC of AIDS.[3] We are dismayed. Sonia is still holding the little angel by the hand.

"And are you being careful?" she asks the boy.

"Girls don't interest me! I work in a store for tourists and want to be able to afford school."

"But if you have girlfriends later on?"

---

[3] See *Abstinence, Be faithful, Condom or Death*, vol. I, p. 284.

"Oh, I'm not crazy, I don't want to die, I will take precautions! And then, my dream is to marry a muzunga, so I have nothing to fear..."

The grandmother motions to us to come inside. And disappears into the night. Soon a sinister crack! resounds. Augustino chortles.

"Tonight we will have chicken!"

We leave in our wake a carnage of chickens. Everywhere we go, a chicken dies. Sorry face on our heads. The chicken loses his as soon as he sees ours. For the third time today we are dumbfounded. It's because they want to honor us. I pretend to scold the grandmother when she returns after her ill deed: "You're being unreasonable! We don't need that, we had everything we needed."

And she replies with an innocent gesture and full hands: "If you deprive me of the possibility of offering you a chicken, what do I have left?"

And this old woman whose name we do not recall and scarcely her face, which merges with so many others in fiery pupils ringed with wrinkles, also reveals to us that the last power, the last dignity of those who have nothing left is to give, to receive in one's home. And that it would be wrong to deprive them of that dignity. Westerners often ask us how we manage to compensate these folk who invite us or feed us. From this day on, we answer them: "To those who ask, we give; from those who give, we accept." And if we have to be more precise: "If you invited a millionaire to your house, would you present him with a check at the end of the meal? Our African hosts, however poor they may be, are like you."

All evening, we chat by the fire, about development, politics, society. In constant contact with tourists, Augustino has constructed a fabulous and false notion of Europe. He is stupefied to learn that Europeans too can die of AIDS. That we also have fields, cows, countrysides and poor people....But these ones have a roof overhead and a television set....He thinks it isn't possible to get to Jerusalem on foot. Sonia rejoins: "But Augustino, we have just done seven thousand kilometers on foot, we are halfway there, all we have to do is do the same thing; so it's possible!"

"Yes, but there are still seven thousand kilometers ahead of you..."

True. Implacable logic. What remains to be done is harder than what is done. And yet, it is not the overall task that impresses us, we don't even think about it – snails are nearsighted – it's the detail, it's the bottom of the Rift with Lake Natron, the furnace, the thirst, the reaction of the Maasai, the lions, the detour around the lake, the illegal passage over the Kenyan border. Our next two hundred kilometers are what impress us. This little chunk of road is already in itself an expedition. Specialists of Arusha have told us that this stage was impossible without logistics, guides and porters. So the north of Kenya, Lake Turkana, the Omo valley, the mountains of Ethiopia, the Sudanese Sahara, the Nile...is all very theoretical, in a few thousand kilometers. Maybe one day!

In the house, the smoke rises toward the thatch, which absorbs it slowly; the grandmother makes slow, small gestures. She is never idle. It's the fireside choreography. The most commonplace objects, aluminum lunch pails, plastic jugs, dirty rags and wooden spoons are illuminated by the redness of the flames. Rehema has gone to sleep on Sonia's lap. Under neon light, this misery would be much sadder. But we are well-fed, we are warm, we relive in the present, being alive at each very second. We are comfortable. Already the fleas have begun their great nocturnal labor. The goatskins on which we are seated are infested with them. Every time we jump at a bite, Augustino, his grandmother and some neighbors who have appeared from out of the night break out laughing, repeating endlessly: "*Kiroboto, polé kiroboto!*" (Fleas, sorry, there are fleas!) That's so funny, you know, muzungus getting eaten by fleas! It brings you closer together.

Another routine that we resume with the first evening: visits by the neighbors. They file by, enter, greet, sit, marvel, ask the same questions, to us directly, not to our hosts, that wouldn't be polite, so we repeat. Exhausting. A true traveling salesman's job. Except that we have nothing to sell. Just to explain what we are doing here. Why we want to share this lack of comfort. To encounter. To understand: *"Kuku tana na watu. Kwa ku-elewa."* And there they opine. They are satisfied. Our hosts then chime in with anecdotes: ostrich races in South Africa, rhinoceros charge and fly soup in Malawi, the lions of Rungwa...and they have fun all evening. Thus are we cradled beside the fire.

This is the moment I choose to record the day's impressions in my notebook. I light my mini-headlamp. A cry of terror! One of the neighbors squatting beside me has leapt to his feet. Turning my head toward him, I blind him; a frightened grimace – he falls backward and decamps in a din of pots and overturned bodies. Delighted Weebles, the witnesses make fun of the deserter. Augustino, between two fits of coughing set off by his laughter, explains to me that the oddball thought the light was coming from a third eye in the middle of my forehead....After Frankenstein in Malawi,[4] here are the X-Men! When things have settled down again, the gazes regroup now around the blue lamp over the white page, and respectful murmurs accompany the scratching of my pen. During this time, Sonia, at the other end of the hut, is unfolding the stakes of our mosquito-net tent, drawing other curious pulsating pupils to her. We go to sleep completely bushed after this day so short, so long. This day so poor, so rich. Africa Trek has indeed resumed.

---

[4] See Vol. I, p. 339.

2 Ngorongoro, Heart of the World

TANZANIA

W e are climbing into the jungle. The road has been snaking along for an hour. The recent rains have made it slippery. The motor balks. We very quickly reached the park gate this morning. The night was eventful. Leaps of carps in our sleeping bags against leaps of fleas in the tent. An hysterical rooster that, beginning at four, blew in my eardrums point-blank. Augustino disappeared without waking us, considerate and disappointing at the same time; emotional farewells to Rehema and her grandmother. Final kilometers uphill to Ngorongoro Park, on an empty stomach. We had to explain to the stupefied sentries that we were invited by the park authorities to film Olduvai Gorge, on the far side of the volcanoes, at the gate of the Serengeti Plains. They have been informed. That much is good.

The park director, Bernard Murunya, is awaiting us at the headquarters, but there is no way to get there on foot. "There are wild animals, you know!" We know. But that's the rule. We need a vehicle. All morning we have therefore cooled our heels watching the cars and 4x4s of the tour operators go by. There is indeed something good about organization. But our particular wealth is time. We had to wait. The director's car was maybe going to return from its overhaul in Arusha. Maybe.

It finally came late in the afternoon and carried us off. Simple, finally, you just have to wait. The jungle goes past. And we search, feverish and incredulous, for traces of wildlife in this forest. An elephant here? Could that be? A buffalo lying in wait in this foliage? Samuel, the director's driver, opines: the other day, coming back down at dusk, he passed a leopard here.

The road twists and turns. The suspense grows as we climb, we shouldn't be too far now, the road takes a tangent toward an opening to the sky, the crest comes, there it is, Samuel parks. Turns off the motor. All of a sudden there is immense space, the void, the cavity, the abyss. Under the shock, our lungs swell like airbags. Before our eyes it's all there, the lost world, the Garden of Eden, perfect, circumscribed by the raised edges of the Ngorongoro crater, wow! Breathless.

A rising wind rustles our hair. So much beauty, the gaze loses itself. It is too far, a thousand meters below, giant belvedere! Lake Magadi shimmers like mercury, puddles of yellow flowers and puddles of green grass are woven into a giant vegetal puzzle where the shadows of clouds run like black sheep that have come to graze in paradise. Chiaroscuro. The edge of the crater is ringed with clouds that play with the light, sowing titanic shadows on the foothills. Excess. Our eyes avidly look for wild animals. Nothing! Everything looks deserted, virgin and abandoned. Then Samuel indicates to us: "Look at the little bugs down there!"

Black aphids, scarcely visible on the yellow carpet bordering the lake.

"Quick! the binoculars!"

Sonia focuses and muffles a cry: "Look, Alex, the aphids have big white tusks..."

Metamorphosis. Space dilates again with the change of scale. It is peopled by a multitude. The carpet is teeming with minuscule "bugs."

Samuel breaks the charm to remind us of our appointment. "The director leaves at five, we've got to get moving."

The road follows the crest to the west. We are still in shock. Samuel brakes suddenly. He has seen something in the grasses. He puts it into reverse. In front of us bolts a nervous buffalo. He too stops, turns around as if to call to his companions. In a bound, he crosses, followed by his herd.

"You see why you can't walk here! You only see buffalo at the last moment and they are extremely dangerous."

Bernard Murunya greets us in a freezing little office. It is very cold at the crater's summit. To warm us up, he tells us of his trips to Paris, of his wife and children who live in London, of his administrative problems. He hasn't enough game scouts to fight the poachers, no cars, no heat. Everything around us has a feel of the 1970s. The crushed velvet of the brown couches, his Formica desk, ugly four-color posters with pretty tourists in mauve shirts decked out in goggles. Time seems to have stopped thirty years ago in the African administration.

"Dr. Masao is not at Olduvai, he went yesterday to Arusha to take delivery of some materials. You are going to have to wait for him. I am very sorry, I have no infrastructure to receive you."

"You know, we can sleep on the ground, in a corner, in our tent…"

"We are at 2500 meters; at night the temperature drops by ten degrees. You are going to freeze. Besides, leopards are moving into the surroundings. Of course there is Crater Lodge nearby, but a night there is eight hundred dollars…"

In South Africa, in the *Getaway* magazine where we had read an article about the Liliekloof valley and the San frescoes, we had fantasized over this extraordinary hotel and had said to ourselves:

"If we get that far, we will celebrate by breaking the piggy bank!" We are here. And we have no desire at all to break the piggy bank. From Arusha, we had sent an e-mail to its directrice, endowed with a genuinely South African name, in case she might wish to invite us. No answer. Might as well ask her directly. We call her.

"You are the French hikers? Sorry, I didn't answer. Where are you?"

"Right nearby, at the headquarters, and we can't sleep here."

"Come on over, we'll work something out."

Those amazing South Africans. Open sesame! Crater Lodge is the very best in hotel kitsch, with an unequaled luxury of refinery. The decor is fairylike, African baroque, safari style revised by Gaudi,[1] colonial phantasmagoria spruced up with a few Italian excesses. The statues of primitive art thus stand next to Venetian crystal chandeliers, and armfuls of roses clash with the cold hardness of pure stainless steel. Tonya Siebert greets us with crystal goblets filled with orange juice and warm towels scented with rose water. She offers us a free night: "It will be the icing on your African cake. I know what you have been through. I have done it by car."

The panorama opens onto the bowl of the crater, the roundness is perfectly shaped, the curves regular, the thatched roofs and tall chimneys of the apartments scattered through the jungle point through the branches, downwards. Two elephants are foraging before our eyes among the huts.

"Final recommendation: do not move about alone and do not leave the trails; there are right now buffalo around. Enjoy it!"

Our apartment is on pilings, its roof in woven Pandanus leaves is an inverted corolla in which shines an enormous crystal chandelier. An imperial teepee. The bay window is fringed with heavy purple silks. In the grasses, to welcome us, a serval is frolicking. Beginning with Naughty, the breeding serval of Moholoholo, and Port

---

[1] A famous Catalan champion of the *art nouveau* era.

and Starboard, the little orphans of Nchalo,[2] we are crazy about servals. The dark hardwood flooring embellished with Persian rugs leads to an old-fashioned bathtub. The large faucets are soon drawing a scalding bath for us. The toilets, for ultimate refinement, are set into a Gothic pepper-box boasting a little window facing the crater. Imperial pee. There aren't enough superlatives to describe everything. When we leave for dinner, we pass grazing zebras in the night. In the dim light, there can be no doubt that they have white stripes! The sequel is a festival of courses, majordomo and white gloves: cream of tomato with bell peppers, seafood cassoulet, a mixture of lobster, crabs and other marine mysteries in a peanut sauce spiced with curry, braised lamb on a bed of green asparagus, the whole accompanied by a nice Cape wine under the rococo-stellar paneling of the dining room. Let's not mention the terminal crêpe Suzette. A crêpe Suzette in the very heart of Africa! That is luxury: to bring improbable dishes from the four corners of the globe and combine them on a single table. We are swimming in an anti-Africa Trek....Why wonder at that? Because despite all, it is our trek that has opened these doors as it has opened those of the most modest hovels; because it is one night of folly in three years of deprivations. A present which we accept with the same joy that we have accepted a poor, life-saving hut after a day in the bush. Walking leads to everything.

As she drifts into sleep, Sonia whispers: "You remember last night's fleas?"

At dawn, I am trapped. Pillows do not work for me. As at the Louws, at Fée's, at the Greens', at the Royal Livingstonia or at Gez Bester's. My body refuses nights of comfort. A raging pain in the neck. Forced rest. The crater flouts us, playing hard to get. No way to go down there today. Late in the afternoon, we return to see Bernard. Dr. Masao won't be there until day after tomorrow.

---

[2] See vol. I, pp. 182 and 281.

Yet we must go to Olduvai! And it's difficult to ask Tonya for two more nights. At this moment, a guy comes in with a paper to get stamped. By the time Bernard has taken care of it, Sonia notices the emblem on his T-shirt: "Tanganyika Expeditions," the company where Frédéric Mendonca, who had offered us the Kili, works.

"You have a camp in the crater?"

"No, not here, on the way to the Serengeti, near Olduvai Gorge…"

We call Frédéric. What luck: he is there.

"Yes, we have a tented camp on the other side of the Gorge. You want to go there? It's good timing: there is nobody there right now. And tomorrow, if you want, I will make you a deal on a descent into the crater, and you will see Dr. Masao afterward; it only takes ten minutes to get to the Leakey camp…"

There really is a hiker's god. It's crazy how things happen when you put yourself in a situation to let them happen. You have to be alert, recognize them, respond to them. Life carries us as much as we lead it. To charge head lowered is to run into a wall, to let yourself be carried is to go nowhere, that is not living, it is taking it easy. Between the two, there is Adventure. And Adventure is the cornerstone of each of our days. It's more a state of mind than a state of fact. You just have to leave a little room for it. Not plan everything. Some call that nonchalance, others who have never had anything happen to them call it Luck and make a new capricious and pitiless god of it. Now here, now not. We prefer to see in it, in doubt and in secret, an immanent goodwill in things that conspire to help us. Very discreetly. But present and permanent. Spiritual. And which likes a little fun.

After warm thanks to Tonya, we set off with Victor for a descent on the other side of the crater, toward the Serengeti Plains.

Just as Ngorongoro seen from above was circumscribed vastness, this panorama is infinite immensity. The yellow waves to the horizon suspended from the sky. A uniform, endless frame in which so many animal stories have been filmed, so many little dramas, which we have all watched rise and fall in the documentaries on the African fauna, on the migration of the wildebeest, the return of the rains, the family of hyenas, the struggle of the cheetahs or the birth of gazelles by the thousands, these crunchy snacks of the plains: to go down to the Serengeti is to penetrate into the world's largest studio, except that here the walk-ons play day and night since the dawn of time their minuscule score in the symphony of life.

On the straight road, Victor drives flat out, raising an enormous plume of dust: "We have to get there before sunset, so you can observe it from the top of a *koppie*[3] with one of the guards from the Maasai camp."

On our right, a signboard announces the Olduvai Gorge and the site museum. We turn left in the direction of a small pyramid of rocks situated between the plain and the foot of the titanic volcanoes.

When we arrive, Kadogo Lerimba, a short, jovial Maasai, is waiting for us. We immediately start following briskly behind him. The summit of the rocky eminence that overlooks the plain is twenty minutes away. A singular race against the sun begins. As if one must not arrive late for this eternal Mass of nature. After an expanse of grasses glowing red in the low sunlight, we start climbing on the boulders, weave our way between the sisal and bushes, end up on all fours, and chase off a band of baboons that had taken the front-row seats and withdraw with loud cries of protest. On top, the rock is smooth and warm. The plain flat as the sea. An ocean of moving grasses. Kadogo's red toga stands out on the evening gold. Straight west the sun begins its descent in ruby sheets. The rubicund clouds swell. The shadows of the rare acacias that dot the savannah at our feet stretch and yawn before the great sleep. We let the silence fall with our contemplation. A fragrant breeze of honey and warm grass infused by the twilight

---

[3] An outcropping of rock, from the Afrikaans *kop*, head.

surrounds us. Kadogo begins to sing a Maasai lament made up of guttural vibrations, a solemn salute to the dying sun in the bloody carmines of the horizon. Mass has been said. We go back besotted with beauty.

The camp is up against a small mass of round rocks that rises in the middle of the plain surrounding this arm of the Olduvai Gorge. In front of our cotton khaki tent, a little deck opens to the east onto an unobstructed view: the chain of volcanoes with their summits made purplish by the nocturnal kiss. A small table in bleached wood and a chair are there to collect the inspiration of day's end by the light of a hurricane lamp. Behind, up against the rock, the copper shower handle and its oilcloth water bag rinse away the dust from the road, and our fatigue. Each tent is isolated by boulders and *oldupai* foliage, a name given by the Maasai to wild sisal (*Sanseveria*), which stand like the thick blades of a bouquet of spears. This is straight out of *Out of Africa*. We willingly allow ourselves to be possessed by the mirage. Suddenly, Sonia hails me with a whisper: "Alex! Come look at this!"

I gently push aside the piece of canvas. Through the fold we can see, emerging from the wall of oldupai, two adorable slender-legged dik-diks. They are one of Africa's smallest antelopes. The doe is like a Yorkshire. Huge eyes full of black water, a humid nose and a puff on top of its cranium, they stare at us, immobile, for a moment, still as pointers, their hindquarters lowered into starting blocks, and take off in three rabbit bounds toward the oldupai grove opposite. In the vegetal spears, the dik-diks are safe from the hyenas.

Our excellent dinner is embellished by a facetious genet, a gorgeous little spotted nocturnal weasel. It is so cheeky that it is all but in our plates. Victor comes by: "Ah! I see you get along with genet Jackson. It's our mascot. Don't get too familiar because it will end up in your tent for the night. Tomorrow, we leave very early if you want to be among the first to go down into the crater."

Before I go to sleep, I go sit cross-legged on a naked rock

that rises like a prow in front of our ship of tents and life cutting through the night. The gorge sends flows of blue night to my feet. Sweet nocturnal breath caresses my naked torso. The volcanoes Lemagrut and Olmoti stretch into space a black horizon line that meets the lip of the Ngorongoro crater. From this black arc slowly emerges a full and serene moon that sows light on the valley of time, the gorge keeper of the secrets of our past. To the right, the Southern Cross, to the left Ursa Major, and always that eucharistic moon raising its peaceable power heavenward. Contemplation borders on meditation. From the depths of night ascend the three-toned lowing of the wildebeest grazing on the plain. They are fattening up before the great departure. A flight of lost plovers rends the veil of the still night – ki-witt, ki-witt, ki-witt. On this granite, I still feel the heat of an Australopithecus that came here to sit three million years ago to keep watch and assure the safety of his herd or ponder in fright the red glow of an eruption on the flanks of Makarut.

At dawn, the next day, we return to the east, to take on the volcanoes. As we are climbing, we pass some strolling Maasai. They have a sacerdotal walk, blood red splotches in the yellow of the landscape. From the pass, the slope is vertiginous to get to the bottom of the crater. A horrible gate, brand new: the control of vehicles and permits. Two young Maasai, comely as stars, tempt the tourists. Lower the window? Frame it up? The image is perfect of the proud shepherd against the background of the crater. The index finger itches terribly. In the car in front of us, one woman succumbs. The young Maasai rushes at her with his hand outstretched. Panicking and blushing with shame, she quickly closes her window as if she were going to be shot. The charm has evaporated. Mutual disappointment. This is not where the encounter will take place. The walk down is marked with enormous euphorbia, cactuses that raise their thorny chandeliers into the blue of the sky. It's all much too ideal, it looks too much like a stage set to contain real wild animals. And yet, we are scarcely at the bottom of the crater than we are greeted by buffalo, pug snouts and smelling of musk, scowling under their triumphant horns of which the gleaming points are – along with their eyes – the only things that shine. Real legged lumps of mud, these bovine tanks looming up from the depths of time are quietly grazing as we go past. A little farther down, there are wildebeest spinning in the grasses. The bearded males try to isolate the females on the run to form harems and charge each other with great clacking of horns. These do not leave the crater, do not migrate with the others; they have found the paradise of eternally green grass, why should they leave it? Meuh, muuu, monh, mhu, they bellow and they wail in canon to compose the sound background of the crater. It is this entrancing music that you take away with you forever; it comes back with every picture and every memory.

We drive toward the salt lake where a brook pours itself forth. This is the place which thousands of pink flamingos have chosen to remove the salt from their feathers. Pressed together, they shake noisily in the fresh water tributary, suddenly stand up on top of their long legs and start over again, in a comic elevator motion. Further along, in tight rows, groups of dark pink males follow light pink females, and these courting companies move, in this sea of feathers, like waves of cotton candy in a shivaree of beaks, necks and cries. A moving surf, living agitation, the assiduity of these gentlemen expresses itself with dignity, head held high, then head lowered, the fine feet pawing in the waves, all intermixed in a phalanx of red noodles bowing, standing at attention and handkissing at the same time. Nearer to the shore, heads under water on the end of a long, slender neck, the flamingos dance *Swan Lake*, knitting their entrechats in the clay to filter from it the *substantifique moelle*,[4] and make a sublime choreography of their meal of animalcules.

---

[4] An expression borrowed from Rabelais's *Pantagruel*, meaning substance-full marrow.

Jackals prowl trotting among the feathers of the tutus glued to the clay of the banks. They dream of a flamengo drunk on spins, spirals and spirulina, too giddy to fly away. We are soon driving in tides of yellow flowers (*Bidens taitensis*) so dense that the sun wallows in them the way Narcissus does in his reflection. They invaded the crater only a few years ago. A bad seed brought by the wind. And bad news for the wildebeest and other ruminants, since the stalks are too tough for them. Each hectare conquered by the yellow tide is a hectare of grass lost. But we are in the merry month of May and nature is bedecked in all her charms. It is within this jewel box that our first zebra manes spring up. Against the gold of the flowers their stripes cry out; they are too sharply outlined – the gaze labors to bear the violent contrasts that vibrate in the waves of light. By day, no shadow of a doubt, they are white with black stripes. They graze, clash, then two by two give each other somnolent caresses, standing head to tail at neck level so each can rest his painted muzzle on his buddy's back. Suddenly they bolt, bucking and sputtering and, with their wild manes and their kicking, bring a bit of folly to the great order of the plain.

From this ocean of flowers emerges a squadron of elephants that forges through the waves of petals with their senatorial gate. Black and ashen, massive and rough, they trample the frail grains and, with their insouciant trunks, rip out huge bouquets to be crunched between their teeth, and their pachyderm chops become coated with fragrant juices. Vessels of flesh gathering nectar among the bees, they brush past without seeing us, puny insects, and pursue with measured steps their rounds in the crater. Only a wake remains of their slow-motion passage...

All the actors are here. Close to twenty-five thousand large mammals, Victor assures us. The arena is fifteen kilometers in diameter. Paradise is large and small at the same time! They are side by side, try to avoid each other or on the contrary to seek each other. A soup of free electrons that play their whole lives at Darwin's great law. It is the oldest game and the simplest, it has two rules and no more: reproduction and natural selection. But in Ngorongoro, everyone cheats, there are almost as many zoological enigmas as there are species. They all have some bizarre behavior in paradise. For example, we learn from Victor that there are nothing but male elephants here. The females and the young never come down into the crater, the herds remain in the Oldeani forests. Yet the males do not come here to fight. Maybe it is rather to have some peace among the daisies, like old Brits in their clubs? The great absent one in paradise is the giraffe. Is it because with its long neck it already lives in the sky? Legs too long to get down into the crater? No. There are probably not enough acacias here to graze on.

Victor continues his rundown: "There are about a hundred lions and four hundred hyenas, each with their own territory; this is the highest density of predators on earth. Here the dominant males wear a black mane and do not participate in the hunt, they leave that thankless task to the females. Three thousand buffalo have returned since the departure of the Maasai, who are no longer allowed to live in the bottom of the crater, only to bring their cows down to water, near the access ramp, in order to take advantage of the proximity of tourists to pay for photos..."

"No one has ever lived in the bottom of the crater?"

"Oh, yes! The first inhabitants were Iraqs, a Cushitic people that came from Ethiopia and which you met, I believe, in Mbulu. Did you not tell me about a lovely Iraq princess? Madingo?"

"Yes, Madiako! We will never forget her sweetness, her beauty, her kindness....But she was married to a Barbaig chief..."

"Precisely! The Barbaigs, who here are called Datogas, are a Nilo-Hemitic people that came about four hundred years ago from southern Sudan and forced out the Iraqs. A century later some cousins arrived, the Maasai, with whom they have never stopped fighting, finally to yield to them about a hundred fifty years ago. Ngorongoro purports to be the name of a group of valorous Barbaigs whom the

Maasai are supposed to have defeated in the crater. The Maasai call the Barbaigs *Mangatis*, which means 'respected enemy'…"

"And then?"

"In the nineteenth century, the Germans colonized Tanzania. The Siedentopf brothers then forced out the Maasai and divided the crater in two, one part for fields and the other for livestock. The ruins of their farm are in the northern part of the crater. They were the first to get ostriches to reproduce in captivity and made work animals of zebras. Can you see the crater transformed into a circus! All they needed was a Big Top. But they had all the trouble in the world: the Maasai pilfered their livestock. At the end of the First World War, with Germany's defeat, the British came in. They made the crater into a hunting reserve. But it was only in 1948 that the place became a protected zone and the Maasai were denied access to the crater."

"And now?"

"Since independence in 1961, the Maasai have obtained the right to come and go, but they were forced more and more to settle down. Even their right to come with their herds into the authorized zone of the crater is more and more contested, because of the diseases that can be transmitted to the buffalo, tuberculosis in particular. That is a matter of tolerance and will soon be suppressed."

After a pause, Victor continues: "In fact, everyone is fighting for the same thing here. And that is the secret of this paradise: water, the marshes and the springs filtered all year long by the lava from the surrounding volcanoes. There is even a considerable herd of hippopotamus in the Gorigor marshes. This permanent fertility brings with it an extraordinary phenomenon: the involuntary collaboration amongst herbivores."

"Against predators?"

"No. For pasture. The elephants and buffalo get first priority: they pull up the tough plants. Torn up and trampled down, they send up shoots of which the zebras and hippopotamus are very fond. When the terrain has been cleared off and enriched with the manure of the first users, fresh grass delights the wildebeest – they graze it clean. After them come the gazelles, who have thin lips to finish the mowing. When there is no more grass, the tough plants take over again. The cycle lasts more than a month. Without it, the gazelles could not live in the crater. Here, we understand what the word ecosystem means.

We are rolling briskly along, invisible witness to the great game of creation, when Victor stops cold. At our wheels, lying in the grass, off the shoulder, visible only when you are about to step on their tails, lions. Adrenaline queasiness. I discover that I hate lions. A hatred from visceral fear, panic in the guts, intravenous anguish. I know a little about them. We have seen in Rungwa what they can do. Not the big paunchy stuffed animals made drowsy by the sun and digestion. Killing machines. And there he is, the young bastard, piercing me through and through with his yellow eyes, cruel and empty. I yield, all hairs bristling: gooseflesh…like a wimp! I no longer dare look in his eyes. He begins to skulk around the car. Another car joins the celebration. Everyone is laughing. Not me: the vehicle is completely open. What is he going to do? I can still see Joseph's arm[5]. His tail is knocking against my door, making my head resonate with fear, then he tries to climb onto the hood. Victor starts the engine. That puts him off, he doesn't like the vibrations. He is eaten by flies, all moth eaten, clawed, bleeding – surely a foul character – he yawns with his toothy maw. How many times have we crossed their trail in the Rungwa forest? I can't get over it. I'm a leophobe. They were not far away, invisible in the grass. But there. Always there. Spirits of the bush…

We leave the crater replete with contemplation. But make no mistake about it: at nightfall, it all becomes pursuit, struggle with bared teeth, beak and nail, hooves flying, massacres and carnage,

---

[5] The story of Joseph, who miraculously survived a mauling by a lion, is described in Vol. I, p. 390.

guts spilled and newborn munched. Eat or be eaten, such is the law of the bush. Never forget that!

Back on the way to Olduvai camp, we pass a white Land Cruiser; Victor cries: "That's Professor Masao's car, isn't he the one you were to see?"

In an instant, in the open savannah, we change cars and wave farewell to Victor.

CHAPTER 2

Olduvai, the Valley of Time on the March

TANZANIA

For eighteen months, we have been magnetized like a needle toward the North Pole by one of the most important pre-human vestiges, which is also a bit at the origin of our "walk in the footsteps of Man": the mythical sequence of the Laetoli footprints, simple steps of Australopithecus left in the mud three and a half million years ago. A boneless fossil. The true site is forty-five kilometers from Olduvai Gorge, on the slopes of the ancient volcano Sadiman, in the south of Oldeani, but it was covered with a thick protective layer of sand and clay. The little museum of the gorge has a faithful reproduction of it. Dr. Masao drops us off there.

"To meet me at the camp, all you have to do is cross the Gorge on foot with the conservator, since he lives with us, but all the same look out for elephants: every evening, they come down the gorges to the water below."

We are greeted by Ozias Kileo and John Pareso. We had called them from the office of Bernard Murunya, and they have the authorizations for filming that we must give to Dr. Masao to have the right to film his activity.

"How many footprints have you left on African soil to come look at these?"

"Several million…"

We enter the museum, round a corner, and there they are! We are deeply moved. Silence. It is a vertiginous plunge into our origins, a testimony of strength and precariousness, so far from us, so near to us. All the contradictions of the world imprinted in the mud, about a billion two hundred eighty million days ago. These imprints have traveled an eternity through time – an immobile voyage – and there they are in the present, before our eyes! "Arrow and axis of the universe," said Teilhard de Chardin. There are only a dozen footprints. So little. But immense. The first footsteps of Man. But what man? Who walked in Laetoli?

John Pareso breaks the silence and, like a tracker, makes the footprints talk: "As you see, there were three of them…"

"Three? But there are only two parallel trails."

"Apparently, yes. We can easily see the small trail of a child, on the left, but look at the large series on the right, here, at the height of the big toes. Then on the other, at the height of the heel, you see the double footprint? There is a second individual, slightly smaller, walking in the steps of the preceding one. On that footprint there, we see clearly two series of big toes superimposed.…Thus striking us like a slap in the face is a proof of intelligence: no animal deliberately walks in the steps of another. If he does it, it's by accident. Now here, the accuracy excludes chance."

In the petrified mud: the trace of intention.

In play? Idly? The way a kid watches his feet against boredom?

John resumes our dialogue with the casting: "Let's put it back in context: the Sadiman volcano, on the slopes of Oldeani, has just spread a layer of ash over the whole region, the landscape is lunar, desolate, the trees are on fire, the fruits are trapped in the charred layer, all the herbivores have fled. Over there is a hipparion, a small horse with three toes instead of hooves; here is a deinotherium, a small elephant which is also extinct; the streams are choked with mud – all the more since it has rained and all this ash has been transformed into a sloppy carpet that hides traps of lava, holes, pitfalls."

"But where were they going, then?"

"Our three individuals are fleeing; they are leaving this hell, they are hungry, afraid, at the mercy of the surviving predators, which also are hungry and thirsty. Thus, in all probability, the individual walking in the steps of the first, smaller and weaker, was doing it for security, by instinct of self-preservation. Where the stronger was walking, he did not risk sinking into the mire or hurting himself..."

And we see one of the first pre-human families walking by, like three phantoms.

The man breaking the trail, and the (already!) prudent mother following her husband, holding her child by the hand! Pre-human? The dating speaks of Australopithecus. And yet, the footprints are in the line of march, so these Australopithecus – but were they Australopithecus? – did not walk like ducks, swaying their hips, as the locomotor analyses say when speaking of their pelvises and hips. And besides, the print proves a completely erect stance, with the weight on the heel and the thrust in the big toe. We are far from the stupid simian cliché that gets pasted on Australopithecus, whose cranium does not exceed 450 cubic centimeters. So who was walking at Laetoli? At such an early date, the Australopithecus are the only candidates, but the debate remains open. John takes us next to the edge of the gorge, opposite the "castle," a vestige of the plateau that rises like a tower isolated by erosion and all the strata of which describe a whole palette going from red to gray. How often have we seen this landscape in our history or natural science books? Olduvai, Olduvai! I repeat this name under my breath like an "Open, sesame" to so many mysteries. John deciphers the panorama for us.

"Each stratum can be read like the page of the great book of the history of the world over the last two million years. Nothing older can be found here than the base of black basalt which you see at the very bottom of the gorge, in the dry bed. Erosion stops there. The rest is made up only of layers of volcanic ash deposited successively by the Olomoti, Lemagrut, Makarut and Ngorongoro volcanoes. On average, this book, this cake, measures one hundred fifty meters thick. Don't forget that the Ngorongoro is a caldera, which is to say a collapsed volcanic cone, which two and a half million years ago was at least as high as Kilimanjaro…whence the thickness of the layer deposited throughout the Serengeti to the west, under the prevailing wind. That ash was very fertile, and there was plenty of water: indeed we find in these layers the fluctuating banks of a vast paleo-lake teeming with life which was suddenly eradicated by an eruption, and then reappeared.

"Why is the upper stratum red?" asks Sonia.

"Because of the last eruptions, which were richer in iron oxides, and on the other hand very poor in fossils. It is in the lower layers, the gray ones, clear at the bottom, called Bed 1 (−1.8 to −1.2 million years) that the Leakeys found remains of an *Australopithecus boisei*, including an extraordinarily complete skull in 1959."

John pulls a casting of it from his bag. Finally we can see what the famous OH-6[1] looked like, this *robustus* that Friedemann Schrenk had described for us in Karonga (he for the present has found only a few teeth). It is, indeed, sturdily built. A pronounced sagittal crest to anchor powerful chewing muscles. The molars are huge, whence its nickname "nutcracker" or "megadont," the brain remains small (500 cm^3) despite an enormous flat face. Everything confirms a portrait of a placid, good-natured vegetarian, certainly not outstanding for intelligence but doubtless able to terrify other hominids with its anger – for such is the great contribution of the Olduvai site: it is the first to have provided the proof that vari-

---

[1] Scientific classification: Olduvai Hominid no. 6.

ous species of hominids had coexisted, where it had been thought before its discovery that they had succeeded one another.

John continues: "When Louis and Mary Leakey took over the digs, they found stone tools. At first they believed they had been made by Australopithecus, which would have been an unprecedented discovery, but very quickly, in the same layer, they found more slender bones that corresponded to no known species, hand and foot bones very human in appearance as well as a jawbone with teeth smaller than those of the Australopithecus. Everyone was very excited! Finally, they found cranial fragments allowing them to deduce a volume of over 600 cm^3. The relationship between brain development and the making of tools was quickly established and the new fossil was named *Homo habilis*, adept man, the artisan of the Olduvai tools: the first man.

"That *homo* was surely omnivorous and opportunistic, not hesitating to try carrion when the occasion arose. Most of the tools found are smooth stones arranged to break bones so as to suck the marrow from them, and rough, sharp fragments for cutting things up: these artisans created a genre, the Oldowan tool, the stone for which, not found at the site, came from somewhere else. Which implied travel and exchanges, therefore knowledge and communication, two other teats of intelligence. It was only much later, in the 1970s, that Richard Leakey, son of the aforementioned, found further north, on the banks of Lake Turkana, a complete skull of *habilis*, confirming for a while his parents' discoveries."

In late afternoon, we cross the gorge on foot with John. We are between Ngorongoro Park and Serengeti Park. It is strictly forbidden for any man with exception of the Maasai to leave his vehicle. It costs the unhappy offender the equivalent of three hundred euros' penalty to dare set foot on the soil for an urgent call of nature behind a bush. Thus it is with secret jubilation distilled by transgression that we descend freely into the gorge. On the way, John comments on the deposit layers, unearths here a pygmy hippopotamus toe, there a bit of deinotherium tibia: "That was a very prevalent elephant here, a little smaller than the present elephants, with tusks attached not to the skull but to the lower jaw, so they were bent downwards, but...ssh! Look what's coming..."

Silently, slightly below us but already much too close, emerge elephants raising a trail of dust from the bottom of the gorge. A half dozen of them. Within a stone's throw. On little cat feet.

"We crouch down and don't move!"

The scout has spotted us with her little caramel eye, she trumpets, flaps her ears, turning her head towards us, and swells the base of her trunk. The echo of her cry is still resounding when she thunders a second one, deafening. John whispers: "If she charges, we climb up the slope, it's too difficult for her, she won't follow us. But I think they are going to go away."

And indeed, the second signal was to accelerate. Now they are rampaging off, in a tight pack, their trunks out front and ears rowing. They are carried away in the turn behind an opaque wall of dust like big, gray octopi behind their cloud of ink. Whew!

That evening, we lodge under the tent in the famous Leakey camp with a team of American amateurs who are digging under the direction of Professor Masao, in the framework of an Earthwatch program. It is magic being here. It's like gleaning crumbs of the great adventure of the century, it's like visiting Albert Schweitzer's hovel in Lambaréné or what remains of the *Calypso*[2] in the port of La Rochelle. The buildings show the ravages of passing time, here too, while hovers the memory of Louis and Mary Leakey. Their story is one of unbelievable perseverance. On the advice of a German butterfly hunter who had been the first to visit the gorge in 1911, in 1931 Louis Leakey organized a first expedition. From the first day they found huge numbers of stone tools and artifacts, and they were euphoric. Then the gorge played hard to get: it would take Leakey twenty-eight years of painstaking research financed by

---

[2] The famous research vessel of Jacques Cousteau (1910–1997).

private funds before the major discovery: the skull of *boisei*...named after their main sponsor. In the valley of time on the march, the digs can only march forward with time.

Earthwatch is a typically American institution, born of the principle that, in a liberal society, science must find other resources than the government. The inverse of the French policy – with the consequence that the CNRS[3] and its researchers often wait long years for the funds needed for field research to be made available. Thus, respecting a charter based on sustainable development and local initiatives, Earthwatch underwrites the research of a hundred thirty scientific expeditions distributed among forty-seven countries, for an annual budget of sixteen million dollars, thanks to the participation of amateurs under the direction of experienced scientists. It is thus possible to participate, among other things and according to one's affinities, in the rescue of Philippine leatherback turtles, in the identification of Inca sepultures in the Andes or in the census of threatened parrots in the Cuban jungle. With Earthwatch, for three weeks – and all the same in exchange for two thousand five hundred dollars per person – people like you and I can lend a hand to science and scientists of countries too poor to afford the luxury of research, even if they are twinned with Western universities. Thanks to this means of support, Dr. Masao has been resuming his digs each year at Olduvai for more than twelve years, training and remunerating twenty or so Tanzanian students, technicians and scientists. Without these enlightened tourists, he would be vegetating in his office in Dar es Salaam, or inventorying the stockpiles from the 1950s. The dozen participants are a motley assembly of persons and characters.

Peggy, a seventy-year-old American, postal retiree from a small town in the Middle West, has come to realize a childhood dream: "Since I recovered from cancer, everything has become possible! I had missed my calling as an adventurer, here I am catching up

---

[3] Centre National de la Recherche Scientifique, the main government organ for research support in all fields.

on time. Now isn't that a good definition of paleoanthropology? Catching up on time!"

Mike is bald, ruddy-faced and roundish, with sports-corrective Ray-Bans and a thick mustache: "I sell insurance. And I am taking a big risk by coming here! When I get back, I'd better tell my wife that I enjoy just as much spending vacations with her and the kids on the beach....But for me, even if it means making sand patties with a shovel and rake, I think this makes more sense here..."

Debbie is a horsey, gossamer, heliophobic Englishwoman covered in cream, long sleeves and a large, soft hat. She was a pharmacist and lives in a little, damp cottage in Sussex with her cats and muffins. Her passions are philosophy and Shakespeare: "I come here for the origins of intelligence! The click, the spark, the first broken flint! The *habilis* who lived here were pioneers! They had to invent everything! Try as they might with their thousands of sparks and broken stones, they had to wait almost a million and a half years for that same spark to start a fire! You realize how slow their world was? A million and a half years to breach the few centimeters between a spark and a little tuft of dry grass with a little tinder dust on it....Then you can picture the distance between that stone – she holds up a shard found during the day – and *A Midsummer Night's Dream*! There was such an acceleration, these last thirty thousand years....The first *habilis* skull found here, OH-24 – not a very sexy name – has been renamed Twiggy, like a top model from the 1960s, who had a small head and big eyes. That's my cat's name, too! So picture me here, someone who is absolutely insignificant, me being associated with a capital discovery for all humanity? There's no price you can put on that!"

For a certainty, Peggy, Mike and Debbie are more useful and more happy here than in Coney Island, Cancun or Bali.

The next day, we follow them into the gorge, these touching little retirees making sand patties with their trowels, scraping the earth in the burning sun, with tools scarcely more sophisticated than the ones invented in this very place two million years ago by those first men who were off to the remotest regions of the world. There they are, sitting on the ground, in silence, conscientiously sorting with large sieves the sediments drawn from the two trenches of one square meter each. Two square meters for this year! It makes you modest. The gorge is forty kilometers long....At this pace, time may advance for a long time yet at Olduvai. But the faith of the bone hunter inspires them. Their day's crop? Crocodile teeth. The same as yesterday, but blackened by fossilization.

Peter, a young Tanzanian student on spade duty in this magical square meter from which everyone hopes to extract a nice complete skull like a gold ingot from a safe, hails us softly. Feverishly, Masao rushes over: a new find? The sacred flame illuminated for an instant in his pupils goes out.

"A bird bone. Look at it! It's hollow. That's how they can be recognized. This was already a pink flamingo, a little smaller than today's. That's how we see that the evolution of men, even stretched out over three million years, was more rapid than that of all the other species."

We climb a bit higher in the gorge, reascending in the great book of time to admire the setting. Way below, in a dried-up turn, our friends are excavating, hunched down, tiny in space and insignificant in time, intent on their quest of roots, and we seem to see a group of *habilis* busily at work on the carcass of a large saurian.

Return to the Heart of the Rift

TANZANIA

R eturn to the nitty-gritty of the trek. No more frolicking in paradise. Our benumbed pedometer is delighted to get back to its metronome function, in time with our steps. It is a little apparatus which I attach to the waist strap of my backpack, on the right side by my hip, and which contains a little hammer held back by a spring. At each stride the spring stretches and the hammer contacts a little printed circuit that records a step. You only have to have entered in advance an average length per pace. Mine is 77 cm. A little more in the morning, a little less in the evening. And the pedometer, simplest thing in the world, just adds these 77 cm's all day long, converting them to kilometers. I verify the calibration of this stride, not by measuring it on the ground, but by using kilometric milestones on the rare occasions when we find them. Set at 77 cm, the round kilometer comes out within ten meters more or less of the next kilometer marker, depending on the terrain. The precision of this apparatus increases with the distance traveled. That is a statistical law. Over five kilometers, there will be a small margin of error, which will be smaller after fifty kilometers, and insignificant after five hundred. At the 5,000th km, or at the 7,000th km, it's not worth thinking about, and you rack up with satisfaction the kilometric harvest of the day.

The pedometer helps us walk, it brings a little precision to the falsity of our senses, a little sense of duty when the pause or the nap is good, when the backpack is too heavy and the temptation to stop too early is too strong. A glance at the little LCD tells us whether we have walked far enough or not. There is no rule, sometimes we are satisfied and tired out after a day of 30 km, sometimes we are disappointed after a day of 42 km. One of the principles established by experience is to try not to stop for lunch before the 20th kilometer, knowing that we always walk less far in the afternoon, and that the day is earned in the morning, there's no point in hurrying.

I feel it beating on my flank when we fall silent, when a space opens up between Sonia and me, when the trail is hard and the effort requires our full concentration. Its pulsation keeps me company like a little clockwork, like a little fuel cell that powers my biped robot carcass. The pedometer is also our censor, distributing, according to the day, good points and bad grades. And when the sun presses down on us, when the landscape repeats itself endlessly, and the mind wanders a moment only to fall an hour later on the same bush, the same stone, with a sinister feeling of *déjà vu*, we hang on this little box: yes, we have indeed made progress; no, we are not walking in place; yes, the evening halt is getting here, at the 35th or 40th kilometer, no matter where, as long as it is with someone. This little toy makes surveyors out of us, it is the landmark and the marker, the carrot and the stick, it contributes its indispensable tick-tock to our moments of doubt, as long as it is clicking we are moving forward, as long at it is beating we are alive, and each pace racked up makes of our trek a quest, a capital of space so we won't lose our heads. Thus this little plastic creature, this electronic mascot, saves us from wandering and bankruptcy. Don't leave home without your pedometer!

From Mto wa Mbu, at the foot of Kitete, we split straight to the north, to the heart of the Rift. We went back to greet Habiba on the fly. Third time's a charm. She has become one of our friends and benefactors without whom our steps would have no meaning. It's good to know they exist. We are walking for them too, in their memory and to sustain their memory. Such is the stuff of our lives and our trek.

At each re-departure, the same intoxication takes hold of us. For us it is a return to simplicity, to happiness, after the complexity of human relationships, the losses of time and urban numbness. Overeating and comfort was exhausting us in Arusha. We were drained after a ten-hour night, tuckered out after a day at the computer, famished in the evening without burning any fuel at all, and we wondered how we managed to keep going with five hours' sleep, forty kilometers in our feet and ten hours under the sun, with nothing but a small noodle soup under the belt. This contrast is a mystery to us. The great fatigue of the sedentary. We are not the same in town and on the road. The sedentary life deadens our minds and bodies while the trail sharpens them. And in the last month our filming, appointments, car trips, the organization of the vacation in Zanzibar, the ascension of Kili, the visit to Ngorongoro and Olduvai have brought us to our knees. These side-trips have been amazingly "stressogenic" in comparison with hiking. Traveling as a tourist is debilitating! More than we can handle. We would never have been able to cross Africa hitchhiking or using local transportation as many Anglo-Saxons do.

When we run into them, they describe to us their daily lot: they disembark winded at night in armpits-at-the-end-of-the-world after multiple stages, must endlessly negotiate the price of everything, talk about nothing but money, keep an anxious eye on their backpacks and belongings, meet only people who want something from them, eat bad sandwiches and warm Cokes on the run, are constantly alert for the next departure of the transportation on which they depend to keep going, not really knowing why they keep going, hang on the magic names of the "other features" listed in their two-pound brick of a fashionable guidebook, are harassed in the tourist traps by youths waiting for them at the bus stop to herd them into "guest-houses" or guide them forcibly to such and such a curiosity where they will find their peers equipped with the same guidebook and sporting the same stories of pickpockets, swindles and sleepless nights...

But it only takes a few steps to be free of these perils, of these informal circuits that already are exploiting and corrupting informal tourism everywhere on the planet, the tourism of backpackers and their praiseworthy and sincere, but always frustrated intentions of encounters with other cultures and the peoples of the countries they are crossing.

Thus, at a time when we are taking on incontestably the hardest stretch of terrain since we started, we are worn out. It has only been a month since Sonia recovered from her malaria. But that's not important: walking regenerates us. Also a return to the open Rift, which we have been following, in its sutured part, since Malawi. Descending the escarpment, we enter *ex abrupto* Maasai country, harsh and dry, dusty and flat, a thousand meters below. Heat and light. And indeed, without transition, there are the Maasai, everywhere, so different from the other Tanzanians. We pass them agape, as in a dream, so exceptional are their costume, their gait and their sprightliness. They are more genuine and beautiful than nature. Too beautiful not to be real. We were expecting a little anxiously to pass a few ethnic clowns disneylandified by tourist manna, and here we are confronted with something extremely strong and structuring: a resistant unity and cultural identity. Even if we know nothing about them. It's like that, it hits you in the face. Lords. Neither haughty nor superior, cheerful and at ease, even joyful.

In the region, Mto wa Mbu is their great trading center and meeting point with Tanzanian institutions and other Tanzanians.

Outside of Mto wa Mbu (the brook of mosquitos), there is nothing but Maasai, north and south, in a territory half as large as France, straddling the border between Tanzania and Kenya, accessible by no road and counting very few trails, schools, or dispensaries. To avail themselves of these services, far from their remote villages, the Maasai have to go outside their domain. Police and justice do not venture onto Maasai lands. For all Tanzanians, it is a *terra incognita* full of mysteries and perils, big cats and "savages." The only foreigners to go deeply inside are ethnologists and humanitarians. As for tourists, they always go to the same places, in proximity to the road to Arusha or Nairobi, and only "meet" the "Maasai" whose trade that has become...

All that is not very reassuring, all the more so that they are not reputed, and it's easy to understand, of being very welcoming to Westerners, whose cameras, camcorders, morbid curiosity and presumption, stress and hurriedness they no longer tolerate.

To stave off our apprehensions, we walk, walk, walk, without speaking, without marveling at all these adornments, these red togas, these jingling jewels – necklaces of large, colored disks, earrings mounted like pendulums – at the women's shaved scalp and proud carriage, at the martial bearing of the men whose arsenal – club, sword, spear, staff and shepherd's whip – does not appear to encumber their hands.

Our objective is to plunge as quickly as possible northward, to get beyond the zone where we could be taken for lost tourists, to go more deeply into territories where human relations have not been corrupted by the too-frequent passage of muzungus. We call that "getting backstage of the decor." Decor meaning what the travel experts and agencies oversell. The phenomenal aspect of the world, its postcard side. Its secrets, though, are in the reverse side of the decor, in the hearts of men. Each time we resume our trek after a long pause, we must get back to the reverse side of the decor. The salt of our trek, all the interest of what we are about, relies on that.

Today, this passage is quickly accomplished. As soon as we have left Mto wa Mbu and its dirty metal-sheet camps, we are in an arid, dry steppe bordered on the left by the vertiginous wall of the escarpment. It's simple, we have only to follow the wall northward. Ahead of us, in the distance, stand the first baobabs we have seen in a very long while, since the banks of Lake Malawi. We keep them in our sight all morning. A few antediluvian Land Rovers converted to pickups pass us by, crammed with standing Maasai, whose arms, spears and red togas make them look from afar like giant bouquets of roses. At the foot of the baobabs spreads Selela: the first shop, run by Somalis. It is prayer time. The Somalis are the Maasai's grocers. It is they who sell them the electric batteries for their radios and their *made in China* flashlights, who unload on them the horrid basins in fluorescent-colored plastic, red *made in India* fabrics, Kimbo cooking oil *made in Malaysia*, *ugali*, Simba matches, tea and sugar they need. They are the only ones who can stand the heat and dust of the Rift bottom. Mohammed has finished his prayer, and comes toward us from the back of his shop.

"Where are you going? Are you lost?"

"Not at all, we are going north."

"To Lengai?"

"Yes."

"Impossible! It's three days' walk....There is no water, very few Maasai, and far from the road..."

"*Wali maharagwé waïzekani?*" (Can we get some rice with beans?)

He smiles.

"*Waïzekani.*" (You can.)

A plateful soon arrives on dirty dishes. Ideal for plugging the gaps. The onion which we eat like an apple spices the blandness of the starch. Impossible to swallow without a drink. The teas don't do the job. Mohammed has given us a big bowl of warm, murky water, somewhat brackish. The salt from the Rift floor, the water of our coming weeks. Sonia laughs.

"It's like swallowing the water we gargled with for sore throats!"

It's that exactly. What would I do if she were bitching? If she were complaining? If she all of a sudden rose up and said: "I've had enough, I can't stand this filth any more, it's more than I can take, I'm going home…" I would have to expend the little energy I have left trying to persuade her, I would begin to have doubts, I would have scruples.…She is happy about everything, never complains. And yet, I can tell she is preoccupied, tense, as I am, facing the unknown that is opening before us, spiked with tests and pains, but punctuated, in our hopes, with purity and authenticity. She has confidence. In me, in us, in our trek. I tend to take all that for granted, but, when I am myself weary or anguished, as at this precise moment, seated on the ground under this metal sheet frying in the sun, I am suddenly aware of the exceptional nature of her character. Then I choke up, begin to sniffle and look at her, mute and blissful. Speechless. She knows my little act: it moves her every time like an overburdened mother who realizes that her children have not forgotten her birthday. Between us, almost every day is her birthday. A peach.

We have taken refuge in a shed the walls of which, made of drying racks, let the air through. The metal sheet above our heads radiates with heat like a hotplate. The relative shade makes us realize how white the light is outside when the sun is at its zenith.

"What will we do when there is nothing and no one to protect us from the sun at high noon?" worries Sonia.

As always, digesting *wali-maharagwé* provokes a gentle somnolence in us which we take advantage of to catch a nap and let mid-day hell pass. Mohammed, our Somali, brings us plastic mats decorated with proud dromedaries. He appreciates the confidence we show in him. And the time we are taking to rest: no White ever did that before.

Just before drifting off to sleep, Sonia, flushed, tosses me a bone to chew on: "This place reminds me of the biltong drying sheds, in South Africa, where shreds of meat were hanging under a hot-air fan. The only difference is that here we are not protected from the flies."

When we awaken, we are drenched with sweat, panting, glued to the dromedary on the plastic mat, blinded by the light outside. To be able to sleep we had to put our scarfs over us like shrouds. Impossible to sleep with a fly on your nose. It is a nightmarish vision to see your wife draped like that. All is silence, burnt out, exhausted. Go out into that furnace? I whisper to Sonia: "We have awakened in the Sahara! While we slept we have leapt four thousand kilometers forward!"

"Don't dream. We might not yet be there a year from now."

We set out again, head in the oven, to a sardonic smile from Mohammed: "*Haiwazekani!*" "Impossible," he repeats, "just wait for tomorrow's Land Rover..."

By dint of walking so long to the north, we have learned to divide the sky and the path of the sun into four quarters; the two in the morning, on our right, are devoted to walking, we do not look at the sun, we know it is coming from the east, from the right and, beginning with the second quarter, about nine thirty, when the right cheek begins to tingle under the UV, we tilt our hats to protect a maximum of skin surface. That is the best protection. No cream can stand up to sweat. They all increase perspiration and keep you hot. Sweat in your eyes is not pleasant, but when it's mixed with cream the chemical sting adds to that of the sun! And since cream has an annoying propensity for attracting dust and dirt, you are in for ferocious irritation. All we use now is Decléor chapstick SPF 15 applied to points where the sun's rays are concentrated. The glycerine in the stick resists sweat much better than creams and attracts less dust. One stripe on the nose and, when the albedo[1] is very strong, two stripes under the eyes. To protect our arms, we unroll our long sleeves at the beginning of the second quarter. We try to start walking again before the end of the third,

---

[1] Reflection of solar energy from the ground.

when the sun is beginning to decline on our left, toward three thirty, even if it is still hot. The hat is then angled to the west and the eye is riveted to the horizon, straight north.

I carry in my hand a five-liter plastic jerrycan in addition to our three personal liters. It is heavy, but it is the key to the steppes that stretch before us. A minimal security if we don't find anyone tonight. Mohammed was unable to inform us, he doesn't know the Maasai villages scattered through the Rift. Most of them, moreover, aren't found on any map. The road is soft, powdery, steps are heavy, muffled by this brown plaster. They raise little clouds that go pof! pof! pof! at each stride. The dust gets into everything, into your socks, mixes with the sweat running down your calves in blackish trails; the bottoms of our legs get covered with volcanic ash. Every five minutes I change the jerrycan from one hand to the other to balance the strain on my back. We advance, we are happy. There is nobody at all around. Every now and then we see bunches of guinea fowl that cackle noisily at our approach and disappear in tight rows, single file, with a comic way of flattening their two sides while rounding the back, pulling the head in and hiding the feet; a gait that makes them look like black disks rolling through the bushes at ground level. Suddenly, we come upon an ostrich. We see it from behind, a big ball of black feathers with a reddish rump, perched on two stilts. With one movement, it lifts its long neck, turns its head, takes a few slow steps, unfolds its short, white wings; it doesn't appear worried, looks us over gently and, at some mysterious call, hightails it away, its head held high and stationary. Its gait is unreal and light, its head floating above the body, and yet the ground resonates under its strides like a drum covered with velvet. Sonia is moved to tears.

"Our first wild ostrich! I would never have imagined it would have that effect on me! Yet we saw dozens of them in Ngorongoro! Not to mention the breeders from South Africa! Why is this one so different when we are on foot...?"

What is true of ostriches is true of every form of encounter, and also of men. Walking magnifies and embellishes everything whereas the auto trivializes and falsifies everything. The auto reifies the world. It is an intermediate state between television and reality, just a little less comfortable. Walking brings a different gaze, direct from the scene; it isn't the object that changes, it's the way it is approached. It does not make things more authentic – the ostrich is still an ostrich seen from a car – it makes them more real to us, more experiential. It metamorphoses the walker, not the ostrich.

There it is! The sun is no longer the enemy, it has indeed entered its fourth quarter. This is the most beautiful time of day, the golden time. We take off our hats, the accumulated sweat on our brows suddenly cools in contact with the surrounding air. The day will be shorter today. We are at the bottom of the Rift and, to the west, just above our heads, rises the imposing massif of volcanoes culminating with Olmalassin at 3650 meters. It looks real soft with green, damp jungles where the bottom of the Rift is so dry and burning. No sign of human life here.

"Yes there is! Look! It looks like two men! Over there!" exclaims Sonia.

Between the scrubby acacias, two silhouettes slowly advance, we stop, one of them turns.

"Kori bustards! The biggest flying bird in Africa!"

We approach them, they walk along nonchalantly. The tuft lying on top of their heads counterbalances to the rear their heavy, pointed beak. It gives them a hammer profile. There is nothing of a crane or a marabout about them, no remarkable colors, they remain discreet under their large ash-brown feathers. In the world of birds, the smaller one is the more nervous; just look at the hysterics of the hummingbird. The bustard, with its fifteen kilos, moves with stately restraint. Its long neck seems to be a heavy feathered trunk that's like an accordion when the head retracts. Free and proud, as if they were conscious of their rarity, they work this pebble seed bed dotted with golden tufts. Suddenly, one of their necks swells, letting go a deep, cavernous cry that sounds for all the world like the call of a lion. Now it begins to run, slowly unfolding its broad digited wings, accelerating over an interminable distance to lift off barely with supple strokes of the wings, in slow motion. It is still skimming the ground, so hard is it to get airborne! What an effort! The bustard is an extreme bird. The other one, more laconic, did not have the energy to fly away.

We are getting deeper and deeper into surroundings that are more wild with every step. After the bustards, Thompson's gazelles make their appearance, all over the place, as if by enchantment, grazing amongst the stones like goats. But free goats, with no shepherd. The sun will soon begin to flirt with Olmalassin. We are dead tired but drunk with silent joy. We will not walk at night, we will not look for anyone, as if the solitude allowed us to enjoy this virginal beauty better, without men, as if to justify carrying the jerrycan, as if to test our ability to survive in this new world. The sunset finds us walking among prancing zebras and hordes of gazelles. Therefore the predators are not far away, we'd better find a shelter. Esthetic apotheosis. They block our path, start, take off in a quarter turn, spluttering and clacking their hooves, their thick manes brushing the evening air. We are in seventh heaven.

"How far are we going to walk?"

"I don't know! It would be nice to find a *boma*, even an empty one..."

"Isn't that one there?"

"Yes it is! Great!"

Appointment kept, no waiting around, right on the dot, an abandoned boma, a circle of thorny shrubs that protects the livestock from wild beasts. Our trek seems to be ruled like music paper, programmed. We have no explanation. The boma is there, obviously enough. To thank us for having risked it. The interior of the circle is divided into cells, so as to separate the cows from the goats. We clean out one of them and set up our anti-mosquito shelter. I go back out to find some firewood. Some curious zebras have come in close. They know that danger never comes from the bomas. The Maasai do not hunt. When I go back in, I close the barrier behind me with a big pile of branches. Night has fallen all at once. The fire is soon hissing, lifting skyward its blue trail of smoke while the stars one by one turn on in the sky. At ten-thirty, we are dead to the world, tranquil behind our thorny rampart.

The Maasai of Irkong

TANZANIA

A wake before dawn, we have taken up again our routine of porridge and tea, folding the tent and getting started while it is cool. The night was good and mild. We have only a little water left in our bottles. Soup, nighttime rehydration, porridge, tea and a little cat-like clean-up have taken care of the five liters from our jerrycan. What is urgent is to find some water. We take to the track that winds among the acacias and walls of tall grasses. We are going north alongside the Ngorongoro Park, destination Kenya via Ol Doinyo Lengai, the sacred volcano of the Maasai, and Lake Natron, which, at 609 meters elevation, is one of the lowest and hottest points in the Rift. The road leads into a thick carpet of pulverized volcanic ash outpoured from the surrounding volcanoes. We sink in it ankle-deep, it seeps into everything and rises in a plume behind us. However this same ordeal allows us to spot the moving herds of goats in all directions: the shepherds are heading for pastures, raising large clouds in their wake. The Maasai villages, the *enkangs*[1] and *manyattas* were not very far away, a few

---

[1] An enkang is a Maasai village surrounded by thorny bushes, grouping several families, often a single patrilineal clan.

kilometers toward the foot of the mountains. That seems close in the morning, impossible to reach in the evening. The estimation of distances is a function of one's state of fatigue.

"That's good to know, if we want to find some Maasai, we just have to leave the track and go toward the hills."

"For now, we need water, and I hope we will find some before Engaruka, since it's twenty kilometers from here."

The temperature is rising fast and, with the sun, here come the first flies. They throw themselves at us, starving after their night of silence and immobility, and absorb at the source the first drops of sweat pearling on our brows. Minute by minute the specter of thirst is growing – already encountered at the time of our painful episode from the Mozambique border. Conversation goes slack, steps become heavier, the landscape less interesting, the zebras in the distance unnoticed. Nothing has any importance in the eyes of thirst except water. We are quite aware that we are not about to die there, but the lack of water is just unbearable, warps all the senses, distorts reason. Three tall Maasai have joined us. Not necessarily friendly. After the usual salutations, the dialogue dries up quickly. They walk much more lightly than us, ascetic and perched high on solid legs, dry as wood. Their earlobes are exceedingly elongated into a thin loop of flesh where hangs a little copper weight that swings with each step. There again, our contemplation quickly stops, restrained both by reticence and by thirst. A truck in the distance on the road. Stopped. Unnoticeably, we have stepped up our pace. Is the driver about? Does he have any water? Yes, there is someone, Yes, we seem to make out a white cube near one dismounted wheel, a plastic jerrycan....Their truck has been broken down for three days. They have just received from Engaruka a jerrycan of fresh water. All at once everything seems simple, our hiking companions seem friendly, and a lot of details in the landscape that we hadn't been noticing jump out at us. Thirst reduces the field of vision, reduces man. We swallow in one gulp the few kilometers that separate us from Engaruka, where a river flows. It descends from Empakai; for centuries it fed a mysterious civilization that has now disappeared, of which the only remains are terraces on the Rift slopes, low stone walls and canals. A civilization from before the Maasai and before the Bantus, who built their houses of stone, a unique trait in the region.

After a nap by the river, we set out again off road. We have been warned: it makes a large detour and goes through no Maasai village. So we must cut straight across the plain, following the volcanoes, if we hope to run into any. The orientation is simple, we have no need of a GPS or compass. All we have to do is to line up these titanic markers that will provide the framework for our coming days in the immensity of space: Olmalassin, Empakai, Kitumbeine, Kerimasi. They will oversee with their tutelary status our progression toward the mountain of the god Enkai, Ol Doinyo Lengai. Though we will never be lost, we will never know where we really are. All we need to do is to go to the foot of these milestone mountains to find men and animals who converge like shadows in flaming dust towards *enkangs* lost in the grandiosity. That's the program. The rest is Adventure.

More than ever, we are walking with gazelles. They don't even see us. This difference in behavior is extraordinary. During our walk through the Kruger Park, in South Africa, we had very close interactions with elephants, rhinoceroses, and lions, but we had not seen a shadow of the tail of the least springbok, the least gazelle. During the thousands of years that man has been a hunter, the antelopes have learned to perceive us before we spot them. The vibration of a biped on the ground? The scent? The sound? One day, perhaps, we possessed these faculties. At the distant time when we were just prey. Since then, our senses have been replaced by intelligence and tools. It's this capacity for fleeing and fearing man that all herbivores have developed which we had deduced throughout the five thousand kilometers covered in the Rungwa jungle, in Tanzania, as we had seen the fresh traces of everything but never their owners. To us it was like passing through a bush peopled by phantoms and threats – which were finally embodied by the Mitundu lions and their victims. Here, around us frolic Thompson's gazelles, Grant's gazelles, zebras and antelopes. How can such a difference in behavior be explained? The key to the mystery is not in the animal kingdom. These animals have learned not to fear man. For centuries, the Maasai have lived in harmony with them. They are strictly forbidden to hunt. It is one of their supreme taboos. Every crime committed against nature is punished since they fear above all the revenge of the elements. It is not a matter of superstition, but of the conviction that nature is the fruit of a fragile equilibrium in which man is but one factor among others, capable of disrupting its harmony. A Maasai who ate wild flesh would instantly be eliminated or excluded, and his family covered with shame for several generations. It's as simple as that. That is why the Maasai territories are so full of game, whereas in the Bantu territories and everywhere else in Africa wild species survive only in game reserves, protected from poachers by the law and armed patrols. Here, the simple presence of the Maasai suffices to dissuade the poachers. They would quickly be trapped and executed without further ado. The animals who scarcely raise their heads when we pass seem to know that.

We are walking in the paradise of harmony between men and nature. Here among the Maasai the pact has not been broken. Man has not set fire to the brush,[2] has not been banned from paradise by original sin, has not tasted of the forbidden fruit, has not stolen the Promethean fire, has not become "master and owner of nature," has never said: "This land belongs to me!," has not answered to the call that says: "Be fruitful and multiply!" The Maasai society is necessarily balanced, it has no impact on the ecosystem, you can see that in the landscape, and deduce it from animal behavior. The Maasai are the inventors of primal ecology and of the first ecology.

---

[2] See the creation myth in Malawi, vol. I, p. 303.

This is what we are saying to ourselves when we realize that among the gazelles there are now cows and goats and that they are all walking in the same direction we are, converging towards an identical vanishing point, straight ahead, in the fold of a small hill. These herds – hundreds of head – still very far from the vast plain, seem to move on their own.

"No! Look behind us, there is a little kid skipping along…"

About yea-high, a small, completely naked child, hardly taller than the grass, is driving these tons of muscle and flesh with the whistle of his frail whip. He is all alone. We are flabbergasted. He holds onto the tail of one of his cows to speed it up, lets her go to grasp another one, comes back around passing under a bull, as spritely as a goblin. Little by little, his herd, stretched out over four hundred meters, gets closer to us. We are at the foot of Kerimasi. These herds are surely coming home to an *enkang* hidden by the undulations of the terrain. We let ourselves go with the flow. Two Maasai standing on top of a talus pretend not to see us. We greet them from a distance. The response is timid, restrained but smiling.

Soon carried into the fold of the hill, we climb somewhat among the bleats, jingling of bells, bellows, whistles, scraping of hooves against rock. Men and cows carry the weight of the day, their bodies stream with encrusted sweat. At this moment there floats in the heart and the pleasantness of the air a serene weariness at knowing the stage of the day. Time slows so it can be savored intensely, the golden time of work done, space covered, deserved rest. The gaze of the Maasai, who have appeared as though by magic behind their cows, is pacific and restrained: if things are to happen, let them happen, they seem to be thinking. They know that we are going to speak to them but don't hurry anything. They leave the initiative to us. Modesty and tact.

We soon reach the summit of a shelf. The view over the plain is breathtaking. In the distance, giraffes march in slow motion, around us Maasai pop up all over the place, women bent over udders to draw a bit of life from them, little girls accompanying other women bent double under the burden of a calabash filled with water, wedged into the curve of the loin and attached to the forehead by a broad leather strap, and naked, ashen children running in all directions amongst the goats.

There, now! We stop at a fair distance. And wait. We are going to get to speak. Two young proud and martial morans,[3] putting on the appropriate expression, come to check us out while the theories of amused children are already babbling around us. I speak first, giving a try to our Maasai survival kit, mixed with approximate Swahili: *"Sopa!"*[4]

"Ipa!"

"Inaïtwaje?" (What is this place called?)

"Irkong!"

"Inchoki airag enkaji tara kaorié?" (Could we stay with you for the night?) *"Aramanayé tarongadiek inkoapi poakin."* (We are crossing all Africa on foot.) *"Sisi muzungu wachungadji, parrimangat olashumpaï."* (We are White nomads.)

It takes no more than that to turn the village upside down and, in a flock of naked bodies, laughter and friendship, seized by this wave of life returning to the fold, drowned amidst the fascinated gazes and cows' behinds, in the middle of a cloud of flies and dust, in the pungent odors of cow dung, soot, sweat and milk, we enter the life of the Maasai people.

The setting sun sets fire to the dust raised by the animals' hooves. The villagers perceive us at the last moment through this cloud of gold and fire; their cry of disbelief brings the neighbors running. Soon there are a hundred jovial, overcharged souls escorting us slowly; it's a tussle to come look us over and take off again with a burst of laughter. We go through a few huts, maybe twenty, they are distributed in a circle, on the periphery of the village, on the

---

[3] Age group of "warriors" who protect the tribe, in a sort of military service, more social than military.

[4] "Hello!" To which you reply, "Ipa!"

edge of the outer enclosure and separated from each other by small private paddocks. In the center of the village, there is a large circular enclosure which also is subdivided into quarters. The walls are made of inextricable entanglements of thorny shrubs. The cows that accompany us stop when we reach their pens, as a car parks. Starving calves immediately come out of the houses and greet their mothers with capers that add, if it were possible, to the confusion of our tour. A thick cloud of flies envelops us. You drive them off in a permanent ballet of arms and hands. It is a slow, collective choreography, indissociable from life in a community and the return of livestock. An echo to the swinging of the cows' tails. It's really unbearable only when your hands are busy, in particular if grasped by avid and friendly kids. The crowd ferries us to an old wise man seated before his mud house. He stoically watches us coming. We repeat timidly to him, with our hearts in our throat, the necessities of our journey. The crowd has fallen silent as by a charm. Serious, he looks us over carefully, askance, then decides and calls out to someone, in a hut behind him.

"*Pakiteng!*[5] *Kori Olorika! Inkukurto!*" (Bring a stool and a gourd of milk!)

The thin voice of a young woman replies. Now she emerges from the entrance corridor of the house, doubled over, holding in her hand a stool and a gourd nearly a meter long adorned with beads. When she stands, her panoply of necklaces jangles noisily on her chest. The shimmering facets of her earrings mounted like little mobiles swing with her every movement. We are fascinated by such beauty. Seeing that there are two of us, she goes back for a stool for Sonia. The old chief's skin is shriveled like an old elephant hide, the ridges of his bones stand out along his folded limbs, in which tendons and dry muscles quiver. His knotty joints unfold like a strange mechanism; the hollow ribs and salient

---

[5] This means literally "my cow" but also "my wife," or yet "my brother"! The Maasai name for themselves is *inkishu* (cows). Hence a consubstantial affection with their animals.

clavicles speak of the rigors and sobriety of his life. From a knot in his *karasha*, his red toga, he takes a leather purse with blackish balls in it and hands me one.

"*Timbaku?*" (Tobacco?)

I politely decline. He wedges it between his lower lip and teeth, on the side. The purpose is not to chew it, but to salivate and swallow the tasty juice. The excess is spit out between words in a thick, precise stream. Everyone watches him religiously. A fiery gaze above cheeks folded into deep wrinkles and excessively elongated ears completes this ascetic portrait. Only his scalp is smooth. The Maasai say that the larger the ear hole, the greater the aptitude for hearing, and therefore for wisdom. His hang onto his shoulders like two old socks with holes in them. There is much kindness and gentleness in his gestures. He extends the gourd to me.

"*Karibu! Kulé Naaoto!*" (Welcome. Here is some clotted milk!)[6]

"*Aché naleng!*" (Thank you!)

When I uncork the inkukurto, a powerful odor of smoke, acrid and hot, rises into my nostrils. How can fresh milk smell like fire? I apply my lower lip to the extremity of the long squash which I lift, my movement being a tiny bit too rapid, the surge of whey showers my face, the whole village explodes in laughter. I cough. I am embarrassed. Sonia seizes the opportunity to berate me and cuff me on the head, which redoubles the laughter. The village is having a ball. I have it all over my neck. The flies swarm onto me. Yet the opening of the inkukurto is scarcely larger than a bottleneck. You don't see it coming. Belatedly cautious, I lift the bottom of the gourd slowly. Everyone watches for my reaction. The milk comes little by little, slightly lumpy, strongly smoked, dense and rich: Maasai yogurt! A true delight! Glug, glug, glug! The audience waits. My beaming face triggers a new round of laughter. Here is our second and strong impression: the Maasai are always having

---

[6] Fresh milk is called *kulé naïrowua*.

fun, laughter seems to be part of their language, so often does it punctuate their long, unintelligible tirades.

For our benefit, chief Olkuma admixes Swahili and Maasai. Pointing to the great central enclosure, behind us: *"Emboo kubwa! Mingui mbuzi. Mingui inkishu!"* (This is a large enclosure, we have many goats and cows!)

"Mingui sana! Mzuri boma mzee!" (Yes, Venerable! Very many! It's a beautiful village!)

The herd is perched on a dome constituted year after year by the piling up of manure and dung. That is how you guess the age of an enkang, for the houses, the *enkaji*,[7] are remade every year. Their oblong structure is constructed by bending slender trimmed rods, tied to each other like crossbars. In the long direction, other stems are woven and intertwined on a fence of slim pickets to rigidify the whole like an upside-down wicker basket, ready to receive its cement of cow dung mixed with dried grass and ash. The sun crackles this smooth surface, which then blends perfectly with the landscape.

Night has fallen. Nightjars pirouette just above our heads, gorging themselves on flies. Sonia marvels. The laughter of the aficionados just starts up again. The crowd has little by little dispersed, going about its business. Olkuma shows us the small enclosure adjoining his enkaji. His house is too cramped for us to be able to install our tented mosquito net inside, also too smoky. So we pitch it right next to it, outside, under the heavy fire of a hundred gazes. The little blue bulb of our headlamps hypnotizes them like cobra eyes. Forming a tight circle around us, the morans hanging onto their spears never have enough of watching us and comment with whispers and laughs at our slightest little gestures. No way to pick your nose, no way to get undressed. This lack of privacy no longer bothers us, we are the show, voluntary actors in a sharing of which

---

[7] This term is exclusively Maasai. The generic term for this type of mud hut would be *tembé*.

sacrificed intimacy is the price. In Africa, the guest is king, so there is a *coucher du roi*...[8]

It's seven fifty-five. It's pitch dark. A feeble light flickers at the entrance of the enkajis; laughter and muffled murmurs which pour forth from them continue long into the night, as every night for centuries. In the sky, straight overhead, an airplane passes with its blinking red lights. So near. Already so far from us. In another world.

---

[8] The king's retiring ceremony in pre-Revolutionary France, attended by select members of the court.

CHAPTER 6

Ol Doinyo Lengai, God's Mountain

TANZANIA

W hen we awaken, everything is sadder. That's the way it is. The flies more unbearable, the excitement of the children less kind. The night was rough, ten meters from a rutting billy goat in heat. The poor she-goats, shamelessly raped, bleated with horror all night....The bastard! We get it! It's easier for him when they're all piled into an enclosure than in the green prairie. What a mistake to have forgotten earplugs! I was within an inch of plugging my ears with two fresh, round goat turds...

We've got to get going. We leave without eating. Last night's noodle soup is already a long time in the past. The landscape is yellow and undulating at the foot of Kerimasi. We cut across the volcano foothills, optimizing an itinerary not too low so we won't have to go too far around it, and not too high so as not to go constantly up and down in the ravines that drop down from the steep slopes. Gazelle skulls and hyena poop, white as quartz, remind us that we are indeed treading lion territory. They often come down from Empakai and Ngorongoro, we were told. The landscape is indeed ideal with its observation posts and steep hills well-suited to setting traps. We walk on the lookout with our walking sticks. We also are wary of the snakes that must be teeming in these dry grasses. A light wind makes them sing, which covers the rustle of their flight. We have neither anti-venom nor serum. Only the White Fathers' "black stone." We carry it a little like an amulet even if Father Raphael Romand-Monnier of the Mitundu mission[1] had asserted that thanks to it he had saved the life of two persons. The method is simple, he told us: "All you do is apply the stone to the bite, making it bleed, after tying the limb, then remain still as long as possible while drinking lots of water. The stone then absorbs the venom and decomposes." He had told us about a third victim who succumbed after running toward the road to find a car instead of waiting for the venom to be neutralized by the stone. Lack of faith. In the stone. I have it in my pocket and rub it occasionally to ward off fate. It is not a stone, by the way, but a bit of burnt cow bone, impregnated with a secret substance the formula of which comes from Indian Ayurvedic medicine. Some nineteenth-century Jesuits, in the midst of an inculturation experiment in the ashrams of Kerala, received it from yogis and snake charmers and bequeathed it to Monsignor Lavigerie, founder of the order of Missionnaires d'Afrique. For want of better, when in doubt, you carry it with you fearful of having to entrust your life to it. But all we see is field mice running away from us, not the least snake; is the black stone acting like a charm?

We pass not far from some bomas and enkangs lost in the yellow of the grasses, places of life whose names appear on no map. They are the geography of a nomadic people, of families assembled in the heart of thorny enclosures so discreet that they could not be found unless you listened carefully, to locate the bleating of the goats.

We are walking straight ahead, all alone, all day in the tall grasses; the rare morans we have passed do not believe their eyes.

---

[1] See vol. I, p. 388.

We read in them interrogations without answers: A couple alone? Where is their guide? There are lions hereabouts! Didn't anyone tell them? They don't even have a spear! How do they know the names of our mountains? They are here for the first time and they know the landscape, the paths, know where they are going....Sorcery! They take us, with a telling gaze, to be sorcerers, great hikers, Maasai olashumpai.[2] Respect and laughter! And we for our part faint away at their hairdo with long braids pulled together and buttered with red ochre, their jewels, their ankle and wrist bracelets of little beads, their serene pride, their joyous purity, their candor, their warrior attributes, their calm nonchalance, their deprivation in a space suited to them. They are each time encounters of the third kind, magic and unreal, joyous and contemplative. Pure, unfettered Africa Trek.

Exaltation carries us more than the few biscuits swallowed along the way. We soon drop exhausted under an isolated acacia, with an excellent view of a vast, deserted prairie. Sonia is tomato red. Slumped. She hasn't even got the strength to take off her backpack. She is panting like an old lion. The shadow afforded by this flat-top tree is entirely relative but it nevertheless makes an enormous difference. I glean branches fallen under the limbs, and, harder, go looking for stones for a hearth. When I return, Sonia is still in the same position.

"My head is a little warm. I have the impression I've almost got sunstroke..."

"Are you hungry?"

"Not even..."

"Then that's what it is! Take off your backpack and cool off with a little water..."

"You mean with a little hot water from the plastic bottle?"

"It's evaporation that makes you cool, not the water..."

And there we go into physical considerations about the

---

[2] White, strangers in Maasai.

expansion of gases, the reasons why the Mediterranean cools when the Mistral is blowing, how refrigerators work...

"What? You mean you can make cold by making heat?"

"Yeah, sure. That's how it works in your refrigerator! Can't you tell that you feel better with this light warm wind on your drenched shirt?..."

During this time, I have cleared the grass for a hearth. Wouldn't be a good idea to set the prairie on fire. My mattress stood sideways serves as a windscreen. At high noon, when we are no longer walking, the silence of the savannah is deafening. Sonia, her eyes fixed afar, is vaguely worried: "I would be more reassured if there were some gazelles grazing quietly in this prairie....These huge, empty expanses make me a little uneasy..."

"Yes, but if there were gazelles, that could attract lions..."

"Unless the gazelles have sensed something in the vicinity and have decamped..."

"OK! But look, there are no gazelles here, so what would a lion be doing in the vicinity?"

"I don't know, run into us..."

Surreal conversations fanned by sun and hunger, imagination and the unknown. We feel dawning in us the small universal anxiety shared by all preys, and with which our ancestors must have lived for hundreds of millions of years. It re-emerges from the limbo of our cortex where it was sleeping in a loop of gray matter, a feeling both disquieting and exciting at once, always present, like a little lantern, like a little resurgence of energy for watching, smelling, listening and rediscovering bits of a sixth sense for danger which our species must once have had. We are on our guard. The noodle soup is ready. Lifting my head after each spoonful, I catch myself unconsciously scanning the landscape....The pseudo-nap that follows is not very restorative.

In the afternoon, Ol Doinyo Lengai heaves gently into view, step by step, behind the slopes of Kerimasi, then finally becomes completely separate from it. We soon have it in our line of sight, symmetrical and lordly, with its bald summit whitened by carbonatite ash – not surprising that the first explorers described a snow-capped mountain. The archetype of the pyramidal volcano, rising from the savannah. But it is still far away and we are wandering into ever higher grasses that finally block our passage. It would be a big mistake to think that these open spaces are easily crossed. The prairie conceals numerous snares, ravines, holes, traps. There is a great variety of grasses in the savannah: supple ones, rough ones, slim stalks, cutting leaves, scratching leaves, golden plumes, rose tufts, treacherous grains with hundreds of seeds that are so many darts to stick in your socks, then in your skin until they impede walking. And here before us, walls of elephant grass, tentacular, abrasive, impenetrable. We struggle for a whole hour, we get scraped, sweat, swear and finally fall back on a dry river bed which, though it lengthens our walk, spares us needless suffering. The black sand, hot and heavy, takes over and tortures our calves while the lack of water is becoming noticeable. A large snake has also descended into the arroyo. We follow its trace for five kilometers! It is moving straight ahead with the regularity of a bicycle tire, as if it knew perfectly well where it is going. In this sun and serene nature, never forget that death is two paces away and that the prairies are teeming with vermin. Thanks for the reminder. The sun anesthetizes vigilance. We ought to leave the river bed and try going through the grass again. A little cookie pause. When we are about to set out, we see two warriors dressed in black emerge above us. Seen no one this afternoon. Apparition. In this desert, everything becomes singular. Improbable. Are they following us? Once we're over the fear of being trailed, I recognize two young circumcised men in their ostracism garb. It is part of their long initiation ritual that will qualify them to pass into the moran age group in the service of the community. Aged from eight to twelve – younger and younger to avoid going to school – they are left to themselves for six months in the bush among the wild beasts as apprenticeship for future warriors. They learn about Maasai botany, traditional medicine, poetry, morality, spirituality. In place of a headdress they have extraordinary architectures of shoots, strings and ostrich feathers on their heads and on their faces masks painted white, finely tooled in geometrical motifs. Enough to impress the evil spirits of the bush. They are thirsty. Normal, the Maasai are supposed to carry nothing but their weapons. Rationed ourselves, we sacrifice a few swallows to them, they tell us about a shortcut. And we leave them as we met them, by the simplest of magic. For they needed us. For we needed them.

Camp at the foot of Lengaï, Thursday 11 July 2002, day 560, 36 km, 7115th km

Day is fading and we are reaching the foot of the giant: Ol Doinyo Lengai, the mountain of the Maasai's god. To each night its volcano. Its steep flanks are hollowed out with regular furrows eroded by rain flow. That gives it a classic high-fashion draped look. We will not go further, this evening, we are bushed. No livestock, no dust, no boma, no enkang hereabouts. Men have always feared the growling mountain. A giraffe flees in front of us. We pitch our shelter amid the tall grass. The heavy gold of the setting sun gilds everything. We only have two liters left. To hold out until tomorrow, that's tough. We sacrifice one to rehydration. Night settles in around our minuscule campfire, full of the rustling of grass in the wind. With the soup, life enters by hot gulps. Tomorrow, before noon, we must find water. No choice. We are drunk with fatigue and sun.

All is calm when the laugh of a hyena resounds under the stars. To instill fear. Then another. To make the heart beat. And a third. To swell the terror. We are petrified. The silence becomes anguish, expectation. In suspense, we monitor the cries of the bush. Fear. It's ridiculous, but it's fear. Real, raw, animal fear. We didn't find a boma this evening. Nothing separates us from these beasts endowed with the most powerful jaws in the animal kingdom. I recall the testimony of Mike Van Sittert,[3] who, lost behind enemy

---

[3] See vol. I, p. 116.

lines, during the Angolan conflict, had walked four days and four nights in the bush: "The worst, at night, is the hyenas, they don't quit. We were obliged to attach ourselves in trees with our belts. I had a buddy who fell and ended up sleeping on the ground. A hyena tore off his face and ran off with it into the night, I can still hear his cry..."

And our hyenas reply to my anguish: Ha-oup! Ha-oup! We coil up in our mosquito-net dome. Laughable bastion. I arm myself with my walking stick, my tear gas canister, our distress flares, and patience. And what distress! I feel naked and watch without interruption through the fine mesh of our mosquito screen, the only opening through which a potential salivating face could present itself. No shuteye for me tonight. The wind brings me by waves the sinister cries, modulating the surf – sometimes whispering, sometimes strident. Are they closer? I have the impression they are circling us. Have they smelled us? Not yet! We are downwind from them. My soliloquy with shadows continues through the interminable night.

Suddenly, in a longer lapse of time, resounds the cry of the lion....Panic! Another. Yet it is not exactly the decrescendo cascade so often heard in South Africa: a single cry, relatively short. I try to convince myself that it is in fact a bustard, maybe even an ostrich, since their calls resemble the lion's. When in doubt, you freak out. This is the first time we sleep alone in lion territory. But the hyenas return to dispel my doubts. Beside my head, I have placed our photo tripod against the tulle, telling myself that the beast will first have to overturn it before it gives me its fatal kiss. Derision, derisory. I am flipping out, and turn and start at the slightest sound. All night, I self-inject big squirts of adrenaline in my veins. Each time, my heart goes ape and I hear its muffled resonance in my rib cage. I don't manage to listen to reason. My only consolation is the adorable snoring of my beloved.

At dawn, I am drained by all these battles with phantoms, with myself. And yet...I inspect the landscape to be clear in my own mind. Nothing! Much ado about nothing. A little morning pee. I fill my lungs with pure air and relief, and return to my little business. Suddenly, in the dust, a hyena trail leaps out at me that stops cold. A huge one. It veered into the grass after taking a whiff of us. My turn for laughter…a forced laugh.

Freed of our nocturnal tribulations, we walk across a vast yellow pediment toward the base camp of the volcano Ol Doinyo Lengai. A plume in the distance is coming towards us. A Land Rover. Water, maybe. It stops beside us. A little man hunched over his wheel exclaims behind nearsighted glasses: "Zo! You taking a valk?" (distinct German accent).

Travelers' luck! We have happened across Jorg Keller, geologist at the Freiburg University, a Lengai specialist and old friend of the late Maurice and Katia Krafft.[4] Besides, he has water. Normal! He will rejoin us in a while for a little talk about carbonatite lava. "I'm going hunting for stones for my collection…" he explains before leaving us.

Engaré Sero camp is at the foot of the Rift, which here has the form of an impressive straight cliff three hundred meters high and twenty kilometers long. Right behind the tents, this fortress is cut through to its base by a river that springs from a cleft in the escarpment: a crystalline miracle in the middle of the desert. A bath. Even slightly salty, so much water amidst such aridity is a blessing. At day's end, just before leaving to climb the Lengai, Jorg, who has returned from his collecting, comes to brief us: "You are going to see that this mountain is a genuine marathon, six hours of continual effort, a slope that just gets steeper, not a single flat meter, and you end up on all fours! But it's worth it for the lava flows: the Lengai is the only active carbonatic volcano in the world. It produces black lava devoid of silica, and that is why it is not red and is very liquid. The Kraffts measured it at 500° C. It's the coldest lava in the world! Elsewhere, basalt lavas are at 2000° C. Another unique phenomenon: the whitening of the carbonatite

---

[4] Famous French volcanologists.

is not an oxygenation but a reaction with atmospheric water; it dries out very fast and turns into a white powder – sodium carbonate – which is why the cone looks like it's covered with snow. One piece of advice: when you are in the crater, make an extra effort and push to the summit, you'll be glad you did!

We leave the dear man there and start out on a moonless night with a Maasai guide, Mtui. Sonia has had a very sore knee since our return down from Kili. She is afraid of being a hindrance. She also fears compromising our passage through Natron toward Kenya. I try to reassure her. A good soul has lent her two knee supports.

It is eight-thirty in the evening when we begin the climb along a narrow trail in the elephant grass swept by a wind that could make a pachyderm take off. Slow but sustained rhythm – of high mountains. We walk in silence. Sonia is in the lead, right behind Mtui. As the strength of a chain is that of its weakest link, the slowest hiker or the most vulnerable, the one who limps or has blisters, a tendinitis or a colic, must always be in the lead. Instead of ball and chain, he becomes the metronome. If he makes it, everyone makes it. An hour of peaceful declivity later, the slope increases. The trail becomes an ashen track, more and more vertical, lined with stinging grasses. The breath grows more shallow, the feet go to work. All about is darkest night where gusts of wind roar. The only space that counts is the part my head lamp illuminates and Sonia's feet ahead of me. Concentration. The higher we go, the thicker, the harder it is, and the softer is the path. Effort management.

At ten-thirty, the ash gives way under foot. You try in vain to find a foothold. You have to get used to it. Like a powdery slope. Find another rhythm. A second wind. We trudge like this for an hour, then the track becomes a narrow passage, congested with round stones that disappear under foot, *absorbing* all the energy: a guaranteed pitfall! Thus we advance in unstable equilibrium, focused on a single concern: to remain on our back legs. The wind cools the sweat pearling on the brow. In a thousand meters, we have lost 5° C. And that continues, the rest is still there, more and more vertical, stretching overhead.

Gravity is slowly winning, everything flows, everything flees, the soil thins, earth and grasses yield ground. At twelve-thirty, the bone of the mountain appears at times in the distance: finally a few shots. The passage is sometimes so deep that it is a trench, a corridor of rockslide where we all but crawl, legs apart to get a hold on the bare edges, going from one to the other. I catch up with Sonia, taking care not to put my feet where hers have slid. That is the advantage of followers. By trying to spare her knees, she chooses less secure toeholds. I keep the corner of an eye on her, push her from behind in difficult passages. She makes no complaints. Noble.

The wind has suddenly ceased, yielding to the muffled high-altitude silence. From time to time, we are brushed by flights of pink flamingos. Their cry is strangely reminiscent of the electronic babble of droid talking to a fax machine. They are going from Natron to Ngorongoro or vice versa, traveling only at night to guide themselves by the stars and foil the attacks of birds of prey. The mass of the summit is dimly visible against the twinkling dark. It is one o'clock in the morning when we reach the bare, adherent rock: great flows of lumpy conglomerates. The ascension is becoming heady. You place your feet as when scaling a mountain, look for a foothold, using your hands, what was awkward heavy labor now becomes a dance with points of traction. The void is there, in the night, but vertigo fades and all you see is your feet. We climb ridges impregnated with sulfur, soda, and pungent forge odors. Mtui, in sandals, climbs like a young goat.

Just before the summit, in the final passage, he stops suddenly and, his face against the wall, begins a hoarse chant. He scans a vibration beyond time, a guttural prayer underscored by a shaking of the head, an open sesame to gain access to the territory of the god Enkai, he who gave the Maasai all the livestock in the world[5].

At two o'clock, the lip of the crater embraces us all of a sudden, revealing to us the unthinkable: the moon! We are on the moon in a moonless night. Everything is white and flat under the stars, ashen, enigmatic and dead, circular and sidereal. Little craters, pointed cones. From the depths comes to us the breath of the volcano, it belches, it spits, it vociferates in the dark. We remain on the edge of the crater. Fearsome crevasses gaping over the earth's entrails defer deeper exploration until dawn. We are overwhelmed with fatigue, this is our third night without sleep. We unroll our sleeping bags right on the carbonatite gound, heated from below, and go to sleep lulled by the droning of Enkai.

At dawn, everything appears even whiter. From the crater's lips a red sun surges on the horizon like an eruption. The wisps of smoke light up mauve, draperies of gas and vapor dance in the first rays of day. We head for the large cone, at the crater's center, which raises its drooling black mouth into the pink sky. Blorff! Tchouff! Flourp! A splash of lava, followed by another, at irregular intervals: metronome of Earth's guts, a fantasy of Titan. The volcano breathes, utters, pulses its rumblings, sneezes out its Vulcanic snot. It flows in broad, black flows that crunch and pucker at our feet as they cool. These flows can be dated by their color. The black ones are at most two days old. The gray ones, between three and five, the whitened ones, over a week. That gives an idea of the rapidity of its growth. These flows are so fluid that the bottom of the crater remains flat. The level rises as in a kitchen sink. Simple. This genesis of the world, this mountain in labor accompanies its parturition with a crystalline groan, the clinking of lava: a song of ground glass, charcoal stirred by the hand and wind in a sonorous mobile.

Sonia, never short of ideas, fetches some slices of bread from her backpack: "What if we toasted them?"

---

[5] They believe our livestock is just some that got lost in History.

She tosses one of them on the carpet of black lava rolling slowly before her.

In three meters it is smoking. Deftly, with the point of her walking stick, she flips it over and goes to wait for it a meter further down. With the same motion she recovers her toast; a puff of hot air suddenly undoes her hair: "Whoa! A little closer and I was toast!"

I film the scene. She comes back toward me: "So we have perfect toast, done on both sides, ready for consumption!"

With backlighting, the sunlight illuminates the browned slice. I worry: "Doesn't it smell a little too much like sulfur?"

She inspects it at the end of her long nostrils, then bites jubilantly into it. "Not at all! It's delicious!"

Mtui resumes his song with his god. Atmosphere. The summit is on a raised edge of the crater. We religiously begin the climb on a gentle incline. We are not the first, this morning. Footprints in the white ash – a porcupine, and there, a leopard; the second was following the first.

"*Mtoto Chui?*" (It's a baby leopard?) I ask Mtui.

"*Hapana Mtoto!*" (No, there's no young one.)

"*Lakini hapana kubwa?*" (But he's not very big?)

"*Ndiyo, kubwa!*" (Oh yes, it's an adult.)

A surreal conversation in the ash of the trail. A leopard at 2900 meters, in this carbonic snow: the guardian of Enkai's forges. It is the equal of Hemingway's mythic leopard in "The Snows of Kilimanjaro"! We were sleeping beside him; the spirit of the bush was prowling around us...

From the summit of this pyramid of the ages, we can survey two million years. This volcano is the youngest in the region, the massif's lastborn, the finest belvedere in the world on the Rift. The landscape is slashed by the scars of time. To the west, the Gol Mountains, random surface remnants of the old granitic bases of Gondwana: three hundred million years. At their feet, in the north-south axis, the immense Gregory Rift[6] and its black cliffs: sixty million years. Behind us, to the south, an amalgam of craters that delimit the Ngorongoro: Empakai, Olmalassin, Olomoti, Oldeani, Lemagrut, an enormous mass of ash extruded from our innermost depths between three and forty million years ago. To the east, very far into the sun, the bald scalp of Kilimanjaro, the dark head of Meru, the table of Ketumbaine and the fine cone of Kerimasi. To the north, Lethean mists float on the mirror of Lake Natron, with the imposing Gelai volcano to one side: the extension of our itinerary. At the end of the lake, the Kenyan border. Mtui begins a warrior's dance in homage to Enkai, the creation principle of the world. Draped in red, like a cherry atop an immense cataclysmic cake, he sings in a sepulchral voice a psalmodied droning in order to become one with the mountain. In our hearts plays *exultate jubilate*.

At the camp, we meet up with Jorg Keller again.

"So, how was it?"

"You were quite right, the summit made all the difference!"

"You know, the last offspring of the Rift has not spoken its last. It has erupted three times in the last century, there is no reason why it should not erupt sometime soon. The last time was in 1966. The entire region was covered with a layer of white ash: hundreds of Maasai died as well as ten thousand cows. In 1967, during our first expedition with Maurice and Katia, the bottom of the crater was a hundred fifty meters lower. Since then it has filled up, and you see that it is spilling over in three places. That makes an incredible cork! Did you see the fissures?"

And almost jubilantly: "It's going to blow up just by connecting the dots!"

Suddenly his laughter subsides, and our friend confides in us:

---

[6] From the name of a Scottish geographer, John Gregory, who originated the concept of the Great East African Rift in 1890.

"That reminds me of a funny scene with Maurice; he had burned his shoes in a fissure, and said to us: 'I would like to be reincarnated as an asbestos mole to go dig in volcanoes' guts,' and Katia replied: 'For me I would rather be an asbestos eagle to fly over the eruptions.' Today I pray they may have obtained satisfaction. We had only to cross the Rhine to get together! We made little dinners for each other. Ah! the Lengai, it's also the memory of beloved persons we won't see again..."[7]

Behind his thick lenses, the two little blue nuggets of the stone collector with a heart of gold are like pearls in crystal. Thank you Jorg.

---

[7] Maurice and Katia Krafft were killed in Japan in 1991 by a burning cloud from the volcano Mount Unzen.

CHAPTER 7

Natron, the Lake of Hell

TANZANIA

Lamendea, Maasai enkang, Monday 15 July 2002, day 564, 36 km, 7204th km

We break camp an hour before dawn and set out toward the north and the Kenyan border, Lake Natron and the unknown.

Natron. A foretaste of the deserts. The sweat of the world, rinsed with volcanic ash. Laundered. *Natrium*: German sodium. Alkaline lake, paradise of pink flamingos – their nesting lake. It is one of the names on the map that struck the most fear in our hearts. And it is there before our eyes. Flat, infinite, mixed with sky. Real and virtual. We intend to go around its right side. In the distance, Shompole, an old volcano, at the bottom of the Rift, marks the Kenyan border. Between now and then, a hundred kilometers of uncertainty. No way to collect precise information about the flanks of the Gelai volcano, which is on the east side of the lake. One thing is certain, there will be very few Maasai. Will there be water? That is the key to getting through: find water. The lake water is a fearsome poison. Mount an expedition? Enlist donkeys and guides, buy ourselves a minimum of security and peace of mind? I think back to the other night's hyenas....No. Africa Trek has no safety net. Bring on the sleepless nights, the hunger, the thirst, the fun-filled agony of the unknown!

An exhilarating departure at dawn, with maximal autonomy: eleven liters of water. Two bottles of one and one-half liters each. I am carrying the five-liter plastic jerrycan in my hand. Sonia will take over when I am too tired. We leave the striped, black escarpment to the northeast, across a yellow plain that stretches forever, punctuated by little black cones. We follow dry beds, snaking between these pivots to avoid the grasses. In any case, all beds lead to the lake. Between the ripples in the terrain some ostriches spring up on our left, gossips all ruffled in feathers, get upset about nothing, take off at top speed; on the right, a little farther away, a column of a hundred zebras or so blocks our path on a gallop, raising a curtain of ash that is carried away by the wind; in single file, in front of us, some disoriented wildebeest whirl about in the dust. A jackal comes and trots about alongside us while the sun sunders the clouds above Gelai in glory, painting the sky with its golden rays unfolded like a fan. Intoxication and freedom in the fresh air.

Our azimuth soon converges with that of two morans who popped out from nowhere. They are apparently going in the same direction we are, toward the angle of the southeast shore of Lake Natron. These are initiates, draped in their flamboyant red toga, armed with a spear, a double-edged sword, a club, and a staff. They come up to us with no hurry or timidity. Their names are Paulo and Maya. Guardian angels, sent by ours. They are younger than their appearance, from a distance, would make you expect. We inform them of our intentions. It doesn't seem to impress them. We set out together, improvising a course in the Maasai language. Paulo has been to school, he can speak Swahili and bits and pieces of English. He is tall and svelte, he does not have pierced ears and does not wear the traditional braids. I question him.

"At the government school," he replies, "they tell us that our culture is bad, and that it is bad to have your ears pierced..."

"And what do you think?"

"Here, it bothers me to be a bit different from my brothers,[1] but when I was in school, they would have made fun of me if I had had pierced ears, they would have called me a donkey, since the ears of a donkey are notched so they can be recognized. One thing is sure, I am happier here, dressed in *ol karasha*, with my spear and my brother. I feel at home."

"Is Paulo a Christian name?"

"Yes, in my family we are both Christian and Maasai, Enkai is the god who gave us all the livestock in the world, and Jesus is his son: the chief of shepherds, the good shepherd of all humanity."

His "brother" Maya is a skipping little squirt who is wearing the traditional braid gathered in the back into a point. His temples are shaven very high and on his forehead a little fringe comes down, also pointed. His ears are deeply notched. The loop of flesh thus created is weighted down by two copper nuggets that swing on his shoulders at each step. He has more jewels than Paulo, he has not been to school and is not a Christian. He believes only in Maasai wisdom. He conceives a friendship for Sonia and instinctively places himself to her right as if to protect her from danger, as a bodyguard would do in a crowd for a star. My star.

With these friends, we learn that the red toga is called a *karasha*, that the morans' spear is called an *eremet*, that the club is an *orinka* and the sword an *olalem*. I ogle the latter, the singular form of which is nothing like the *made in China* pangas or *diamond* machetes that you find everywhere in Africa. The end is broad and rounded, giving weight to the blade sharpened on both sides, which tapers, narrowing towards a handle no wider than a finger, in a sheath made of gut. The straight scabbard is covered in burgundy leather that matches perfectly with the karasha. Our young Cerberi, wearing tire sandals, step right along. The wind whips their tunics, tied

---

[1] The Maasai "fraternity" is based on age groups and not on blood lines. The true brother is the one which whom you have been raised, and not the one with whom you share a father.

on one shoulder like Roman togas and attached at the waist by a belt. Over it, they cover themselves in another burgundy checkered sheet. The ensemble is not a product of chance, it is the result of constant esthetic attention. They are fascinated by Sonia, her blonde hair, her freedom, her strength, her "masculinity" – the morans live in manyattas, men's bomas installed somewhat back from the villages, where, for the three to six years they spend with their age group, they have not the right to associate with the girls.

Lengai lords it over this countryside. We soon reach the dried-up banks of Lake Natron, with its variable geometry. It began to recede at the end of the rainy season; by now it is reduced to its minimal size. Millions of footprints exfoliate the dry, crunchy sludge under our feet like potato chips. Far from prying eyes, Paulo and Maya willingly lend themselves – one time doesn't set a precedent – to the image game. Proudly even. We are in seventh heaven. In the six days we have been in Maasai country, the only pictures we have taken are of landscapes....

Sonia comes and unfastens the tripod attached by Velcro to the outside of my backpack, and while she sets it up, I get her camera out of her belly pack, make sure the lens is clean, and disengage the autofocus. We screw the Nikon onto the socket and put the tripod in place. The frame is splendid on the Lengai background. I zoom with the 28/200 to make the volcano larger in the lens. I move back the plastic jerrycan so it won't ruin the photo and ask Sonia to take her place about fifteen meters away, on the left edge of the frame. I then ask her to take a few steps forward to estimate where we will be when the shutter takes the photo, for we do not want a static picture but a dynamic one. I then ask her to stop, so I can focus on her. And I reframe in function of that. Already Paulo and Maya have no idea what's going on and laugh under their breath. It's in such moments that Sonia and I have disagreements, when the sweat is running into my closed right eye, when my knee on the ground hits a pebble, when the weight of my backpack prevents me from leaning forward over the camera, when a fly is buzzing around my nostril, when I am too tired to make myself clear and she gets annoyed at my contradictory instructions: "Move back, move up, to the right! No, to *my* right, which means to your left. No, that's *your* right! OK, stop!"

When it is sharp, I set the camera to "aperture priority" and I bracket until I get an acceptable shutter reading, 1/125 or 1/90, not difficult in such luminosity, all this to obtain maximum depth of field and therefore maximal sharpness. I then check with the depth of field button whether the background of the Lengai is good and sharp. Perrrfect! Don't move. In automatic mode there would be too great a risk of the camera focusing by itself on infinity or snapping the shutter too soon, which would reduce the depth of field and the chance we would be in focus. Taking a picture is easy after all...

Now that everything is ready, the hardest part remains: explaining to Paulo and Maya what we intend to do, then do a dry run to see whether they have rightly understood; return to the camera, count to ten, start walking at seven or eight, when I join them, tell them: "When we start, you start! *Kutembéa twendé!*" – stay lined up, so we won't overlap in the picture, don't look at the camera but straight ahead, as if everything were normal, and return to take our places at the starting point for a second try. Super, they have understood! When all is ready at least ten minutes and a few hundred calories have gone by. And nothing yet has been done. And the photo is not yet taken. So I go take my place behind the camera, which is set up fairly far from the scene since long lenses are more flattering, warmer, and denser on the principal subjects: the four of us. But that means I have to sprint to be five or six seconds later in the axis of the walk at their sides. I set the delay to ten seconds, press the button and rush to my position while counting out loud. With a wink I indicate to Paulo and Maya that this is the moment, that we finally can start walking; out of the corner of our eyes we check the blinking diode that announces the end of the ten seconds by ceasing to blink, two steps later we hear the fateful click of the curtain, and now, we have to try in a flash to see ourselves from an outside point of view to picture whether the collective composition was right, that I was not hiding Sonia, that Sonia was not hiding Maya.

Sonia confesses: "At the instant it clicked, I looked at Paulo because he was looking at the camera..."

"We have to do it over!"

And we do it over. With a digital camera we could have a look at the photo and avoid doing it several times, but we only have a classic slide camera, so it's a question of feeling. Good or not good? So we start over as many times as our physical state allows, as many times as our morale permits, proportional to our humor: ten times if we are hypochondriacal, three or four times if we are nonchalant. This morning with Paulo and Maya is different, we are sure we have our cover shot, we pass sixteen times in front of the lens....By the end it's no good in any case because our two buddies are doubled over with laughter, very much thinking, "The Olashumpaï are truly all nuts, even the ones who walk!" Once the photo is taken, as the framc is already in place, we repeat the same thing with the movie camera for our films. While we're at it! But that's less difficult; we can control the shot, the autofocus takes care of the sharpness, the shutter the light, and the sequence lasts fifteen to twenty seconds. So that is merely a formality, except if we have a text to include and we have to set up the mike, its hood to absorb the wind noise, and avoid a slip of the tongue at the moment of the shot.

Halfway through Africa Trek, we have taken as many photos as kilometers covered, more than seven thousand, but fortunately not all with the timer, which is to say how familiar we are with that little exercise, and to say also to what extent we work, sweat and run in all directions. Most travelers and adventurers today do not bother with such exhausting gymnastics, this equipment, and it's easy to see why. They have professionals sent from their capital city to spend a few days along their itinerary to carry out impeccable work with much better equipment. How right they are! But we are not yet ready to make that sacrifice of our creative freedom. Taking pictures is also part of the adventure.

Before us, in whirlwinds of dust, wildebeest are prancing drunk with freedom madness. An overly large, frowning head, hiding two small eyes, close together, a little silly-looking, beneath little horns sticking up, and mounted on a thick torso that extends toward a ridiculous rump. Their awkward gallop makes their hunchback silhouettes hiccup like running old men, you can't tell whether they are gray, beige or black; the hair of their little goatee matches their tattered mane and bushy tail. It all adds up to a bizarre chimera, but they are wildebeest, who are such appropriate symbols of these eternal, primitive spaces. Pink flamingos quiver in a mirage, on the lake, far away. The reflection cuts off their legs, and makes for a pink horizon floating on a coat of mercury, out of which a shivaree of feathers rises in waves. Our Maasai friends are singing.

Maya suddenly stops in the middle of nowhere. "*Amekufa simba hapa kwa kumi na mbiri morani, umekula yangu mbuzi.*" (I killed a lion here, with twelve brothers. He had eaten some of my goats.)

We immediately see this scrawny fourteen-year-old with new eyes. Not everyone has the luck to own a Playstation....An hour later, we climb up from the banks of the lake toward Gelai, an immense extinct volcano on the east shore of the lake, which we are going to follow for two days.

The trees have made their appearance, *lahai* acacias, with their parasol branches and red trunks, and *seyal* acacias with impressive double thorns. Rather than continue northward alone, we follow our friends; the sun is beginning to hit hard and they know where they are going. We soon perceive animation, goats, morans. One of them is escorting through the grass two Smurfs in navy blue uniforms returning from school. For this too is the morans' mission, they are at the service of the community and must assure the protection of children, women and livestock against wild animals. Something is troubling Sonia.

"A school, here?"

"Yes, it is the Romani enkang."

"Romani?"

"Yes. Here, everyone is Catholic."

!!!

We soon come to a small enkang inhabited by only one family. The architecture of the hut is not the same as elsewhere: this one is a two-story bark cupola on piles, better ventilated; the ground floor for the kitchen and storage, the upstairs, like an igloo tent, for sleep on cowhides. Maria, a splendid, tall Maasai, whose ties to Paulo are unclear – is she his mother, his aunt or his sister? – greets us in the shade of a tree, in her boma. Heavy plates of beads circle her neck. In her cut earlobes are hooked unbelievable architectures of earrings embellished with little chains on the ends of which dangle metallic facets that animate each movement of her head with innumerable reflections, like a lure. Her shaved scalp accentuates the depth of her somewhat emaciated gaze and her straightforward smile. We pause to chat under this tree, with this splendor from another planet; we are happy. When everything is more calm, at the white sun hour, we gulp down some noodle soup, which makes us sweat great drops.

We are told that further north are hordes of lions, no path and very few enkangs. And we have no spear. I try to buy one when Maciar, a fierce warrior with a scarred face, joins us under the tree. He is to go to Kenya. He was awaiting another moran before leaving, but accepts the idea of making do with two *olas-humpaïs* nomads. We let the solar fire pass and head off again. Paulo and Maya have disappeared. It bothers us somewhat to leave our friends behind this way, but that is only an old western cultural reflex: why, indeed, say *au revoir* when you know you will never meet again...? The Maasai separate without ado, but on the other hand exult with joy at reunions and for long minutes repeat to each other extravagant formulas of civility that go back as much as seven generations!

We are walking due north with Maciar, following the wild

shoreline. Life is teeming. Flocks of seedeaters, small gregarious sparrows, pirouette in dense clouds, like starlings, hares take off under our feet, when it isn't bolting quails that makes us jump. Innumerable limicoline birds jabber in the slime, ducks, geese, wading birds, sacred ibises, the whole avifauna of Africa has chosen to meet at the Lake Natron banquet. Fluorescent green bee-eaters pirouette in the grass tops like swallows. Across the trail rectilinear streams of about five hundred meters in length spring forth from the hot alkaline springs that carve their way toward the lake through the dried silt encrusted with salt. Fish are teeming there, which herons spear and kingfishers dive-bomb; a martial eagle takes flight at our approach. It is neither rainwater nor filtration water. It is a mineral water that comes from the Earth's entrails because of its heating and dilation. It is nevertheless crystalline. I taste a drop on my tongue, Maciar makes a face. It is very salty and laden with unknown minerals, at the temperature of hot tea. How do the fish that we see abounding everywhere manage to live when the lake is lethal to them? They cannot go there. That means that their ecosystem, their world, is this five-hundred-meter stream? For how long, how many millennia have they been reproducing thus? They look like the cichlids of Lake Malawi.[2] We go on, quite bowled over by this miracle of survival and adaptation...

In the declining daylight and the golden feathertops of the blazing grasses, we once more mix in with herds of zebras and gazelles which, at night, gravitate toward men to get away from the big cats. That is a spectacle we never tire of. We are conscious of treading a world that knows not the rifle. Animals bolt when we approach, and stop fifty or a hundred meters further on; this little game of stop-and-go goes on and on. The minimal tolerated distance is that of an arrow's flight or the acceleration range of a

---

[2] See vol. I, p. 312. We have since learned that it was *Oreochromis alcalicus grahami*, a one-time freshwater variety, which over time adapted to the very alkaline scalding water.

big cat. That is the standard of this space. It is prehistoric. At the outer limit of that reach, game feels safe.

His ears alert, Maciar soon has located an enkang; herds and girls are converging on it, following a ritual with which we are becoming familiar. In this hostile world, hospitality is natural, that's obvious. One can also tell that these particular Maasai receive few visits. For the handful of children present, we are the first olashumpaïs. They are fascinated. We are indeed backstage of the decor, at thirty-six kilometers from the Engaré Sero camp, where thousands of olashumpaïs come calling every year. The world, more and more covered by the global web, by the network of roads, the mesh of threads, the information channels, the trading axes, remains enclosed, virgin and wild. To find adventure you only have to walk between the threads, between the links in the net.

"What is this called here?"

"Lamendea."

Lamendea....Wherever there are men, the earth has a name. We are walking also for that, the poetry of topography. How many local names have we recorded this way? We recite them to our guests by order of distance, they always know the first two or three, rarely the following ones and are delighted that we should not have forgotten the closest ones, since they understand that we will not forget Lamendea. We put up the tent in an abandoned enclosure. Night has fallen. Rice with onion chunks and carrot soup tonight, after some restorative tea.

The bag of rice tears. Maciar, squatting beside Sonia, helps her silently, and I watch their hands peck in the circle of light from our headlamps, busy saving the magic grains of this cereal come from elsewhere, from a world where the fields are lakes. And from this harvest of rice grains, from this black hand and this white hand gleaning grams of life, from this harmless and silent scene emanates a violent poetry. A crescent moon rises over Gelai, a jackal yelps, the fire hisses, the water boils, the drum of zebra hoof-beats echoes around us in the bush, night settling in.

Sesaï, Maasai enkang, Kenya, Tuesday 16 July 2002, day 565, 50 km, 7254ᵗʰ km

This morning, at dawn, we are walking in the footsteps of lions. Not phantasms of lions on territories where they are maybe there and maybe not; real lions, really present! This is the seventh time. Still can't get used to it. A whole pride. It isn't far away. Fortunately, we are with Maciar. Our warrior studies the landscape with his built-in scanner, sniffs the wind and comes and points his sharp eyes into the dust. So many footprints that he can't make heads or tails of them. A right forepaw left there during some stomping around is the largest footprint we have ever seen: terrifying. And it is fresh. The decor is typical, they could be anywhere. We advance together. In doubt, I have drawn my flares, a way of getting used to the idea. Like a cowboy from a low-budget movie, I simulate a firing stance, arms extended, trigger set, accompanied by Maciar's overt laughter, just trying to exorcize my fear. He walks with a swaying stride, like a punk, perched on cricket calves. He seems to know the slightest details of the landscape, to recognize the tiniest pebbles, where we see nothing at all. He inspects everything, continually, like a wading bird pecking grains in a field, methodical and concentrated. He goes faster than we do but stops every fifteen minutes under an acacia to wait a minute for us, seated on our jerrycan of water which he is carrying to help us. And when the distance increases, our unease increases too. Intermittently, we cast a glance over our shoulders. I am last in line. Sonia catches me looking: "Are you afraid?"

"Yes! Beyond shame, yes!"

I shouldn't let her see that, since she is afraid of my fear. But there is no reason I should be scared still all alone. I could hide this fear under some pretense, but no, I know fear is salutary. It is the tension that keeps our senses alert, prepares us for the worst, for attack, could help us brave danger in the calmest way. Fear is a survival reflex. To fear nothing is to be suicidal. Sonia tries to reassure herself: "Lions apparently can tell the difference between an armed

Maasai and a Maasai without a spear, and are deathly frightened of armed Maasai."

"Sure! Maybe...we'll ask them..."

We walk in silence. As the hours go by, the level of our water bottles and the jerrycan that Maciar is carrying is dropping. However we ration ourselves, it is hot and rehydration is indispensable. How are we going to find some water? We thought we understood, in last night's discussions, that there would be nobody between here and Kenya. Nonetheless, another Maasai came with us by enchantment. They know each other. It's a little hard for us to understand them because Maciar only knows a few words of Swahili. They talk about lions. The other guy seems to have seen them. My heart skips a beat: *"Iko wapi simba?"* (Where were the lions?)

"Simba lala karibu njia, chakula punda milia usiku!" (They were sleeping close to the path, they ate a zebra during the night.)

They had drifted off near the carcass of a zebra, their bellies full of meat, within a stone's throw of the trail. They watched us go by; we had not even seen them. A hint of something in Maciar's eye, like a flash of retrospective fury and fear, makes me think that he knew, that he had sensed them but hadn't said anything to us about it. From afar, they might have sensed our terror. So the lions really fear the Maasai like the plague. Maybe they crouched in the tall grasses because we were passing by.

Towards noon, our two guides seem to be leading us astray on a rocky platform radiating heat. They have a big powwow, discuss the orientation, look for a passage between the blocks of burning stone, until the moment when we come across a dry river bed carved into a small gorge. The companion whose name we don't remember begins to dig in the gravel with broad movements of his hands held flat. It goes faster than we expected, and, at fifty centimeters, water appears, life. It is indeed captive water. Rainwater that has stayed here on this rocky base, in this mass of fine gravel, since the meager rains of last year. I film the scene, Sonia comments: "OK, it's not really a problem, it's just a little brown..."

I jump in turn into the hole, with our Platypus bottle.[3]

"No, no, look, Sonia, there is clear water here. Nice water filtered by volcanic sediments, it's Volvic!"

For millennia, men have been doing just this: filling *guerbas* with water, except that ours is plastic.…We leave with light hearts and a heavier backpack. The heat is torrid today, since there isn't any breeze, not a hint of fresh air. Lake Natron is like oil. Scattered flamingos hem in pink the mirror of the banks. We walk without stopping in this heat, like the damned, for the other Maasai has confirmed before disappearing as naturally as he had appeared that there is nobody before Kenya. Sonia wonders. "It's unbelievable! It's as if that guy had turned up just to find us some water…"

Right in the middle of the afternoon, beaten down with heat, the head numb, hypoglycemic, we beg for mercy; the Maasai are walking machines, honed for endurance, light, limber and speedy. They can walk a hundred kilometers without drinking or stopping. In the emaciated shade of a commiphora and before Maciar's eyes, we make quick work of some noodle soup. He doesn't want to taste it, he points at the noodles and makes a face: "*Vidudu!* Ugh! *Vidudu!*"

We don't know this word. Sonia looks in our little Swahili dictionary and soon exclaims: "Worms! He thinks they're worms!"

We laugh to our hearts' content. We set off again on a plateau along the Lake, toward Shompole, a little volcano planted in the middle of the Rift, which is getting surely closer. We soon have an open view over the lake. We can finally appreciate the pink tones, due to the presence of a microscopic alga. The successive shores of the lake, each time reduced by the drought, have left white haloes of salt that fringe the perimeter like the motifs of a giant agate. In the middle of the lake, the conglomerates of chloride and sodium carbonate resemble coral reefs on a sea of blood. An absolutely striking spectacle, beginning and end of the world, universe of

---

[3] Very handy collapsible plastic bottles that can be flattened when empty.

eruptions and cataclysms in a nature still far from being appeased. Despite the fatigue, we step up our pace. Maciar seems to want to find a boma at any cost, he knows the price of sleeping in the open. Despite that, at the fortieth kilometer, night catches up with us. He perseveres. He wants someone. A half-moon is a help. Meanwhile we lose the path, find it again, lose it again, look in the dark for goat footprints that would betray the presence of men in the vicinity. Like a bloodhound, he has his eyes riveted to the ground. The moon, still low, reveals precise little reliefs left in the fine dust. He recognizes the footprints of morans' sandals by means of their degree of wear or the model of tires from which they were cut. Very quickly, this becomes a game among us. He gives them names, pretends to recognize buddies. When he has a trail, we follow it for several kilometers, notably the footprints of a guy whose right big toe, doubtless misshapen or broken, sticks out of the sandal and prints itself very clearly on the ground. That one is betrayed by his footprints. In the sky, straight up, ever this nocturnal airplane that passes, blinking, each night a little later. It is eight-fifteen, we have been seeing it for four days. It must be the Dodoma–Nairobi. Is it late? No, we are advancing by five minutes a day…

While walking thus in silence, we trigger precipitous flights in the bush. We recognize the animals, without seeing them, by their sound signatures, the trot of zebras that take off with a quarter-turn, the giraffes, with their heavy syncopated rhythm, that stop and start again, the flurries of gazelles, they all make our hearts shudder. We advance madly. Maciar is even more stressed out than we are. A bad sign. It is true that he has not swallowed much today, a few cookies and pieces of candy that we gave him. That's not much. He must be starting to hallucinate about a nice *inkukurto* of smoked milk. I have got out my lighting flares again. You're never prudent enough. Sonia would rather stop anywhere. The hyenas don't keep her from sleeping. We forge ahead in the blue night inhabited by shadows elongated by the moon into crooked specters.

We advance like robots on automatic pilot, our attention

flagging, behind our mad trailblazer, when suddenly he stops before a smaller footprint, smoother and oblong, finely striped crosswise on the path: "A hairless cow!"[4]

He is euphoric. If there are women hereabouts, it means that the enkangs are not far away. We start walking again, more vigorously. Soon after, he listens carefully with his long-lobed ear and, in the emptiness, seems to hear songs and conversations. That's it, we say to ourselves, we've made it, but it goes on and nothing happens. On nights with viscous moons, sound carries far. A half-hour later, we finally reach, exhausted, the palisade of wood and thorns of an enkang. A quick glance at the pedometer: we have gone fifty kilometers. We hear soft voices in the enkaji, Maciar says timidly: "*Hodi!*"

This is the way you announce that you are outside. No answer. I repeat, a little louder: "*Hodi!*"

Silence and stupor inside. They have recognized my bizarre accent.

"*Karibu!*" replies someone, who immediately comes out.

A giant Maasai, head shaved and fine teeth. He bursts out laughing when he sees us, pale in the moonlight. Our two compatriots quickly exchange salutations and accounts of the day, rapid-fire, punctuated with salvos of laughter; the whole household has come out of the enkaji to see the olashumpaïs. When the pace slows down, I ask our host: "*Kenya hapa?*" (Are we in Kenya?)

"*Ndio! Enkang Sesaï.*" (Yes, the village is Sesai.)

Without realizing it, under the stars, at the foot of Shompole, as in the days when there were no borders, we have entered Kenya. Our sixth country. Sonia exclaims: "Three countries from now, we will be at Israel's door!"

"No! Not already!"

"Oh yes: Ethiopia, Sudan, and Egypt!"

"It's true....But it's a lot to take in..."

---

[4] One of the ways of designating women in the Maasai language.

Our hosts chuckle, hearing us speak a mysterious tongue. And at our ritual – it is our custom to embrace when we have crossed a border, something that is not done in the Maasai culture. Instead of being shocked, our hosts are rolling on the ground laughing.

"*Karibu! Karibu!*" (Come on in! Welcome!)

The big guy pulls back with one hand the big thorny branch that closes his enclosure, slapping his thigh with the other. It's party time tonight in Sesai!

Before we set up the tent, we are invited into the enkaji. Right over the threshold, the little corridor makes a turn, so you can't see what is going on inside, any more than light can enter. The central room with its fireplace is surrounded by cells separated by partitions. Each one is a bed of branches covered by superposed cowhides. We have been shown to one. The leather is dry and smooth, shaved of its hair; it crackles and grates under our weight. Large branches are burnt at one end; they encumber the ground and everyone must step over them to take a place around the fire. With a precise and subtle movement, the lady of the house separates two pieces of wood the points of which had come together when I stumbled into them, so as to relight the flame extinguished by my awkwardness. The small space is quickly filled with smoke, since there is no evacuation means. The mud roof being hermetic, you wonder by what miracle we are not all asphyxiated. You never stand up for very long in an enkaji, with the smoke swimming in thick sheets under the ceiling. The temperature rises fast. The mother fixes us some very strong black tea, soon followed by an *inkukurto* of *kule naïrowua*, fresh milk sweet as honey and scented with violet. While manipulating her objects, she sings; her lovely round face turns golden each time that, coming out of the shadow, she exposes it to the fire. We do not tire of looking at her. Her necklaces hang, her earrings and bracelets jangle in unison, her toga comes loose. Her stool is a small rusted can turned upside down and unstable, the utensils are scattered around on the ground, the walls are dirty and sooty, encumbered with clusters of gourds and spiderwebs burdened with soot but, like an orchestra director in this dark and cluttered room, she remains neat, skilled, her movements slow and efficient at the same time. A sublime domestic dance. Now she grabs a long, empty gourd behind her, turns it over, makes sure by tapping on it that it has no dust in it, and pours into it a big handful of wild olive pits. Using a small plier, she grasps some embers which she then inserts in the narrow neck, then using a long stem, stirs this strange mixture in the bottom of the calabash for a long time. A young Maasai strings us along: "The purpose of that is to sterilize. That's what gives *kulé naaoto*, our traditional yogurt, its smoky flavor."

We sing late into the night with this cheerful, hospitable family, sharing stories of lions and malaria, telling of Lengai in front of batteries of pupils twinkling in the dark, for no one, in Sesai, has been to its summit.

The night is fair and gentle. Tanzania, that land so feared, so beloved, is over. How far now is the southern border with Malawi! When we said to ourselves: "And what is on the other side? There is Kili!" How many kilometers behind us, how many turns of events, how much has been learned! Even more than in descending from Africa's summit, we have the feeling tonight that a page is turning and that we have taken a giant step.

This morning, we are in a hurry. The children of the family also, who are being washed before putting on their school uniforms. Royal blue is here replaced by green shorts and a yellow shirt. Like all the children in the world, they balk at getting cleaned up, struggle when their mother insists they blow their nose or clean their ears. A young mother is nursing her two sons, one of fourteen months, the other of two years. To each his breast. The two babies then cuddle and caress each other. There was another billy-goat tonight, but my sleep is apparently becoming selective since I could hear him without it awakening me. We are in a hurry to get back on the road, since we are one day late for an appointment with Alexandra,

Sonia's younger sister, who has come from France to share a few kilometers with us in Kenya. At Shompole, our first Kenyan village, we look for a car to go get her in Nairobi. Since we entered the country illegally, we must also get ourselves regularized. There are no cars expected today. We are stuck. We have to wait.

As we are strolling through the market, observing the differences of costume between the Tanzanian Maasai and the Kenyan Maasai, two green Land Cruisers come flying into the village. A handsome kid with the arms of a dock worker, the suntan of a brawler and an Ultrabrite smile, comes bursting into a greasy spoon, soon right back out and heads for us: "Do you need any help?"

We give him the résumé. He can't believe it, calls his boss Anthony 1 (he is Anthony 2). The solution is quick in coming:

"We are going to Nairobi tomorrow, in the meantime, come get rested, we have a lodge on the escarpment, near here; it's a privilege to have you…"

Is life not even crazier than the craziest of novels? Walk! Everything happens.

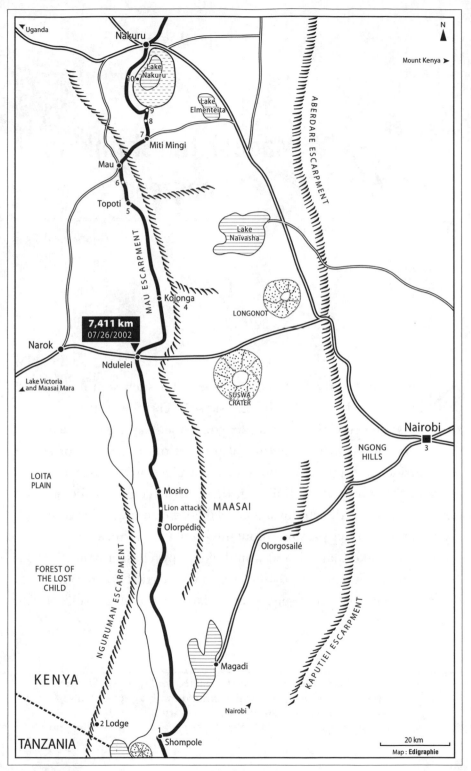

South Kenya

CHAPTER 8

Magadi, the Shrinking Shagreen[1]

Nairobi on the fly. Just enough time, after such solitude and deserts, to be terrified by the skyscrapers, the traffic jams, the horns concerts of the *matatus*[2] going mad, and gather with Alexandra and Baptiste. The time also to get our passports sorted out. Anxious and guilty, we presented ourselves at the thirteenth story of the Immigration Building, right in the center of the city, before the highest director available: "Hello, we entered your country illegally, without passing through a border post, between Lake Natron and Lake Magadi, and would like to purchase a visa…"

"No problem. I am exactly the person you need. Take this paper downstairs and pay the twenty-five dollars for the visa. Welcome in Kenya!"

??!!

---

[1] In Balzac's 1831 novel *Peau de chagrin* (translated as *The Magic Skin* or *The Wild Ass's Skin*), a magic shagreen, which embodies its owner's lifeline, has the power to grant wishes, but shrinks with each use.

[2] Collective private taxis, intended for eleven people but often carrying more than twenty.

Never seen such an easygoing country. Never got a formality taken care of so quickly.

We return quickly to Shompole to resume the thread of our trek. We are not too fond of this sort of "trafficking" with our operation, but could not ask Baptiste and Alexandra to meet us in the open bush. And it is wonderful to have visitors. It helps us to hang in there. The greatest sacrifice in this sort of travel is family. Having them come is a good compromise since we do not wish to go back to France, interrupt the adventure, cut it into slices. It seems important to us to walk out this itinerary "in the footsteps of Man," from his origins to now, from the Australopithecus to modern man, in a continuous process, to replicate symbolically the first trip of the first men at this beginning of the third millennium, not to give in to the current penchant for mocking space to fill the time, since we want to mock time to fill the space, cover it, live it: to restore to space a time on a human scale. Nor do we wish to succumb to the song of the media Sirens who sing to us this well-known air: "Your films don't sell without you, we are beginning to forget you, you ought to come back and do some promotion..." No, no, and no!

Under a leaden sun, we take off from the greasy spoon where we met Anthony 2. Anthony 1 has asked one of the Maasai whom he employs in his nature reserve to accompany us. For one thing, he feels responsible for us, and for another he has had the idea of proposing to his clients a little hike in the bush and wants to try out the qualities of a potential guide. We offer him the perfect opportunity to be his hiking guinea pigs. In passing, he had shown us from the car three lionesses perched like leopards in a huge fig tree...

John Masikonté Ntiiti is delighted to walk with us. He must, in any case, go spend his one-month leave with his family which has a piece of land on the escarpment of Mau, two hundred kilometers farther north. He speaks perfect English: "No road crosses these Maasai territories, so normally I am obliged to make an immense detour through Nairobi, to change matatus three or four times;

that takes me at least two days and I detest it! Besides, on foot it will give me the opportunity to go through remote regions I don't know. All things being equal, I would rather walk than garden."

"Aren't you guarding the game reserve?"

"There is nothing to guard here. The animals are safe, no poacher would risk it in this vicinity. In fact, at this moment, I help in the gardens and kitchen gardens, since almost all the vegetables consumed here are produced here. I have a degree in greenhouse agriculture with a speciality in micro-dripping.[3]

"But I thought the Maasai were not allowed to work the soil?" asks Sonia.

"Today, we no longer have a choice. It is better to learn to do it ourselves on a small scale, using an up-to-date technology that allows us to grow products rich in vitamins, like tomatoes, carrots, parsley or onions, than to import Kikuyu or Kamba workers who would come settle here with their families, create villages, end up tilling their own parcels, letting their goats loose and upsetting our society's fragile equilibrium. In any case, we are not about to plant corn or wheat in these deserts, so it isn't really agriculture, it's more like gardening.

I sense that our walk with him is going to be fascinating. He incarnates the paradox of a traditional society that wants to remain so without at the same time being relegated to the role of poor relative in a society blinded by the mirages of modernism. And he is finally going to answer the numerous questions we have asked ourselves in the course of our sojourn with our Maasai friends of Tanzania, with whom the conversations were limited to the vital minimum.

The bottom of the Rift, in the Magadi plain, is one of the most hostile places on the planet. The shock is harsh for Alexandra and Baptiste, who have just arrived from Paris. One is a travel journalist, gracious as a tiny squaw with large brown eyes, and the other

---

[3] Drip irrigation (watering by means of a drop-by-drop system that saves water).

is a lieutenant in the merchant marine, debonair blue eyes and a smile on his lips, even if he is more accustomed to being at the helm of a supertanker than slogging through the desert. But I am not worried; with John, we are in good hands. What intellectual comfort to be able to rely entirely on someone! A guide! This is the first time that has happened in seven thousand kilometers.

We five set out northward, circumnavigating to the right a dense forest thick with thorny bushes. John is bearing a moran spear which he holds on his shoulder, a fine red karasha, an olalem and a club. To serve as a gourd, hooked to his schoolboy backpack, he has a little round, red calabash. He too walks in traditional sandals made from a tire.

"Yesterday a horde of elephants and buffalo by the dozen were spotted foraging near the Ewaso Ngiro River. It's better not to encounter them!"

To the left rises the imposing and interminable Nguruman escarpment, which we are going to follow north as far as it goes. It will be our safety railing. It is there that the mythical "forest of the lost child" is located, the spiritual center of the Maasai culture, and an important political issue. On our right spread the whitish and pinkish expanses of the Magadi salt marshes. The water still free seems to be so laden with minerals that it is viscous and black like a tinted glass. A few flamingos dance on this mirror like skaters in training. John comments: "You aren't going to believe me, but the sodium carbonate has been commercialized here for sixty-five years, and the deposit is growing!"

In the distance, the chimneys of a large factory disfigure this virginal landscape.

"In fact, more than four thousand tons of natron are deposited here every day by percolation from the alkaline water: the deposit is endless."

"What is sodium carbonate used for?" asks Baptiste.

"It is an indispensable component in the manufacture of glass; once transformed, it is called soda; three hundred thousand tons are exported per year to the entire world! Unfortunately, as Maasais we get no benefit from this wealth exploited on our territory."

Towards noon, we pass a fisherman's cabin. Its occupant is putting a strange variety of prehistoric catfish out to dry: lungfish, fish capable of surviving in the slime between two rainy seasons, since their branchiae are supplemented by small lungs. He has smoked them; they are dry and golden. We take a few for the coming days. John makes a grimace of disgust: "You're not going to eat those things, are you?"

"Sure! Smoked fish is really good," suggests Alexandra.

"Not for the Maasai, it's like eating snakes."

All day, John reveals to us secret aspects of his culture, an extremely complex one. We speak of initiation and excision rituals – which we will not see, since it's not the season – of the *eunoto* that celebrates the end of the morans' "military service," so much so that, not noticing the time going by, we do not realize that we are dehydrated. The evening finds us all knotted up in cramps and pains. Baptiste is already limping on a big blister, but doesn't lose his smile. John lodges us in the enkang of one of his aunts. We collapse from fatigue. In the reddish moonlight a flight of pink flamingos goes past heading south.

Olorpedio Enkang, 24 July 2002, day 573, 31 km, 7347th km

This is our third day walking with John. He remains inexhaustible. The landscape is bleak and flat, hot and dotted with emaciated acacias. The Nguruman escarpment, far to our left, isn't enough to beautify our daily fare. We trek from enkang to enkang, each time provoking surprise. As a sign of respect to the elders, children come in a procession to present their hot skulls to us so we can place a hand on them, as for a blessing; while so doing, they whisper to each other and have trouble refraining from their charming chortles. They have never seen any Whites. John's presence facilitates things, since he introduces us and constantly deciphers, but also creates an enormous gap between us and the Maasai we encounter.

We become in a way spectators of our trek. The relationships are less close, he always finds a way for us to sleep outside, or isolated from people. We discover group life. There are five of us; we indeed form a group. A small group for sure, but that changes everything. The welcome is no longer the same, the exchange is more distant. We need to be more autonomous. Sonia and her beloved little sister talk all day long. They have never experienced such a long separation. There is time to make up for, so many stories to tell.

The Maasai costumes have changed. Here the karashas are more varied and colorful than in Tanzania, where they were all more or less the same type. Here there are more cottons imported from central Africa. The severity of the blood reds is often dressed up with fabrics with big flowers in garish colors or, even more daring, the famous red toga is replaced by a pink, canary yellow, or apple green sheet. Sonia expresses her astonishment to John.

"You know, the Maasai style evolves, we have not always been robed in red. Look at photos of the 1960s and 1970s. At that time, we were all wearing chestnut, leathers or dyed fabrics with natural ochres. The red dates from the 1980s, from the importation of Indian fabrics. It is true that we like red, but our culture is alive and inclusive, as are the necklaces or bracelets; the codes and combinations are endless, it's like fashion in your country, and it comes back in cycles! There are only certain parts that remain unchanging."

The heat is becoming overwhelming. We are walking on scatterings of little blocks of lava dispersed on ash covered with yellow grass. It has the odor characteristic of saunas, with this touch of vetiver contributed by the dried grass.

Seated on a knoll, a moran waves to us. We go over to him. He has an eye really messed up by an acacia thorn planted directly in the white part, now red. He asks us for medicine. The thorn is still there, so it seems. I can see a segment of it above the surface of the cornea. I am afraid that, if I touch it, the eye will explode and empty all at once, the way Irene's hand had in Makoumba.[4]

---

[4] See vol. I, p. 338.

"How long has he had it?"

"A week…"

"If he doesn't go to the hospital, he's going to lose the eye."

We leave him some eye drops and some Diantalvic pills. What else can we do? We too are on reprieve. Here everything is aggressive, the plants, the sun, the dusty air. Today, the latest discovery of Africa Trek is speargrass: a vicious grass the seeds of which are little arrows equipped with tongs and barbs that work their way into stockings by the hundreds and go in deeper with every movement toward the flesh. When they have found it, they burrow into the dermis and intend to stay there. The torture is unbearable and immobilizes us every kilometer. We must then pick them out patiently, shredding our socks. In comparison, the prickly heads of burdock and other scratchy hairs are angelic velvet.

Sonia remarks: "It's not surprising that Maasai grass should be armed with little spears.…Either we need gaiters or we need to walk in sandals, like John, but that would mean exposing ourselves to all the other scrapes and dangerous acacia thorns."

Suddenly, while we are busy with this fastidious exercise, she raises a finger in the air.

"Didn't you hear the sound of a spring?"

"You're dreaming. A spring in this desert?"

John returns from behind a bush.

"Yes, there is a faucet nearby…"

"A faucet?"

We rush to the spot. The vision is surreal: alone in these desolate spaces stands a faucet like a cobra on its tail that fills a little round lake. No settlements, no settlers, nothing but desperately dry savannah and this faucet filling a lake.…We burst out laughing.

"What's funny?" asks John.

"Who made that?"

"It's an Italian NGO. They brought a pipe down for fifteen kilometers from the Nguruman escarpment. To provide water for the cows."

"But why not fill troughs when the cows are here and close the faucet when there is no one? Or else install the faucet in a village?"

"In the Maasai culture, we consider that we don't have the right to arrest water or to appropriate it to ourselves, it belongs only to Enkai. Otherwise it would create jealousies. Besides, sleeping water is full of diseases, not running water. There is no one here because the enkangs never are allowed to install themselves closer than three kilometers from a spring, so that all the villages will have equal access to it. And that is just a spring brought here by a pipe."

"But all the same, you could save water, shut the faucet..."

"It's broken."

"What if it gets repaired?"

"It will immediately be broken again for the reasons I just gave."

"But you, the specialist of drop-by-drop, what do you think of it?"

"Oh, that has no connection, that's for the cows!"

We see three today of these cornucopias pouring their precious manna into the volcanic ash. If you think about it, in any case this water that comes from Nguruman and the forest of the lost child has but one destination: Lake Natron.

A little farther on, our eyes are attracted by a dark fabric oscillating in the bushes.

"What's that? A scarecrow?"

"You're closer than you think, it's a tsetse fly trap."

A cone of indigo canvas over a wasp trap filled with a yellow liquid is slowly agitated by the hot wind.

"Is it honey?"

"No! Cow urine, that's what the flies like. As well as the movement. They think it's a cow, go under the skirt and come up to get trapped in the bottle. The tsetse flies are a plague. It is very important for us to eradicate it. In the Magadi district, there are more than three hundred apparatuses like this paid for by German veterinarians."

"And what is the Kenyan government doing?"

"Don't bring it up, it's our worst enemy! The Ministry of Agriculture wants us to change our traditional livestock for Brahman or American cows."

"Why?"

"They produce more milk and meat. But they are not resistant to tick fever; that way, they can sell us anti-tick products on credit and make us construct sanitary footbaths in this desert. They call that development! Certain Maasai have tried, but it takes so much investment on their part that they have to sell their livestock to pay back their debts and disappear to the benefit of the big breeders who are in the political rackets, and employ Maasai as cowherds. You talk about development! To prevent us from owning a small herd is to steal our freedom from us and kill us. The whole economy of our society is based on it. Without herds, there are no more Maasai. When you want to buy livestock, you can't get credit except for exotic cows, not for traditionial cows, whose origins and breeds are not recognized. In fact, they want us to cease rivaling the Kikuyu ranches and, in time, divide the whole Maasai territory into private lots."

"That would be the death of your culture, no?"

"In fact, the government would like to displace us into reservations far from the wild animals and our cows, make us fodder for the tourists and dispossess us of our lands. They attack our 'tribalism' for political ends, while exploiting our culture in the form of folklore expurgated of ritual meaning. We just want to live on our land as we wish. We do not want to own the land, it belongs to all Maasai, we do not want the land of the Kikuyu or other tribes, we just want to go live freely on our ancestral lands with our cows, that's all. A Maasai needs space like the birds that fly in the sky."

"But," asks Sonia, "what could they do with this land?"

"They want to divide it into intensive ranches, but they don't know that it is much too fragile to support such pressure. Guaranteed desertification. Besides, there is no water. It's absurd! Rubbish!."

We look at the landscape around us. Hard to imagine barbed wire dividing these desolate spaces where it rains only a few days a year, into grids. And what would the Maasai do separated from each other, taken away from their community life? What would the morans do to live in their manyattas? What would be the role of the old wise men? So many questions that follow on each other.

"And what is the Maasai secret for managing this fragile ecosystem?"

"We are not numerous, we control our births and we constantly move our herds around. That way, the grass grows again for the next ones. We have another proverb that well illustrates this philosophy of sharing: 'The grass belongs to no one.' The number of head is a function of the family size. What good would it do us to have too many cattle? We do not capitalize the cows. It would be suicide. We can only have one when we are married, and everything is regulated by the authority of the elders. Too many cows would place our cows in peril. We are the only ones who can live in this arid world. Traitors, attracted by the lure of profit, have sold territories that did not belong to them. In so doing, in the long run they lose everything and go to swell the ranks of the destitute piled up in the Nairobi shantytowns. I don't feel sorry for them, they deserve to be killed."

Sonia interrupts us to point out that we have lost sight of Baptiste and Alexandra. We wait for them. They arrive, limping a little. Baptiste's blisters are not doing well; he is walking on nails, but suffers in silence, with humor and detachment. Great class. It is time to find an enkang and have a lunch break.

Under the Forest of the Lost Child

KENYA

We approach an immense parasol acacia. In its beneficent shadow are seated an old man and a small group of newly circumcised young men.

"He is a wise man. He is teaching them what they must know for the long initiation which will make morans of them. They are under the counsel tree. Each morning, a wise man comes here and waits for people who have problems to solve."

At our approach, the old man rises slowly on a stick and dismisses his flock with a wave of the hand. John speaks to him respectfully for a long time. The ancestor opines and punctuates each of his young interlocutor's sentences with a little "Eh!" of approval. We had already noticed this detail among the Barbaigs. Every monologue thus becomes a dialogue. With a sign, he orders a small boy in black to fetch us some water for our noodle soup and another to light a fire between three stones. Then he motions us to sit down with him, opening up with a broad, benevolent smile.

John turns toward us: "He has seen Whites only three times in his life. The last time that Europeans sat under this tree, it was during the English period, when he was a young moran. He is very happy to see you. I told him what you are doing, and he is very impressed."

The moranillos have returned. The water begins to boil. The old man watches me pouring the contents of the packets into the water with a disapproving whistle.

"What's the matter. He thinks these are worms?"

"No! He says that your wife should be doing that."

I burst out laughing. Sonia, Alexandra and Baptiste are already sleeping. The bush is anesthetized by the heat and light. Not a breath of air, not a sound disturbs this stifling silence. John breaks it with a glacial slice: "For three nights they have been hearing lions in the vicinity, he advises us not to sleep alone tonight. He also says that they are the last inhabitants in the Magadi valley, there is no trail to the north, that they have no contact with the northern Maasai because they belong to different clans. They are even rather enemies..."

Stretched out on his right side, the man lays his head on a tiny wooden headrest and observes my anxiety. In one movement, he takes the lobe hanging from his left ear, raises it and puts it like a rubber band behind the pinna, so it will stop tickling his neck. He has chestnut irises with pale blue circles around them, like many old Africans. He tells me that he misses the time when the Whites administered the country, since they were more tranquil and managed their own affairs. Today, he says, the Maasai are divided by politics, they tear each other up.

All at once he hands me his club and a long staff from the same source. John's eyes are opened wide. I do not know what that means. I question him with a glance.

"He is giving you his symbols as chief, it's a great honor! This straight club with a small head is called an *olkuma orok*, and the staff an *ésiré*."

I am bewildered and sputter: "Why?"

"He wants you, by your trek, to bear witness to our plight..."

When we leave, the depth of this gaze long remains in my memory. John understands my impression. "Among us, when we meet someone like that, we say that he has cast a shadow on us, like the counsel tree, which means that he has done us good."

"Among us, it's the reverse: someone who casts a shadow is someone who does some harm..."

Since this morning, the terrain has been rising little by little toward the Nguruman escarpment. The Rift floor is over. Rocks are appearing, with deciduous trees. As we go, approximately north, we resume the interrupted conversation; decidedly John is a mine of information. I contest the wise man's final argument.

"It was all the same during the colonial period that the dismantling of the Maasai territory began..."

"Yes, but it accelerated after independence. We lost the Mau escarpment, the Maasai Mara, the Athi and Kaputiei plains and, now, they want to take from us the Loita plains and the forest of the lost child....We won't let them get by with it!"

"The forest of the lost child?"

"It's an intact primary forest that extends just beyond the crest of the Nguruman escarpment, above our heads, and in which take place rituals that are very important for us. The medicine men find plants there, the prophets we call *Laibon* speak there to the spirits and make oracles, the elders meet there to pray to Enkai, the circumcised are gathered there for lessons on life in the wild and botany. It is our spiritual heart, our Vatican in open country. And the authorities want to force us out to make an umpteenth natural reserve, whereas if we leave it, it will rapidly be emptied out by the poachers. Protecting the Serengeti against poaching is easy: they are plains. Protecting a forest is much harder. They want to take our last sanctuary from us.

"In fact, it is only in the desert now that you are at home?"

"That is the only thing we have left and they want to take it from us. In 1850, the Maasai territory extended from the middle of Kenya, toward Lake Nakuru, to the middle of Tanzania, over more than a thousand two hundred kilometers, with plateaus and escarpments on both sides of the Rift. It has shrunk so much that it is now no more than three hundred kilometers in the bottom of the Rift. And they call us invincible warriors! We are rather incurably foolish pacifists."

"How do you explain this reduction?"

"First, around 1860, there was a bovine plague that ravaged our herds, soon followed by a smallpox epidemic that came from Somalia, and killed half the Maasai. That is when Great Britain and Germany divided up East Africa, with one great stroke cutting Maasai lands in two (Kilimanjaro thus ended up in Tanzania because Queen Victoria had just given it 'as a gift' to her nephew Emperor William II). The British colonists chipped away at our cold, wet territories on the high plateaus, then, on decolonization, the government forced us off the reserves it had created for the tourists. Since then, it takes terrain everywhere because of the demographic pressure of the other tribes, the Kikuyu, the Luos, the Kambas or the Luyios, who come from every corner of the country because they were told there were still wild lands here. Statistics that have been kept secret even say that we became the minority in Maasai territory. In Kenya as in Tanzania, all we have left is the bottom of the Rift! Kenya is very unkind to us, since we saved it from the slave traders..."

"How was that?"

"No slave caravan was ever able to cross Maasai lands. We always attacked the Arabs of the Swahili coast who ventured into our territory and beat the Somalis. We liberated thousands of slaves; all Kenyans have benefited from this protection. Nairobi moreover is a Maasai name that means 'the little cold-water stream.' In fact, we suffer much more since independence. The English had understood that they would not change us; they admired and respected us, whereas our Kenyan compatriots disdain us and consider us backward. Every time I go to the city, there are people who make fun of me, act as if I drink blood, rape little girls, cannot read, am a pagan – although I have more diplomas than they do…"

"And yet, I have heard that Prime Minister Saitoti is a Maasai, doesn't he defend your interests?"

"What shit! The name is phony. He is not Maasai. In fact, his name is Georges Kinuthia, he is a Kikuyu and can't speak a word of Maasai. He was parachuted by Moi into our district, but we never voted for him; he is here to provide tokens of good conduct to the international community, but, under cover of national reconciliation, he controls and crushes us."

By dint of discussion, we have not realized that the terrain was rising. Turning to wait for the three others, who also are lost in discussion, we survey the landscape we have covered in the last four days. Far away, about a hundred kilometers, scarcely visible in the heat mist, Shompole appears tiny in the middle of the uniform, dirty yellow Rift that rises towards us like a ramp. Baptiste calculates: "You have to cover about seventy times that to finish your trek! Since we have done it in four days, you should make it in a year…three hundred twenty days."

"Are you sure you are saying that to encourage us?" Sonia asks ironically.

John is tense. There is no longer the slightest path, the slightest animal trail. We are treading in grasses so tall that they caress our chins, weaving among the acacias of which the low branches seem to be there just to tear our sleeves. The pace slows, we follow each other step for step, the conversations have ceased, John has unsheathed his olalem and is blazing a path in the biting vegetation. Our only certainty is that we must walk due north and find someone for tonight. Around us, there could be lions everywhere. Behind the gray, clawing foliage, we hear zebras take flight. Yet there is much less game than on the Tanzanian side. These last days, we have relatively speaking seen none. Above the clumps of bushes suddenly appears and disappears an enormous giraffe head. It stops at a hundred meters and watches us. A partial clearing allows us to admire its coat. Sonia remarks: "It's strange, it doesn't have at all the same design as the giraffes in Tanzania."

In wonderment, I exclaim: "A Maasai giraffe! Normally they are farther north…"

Indeed, its coat is not decorated with the classic orangish polygons fringed in brown against a white background, but with ash-brown jagged spots with sizes and forms distributed in unequal flakes. Its camouflage is more effective.

A little further, the trees broken off half-way up leave no one any doubt: elephants. John stirs the dung with the point of his spear.

"It's all right! They were here a week ago. One thing is certain, no one ever comes here….Keep your eyes peeled, there could be buffalo in the vicinity. And if we don't see them before they see us, we're dead."

Progress is harder and harder. The chaotic relief doesn't help. The vegetation increases with elevation. We are in a no man's land, between two zones of influence. South of this forest, the Maasai face Magadi; to the north, Mosiro and Narok. The strangest part is that the two clans have no communication between them, no link, no exchange. Not even a trail for moving livestock. Nothing. Mystery. We have to make the junction before nightfall. We are not loitering. Despite that, we meander for a long time, until dusk, pawing the ground in the tall grasses, struggling with the "wait a bit" acacias that try to hold us back with their thorns curved like hooks. Finally we find a trail. John's face relaxes. If there is a trail, there are men. Indeed, we soon come across a wood cutter astonished by our appearance. He leads us to a small temporary camp where his companions are awaiting him. A cowhide is stretched on the ground, held in place by small stakes, ready for tanning. Sonia attracts my attention: across its rump, we see four cutter slashes.

John turns toward us. "An old, solitary lion attacked them last night. Those are the most dangerous. He killed this cow. The four claws are signs of his attack from behind. They managed to wound it in its hind foot with a spear, but he got away."

The fellow has a wad of tobacco stuck behind his ear, which I had first taken for a big wart. He takes it, rolls it between his fingers, breathes it in the way you would a Havana, and puts it back meticulously. Night has fallen abruptly. We sit around a large fire. The bush rustles with a thousand crickets in the dark. A large inkukurto of smoked yogurt makes the rounds, restorative. Awaiting our turn, we conscientiously extirpate the speargrass seeds from our socks. We are all overcome with fatigue, our ankles bleeding, our legs flayed, our shirtsleeves shredded, our hands clawed. Baptiste's feet worry us. They are now just one oozing, bloody blister. The poor guy begins to grimace, his morale begins to fade. We play a little recorder around the fire to spread some balm on our trials of the day, and sink into sleep.

On opening my eyes, before dawn, I see John sitting near the fire, draped in his red toga and leaning on his spear. He has watched over us a good part of the night, fearing the lion's return. His eyes fixed on the flames, his hands highlighted in gold, hieratic, he meditates. Since the beginning of time men have kept watch like this over their fellow men. To sleep in the bush is to leave seventy kilos of warm meat at the disposition of hungry fangs. Daylight appears at the tip of his spear, his mission is accomplished. He pretends not to have suffered. I get busy right away with the porridge. That is my morning mission. To get Alexandra, who has a holy horror of this gut paste, to swallow her fuel. I try every stratagem, sugar, chocolate, honey, raisins…she rails as she chokes down three miserable spoonfuls of it.

Sonia encourages her. "Force yourself, my sweet! You think I like it? It is the only way to make the distance, otherwise, at eleven in the morning, you are going to collapse. The equation is simple: a bowl of porridge is enough fuel for twenty-five kilometers or five hours of slogging.

As we resume walking, John tears off a branch of a small shrub, removes the leaves from it, and cuts it in sections with his olalem. He hands one piece to me.

"*Enkiké!* This is the Maasai toothbrush, watch how I do it."

With the sharp side of his blade, he strips the bark off two centimeters at the end of the branch and starts chewing it, absorbing the juice of saliva and sap. Soon all that is left is a small brush of fibers which he applies attentively between his teeth, rubbing the gums well. We try. The branch has a vague clove taste.

"So that's your secret for having such white teeth! A sugarless diet with meat, blood, milk...and this miracle toothbrush!"

"Where have you seen that we ate meat and drank blood?"

"I don't know, in the press, that's what they say about you..."

"You have been in Maasai country for three weeks, how many times have you eaten meat?"

"None..."

"Those are stupidities that they peddle to emphasize our tribal, backward side. You see the cliché: 'The fearsome Maasai, who feed on warm blood and raw meat, like lions...' We only rarely eat meat. We are forbidden to eat chicken and eggs. A goat about every two months, and even then very well cooked! As for cows, they are our bank accounts, we try not to touch them. We sacrifice them only for our rituals, births, deaths, marriages, circumcisions, and the famous *eunoto* which takes place every seven years....It is on that occasion – the only one! – that the initiates drink a swallow of the blood of the sacrificed bull, to enter into the world of adults. That happens once or twice in one's life! Personally I have drunk blood only once. But you, in France, apparently you eat a blood sausage, it that true?"

"Oh, yes! We call it boudin....It's made with clotted hog blood..."

"Yuk!"

"No, it's really good. We eat it with our *ugali* of potatoes and applesauce, a delight..."

We review, salivating but accompanied by John's cries of disgust, the marvels of our gastronomy: snails with garlic, frogs with parsley, oysters with shallots, sweetbreads with morels, brain of lamb with lemon, kidneys with mushrooms, andouillettes, snout with vinaigrette...

Sonia takes the ball on the bounce. "Mmmm! A nice, well-chilled *museau vinaigrette*!

"Pig nose? But that's disgusting! Have you seen the use he makes of it?"

And John breaks up laughing.

"So who are the savages?"

The road to the north has slowly broadened. The first tire prints appear, the first villages, we are in the other zone. People join us for segments of the itinerary. In Africa, as soon as someone is walking, there are people to group around him like the wagons on a train. There is soon a small company of us. I am bringing up the rear because I have spent some time ridding myself of spear-grass seeds. I am walking even with a ravishing adolescent who skips along, pushing two asses in front of her. A mischievous nose over a fleshy mouth, she casts glances at me which at first I take for fascination until I understand she is making advances toward me. I am blushing in the sunlight. What does she have in mind? For us to disappear behind the bushes and fall ardently upon each other? She continues to hum as if nothing was up, whipping her asses in the butt with big swings of her switches accompanied by bursts of laughter. Giddy and incredulous, I hold some of her unequivocal gazes and she starts licking her pretty lips. I am a little ashamed, step up the pace, but she doesn't want to let go of me. And then she takes her round, firm breast out of her tunic, adorable with her black nipple, and starts gently fondling it. That's too much for my resistance, I flee as fast as I can before the thundering laughter of my pretty wench....Quite taken aback, I go past Sonia as if nothing had happened and join John in the lead. When I turn around, the maid has disappeared. I tell him what just happened to me. He explodes laughing.

"My friend, with your chief's orinka, she took you for an initiate! Every moran has his mascot, his little protégée in the tribe. He is allowed to have sexual relations with her as long as she is not excised and fertile....In general, it's only fondling and oral caresses."

"That's not pedophilia?"

"Oh, the big words! With us, everything happens younger, the morans are not adults either. They live with other boys in the manyattas a little like in boarding schools, so they have girlfriends. The girlfriends are younger because after their first period that is formally forbidden. They must break it off. The greatest of sins, in our culture, is to become pregnant without being married. After eunoto, the moran, now a man, will marry and can have sexual relations only with excised women, whether his wife or not. All this system is meant to prevent morans from going to see married women, because in that case the husband would have to kill or ban him."

"Did you too have a mascot?"

"Yes, but I never touched her! I am Catholic so I preferred to violate the other taboo: I had relations with mature women before my eunoto, which is much more risky!"

"What about AIDS in all this?"

"That's a real drama in our community. Many youths no longer follow the moran training, or else they go study in the city and have sexual relations with Kikuyus or prostitutes of other African countries. They come back with AIDS and pass it on to the married women. Whole villages are wiped out from the map. The casualties are heavy, especially among the more traditional Maasai, since the adults of the same age group are quite free: there's no problem for a man to go with the wife of a brother of his age group if he is not home, or if his own wife is pregnant, since for nine months he is forbidden to have relations with her under threat of being lynched by the other women."

"What about condoms?"

"I use them because I insisted on complete circumcision...so it works....The others can't..."

"??? Uh....Sorry I don't get it, but why?"

"In traditional Maasai circumcision, the circumcision is partial, they leave part of the foreskin hanging under the scrotum: it's called the brake, and it allows you to be vigorous like a bull, but because of it the condoms break. So they can't use them."

"Sorry, I'm out of it..."

"I see you have not often seen bulls mounting cows! There are no preliminaries, it goes very fast and it's very violent. Among us, a man considers himself very powerful when he does that. Whereas for you, the gentler it is, the longer it lasts, the more satisfied you will be. And I agree with that concept, so I asked for complete circumcision and I can have longer and protected relations. In the more modern villages, they all ask for that, because of the new religions."

"So you are Maasai and Catholic?"

"Yes. I try to respect both teachings a little. There are plenty of other churches, mostly American Protestant ones, but they don't let us remain Maasai, they want us to change our clothing, to live in cement block and corrugated steel houses, to abandon our initiation rituals, the long hair of the morans, ochre, the dances, sacrificing cows, the advice of our medicine men. Besides, I don't like their sermons, they yell too much, they forbid us to drink Tusker[1] or traditional beer. Whereas my Catholic priest is himself a Maasai initiate; he lets us do almost anything except certain things we have to change."

"What, for example?"

"Well, for one he is against excising the young girls. He says we

---

[1] A well-known Tanzanian beer; with an elephant with fine tusks featured on its yellow label.

can conduct the ceremony after the first period without the excision ritual, that the symbol is enough to make a woman of her. He is willing to allow us to have mascots, but doesn't want us to touch them. He is not against circumcising the boys, but insists it be complete. Afterwards, we must be faithful to our wife, but I am not yet married....Also, he is against removal of the lower incisors..."

"What's that?"

"A tradition linked to tetanus. Thanks to the hole made through the teeth, you could continue to feed someone whose jaw was tensed up by tetanus. Hence, the elders believe that it staves off tetanus. Today, the government wants us to be vaccinated. What I like about the Catholics is that they don't ask us to change our clothing, they let us live in our mud villages, initiate the morans, perform the eunoto, and participate in all our collective festivals; they just ask us to make moral adjustments. For example, we are required to have cemeteries."

"There were none previously?"

"No. We left the dead in the thickets, and the hyena came and ate them; it was more clean, and then we were less afraid for the spirits. If the hyenas didn't touch them, it was because the deceased person had committed sins. The heirs had to sacrifice cows for the village. Today, we don't know any more; we bury them to the west of the villages because that's the direction of the land of the dead."

"Really?"

"Yes, in our tradition, the east that proclaims the new day brings life and happiness, luck and prosperity. The west, on the other hand, is the direction of evil and death."

"It's unbelievable, you are not the only ones who think that.... So do the Egyptians."

"Yes, I know. I have even heard that, being originally from the south of the Sudan, our ancestors could have been influenced by the Nubians in contact with Egypt, which would explain quite a few of our traditions, our weapons, our karashas, excision, our shaved heads, our system of age groups..."

We remain silent on this historical fantasy and meditate on the universal roots of cultures. Egypt, forged on the banks of the Nile, and the Maasai country whose spinal column is equally structured by a north-south axis, the arid, thankless Rift.

We have lunch in a government school surrounded by hundreds of Maasai and Kikuyu children. In the villages constructed along the roads, the populations are mixed. In the bush, not yet. That is why the plans for roads and bridges of those who are obsessed with development are a threat to the Maasai culture. Baptiste and Alexandra are are worn out. The runs and blisters. It's time to get there. Should be tomorrow.

Ndulelei, Friday 26 July 2002, day 575, 29 km, 7411th km

Night has not made anything better. Poor Baptiste is paralyzed. His raw flesh is torturing him. Like the granite Breton he is, he does not complain but his spirit is no longer in it. He resumes the walk, gritting his teeth and hanging in there. Alexandra on the other hand demonstrates remarkable resistence. Those Slovaks, you know, they're solid material. Okay, I know, she weighs thirty kilos less than her man. The advantage of small formats.

As I hit the road I am thinking of *Homo habilis*, who was no taller than one meter forty, of Boisei, who must have weighed as much as a gorilla, and of *erectus*, who was not over one meter sixty. The world was conquered by light men. Not by strength. You only have to see John's cricket calves and skinny legs pulsing in front of me. He is neither scrawny nor emaciated, he is built like that, honed for walking, lanky and light. Behind, with my short legs and broad Norman torso, I must compensate by taking great strides. It's become my habit. My frame is that of a peasant or a northern sailor, not of a hiker of the high steppes. While we are crossing though our first cornfields since Karatu, John enthralls us with lion stories. He tells us how Entekei, his moran partner, woke up one day with a bound, while they were sleeping side by side in their manyatta, to go completely naked to the rescue of one of their cows which had been attacked by a big cat. A leopard had sprung from a branch within the enclosure. At the second when he was going to leap at the cow's throat, he had turned his yellow eyes on his friend bursting in and had taken a large stone on the mouth, which had broken his teeth; it almost overwhelmed him with pain; he tried to flee but couldn't clear the thorns; he was running in circles in the enclosure, and the deft Entekei had finished him off by throwing another stone right at his head. John, all excited, seems to be reliving the scene.

"In our culture, we think it is better to be wounded than not to defend one's livestock. If a guy flees before a lion, one day he will be eliminated by his age group, which will disguise it as an accident, or he has to go away, since he has become useless to the community. He has broken the pact. In all such cases, it is better to face up! It's like the story of what happened to that group of morans during their initiation; they were tracking a lioness when she turned on them and charged: the moran in front threw his *eremet*,[2] but too soon; the lioness dodged it and grabbed his arm; one of his buddies came up with his olalem to defend him, but unfortunately, at the last instant, the lioness turned around, and the blade cut the moran prisoner's arm clean off. The guilty man, in shame, then took flight. The lioness returned to the attack against the wounded man who, with his viable hand, hit her an enormous blow with his club in the eye, smashing her skull. She died on the spot. He was carried in triumph throughout the region; he forgave his buddy, considering it wasn't his fault. If the wounded man had been killed, the deserter would have been eliminated." Next John tells how the morans' eremets must be sharpened and anointed with blood before they can be planted in the soil in front of a house.

Then he fulminates: "In any case, it's too easy to kill lions

---

[2] Moran's spear with a meter-long blade.

with spears. Today, the morans take pride in killing a lion in direct combat. Last year, something really extraordinary happened. A group of morans was pursuing two large males. One of the runners was going much faster than the others, and soon found himself alone; the lions, perceiving this, turned on him; fortunately, there was a tree nearby, and the moran used it as a shield: the first lion attacked from the left, the warrior leapt to the right of the tree; the lion anticipated this and changed his path to go to the right, but doing so did not see the blow coming from behind the tree: the moran killed him cold by smashing his skull with his club. The second lion immediately charged on the right side of the tree, the moran did the same thing but in the other direction, he protected himself behind the tree by leaping to the left, so the lion attacked him on the left, but there again he didn't see the blow coming. In ten seconds, the man killed two lions by hand! For three months, he did the honors for every woman in the region...he found, nine months later, that all births were being attributed to him. And the husbands were proud to say that they were having children of the hero!"

Five kilometers before the Ndulelei crossroads, a pickup stops alongside us. We decide to foreshorten Baptiste's sufferings. He climbs in and goes to wait for us at the crossroads. An hour later, we find him asleep under a tree, in front of a half-dozen banana skins. On the asphalt road, trucks roar and buses dodge the potholes; the traffic is heavy in both directions. This is the first road we have crossed since the one in Ngorongoro, four hundred eleven kilometers back. It leads to the Maasai Mara. We have gone past the latitude of Nairobi; we decide to make a side trip there.

It is time to leave John. He carries on in a minibus toward the Mau escarpment, where he owns a few hectares of land that contradicts his indictment of private property and land distribution that he deployed for us. A few rare Maasai were able to keep their properties, up there, but by adopting the lifestyle of the other tribes. John juggles his two existences. He tries to make the two models cohabit. How can he do otherwise to preserve the Maasai world from being swallowed up in the acculturated mass, and also without sectoring it in its tribalism?

We are moved in direct proportion to what we have shared with John. He is the African who walked the longest with us, the one with whom we have had the best understanding, and the best exchange. He was for us the ambassador of his people, the interpreter of its distress, its being torn between two worlds, between two eras. And yet, as an individual, he seemed to us to incarnate a happy medium between the nostalgics of the "it was better before" and the leveling extravagances of ideological state modernism. He proved to us that one could be Maasai and modern at the same time. That Maasai culture was indeed alive and had much to say to other cultures in terms of ecology and wisdom, spirituality and management of resources.

Before leaving us, and by way of a gift, John gives me his olalem.

"When I am no longer with you," he says, "I shall be with you. Good luck, when you resume your trek! There is a Maasai proverb that says: 'Only the eye that has traveled is wise.' You are true Maasai olashumpaïs. Farewell, my friends."

CHAPTER 10

Orphans and Ivory Prohibition

KENYA

I n Nairobi, thanks to the hospitality of a young volunteer from Alcatel, Arnaud Thépenier, we can begin writing up the first part of volume I of our African adventures. Indeed, faced with the quantity of anecdotes, encounters and lessons drawn from out trek, Nicole Lattès, our editor at Robert Laffont, agreed that, for one thing, it would be a mess to cram all this wealth at any cost into a single work and that, for another, it would be better for us to start writing as soon as possible so as not to lose the substance of the initial discovery. We have indeed been slower than planned. We went deeper into things, to the heart of stories that were confided to us. Day after day, our adventure "in the footsteps of Man" became more human than sporting. The farther we went in Africa, the more the continent seemed to us to grow. Planned from Paris, our trajectory was supposed to last eighteen months for about ten thousand kilometers. But kneeling down on the famous Michelin maps numbers 954 and 955 with a curvimeter in hand, we were still far from the realities. The reality is here: in twenty months, we have covered barely more than half of our route, and the hardest part is still to come. For a long time we have taken the pulse of Africa. Our time has become space of freedom and expression, encounters and sharing. We no longer count it, we devote it.

So, two months' pause, which we use to prepare the rest of our itinerary, order new shoes, recharge ourselves, replenish our vitamins and mineral salts, and retrace in writing our journey in South Africa thanks to the fantastic welcome we received there. In addition to writing, we organize appointments and filming sessions.

Arnaud does not do things halfway. Laure, his adorable fiancée, mounted on springs like an imp, makes sure we want for nothing. We are fawned over. They let us use their guest room with its vast king-size bed, in which I set up a little office. While I write, Sonia rereads, annotates, trims, adds flowers to my deserts, sensitivity when I am too technical, humility when I am boastful, heart when I am too blunt. Our writing is bicephalous. As this adventure would without her be only sweat, this book would be flavorless. We also have much work to do on our visuals. Sonia "derushes" about forty 42-minute tapes, reconnects with our producer and with Florence Tran, who takes delivery of all these videos in France while we are walking. With our articles, our chronicles and our editing instructions, she puts together the first three films based on our 156 first tapes each with 40 minutes of rushes, for a total of 6,240 minutes of videos. A big job. And to think we don't even know her; she joined the project while it was under way!

Nairobi is a dangerous, ugly city, polluted and materialistic, violent and expensive. The reverse of what motivated our trek. Some refer to it as "Nairobbery." We remain closed into our apartment, in the Blackrose Residence near the Yaya Center, and enjoy the joys of sedentariness: intimacy, silence, cleanliness. During our stay, we meet three important personages: Louise Leakey, Nigel Pavitt and Jill Woodley. The first is the granddaughter of Louis and Mary Leakey, the daughter of Richard and Meave Leakey; she took up the family torch of paleoanthropological research in Kenya, notably at

Koobi Fora, on the banks of Lake Turkana, site of the very important dig which we hope to visit. The second is a renowned photographer who has long worked in Turkana country and knows the country like the back of his hand; we need some tips. The third directs Daphné Sheldrick's baby elephant orphanage, situated on the edge of the Nairobi national park, near Karen, a classy suburb of the megalopolis named after the famous baroness Blixen. Here, alleys of jacarandas and tulip trees line the streets; in the distance, to the west, the Ngong Hills lace the horizon. We do not long resist the idea of seeing the little elephants.

One morning we have an appointment at eleven to film her little wards nursing. Jill, married to a Frenchman, speaks French fluently. She serves us tea in her home, a simple house opening onto the bush, with a feel of African adventure, a house full of the goings and comings of birds and little visitors eager for muffin crumbs. Suddenly, she looks at her watch and exclaims: "Quick! We have to go! Those little devils are very punctual!"

Ruled like music paper, six baby elephants come out of the bush with no warning, escorted on the run by their trainers. Before the landscape of the national park, in an open space of blood-red laterite, the bottles full of milk are waiting. It's a stampede! One behind the other, they run feet forward and ears flapping, trunk swinging around in front of them in great excitement, a feverish train the cars of which quickly detach in a shivaree of trumpeting, swinging of ears and stamping of feet. The spectators are delighted. Real toys! After the ruckus and the fear of being forgotten, after an overturned bucket and a great annoyance noisily expressed, each baby has found its trainer and sucks up with delectation two bottles of two liters each, with swooning eyes and their trunk rolled around the nursemaid's neck, or lying back in an ecstatic posture. Slurp, slurp, slurp! Jill watches all of them with maternal solicitude.

"This homemade milk took more than twenty-eight years to perfect. Cow's milk is poison for elephants. We begin with a pasteurized powder to which we add mineral salts and vitamins as well as soy milk, but I say no more, the rest is a secret!"

"How did they come to be here?"

"There! The little elephant with ears three-quarters notched, that's Burra. His family was on its way between the Tsavo-West and Tsavo-East parks, where a tribe of Kambas has settled illegally, setting nooses to snare whatever comes by. He was eight months old when he was brought to us, mutilated, emaciated, traumatized: the iron wire of the snare was buried several centimeters in his neck, the muscles were cut as well as this part of his ear; he could no longer raise his head. He's been here nine months, and now he is in great shape!"

Sonia asks: "But why do elephants not avoid contact with inhabited zones?"

"Elephants move about on migration routes thousands of years old which they preserve in their memory. It is men who settle on their path. In cases of territorial conflict and demographic pressure, the elephants always lose. There, for example, you have Thoma, a little female who was left after her family ravaged a field near the small Thompson Falls park, in the Aberdares. The elephants there developed a nocturnal life so as not to be bothered by men. But Thoma, left behind, became the scapegoat of an irate population, she was attacked by spears, machetes, and the surly crowd led her to the Nyahururu prison, where she was incarcerated behind bars. I don't know whether you can picture the scene! When we got there, she was in her death throes, lying in a sea of blood, seated on wounds inflicted on her behind. She hovered for a week between life and death, without sleeping, she had terrible nightmares! Happily, she was not vomiting her milk, else she would have died. We treated her with strong doses of antibiotics, adding silver powder to her milk to strengthen her immunity and homeopathic chamomile to calm her. She is the same age as Burra and, at present, she seems to have forgotten everything. God be praised!"

Sated, full, the group scatters before the little pond of red mud.

One by one the elephant calves test the temperature with the tip of their extended trunks, then put forward a timid foot before throwing themselves completely into the scum with unadulterated joy.

"Oh, look!" Sonia exclaims. Thoma is pushing the little cutie into the water over there!"

"That is Solango, the smallest of the band, but not the least tough! He was found at only two months, trapped in a well, his ears completely burned by the sun. Under the flaked-off skin, he was pink as a piglet. He is the furthest behind, but believe me, one day he will be a dominant male…"

At that moment, having barely escaped the forced bath, now he is chasing a warthog as big as he is, ears fully deployed, tail in the air and his tiny trunk trumpeting like a raging trombone. His duty once accomplished, he comes back and jumps immediately into the pool, splashing the five others. Which triggers a total frenzy. On their sides, the elephant calves begin to swim the Indian breaststroke furiously in place, sending mud flying ten meters all around. The scene is apocalyptic, the red elephants are unbridled, Seraa takes a duck dive, then comes out covered with mud, Solango climbs on Thoma's back to roll backwards, making a horrendous bomb. The tourist crowd is in stitches. A real Barnum show, but one hundred percent natural.

Jill gloats: "The calves need to play, to be happy. For us, that is the best indication of their health. That is why they need to be in a family. At night, they sleep in cubicles with their trainers. Each of them has three to avoid creation of too great a dependency between them. Training them is a task of every moment, twenty-four/seven. Finally, you know, Seraa, Soslan and Solango saw their families slaughtered by poachers; they have nightmares, that's why they must be surrounded with particular care and love. Sometimes they even experience depression!"

"Do you lose many of them?"

"The little ones often come here is such a state that they allow themselves to die of hunger or do not recover from their wounds.

We have about 40% losses. At four months, they get their teeth, which gives them terrible diarrhea of which they sometimes die, so fragile is their metabolism, and destabilized by the traumas that brought them here. At Tsavo, where we take our protégés once they are too big, we have three elephants who lack a trunk, can you imagine what they look like? They look like giant pigs; they lost them to machete blows! Hard to forgive man for in these conditions! Especially when you have an elephant's memory..."

Out of the water, our elephants, copper-colored from the mud, embark on rolling in the clay soil. Accompanied by gales of laughter. Solango crawls like a soldier to scratch his stomach. Burra, his great buddy, comes to butt him with his head, as if he were jealous of his success. He is promptly stopped by his trainer, who reprimands him in a thundering voice with his index finger raised. The other retreats, trunk raised, ears flared, then turns as if to say: "Okay, so what! There's no harm done! Just wanted to have some fun!"

Sonia follows with: "And what do you do when they're not good?"

"The guards and trainers must incarnate the authority of the group so these calves can one day be reintegrated into nature within the existing herds, since that is our principal objective. They must therefore learn to behave themselves. For extreme situations, where we might sense that an elephant's character is getting out of hand and endangering the lives of the trainers and other elephants, we have a little apparatus that sends weak electrical currents that are quickly interpreted as a punishment, immediately followed by great consoling caresses. Happily, we only rarely have to use it."

"You don't reward them with goodies?"

"Never! That would be their undoing. Our elephants feed only on foliage collected in the bush so they will not acquire a taste for vegetables or fruits. We have seen elephants bash in cars or flatten houses solely because there were oranges inside. An animal which has had fruit casually tossed to it during a safari is on a death sentence with reprieve. Sooner or later he will get himself killed in an orchard."

"How long do you keep these calves here?"

"After two years, they are progressively weaned and led to our ranch in Tsavo, where they are absorbed into the groups of semi-adults who have preceded them. There they take long trips into the bush with their trainers, come across the scent markings of wild herds, sometimes meet some, spend the day with them and return at night to the fold. The miracle is that they are very well accepted. One day or another, it depends on the individual, they find the contact with elephants more stimulating than with men and are integrated, one by one, into the Tsavo families."

"What explains the differences in integration?"

"Those that we have had as babies tend to remain close to us while those we recuperate at one or two are very quickly integrated. In the end, of our forty adult or adolescent orphans, twenty-four are still dependent on our ranch, but under the authority of an adult matriarch who voluntarily refuses to return to wildlife to take care of them. It is incontestably a sacrifice on her part. At present, it is Emilie who holds this position, having recently replaced Malaïka. Sixteen others have achieved their integration into wild herds. They come from time to time to present their new progeny to their trainers, whom they will never forget."

Their dirt bath over, the calves delicately strip the leaves from branches two meters from the dumbfounded tourists behind their security rope, then go tranquilly to a place in the forest where they will spend the afternoon in the shade, in the company of their trainers.

Jill turns to us: "Since you seem interested, why don't you come for lunch? At two, we are going to transfuse a very tiny calf a few days old with blood we drew yesterday from Thoma."

"What happened to it?" asks Sonia.

"We got it yesterday. This little female was found mired in mud in the Meru park. She didn't even have the strength to get herself out. She has been made completely anemic by a terrible diarrhea."

At two, Jill leads us to the edge of the forest where the sick calf's trainers have stretched blankets between the bushes to create some real shade. The little elephant lies on her side under a small blanket, a damp cloth over its eyes, its tiny trunk contracting and relaxing to the rhythm of the soft snore of her respiration. Amos, a young and very moved Kikuyu, is keeping watch over her: "Wendy probably didn't get enough milk in her first forty-eight hours of life. The first milk contains a level of colostrum that is indispensable to the constitution of good immunity. Once that time is past, they usually die of dysentery or septicemia."

"What do you think happened to her?"

"Either the herd was disturbed and fled quickly, leaving her behind, or she is a twin. It often happens that mothers abandon one of the calves if they sense that they will not be able to nurse both of them, especially in periods of stress that elephants go through."

"Do you think she'll make it?"

"She doesn't have enough antibodies, that's why the milk we feed her gives her diarrhea. We counter the dehydration by adding mineral salts to her milk but that doesn't get us anywhere if we can't cure her!"

The veterinarian arrives with his precious bottle of plasma. He immediately sets to work. The vein in the foot is resistant; he turns to the ear, very well supplied in veins. The needle makes the poor thing awaken with a heart-rending cry and try to get up, but the anesthetist loses no time putting her back to sleep. The vet quickly sets up the transfusion: "Thoma's blood has been centrifuged to take only the plasma, rich in platelets and antibodies. Since we do not know blood types for elephants, suppressing the red and white cells lessens the risk of rejection. With this she should make it!"

Once on her feet, Wendy teeters a little, cheers herself up by playing between our legs, like a rugby hooker in a pack. Then she begins to shoot into a truck inner tube; a real terror. Amos tries to calm her down, no use, she is eager to get herself worked up. When she is tuckered out, she returns to her mattress and falls in a heap. Sonia, who has adopted the good habit of taking a nap every day after lunch, takes advantage of it now to replace Amos, lie down beside Wendy and soon join her in the arms of Morpheus.

Amos whispers to me: "Wendy in Meru language means 'hope'!"

If you want to be godparent to an orphan elephant, it will cost you no more than fifty euros a year. Find Soslan, Burra, Solango, Thoma or the newcomers at www.sheldrickwildlifetrust.org.

To feed our reflection on the fate of elephants in Africa, Jill had the good idea of inviting us to the private screening, at the Nairobi museum, of the latest film of Simon Trevor, a renowned animal cinematographer, who notably created the animal scenes in *Gorillas in the Mist* and *Out of Africa*. The preview of *Wanted Dead or Alive* takes place before the representatives of CITES (International Convention on Trade in Endangered Species) who come from the African countries concerned by the argument over the re-opening (or not) of the ivory trade. Among the strongest opponents of this re-opening is Richard Leakey, former director of KWS (Kenyan Wildlife Services) and instigator of the absolute moratorium put into place at the beginning of the 1990s.

The film begins with elephant charges. One after the other. Impressive. The commentator's voice asks: "Why?" Aggressiveness? Hostility to man? No! Fear! The elephants of Tsavo Park are still afraid. They are just getting over the waves of massacres in the 1970s and 1980s, which saw their number drop from forty-five thousand to a few hundred. The eldest who were lucky enough to survive the massacre remember and remain irrepressibly mistrustful of men. Over the long term, the whole elephant society, with its hierarchy, initiations, and structures, which was destabilized, gives rise to a category of hooligans, dominant ill-integrated, ill-raised males, that are finally referred to as "problem elephants," especially when they come closer to farmlands. They long remain solitary, unable to accept the authority of other males, creating havoc in the herds. These psychological traumas are just beginning to fade, the herds to find their generational equilibrium and their place in an ecosystem that needs them, and here are the countries of southern Africa militating for lifting the embargo on the ivory trade, a measure that would instantly start the carnage going again.

The simple mention of this possibility has pushed the poachers to anticipate the future and cost about sixty elephants their lives in Kenya in 2001. Simon Trevor's film returns in detail to one of the sinister slaughters: thirteen elephants eliminated by Kalashnikov by two Somali poachers in the north of East Tsavo. In the course of the films, we follow the tracking of the two killers, organized with teams of rangers dropped by helicopter at strategic points in the park thanks to GPS. Trackers follow their traces on the ground at the risk of falling into an ambush. Campsites are found, the ashes still warm, then the tusks, buried in their flight, then an abandoned anti-aircraft rocket and grenades. Aware they were being relentlessly pursued, the poachers disband. A team of snipers is dropped near the only water source in the region. The fugitives however do not take that direction. They appear to escape. However, one night, against all expectations, they make a right angle turn and head for the pond, where they meet death at the hands of the ranger lying in wait....Thirteen elephants, two men....The commentator wonders: why all this blood spilt? Poverty? Elephant overpopulation? Ecological disasters? No. Just that the rumor was about that certain ivory stocks might be sold on a case-by-case basis by the new CITES convention...

After a concluding commentary, we have the good fortune of being able to interview Richard Leakey, who has come to support the arguments with his rhetorical skills.

"For you, a door has to be open or closed? There can't be a compromise or case-by-case solution, given the overpopulation of elephants in certain countries in southern Africa?"

"First you need to know that Africa cannot live without elephants. They are indispensable to the ecological equilibrium of the bush. Second, the very idea of overpopulation is an absurdity.

Only man has that tendency. Elephants have natural cycles of birth control fixed by the limits of the ecosystem they inhabit. They manufacture the landscape, shape it, and are shaped in return by nature. Where there are too many trees, they clear space for the return of grassy spaces, where there are not enough trees, they plant more by carrying the seeds in their manure. If resources are lacking, the females are infertile. And droughts take care of eliminating excess populations. There is no need to organize sanguinary safaris! The truth is that the elephants are never an ecological problem, but that certain ill-intentioned men are trying to make of them a social and economic problem. They talk about elephants only when they enter into conflict with men. Which, most of the time, happens when men invade their territory and transform forests they have burned into fields of very low productivity. In the first place, it is financial interests that remain the principal force behind the debate and the primary argument for the reopening of trade in products derived from the elephant. The selective culling proposed by Zimbabwe and Namibia creates a market, an economic circuit that will always demand more, that will not be content with quotas, that will respond to the laws of the market. The leather is sold for high prices in Japan, the meat is transformed at little cost into dog food, the hair feeds the making of bracelets and other horrors sold to tourists, the feet become vile stools, not to mention the ivory, transformed by Asians into buckets or other pathetic trinkets."

"Are there no leaks in the present apparatus, which are nevertheless officially very restrictive?"

"We are in fact on a bad slope. In 1989, CITES had placed elephants in appendix 1 of the fully protected species' list with an embargo on all ivory trade. The price of ivory had then fallen dramatically as well as the motivation for poachers. I was behind the destruction of thirty tons of ivory to demonstrate that ivory had lost all value, and that to retreat was impossible. President Moi was intelligent enough to accept. In the last ten years, the growth in tourism has demonstrated that a living elephant brings in much more money than a dead elephant, and benefits the local communities and governments rather than the mafias and corrupt functionaries. But to answer your question, the day after the inauguration of the moratorium that slipped the subject to appendix 2, Hong Kong was selling its stock to the highest bidder. That satisfied the Chinese market for a while, but fortunately did not relaunch the global market. However, never forget that we are in a logic of exchanges globalization, and that the ivory of a Zimbabwean, Congolese or Kenyan elephant has the same value. We can't pretend we can kill an elephant in Namibia without mortgaging the future of the ones living in our Kenyan national parks, and provide a living for hundreds of thousands of Kenyans. Those who pretend the contrary have a financial interest in the matter. They are liars. We must have a very firm global approach, or else we will fall back into a drastic cycle of eliminating elephants. Ten years was just enough time for two generations to come into being. In 1997, the CITES convention that took place in Harare, in Zimbabwe, scandalously went around the moratorium by granting Zimbabwe, Namibia and Botswana the right to sell their ivory stocks to Japan, even if elephants remained in the appendix."

"How did they manage to do that?"

"They pretexted their poverty and starving population. The tender chord! Who are they kidding? Who would dare to believe that the poor population benefited from that outrageous transaction? In April 2000, the southern African lobby in favor of reopening gained more ground, even if they all recognized that the debate had reactivated poaching where the elephant populations had been naturally stabilized. Their position was to forbid all trade in elephant products, including live elephants, with exception of ivory stocks from elephants that died a natural death.... Blatant hypocrisy! Taking these negotiations for a *fait accompli*, Zimbabwe in June 2000 sold huge quantities of ivory to China.

We are trying to explain to the CITES representatives in the room tonight that the laws of the marketplace apply without discretion: once there is demand, the supply cannot be controlled, since they are wild animals. In 2001, Congolese ivory coming from the civil war was intercepted in transit to India, Thailand, Belgium and Egypt. Tiny tusks from the equatorial jungle, and thus taken from a threatened species....CITES, which ought to control the outlawing of all trade, largely failed in its mandate. Its loss of credibility will play against the saving of elephants in the negotiations we have yet to hold."

"In what way are elephants indispensable to Africa?"

"Take the example of Tsavo. That region became a park solely because it was a semi-desert, unsuitable for agriculture and even for the extensive breeding of pastoral tribes. The lesson to draw from the experience is that the near-disappearance of elephants late in the 1980s entailed that of other animals, antelopes, and predators. The whole chain was affected. On the one hand, because elephants clear grass spaces by taking down the surplus trees; on the other hand because they dig water holes and keep them supplied by trampling and compacting their clayey base, they waterproof the ponds, which makes them hold their water longer. One study showed that three kilos of manure contained as many as 9000 insects, which benefit birds and other insectivores. Dung beetles bury their balls and fertilize the soil. Elephant carcasses maintain the whole chain of carrion feeders. After the disappearance of the elephants, the bush became dry, poor, impenetrable and deserted. Elephants open trails that benefit everyone, they are the gardeners of the bush."

"But human pressure on the environment is growing and the elephants' space is shrinking..."

"Thirty years ago, Africa had three million elephants. No one ever talked about overpopulation. Today, it is down to two hundred fifty thousand, a figure that will still drop. The principal causes of conflicts with men result from the small size of the parks, which pushes the herds to look outside for food. In the Samburu reservation, for example, some groups move between two parks during the night. They can do much more damage on the way. The satellite tracking of a large male, which you saw in the film, is very revealing in this regard."

"Then what solution do you propose?"

"What we have here is a management problem. In its current state of development, and taking account of the social, economic, and political factors, Africa is not ready to control a reopening of the trade, even if very well regulated and sectional, on elephant products. Otherwise, the elephants are condemned, and with them entire parts of these fragile economies.

"The elephant problem is but a tiny little part of a more general problem that is taking on alarming proportions: that of bush meat. Finally, the lot of elephants is not too bad compared to ordinary game. The growth of bush meat poaching has become the rangers' top preoccupation. The constantly growing pressure on the natural milieus of populations affected by endemic poverty leads to this blind predation that destroys game around the national parks, not to mention communal or tribal zones....One example: the train line from Mombasa to Nairobi includes about fifty stations. In a radius of six kilometers around each station there are as many as a thousand snares! The meat goes directly to the shantytowns or restaurant tables of Nairobi. Every day, in the course of their patrols, our rangers dismantle between a hundred and three hundred snares, which have killed sometimes from three to five animals in several days, thus unsuited for any consumption. Wiped out and wasted."

"But then how can this scourge be fought?"

"On several fronts. First, given that the human species is spreading, we must trace more precise and definitive boundaries between zones with or without animals, and between zones with or without men. All the problems come from the simple fact that the poachers come into the parks, and that animals go out. To prevent that, there is only one solution: enclosure. On one side men, on the other animals. Death for the man or animal that breaches the limits. This policy is indispensable once a country develops demographically and economically. It answers to a rational organization of space. Short or medium term, there is no other solution for Kenya. This model works very well in South Africa, with Kruger Park, notably, where poaching is nonexistent.

"Secondly, we have to put a spotlight on the guardians of these rules: the rangers. Four hundred armed rangers, for the country, is not enough! And more than soldiers who can kill poachers, as we saw in Simon Trevor's film, they must be ecological professionals able to become active conservationists. We must at least double their number and their vehicular means. With an enclosure, their work would be more effective, since they will know where and what to oversee. Third, education remains a priority axis. It is the next generation that will decide whether or not there is room for wild animals in Africa. There are not yet enough African children in the parks. These are becoming sanctuaries for foreign tourists! Little Kenyans need to have the feeling and pride of knowing that these living animals belong to them, that they constitute their patrimony for the benefit of the nation and the entire world.

"Third point, let's face it, is a simple fact: the population needs proteins. If it does not have the means of obtaining them, we will not impede it from seeking them in the bush. This country possesses a fortune in livestock and tribes whose only occupation is raising it. This wealth is not managed. There are neither butcheries, nor slaughterhouses, nor large-scale distribution networks. The overproduction of beef and sheep is a reality, with its well-known consequences: overgrazing, erosion and drought that decimate the herds that ought to have been sold. Everyone loses. And on the other side, the demand is there, insatiable and blind, ready to destroy the entire fauna. It's a stupid paradox. Between the supply and the demand there lacks a network for the transformation and distribution of meat. That is in my mind one of the country's great economical and social issues, to which the new government will have to give its attention without further delay.[1] I wish it well."

---

[1] When we were in Kenya, the country was preparing for presidential elections which were to decide on the successor to Moi.

CHAPTER 11

The Bwindi Gorillas

UGANDA

A side-trip is not really reasonable. It answers to a simple impulse: we have to go there! Shouldn't we stick to our way and to our steps? Doesn't it bring into our adventure some touristy interferences? Who cares anyway? We're free and for us it's a bonus and a reward. In general, we leave capitals when we itch to leave them. Always for a threatened little corner of paradise that we are not sure we will find on some future trip. We have not abused side-trips, one per country: Mrs. Ples in Johannesburg, Victoria Falls from Harare, the tigerfish of the Zambezi, the dolphins of Zanzibar, the Eden of Ngorongoro and now the mountain gorillas of Uganda. Only African gems. Two days to get there, two days there, two days return, two thousand kilometers straight west in a bus going full out, and 500 hundred dollars each for the right to remain seated for one hour in the rain before a group of gorillas – if we're lucky – that is decidedly not reasonable. But after walking 7411 kilometers "in the footsteps of Man," we want to walk in the footsteps of our cousins to see if they are as distant as all that. George Schaller, a pioneer in the study of the great apes, used to say that no one can look a gorilla in the eye without the gulf between us being suddenly filled in, and without recognizing the gorilla there is in each of us.

Entering to the north of Lake Victoria, we pause to remember John Speke in Jinja, on the bridge over the Ripon falls, today buried under fifteen meters of water by the lake formed by a dam on the Kagera River, which he intuitively declared, following a series of epics marking the exploration of East Africa, to be the source of the Nile, since they were the outlet of the great lake. History later vindicated him even if he had not demonstrated it scientifically. For that he would have had to make the junction downstream towards Gondokoro on the White Nile, a British post in the extreme south of the Sudan opened by Samuel Baker, the discoverer of Lake Albert. The Royal Geographic Society never forgave him for this negligence and the din he provoked by his shattering revelations that opposed him to Burton. He quite opportunely found his death in a hunting accident the day before a public debate on the question. At the same time Livingstone was obsessed with finding the sources emerging from Lake Tanganyika, whereas Burton opted for the mythical and evasive "lunar mountains" which Stanley would discover only in 1888 in Ruwenzori. One must never be right before everyone else and especially not against the opinion of the "specialists."

Seen from our bus windows, Uganda appears to us quite active and in full sway of economic recovery. At the stops, legions of hucksters offer us through the windows huge grilled chicken thighs, liver brochettes, juicy fruits. A perfume of effervescence and prosperity floats in the air, which we are encountering for the first time on this continent. Numerous indications and signboards reveal the return of foreign investments, the return of confidence. Everywhere people are busy, the rich, fertile fields are alive with the colors of farmworkers, green hills are peopled by magnificent Ankole cows with enormous horns, eucalyptus groves, enclosures, straight-rowed kitchen gardens and fields and terraces bespeak

good management of the wealth and the territory, of the fructi-
fication of favorable conditions. We are no longer in East Africa!
In any case, not in the one we know. The tropical richness diffuses a completely different ambiance. Laughter, labor and fertility, for a small country recovering from thirty years of nightmares.
Nothing in common with the ambiance of Kenya, made of politics of patience and political disarray, with that of Tanzania, made
from dignified, laborious poverty, or of Malawi, made of powerless insouciance. All that is awfully subjective and reductive but it
constitutes the framework on which the knowledge of a country is
woven, and good examples are too rare on the continent not to be
mentioned. Unhappily, we have not the leisure to hike from West
to East and deepen our understanding of Uganda, for we are hiking northward only and we must soon go pick up the tracks of our
trek to Nairobi.

We are going up a steep slope in a massif of dathuras. Their
white bells, like giant bindweeds, sway softly above our heads
when we force a way through the foliage, and release great drops
of condensation.

With elevation, this deep valley of the "impenetrable Bwindi
jungle" appears to us in all its magnificence: a canopy whirring with
insects from which surge majestic shafts extending their branches
into the sky to catch scarfs of mist hanging around. A blue tou-
raco with its red wings paints a vivid trail through this verdure
all knitted with liana. Sonia is enthralled by this flying jewel. She
did not imagine a bird could be so beautiful. Welcome to Bwindi!
We climb. It was right here that in March 1999 eight English and
American tourists were hacked to pieces by Congolese rebels. The
Zairean border is five kilometers away, the Rwandan twenty-five:
the gorillas really chose the wrong spot! We are in the extreme
southwest corner of Uganda. It was just on the other side of the
massif, in the Virungas mountains, that Dian Fossey, brutally murdered, was buried in the midst of seventeen gorillas. The approach
to these survivors and the knowledge of their behavior are possible

only because of the fabulous documentation which she was able to assemble between 1967 and 1985. Today, our safety is assured by three armed soldiers. They walk at the end of the column.

This Bwindi jungle is perched between 1100 and 2600 meters, over 331 square kilometers. It is a survivor of the climatic changes that occurred at the time of the Quaternary glaciers, which explains its unbelievable diversity: three hundred twenty-five kinds of trees, three hundred species of butterflies, more than three hundred fifty different birds. By way of comparison, a temperate western forest has on average fifteen kinds of trees, twenty species of butterflies and forty of birds! Since 1994, it has held world patrimony classification by UNESCO. Its finest treasure is the mountain gorillas: half of the world population, or about three hundred individuals. The other half shares a trans-border zone situated between Mgahinga park in Uganda, National Volcano park in Rwanda, and the Virungas mountain park in the Democratic Republic of the Congo, whence a greater difficulty of access and protection against poaching.

Among the three hundred individuals at Bwindi, about sixty primates in three groups have been acclimated to the presence of man and can therefore be approached. There is the Mubare group and Habinyanja A; ours is called Habinyanja B. The mountain gorillas, *Gorilla gorilla beringei*, get their name from the first Westerner to have discovered them, in 1902, the German Oscar von Beringe – taking advantage of his good fortune to bag two of them. Strange honor. Above us, on the hillside, the trackers are at work. They are trying to identify the direction which the group took this morning. For these gorillas are not territorial; they move a kilometer or two every day, and soon we are climbing the slope on all fours; our guide, Julius, opens a breach in the green wall with his machete. Suddenly he turns toward us: "They slept here last night!"

In the tall grasses, we see a sort of nest of gathered leaves, embellished in the center by an enormous excretion...

"This was the nest of the silverback, the dominant male. He defecates in it when he leaves it. This nest will never again be used, gorillas make a new one every night. A glance at the nature of the feces lets us follow the health, or the morale, of the group. When they are stressed, they are all colicky!" We resume our progression on the trail opened by the gorillas and are soon at the crest. Everywhere along the way branches and tree trunks have been stripped of their leaves and bark. Their passage leaves traces. Walkie-talkie pause. Julius calls. A crackling sound answers him, followed by a few words: the trackers have spotted the group on the other side of the hill. We start an acrobatic descent on thick branches so tangled that we do not touch ground, we slide along these vegetation domes, struggling not to fall through. Whence the value of having four hands. It is in this uncomfortable position that Sonia, petrified, attracts my attention by a mousy squeal; I raise my head, and there, seven meters from us, in the middle of a gap, I see a very surprised little gorilla, suspended from a vine by one arm and one hand, looking at us askew with his large black eyes full of gentleness and query. And time, and my breath, and my unstable equilibrium also remain suspended by interminable seconds which the baby breaks off by disappearing without haste into the foliage.

So true, so close, so baby, so cuddly!

Five meters from us, a large, thick plant moves. One step more and we would have run into the silverback. He is there, on his back, surrounded by a cloud of gnats, conscientiously skinning, like a fat grandma a candy wrapper, a branch of bamboo. He turns his head, rests his gaze on us and plunges back into his task, applied and concentrated, as if we did not exist. In a thicket he would not seem so enormous; it is only when his arm extends over his head to break off down another branch that you realize his bestial strength. Goodbye Schwarzenegger! Despite his enormous canines, which we can see under his amazingly mobile lips, able to grab delicate leaves adroitly, gorillas are exclusively vegetarian. Their diet includes nearly sixty plants, with a predilection for rhubarb, wild celery and bamboo shoots. The turgescence of these plants allows them to drink very little. When our silverback rolls over on his side to reach a tender green bough, we can see his enormous round belly. Unlike other vegetarians and other monkeys – the colobus for example – gorillas have only one stomach and, like us, a very long intestine. The apparatus is neither very well adapted nor very efficient for digesting plants: so they must ingurgitate up to twenty kilos of them every day to get enough energy from them. That is what gives them this bloated aspect and explains their constant flatulence, a concert of farts and growls, whistles and whines.

A young gorilla comes over and rolls down beside the patriarch; he pushes it gently away as if to say: "Go play somewhere else." Little by little, cracking branches makes us realize that the gorillas are all around us. The jungle shudders with little earnest mastications. Our hearts are pounding. Julius motions to us.

"Pick branches and pretend to chew, we are being watched.... That will relax them. Laid back and nodding, our eyes pointed at the sky and our chins jutting out, we lend ourselves to the game. Tranquil is the life of the gorilla when he is not pursued by poachers....Sonia whispers:

"What a good gorilla you make, Alex! You'd think you'd been doing it all your life..."

(Fart.)

"Okay, okay....Don't do too many all the same!"

The silverback just disappeared. The rustling increases, and at some mysterious signal the group starts to walk. Julius anticipates the direction; we get ahead of them, intercept them and take positions below them, on a path. One by one they emerge, pass in front of us, pause a moment five meters away and slip into the green sea. The most curious of them is the baby. He takes a few steps towards us when his mother, alert, catches him up unceremoniously. He utters a cry. In the greenery, the silverback stifles a growl immediately followed by a chest-thumping that resonates like a conga. First warning! Now he is climbing into a huge fig tree to follow his family's progression. His prominent dorsal muscles gently pull on his arms thick as treetrunks; on his back, the silver-gray corset contrasts starkly with his jade-black fleece.

Julius whispers to us: "This group is very small, there are only seven gorillas because it is recent. Mirumba, the silverback, created the Habinyanja B group with two females two years ago, after revolting against his brother, the silverback of Habinyanja A. The dominated males remain in the group as long as they don't challenge the silverback. But at the slighest opportunity, the adults of both sexes (a period of life which they attain between eight and fifteen years of age) try to free themselves from his domination. That usually happens when two groups meet. Standing on their hind legs, the silverbacks then deploy their entire arsenal of intimidation, mock charges, muscle display – the most famous one being drumming their chests – in order to preserve their flock or seduce members of the other group. In fact, these dominated ones take advantage of the confusion created by the battle of the titans to effect transfers and kidnap females. If a silverback is driven out, the new dominant male claims the females but systematically kills the babies before impregnating his harem, to preserve his genetic heritage. For His Honor has an acute awareness of his paternity!"

Soon, the whole group is in the fig tree. Each one at the end of a branch, they look like huge ripe, hairy fruit. I swear like a sailor because the position is not easy to film: all I see is their backlighted rear ends, and all my dreams of interactions evaporate. The stars snub our lenses. Oh well, that's the way it is, and it's all right. The silverback stretches out on a fork and picks fleshy leaves like a dilettante. Time passes tranquilly. The gorillas are not in a hurry, they are doing their three times eight: sleep, eat, move. One after the other, they cast detached glances at us.

Julius explains: "It takes two years to accustom the gorillas to our presence. Come rain or wind, someone comes to see them every day. At first, they disappear in a great crashing of branches, then, little by little, they don't flee as far, until they allow themselves to be approached. We coax them with vocalizations, we calm them by aping them, we move away when the young ones come toward us and we always respect a minimal distance of five meters."

Closer to us, the female delouses her little one while he is busy nursing. The tiny hands are hooked into the scrawny breast and press imperceptible contractions on it. The mother doesn't like that and, between two lice, pushes his hands away and utters a squeal: "Stop that now, it hurts!" The children cling to the adult for the first six months, then set out to discover the world. Fertile at ten, the mama gorilla spends her last forty years either being pregnant or mothering. A sinecure! As she doesn't wean her child for two years and gestation lasts eight and a half months, she can give birth to ten or so little ones in her lifetime. That seems a lot, but one gorilla out of three does not reach the age of six. The babies pay for the silverback challenges, fall from trees, catch respiratory illnesses or dysentery. A visitor with a cold or an illness will be refused access to the gorillas' territory: sharing 97% of our genetic inheritance, they are susceptible to the same germs we are.

After denuding all the branches around him, our silverback takes a snooze with his arms crossed behind his head, his legs sprawled out. A young female takes advantage of this to approach him. She comes down from her branch along the trunk and gets on the same one with the large male. He sizes her up out of the corner of his eye. The female comes even with him and, extending her fist, taps on the sleeper's shoulder with a groan.

Julius is amused: "It's an invitation! The only such case in the animal kingdom, with gorillas it is the female that makes the first move. Not like with us! You are lucky to be able to observe it, they are receptive only three days a month."

But the big lug doesn't seem at all interested. The poor, whining female tries five times before the sire deigns to honor her. He does it as one goes to the front, reluctantly, and as one comes out of a trench, uttering great cries. It is done very quickly – a combat on a balancing beam, a sumo hold, a black, steaming locomotive heading full speed down the rails. The jungle falls silent. His duty accomplished, he falls back onto his fork and pushes the intruder with his foot, who goes back to her lunch on her branch, as if nothing had happened. Big blasé!

The time allotted to us has expired. Julius has already granted us fifteen extra minutes! He intimates that we should come down. While we are retreating, the silverback awakens and seems himself to want to move. He is the first to come down out of the tree, in his slow, dominant manner. He seems be taunting us: "The visit is over! Finally we'll have some peace." The temptation is too strong; it is the perfect opportunity to get some closeups; we backtrack. At the foot of the tree, we can't see a thing. The gorillas have dispersed. Only the female remains. She is waiting for her little one, who insisted on getting down by his own means. Like a mama at the foot of a climbing wall, she follows her pipsqueak's slightest movement. Suddenly, instead of descending, the scamp gets onto a branch that leads toward Sonia. The female is taken aback, the little guy is within a meter of my wife, who backs off without brusqueness. He dangles there and stares at her greedily. It leaves Sonia trembling with emotion, a magic moment, frozen, eternal, an encounter of the third kind! Between the two of them a current passes, the gulf detailed by George Schaller (see p. 136) is filled in!

A raspy cry suddenly breaks the charm, followed by the chest-drumming of the uneasy female. To prove she isn't kidding, she grabs a shrub and shakes it like a plum tree. Sonia makes a strategic retreat while the little one obeys. He was our first vision, he is the one we will take away with us. The future and hope of a disappearing species, who asks for nothing other than a protected forest.

That protection is costly, in the face of human pressure: $500 apiece for an hour's observation. Conservation too obeys the law of supply and demand; the ecotourist must bring in more than poaching for the gorillas to survive. At Bwindi, everything is being done so the surrounding populations will be aware that they possess an inestimable treasure. Unfortunately, the government risks killing the goose that laid the golden eggs in using it to finance all national parks indifferently – to the great disadvantage of the local communities, which are very involved in the protection of the gorillas and their habitat. The sustainable development syndicate of Buhoma receives only $1.50 (10% of the park's entrance fee of $15) instead of the $25 (10% of the tracking fee of $250) originally planned. The nuance is great and dissatisfaction is increasing. That is why, if you want to share this dream hour, this plunge into the origins of our humanity, we encourage you to sleep in the huts of the Buhoma Community Campground in preference to the five other more prestigious lodges. It will cost you $10 instead of $200, and your participation will go 100% to the conservation of the forest of marvels. The park takes only twenty visitors a day for the three groups of gorillas. In going over the register, we counted 3776 over the last three years, eighteen of which were French – "Shame on us!" Hurry! All reservations must pass through the offices of the Uganda Wildlife Authority in Kampala.[1] To go see them is to save them.

Back in Nairobi the "megalopolluted," Sonia undertakes contacts with the Ethiopian authorities to obtain a special authorization to enter their territory via Lake Turkana and the Omo Valley, right in the Rift, and not through the border post at Moyale. For there is only one way to go to Ethiopia, and we don't want to take it. For one thing, it crosses the bleak Chalbi desert, without water, villages, or people, and for another bandits from Somalia attack convoys of livestock trucks coming from Ethiopia and the jeeps of the overlanders[2] driving through Africa from Cape Town to Cairo. Our three South African friends, who had undertaken before us to cross the entire continent unaided (and still hold the world record for it), had been entirely despoiled on that road by those fearsome *Shiftas* as they left Marsabit.

The terrifying story of Bruce Lawson constantly recurs to us: "It was night. Our igloo tent was pitched in the desert. It was so

---

[1] See references at the end of the book.
[2] Travelers, often British, who cross the continent in a vehicle.

hot we were all three in our undershorts. Our lamps were lit; it is certain our yellow dome must have been visible from a long way off....When we lay down after putting out the lamp, a burst from a Kalashnikov ripped through the tent above our heads: hell had descended on us. Then they shouted things that were incomprehensible. We fled through the hole in the tent and ran madly into the desert. From a distance, we witnessed the ransacking of our camp: they were after our passports and money, but that was the only thing we had been able to save. We were naked, with our fanny packs. When they realized what had happened, they began to follow our trail. We saw them light their lamps from time to time to find our tracks in the desert. During my military service in the special forces, I had learned that, in this situation, you have to zigzag. We could see them backtracking, starting forward again, firing into the air to intimidate us; this little game lasted all night. At dawn, they had disappeared. Nothing remained of our things but debris. When we were back in Nairobi, it took us two months to get over it before we could set out again, this time with an army escort, which followed us step by step from Marsabit to Moyale, for two hundred kilometers..."

Our plan therefore is to remain at the bottom of the Rift, in contact with the tribal populations, and go by way of Lake Turkana, where we hope to be able to meet with Louise Leakey on her dig site.

One day, Sonia returns radiant: "The Ethiopians accepted: we have just received a letter signed by their Minister of Tourism. He grants us an exceptional authorization. Look, here it is! Another good piece of news, I also succeeded in catching Louise Leakey just before she flew off in her little airplane. And guess what? She is going to manage to be there when we are at Koobi Fora!"

In the meantime, we meet Nigel Pavitt, a retired British officer, who has an excellent knowledge of the terrain from having crossed the Turkana country in every direction. He is reputed for his precision and meticulousness. A distinguished member of the Royal

Geographic Society, he is famous for his photos of East Africa. He gives us some advice.

"Up to Kapedo, to the north of Lake Baringo, you're okay, there are people everywhere. After that, you are in theSuguta Valley, dry and dead in this season: there is not a soul for a hundred forty kilometers until Lokori. It's a zone of tribal war between Pokots and Turkanas, a no man's land. When they see each other, they fire. But right now, as there is no grass, it's rather calm, you should have some chance....Along the way, there is nothing but a hand pump from the 1930s, in the destroyed village of Napeitom. Last I heard, it still worked. After Lokori, same thing to Lake Turkana, but beginning there you have two hundred kilometers utterly off-trail along a dry river bed where there are Turkana tribes that dig wells in the sandy bed. I think they are very friendly. If you can manage to hike from well to well, you should be all right. In forty years, I have only heard of one Westerner, an American, who risked it alone, but he had a little caravan of three camels coming from Samburu." And Nigel concluded, in very British manner: "What you intend to do there is not impossible, but very daring."

A few days before returning to Ndulelei to pick up the trek where we had left it, at our 7411th kilometer, at the house of our friends Laure and Arnaud Thépenier we meet Patrick, an expatriate.

"You are not the only ones to be crossing Africa on foot," he declared. "Yesterday, a customer told me he had run into a colossus of a man who has been walking for three years and preaching in the shantytowns..."

All together we exclaim: "Harald Bohn!"

That's our Norwegian giant, whose steps we have been following since the homes of Rick Becker and Nico Steinberg in South Africa,[3] where he had passed respectively one year and six months ahead of us. This is too much! Third time's a charm! Since then, we have heard no more about him. This time we have caught up with

---

[3] See vol. I, pp. 49 and 137.

him. We ought to meet him. Patrick specifies: "If I have understood correctly, he is at a campground near the city center. There must not be many, so it shouldn't be too difficult to find him."

The inquiry is quickly made. We find the campground, go there and ask the director: "Where is the hiker's tent?"

"Over there, in the corner. You're in luck, he just got back from the Mathare shantytown. It's crazy what this guy is doing! You know him?"

"Somewhat..."

We present ourselves at his tent and call him in a cavernous voice: "Harald Bohn!"

He has no more stuck his head out of the tent than two frantic Frenchmen throw themselves at him. We have so many things to say to each other, so many memories to share! Few people can truly understand what we are going through. He is one. His plan is a little different from ours, but we have much in common. He is packing much more weight than we are and is not following a straight line; he goes wherever prayer and the members of Christian communities call him. He remains to pray with them for several weeks, tries to solve their problems and reinvigorate their initiatives. He is a spiritual visitor in the Lutheran style. He is tall and impressive as he has been described to us, with the eyes of a lamb of evangelical gentleness. In three years, he has had the time to know a few disappointments. In Transkei, he almost got himself killed by the owner of a guest house where he was sleeping.

"I was dreaming that she was over me with a knife, I opened my eyes, and she was indeed there, with bloodshot eyes, bent over my bed with a raised knife. I calmly said to her: 'Go ahead! Do what you have to do!' She melted into tears and asked my forgiveness. She had had a fight the night before with her husband, and someone had come to warn me to get out of there. But I had stayed."

We are petrified. We had gone around Transkei on the advice of many South Africans. He, knowing perfectly well what he was doing, had decided to go through it to respect the words of Christ: "I am come not to save the righteous, but sinners..."

More recently, passing along the Kenyan coast between Tiwi Beach and Diana Beach, near Mombasa, a great center of sexual tourism, soft drugs and new "Goa" of the backpackers,[4] he was assaulted.

"I was walking on the beach road, carrying my big backpack, when three guys came out of the thickets with *pangas*.[5] Without even asking me anything at all, they began to beat me. Since I am nonviolent, all I did was defend myself, I dodged several blows, but they surrounded me and I didn't see them coming. Fortunately, they were not very big and I could hold them off with my long arms. It was surreal, they were not shouting and I said nothing. It all happened silently. I had nasty slashes on both arms and on the head, I was pissing blood and I could see the fear in their eyes: they did not understand why I was not running away, why I did not fall, why I did not cry out; it's easy, I was reciting an Our Father. A *matatu* came out of nowhere, stopped beside us, the door opened and hands literally plucked me from the ground. I was saved! My good Samaritans took me to the Mombasa hospital, where they sewed me up. The poor blokes! I forgave them, I pity them, they probably needed money to buy drugs..."

We are chilled. That is what so far we have been spared. That is why we try to avoid urban zones. How would we react in such a situation? When I tell Harald that, like us, he ought at a minimum to have a tear gas canister, he replies: "But I am not worried, your things are just gadgets, I have the best protection possible." The madness of a sage, the faith of a prophet.

When the time comes to set out again, mindful of all these uncertainties, all these challenges and improbable meetings to come, we have written up the first 214 pages of our first book. The work is well along. We have ended this writing period by describing

---

[4]   Goa is a place where backpackers go to smoke hashish in India.
[5]   Machetes.

our arrival at the ruins of the Great Zimbabwe on 11 September 2001, exactly a year ago. Our plan is to finish the last chapters in Ethiopia, where our friend Jean-Claude Guilbert has been awaiting us for two years...

12

The Mau Escarpment

KENYA

The resumption is hard. As usual. To stop for more than a week is to start all over again. Too many steaks in Nairobi. The suntan has worn off. Where are the proud hikers who have covered 7411 kilometers? Reset. Go back to Go. It's as if we had never walked. Our friend Naeem Omar, from Nelspruit in South Africa, has sent us *in extremis* some new shoes and some halal *biltong*[1] via DHL. He swears by it. It is his duty, he says, to provide us our shoes, because we are walking toward Jerusalem. He sees in our walk "in the footsteps of Man" a pilgrimage, a *hadj* toward the eternal city. We are also walking for him.

On the way back to Ndulelei, we ride on an asphalt road that is completely stove in. The potholes are cauldron holes. The buses and trucks zigzag in an infernal rodeo, the windshields graze each other, the rearview mirrors all but touch, the wheels skid onto the shoulders, giving all these rolling tombs an impressive cant. We are scared stiff, our backs like jelly, holding on tight to the handles in front of us. We have lost the habit of speed. Gritting her teeth,

---

[1] South African recipe for dried meat.

Sonia rails: "We would really look stupid if we were crushed in a bus while pretending to be crossing Africa on foot…"

I complain about the awful quality of the road to my neighbor, an impassive Kenyan, in a little tight suit with a little leather briefcase on his knees. He replies: "Yet you have paid for this road. European money has been sent to the Equipment Ministry, the Indian contractors are ready, the asphalt has arrived from the Middle East, the gravel is in stock.…But it doesn't get done…"

"Why not? It's all the same a strategic axis for the whole country, the road that goes to the Maasai Mara, isn't it?"

"That's exactly why it doesn't get done."

"I don't understand."

"Think about it! To whose advantage can it be for this road to be stove in? How do tourists get to the Mara now? Most of them by plane. What you don't know is that two of our ministers, Olé Ntimama, in the president's office, a Maasai by birth, and Nicholas Ono Biwot, of the same tribe as President Moi, Kalingin in other words, personally own several airplanes, Cessna Caravans of Kenya Airways, that every day fly several round trips to the Mara, carrying hundreds of tourists. At a hundred dollars one way per person, it's a juicy traffic. These men have no interest in seeing the tourists go to the Mara by car or bus.…They would rather keep the money to redo the roads that lead to their private properties…"

"How do you know all this?"

"I work at the Equipment Ministry.…But fortunately, this time, Europe is not going to let it happen, the funds can only be used for this road. So the ministers yell about colonial interference. Your mistake is to have trusted our leaders for forty years.…But that will change, the people are tired of it and will soon be heard from. The African Renaissance[2] will come from the people, not from the governments![3]

---

[2] A concept fashionable in pan-African political circles, according to which there is a liberal, imperialist plot that willfully perpetuates the continent's problems the better to exploit it.

[3] We left on 5 October 2002; the presidential election was to take place in December.

From Ndulelei, we leave intuitively in a northerly direction. The sensation is heady. To have no cares except to go freely forward. This freedom that has been inspiring us for twenty-two months. We cannot set a precise goal for ourselves nor a deadline because we know neither where we are going nor how we are going to get there. Our sole obligation is to walk northward and to meet unknown Africans. That would fill many with anguish but it relaxes us, our immediate future is not in our hands. What would stress us would be to be forced to stick to a plan, to be expected somewhere. With this kind of hike, we reconnect with a double feeling, the satisfaction of accomplished work, behind us, and the call of the unknown ahead. The effort and a full life, in slow motion. Everything becomes a surprise, everything becomes an adventure. Even and especially the simplest things.

Lungs dilated and a smile on our lips, we slowly climb the Mau escarpment. It is a prolongation of the Nguruman escarpment, which we were following further south. Still this western lip of the Rift. A day of ascending in the sun, but, with elevation, we reach cool air. At the end of an alley cut through a cornfield, we come out at the crest. The view of the Rift blows you away. The immense collapsed trench is clearly legible; its tiers descend like steps all the way to the bottom. Between the Longonot volcano and the Suswa crater, the road to Nairobi stretches straight on the plain. All the way at the bottom, gangly, microscopic giraffes autograph the landscape. At Kojonga, at the top of an interminable steep-sided trail, we are greeted at the home of Joyce Kojay, director of the school. All the teachers in the country have been on strike for more than a month.

"Our bonuses and our overtime have not been paid for five years! How do you expect us to raise the country's children on seventy-five euros a month?"

Kojonga is a wooden village perched on the escarpment. Its inhabitants are all displaced persons from various tribes: Kikuyus, Luos and Maasai who have settled, often married to women of other tribes. They came here in 1988, after violent conflicts that opposed the traditional Maasai and other populations that had settled progressively on their territory. Here they have cleared everything and survive on small plots of land. Joyce is a large, jovial matron who takes in abandoned children, serves soup for pupils who cannot pay the board and provides comfort all around her.

"My husband left. We had an authority problem. He could not accept my standing up to him. One day, he was going to lay a hand on me, so I threw him out....Since then I feel so free! You know, African women can very well do without men. Especially here. The men are alcoholics and idle. There is no work except harvesting potatoes."

Topoti, Monday 7 October 2002, day 648, 36 km, 7501st km

On the escarpment, the forest has been recently destroyed. Half-plucked tufts of trees here and there are resistant, only the largest, the ones the woodcutters could not take on for want of appropriate tools. Besides, they respect the old ones. The furrows adorned by potato sets are rich and fertile. The air is chilly. It is a health walk. Our passage on this byroad arouses a veritable frenzy. The people come and greet us at their threshold: "*Karibu chae, karibu pumzika...!*" (Welcome to tea, come rest a bit!) The last recorded White is a missionary who came through by car six months ago. To think we are within thirty kilometers of the road to the Mara, taken by all the tourists who haven't the means to fly there! Another reverse side of the decor...it's never far away. It suffices to go to the out-of-the-way places where there isn't anything to see, only men to encounter. We walk due north on the crest. On the right, the sheer cliff of the Rift, and at the bottom Lake Naivasha surrounded by huge expanses of greenhouses; on the left, the undulations of the slopes that descend towards Narok, the Maasai capital, on which stretch the most impressive grain plantations we have seen since South Africa: regular verdure as far as the eye can see. A shock! Real fields! Opulence! It is therefore possible.

At noon, we happen to stop before a truly little old house

planted on the edge of the escarpment, in the middle of a green lawn surrounded by enclosures. The vision is so improbable that we are persuaded a European lives there. A prioris are tenacious, especially when they have been "a-posteriorized" over nearly two years and thousands of kilometers. So there! Serves us right: Nahason Naïja welcomes us. We are joyful. We adore encountering the exception that confirms the rule. It is the proof that everything is possible and that the predictive field can be thwarted by the fantasy of existence and human freedom. Nahason grows potatoes on a plot of five hectares which he owns.

"In fact, I was the assistant veterinarian in a Naivasha milk factory; I thought I could start a business on my own. Big mistake! I bought several milk cows and settled here, because there is a good demand for milk among the planters. In three years, all my cows died, I don't know why, maybe the elevation, the cold nights, an unknown disease, I don't know, but I can tell you that I miss my pay!"

"Then how do you manage to live here?"

"I have my potatoes, but they don't bring in anything; I still have two cows for my personal consumption, and besides that I work from time to time in the barley and hops plantations of Narok."

"It's not wheat?"

"Not now but, indeed, in the colonial period, these thousands of hectares had been opened for raising wheat for export – since we didn't eat bread. Today, the harvest is destined for the nationalized Kenya Breweries, the country's largest factory. We make beer with it."

A question of priorities....Drink or eat? In any case, wheat comes free from the United States or the World Food Programme. Here as elsewhere, to put the people to sleep, the government replaces *panem et circenses* with a *vinum et circenses*.

"We were displaced here after the riots and pogroms that occurred during the last two elections, at the end of the 1980s; we were driven out by the plains Maasai, themselves exiled from Naivasha by the great flower plantations, which flood the world rose market and empty the lake. We needed land to survive; so we planted potatoes here. The problem is that the production everywhere reaches the market at the same time and the prices collapse, not even covering our costs."

Nahason and so many others are educated and unbelievably cultivated.

"Never forget that we African people are alone in the world. No one helps us as individuals, even if our countries are permanently subsidized. In Europe, your society is generous, education and hospitals are free, you have social security, unemployment insurance, electricity, running water, roads, you help each other without knowing it, your taxes come back to you in the form of advantages. Here, we have to pay for everything; the taxes go up but entitle us to no advantage at all; they pay for the ministers' Swiss bank accounts. Myself, if I can't work, I die, and my family dies."

We developed a great admiration for these African men of every country, braced against adversity with serene resignation. They have left ideologies aside. They do not believe in the extravagances of the cities, they are pragmatic. For a long time we have known that they are not lazy. That their misery is not geographically or climatically predestined, either. That isn't also the result of imperialist aggression, no more than a consequence of the colonial era. It is just a problem of management. Nahason seems to be reading my thoughts.

"Well run, Africa would be the richest continent on earth. We have everything here, and all year. I have a friend who did his veterinary study in Russia. He was in Siberia. He told me it was hell on earth. Nature is dead for more than half the year. Do you think it's easier to live in Siberia than here? And despite that, Russia is much richer than we are. The truth is that our government is incapable of creating jobs, plants, factories, an economy able to employ workers."

"Do you miss the time when you were paid wages?"

"You bet! You know, there are three sources of work for the

educated in this country. Public service, but there, if you are not Kalingin, the tribe of President Moi, you have no chance; the U.N., which employs four thousand people in Nairobi, many of whom are expatriates from the world over; the NGOs and foreign companies. Our government is uninterested in developing the country. Only the Indians, the churches and the NGOs are involved in development, but too much money is diverted. We are the fifth most corrupt country in the world. We want change!"

On the eve of the presidential election, everyone repeats the same mantra: change. Old Mzee's[4] power is used up and violently decried. Will he yield to an alternative? Everyone is doubtful. Nahason pursues: "He wants to impose Uhuru Kenyatta on us, the son of our first president: he is a former drug addict, alcoholic, with no past, no qualifications, who has never been able to grow in his father's shadow. He will only be Moi's puppet, we don't want that masquerade."

Along our path, all the Kenyans we have met have expressed comparable feelings, proof of amazing political maturity. But Nahason concludes pessimistically: "Unfortunately many young people have no identification card, the necessary condition for registering to vote, and will be refused access....In any case, the government will cheat, or at the last minute buy out the opposition candidates."

A story to follow at the end of December. Where will we be?

The next day, we are going through burning bamboo forests. Our map shows a state domain. All of the primary jungle of Mau is going up in smoke – moreover this jungle isn't even on our section of map any more....Other people came to settle here on these wild clearings to plant other surplus potatoes. Man must eat. Here unfortunately there is no human development without ecological disaster. And no ecology without a hint of misanthropy. Nothing can contain the demographic pressure. It is stronger than all the

---

[4] "The Venerable," a surname given to Daniel Arap Moi, president of Kenya from 1978 to 2002.

fine ideas and good feelings, the pretty flowers and little patches of virgin forest.

We redescend the escarpment even with Lake Nakuru into a suddenly intact and radically different forest. A thalweg is cleared to provide enclosed pastures at the bottom of a gently sloped little valley. The barbed wire is rusted and the stables speak of a distant era when livestock was abundant. On both sides the tall heads of mountain pines and centuries-old spruce rise on the hillsides. We could be in Switzerland, in Slovakia, in Romania or in Arkansas, but not in Africa. Sonia exclaims: "Here and nowhere else is where I would come settle if I had no land. But there's not a living soul… a mystery!"

A young man is walking with us. His name is Simon, he is a social science student in Nakuru on his way to Mau. We share our astonishment with him.

"It's normal. It's a private forest here, a former colonial domain given intact to the Maasai to compensate them for the losses of territories to which they have been subjected. They drive out at the tip of their spears anyone who wants to settle here and elimi-nate the field-clearers who dare to go after the trees. The Maasai have an immense respect for forests but don't inhabit them. I know the family that runs this one; they cut one or two very large trees each year at remote points, when they need some cash to buy livestock."

"Why don't they come live here?"

"They don't like to live in the forest; their cows would catch bronchitis because of the cold nights…"

We pass by a large ruined building that looks like a Swiss chalet, with a shingle roof falling off the remains of the caved-in frame.

"This is the former British sawmill. All the trees here were planted by the English. And no one has touched anything since they left. Beginning at that stream over there, the forest belongs to President Moi."

Indeed. The line is clear. Power-saw massacre, as in the great

Canadian North. The hill is naked, scattered with a macabre jumble of stripped branches.

"How long has it been like that?"

"Five years now."

"And they are not going to replant it?"

Simon bursts out laughing. "Replant? That is much too expensive! And what for? The old Moi will be dead when the trees are grown, so he has no interest in it."

That night, at Miti Mingi, we come to a halt before another stone house lost in a field. Lots of glass, a bay window, a plywood roof covered with asphalt shingles and dormer windows: a house nicely reminiscent of the 1950s. We are going to see. A roundish mama greets us in the doorway.

"Are you lost?"

"No. We are going to Nakuru. But it's too far for tonight."

"Are you out of money?"

This is the first time this question has been asked us so directly. I hesitate before replying: "No. But we are walking so we will meet people, and we saw your fine house, so since night is about to fall, we thought maybe we could sleep in your garden…"

She bursts into laughter. A powerful, loud laugh, full-throated, that makes her generous chest heave.

"*Karibu! Karibu!* Trust Anastasia, you aren't going to sleep outdoors tonight!"

When we start to enter we have a shock. The house that from a distance looked so well-kept is in fact occupied by squatters, it has no water or electricity. The living room has been transformed into a corn granary. There are pallets along the walls and the middle of the room with caved-in wooden floors is filled with huge jute sacks full of corn from which Anastasia on the ground sets to work removing the grain. All over the walls, kitsch fluorescent posters of Jesus, the Virgin Mary and shepherds surround old frames where sit enthroned a handsome young man with slicked-back hair in a becoming uniform and a beautiful young, delicate woman in a lace dress. Anastasia spots our bewildered glance.

"That was my husband, he was a military man, and I..."

She stifles her laughter with a smirk meaning that she was about to say something stupid. There are all sorts of odds and ends in the corners. We plunge in to help. Night falls. The dogs have come to see what's going on, closely followed by a gaggle of children, and then the neighboring women. The consecrated ritual begins anew. It is part of our daily routine. And our video camera will unfortunately never capture that backstage activity. It is made up of repetitions, greetings, laughter, sore feet, grime in the joints, pressing desire impossible to satisfy, sticky hands and torn nails, rotten teeth and fetid breaths, shoulder pains and wet shirts that cool with immobility, crusted with salt, with embarrassing odors and dirty socks, discomfort and absence of intimacy. And Sonia bears it all with a smile, even happily, as long as idle, noisy men don't break in. Now this evening there are only industrious women, well-behaved children, a hen coiled up against a sleeping cat. So all is fine.

Anastasia, in the golden light of a candle, asks us with her imperturbable simplicity: "What have you done wrong? What sin are you atoning for to want to suffer so?"

It's our turn to burst out laughing. We explain to her that we have nothing significant on our conscience with respect to higher powers, and for us that this trek is a passion, a job, our life, all at once. She remains doubtful.

"You have no children? That's why you're walking! To ask the Lord to give you children..."

We do it again, doubled up. Anastasia is really extraordinary. She finally reveals out loud what thousands of Africans must have thought *in petto*, pretending to believe our line. It is no doubt an idea only of the well-off to be willing to do without everything, willing to get fleas and live with no thought for the morrow for the simple pleasure of meeting people, of being here with Anastasia. And maybe one can't understand a process of voluntary renunciation and deprivation as long as one hasn't attained material comfort. I don't know. I no longer know. I only know one thing, and that is that we are happy with this big lady with a heart even bigger than her mammaries. And that she is happy to have us in her place.

Sonia explains: "If we had children, we would not be able to hike in Africa. Where would we leave them? With our parents? With our brothers and sisters? It doesn't work that way where we live! There you are responsible for your own children; life in the extended family no longer exists!"

And she replies with her contagious laughter: "So that means you never make love?"

Always her unbelievable straightforward candor. We think we come to study her, hear her testimony, and it is she who examines us.

"Oh yes, occasionally, but I take the contraceptive pill..."

"But didn't you tell me you were Catholic? Our curate says taking the pill is like an abortion..."

And there we go into discussions on free will, personal conscience, respect for others, family planning, and the fact that the African churches are often more royal than the king, caught between the ideal and reality, the difficulty of maintaining a single line for all modes of life and all economic levels.

Sonia reassures her: "No, Anastasia, taking the pill is not an abortion. I believe, on the contrary, that it makes it possible to avoid many abortions."

1. Benjamin Salbé, Desmond Rotitch, Emmanuel Toroititch
2. Susie Mills, Dr. Brooks Childress, Wim Van der Bossche, Jenny
3. Hélène Momoï
4. Thomas and Jane Nanok
5. Clarkson Ekouleou, Robert Ignolan
6. Padre Rico

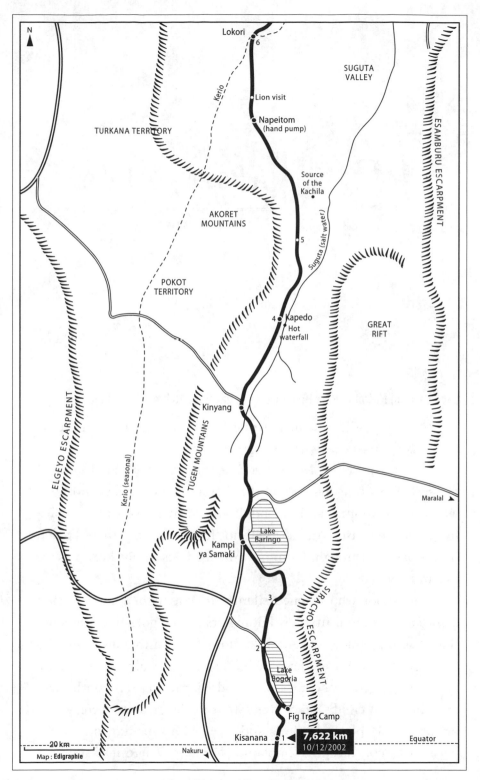

N

Lokori
6

SUGUTA
VALLEY

ESAMBURU ESCARPMENT

Lion visit

Napeitom
(hand pump)

Kerio

TURKANA TERRITORY

Source
of the
Kachila

AKORET
MOUNTAINS

5

Suguta (salt water)

POKOT
TERRITORY

4 Kapedo
Hot
waterfall

GREAT
RIFT

ELGEYO ESCARPMENT

Kerio (seasonal)

Kinyang

TUGEN MOUNTAINS

Maralal ▶

Lake
Baringo

Kampi
ya Samaki

S/RACHO ESCARPMENT

3

2

Lake
Bogoria

Fig Tree Camp

20 km

Kisanana 1 ◀ **7,622 km**
10/12/2002

Equator

Map : **Edigraphie**

Nakuru

From Harrismith to Messina

CHAPTER 13

A Rosary of Lakes

KENYA

Lake Nakuru, National Park Headquarters, day 650, 10 km, 7540th km

"Why come and form such strong bonds only to leave the next day?" says Anastasia, when we say goodbye.

We have no reply. Maybe so that the next day's attrition will not sully the strong memory of the first moments. In a year or two, when our adventure and our book are finished, we will not have forgotten Anastasia. And she will not have forgotten these French hikers passing through. From now on she lives in our hearts as we live in her head.

A neighbor who listened silently to last night's conversation comes along on our first few kilometers as one goes to confession. She is accompanied by Peter Likomo, a tall, thin young man who has pastoral duties in the parish. And as we walk, as often, we become engaged in a course of sexual education. Six months ago, after her sixth child, Nancy Rose went in the greatest secrecy to a private family planning clinic and received a subcutaneous, semi-permanent contraceptive implant, Norplant. There it is she who

is improving our education, for we didn't know about this procedure. Since then, her husband, satisfied, no longer cheats on her,
and does not risk bringing AIDS into the house. She is afraid to
speak to the curate about it and wants to know how we feel. We
assure her by saying that she has made the best choice and that it
is nobody's business but hers. And that, if she is ill at ease about
it, it's just that she is ahead of her time.

The international campaigns against AIDS are no doubt too
focused on condoms – which most Africans are reluctant to use –
and have neglected women's contraceptive procedures that would
allow men not to go hunting outside what they could find safely
at home; to experience sexuality as a couple without the risk of
procreating when they believe they have enough children for their
resources.

That too is why we walk. To learn certain practical realities at
the source, to see the world with the other end of the spyglass.

At the gate of the Nakuru National Park, we wonder which way
to go around it when a white Land Rover comes up to us. The sign
Rhino Rescue, a British NGO, covers the hood. A little man with
glasses gets out half surprised and half suspicious.

"What are you doing there?"

"We don't know which way to go around the park, but perhaps
we could cross it on foot with a ranger?"

"Are you kidding me? Are you journalists? Don't you read the
newspapers? We've just had two rangers eaten by lions, so that'll
be enough for this week..."

We have bumped into Pius Mulwa, the conservator of the
hundred and sixteen rhinoceroses of the Nakuru National Park.
We tell him about our last twenty-two months, and he starts to
smile. When we tell him about our lions in Tanzania and our rhinoceroses of the Kruger Park, he gets excited: "What, you know
Johannes Malan, of Game Capture?[1] He's the one who sold me our

---

[1] See vol. I, p. 165.

black rhinos. Here they had all been poached. And you have been walking all that time? You must be crazy! But sorry, even for you, it won't be possible to cross the park on foot; on the other hand, I will invite you to my place in the center of the park, and tomorrow I will drop you off back here, all right?"

By dint of living through wild coincidences, we end up thinking everything is normal. In the park, all is lovely and calm. We go through a fine forest of *xanthophloea* acacias with trunks yellow like plain trees, with immense fans of branches under which scads of impalas graze peacefully. We have already forgotten how virginal and poetic is a space without men.

Pius gets back to his rundown. "We have just put down the whole lion pride. A dozen of them had tasted the rangers. The rumor got around that they had committed professional mistakes, that is absolutely not true. The first incident took place in full daylight, between the main gate and his car. The man went five meters! The lions were lying in wait in the grass, right there. They could have got out of the park, but had no desire to do so, they wanted to dine on my bloke. The second incident cost a woman her life, the next day at dawn, right in the middle of the compound, between her house and her kitchen: barely three meters! She was going to fix her baby's porridge. The truth, which no one wants to admit, is that we border on the city of Nakuru, second largest in the country, and the lions have become accustomed to human flesh..."

We are beside ourselves.

"How? From cadavers?"

Pius makes a face. "Almost....You know, AIDS kills twelve hundred people a day in this country, at least 20% of the population is infected, that makes more than six million people. The HIV-positive women who already have six or seven children get rid of their fetuses or their newborn by throwing them over the park fence, where the police will never come to look for them. I know, I bury more than three of them a week on average. Recently, we hardly find any at all, but the lions are always lounging in that area. As if they were waiting for their food....The only thing that will save this country is the contraceptive pill!"

"Strange enough, we were talking about it last night and this morning with people on the way, and we were coming to the same conclusions."

"Well for me, I wish someone had told me about it sooner. I am HIV-positive and my first wife died of it."

We are dismayed.

"Take it easy! I have a second wife and just had a child. God be praised, neither of them is infected."

We come to a sort of metallic prefabricated building dropped there like a wart on one of the world's prettiest faces. Husna Abdallah, the young wife, comes to greet us with the baby.

Over a cold beer, he talks about his job. "In ten years I have succeeded in wiping out poaching around Nakuru thanks to concentrated work by the local communities and Rhino Rescue, which builds them schools, dispensaries, pumps. The money given for the protection of rhinos is not spent on weapons and materiel for reprisals or dissuasion but on improving the living conditions of the local communities. If a rhino is killed, everything stops, the people know this. Thus they see the direct interest in fighting against poaching and do the policing themselves. Nothing is more effective. But before all that can be put into place, I still had to have an iron fist. I pursued the guys into their own villages; when they escaped, I had their families imprisoned until they surrendered, I was shot at dozens of times. When I caught one, I can assure you he didn't do it again. The real problem was the supply lines of bushmeat that had to be dismantled as far away as Nakuru and Nairobi. What I did, no White Kenyan could ever have done..."

"Really? Why's that?"

"Because he would have been accused of racism! But thanks to that, in this park, which is one of Kenya's smallest, I have sixty-five black rhinos in the forests overlooking the lake and fifty-one white rhinos on the plain. The tourists are sure to see some."

As we border the park on a dirt road following its outside perimeter, we observe several results of this positive mutual assistance that benefits everyone. In one school, we meet Spencer Gelthorpe, a hyperactive British sexagenarian, who turns to Sonia as if he had seen an apparition and says to her in the guise of a compliment, most impressed by her beige skirt and straw hat, "Meryl Streep, I presume?"

He is rebuilding an old 1946 Lister Monocylinder that pumps water from a hundred fifty meters deep. He tells us about it with tremors in his voice, vaunting the merits of the impressive couple produced by the very heavy iron shuttlecock and the robustness of the four-cycle monocylinder boasting two valves – which requires next to no maintenance – and the advantage of belt transmission....Nothing is forgotten, a true devotee. The drill was paid for by English donors who sponsor the park's rhinos. The school is the only water source in the area. It was constructed in 1998, in hewn stone, to replace a mud building that today has become a stable, with the cows providing milk that is distributed to the schoolchildren. An ecology awareness program is integrated into the education. Every Monday, the children join a reforesting initiative. The dispensary was built in the same way, and the wages of the permanent nurse are covered by Rhino Rescue. Spencer is everywhere. He is very affected by what we tell him about the deforestation of the escarpment.

"It's a collective suicide. When I came here, the village's two rivers were permanent. Now they are seasonal. Last year, they did not flow at all. In 1988, this agricultural slope you see was a virgin forest that provided water for Lakes Nakuru and Elmenteita. Their level drops a little farther every year, endangering the life of the pink flamingos. And if we had not come to make this well, where would all these people get water? The government does strictly nothing for them..."

Leaving Nakuru, we travel fifteen kilometers of asphalt, the first in two thousand kilometers. From Malawi to here, we have always walked on dirt trails except twice five meters, to cross two roads, the road to Ngorongoro and the one to Narok.

Kisanana, on the equator, Saturday 12 October 2002, day 653, 26 km, 7622nd km

By jumping. We pass it by jumping. The equator. Under a rainbow. Over our walking stick placed on the ground to represent the imaginary line. With this little symbolic bound we pass, lost in the open bush, into the northern hemisphere. The only map we have is a rumpled photocopy of a 1950s document. But the equator hasn't budged. It passes precisely across the top of this little hill, on our right. It's only one more step, but for us it's a giant step. And still that improbable rainbow that smiles on us against an ink-colored sky to the north. We embrace to the mocking laughter of a yellow-billed hornbill.

This morning, we have left the blacktop and happily rejoined a trail and are with each step going deeper into an arid bush. We're finished with coolness until Ethiopia.

This evening, we find refuge with three nurses at the government dispensary in Kisanana. They wanted to be doctors. They weren't allowed access to the exams since they could not pay the bribe demanded. They are squatting in an unhealthy building. We pitch our tent in a dusty, empty room. Benjamin Salbé soon comes to fetch us to share a dish of *ugali* garnished with *sukuma wiki*, boiled cabbage leaves, since they do not have the means of buying themselves meat. On the walls, trails of blood bespeak nights tormented by mosquitos angrily smashed. On the posters, les Bleus[2] and their triumphal 1998 victory serve us as ambassadors. The nurses speak at length to us about our French society, open and generous, that gives Africans their chance. They marvel at our social system, complain about theirs.

---

[2] French national soccer team.

All day we have seen, alike around each large African city, and like before Blantyre, in Malawi,[3] a noria of coalmen riding bicycles, bringing fuel into the cities after burning the surrounding forests.

Benjamin explains: "The government keeps on raising the price of paraffin, instead of subsidizing it, and they run publicity to get us to use burners to cook with. But as long as coal is cheaper, since it isn't taxed, the forests will disappear. There is no alternative. Sustainable development makes me laugh! In Johannesburg, at the Earth Congress, no one had this idea which is so simple: subsidize paraffin. I'm telling you, development is just a business."

Emmanuel Toroititch carries on: "The clowns! They recently celebrated the centennial of the railroad that goes all the way to Uganda. Even Museveni[4] was there! What were they celebrating? A disaster. The train hasn't been working for eight years. My father was a trainman. Everything is broken. It would take millions of dollars to make it operational again. And Museveni needs trains to unblock his country. They did that to influence the World Bank. Our leaders wanted to skip all the steps and not go through the industrial era. Our country only survives thanks to colonial agricultural heritages, tea and coffee, and that is what's killing us! For forty years, nothing has changed, everything has continued to deteriorate. We no longer have the knowhow to maintain the trains. All the spare parts have been used, nothing has been replaced, thought through again, anticipated. So with one hand they beg, and with the other they rap those who give. A Maasai prophet had foreseen the arrival of the Whites on an iron serpent spitting fire, he had not foreseen that we would break it..."[5]

Desmond Rotitch, in despair, takes the ball on the bounce: "We have been here for four years. They don't want to send

---

[3] See vol. I, p. 278.
[4] President of Uganda.
[5] The *Laïbon* (prophet) Mbatian had predicted in an oracle the invasion of the Whites and the loss of high plateau pastures. Moreover, he had seen an iron serpent spitting fire throughout the Maasai country up to Lake Victoria. He died five years before the line was built.

replacements, or supplements; we still have no electricity, no vac-
cines; they promised us building refurbishments, we have seen no
one, we are chronically short of medicines. When it is serious, we
pack people into a matatu for the Nakuru hospital. Two months
a year, fortunately, an English nurse comes as a volunteer with
medicines and materiel for a vaccination campaign. The rest of the
time, we are of no use..."

Things are bad.

"Moi is detested everywhere in the country, we do not want
Uhuru Kenyatta, we will all vote for the Rainbow Alliance (NARC)
and for Kibaki. Even if he is a former vice-president, was eight
times a minister in a KANU government, he represents a change.
There can't be a democracy without change. The United States
changes every four years, you every five, whereas here KANU has
been in power for thirty-nine years, and it is twenty-four years
since Moi replaced Jomo Kenyatta. And they want to give us
another Kenyatta to continue with their racket? Never! We didn't
free outselves from the Queen of England to fall back into a dynas-
tic monarchy....If Moi cheats, it will be revolution! He is so hated
that he can't even travel in the territory. Last weekend, he went to
Eldoret for a rally. A guy in the crowd called out to him, and things
degenerated. The presidential service of order fired into the pile,
there were three dead and a dozen wounded, the president had to
flee under a deluge of stones....We are very uneasy about these
elections..."

In Olkokwe, the following day, a short walk off-trail brings us
to the abrupt edge of the escarpment and the primeval panorama
of Lake Bogoria. Immense and wild. Beauty to take your breath
away. To the north, the empty bush extends as far as the eye can
see. Wedged between a raised fold with a gentle slope and the foot
of the Siracho escarpment, this green lake extends lengthwise; it
was its discovery that inspired in John Gregory, a Scottish geologist of the late nineteenth century, the very concept of the Great
African Rift. From here it all looks transparent: this immense valley

was not produced by erosion but by a collapse that occurred along the lines of tectonic faults. Lake Bogoria is one of the thirty lakes that punctuate the Great African Rift, from Ethiopia to Malawi, at various elevations, going from Lake Turkana, situated the lowest at 365 meters, to Lake Naivasha, the highest, with its 1883 meters of elevation.

We descend and put up the tent on the south shore of the lake, at Fig Tree Camp. Enormous wild fig trees, heavily buttressed, make an entwinement of branches and vaults, pillars and arches over our heads, where noisy baboons are milling about. A vegetal cathedral. We conscientiously surround our little tent with thorny branches in preparation for the coming night: we are in a natural park and hyenas are not far away.

Scattered on the smooth lake surface jabber myriads of flamingos. A turtle is strolling down the shore. A few paces from there two geysers are blowing like valves, giving away the humors of the earth's entrails. We go bathe nude in a stream of crystalline water coming down from the forest. Jungle ablutions are not very relaxing. It's amazing how vulnerable a Westerner feels when he is naked. We are on the lookout. A baboon cry makes our hair stand on end. Tree roots crawling toward the water become snakes, a little branch ferried by the current into my back makes me jump. It is only when I put my clothes back on that I can enjoy the scene: Sonia bathing, like an African woodland nymph, her harmonious contours, her welcoming curves, the ballet of her hands dancing with crystal, a Diana of primitive times disdaining for a moment her bow and arrows. The only darts flying in this mossy undergrowth are Cupid's.

The night was eventful. The baboons squatting in the branches above our heads were hunted by a leopard. Their cries of alarm long kept us alert before he attacked them. We clearly recognized his growl, reminiscent of the saw stroke ripping the night veil. Panic. Commotion provoked by the charge. The heavy fall of two bodies on the ground and the violent fray that followed petrified us. The silence that succeeded froze us for the rest of the night. A leopard is never far away in the great African sleep. The loss of one of their number does not seem to have traumatized the baboons, with whom we had to contend vigorously to save what could be saved of our breakfast. The bag of sugar soon found itself perched on one of the highest branches, triggering a general brawl among the primates.

It follows that we are not very valiant today. The torridity is overwhelming. We stop soon under the meager shade of an acacia and watch thousands of pink flamingos go by, skimming the water. A little fire, a little soup and photo session. In a methodical ballet, in closed ranks, the artists hem the banks with a pink ribbon and, head down, with their curved-up beak filter their ration of spirulina at the surface of the alkaline waters. Whereupon four Westerners slathered with sunblock come by in a little inflatable dinghy: an Earthwatch team studying the flamingos. It is the second we have run into, after those of the Olduvai Gorge. Great! we think. We are going to learn a lot about flamingos...

Susie Mills is a pretty, blonde English biologist whose mission is to gather water samples for studying the spirulina, that phytoplankton shaped like a little microscopic spring that the flamingos feed on. Dr. Brooks Childress, an American, assisted by Wim Van der Bossche, a Flemish ornithologist, bands birds so as to follow their movements.

"We don't know anything about flamingos!"

Scientific humility. They want to know what are the relations between the various Rift populations and whether their movements occur in regular cycles. Why, from one year to the next, do the numbers vary? We find ourselves this evening at their camp. Brooks invited us with a wisecrack. "Two birds more or less at the table,[6] what does it matter?"

---

[6] The authors' last name "Poussin," means "chick" in English.

On the way there, we pass by the lake's innumerable hot water springs and geysers. Beyond the curtains of vapor, in the mists of the boiling streams flowing towards the lake, to the breathing of Moloch spat through these bottomless fissures, ballets perched on their paintbrushes dance, and bouquets of choreographed necks unfold like the hands of prima ballerinas. Others take themselves for swans and cruise nonchalantly on the water's surface, like petunias ferried by the wind. The setting sun bathes the escarpment in carmine, the show goes on and on, eternal, African, and suddenly, with one feathery impulse, one wingbeat transmitted like a gust of wind and taken up with a thousand cries, quadrilles and minuets, dancers and tutus take off above the wisps of red mist. The flamingo ball has left for other nocturnal banquets.

At the camp, we make acquaintance with a few other amateurs who have decided to donate time, money and passion to advance science and help young Kenyan researchers to pursue their studies. Jenny, for example, is a young Kikuyu biologist from the University of Nairobi. She assists Susie in recording and processing the data collected on the spirulina she's gathered in the field. She cannot accompany her on the Zodiac because she is in a wheelchair.

The dinner taken in common in a tent is high flying. Gordon Thomson, a banker from the City in London, the double of Magnum, with a walrus mustache and Ray Bans screwed to his nose, is the live-wire of the band. "On the program tomorrow, counting the feathers of young males. It's my speciality! I spend my time fleecing people!"

We decide to remain and shoot their work. Brooks warns us: "You can't film the way we catch the flamingos, since we don't want to give our trick to the trappers. Do you know how much a live flamingo can go for, for zoos and other private reserves? Hold on: two thousand dollars!"

An hour before dawn we are on the water with Susie. She has a doctorate on a cavern-dwelling hermaphrodite salamander from

Norway that changes color when it changes sex – funky isn't it! Not surprising if we didn't understand it all. On board is also Yaqing He, a cute young Chinese translator from Hong Kong whom one could more easily picture in a dark suit at an international colloquium on the deregulation of interbank exchanges than on all fours over boxes of Susie's samples, in the muddy-smelly bottom of the Zodiac.

"Susie, lend me your knife, I've bent my nail and can't get this label off!"

In fact, what we are going to do is very complicated: the idea is to gather before sunrise samples of water at several points on the lake, first at the surface, then at depths of 5, 10, 20, 50, and 70 centimeters. Why 70 centimeters? Because that is the length of Susie's arm. There she is in up to the armpits when a little wave fills her mouth with water.

"Ugh! disgusting! Dishwater....Spirulina can only develop in warm, alkaline water with certain salts and other minerals."

Susie explains to us the object of her research. "This phytoplankton, full of chlorophyll, proteins and vitamin C, changes depth according to the hour of day, the sun exposure and wind velocity, which determines the birds' feeding. For example, we'd like to know whether a windy, cloudy season, therefore poor in spirulina, will have repercussions on the number of flamingos that return the next year. To proliferate, this little vegetal source needs calm water and a good deal of sun. And it's only in those conditions that the flamingos can be properly nourished."

For each flask, Yaqing notes the speed and direction of the wind with an anemometer, our position on the lake with a GPS, while Susie plunges her arm to the required depth.

"In a little while, in the camp lab, Jenny will do counts with the binocular magnifying glass to determine the different densities of spirulina, and enter it all into a computer."

Sonia is enthralled. "She's going to count them one by one? But there are millions of them!"

"No. For that she uses a millimetric grid. She counts the units of spirulina in a square millimeter, then multiplies the figure obtained by a thousand to get the density per cubic centimeter."

We get back covered with salts, our skin dry and cracked, eyes red and mud to the knees, while dawn is lighting up a fluffy cover of dappled clouds. We get here just in time for breakfast, then leave again to catch some flamingos.

The device is very quickly set up. Not complicated, but that's all you get to know! Everyone comes back and hides behind the cars. Wim watches in his telescope a candidate group to come get caught. There it is coming, the flamingos are walking on the banks in a compact group. Suddenly two or three of them find themselves hooked by one foot. The others flee. Our apprentice flamingo hunters run toward the shore.

Pamela is a housewife under fifty. The famous housewife! We have finally found her! Not where we expected. She is in shirtsleeves, an oilcloth apron in front. Why an apron? Because, the minute they are stressed and before each takeoff, flamingos jettison ballast....She comes back smiling, with tangible proof of the phenomenon.

"I thought I was well protected, but he got me right under the armpit! Yuk!" Brooks, Wim and Gordon now turn to weighing each bird and counting their alar feathers, in order to find out whether the molting cycles correspond to the richness of nourishment or solely to the age and the hormones unleashed by the reproduction season. Then, they proceed to band the two feet – with a little permanent band that can only be recovered when the bird dies, and a fat band in orange plastic that can be sighted with a telescope, bearing the two letters KA for Kenya. Finally, Wim, a specialist in stork migration, attaches to the back of the more robust specimen a little box fitted with a solar panel and an antenna that emits a beep every five seconds, which is captured by three satellites that make it possible to triangulate and therefore follow its movements. And our cyber guinea-pig flamingo takes off again, belly to the ground then skimming the water on which his mirror image makes him double.

Lake Baringo, Friday 18 October 2002, day 659, 34 km, 7729th km

We leave the team at dawn. Scarcely have we begun than a cry is heard behind us: "Sonia!"

Jenny comes up in her wheelchair. Sonia is embarrassed.

"Sorry, Jenny! In our hurry, I forgot to say goodbye to you."

"It's not that....I was in my tent, I have a little something for you..."

I see them step aside and talk eye to eye. Sonia takes her hands and kisses them tenderly. When she comes back toward me, her eyes are full of tears and her throat knotted. No one has noticed anything. We set out again. After a few moments, she finally breathes out and explains: "She gave me this shell, asking me to take it as far as possible and leave it in the prettiest possible place, that way, she said, she can travel a little with us. We'll have to write her where we have left it so she can dream she's been there too!."

Return to solitude. To silence. To the interior dialogue. With the coming of day, the heat is horrendous. Sonia's thermometer reads over 45°C. For Turkana, we will have to take a donkey or two and enough water. Otherwise we will never make it. Everything is dry and bare. Heat and light. We pass an occasional emaciated inhabitant running to take refuge in the shade of a tree or a shack to wait for the day to be over. Just so do we land in a little hovel of corrugated iron, suffocating with heat. Sonia is scarlet. At the brink of sunstroke. Under the iron, it's not even worth thinking about it. A solitary, shriveled acacia sheds some patchy shade. At least air passes under it. We wait in silence. Sonia is curled up on a sort of china hutch or display, a meter off the ground, and I lie down balanced on a narrow bench. The sandy ground would be far too hot. She is panting like a sick pup. Wait. Nothing else to do. Nothing to hope for from this anus of the world. A great moment of solitude. Children pass. Nice. Don't have the energy to bother us.

Suddenly, a little voice speaks in French: "Bonjour!"

A voice. I'm dreaming. Now I am hearing voices. Delirium threatens.

"Bonjour!"

We start. A little girl is standing there, dressed in pink, guided by a little friend. She is blind.

"Bonjour! Je m'appelle Hélène et j'ai douze ans[7]..."

She tells us how she was taken in by French Sisters at Eldoret, from whom she learned braille; she speaks to us of Paris, describes the Alexander III bridge which she has never seen, the Eiffel Tower, Notre Dame. Sonia weeps silently.

"Why are you crying?" wonders the little barefoot princess, our angel with the lunar eyes.

"I am so happy to meet you. You are marvelous and I am proud of you. Your parents are very lucky to have you."

"That's not what they say..."

"They are wrong. You are the smartest little girl that we have ever met in Kenya. And if you could see, you would know that you are very pretty."

She breaks out in a broad smile and goes straight to Sonia's arms for a hug eternally inscribed in our memories.

Where are you today little princess?

In the evening, still under the charm of that magical encounter, we reach Lake Baringo where French friends, volunteers in Nairobi, led by our faithful Arnaud Thépenier, meet us to spend the week-end at Roberts Camp in Kampi ya Samaki. Saucisson, camembert, red wine....We spend wonderful evenings before plunging into the great northern deserts and the hostile immensities of Turkana. We try in vain to buy two donkeys in the village. Farther north, we are told, farther north....One evening, while we are feasting by our campfire, a German tourist is chewed in the dark, fifty meters away from us, by a hippopotamus. She survives with only broken ribs,

---

[7] Hello, my name is Helen and I'm twelve years old.

one lung punctured and one arm gored. She went looking at the moon with her boyfriend. How romantic! They found themselves face to face with the female and her young. At Baringo, you can bathe amidst the crocodiles, they have never bitten anyone, but do not dance the farandole with the hippos....To each lake its dangers. The *Fantasia* of Baringo is not that of Bogoria.

CHAPTER 14

Suguta, Death Valley

KENYA

W hen we leave Lake Baringo we spend two days on the margins of Pokot country, another derivative of the nilo-hemitic peoples with pastoral traditions, common origins but ancestral rivalries. The lifestyles and traditions are largely the same, but the distinctions of identity are irreducible. They never compromise on costume; each tribe distinguishes itself by a very precise decorum, a uniform that marks its identity. A Maasai is not a Samburu any more than a Pokot is a Turkana; even if they share the same condition and sometimes the same language. Not their territories. Not their pastures.

You can't understand these peoples if you don't understand that livestock is the spinal cord of their whole existence, the structure of their thought. Bank, pantry, symbol of power, of fertility, arsenal, soulmate, spirituality, work, pastime, spectacle, subject of conversation, of poetry, of song, exchange currency, reason for existing, for loving, for fighting and dying, livestock is everything, and there is nothing outside of livestock. I have livestock therefore I am: that is the pastoral *cogito*.

Among the greatest feats are, of course, the theft of a neighboring tribe's livestock, the invasion of enemy pastures, and murder. Principles that are hard to reconcile with a society of law. The Pokots are the most feared for their military achievements against the Karamajong of Uganda (another nilotic pastoral tribe), the Samburus and the Turkanas. They have entrenched themselves on the western escarpment, to our left, whereas the Samburus are on the eastern one, to our right, and the Turkanas between the two, at the bottom of the Rift, around the lake of the same name, straight ahead of us. During the rainy season, the pastures of the Rift are coveted by all. Samburus and Pokots fight over the Turkanas' grass, when they are launching lightning raids to divert the herd of a sleeping shepherd, the heroic act par excellence, rewarded by the highest honors: access to all the women in the tribe, remuneration in kind, notable status within the group, entrance into History. All that is going on at this, the beginning of the twenty-first century.

Lost in the bush, Thursday 24 October 2002, day 665, 35 km, 7792nd km

We walk two days in Pokot country, between Loruk, Kinyang and Kapedo. People talk to us in very bad terms of the Turkanas. Only the churches try to soothe our minds.

The Anglican pastor of Kinyang, himself a Pokot, reassures us: "In any case, you have nothing to fear, you have no cows and there is no grass at the moment, it's a time of truce. Nevertheless, there is a no man's land between Kinyang and Kapedo. Above all do not walk there with a Turkana because you might get shot at..."

We inquire about water.

"There's no point in carrying water for the first ten kilometers, you have the village of Nakoko on your way."

Confident, we therefore leave with one and a half liters. On the way, we pass beautiful Pokot women. They are wearing huge flat leather necklaces adorned with wooden beads and coated with buttered soil. Under this wide disk, wider than all the Maasai necklaces we have seen, the bust is covered with a most attractive breastplate of colored beads. Leather skirts decorated with beads and copper earrings rolled up like springs consummate the ornaments – not to forget a head shaved on the side and the back of the neck, with a lock of little buttered braids rolling on the forehead and the temples, giving them a funny muppet look. Another common point with the Maasai: the two lower incisors are pulled. The "modern" women, who are wearing T-shirts under their necklaces, have found a practical solution for nursing without undressing: two holes even with the nipples. The men are not very pleasant. They cast mean glances at us, the Kalashnikov on their shoulder and the always-present headrest in the right hand. They are all dressed in a khaki canvas jacket girded with a tight belt on a very short red loincloth that sets off their long, long legs. To crown this original appearance, they wear, posed on the head, a little green hat in cotton adorned with a feather. A caricature of an Austrian game warden – but more fearsome…

After ten kilometers, out of water and energy, we still have not found Nakoko. Night is falling. Not a soul in sight. We walk in the darkness. Nothing. No water to cook our noodle soup with; throat raspy and tongue thick, we are step by step entering the Great Moment of Solitude – a GMS in our jargon, is a moment when the fact there are two of you provides no comfort. Each remains with his/her little pains. You can't be thirsty for the other, you are thirsty, that's all. Got to make camp. No moon. An inky, silent night, heavy and dry. Not a breath. We go to sleep without food, saving what's left in one bottle to start with tomorrow morning. We ration ourselves one swallow per hour. I drink little in the daytime, about two liters, but I usually need a liter of nighttime rehydration and a liter to get going the next morning. It keeps me awake all night. The sixty minutes are an infernal countdown for the next gulp, hot and soapy, which I hold in my mouth as long as possible before swallowing it, full of saliva and bitterness. The sand is hot under our backs. We sweat our last drops of water. Sonia suffers less. She's a real camel. And she sleeps besides, the lucky dog!

About one in the morning, in a semi-sleep, I hear women passing on the path with donkeys and water tanks. The sound signature is unequivocal. I rush out to ask them for some water. In an uncontrolled shriek of terror, they vanish into the night in a second, carrying with them my fantasized swallow; in my hurry I forgot that I was in my undershorts with my headlamp on my head. They will doubtless tell about seeing a phantom leap out of the night, a horrible white ghost, a cyclops with an eye of fire, thirsty, crying desperately in the dark *maji tafadhali!*" (water, please) and everyone will make fun of them!

The next day at dawn, we must reach Kapedo. These kilometers seem to us interminable. Head numb and legs trembling, we realize with an acuity never before known in twenty-two months how fragile we are. Zimbabwean reminiscences. After seven thousand eight hundred and six kilometers you think you are up to anything. Yet thirty-four kilometers, without eating and in intense heat with one single glass of water, are enough to wipe out the most experienced hiker. We are as vulnerable as the first day. "Nakoko or never believe blindly the directions locals give you": they do not have the same modes of orientation, of location, not even the same notion of kilometers and…they know where the water is. A little fellow is walking with us. He has a bow and arrows. He speaks neither English, nor Maasai, nor Swahili, but understands that we are thirsty. He points in the direction of Kapedo, on the trail in front of us. Thanks, we know that! Meager consolation. We're going, we're going! That's all we're doing. At the fourteenth kilometer, after three hours' walking, the village of rondavels and square houses with tin roofs finally appears.

Thomas and Jane Nanok are our first Turkanas. Living at the entrance of the village, they save us with big glassfuls of pure, cool water. They are drawing it from a plastic jerrycan covered with heavy canvas of wet jute that cools water by evaporating in the shade. The bush refrigerator. In a few seconds, it is all gone, the pain forgotten. Beatitude. It's as if we had never suffered, never been thirsty. You only suffer in the present. Once you have filled up, everything's all right. So stupid. So vital.

Thomas is a Protestant pastor in training, of some complicated evangelical denomination the name of which I immediately forget. It's crazy! We have the impression that all the people we run into are more or less pastors, catechists, deacons or beadles. We're not doing this on purpose. Africa is much more Christian than we thought. We imagined it more animist, murky, hostile. And I now reflect that all these folks who welcome us, for nearly two hundred days now, aren't doing it by chance, nor by self-interest, nor by lay humanism – an urban notion of the well-off – they do it by, for, thanks to and because of their faith. And they express it to us. They invite us, take us in, help us, because they have a living faith, because they have heard on the previous Sunday morning at mass or service such and such a word of Christ on welcoming strangers or on charity. The anti-clericals notwithstanding, it is a fact, it is a thousand facts. To live this one day at a time, far from our western bad conscience, gets rid of our hangups with respect to our Christian cultural roots made somewhat intricate by Europe's old history and religious crisis.

But the news is bad. Thomas briefs us: "Kapedo is the last village before the desert of the Suguta valley. You have a hundred twenty kilometers in front of you without a living soul, water, nothing. Between us and the Pokots, this is no man's land. A war zone. Impossible to get to Lokori and the Kerio valley on foot, you are going to lose, there are lions and, if you run into a band of Pokots or Somalis, I wouldn't give much for your skin."

"If we find two donkeys to carry water, it ought to be playable!"

"The Turkanas here have no more donkeys or livestock; they have all been stolen by the Pokots. Kapedo is an administrative center with an army post that makes them respect the truce, that is why you will see Pokots and Turkanas here together, but don't trust it, the reason is that the village is the only place where the Pokots can come buy or sell things. Past the last house, the war begins again. I am going to speak with the school director about it. He has Pokot friends. But I don't have much hope."

We spend the next day with Joseph, director of the school, negotiating two donkeys with a Pokot who makes us turn into donkeys ourselves. He first brings us a female that ten seasoned shepherds take ten good minutes to immobilize, while its panicked little one kicks in all directions. No chance. I can scarcely see myself running a hundred twenty kilometers after a hysterical she-ass. Then he brings us a knock-kneed nag that nothing can make go. Ten minutes and many blows of a stick later, the poor thing had gone a hundred meters, her ears folded to the rear and her tail between her legs. We are befuddled. With the passing hours, the price of the pearl of great price rises. It arrives in the evening: a donkey, calm and well trained, docile and cooperative, which I lead with brio to the villagers' laughter. Faced with such success, the seller changes his mind and disappears with his marvel. A last Pokot finally comes with an old donkey that seems to know everything about the human race. He looks me over with its large pessimistic eyes. We agree on a price of 4000 shillings (70 euros) with complete equipment, a tether and a saddle to which we will fit the two ten-liter water jerrycans that we have just bought. When our Pokot comes back in late afternoon to conclude the deal, the bill has gone up by 1000 shillings. Our Turkana friends are scandalized. I compromise at 4500, asking my interlocutor to do the same, but the proud Pokot replies: "This donkey is my son! It's 5000 shillings or nothing!"

And he turns his heels with the jackass and our day lost. Joseph has a forced laugh.

"Those Pokots are nuts! The price of a donkey varies from 900 to 2000 shillings maximum. With 4500 shillings, he was breaking an historical record, for that price you could have had four....He must really love that son of his..."

We have to change our plans. Sonia is delighted, she detests being the stooge on duty and could ill picture herself running all the time after the headstrong nag. Not to mention the attraction that a donkey can be for an hungry lion. Back at Thomas's, I ask Joseph: "Someone told us about Napeitom, and a hand pump…"

"Indeed, it is beside the road. The village no longer exists. But at this time of year, it is probably dry."

"How far is it?"

"Two-thirds of the way there, about eighty kilometers."

"We could be there in two days. Plus a third day to get to Lokori. The hardest part will be carrying water for the first two days: five liters each besides our three personal liters, that's sixteen liters for two for two days and eighty kilometers, its sober, it's heavy, but it's playable…"

"Unless you find the spring at Kachila…"

"There is a spring on the way?"

"Yes, it's a secret spring, in the Lomelo mountain. Very few people know about it and it is hard to find. Listen carefully: after five hours' walking you will find yourselves between two hills. At the top of the right-hand one, there will be a tree that looks like a man lifting his arms to heaven. Well, at the foot of that mountain, by going up a little gorge, you will find the Kachila water source. If you don't find it, you can never walk all the way to Napeitom, you will have to come back here, or you risk dying. If you find it, you will have no more problems getting to Napeitom, but be careful, it's a dangerous spot – all the bandits who cross the desert know about that well and come refill there. Finally, if there is water at Napeitom, you will get to Lokori without obstacle."

That's a lot of "ifs" for an initiatory path that sounds like a parable. Before he leaves us, he adds this: "Oh, yes! I almost forgot.… Just before Napeitom, there is a fair valley that is called Nasekeng; you can't miss it, it looks like an oasis with a few doum palms. Above all, do not sleep there: that is where lions hunt at night, on the dry river bed."

The departure is tomorrow, at two in the morning, without

donkeys. We go console ourselves for this weighty decision under the extraordinary hot waterfall of Kapedo. A salt cataract ten meters high, from the flanks of the Selela volcano, plunges from a fractured plateau in a 60° C curtain and bubbles in sorcerer's cauldrons like a divine jacuzzi. Under the ferocious shower, I sing myself hoarse with an opera aria that delights the children who have come for front row seats at the muzungu bath! The spot is unique in the world: as at Victoria Falls we discovered "God's jacuzzi," here we baptize Kapedo the "shower of the ancient gods." When we return, Jane has taken to bed with a forty-degree fever and is shaken with tremors. It's a malaria bout. Thomas admits that she is pregnant and he cannot give her quinine. Sonia is troubled and seems to relive her own suffering. She gives him some Doliprane to bring her fever down.

Jane is concerned for us. She would prefer we stay here. Sonia takes her hand. Between two groans, she finds the strength to murmur: "But why do you have to walk? Is it your government that orders you? Are you paid for that?"

People often make this same strange remark to us. Sonia replies gently: "No, Jane, it's because we want to be free, free to meet women like you....Because it makes us happy! Our government doesn't even know we are here, and no one is paying us."

"You mean you are doing it for the love of us?"

"Exactly, Jane, it's exactly that, out of love, but sleep now..."

Before she falls asleep, she takes off a big traditional bracelet which she puts on Sonia's wrist.

Somewhere on the trail, Sunday 27 October 2002, day 668, 40 km, 7848th km

At two in the morning, two Turkana *askaris*,[1] well armed, come to get us to escort us the first day – the head of the post had gotten wind of our departure. They belong to the tribal militia armed by the government. It is a relief for us but also a source of worry: we

---

[1] Generic term given to guards, guardians or soldiers.

187

have been advised several times not to walk with Turkanas in this conflict zone. Their mission is to get us across that very zone where the Pokots tolerate no incursion and shoot on sight. Thomas's aunt and cousin were killed like rabbits six months ago by Pokots from Akoret, an isolated village in Turkana territory. For no reason. In any case, it seems we have no choice. They also will help us find the Kachila spring. Emotional farewells. As usual. We always leave behind a little of our heart, but fortunately love does not divide: it multiplies as we meet new people, it gives us wings.

Conscious of undertaking a key passage on our itinerary, but confident and carried by all the Kenyans who love us and whom we love, we set out in the night with Clarkson and Robert contemplating the uncertainties of our program for the next three days, and the following ones...

Under the moon that turns the world blue, we walk in silence. Their two dissimilar silhouettes stand out on the indigo background of the desert. Clarkson is filiform and very tall, Robert is gaunt, short, knock-kneed, with something vaguely Asiatic about him, a hint of Khmer Rouge. No doubt his slanty eyes. The former speaks a little English, the latter not a word. In any case he doesn't talk at all. The only similarity between these Cerberi: the G3 long-range assault rifle carried on the left shoulder and the five-liter water jerrycan in the right hand. One for today, the other for us, tomorrow, when we will be alone. Clarkson is anxious. He fears an ambush. He suggests we make as little noise as possible. He scans the bush and the shadows on our left. The African night utterly absorbs us.

When day breaks, we have gone seventeen kilometers and passed the dangerous zone of Akoret. We are bordering the phantom village of Lomelo: "Forty-one Turkanas were killed here in 1999. My father was one of them. Now I live with my father-in-law, in Kapedo. The village had to be abandoned."

With the sun, the heat rises fast. We are in the Suguta valley, the Death Valley of East Africa. Knowing neither whether there will be water at the Kachila spring, nor whether we will find it, we save our five-liter jerrycans. To the east, a bevy of volcanic cones aligned at the foot of the Samburu escarpment creates a succession of decors where the lacy shadows decline from black to gray in the already white sunlight. The trail is powdery and ashy as at Lengai, the savannah scattered with footprints. We quickly come across those of a lion. This is the ninth time. Clarkson looks all about. We're safe with the G3's. But tomorrow? I reject this anguish for later.

After five hours, we have almost covered the twenty-five kilometers indicated and there is not the slightest hill to be seen. I raise this concern with Clarkson.

"I don't know, I don't know the Kachila spring..."

My heart leaps in sudden anguish, I give no sign of it to Sonia. *Alea jacta est*. We must find the spring on our own....Happily, five kilometers after the fork at Lomelo, Joseph's quasi-biblical directions come to life. There is only one hill that has a tree on its top. It soon salutes us like a Golgotha. We leave the trail and search among the basalt cliffs for the bottoms of little gorges. A good sign: green trees. Next, many birds. Flights of doves clack in the wind. The spring can't be far. We pass a rockslide and suddenly we see it, murky and sullied with feathers, apple green against black rocks. Our relief is immense. We will be able to walk tomorrow toward Napeitom. A wild olive tree offers us the necessary shade to spend the seven hours' wait until the sun finally begins to go down. Robert goes to a position at the top of the opposite cliff to stand watch in case we were followed. I prepare the tea while Sonia stretches out our double roof as a dais. The culture fluid is so green and so laden that we boil it ten full minutes. The hours pass in conversation. Clarkson tells us about the Pokot raids. With his fierce hatred, barely softened by his Christian feelings. He has killed four Pokots....He speaks of the dead with fixed gaze, eyes looking nowhere, his neck wedged by his headrest. Remorse.

The doves come down by whole flights to the edge of the green puddle to take off again with a few drops of life. Shoving and confusion, group strategy to perturb a possible predator. Later, it is a swarm of bees that swoops down on the swamp. The entire gorge buzzes with their frenzy. Threatening sentinels circle above our heads and inquire about our intentions. We don't move even a hair. When the queen is sated, the swarm takes off again with the ruckus of a helicopter.

"Whatever lives within thirty to fifty kilometers comes to drink here, the lions, the leopards, the baboons, the gazelles...the bandits, to each his turn, that is why the longer we stay the more dangerous it is."

Robert has returned for the soup. He crouches at the foot of the olive tree and polishes his assault rifle. When he has finished, he runs his right hand through Sonia's hair. Once the furious astonishment has passed, I suddenly am brutally aware of our weakness – we are so far from everything, at the mercy of these two killers. Clarkson chuckles. The pressure immediately drops. He translates for us: "It's the first time in his life he has seen blonde hair. He is very impressed!"

"Does he think it's pretty?"

"*Mzuri Kabisa, kama dahabu!*" (Super pretty, like gold!)

To extricate herself from this slippery slope, Sonia takes out her travel notebook full of drawings, poems, recipes and prayers given by our hosts. What interests them more than anything is our family photos. It is very important for them to be able to link us to brothers, sisters, parents, and discover how we look spiffed up on New Year's Eve, or on the beach with nephews. They marvel at details we don't even see any more, the green grass, the white hair, the crystal glasses....Clarkson is translating to Robert when he suddenly stops at a photo of my paternal grandparents: "*Bibi ya Babou, mwaka tisini na moja!*" (That's his grandmother and his grandfather. He is ninety-one years old.)

Robert is floored. He did not know it was possible to live so long. Sonia bursts out laughing.

"Your grandmother is Bibi. And your venerable grandfather is Babou. You'll have to tell them that!"

The peak of success is reached with a watercolor by Sonia's father, done during his trip in Malawi, which pictures an African bestiary on our heels. It must be said that Claude is a wonderful draftsman. Clarkson loves it: here the laughing gorilla, there the enraged rhinoceros stepping on the leopard's tail, and, perched on the giraffe's neck, the comical monkey throwing a coconut at us. They bend double, turn the pages and turn them again, describe everything aloud, want to see it all. Our two killers revert to childhood and drive out their demons, fascinated by a drawing.

At four-thirty, we leave for more than ten kilometers, to get a head start on tomorrow's day. Everything is yellow. The landscape is disordered. The reading of space is unclear. Where is the trail going to come out of this confusion? When we get to a clearing, Robert, before we have time to react, shoulders his gun and aims at a gazelle. The crack rips the sky and echoes desperately for a long time in the yellow valleys of the setting sun. Missed it. He did not like the noodle soup at noon. We keep on for two hours after sunset. Exhausted, at eight we pitch camp right on the trail. No risk of being run over, the last car came through last month.

To see me, after forty kilometers, bustling about the tent, the fire, the soup, the dishes and the tea, Clarkson, amused, ventures: "Alex is a very sharp muzungu!"

I appreciate the compliment from a Turkana warrior. The breath of night caresses with liquid balm the burns of the day.

Our sleep is short, at three o'clock we are afoot. It is now that we separate. Our warriors return to Kapedo with one of our five-liter jerrycans. They are worried. "Without you, the Pokots will not hesitate to shoot at us."

Clarkson is going to get married in two months, we present him with our best wishes and give him something to buy two rings with. Quite moved, he hugs us for a long time.

"*Mungu akubariki Alex na Sonia!*" (God be with you, Alex and Sonia!)

"*Mungu akubariki Clarkson!*"

We watch, motionless, our ferocious askaris being swallowed by the night.

Before us solitude, lions, thirst, the unknown, the countdown with the sun, the trail, life: find Napeitom. I am carrying our five-liter jerrycan, and three and a half liters in my backpack, Sonia three and a half liters – we remember Nakoko's lesson. It is quite sufficient. Unless Napeitom is dry....I keep my flares at hand ready to spit out their balls of explosive fire. Lions hunt at night. This is the tenth time we are walking in the footsteps of lions. You still don't get used to it. We plod on. Without talking much. Without meditating much. Concentrated on the song of the desert, on the victory of each step, on the thread of time and space that is ours to wind on Fate's distaff . At this point, we are embarked. There is no going back. Salvation lies before us. There is a sort of wild tension in the air. Dawn comes too soon for my taste; it frees us from fear of the lion but grinds us down with its sun. We escape one bite to undergo another. Hypoglycemia catches up with us; the last stick of halal biltong from our friend Naeem reinflates us as we walk.

Before us extends an interminable ashy plain dotted with thorny bushes. There are vortices crossing these expanses spinning their columns of dust. Dust devils, the English say. They are fearsome. They are the only "living" thing we have seen since last evening's gazelle. With the heat the anguish increases. Sweat is water escaping. We are a two-legged pocket of liquid which the thirsty desert is waiting to absorb entirely. It's drop by drop from here on. We leak. Everything comes out, salts, juice, sweat, strength. We flee. The bitter observation of a boat that is sinking in black sand. Don't drink too much. One swallow per hour. The only way out is straight ahead. The struggle between the mineral and the living is engaged. Unequal. Stay together, watertight, concentrated, calm. Therein lies our salvation.

According to my bit of map, at the twenty-fourth kilometer we ought to have found the hand pump. But nothing. We push on for two kilometers. In other words, twenty-four minutes later. It's not nothing, twenty-four minutes, when you are beat. In vain. It is too hot. We are exhausted. To continue is to court sunstroke. We abdicate. No shade. Emaciated acacias. We put up the tent. Wait. Tension. The mopane flies immediately crash the festival, go after our nerves. Sonia loses hers.

"How do these bastards manage to live when we are not here?"

We pull on our head netting. Since the insects are interested only in our faces and the heat is beastly, Sonia undresses. Here, no risk of being seen, we are desperately alone. Not a whiff of air. Deathly silence. I get busily at the soup, then the tea. The flies go nuts. The water vapor intoxicates them, they dive by the dozen into the mess kit to get boiled, like moths in the flame of a candle. Impossible to prevent them. All it costs us is a fly tea. The heat is unbearable. No way to recuperate. All of a sudden I realize: "Joseph had told us not to stop in the valley before Napeitom, do you remember? I noted the name on the map, there it is: Nasekeng, you know, I think that's where we are."

Ideal for taking a nap. Amorphous and defeated in advance, I long watch out of the corner of my eye, in my apathetic lethargy, the spot where a lion might appear. A horror film. Uneasy, we decide to cut the torture short and, taking advantage of a little cloud masking the sun, we set forth again. It is only two o'clock. This is much too early. A little wind has come up which dehydrates, but which also, happily, cools. Second round: to find Napeitom.

Two hours later, in heavy iron, it appears all of a sudden, as enigmatic and improbable as the black monolith in *2001: A Space Odyssey*, a colonial vestige that has survived the devastation: the hand pump. We rush to it. Countdown. I don't believe it. In ten seconds, our destiny will be settled. Ruins of shacks attest combats. I turn the wheel, the handle, the pipe belches and belches again.... Nothing. My heart accelerates. I persevere but get nothing out of the beast other than hollow gurgles. It balks, sighs, burps, then, suddenly, all at once vomits up some life. Hot, salty water. The closest fluid to blood. We shout with joy and fall into each other's arms. We have just won Lokori and our three days in the desert. Hallelujah! We chow down on porridge, and grant ourselves a luxury: a naked shower beside the trail right in the middle of the desert. Refreshed, we take off again for eight kilometers before nightfall.

At dusk, as if destiny were fooling with us, lion prints, which have been haunting us since yesterday morning, reappear. Not too recent. But not reassuring for that. A large, lone male. The most dangerous for man since they are old, since they are hungry. Though we know that makes no difference, we walk five minutes farther and set up the tent on an open space. With my Maasai sword I cut seven acacias which I use to surround our tulle shelter. Sonia gathers a supply of wood that will hold out for our short night. Soup, orange verbena tisane. It is urgent that we sleep. Behind our ramparts of thorns, we say to ourselves that we will at least hear death coming. I put a double thickness downwind. That is where the potential predator will come from. Unbelievable how one can be pragmatic in the face of danger. Not an insect is rustling in the desert. The night is cottony and mute. We go to sleep on our guard. I keep my flares at hand. My olalem is planted in front of the tent, the proud Maasai double-edged sword. Superstition is a therapy against anguish.

At one in the morning, a very close groan makes me leap up. Headlamp on, flare engaged, I rush out of the tent shouting. A heavy sound of flight. Two fiery eyes in the night. Fucking lion! He stares at me and leaps in the night. Gone! More curious than hungry. The isolated old male. Thank God! My heart is beating so hard it echoes in my ears. I have the palsy of the sheep in my legs. It won't happen today. Pokots and predators are afraid of white phantoms. Our second encounter after the Kruger ones; and the eleventh time we have seen footprints. Sonia awoke at my shout. Her calm leaves me speechless. I am really a wimp. I put more wood on the fire. A hell of a fire! I light the bloody night and salvos of firebrands climb to the stars. She goes back to sleep. Not I. I stay awake until two. Reveille. This morning, we will not make the mistake of setting out without food, even if Lokori is within a sole's distance.

En route, our headlamps scan the shrubs like an aerial defense battery looking for damned yellow eyes. We perfect a protocol for reaction in case of an attack. Derisory derision. But you have to keep busy, and then, it conjures fear, lulls it with illusions.

In six hours and thirty kilometers, we win the wager, with a good surprise on arrival: the Kerio River is at flood stage. It must have rained a lot in the Tugen hills. Water, trees, men: our descent toward Lake Turkana is looking good. Lokori liberates us from Death Valley. I am on my knees. The tension lets go. Sonia is regal. God how she impresses me! Her hair is floating in the wind, this morning she didn't have the time to braid it. A Mexican missionary, Padre Rico, wearing a Stetson, Ray Bans and cowboy boots, welcomes us at the bottom of a Sierra Madre. Desert magic!

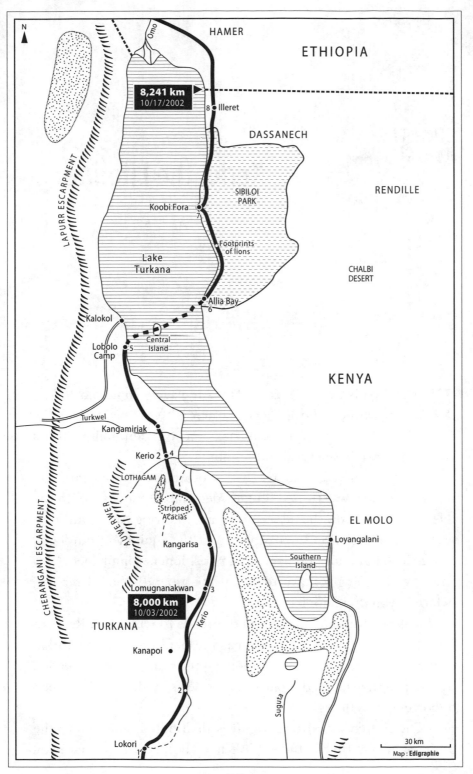

North Kenya

Kerio, the Lifeline

KENYA

Father Rico is new in Lokori. He is replacing some old Italian Fathers who can no longer stay here all year because of the heat. He speaks to us of his problems of adaptation, rolling his *r*'s with unbelievable sincerity and humor.

"When I arrived, I almost had a heart attack! On Saturday night the chapel was turned into a video club. Ay, ay, ay! With the television placed on the altar. Ay, ay, ay! Showing American films with sex and violence. Impossible! I put the equipment outdoors. Since then, I am not popular....The parishioners complained: 'But Padre, we're going to have to sit on the ground!' 'So?' I replied, 'what do you do at home?'"

He is poor among the poor and intends to remain so. Reset to Christian basics. He is trying to teach responsibility to the Turkanas, who are used to receiving food supplies and to being spoiled by the paternalism of the old Italian priests, and have developed opportunistic reflexes.

"The church is full when *ugali* is distributed, and empty the other Sundays. Isn't it funny? We have become an official relay for distribution since the FAO (Food and Agriculture Organization of the United Nations) is sure that here at least, we do not sell the corn flour to the people! In short, this conflation worries me terribly. Last Sunday was the monthly distribution. The chapel was full to the gills and everyone wanted communion. I was very impressed. I was accusing myself of judging them a little too fast, but when, after the mass, I asked a few of them why communion was important to them, you know what they answered? 'We like the White people's bread...' Ay, ay, ay!"

He can't believe his ears. Day after day, he discovers even better ones.

"In Mexico, the priests' problem is that everyone wants to give us things! Here it's the opposite. When I go into the bush, they hear me coming and take a position on the road to go part of the way with me. When I ask them where they are going, they tell me: 'I don't know....I heard the car and thought I would go have a drink in the village.' Ay, ay, ay! Or there are some who wait for me on the road with their mats and baskets to sell, their harvest bags, a goat, their jerrycans, so I will take them. Hey, I am not a taxi, you know! Ay, ay, ay! How funny they are. The other day, I was mired in the mud, with passengers in the car. You think they would help me? They waited, in the back, for everything to be fixed. When I asked them to help, they paraded off. They all had other irons in the fire! Ay, ay, ay! Then I saw some donkeys going by and asked if we could use them to get the car out. One guy who had stayed with me became indignant: 'Donkeys? Are you crazy? We respect our animals! I'll go get some women, they are less difficult to order around.' Indeed, twenty or so women came and got the car out of the rut. Since that story, I pick up only women hitchhikers. And here's another good one. In Kapedo, where you came from, we have a project for a primary school. The other day, I went there with construction materials. When I got there, the parishioners asked me: 'But where are the workers?' Ay, ay, ay! I replied, "But who is this school for? Whose children are they? Mine, maybe? If

you don't want it, *no problemo*, I'll go back with all the materials!'
The little pets, they ought to roll up their sleeves! They understand
that with Padre Rico, they have to put in some hard work! *Esta loco
aquí!* In the villages, children run up and ask me: 'Padre, padre,
what are you bringing us today?' 'But...nothing!' 'Then you can go
home, you are a bad priest!'"

And Father Rico cracks a big smile. He's laughed himself out.
He keeps repeating that merciless reply to himself and ends with:
"Ay, ay, ay! There's work to do! We have to start all over. We behave
like gringos here. Faith is a liberation, not a servitude. Every day, I
tell them: 'Help yourself, and heaven will help you.' *Madre mía!*"

At Lokori, by Padre Rico's satellite e-mail, we learn some good
news. Louise Leakey can come to Koobi Fora, but unfortunately
it's on the other bank of Lake Turkana. Indeed, the Kerio valley
which we are planning to follow runs into the middle of the lake's
western shore, whereas Koobi Fora is right opposite, on the eastern
shore; so we will have to cross it....But Louise has a solution to
every problem, one of her friends, Halwign Scheuermann, awaits
us in a tented camp set up on our side of the lake: "In principle,
Halwign will take you across on one of his boats, but if that doesn't
work, don't worry, I'll come get you with my little plane." So we
have a new target toward which our minds are magnetized: Lobolo.
It's only a name, and it isn't written on any map, but in our hikers'
jargon we call that a "carrot"!

When we leave the mission we have a very strong feeling of landing on another planet. Somewhat the same atmosphere as in Mto
wa Mbu, on the edge of the Maasai territory. But we are better
armed: in Nairobi, we devoured the book *Turkana*, by Nigel Pavitt,
and know much more about the Turkanas than we did then about
the Maasai. The only thing we have to fear, Father Rico cautioned
us, is bands of Ngorokos, young men who have lost their herds
or been driven out of their tribe for various reasons, and live by
plunder and extortion. But there too, during the dry season, they

migrate toward the cities. By way of farewell, he gives us a secret password.

"You know why I get along so well with the Turkanas? They have an expression that means exactly the same thing as 'Ay, ay, ay!' and it's *Hoy tokoy!* They use it for everything. Whether it's pretty, it's good, it's painful, it's hard, it's nice….It's always *Hoy tokoy!*"

This time, there is not the slightest trail. We are entering a world where automobiles do not venture, where will have no recourse. We are betting on curiosity: the tribes that have settled along the Kerio bed never see anyone pass who isn't a Turkana. Our sole security, our sole safety rail, is always to keep to our right the green snake of the Kerio, which blazes its tunnel of vegetation in the desert, heading due north. The river itself is drowned in an inextricable jungle penetrated by no path, an uncrossable entwinement of roots and tortured tree trunks, thorny foliage and shafts of magnificent acacias lost in masses of tightly packed doum palms. So we are following the water but have very little access to it. It is above all psychological security. From time to time, however, there is a loop in this seasonal stream that breaks the vegetal stranglehold to flirt with the desert. The herds converge on these meeting places with life to drink as if to refill their blood with the heavy red slimes ferried by the current. We just have to follow the animal trails to find the fords. That is where we make our pauses, go bathing and enjoy the coolness, like hippos, with water up to the nostrils. And that is where we have our first encounters. One day, we are slumped in the shade of a doum palm for our midday halt when three pretty girls with firm breasts come to fetch water in the holes they dig with majestic movements in the sandy banks. *Hoy tokoy!* The water is too laden with sediments to be drawn directly from the river. I approach them quietly with my bottle to study their technique. When they see the color of the liquid and the sediment deposit at the bottom of my container, they laugh and mock my inexperience before showing me how to do it. About a meter from the river, they dig by hand in the sand of the bank a hole having the diameter of a plate. They lean on the other hand, fairly far from the hole, taking care that the pressure of their body does not make the fragile edges of their little well collapse. Seated on the side, they use a graceful twist of their slender torso. The deeper they go, the broader is the movement and the more it makes the tapered muscles stand out on their fine brown skin dripping with sweat. Their only piece of clothing is a leather apron weighed down with steel rings, and an unbelievable piling up of disks of beads set around the neck, which form a sort of multicolored display on which their head is placed, like a fine fruit on a fraise. The whole is richly buttered with animal fat mixed with ochre, which drips gently down the furrow of their backbone, between their two spindles of dorsal muscles. My little well-digger begins to sing as she buries her arm up to the hilt in the ground. Her head coated in red ochre is closely shaven, except for a crest of little stiff braids that roll onto her upper temples with the back-and-forth of her drilling. Finally she sits up, smiling, and steps back a little to allow me to see the fruit of her labors. At the bottom of the pit, wider and more flared than the orifice, shimmers a silver disk of pure water in which my face is reflected seventy centimeters beneath the river level. The meter of sand that separates us from the chocolate-brown river water thus filters out the particles. *Hoy tokoy!* My wonderment makes them laugh. With a dry, scraped-out gourd in the form of a ladle, they nimbly fill their calabashes strapped into carrying thongs and take off with a swaying stride on the sand of the river. I gape and ogle at the departure of the rounded rumps of these aristocratic nymphets, trimmed in back in soft leather trains decorated with beads.

When I return to Sonia, she teases me: "So, weren't you cruising a bit? You think I didn't see your little game!"

"*Hoy tokoy!* Perfectly well! I was dredging the sand by the river so your noodle soup wouldn't make you grit your teeth, my love…!"

With water, these little corners of Africa appear like primal paradises. We let the time pass blissfully. It's the sun time. We don't want to steal its show, let it have the spotlight, we will wait 'till it's tired. The Kerio bubbles gently and lulls us to sleep. There is no disturbance, we could be at the beach, on a desert island. On the other bank, whole trains of camels file past like ships and disappear in a stately crunch into the massifs of doums. A little later, whole herds of goats shoulder their way noisily on the same stretch of the bank. Capers and ruts, sounds of suction and lapping. Little naked shepherds throw a few well-aimed pebbles and go away with the shivaree. No one bothers us. The children are nice, not excited. They wave to us from a distance, but none comes to disturb our peace. This is the first time it happens since South Africa. Father Rico had told us so: "You can believe the people are distant because they do not come to you spontaneously, you will sometimes have the impression that you are invisible, but that's their way of expressing their respect. That's the way they are. As long as you don't make the gesture of going to them, they will act as if they hadn't seen you!"

In the evening we head with dead reckoning into a vast forest of timeless acacias, simply attracted by children's laughter. The impression of an African Brocéliande[1] peopled with malicious goblins, full of knotty trunks, charms, shadowy zones and ancient spirits. We soon come upon a village built in the shelter of these large trees. A cluster of girls is having fun trying with very long poles to knock down from the foliage shells and pods of acacia seeds for their goats, since there is nothing to graze on with this dusty soil. This is our first undergrowth village. Thus bathed in filtered light, it diffuses an immense charm. The hemispheric huts are perched on piles. Stripped branches are placed there to serve as a ladder.

Our intrusion provokes no stress, no amazement, the girls have kept their noses in the air. As prescribed, we stop a good distance

---

[1] Ancient forest in Bretagne, believed to be the setting of the Arthurian legend. Thick and humid, full of hidden glens, its magic and mysteries make you meet Merlin, the Lady of the Lake and the Knights of the Round Table...

from the huts and greet a man seated in front of his hut. He rises slowly and comes to us.

"*Ajiok!*" (Hello.)

"*Ajiok onoï!*" (Hello to you.)

Bernard Katoi knows Father Rico, he mumbles a few words of English and Swahili. His skull is capped with a shell of smooth clay pressed into his hair. His ears are not elongated like the Maasai's. They are merely pierced; five centimeters of steel chain are hanging from them. His only ornament is a bead necklace. He sits balanced on a multifunction headrest and invites us to sit on a bed made of ropes. From a small metal box he takes a pinch of brown power which he spreads on the top side of his index finger. He pinches one nostril with his thumb while he noisily sniffs in the blackish line.

"*Timbaku. Unataka?*" (Tobacco, you want some?)

"*Hatutaka, asanté sana.*" (No, thank you.)

On his belt he carries a club the peen of which, mounted on a wooden handle, consists of the smallest gearwheel of a Land Rover gearbox. While I am wondering at this techno-medieval weapon of modern times, he spots my olalem. We tell him about our crossing of the Maasai territory, achieved without obstacles, about the morans, our strong impression, *Hoy tokoy!*...

He retorts: "*Hoy tokoy!* The Maasai are effeminate. They sit on the ground, like their wives....Besides, we reject excision and circumcision. Akuj, our god, is against mutilations. It's only if we kill an enemy that we are to be scarified – if you see a Turkana with many small scars on the shoulder, look out for him, he might be dangerous..."

We put up our tent between two round huts. The night comes quickly. All has remained calm. We have been able to go quietly about our business, taking advantage of the golden light of dusk to take some magnificent portraits without starting a riot or eliciting resistance. The women are cheerful and gay, not hostile. Some of them are wearing, hooked to the top of their ears, aluminum plates in the form of leaves cut from old mess kits, pierced and decorated with veins, that look like lids to their external ears. The most mature wear large white shells hung from their mass of necklaces. From the hole in their lower lip comes a small tongue of curved copper that falls just under the chin like a pharaoh's goatee and jumps around frenetically when they talk. Those who lack this ornament fill the hole with a little wooden cork so the saliva will not drain out through it. Others finally have the whole rim of the ear riddled with metal rings like punks, a resemblance all the more evident for their shaven heads and their Mohawk crest. Around the fire, the village children regroup, naked as worms, their bottoms in the dust, lined up, legs at right angles, and sing high-pitched songs carried by the rumble of the tomtoms. Their white teeth shine in the semi-darkness. Their little hands clap in rhythm. The soles of their aligned feet are bathed in orange by the flicker of the fire. God how cute they are, these little toes all in a row! I film the scene with enthusiasm. To get more light, Sonia has lent her headlamp to a little girl who entertains herself by illuminating her face with it. To another she gives a candle. The child's eyes riveted on the flame and her hand placed as a screen bring to mind the Jesus of *Saint Joseph the Carpenter*, the intimist painting of Georges de La Tour. Synesthetic magic. *Hoy tokoy!* is it beautiful! The other little girl lights up her face with the lamp that makes her blue. The composition is perfect, we are delighted, carried away by waves and responses, in a surf of dissonances and syncopated stanzas, and all these strident voices, all these hands beating the soul of a people, all forming, for us, one single body, simple and beautiful, singing with one impulse under the vault of the trees through which penetrates the diamond-like sparkle of the stars and the volleys of satellites carrying the cacophony of the world.

"*Aboudia Aboudia Aboudou…*"

We don't know what that means. Little does it matter to us. For us, it is the magic formula of an evening forever engraved in our memories. In ten years, all we will have to do is murmur "*aboudia*" to bring forth, like a genie coming out of its bottle, our Turkana village and its inhabitants. And suddenly, in one of those visions with which African nights are so fertile, the round forms, the dancing flames, that simple harmony make us think of a village of trolls, of cosmic teddy bears or other Jedi knights that one sees in science fiction films. We are indeed on another planet. *Hoy tokoy!*

Hard to leave it the next day. We are within an inch of staying forever. The tyranny of the trek. We leave late. A short day. Walking straight all day through the desert, without a pause. What you shouldn't do. We review in our heads the images of last night. Sonia has opened her umbrella. No, it's not a joke, she is using it as a parasol. It's a world map umbrella which she bought at the Yaya Center in Nairobi. It allows us to situate Africa on the planet. Africa is so large, indeed, that on school maps it is often shown alone. On our parasol, it floats among the other continents on the blue of the sea printed on the blue of the sky above us. With an indelible felt pen, we have traced our path from Cape Town to Kenya; that allows us to explain our itinerary. From functional, the instrument quickly becomes pedagogical.

Often a hill hides the Kerio or else a meander takes it away from us. We lose our safety rail, our Ariadne's thread, our lifeline. Instantly the walk becomes more tense, more concentrated, more anxious. Umbilical cord and hookah, the Kerio is vital to our bodies and souls. And we keep our eyes peeled at each jump in the terrain to see whether we can spot on our right the return of the green line. It is at such times that we have to pay attention to keeping pointed north. I try to do this using a little gadget compass that Antoine Denaiffe and Maximilien de Dieuleveult gave us in Nairobi. Those two rascals arrived in Kenya by way of Tobruk in Libya, then the Sudan and Ethiopia, on board an old Berliet 4x4 of the 1960s which gave up the ghost on the other side of Lake Turkana, in the Chalbi desert. We pass through many seasonal, abandoned villages. The Turkanas are one of the rare African peoples still practicing nomadism. They load gourds and pelts, poles and utensils on donkeys and go into desolate expanses in search

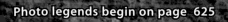

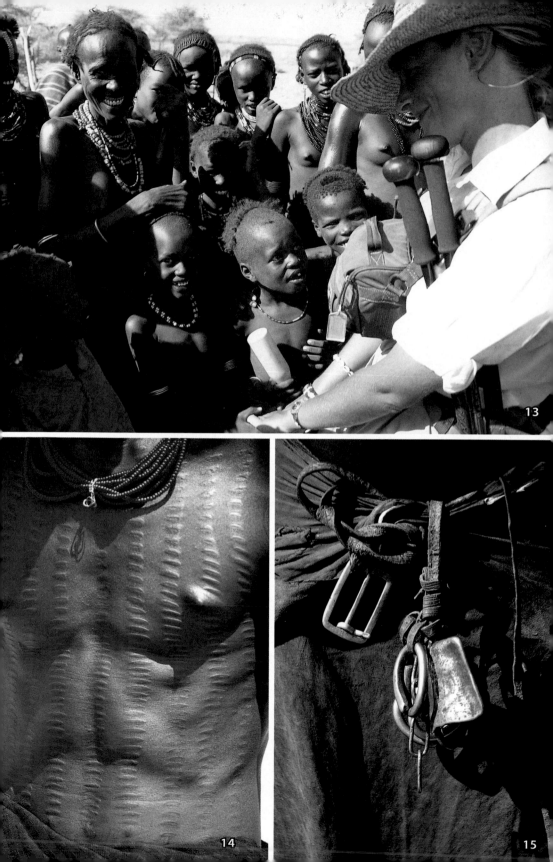

13

14

15

19

20

21

22

23

24

25

26

27

28

29

of better pastures for their camels, their cows and their goats. The installation of a new campground is simple: what is urgent is to create shade. The women assemble the flexible poles into a hemispheric structure which they cover over with pelts. The children can then be protected from the sun, and they can get on with the organization of the camp. In the course of the day, we meet numerous small groups on the move and pass in front of these chance camps, but we are carried off by the trek. They barely lift their eyes to watch us go by. They too are going somewhere. The detours, the social niceties, the greetings and the saliva are too costly in these deserts. Night catches up with us as we are rejoining the Kerio to pitch our tent. Silence and solitude in this "morning of the world." Thus go by our virgin and savage, fierce and primitive days.

Another evening, an hour before sundown, we pass without witnesses, in utter desolation, our 8000th kilometer. For us, it is not a quantitative but a qualitative leap. Every thousand kilometers, we enter into another dimension. As if we are passing a new panorama in an immense video game called "Africa Trek," and by so doing win bonus lifetimes and chances. Sonia is uneasy. We have no more water, the Kerio is far away. We must find someone. While the sun is getting lower and stretching our shadows to our right, we bend our trajectory in the direction where they seem to want to go: toward the river. If there is someone, that's where he will be. It is enough to believe in it. The important thing is not to hesitate, not to zigzag, to walk straight, to trust life, our sixth sense, our angels, whatever! The important thing is to trust. In the dark, at the predicted place, we run into a circular enclosure of woven bulrushes whence voices rise. Do not ask me how we managed to find it. I have no idea. But it is there, and just at the right time. *Hoy tokoy cool!*

"*Ajokonoï!*"

The voices fall silent. I repeat:

"*Ajok!*"

Someone is coming. Sonia whispers: "Shine your light on me and I will shine mine on you, that way they will not be afraid."

An old man comes to the gate of the palisade, his eyes round as billiards. I try on him a sentence of introduction in Turkana which a specialist would surely judge incorrect, but very effective on the terrain.

"*Abouni agnakadien alo Cape Town tana ouné, alossi tikang tolema nilapio, ni tomo arei khangaré, na pei kolong essia Kenya along.*" (We come from Cape Town on foot, we are seeking a place to sleep safely tonight, we will leave tomorrow morning, we are crossing all of Kenya.)

The fellow, gaunt as a charred bine, cracks a big smile and motions us to come in. There is no Turkana word for saying thank you. The nearest formula is "*alakara*" which means "I am content." No need to tell him. Apparently, it shows. We often boast a thank you in Swahili which for the Turkanas is the language of strangers.

Lomugnanakwan, Sunday 3 November 2002, day 675, 33 km, 8004th km

Divine night, lulled by the wind over our tower on piles – an open lookout on the stars, a round eye fringed with bulrushes following the path of satellites among the constellations. At four meters above the ground, we have slept side by side, on a cowskin, in our sleeping bags. Dawn turns the horizon pink, I get up to survey from our eagle's nest the beauty of this *boma* in which we arrived late at night. Mythical *hoy tokoy*!

A tall palisade of bulrushes protects it like a shell from the burning winds of the Turkana deserts. Seven huts huddle together in this oval. The first on the left, near the entrance, is tiny and perched on piles of a man's height – that is the china hutch where calabashes and wooden bowls are side by side with aluminum mess kits and water reserves. The second is open on top, a simple partition rolled like a snail; at its center, the hearth is sheltered from the swirling winds. Then comes our perch, our belvedere, overlooking the boma at the height of the branches of the surrounding acacias. It is a traditional means of fighting malaria, since mosquitos are believed to never fly more than two meters off the ground. Then a lower tower, stocky, well closed up: the granary. Then another hut on piles, raised like a warhead on its launch ramp, with a fine rounded padded strip molded around the entrance to signify that it is the main habitation, and another one yet, this time at ground level, hemispheric, with a wide entrance and a big space that might serve for receiving, and finally a last hut on stilts of which the shaded ground floor, right on the cool sand, serves as dining room.

Our hostess in a pelt dress is already going about her housekeeping chores; she puts away clay pots and wooden bowls, smooths the sand, stores away a spear, a mortar, sweeps up the peelings of doum palm fruits, of which the pulp, sweet like dry figs, is pounded into a granular dough that constitutes the traditional food of the Kerio Turkanas. The huts are made with the leaves of the same palms. Sonia is amazed: "We never got up so late: 6:30! Fortunately, it's a bit cloudy today."

"*Ajok onoï!*" we are hailed from below.

It's our old man. His name is Akim Lorotwakan. We were so exhausted that we barely saw him last night. He explains that he must go with his goats toward a neighboring village. He is gentle. Speaks to us as if we were perfectly understanding everything he says, and indeed we understand the essentials: "There is no hurry, make yourselves at home, I hope you have slept well....When you leave, be sure to go in this direction; you see the big tree over there? That is the way! Straight ahead for three or four days and you'll reach the lake!"

Then he lowers his head, turns on his heels, and leaves as if we had always known each other, as if we would see each other again in a little while.

Getting down, I am going to prepare a porridge for the whole household. Quite often, our hosts to be polite have a taste of it, but give us our bowl back with a scarcely disguised grimace intended for our British breakfast. The exception doesn't prove the rule:

here everyone loves it, and we hear the spoons scraping the metal bottom of the mugs and bowls for a long time. Puppies come and lick the bowls clean. There are always little yellow dogs among the Turkanas. They guard the hearth, protect the children and have another function which we soon discover, dumbfounded: the baby which the mother was keeping glued to her back in a goatskin has just had his morning bowel movement. With a routine gesture she then presents the dirtied bottom of her nursling to the voracious appetite of his little companions. In fifteen seconds, the little butt is clean as a new penny. Among the Turkanas, you don't waste water. Sonia was about ready to throw up. The pup she was cajoling a while ago now decides to come to her after its feast...

"Get away, you filthy thing, don't come near me!"

We resume our walk in the desert. It is good to know that the Kerio is a few stone's throws to the east. It is still flowing straight north toward Lake Turkana. We jump from one trail to another by mysterious switches, dead reckoning, our eyes fixed on the vanishing horizon. Adventure full steam ahead!

Nobody. Freedom. Rubble, sun, camels, palm trees and dry, pure beauty, pitiless and straightforward. Sublime trek. What do we care about the discomfort, the risk, the uncertainty, we are off at top speed, freed from contingencies for a few hours of adventurous tipsiness, we are light, light, so light.

In the arid declivities, on the smooth spread of the sands and clays are placed black pebbles with strange shapes. Heavy and vitreous, they have angles, ridges, curves, and cavities.

"Sonia, guess what! What these black stones are is fossils! We are treading the famous fossil beds – four to seventeen million years old – which surround the lake! At a time when it was three times bigger, lined with tropical jungles, it extended to here, nearly forty kilometers from its banks. *Hoy tokoy!* That's really something!"

Here we find a big toe, no doubt that of a hippopotamus, then there we recognize a crocodile femur and everywhere disks with

complex architectures, fish vertebrae, scattered in the sand according to a chimerical order, like the knucklebones of a forgotten game
which to read it would give the keys to evolution.

Sonia ventures: "Imagine we found a hominid skull, that would
be great, no?"

"*Hoy tokoy!* Besides, it would be the skull of the first frogman."

"No, no, dummy! He could have drowned, like Lucy; and please
stop saying *Hoy tokoy!*"

We proceed for a long time along the vanished shores of this
paleolake, in this cemetery of time with bones polished by the
winds.

In late afternoon an enormous black front hemmed by a white
strip rolls toward us. It raises from the ground flames of golden
sand swallowing the palm trees. The vision is apocalyptic. Coming
from the east, the fantastic scroll, bloated, voracious, comes right
at us. And yet, everything is happening silently, with no rumbles
or flashes: very simply frightening. We run to seek shelter from a
mound with a bush on top. The first lashes of sand hit us at the
same time as the penumbra. The sand passes, crackles, caresses
us, then in gusts, buries us little by little in a pernicious shroud.
Sonia opens her umbrella and we put one of her scarves around it
to make a corolla. I hold one corner in my mouth while our four
hands try to maintain this little makeshift tent. We have put on
our sunglasses to protect our eyes. Through the umbrella, trans-
parently but backwards, we see the five continents and our itinerary, minuscule, eight thousand insignificant kilometers, nailed
to the spot, immobile, hunching down: resigning ourselves to this
storm in the Turkana desert. Our tête-à-tête continues, not exactly
comfortable.

"You okay?" Sonia asks.

"Quite...I have the back of my neck against your little pointed
skull....Anyway, your umbrella-parasol is also a good parasand!"

We can see less and less. We have sand everywhere, in the

mouth, the eyes, all orifices. We hurriedly put on our rain capes because a hard downpour is beginning, cutting down the wind. Rain in the desert! That's all we needed! And in the interstices, rain on top of sand, there is nothing more execrable. No question of getting moldy here. We set out straight ahead in the night in search of life. At the end of an hour, a fire, in the distance. Salvation. We pile in, crouched in a hut, with a whole family of stupefied Turkanas. We are familiar with this little surprise effect, we are even getting to like it. Sonia reads my thoughts: "Back in France we will have to get used to not being noticed again. That's going to be a change for us!"

"Sure! With the face we've got we would scare a ghost!"

The next day, torture takes a form not yet experienced: we get lost in a field of small flaying acacias that are ever more dense. The maneuver, which consists of sidling between the massifs to continue to progress, has turned into a trap. The goats, whose trails we have followed, are able to pass unencumbered under the clawing branches. Not us. We are caught like rats. No way to go back. But which path? I unsheathe my olalem, the faithful Maasai sword, and begin to slash the thorny bushes to open a passage. It is slow and fastidious. Every branch sacrificed wants to tear off a piece of my epidermis. Only the blade sings: it utters a crystalline "dzing" each time it cuts off the hooked members that take it out on our clothing and draw trickles of blood from us. Dzing! humpf! Dzing! Ouch! Dzing! *Hoy tokoy!* We'll have to stop complaining when we are walking straight in the desert, without encumberment. Never forget that there is always a worse situation. The sun, implacable, is having fun at the zenith, I am streaming and exhausting myself in this battle with plants.

Sonia says, to encourage me: "you're like the proud prince in *Sleeping Beauty* in his forest of malevolent brambles!" Then she worries about my gory arms and thighs. No exit. We have to get out. Think. These shrubs experience rains one or two days per year. Since water always streams toward the same spot, they wait right there, parched but patient. Thus the hydrographic network is drawn in the desert sand by the most tenacious plants. We remember an aerial photograph of Nigel Pavitt's book showing these ramifications several kilometers long, like geoglyphs, or rather phytoglyphs. We are in fact in the bed of what Nigel calls *lugga*, not a stream but a "tree stream" which, like all the others, flows towards Lake Turkana, therefore northward. To continue to walk in that direction condemns us to remain closed in to it – a suicide. The shortest way to get out of this flaying hell can only be perpendicular to the feeble traces of drainage left in the crystallized sand, in other words straight west.

All these reflections take us five seconds. So as not to turn in circles, we spot above the foliage to the west the summit of the Lothagam mountain which we keep in our sights, the hope of a world without thorns. We try to cut straight. Our water reserves are gone. I am emptying myself minute by minute of my energy like a Duracell rabbit at the end of its race. My olalem becomes heavier at each blow. As a misfortune never occurs alone, a beetle has entered Sonia's shirt collar; she begins to cry out like a pig being slaughtered – a *paedirus*, the same species that had burned her with sulfuric acid in Malawi. She still has a brownish scar in the bend in her elbow. This time, a red trail blisters her above the left breast. She is furious. After three hours of this ordeal, we begin to cave: how are we going to get out of this fucking *hoy tokoy* shithole? I am not far from blowing a fuse. The impression of running in place. Of having fought with a collar squeezing about my neck. Are we really going to croak here! Because of these god-damned shitty little bushes! In a burst of fury, I head back to the front, cut, swear, belch an energy of despair while Sonia, behind me, tries to recall me to reason. It is in this animal rage, flayed and bloody, bitching and drooling, that I finally come into an open space at the foot of Lothagam. I fall apart. Console myself in Sonia's arms, my shirt lacerated, my legs trembling and striped with blood. What idiocy! Without the olalem we would have been done for.

In the distance, huts and palm trees, men. Seeing us arrive aglow and broken, this Turkana family understands where we have come from and what we have just gone through. They bring us a bowl of water to bandage our wounds and a sorghum gruel in rancid butter to plug our gaps. They are all beautiful and seigniorial. A little girl plays with her wooden doll. It is a little goddess of fertility decorated with locks of hair, beads and pieces of fabric. Her big belly is supposed to inspire in its owner the desire to have many children.

The grandfather, with a hard stone, punches through a broad, more tender stone to make a millstone. Each impact removes a few microns of matter and leaves a white dot. He progresses methodically. It is long and fastidious, but he has plenty of time, and these stones are everlasting. The same ones are found on neolithic sites a thousand years old. His occipital clay skullcap is all leprous, crackled, his hairdo neglected. He wears a labial aluminum cork that looks for all the world like a trumpet mouthpiece. He has two incisors of his lower jaw removed. In the region, everything seems to be arranged so saliva will flow out of its natural cavity: the hole in the teeth, the hole in the lip; a curious tradition, in these deserts where water is rare. Mystery. He carries on his wrist the fearsome war knife of the Turkanas: a metal disk with a cutting edge, worn like a bracelet. The blade is covered with a little leather girdle to keep him from hurting himself. He is fifty-seven. He looks eighty.

The young mother, his daughter-in-law, is nursing, on port side, a newborn, and on starboard, his brother of one, both clinging to desperately empty, crumpled socks. The comfort is mental. For us too. In the shadow of this palm tree, the gentleness of these people is a balm to our hearts. They know nothing about us, and we nothing about them, but they know what counts: be good, be gentle. Life is so hard out here! The wooden bowl in which by turns we dig out gluey, fatty lumps of seeds is of a form never seen before.

The opening is rectangular while the rest is all rounded, the sides, the rim, the bottom. Placed on the sand, that assures it maximal stability. Calabashes are rare and dear, here, and earthenware is too heavy and fragile for nomadic life. The Turkanas have therefore developed an unbelievable knowhow for working wood. Moreover they are all busy carving something, giving free reign to their artistic sense. The quest of beauty in the object is a materialism of a spiritual order which, without a doubt, contributed to making our very distant ancestors into more human men. The first man is perhaps the one who, of two pebbles, chose the prettiest...

"*Hoy tokoy!*"

The old man, distracted by his conversation with a neighbor who came to see what was going on, has just broken his stone with an ill-placed blow. How many hours of work lost? He looks at it, scarcely vexed, not even enervated. It had a flaw. He will begin another, it's not serious, time is on his side.

We part as we had arrived, in the most natural way there is, because they were here, because we were passing by. Turning back every hundred meters, we can long see their arms and hands waving to us like an anemone of love in the shade of a palm tree. The wind caresses us, we let the sun go down and play our dead reckoning game again, one bearing after another, palm tree after bush, which all speak to us of the north in secret: it's this way! It's this way! The malevolent tide of the *lugga* also flows to the north, on our right. It won't fool us a second time.

Crossing the desert off-trail demands exceptional attention. You can't let yourself coast, escape, think of something else. The walk is silent, concentrated, anxious. You don't banter, you don't frolic. The mind becomes an arrow shot at a point on the horizon, held back at every moment by the carcass of the body. It would be so simple to be nothing but sand! Gone with the wind.

We run into a guy with a Kalash' coming out of nowhere and going nowhere. He doesn't even know the word "*mbali*" that means far in Swahili. Sonia is frustrated: "All the same! It's his national language. He could at least garble it, like us." But why? Nothing is very far for a Turkana. Distance is just a matter of time. And they've got plenty.

This evening, we land at Kerio 2, a shantytown put up in open desert, where displaced Turkanas survive. Kerio 1 was carried off by El Niño. Hundreds of people drowned in the middle of the night in this desert by the flooding river. The height of absurdity. Of horror.

Theophilus Loburo is a young student from Lodwar, the capital of Turkana country, and he speaks very good English. He receives us in his home, in a vast courtyard where the most fantastic of lectures is being improvised before a dozen students as thirsty for knowledge as the desert plants are thirsty for sap. They want to know everything. Why are there earthquakes? Why the Rift? Why the wind, the sandstorms, the stars, the moon, day, night, lightning, it's all there. Seated in a comfortable chair, like an African elder, with all this flock at my feet, I use my stick and point out the constellations, trying to remember my physics courses, my readings of Carl Sagan and Stephen Hawking. They are in seventh heaven. Gravitational force, centrifugal force, the Coriolis force, satellites, the speed of light, the axis of the ecliptic, the sound barrier, the expansion of gases, plunge them into unfathomable delights, they drink in my every word.

They are young and uprooted. Straddling two cultures. Unable to survive in one, unable to live in the other. Useless everywhere. They are in suspense, terrified by the complexity and harshness of a world that refuses to open up to them while they have irreversibly turned their back on their roots. Knowledge is modernity's first poison. Gentle and fatal for the innocence of traditional life. They are nevertheless the Kenya of tomorrow.

Two days later, we finally come to Lake Turkana, alongside which we have been walking for over a hundred kilometers already without seeing it because it was hidden behind a backbone ridge of mountains. It is calm and eternal, mineral. Water in the desert, as far as you can see: the Jade Sea! It was the last of the great African lakes to be discovered, in 1888 by Count Samuel Teleki, a Hungarian aristocrat, and the Austrian Ludwig von Höhnel, they too having come on foot but leading 238 surviving porters of the 668 that had left Mombasa fourteen months earlier. We have had the advantage of being light and having a lifeline, the Kerio. And to know that the lake was there. And it is! We have an appointment with Halwign Scheuermann, whose tented camp, pitched at Lobolo, we find without difficulty. Ours awaits us, facing the Jade Sea, over a palm plantation, the sun and peace. Two fish eagles answer each other's cry to celebrate our crossing of the deserts. A shower follows, a bevy of cold beers, a tomato salad with olive oil and balsamic vinegar, accompanying a filet of Nile perch: this is too much! We are at the end of the earth, at the beginning of the earth. We are in paradise. Thank you Halwign!

CHAPTER 16

The Jade Sea and Koobi Fora

KENYA

Crocodilus niloticus, the Egyptian vulture, Nile perch, Egyptian geese, 90% Ethiopian water in the lake....So much data that induce a serious step forward, so many small signs confirming that we are tipping over to the other side of our trek. At night's end, before dawn, the stars also congratulate us in silence: in the north, low on the horizon, and still without its tail, the tip of the *Ursa Major*[1]. Two years we've been waiting for it. A giant step into the northern hemisphere. Last night, the Southern Cross was setting early in austral spheres.

Lobolo awakens, the lake is like oil. In the distance, Turkana fishermen are already at work on their makeshift pirogues, a simple contraption of light, fibrous branches like balsa. Not to walk. To rest. To be here. What felicity!...Everything happens. How does it happen that we are alone? Billions of individuals on earth, and no one in Lobolo...

Today we head for the discovery of Central Island, a volcanic

---

[1] Known also as the Big Bear, the Big Dipper or the Great Chariot.

cone planted in the middle of the lake, at the heart of the Rift; a mountain that seems to float in the white ether. We glide over the Jade Sea towards the mysterious island. On the way, we are trailing two lures behind our watercraft in the hopes of extracting a mythical Nile perch from the brackish waters. Only initiates and fishing lovers can understand the seduction that this myth of a fish exercises: the record specimens exceed three hundred kilos and two meters! The only monsters like them in the world, which only isolated ecosystems, favoring natural selection and endemic gigantism, can produce. The lake contains only forty species of fish but has preserved eight in common with the Nile, the inheritance of a distant era when their waters were interlinked, seven million years ago, before the upheaval of the mountains of the west coast isolated it definitively. Two other species proliferate in the lake, tilapia and a very archaic variety of catfish. The perch hunts, the tilapia is hunted, and the catfish is the garbage man. We watch the rods closely, the tight lines disappear in the greenish waters. I do not like this kind of fishing, it is too passive and too blind, the lake too vast. It is redolent of deep sea fishing! The trout of the foothills of Lesotho are far away, those of the Nyanga mountains, in Zimbabwe, these hand-to-hand struggles with the tigerfish of Cahora-Bassa, on the Zambezi in Mozambique, and the long hours sounding the long line in the depths of Lake Malawi, with a wet butt at the bottom of a hollowed-out trunk. Despite all, the boat is pointed at Central Island and we are searching, eyes peeled, senses on alert, for one of the finest angler's dreams. In vain. Not a nibble. The Nile perch shall remain an unsatisfied phantasm, a chimera. Peter, our helmsman, tells us that it is a threatened species, overfished.

"At Kalokol, there was a Norwegian cannery. The government wanted to move it to Baringo, to favor President Moi's ethnic group, the Kalingins. The Norwegians didn't agree, and they had a week to leave the country. At Kalakol there also was an Italian fish farm, very beneficial to the lake because they sold male tilapias and let the females go. They too were driven out, in 1999; they had complained that the government was not regulating fishing."

"Those departures don't explain why the fish are disappearing..."

"Yes they do. Because today the fishermen have no solution but to dry the catch they cannot sell, stock it, return to fishing to catch fresh fish for very rare buyers, who bring the price down, which causes the overfishing and an enormous mess. In fact, it is anarchy everywhere. And there are newcomers, the Luos, an ethnic group from Lake Victoria. They come with refrigerated trucks to export the Nile perch to Europe and the United States: they are plundering everything!"

Approaching the island, we count eight fishermen's boats operating illegally in the waters of the national park. They go farther away when we pass. Still closer, we observe the presence of endless strings of floaters that ring the rocks: "Those are the long-lines. With those they bait thousands of hooks and run off with all the perch."

While beginning his approach, Peter tells us a lugubrious story. "In the 1930s, Dyson and Martin, two members of the first scientific reconnaissance mission of the lake, directed by Vivian Fuchs and John Millard, disappeared body and soul from the island. We think they were eaten by crocodiles or were drowned in a terrible storm that lasted a week. Since then, their memory haunts the spot, some even say they have encountered their ghosts..."

"John Millard? The British colonial officer?"

"Yes."

"That's incredible! We slept in his house, at the Greens, at Millard near Barkly East, in South Africa...six thousand kilometers back. What a coincidence! And he was the first Westerner to set foot on the island?"

"Surely even the first man, since at the time the Turkanas did not fish and had no watercraft..."

We pass under the sheltered side of the island, along the basaltic organs tinted a thousand colors, land on a beach scattered with fish bones and set off in rockslides to climb the bald cone. On the crest, our gaze plunges into the heart of the crater. The sight stuns us. A lake in the lake! An emerald jewel set in jade. A green lake like a giant oyster fringed in black and pink flamingos. The flanks of the crater reveal the layers of volcanic ash laid down by successive eruptions. Some are gray with black lumps, others smooth and ochre. At the summit of the cone, among the flamboyant concretions, a fissure is releasing whiffs of sulfurous vapor. Two Egyptian vultures come and flirt overhead in these rotten egg odors. They are very white, with black-tipped wings like seagulls, with a hairy head and golden yellow beak. They are able to break ostrich eggs with a rock. Deserts make you ingenious! They suddenly take off, surfing a thermal. In the lake, wisps of spirulina trace green arabesques that sometimes look like toads and sometimes like the veils of a gigantic emerald. Ribbons of flamingos wrap the volcano in their spiral flight toward other feasts and other ballets. A genesis landscape. We descend to see the second of the island's three crater lakes. It is black as ink.

"It's a crocodile nursery. You see them? There! and there!"

Indeed, they are floating like dead tree trunks. By the dozens. Enormous. Among the rocks reside goliath herons, the world's largest. It would seem that to survive in this hell, you have to be big! We return to our boat and resume our crossing of the lake, towards the Sibiloi National Park. We are to meet Louise Leakey tomorrow at Koobi Fora, forty kilometers farther north. The challenge thrown down over a month ago in Nairobi is accepted. She unearthed for us a permit to walk in the park without a ranger or escort.

The director of the Sibiloi Park, Mr. Jorogwe, a phlegmatic type, welcomes us kindly. Everything is run down, the toilets are ruined, there is no vehicle, no electricity, no means for overseeing his park. A punishment. A slammer in hell. Flat broke. He dreams only of a transfer and an office in Nairobi. A dossier lies on the table: "Plan for park rehabilitation," published by UNESCO. I glance at it. Louise, as technical consultant, has initialed each page with a

"No!" or "Unfeasible!" or "Ridiculous!" or "Are you kidding?" The plan speaks of constructing a road on the central island, administrative buildings, of authorizing fishermen to come and rest there, to transform the infirmary into a dormitory for rangers, to pour three hundred kilometers of asphalt in the desert, and the stupidest ideas....Hopeless!

Jorogwe comments: "You know how much the author of this rag was paid? Twenty-five thousand dollars, whereas I earn one thousand two hundred a year..."

Sonia has drifted off. I go out to take in the twilight air. A dozen hyenas laugh as they tear up an unfortunate rabbit. The ruckus they make is wild. An east wind from hell is blowing off the Chalbi desert. Not a tree to slow it down. The park is visited only by a few hundred people every year. It is more than anything a reserve intended to preserve the lake shore from overfishing and crocodile poaching. I think of Jorogwe's discouragement, of the fragility of this reserve when, suddenly, I see three shadows gliding toward me. Damn, the hyenas! They are as close to me as I am far from the camp. Decision. Call out? It's already too late! Turn my back to them? At a sprint, they would beat me. I hastily pick up some stones and take shots at them....They take off like the rabbit they were ripping to pieces....What shit! To go piss under the stars, in the bush, is to risk your life.

At dawn, we follow the lake shore. The east wind is still blowing: the breath of dry death. On the left, the bank laps and quivers under the breeze. God how much better one is close to water! Our hominid ancestors must never have gone very far from it. Thick algae eat the fertile soil; they teem with darting insects which the fish on one side and the birds on the other come to feast on. Life. That's how it started, on primeval banks similar to the ones we tread. Our steps raise a ceaseless variety of limicoline wading birds, which take off into the wind, rising straight up without beating their wings, brush us with their rustling sound, intoxicate the air with their cries before landing again behind us. We surf all morning in these waves of fowl.

In the distance herds of zebras take off. Starts and stops, as with cannon fire, rushes and kicking up of heels, the ground rumbles and the striped charge disappears in a fracas of rumps swallowed up by maelstroms of dust. Topis, reddish and weird antelopes, stare at us with their little heads with comma horns, more curious than uneasy, then, suddenly, answering a collective call, set in motion their swaying gallop toward the desert. We are drunk with space and steps, with azure and life. Sometimes the mud sticks to our soles, at others we must walk around marshes, fight off cuts from elephant grass, but who cares! We advance and come into bare prairies, quivering with heat, open onto infinite Africa. When we get back to the shore, we find it strewn with dead tree trunks aligned at regular intervals to the horizon. As we approach, one by one, the trunks start up with a sharp clack of the tail like a whip, and throw themselves into a frantic sprint to the lake where they disappear in an outboard wake: the famous crocodiles of Lake Turkana. Now rare, they take refuge on these banks of the Sibiloi National Park, where they can reproduce in complete tranquility. I remember Peter's words yesterday: "In the 1980s, people were still eaten by crocodiles, and hence no one fished. In the 1990s, everything was killed, and today there is nothing left!" Even the mythic and distant Turkana is threatened by blind appetite and poor management. It took only ten years to empty it out.

The wind has desisted and the heat catches up with us. Implacable. Not a tree, not a shadow! At the eighteenth kilometer, we decide to go bathe among the crocodiles, on the faith of Peter's promises: "Nothing to fear!" he swore. After some uncertain hesitation, the attraction of coolness wins out over fright. There is very little depth. The crocs' snouts crisscross at a distance, skimming the surface, but here we are fine, as in primitive times, our radiators cooled, rocked nude by the surf, on the soft slime. Alone. We are alone in the world. The multicolored nudity of my Eve lasciviously abandoned to the sun's ardors makes me giddy. There are no grape leaves in Turkana, no forbidden fruit. Her golden hands slide over her milky breast in an effort to get a little bar of soap to lather; a sunburn on her neck makes her utter a little cry. Her body is a chromatic patchwork. The leg is a perfect gradient from gingerbread to chicken breast. The tan on her arms contrasts sharply with the snows of yesteryear. *Le vierge, le vivace et le bel aujourd'hui*[2] remains the foot. It has been so long since we have seen each other naked. We are almost intimidated by it. This trek is an X across our carnal intimacy to the benefit of our fraternal and spiritual intimacy. Our caresses soon repossess these lost territories, in the middle of Creation, under the hot sun, on this bank, before the very eyes of a couple of vultures circling overhead who, enticed, await the outcome of the hand-to-hand combat, of a little side-striped jackal poking his nose around our backpacks, and a Somali ostrich, with its turgid indigo blue neck, coming toward us, head lowered and feathers tousled, deaf and blind to our joy.

It is time to start walking again....We have refilled our bottles. The lake water is just barely potable: salty, with a little aroma of soapy, alkaline muck that makes it taste for all the world like sewer water. Ninety percent of the Turkana water supply comes from Ethiopia by the Omo River, the Turkwell and the Kerio sharing the remaining ten percent; therefore the further north you go, the less salty is the water. Further on in the mud, the heavy and fresh footprints of a hippopotamus and its young one, in the middle of the desert! Indeed we thought we had heard their characteristic snoring vibrate on the water. We had attributed this impression to euphoria. There is nothing to graze on here! How do they keep alive?

The day passes with the kilometers, gallops and flights, the course of the sun in the merciless sky, from right to left, thorough suntan. The backpack becomes heavy as well as the muddy soles. More footprints. Hyenas? No, lions. Twelfth time! Nothing on the

---

[2] Eponymous first line of a poem by Mallarmé: "The virgin, vivid and beautiful today."

horizon. Yet they are today's, may be yesterday's. Can't gather moss here. We have to get to Koobi Fora. Especially since there is no acacia to cut to make a nighttime shelter. In answer to my anguish, a vibration rises in the air, like a muted rumble, a heavy roar….Apoplexy. Nothing in sight. Damned lion. The vibration increases…an airplane! It's Louise Leakey! Whew. Spin around to the south. Skimming along the bank, she is coming at us like a Stuka, makes a tight turn to give us a wave with the two wings and her hand. We fire the booster. Hell with the lions! We sing our joy at the top of our lungs. Two hours later, we reach the Leakey camp, made up of fine stone houses hidden under gray thatched roofs. Louise is there, blonde and elegant, a woman with straw hair, a permanent smile, imprinted on her cheeks by the sun and her *joie de vivre*. She welcomes us with two flutes of champagne against a background of Bach: "You've lost! I've arrived first! I can't believe you made it! You are unbelievable, it took me three hours; it took you five weeks, you are crazy! Vive la France! Chin-chin!"

I think that between the tomato-with-basil-pinenut-parmesan-shaving salad and the garlic leg of lamb we again wept….Walking must develop an axon between the salivary and the lacrimal glands…

Koobi Fora, Wednesday 13 November 2002, day 685, 8162nd km

"Let's go, the Chicks up! We're going swimming!"

Combat disarray. Louise is running toward the lake for a morning bath among the crocodiles.

"Keep cool! They have known me for twenty years…" she shouts as she dives in.

We join her. The pale pink horizon spreads from lake to sky. A pelicans' fleet takes flight with heavy tapping from their feet on the water's mirror surface. They pass like a squadron of furtive bombers but the beating of their wings squeaks in the silence like the rowlocks of an old boat. A purpled goliath heron rows in the air with its huge, heavy wings that flirt with their reflections. Morning magic.

The site at Koobi Fora is inseparable from the name of the Leakeys, a line of paleo-anthropologists who, over three generations, have marked the rise of this discipline with cardinal discoveries. If Louis and Mary Leakey are rather associated with the Olduvai site in Tanzania, Richard and Meave have extensively explored the surroundings of Lake Turkana. Louise has taken up the torch at Koobi Fora, long threatened by ostracism and politics. It was Richard who, in the 1960s, built the Koobi Fora camp with great taste, not far from the fossil beds of the same name, on a sand isthmus that juts into the lake like a prow. Five or six houses with walls of volcanic stone share the site, open to the four winds, surrounded by verandas the low walls of which align numerous vestiges: skulls, shells, strange stones, giant teeth, concretions, fossils, a heteroclite collection gleaned over the years. And in the middle of the living room, like an altar at the end of the holy of holies, sits enthroned the most precious object that can be found in a desert: the freezer.

"We're going to down a breakfast of crêpes Suzette, and before we get to work, I'll show you the park seen from the sky, all right?"

"Oh-oh...crêpes Suzette! Hold me up, Sonia!"

An hour later, Louise is perched on the wing of her Cessna 220 with retractable landing gear, busy bleeding the tanks and checking out the plane. The airstrip is only a "pan," a sort of drained puddle free of stones and vegetation. In other words, minimal and short. Full throttle, Louise releases the brakes, and we're off! Concentrating, she follows the terrain, gets into the wind without fighting the stick, vibrations, acceleration, bumps, the tail rises; gently her hand pulls us off the ground at five meters from the first shrubs.

"*WAAOW!*"

"It's a tailor-made strip!" she shouts over the single-engine roar.

It's straight away the fairy-like quality of Africa! These landscapes that we have been treading for two years take on another, totally phantasmal dimension: there's no longer anything arduous or rebarbative, nothing troublesome or sweaty, we are flying like a *National Geographic* reporter or like Denys Finch-Hatton, the cult hero of *Out of Africa*, in his yellow biplane; better yet, we are flying a dream, we are flying with Louise Leakey....Herds of zebras raise plumes of dust in the desert, in pursuit of lost topis; thousands of flamingos blink like schools of smelt on the mirror surface; we review the monstrous, slumped crocodiles on the beaches; in the distance, cones, tables, dry beds, it all goes by in giddiness and grandiosity. Flight is well-suited to Africa.

"Take good note of your itinerary! That's where you will be passing tomorrow! Right there! There is a big marsh to go around. Here, it's out of the question to cross this river, it is infested with crocodiles. And over there, the rocky promontory, that is Kokhoi. The water is very deep. Don't bathe in it, that's where the lake's biggest crocodiles are found..."

In her helmet, Louise lets loose a swear word: "Look there! That's what I was looking for: livestock. Look at that. Hundreds of cows there, and further on, all those goats! A camp. Then another. Those nomad shepherds have absolutely no right to be there. It's a catastrophe."

Everywhere, in every direction, the herds scatter, frightened by the motor, the shepherds gesticulate.

"I'm going to have to send a patrol. Those animals stomp and ravage the surface fossil beds, not even to mention overgrazing, exhausting the soil, competition with wild species, diseases, poaching....Here the Dassanech shoot zebras with Kalashnikovs instead of eating their cows. If that keeps up, the park is going to lose its UNESCO world patrimony classification, it would be terrible, not to mention the fossil sites that would be lost forever.

Louise's piloting betrays her anger; she is performing the turns and circles of a toreador, wielding the rudder-bar and stick, we lose the horizon and hold our stomachs. After this aerial rodeo number, the landing, even more impressive: a pocket handkerchief, a carrier landing on a dish of black sand. This thirty-year-old bit of a woman is a heroine of rare mettle. Scarcely are we on the ground: "All right, to work! Are we going to do this interview, or not?"

At the wheel of her Land Cruiser, she takes us to an eroded site where geological strata "like a pile of plates" are easily distinguished. Sonia takes her position, movie camera in hand. Louise continues: "One of the principal advantages of Koobi Fora is that there is very little vegetal covering and that the fossils are at surface level. It is also a disadvantage, they are more fragile and vulnerable. Another advantage, the sediment deposits alternate with volcanic tuffs which allow for very precise dating. Given the orientation of the strata, because of the graben phenomenon."[3]

I question her: "Who was living here at that time?"

"Imagine the decor. It was not very different from today's. The lake is to be sure higher, therefore much more vast, the rivers were lined with large trees and bushes, the banks carpeted with thick grass contrasting with the surrounding aridity. There are gazelles, pigs, a few antelopes, giraffes and elephants even, which are now gone, coming to drink in the lake, watching out for immersed crocodiles near the surface. We see three varieties of hippopotamus and catfish. Far off to the north, a violent eruption that occurred in the Ethiopian mountains filled the air with dust. Soon the ash that filled the sky will be carried by the rivers and be deposited in ever heavier layers in and around the lake. By walking around you might have the luck to encounter some groups of hominids, and looking more closely through binoculars, observe that they belong to four distinct species, differing in their height, behavior, nourishment, necessary conditions for peaceful coexistence. The first species, *Homo habilis*, the one from which we perhaps descend, was, we think, about 1.4 meters tall, but we have never found a complete skeleton. He was a permanent biped, his brain had a volume two-thirds of ours, he was surely omnivorous; we have

---

[3] A tectonic trench.

found rough stone tools beside fossilized bones, hence his name of 'skilled man.' The second species is *Australopithecus africanus* which you know thanks to Lucy and Mrs. Ples. Of very ancient lineage, less adapted to walking, endowed with a very small brain, we call them 'gracile' because they do not exceed 1.4 meters in height and had small bones. Next comes the *Australopithecus boisei*, classified among the australopithecines called 'robust' because of his outsize molars, his sagittal crest which serves to anchor powerful chewing muscles that are capable of grinding grains and roots. Finally there is *Ardipithecus*, a very gracile and primitive form of hominid, condemned soon to become extinct. And not to mention those we haven't found..."

As she talks, Louise bends over, auscultates, passes the sediments under the scanner of her alert eyes, picks out a chip of bone here, a stromatolith[4] there.

"What is exceptional about Koobi Fora is the exhaustive geological measuring and surveying that has been done over thirty years' time: we have a good reading of the site and we know where to look. What we lack is time and means: of about fifty sectors, three have been superficially dug."

She stands up and looks at the other side of the lake. "But Lake Turkana is known above all for the most complete paleoanthropological specimen ever found in Africa: Turkana Boy, the best example in the world of *Homo erectus*, the one who began to walk, and left the African cradle – and who already resembles us enormously: 1.6 meters at age fifteen; we estimate that he would have attained 1.8 meters as an adult whereas his contemporaries did not exceed 1.5 meters. He is also the one whose footsteps are guiding yours, if I have rightly understood! It is doubtless he who left the continent. His cranial capacity is estimated at 900 cubic centimeters, which is three times more than that of the australopithecus. His tooth structure is very close to ours. He made his tools

---

[4] Fossil of bacterial or fungal amalgams, signs of ancient slimy bottoms.

and perhaps even had the use of fire, but that is not yet proven. He has been found on the other bank, over there, just opposite, at Nariokotome, in a stratum one million six hundred thousand years old; he is moreover the oldest *erectus* ever found, but he is too far ahead of his time to descend from any of the previous ones, and not even from *habilis* because the latter lived long enough to be his contemporary. In fact, we still haven't found the ancestors of Turkana Boy, which are probably our true ancestors. Everything remains to be done. Everything remains to be found..."

There are as many missing links as specimens discovered, in this evolutionary chain. And it is impossible to pretend that they descend from each other under the pretext that they succeed each other chronologically, especially since, the more the discoveries are refined, the more it seems evident that these populations coexisted. Evolutionary mechanisms and natural selection remain very mysterious, more complicated than it seems. Our genealogical tree is more like a bonsai the branches of which have been endlessly severed and thwarted, than a great oak with harmonious ramifications.

In the evening, we go to walk barefoot on a sandbank two kilometers long that goes far out into the lake, toward the setting sun. The crocs glide into the water as on exercises. The surf caresses the gray sand. Louise tells us anecdotes of her childhood, her first fossil; the timbre of her voice is so juvenile....It's a pleasure to listen to her, we are under her charm; this prow of dunes is her sanctuary – how often has she walked along it! We pass a crocodile skeleton, then a catfish head. Potential fossils. Eat or be eaten. There isn't much else to add, in nature. Further on, imprinted on the sand, the scales of a belly, the curve of a tail and frightening claws. Again a potential fossil. I take from my pocket the half-femur found when we were walking along the Kerio and which I take to be that of a croc. Louise decides.

"A nice Kanapoi croc 4.2 million years old..."

"How do you know where it comes from?"

"The fossil's color. This blue-black tint comes from over there.

My mother, Meave, found the skull of *anamensis* there in 1995. It was a more modern australopithecus than the ones in South Africa or Ethiopia, and yet more than a million years old. It was more biped than Lucy and Mrs. Ples, even if its teeth were less modern. Another enigma! Look there, we have a femur of today's crocodile."

She picks up an object on the beach. Fresh, white, brand new. But identical to mine! Amazing! These saurians have not changed in two million years. Nothing to add. Nothing to take away. They are adapted. Almost perfect. They will survive us. If we let them live. The red sun on the horizon is wallowing in water, a cloud of gracile terns drops onto the clamorous peninsula. We go back. Behind us, on the bank of passing time, our three *sapiens sapiens* footprints are immediatly erased. To each fossil its miracle.

The song of ice cubes in a Coke is a constantly renewed orgasm. And the world could fall apart during the furtive seconds of the first swallows. Beer too, obviously, but there isn't the crystalline clink of ice. The evening wind blows through the dining room. We remake the world over a good dinner. Africa, in these conditions, is nothing but beatitude. A host of dragonflies is attracted by the lamp hanging from a corner of the roof. A ballet of bats fills its bellies with them, flitting by our heads. Geckos also take their share in the feeding frenzy. Their tails quivering with impatience. The cat is lying in wait for either one. Its tail waves gently. An enormous nightjar makes rapid incursions in the halo of light. All this life gravitates around the lamp in a hypnotic dance the prize of which is closing teeth. A bat, doubtless tired of dragonflies, suddenly falls on a gecko and carries it off into the night, we are astonished: a carnivorous bat! The cat leaps and misses the nightjar...he has entered the circle of light like a tiger his ring of fire before being absorbed by the night: nature is an alimentary circus.

CHAPTER 17

The Dassanech of the Omo

KENYA/ETHIOPIA

We leave Koobi this morning before dawn. We have a two-day hike ahead of us to leave the park. Therefore one night inside. Nothing or almost nothing remembered of the aerial topology. Everything seemed flat and simple, straight and clear. Ah, to fly! Walking still remains just as hard. We don't really get used to it. Forty kilometers is never a foregone conclusion, never easy. Sure there are gratifications. There is also a price.

It begins with this lovely beach, for kilometers, planted with yellow grasses, and our bird escorts, ibis, herons, flamingos. I have a weakness for the pelicans, Sonia elects a little black egret that covers the water with the mantle of its wings like a dome to make a shadow in front of it to suppress the reflection off the water and better dart its beak, like a dagger, at its prey. Mysterious, nutritious dance repeated on every step. The grass gives way to cracked, then muddy, earth. We have to go around. We get lost in a vast, uncrossable delta of elephant grass. Got to go around. Then a massif of flaying acacias; we know what it's like; we have to go around. Further on, we get caught in an expanse of plain bulrushes. This time,

232

no thorns but a more and more spongy soil, and varying foliage more and more dense, that prevents our getting through. We have to backtrack, then go around....A storm front then rolls toward us. No way to go around. We take shelter again behind a mound and let the sandy wind pass. Then buckets of rain fall. We set out again. If we're going to be rinsed, might as well suffer it upright! No way to walk straight. We change our strategy, leave the banks and its traps, go inland finally to walk due north. Between two evils, we always choose the lesser. The sun has returned.

We pass the Khokoi promontory and its basaltic organs sheltering succulent desert roses, *Adenium obesium*. This plant is extraordinary. It's like a miniature baobab, chubby and rounded like a pulp bottle set on sharp rocks. At the end of its several arms, it bears magnificent pink helical flowers like those of the frangipani. And yet the *Adenium* looks more like an animal than a tree; it has a bit the air of a lazy walrus on a pebbly bank.

Our progress over all these blocks of lava becomes fastidious. Always this sauna smell, peppery and salty, that emanates from the rockslides. Stay concentrated. Watch out for your ankles. A sprain here would be a catastrophe. Tell Sonia this right away so as not to regret my silence if by misadventure she twisted her ankle before my eyes. Talk to conjure fate.

"Sonia! Watch out for sprains. Imagine the hell of being trapped here, at twenty-five kilometers from Koobi, if you had to carry me, or even the reverse."

"It's incredible, I was going to say that to you! You're stealing words from my mouth."

It happens to us every day. The same stimuli give rise in us to the same thoughts. Unless by dint of living on top of each other, day and night, for so long, we are becoming telepaths. We make monstrous crocodiles four to five meters long flee before us. The way they tear into the water, the snout ahead of them and the tail far behind, one imagines a dog being pursued by a shark. No bath tonight. But we take a shower anyway, a front of black halberds is coming down on us. We continue along a large bay strewn with whitened skeletons. I collect, in the rain, a few crocodile teeth from an enormous skull. The storm ends with nightfall. A flooding wadi halts us. Everything is saturated, muddy. We all the same find a more or less dry place on a hillock to pitch the tent. I slave at lighting a fire then get rid of my muddy shoes to rest in the tent. Sonia stops me, occupied with her onions (for the soup): "You've got to get some water."

"I'm on it."

En route, I pick up my headlamp, the jerrycan and my Maasai sword since hyena cries have resounded nearby.

"Put your shoes on!" she cries like a mother to her son: "Put on your sweater before you go out!" – an injunction that calls for disobedience.

"Don't worry, I'll be able to wash my feet at the same time!"

"Put them on anyway…"

I have already left, lamp off, under the beacon of the full moon. Little thorns torture the soles of my feet, as if I needed that! Just to prove her right. After eight thousand two hundred kilometers, we still have baby feet, tender skin and a soft sole. Coming back, while walking in my own footsteps to avoid the thorns, I suddenly tell myself that it is silly to save the battery like that, that they are made to be used. So I turn my headlamp on, for conscience's sake. Horrors! In a flash, my foot suspended in the air, I drop the jerrycan before making a reflex jump: I was within two big toes of walking on a horned viper. Mortal. Coiled up, ready to bite. At this end of the world. My olalem avenges me for my fright. And my foolishness. The dead head in my hands, *to be or not to be*, I make him spit his venom yellow as honey, sweet like the kiss of death.…I return to the tent, green and nauseated, with this bad good news. Under the shock, Sonia melts into tears. I almost died, today. Out of fatigue. Out of negligence. For not having listened to my wife. Which is the same thing. But why did I turn that lamp on? We hug each other strong, shivering, chilled by the rain, chilled by the night, chilled by fragility. Sonia sobs: "In ten days, it's your mother's birthday. It would have been some present..."

The next day, we reach the post at Illeret, the last Kenyan military presence before the border. It is in ruins. Ahmed Bakari is in charge. Tartar Steppe[1] atmosphere. He comes from Mombasa and for ten years has been reading over and over an English translation of *Les Misérables*. Sonia asks him why. "To understand the democratic process which we still don't have," he replies. "It's a great struggle against evil, against ourselves, and that can only come from below, it doesn't happen automatically, it has to be deserved: we are all Cosettes and Jean Valjeans at the same time..."

A literary conversation in Illeret. We talk about Africa all night. No one knows anything about the continuation of our itinerary. Ahmed has no stamp and doesn't give a damn about our Ethiopian letter. In fact, is there a border? A barrier? Barbed wire? He never went to check, he has no idea. Who said "Tartar Steppe"?

Lost in the bush in Ethiopia, Sunday 17 November 2002, day 689, 38 km, 8261st km

At the eighteenth kilometer, a white milestone planted in the middle of nowhere celebrates our entrance into Ethiopia. It bears an inscription: C51. We write with emotion: "Africa Trek: 8241st km on foot since Cape Town." Three young Dassanech attend the scene leaning against each other. The eldest holds in his hand a sort of boomerang of which he gives us a convincing demonstration. The others have an extraordinary headdress, like a sort of headband made from their own hair, the extremities of which, near the ears, stick up like little buffalo horns. Martians. They look at us as if we were Martians. We are all someone's Martians.

How many times have we said to ourselves: "When we are in Ethiopia, we'll be home!" Understood, nearly there. It was stupid.

---

[1] Famous novel by Dino Buzzati published in 1940.

We are in open desert. At the end of the world. But all the same. With a step in the sand, we pass from the tribal to the imperial, from the Bantu to the Cushitic, from the eternal bush to the realm of the mythic Prester John, the Queen of Sheba, or the Ark of the Covenant: Ethiopia, the land of "burnt faces," according to the ancient Greeks; a generic term that included all the regions inhabited by people with black skin, south of Egypt. No one knows anything about the itinerary to follow. The lake is behind us. The flaying acacias make their reappearance. For the moment, we follow a road that goes due north, we like that. As for water, still no news. We have maximal autonomy and walk without thinking too much. We're not going to stay here. We're not going to go backward. So what do we do? Well, we go forward. The evening catches up with us as we are hearing songs and clapping. We are done in and intimidated. This evening, we need to be alone. We want a peaceful night to assimilate this border passage – a heavy page is turned, begun in Shompole. We are going to go deeper into the bush to find a place for the tent. That gives us more work, I must create our thorny enclosure, go find wood for the fire, find three stones for a hearth, while Sonia is setting up the tent, putting the backpacks inside, unrolling our half-mattresses, peeling the onions for the soup. Sharing the work. That has become our routine. We carry it out in silence, decompressing the day's fatigue.

Blue behind, caressed by the moon, red in front, in the flickering of the hearth, her calmed skin absorbs the night air like a salve. In panties and bra. Crouched like a big cat. A statuary vision, an ancient goddess, strong and pitiless, an Amazon, God how strong she is! I write in my notebook on one elbow, and watch her: "You know what, Sonia? We just passed the latitude of Abidjan..."

"I can barely contain my excitement..."

"I see that..."

Late into the night we are lulled by the men's songs and dances that pulse in the bush like a charm to which the desperate hyenas reply. As far as hyenas go, we are used to them, they don't keep us from sleeping any more.

The next day, we get lost for the second time in two years. The map shows a road to the northwest that we do not find. I look for it in vain, letting Sonia rest under a tree beside a dry river. I walk alone, five kilometers off-trail due east. If the road heads northward, I ought to cross it. Nothing. U-turn. On the way back, I follow my own footsteps. The wear, the sand, the sun and again the sand. Two hours later, I approach the dry river, torn with anguish: how could I have left Sonia alone in this bush? I finish the last kilometer on the run, my heart exploding in my chest, I apply myself to purging my mind of horror visions, Sonia cut to pieces or prostrate or gone, my neurons are working hard, getting all mixed up, I am nauseated, here is her tree, I cry out, she doesn't answer, I scream, I hear a *"oui?"* with as much emotion as when I asked for her hand atop the spire of Notre Dame, after a night of clandestine ascension....I find her at the same place, lying down by this river bed. My love had been asleep.

When we start walking again my legs are still trembling. Love is something. The only road we have unearthed goes west, and the delta of the Omo flows into the northwest end of Lake Turkana, our opposite direction, we who are supposed to be walking to the northeast toward Gingero and Turmi. The flaying bush is too dense to risk it by compass, we have already been there. We resign ourselves to following the road, wherever it may go. In any case, it has to go somewhere. Unfortunately, it is very hot, we are very hungry, very feeble, too fast. Walk. Walk.

About noon an auto comes by. We can't believe our eyes. Nor they theirs. A military patrol, we think. Not at all. A bespectacled Ethiopian gets out, wearing a little bottle-green polo. He addresses us in English: "Are you lost?"

"Yes. We can't find the road to Gingero, which goes north."

"It hasn't existed since the Second World War. It was an Italian road. Last month we found a carful of German tourists. They too were supposed to look for it. They must have gotten lost, run out of gas. They all died of thirst. You did the right thing by not persisting. This is the only road; it goes to Omo Raté, the administrative capital of the Omo valley. My name is Theodoros, I am a governmental agricultural engineer and I would be very honored to welcome you at my house tomorrow. But be careful along the way: for the last few weeks the Dassanech have been at war with the Hamers; seven people have been killed..."

Despite this bad news, we have a ton less weight on our shoulders. The road is the same, not easier, but we know where it is going, and that changes everything. Information is the key to our lightness. As for Omo Raté, it isn't even on my map...

On the way we pass a few Dassanech villages behind thorny ramparts. They all come to meet us. Mutual fascination. We thought we had seen everything in terms of rusticity with the Kerio Turkanas. We were way off the mark. Here, these people have never seen Whites. We are really extraterrestrials, that seems clear. But extraterrestrials that provoke general hilarity. It is fascinating. From every side, they spring up and scream with laughter. Our Swahili is useless. Everything is useless, so direct is the communication. Everything is crude and raw; they are covered with shreds of leather, dust and animal fat. An old woman discovers herself in the reversible screen of our movie camera; she can't get over it. She laughs, points at her own image in disbelief, hits her chest, saying "mimi," takes my shoulder and strikes it with her forehead in an extraordinarily maternal and natural gesture of surprise and joy. We disembark from another planet and already share 100% of humanity. But the shock is too great for us; we do not stop here, despite the invitations. We are too weak. It takes a minimum of energy to take on such encounters.

In the evening, while the bush is turning red, we come to one of these villages. The herds are converging. The men are all in arms. We have planned to walk in the moonlight to make up for the time lost by my reconnaissance to the east, but a little old man with his Kalash' over his shoulder catches up with us. He gives us to understand that he is the village chief – he has two ostrich feathers stuck at the top of his skull. He speaks to us in gestures of the dangers of the night and of Hamer ambushes. He's quite a sight, with his weapon, miming the enemy crouched down, ready to attack us. He deploys all his art. We are convinced. Besides, that's just what we want. Walking in the moonlight without knowing where we are going is no picnic. We accept. The whole village goes back inside behind us. The girls are pretty and delicate; the bowl cut made of little buttered braids and pompoms lends them a showy air. As soon as I exchange glances with them, they start to chortle, holding onto each other, in their dresses of oiled skin that jingle with an assortment of fobs, and come right back to devour my blue eyes.

"Your groupies get on my nerves."

"I rather like that feeling myself."

The boys wear that unbelievable horned headband, with the forehead shaven and stiff ridges on the back of the neck. It's like a helmet of hair. But the *fin du fin* is the little wooden amulet hanging on a bun, on the occipital bone. Great art. Contrariwise, the huts are the minimum imaginable: branches bent down and covered with a matted patchwork of rusty metal sheet, moth-eaten pelts, pieces of bark and withered fibers. A woman kneeling sings as she grinds corn on an oblong stone, flat but subtly concave. With a firm blow with both wrists, she mashes the grains which expire into flour with a soft growl. Her backward-and-forward movements make her necklaces jangle; sweat runs between the elongated breasts that beat against her stomach. The men have white bracelets on their arms. Standing with their legs crossed, the Kalash' on their shoulders, leaning on each other, they observe us. We set up the tent between two huts, at the foot of a little granary perched on piles. Night has fallen. I write, Sonia sews, the goats bleat a lament, little children babble, the full moon rises, I light my headlamp to general joy, a fly bugs me and amuses them. There is a strong smell of rancid butter and dry dung: the essence of Africa Trek. My kingdom for that perfume in a bottle! A cup of goat's milk arrives, Sonia, enchanted, exclaims in French: "*Y a du bon lait?*" (Is there some good milk?)

Shrieks of laughter. Everyone in imitation repeats her cry of joy: "Yadubonlay!"

It even becomes a song, then, in the general excitement, a Saint Vitus dance in the moonlight: "Yadubonlay! Yadubonlay! Yadubonlay!..."

In waves, two by two, face to face, they jump sideways, sliding their feet in the dirt and clapping their hands. Dassanech swing! The little crystalline voices of the children repeat "yadubonlay" like a refrain between the improvised couplets that rise above this more and more dusty melee, to die out in the stardust of the Milky Way. After this frenzy, the village goes to sleep in the eternal, sinister bleating of billy goats in rut.

At four in the morning, our Rambo grandpa with two ostrich feathers awakens us. He wants to guide us as far as Omo Raté. We must leave now if we want to cross the Hamer zone without problems. We break camp and get out. In the lunar light, we dash out silently. Our man wears a short loincloth of the tight-fitting miniskirt variety above cricket's calves and skipping sandals. He forges ahead with short, light steps, waddling his gaunt, black forty kilos. In his right hand he holds his traditional wooden pike as well as a little stool-headrest shaped like a horse saddle, with a patina that has taken on the copper tones of his skin. Over his shoulder, wedged under his left arm, hangs a rolled-up goatskin. On his right shoulder rests the inevitable AK-47, old model, with wooden stock. I follow him closely. The rusty barrel almost brushes my nostrils at every step in a threatening sway. Keep an eye on the trigger. He has a small, nimble and shaven neck, leaving a clay cap to encircle his skull like an eggshell. This is the headdress of the Dassanech warriors. Like a gray cap highlighted in orange, sealed into his hair but divided into two shells by a transverse part. The back section is slightly profiled, separated from the forward part in the form of a tiara. On each of the skullcaps, a rectangular support glued in the dry clay makes it possible to stick in a combination of ostrich feathers. This morning, our man has chosen two black buns that lend him a grouchy smurf look. Thus he easily passes under the branches.

Shooting stars are raining down in the sky. We count a hundred or so. The scene is surreal. Mars is attacking! And we are guided by the mysterious chief of a mysterious tribe on an unknown planet....Our man doesn't have the time to wonder, he watches behind every bush for an ambush. Attentive as a bird whose neck he has, he scans the dawn for any sign of Hamers, signals for pauses with a raised finger, starts up again bent, hands me his goatskin so he will be ready to fire, panics at the rising of a partridge or a group of guinea fowl, takes things very seriously. Only now do I realize that the color of his skullcap matches his gray loincloth with black and orange stripes. He is exceedingly esthetic. He is a complete vision of another age, a mutant drag queen and pretorian centurion; he would be all the rage on a Galliano podium, he's a Dassanech chief.

But things start going bad. He soon gets us trapped in marshes. We flounder like soldiers in the slush. Can't go straight any more, we wind about seeking places where the mud is less deep. It's not hard, you just have to avoid the puddles and move from one tuft of grass to the next. But we are going in circles, Between two tufts, we sometimes get into knee-deep water. We curse like demons. Which makes our feathered scout chuckle. From time to time, in drier spots, vast fields of millet are planted, protected from birds by kids perched on guard towers where they lick the fowl with primitive slingshots. Demonstration. The kid kneads a clay ball, puts it at the end of a whip, and moving it smartly forward, as he would a fishing pole, he lets fly the projectile with awesome precision. Our warrior ballerina talks things over with the nippers and each time continues with more assurance: they have seen no Hamers.

As the hours pass, the density of the population increases and the terrain becomes drier. We have crossed the swamps of the Omo delta. Without our gracile Terminator, we would have got mired up to our necks. At every field corner we come across tiny, clustered huts from which extraordinary quantities of inhabitants pile out: one, two, four, seven, nine…who unfold long legs and extend large hands with broad smiles. The city is not far. They all indicate the same direction. In one of these small crowds, our wind-up centurion disappears without a farewell. He will remain a bundle of mysteries. We reach the burg alone.

The city is a muddy jumble of mud huts and variegated populations drowned in a cloud of flies. We meet our first Ethiopian soldiers. They are impressed by our letter but cannot put the slightest stamp on it to make our entrance onto their territory official: "In Addis!" they tell us. We shall see. Theodoros finds us in a café black with flies. We are celebrating the 900th kilometer since Nairobi in one month and fourteen days. We have not been slouching. No doubt the hardest and densest bit of our entire journey. The key passage that we worried so much over seems to be won.

We soon find the river that gave the city its name, the Omo. Its broad waters ferry the brown silts torn from the Ethiopian plateaus towards the Jade Sea. Commotion on the banks: fishermen are pulling a monstrous Nile perch out of the water. Dripping, glittering, it guns me down with its big orange eye: a bolt of lightning. Its scales are the size of your palm, its powerful opercula the sharp edges of which protect the blood red gills are like bellows in quest of water. Children run up from everywhere, it's the assault of the Lilliputians! The Leviathan is helpless despite its hundred and fifty kilos of muscle; he is already being carried off by a delirious crowd. Never saw such a big fish!

Omo Raté, Wednesday 20 November 2002, day 692, 8 311th km

We fall ill at Omo Raté. Too many flies. Too much shit. We spend the day in unstable equilibrium in a putrid arbor voiding our guts over millions of starving maggots. Theodoros, even though he is a functionary, lives in a depressing hovel. Slept very badly. Mosquitos and howling dogs. Let's get out of here! I abhor these dead-ends that are also the world's shitholes. We decide to leave this very evening: walking at night to take advantage of the full moon, to escape the sun and the Hamer ambushes. Theodoros has warned us: it's a no man's land of eighty kilometers without a living soul that leads finally to Turmi. On the program: a trail, no men, no water, lions. We've been there. Some Slovak tourists who are heading north tomorrow will bring us on their way a jerrycan of ten liters of water purchased for this purpose. Sonia can't get over it: compatriots of hers lost in this dead end. There are only six million Slovaks in the world, two of whom are in Omo Raté! We leave at nine. To extricate oneself from a shithole is always a liberation. In them you always cross hurrying tourists in big chauffeured cars and depressed backpackers. The latter had a rough time of it in Ethiopia. They have all been very ill. They all have had problems with the local populations. We are not reassured. Sonia breaks the silence of the night to conjure our anxiety. Our objective is to reach Addis Ababa for Christmas, where two dear friends, Jean-Claude and Amaretch Guilbert, await us. We have thirty-four days before us. We have been told it is between six and seven hundred kilometers. That should be playable. The lugubrious cry of the nightjars trills in the blue of the night. The air is crystal clear, our shadows are walking by our sides. We would see a lion three hundred meters away. Time to react. Now and then our blood freezes at the hyena cries; we chatter now. We have to keep moving. Bank time and space for tomorrow's sun. Get as far ahead as possible. At one in the morning, at the twenty-second kilometer, we put up the tent under an acacia.

Up at five, without eating. The moon is disappearing. We are on a small rise. The landscape opens to the north onto a huge, misty forest. The trail insists on walking east south-east. I fret and fume. It's the compass syndrome. If we had a GPS, it would be even worse. I would have my eyes riveted on it and a permanent sensation of being lost. It's so useless to swear at a trail, you just have to follow it....Still! When you are walking north, every kilometer south is a kilometer doubly lost.

I spend the morning cursing my compass and suffering from my diarrhea, drop-trou every three kilometers, run to catch up with Sonia. Cataracts in the plumbing. I found Humphrey Bogart ridiculous in *African Queen*. Now, I understand. The bush is crummy, the trail is straight, the sun overwhelming. Our friendly Slovaks pass toward noon in a truck with our water. The only truck all day. I am very weak. Feverish. No juice! I count the kilometers. It starts to rain. In the desert! I can't go on. There will be no moon tonight because of the clouds. And it goes forever and ever. I lose any time frame. We finally plant the tent in the night. Where our legs stopped. I struggle with the recalcitrant acacias to put our protective rampart in place and we drop, exhausted, without dinner. Hyenas are prowling but fatigue carries me off. At dawn, everything is soaked. While folding the tent, an enormous yellow scorpion that kept himself dry under our shelter crawls between our legs. It is fat and terrifying. When I titillate it with a stick, it plays dead. No children about. I spare him as he spared us. Zero calories to waste. We set out in the rain, without eating. In truth, how long has it been since we have eaten anything? How do we manage to live? Keep going. Get to Turmi.

At seven, an hour after our departure, a car, the first in three days, passes us and brakes with all fours. The fellow opens his window: "Aren't you crazy to walk here! Didn't you see the lions?"

My heart skips a beat.

"What lions? Where?"

"Four kilometers back. Eight lounging lions on the trail, near an abandoned campsite. Get in!"

They had come to sniff our camp. Our thirteenth lions. Once more, we decline. He takes us for fools and continues on his way. It starts to rain harder. My diarrhea is calling me. I take advantage of the opportunity to vomit some bile. We keep walking under a downpour. We count the kilometers: 19, 18, 17....Have to hold on. Only three more hours....I hear Sonia, exhausted, sobbing under her rain cape, murmuring: "It's the first time in two years that this walking seems to me completely stupid!..."

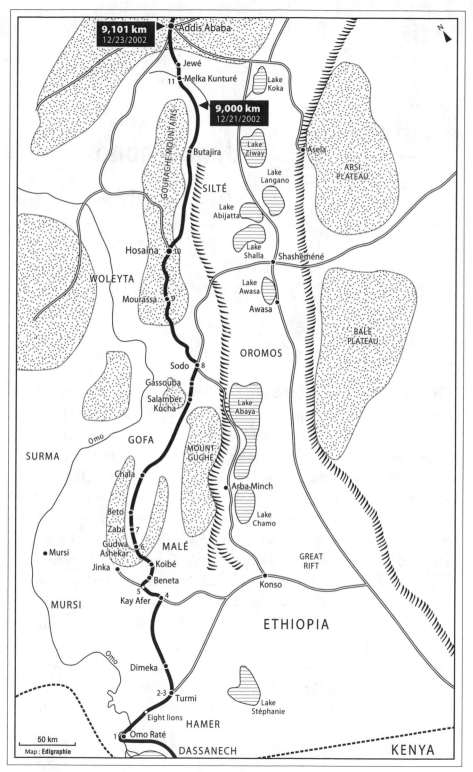

South Ethiopia

Ukuli among
the Hamers

In Turmi, we land in a bar-brothel with rooms in the courtyard. In our death throes. All that for this? This place concentrates all the annoyances that the modern world brings to "early peoples": alcohol, plastic, Nike caps, radios, noise, whores, soldiers, tourists, and us.

For whether we wish it or not, we too are tourists. Different tourists, but tourists all the same. Usually, our advantage is always to be alone, and thus to minimize maximally our impact, or else to be so rare that we benefit from the surprise effect. But here we are neither alone nor rare. Fresh from the neighboring campsite, where they are guarded by two watchtowers and barbed wire, little patrols of Europeans walk about with their battery of cameras and camcorders in search of the slightest cliché. And today is the humanitarian distribution of corn; there is therefore Hamer influence in Turmi. And nice specimens, the one finer than the next. Superauthentic. Butter, ochre, leather, naked breasts, scars, feathers, Kalash'...the whole business. The *faranj*[1] lie in wait around the house corners to

---

[1] Generic term for all white-skinned strangers.

steal photos. Some Hamers flee, others on the contrary come rushing, for here, the click is worth one American dollar. And no way can you sneak by. The warriors take their pose. The ones with an itchy finger, trigger-happy, can be heard a long way away, and then all the loveliest models come running, fight to get in the photo, push and shove, it's a mob, the price of the Hamer takes off, one, five, ten dollars; arms are raised with bills, going, going, gone! The hammer knocks down, the photographer disappears amid cries and gesticulations: from a distance, we think we are watching a group of brokers in the pit of the stock exchange. Defeathered, ruddy and shell-shocked, the poor fledgling reporter flees.

The Hamers, very pleased with their deed, then come to have a drink at the bar terrace, from where we are observing today three or four times the same scene. Is it good? Is it bad? No one asks himself the question. That's the way things are done in Turmi. Everyone is delighted: the tourist who will show his "authentic" photos to his friends, since he paid dearly to come take them, the travel agent in Addis who brought him here, the authorities who open to the world the cultural riches of their country, and the Hamer who can go have a drink with his buddies. Everyone got something "for his money." Fun in Turmi!

Retching in Turmi. We are sick as can be. A rapid visit to the local dispensary confirms that I have dysentery. The verdict of the scale is revealing: I have lost eight kilos in three days. Sonia has it too. She always gets it two days after me, and she is often well two days before me. Her immune system seems stronger.

Sole consolation, in Turmi: Richard Brackett. He is a good-looking Califorian whom we might have taken for a dude if we had not had the luck to spend a few days with him. In surfer's shorts and "adventure sandals," riveted cap to his head over an undershirt that boasts his suntanned shoulders, at first he had not made much of an impression on us. He came to call at our shack: "Is it true that you have come from Cape Town on foot? Man! That's cool! But what are you doing here, haven't you seen the condoms under the beds?"

After a brief inspection under the pallet, we discover with nausea the year's leftovers. We didn't know where that pregnant odor of latex and pepper was coming from. Sonia goes out to puke.

"I can't leave you here, guys! Come to my place, I rent a hut from an adorable lady. You will put your tent beside it, she's got a nice garden."

Richard is a "professional" traveler. For twenty years, he has been traveling six months a year. The other half of the year he lives in Santa Monica, where he puts money aside by taking wedding photos. He has been everywhere. He knows the world like the back of his hand. We share memories of China, India, Tibet, Baluchistan, Iran, Armenia….His particularity is that he comes back every three or four years to the same place with the thousands of photos he has taken and spends six months distributing them one by one to his hosts. The concept is fascinating. He has thus, over the years, made indelible friendship ties with thousands of families on the planet. Turmi perplexes him.

"Four years ago, I was among the first to come here. As soon as the country opened up. There wasn't a bar, just two or three stores, the military post and the dispensary. That was all. The street, there, with the shops and whorehouses opposite each other, wasn't there. The Hamers had never seen a camera at the time! Well, they learned fast: in four years, they have gone from the stone age to union scale for picture credits. I don't blame them. It's the system that does that: everyone wants to see them. The whole world comes rushing to Ethiopia to photograph the 'last authentic tribes.' I'm not telling you about the massacre!"

We resume our conversation about this and that:

"Look! I never travel without this portfolio."

He takes from his bag a notebook filled with photos, but instead of his house and family portraits, we find a killer whale, a penguin, the Eiffel Tower, a Tibetan, the Golden Gate....This guy is really cool.

"When I show them the whale, you know what they answer?"

"No. A fish?"

"Not at all: an airplane!"

"And the Tibetan?"

"Gambella! That's the name of a tribe on the Sudanese border. They are jet-black! That means they have never seen a Gambella..."

And so forth. He is fascinated by their perception of the world and reality. He has false teeth, bulging glass eyes and the nose of a clown, he knows more than one magic trick, with which he attracts the favor or ire of sorcerers. His art of traveling is an approach intended to change the relationship Westerners have with the world. A relationship that isn't commercial. A sharing rather than an exchange. Or else an exchange that is as non-material as possible. He is a specialist in nothing, speaks Hamer though he isn't a linguist, records their music though he isn't a musicologist, writes hundred of pages of notebooks though he isn't a writer, with no plan to publish, takes pictures without a contract for a write-up, just for the pleasure of sharing and the wonderment of diversity. He is an Unidentified Foreign Object who creates in his little corner a new "usage of the world." In two years he is only the second long-term traveler we have encountered, after Harald Bohn. Since he takes his time, he is up to date on everything.

Ababa, our hostess, has the homey kindness of women who, for having suffered, have decided to end their days doing good around them. She rents Richard a little barn with a thatched roof at the back of her land. She agrees to let us put our tent beside it for a modest sum.

"You know you've timed it well, this is the *ukuli* season!"

"The *ukuli*?"

"Initiation ceremonies for the young men during which they must leap over bulls, and the whole day long their families are whipped, you'll see, it's mad! I know there are two in the area being prepared, but the tour operators are already on them and the Hamers are forcing up the bidding. It can be as much as a hundred dollars a head. Fortunately, they are not all like that yet, and I know a girl whose nephew is going to become an ukuli in a few days. The thing is that you never know really when it's going to happen, so you have to wait. If you want, we'll go together. If someone deserves to see that, it surely is you! Tomorrow I will introduce my friend to you, her name is Duk."

She is kneeling before her grindstone like a Muslim at prayer. With her powerful arms ringed with bronze and steel, she pushes the egg-shaped grindstone which crushes the grain against the station-ary mold, with an antediluvian, maternal song that has made the world grow for more than ten thousand years. A nice flat, curved surface, concave and white, makes the motion undulate. I try and succeed, to the surprise of everyone. But Duk doesn't go for it, she feels the coarse grain of my flour with a pout of disgust: "The faranj's flour, it's no good!"

Duk is a Hamer woman in the prime of life. We managed to sneak into her hut without anyone seeing us and therefore are enjoying perfect tranquility. She resumes her swaying rhythm, slathered with butter and ochre, dripping, and the sweat from the effort makes great drops pearl on her back and run down into the hollow of her lower back among the swollen scars obtained by the tormentors' whips during an ukuli last year. Duke's skirt is weighted down by a fringe of metal rings, embroidered with bead squares. The butter and ochre in her hair make red lumps. Her neck is slathered but a necklace of dik-dik phalanges, knucklebones and gris-gris flops against her chest. She pauses a moment, pokes the fire under a stone carafe placed on an ingenious hearth. The set-ting sun filters through the large branches of the hut, projecting multiple rays in which wisps of smoke are dancing – perhaps the ancestors' spirits. Open to the breeze as it is, the inside is cooler and less smoky than Maasai huts. Gourds and calabashes hang by clusters. We are seated on piled-up skins. Duk serves us *chorro*, the juice of unsweetened coffee bark. Watery. That is their drink. From Richard's hands she takes prints of an ukuli from four years ago. She counts her scars. She has many more today. She must have married off other cousins or nephews in the last three years.

Three girls discover the reversible screen on our movie camera. Once the moment of stupor is over, one of them notices that the girl who is moving in the little plastic square in front of her imitates her own gestures; her girlfriends laugh and enter the frame… which makes her understand that the girl she didn't know was she! Screams of laughter. Eyes fixed on her image, her first experiment is to explore with her tongue the hole left by her two missing incisors in her lower jaw. Becoming aware of herself. She only knew herself through other people's eyes. There follows a series of grimaces and funny faces, the last of which is of course a lion.

Duk returns to her grindstone. In her gaze, her panting, her shiny skin, her rounded loins modeled by the leather, her scars bathed in butter, earth and sweat, her heavy breasts, her muscles tortured by the metal, her back-and-forth labor, there emanates something furiously sexual and primitive, heroic and brutal…. Tomorrow, she is going to be whipped at her nephew's ukuli. She invites us to go with her. Thank you, Richard!

We find her early, at the river, in company with a dozen women. They are washing and preparing for the festival, attaching bells to their knees, coating themselves with butter, chewing qat[2] leaves to get themselves in the mood. We fall in behind them, retracking the kilometers of the dry bed, winding through thick brush toward an isolated village. En route, our noisy company blows loudly into

---

[2] A bush the leaves of which contain a psychotropic and euphoric substance. Produced in Yemen and Ethiopia.

cornets to invite the spirits to the festival, drinks barley beer to gain courage, sings its bravura.

"We are lovely, we are strong, we are going to Urgo's ukuli, we are going to honor him, show the strength of his family, the valor of its women. We are lovely, we are strong! Come whip us! You will see of what mettle we are made! We will be worthy of Urgo!"

The village signals its location by the mooing of cows. The father of the ukuli greets us and installs under a shelter of wattle fences built for the event around the huts. The group of women has dashed into the adjoining kraal to dance. In a circle, jumbled single file, they turn counterclockwise, striking their heavy steel ankle bracelets and pounding the ground with their synchronous feet. The drum of the Earth. The thunder of women. Dust flies, ochre spurts, the braids whip the shoulders, the ground quakes, the bodies mingle, the cries cover the cacophony of the cornets. They are unleashed. They form a single corps, tribal. They are all alike, same costumes, same faces, same headdress, so much so that we lose sight of Duk.

In the shaded area, we are seated in company with languid little old men. One of them is seated on his little headrest in such a way that his penis hangs, still, under his short loincloth. Another casually scratches his own, then his nose, and back. They are armed with old Kalash's, gloriously coifed with their clay bun adorned with feathers. They stare at us coldly. We are ill at ease. Our presence does not surprise them. They manifest no excitement, nor particular deference, but undress Sonia with their gaze. They seem to know all about Western women – except a few details. Our grandpa with the exposed dong extends a hand toward her, takes hold of the edge of her shirt at chest level and opens it delicately to look at her breasts. He confirms his discovery to his amused companions: she indeed wears a bra. Sonia is stupefied but easy; the atmosphere has quickly become more relaxed. Except that our old rascal hasn't finished his exploration. Without warning, he fondles her breast. My heart skips a beat. She taps on the hand of the lubricious grandpa like she would correct a scallywag. Laughter all around; mine is rather forced.

"Sonia, suppose we sat somewhere else?"

We get up quietly and go sit further down, still under the wattle roof but among the women. Who knows? Maybe I am going to be fondled as well! I watch our three old guys out of the corner of my eye. They are talking as if nothing had happened, with exception of one detail, under the loincloth, rigid as justice.

Suddenly, the female pack walks out of the enclosure screaming and disappears into the bush. They have seen a tormentor, but instead of fleeing him, they pursue him. We follow. Caught unprepared, the poor fellow searches for his whips, harassed by the women who hold him, grab him, push him around, trap him, ask for blows. He is not ready. The frustrated furies insult him, mock him and go back to their dance and their trance in the kraal; 1 to 0, home run, play beer. The scenario is repeated three times before they take a break and come sit in the shade. On three fires, heavy jars are heating. For several days, barley beer and grain has been put to ferment. From it comes a lumpy, mossy dough that gives off a strong alcoholic odor. Everyone is served some in calabashes. An old woman passes with little steps among the ranks to cut this mush with hot water. Guaranteed effective! Cheered up, the women leave like a single person in the kraal with the firm intention of picking a fight.

The tormentors have come. They belong to a particular age group, corresponding to precise practices and dress codes. Two black feathers attached and maintained on the temples by a headband give them an allure of Hermes. They are splendid and muscular, and hold in their right hand a bouquet of tapered branches, the object of every envy: the whips.

The delirium is at its paroxysm. The tormentors take off on a run toward the dry river bed, each with a group of girls on his heels. Suddenly, the fugitive stops, chooses a pursuer who stands in front of him, one arm raised, eyes glued to his while he polishes his whip, tests its flexibility, lifts it toward the sky, a moment suspended, before bringing it down on the flank and back of the volunteer in a crack with the power of gunfire. Under the shock, the skin breaks in a cloud of butter and vaporized flesh. Not the slightest sign of pain on the victim's face, who yields to the next one. I have lost Sonia in the battle. It's a ruckus! They all want to be first. A girl of nine takes a position before the tormentor who rejects her: "Go away, you are too young, you will try again next year..." A pregnant woman overtakes those awaiting their turn and asks for more. The river bed resounds with detonations in bursts, there is whipping everywhere, everywhere are dares, provocations, insults, the whips fly, the rods crack, the branches break on virgins' backs, the swamped tormentors beat a retreat.

Victorious, the lacerated women go back up to the kraal to sing of their victory. Blood streams on their sides, the swollen skin oozes, and the raw red of wounds on their golden leather cries like vermillion mouths. Not one shows the slightest sign of suffering or weakness. I find Sonia in the ascent, visibly shaken. She has trails of ochre on the face and one sleeve torn.

"Their thing, it tears! I got lashed once by accident. And there was a mad woman who leapt at me to strangle me..."

The scene is repeated all afternoon until the tormentors are worn out. They go to take refuge, lined up under the wattle roof, and the women drunk with glory, beer and blood come to provoke them, throwing themselves with feet together at their knees, pulling on their whip, to ask for more, before being taken away by the indignant old men. "In our time," they seem to be saying, "the tormentors were respected! Have they eaten of the rabid cow, or what?" The tormentors' peace is sacred. Each one plays his role to perfection.

The whole day is spent in these goings and comings, these races and cries, these discharges of whips and adrenaline, these spurts of sweat and blood until the men disappear into the bush. They go to find the *maz*, the boys being initiated this year, who have shaven themselves head to toe and coated themselves in oil blackened with wood charcoal. Forming a caste of the same age group, they are charged with the details of the bull leap, under the patronage of the elders. We find the ones and the others in a long discussion, under a tree. Everything is suddenly so calm! The flux and reflux of the crowd is over, as is the feminine hysteria, the blood has been spilt, honor is saved, make room for the ukuli.

Back in the kraal, we finally notice the famous Urgo, at the origin of this great quake. Stark naked, hair undone and tousled into an enormous tuft, he is seated on a goat skin, in the middle of the enclosure and surrounded with men already initiated. If he is naked, it's because he must be reborn. They press around him, standing, in several rows, to conceal a highly secret sexual initiation, doubled with fertility rites. Through the barrier of calves squeezed together, one can all the same glimpse an artificial phallus placed between the boy's legs, onto which an old man drops copper rings. There is jingling and laughter. How many rings are threaded on? No way to see, nor to know. Wealth and number of children are in the hands of destiny.

When the group disperses, the faces are satisfied. The entire assembly moves toward a large clearing in the middle of which the maz, all shiny and all black, have gathered in a great shivaree all of Urgo's father's livestock. Things are running, bellowing, mooing, in all directions, the women have taken up their trumpets again, the children join in the rally. The maz grab bulls by the mouth and the tail, then discuss, let this one go, catch another in dust ablaze from the setting sun. Finally, eight bulls are selected among the fattest and finest, placed in a row side by side and maintained in position by men placed in front of and behind them. All at once, with no forewarning, the young ukuli springs forward, leaps onto the first bull, over the others in an awkward aerial trajectory, arms above his head and his penis flapping, then disappears on the other side. Acclamations! If he falls, he will be pummeled by the women, the shame and laughing stock of the tribe. We hold our breath. He returns now, jumping on over the ruminants' backs. He makes three round trips unencumbered, he's an athlete! His spindly thighs propel him with no problem over the steaming spines, his footing is firm despite the moving fatty flesh, his hirsute head remains concentrated. The public shouts encouragements and yet we hear nothing more, all eyes riveted on Urgo who seems to hover in slow motion over the bulls; at the end of his flight he touches down, falling into his father's arms. He is a man.

At that precise moment, he is bound for eternity by a sort of soul transfer with the head bull, an enormous, white brahman with wide, rose horns and an outsize hump. Now, he has the right to marry and have children. The crowd, somewhat stunned, immediately disperses. It's over! The sun has just disappeared over the horizon.

This debauchery of energy, this waiting, these rivalries in pride and in suffering, these sacrifices, these long discussions, all this for a few suspenseful seconds....All this to celebrate the entrance of a young man into the world of adults and his spiritual alliance with a bull, token of fertility, wealth and the durability of his lineage. It is all muddled in our heads. We are exhausted. Rinsed. Initiated.

CHAPTER 19

Slippery Steps
of the Empire

ETHIOPIA

"We are really little monkeys!" Sonia declares. We scratch all over.

I burst out laughing. Fleas. We are being devoured. Sonia is covered. The right buttock swollen, beltline aflame, blisters on the ankles. For my part, my feet really stink! A good sign, that means I'm getting my nose back. Still pus in the lungs and both ears deaf. Generalized oto-rhino-laryngological infection, compounded by persistent bronchitis. Erythromycin being useless, I have gone to Augmentin. No good. I still expectorate. Ugh! Ten days this has been going on. Relay taken by my amoebic dysentery. No respite. This country is riddled with germs. And strong ones. We haven't been able to wash since Turmi, over a week ago. And our clothes haven't seen a wash since Koobi Fora, three weeks ago. We have never been so dirty. It's an emergency. My shorts and shirt are stiff like greasy cardboard. Sonia's skirt is a mop.

Since we entered Ethiopia, we have been sick. There are too many flies. Bevies, clouds. Why so many flies? Much livestock. But that doesn't explain everything. The absence of toilets is confirmed every day. This old Christian civilization did not invent them. No house is equipped with them. Not even a hole or a pit at the end of the garden. Nothing. So you have to adapt. Try to do that at night to preserve a hint of intimacy. But where? Anywhere, like everyone. In the alleyways, behind the houses, in the courtyard, in the neighbor's yard, in the field, anywhere. In fact, we soon discover that the bosks of eucalyptus on the confines of villages serve as comfort stations. Instead of the agreeable aromas of turpentine expected, there emanates from them the stale smell of a septic tank. Mined terrain. Always occupied, even convivial, so you put your modesty on hold and vent your colon elbow to elbow with a gawker who takes advantage of you to ask for some T.P. What would he have done without me? Mystery. I'll remember when I shake hands....And the bosk is surrounded: fifty brats and ten idle persons are waiting to trail along with us for kilometers. For Ethiopian roads abound in walkers. At any hour, by hundreds, of all ages. The Ethiopians walk, and they walk fast! Since Malawi, we have lost the habit of walking accompanied. Not that we dislike it, on the contrary, we are walking for that, but it is more tiring. Our Amharic[1] is very limited. In any case, the people here don't understand it well since they are Oromos; they speak Oromo as well as their vernaculars. We don't yet have the keys. To explaining. To understanding. Often enthusiastic and excited, people approach us with long tirades. We try to answer them with the phrases we have taken note of with Theodoros, at Omo Raté, beginning by the standard introductions:

"*Dehna nachu?*" (How are you?)

"*Dehna! Amésséguenallo!*" (Fine, thank you!)

"*Semeh man no?*" (What is your name?)

"*Iskandar na Sonia.*" (Alexandre and Sonia.)

"*Ke yet ager nachu?*" (What country are you from?)

"*Faransi.*" (From France.)

---

[1] Official language spoken in Ethiopia.

Beyond that, it doesn't work at all. Or rather it does, they burst out laughing, then ask the same questions indefatigably. That is why it quickly becomes tiring. We try to get by with admitting *"Algebanyem"* (I don't understand). But that doesn't disarm them, and, when a pest leaves us after asking for money, the probable reason for his intense interest, he is immediately replaced by others. This little game quickly becomes depressing. Sonia is worried.

"It's mad to be walking here without a guide!"

"Why? We've been walking for two years without a guide, we have always managed to get by. Even when we didn't yet speak the local languages. Even among the fiercest tribes. Don't worry, it will come…"

"Yes, but I have a feeling they have never seen Whites on foot and they don't give a tinker's damn about us. Instead of attracting their sympathy, it's as if it rather provokes their contempt."

"No, no, don't worry, it's just children having fun at our expense, that will go away."

We are at the divide that separates the peoples in southern Ethiopia, called "tribal," from the Oromos – Malé, Gofa, Woleyta – that have long since lost their tribal character on their conversion to the Orthodox faith. We thought that human relationships would deepen once we had left the tribal zones for the Ethiopian plateau and its ancient civilization, and looked forward to that. Unhappily, the opposite happens. In the tribes, we knew what to expect. The relationship was crude and lovely, strong and cheerful. Here, everything quickly becomes complicated and violent.

In the villages where we stop, nobody answers our greetings and smiles. Most of the inhabitants are people who came from elsewhere, sent to "colonize" these virgin territories on the steps of the Ethiopian Empire. These "civilized" populations group in tiny new villages that grow along the roads, which are the Ethiopian bridgeheads in the Far South, probably like, in the mid-nineteenth century, the American villages of the Middle West settled in Indian territory. In this context, the slightest pretext is good for getting even. Our arrival elicits mobs that often degenerate into shoving matches, exchanges of cries and blows. In the ruckus, we are constrained to resume walking in search of an isolated house where we ask if we can put our tent.

"*Maref ezzih yichalal? Dunkwan allen.*" (Could we remain here to rest up? We have a tent.)

"*Eichellem.*" (Impossible.)

We experience many refusals. It is absolutely their right. Still, it's the first time this has happened to us. Maybe asking for hospitality is just not done? And we are not sufficiently familiar with the codes, the customs. Perhaps they are in too precarious a situation to invite a stranger. Or are afraid of not being up to it. Or just don't want to....The person who accepts soon regrets because of the uncontrollable mob it provokes, which invariably obliges us to repair to the house.

That is what happens this evening, on the way out of Dimeka; the lady who receives us cannot manage to stop the flood of curious people piled up in her *toukoul*.[2] Her babies begin to cry. The people to laugh. The dogs to bark. We are confounded. Not knowing what to do. Cries. Shoving. So now she grabs a stick and the quarrel begins. A little guy finally works his way in and jabbers a few words of English: "I am teacher English, come see police station."

Things always end up like that. We put the tent in the police parking lot, between two cars, after they have tried to make us pay ten dollars for a room in a flop house in the area (instead of ten birr, or a little less than ten francs).[3] We've been there already! The nights of depressing insomnia in the fetid dampness of a filthy room, on shapeless straw mattresses crawling with vermin, endlessly awakened by groans of pleasure and cries of fury, laughter and alcoholic eructations, slamming of doors and radios spitting

---

[2] Generic term, in Ethiopia, for the round hut covered with thatch. The toukouls are usually larger, more solid and more comfortable than simple huts. The Ethiopians are past masters in the art of their construction.

[3] The birr is the Ethiopian monetary unit, equivalent at the time of our visit to 0.90 francs or about 0.14 euro.

out saturated sonar mush, dogfights and deathly screams. We clear out at dawn. For twelve days, since Theodoros, no one has invited us to his home. We have to get used to it. One day, at Kay Afer, we spot a Westerner in a greasy spoon. To our great wonderment, he is a Frenchman from Cherbourg. Alone. His name is Claude Leterrier. He is a young travel autodidact. Every year he spends two months in India, where he buys silk paintings, miniatures, made with squirrel hair around the themes of the *Thousand and One Nights* and the *Kama Sutra*, which he resells in French markets.

"You know how they go about obtaining that precious hair? They give aubergine to the squirrels and the hair falls out of its own accord! If you pull them, the quality is much poorer, and the detail of the painting also!"

He financed this trip by selling a field full of pumpkins for Halloween. He was even able to buy the delivery truck as a bonus. Claude enthralls us with all his stories but worries us about the next part of our itinerary.

"I've never seen a country like this! I have never seen children so poorly raised! I've been circulating for over a month and every-where it's the same 'you, you, you!' in waves, followed by 'birr-birr-birr!' It becomes unbearable!"

"I know! What we answer is: *'Iellem, iellem, iellem!'* (I have noth-ing, nothing, nothing.) And that makes them laugh. You can't get upset about it, it's a bad habit they'll get over."

"Let's hope! Besides, it's not particularly that which saddens me, it's above all that I cannot manage to create any bonds, to go to people's houses, to create some intimacy. It's the first time that has happened to me. I succeed the whole planet over, but not here. You'd think that doesn't interest them...that they only want one thing: that you should spend. Except that there is nothing to spend on here! No hotels, no infrastructure....In fact, I don't understand at all how things work here, and I am a bit distraught."

Whew! We are not alone. We were beginning to think it was our fault. He doesn't know any more where to go, he just returned from Jinka very disappointed. It is a "tribal city" like Turmi, and its market attracts Mursis, Surmas, Benas, Karos: other tribes of the great Ethiopian South: "The tour operators disembark and grease palms. All relationships are perverted. Everything is bought. Everything is for sale. The White man becomes a commodity, the photo an exchange currency, our presence a problem of rivalries and conflict between tribes. The fiercest and most expensive are the Surma plateau women: they drive off rivals with a stick for ten dollars a picture. I was disgusted. I only stayed one morning. I didn't take a single picture. How do you manage to keep going?"

"It's not easy....But I see time is passing, and we have to get going! Would you like to walk with us a day or two? We'll support each other!"

The three of us leave the village to the north, harassed by children; Claude continues his remarks: "You see, when I go to India, I see children as poor but who don't beg so shamelessly. And when there are mobs, it's just to ogle, it never degenerates. It would never occur to them to offend us. And despite their poverty, you can always share a *dalbat*[4] with them, or stories, jokes, fraternity, you know! Here, I always have the disagreeable impression that they are mocking me..."

"In fact, I think we are among the first independent tourists they have seen, the first 'backpackers,' and they don't understand what we are doing here, wanting to live like they do, eat like them, be here among them."

"And I have the impression that they don't like it. With respect to food, how are you doing with *enjera*?"

"We like it a lot, only it doesn't like us so much..."

Enjera is the country's second religion: a crepe of *tef*, a microscopic cereal the flour of which is mixed with water and left to ferment for a few days. This yields a big, spongy, acidic cake eighty centimeters across served on a large platter, that is used as a base

---

[4] A dish of rice and lentils.

for various concoctions. In the countryside, the choice is limited to *berbera*, a puree of peppers and onion, or *chourro*, a puree of split peas and chick peas. It is a convivial dish, eaten in common most of the time, which each materfamilias prepares in the morning for the entire day. For now, we have seen some only in the greasy spoons, and have not been able to attend its preparation in a family setting. Even if it is very quickly downed, enjera is very social. If someone passes by a friend having a lunch of enjera, he will immediately hear it proposed: "*Enebla!*" (Come join me!)

That happens with us too, rather frequently. We often decline thanking them warmly, but sometimes accept, when we perceive that the invitation is not merely a formality, and is triggered by honest curiosity. *Enjera* is eaten with the right hand, triturating the dough with a little push of the thumb between the fingers, and taken with the tongue from the hand held to the mouth like a shovel. It is polite to chew with your mouth wide open to show your contentment but above all not to belch. Every time the chewing slows, the eater is sanctioned by an iterative and benevolent: "*Bela! Bela!*" (Eat, eat.) Despite that, the conversation remains limited, the language barrier prevailing over the fleeting community of a meal. But we leave with our hearts warmed.

In Claude's company, we rise above the Rift. The devastating heat of the Omo valley is over. Around a little pass, the view over the escarpment is vertiginous. The clouds project immense shadows on it that bring the landscape agreeably alive. The space is vast. We who have been walking on the Rift floor level and far from relief since the Mau escarpment rediscover the third dimension and cool air. We pass a huge herd of cows and steers climbing back up the slope. Claude exclaims: "I wonder what they do with their livestock! In a month, I have seen millions of these bloody cows, and not the least little bit of steak!"

"Arghh! Don't talk to me about it, it goes back to Nairobi! And it's been more than a thousand kilometers we have been walking among breeders and shepherds! Meat is for the rich, in the cities."

Evening comes upon us out in the wild. At Kay Afer, a greasy spoon keeper indicated the hand pump at Mukacha, near which live a family of Benas, another local tribe. We have no difficulty finding the pump: cohorts of girls bent over large round jars converge on it or are returning from it even more bent over. We ask them: *"Oita yet no?"* (Where is Oita?)

Lucky for us, he is as well known as the white wolf. A young boy leads us off-trail to a fine rounded hut of woven bulrushes. The man comes out as we approach, smiling and natural. We do not understand each other, but he has figured out everything. Three tired strangers in front of him who don't know where to go at nightfall. The equation is simple: either "Go away!" or "Welcome!" His first smile was already a welcoming message. His wife soon comes out, a woman of exceptional beauty, holding a nursling in her arms. Like a Hamer woman, Noho is dressed in skins, coifed with braids buttered with ochre and wearing numerous metal bracelets and necklaces. Oita is dressed like all the peasants in poor countries, in colorless old clothes. The only tribal part he has preserved is a few necklaces. For an unknown reason, he has no more livestock; under government pressure, he converted to agriculture, like many tribal shepherds. Theodoros had explained to us that Ethiopia has too many cows. Therefore shepherds receive aid for their settling. We pitch the tent near the hut. With night falls humid cold. For the first time since Tanzania, we put up the fly. We go in for refuge near the fire, in the hut. Noho is boiling water for the *chorro*, that rather bland decoction of coffee bark, while Oita roasts some ears of corn and puts some sweet potatoes in the ashes. Sitting cross-legged, Claude is in seventh heaven.

"For a month I've been dreaming of this moment! And with you, it happens so naturally…"

"Don't believe it! We have been living in this manner for about two years, but in Ethiopia this is the first time. I hope it's going to last. In fact, I doubt it. For the moment we only have been able to get close to the traditional populations. With the 'civilized' ones, it's a fiasco!"

Oita hands me a gourd.

"*Parsi?*"

I smell it. It is barley beer, the local *pombé*. Unfortunately, there is just a little left. We send the kid to get another one with two birrs. Oita is delighted. Claude pulls a harmonica from his pocket and begins some little Breton refrains that lend themselves very well to clapping. In the gentle heat lavished by the fire, we spend the evening singing, playing the recorder, munching corn, sharing our noodle soup dressed up with tomatoes bought in Kay Afer, while Noho goes about her chores; she rekindles the fire, extends the beer with a little water, nurses her baby and sings him a lullaby. Happiness, in short!

Gudwa Ashekar, Wednesday 4 December 2002, day 706, 27 km, 8543rd km

We left Claude this morning at dawn, after a fine day hiking together on a byway, in a rich tropical countryside alongside the imposing Jinka massif which, on his advice, we were careful to avoid. We want to rejoin a road, on the other side of this mountain, which we will try to unroll like a spool of kilometers all the way to Addis Ababa. There are only two footpaths that cross this natural obstacle. One by way of Jinka, the other by Koibé, which we intend to reach for lunch. To get to the capital, cars from the Ethiopian South are obliged to make a detour of more than six hundred kilometers through Arba Minch and Awasa, a long way to the east. For us, the shortcut is the obvious choice: twenty kilometers off-trail in the mountains and Addis at six hundred kilometers instead of twelve hundred, twice as much! We don't hesitate for a second. The Canadian map we have been using since we entered Ethiopia, the only one readily available on the market in 2002, is totally fanciful: more of the names are wrong, all the indications of trails are false, and the placement of the little villages systematically off. As the scale is 1 centimeter for 25 kilometers, our margin of error is huge. We are hiking in artistic vagueness. Only the relief makes it possible for us to locate our position, to recognize such and such a mountain. We therefore draw our itinerary one day at a time.

Claude has left, devoured by fleas. Last night, we ended up with him at the police station in Benata. The day had gone by fine. Not a single child had bothered us. A miracle! Maybe only the places where there are cars of tourists going by are affected by inhospitality? Well, in the mountains, nobody ever passes – cars cannot cross them. So it's going to be marvelous!

We are in a valley inhabited by Malés, extremely nice and affable. We have seen our first Orthodox churches. They are minimal and recent, octagonal, in adobe; the slightly inclined roof is in corrugated iron, surmounted by a strange solar cross and a metal parasol ringed with little mobile disks. Tribal customs are gone. Here, over their light-colored cotton dresses, the women wear large, white togas trimmed with colored braids called *chama*. The men are in short pants and open shirt; their toga, often dirty, is called a *gabi*. They are as black-skinned as the people in tribes, but their features are much finer. This mountain is truly a divide between two worlds.

At Koibé, on the valley floor, before climbing to the pass, an immense governmental dispensary, brand new, has just been opened – a proof that the state is investing in these remote regions. Already the activity of Theodoros, in Omo Raté, had impressed us: he distributed seed grain for free and gave classes in agriculture to the Dassanech to encourage them to plant their own sorghum – or millet – in the Omo delta so they would no longer depend on aid for food. Clever. Simple. Inexpensive. The idea is to allow pastoral tribes vulnerable to bovine epidemics or drought to make the transition to self-produced stocks of cereals. So far he has persuaded eighty-four villages and has, all by himself, launched genuine regional production. It was moreover the mud of "his" fields that we were treading with our Dassanech chief.

We have already seen several of these dispensaries under

construction. For a hiker, these are signs that do not deceive. The numerous new schools, about to open, as well. This is the first time we have seen this in Africa. The first time the work is not done by international NGOs but by the government – according to the same architectural plan, the same method and the same suppliers. Could there be less corruption in Ethiopia than elsewhere? There is no doubt that these investments are financed by the World Bank, Europe or the United States, but to see this money transformed into schools and dispensaries is a proof of good management. Specialists will perhaps be horrified by these empirical evaluations, but we are hiking along African trails, not in the corridors of ministries or back rooms – and what could be more encouraging, in the remote regions, than the sight of a fine dispensary and a fine school that are brand new!

The doctor on duty, who speaks a little English, insists that I stop ingurgitating antibiotics. "You are killing yourself!" he scolds. "What you have is a virus, not bacteria, the antibiotics are just weakening you."

We hit the road again for three hours of climbing on an acrobatic trail that takes us straight to the crest. During the climb I almost pass out. It's true, I am weak. Our first Ethiopian pass. We cross many little mothers in black who bend double at our passage, hand on heart, softly repeating delightfully: "*Acha-acha*"; we do likewise. What a mosaic of peoples! Every day there are new people, new customs and costumes. The habitat is beautiful, the *toukouls* well maintained, with tidy little gardens on the hillside planted in fruit trees. At the pass, the view is breathtaking over the beginning of an immense valley of a Himalayan sort. The steep mountainsides, on the other slope, rise for as far as we can see in a checkerboard of villages nested in hollows or perched on plateaus. The human presence is not of recent date, space is cut up in sections, modeled. This pass where cars cannot go confirms that we are at the dividing line between two worlds, the old and the new, the tribal pastoral and the sedentary agicultural, the millenary animist and the civilizational Christian.

We are swallowed by the descent. On this side, they are still Malés. We pass through charming villages without stopping – we have not done enough walking today; men seated watching the countryside invite us to come rest, a lady offers us some water; we are forced to keep going, the tyranny of Africa Trek! But we are relieved: it augurs well for the valley. Far from the touristic circuits, relations with people are going to be more healthy, more natural.

On the valley floor there is no one. We cross large forests to rejoin the foot of the next slope, where the trail we plan to follow northward is supposed to be. We arrive in Gudwa Ashekar a little before dark. And there everything turns sour. Advance signs had given us to expect the worst. Children had taken off shouting in front of us. Then others, and still others. When we reach the village, there is an ambushing riot that awaits us. After a second of panic, we are absorbed and pushed around by this noisy crowd, which redoubles its *"You, you, you!"* and *"Faranj, faranj, faranj!"* and *"Birr, birr, birr!"*

"Astamari yet no?" (Where is the school teacher?)

In these cases, to cut all excitement short, we ask where the village teacher is. He incarnates authority, since every day he has the children under his cane, and is the most likely to speak English or understand our tourist Amharic. Happily, the school is not far away, and we are taken from the crowd by Stephanos Astakté, a tall teacher with natural authority who has soon dispelled all these little people. He welcomes us in his home, a small lodging with a mud floor that goes with his job, and introduces his wife Andenet.

"I've been here for eight years and you are the first Westerners I have seen venture into this dead-end; that's why everyone is so excited."

"What does *'Faranj, faranj, faranj'* mean?

"Did they say that? Along with 'you, you'? I told them not to say that! They go begging in Jinka, on the other side of the mountain. *'Faranj!'* is a not very nice and derogatory way to address white-skinned strangers. It's as if you called out to me saying: 'Hey you, the Black one!' You know where that word comes from? From the French in Djibouti! The first White strangers who came in large number to the region....They were called *frengi*. I know it's obnoxious, but please don't take offense, they are only children..."

Andenet is gorgeous. A fashion engraving. Moreover, this seems to be a constant: Ethiopian women are stunningly beautiful. She is very attentive to Sonia and me, I can't help staring at her covertly. After a dinner of *enjera*, and while she artistically prepares a traditional coffee, the famous *bunna*, we remake the world with Stephanos. He is from the north. From Tigray. Very far from here. He enlightens us on the country's political situation. The new government in power since 1994 is a coalition of resistance Oromo and Tigray parties united against Mengistu, the "red negus," the despot who terrorized the country for seventeen years. He fled to Zimbabwe in 1992 after a bloody civil war.[5] Stephanos is fascinated that we should have passed right by the tyrant's house,[6] and come all the way here on foot. Regrets that the most recent attempt to assassinate him at his tennis club failed. Concludes: "That man is protected by the devil!" He confirms to us the significant investments in these remote regions, previously neglected by the central government which was traditionally in the hands of Abyssinians of Amhara origin, is very pleased by the national reconciliation, but sees dangers afoot of excessive regionalism, especially in the teaching of languages.

"That's why the children speak the national language so badly around here," he affirms.

Rain is starting to fall. The sound on the corrugated iron interrupts our conversation and casts us into the arms of Morpheus,

---

[5] Mengistu Haile Mariam, instigator of the "Red Terror," to be found guilty *in absentia* of genocide by an Ethiopian court in 2006.

[6] See vol. I, p. 246.

right on the ground. Before he leaves us, Stephanos comes to apologize: "Forgive us for receiving you so modestly…"

"Stephanos, this is paradise to us! Thanks to you, we can finally talk, understand, learn…"

CHAPTER 20

Sodo Maso

ETHIOPIA

At dawn, Andenet is already at work, outdoors but under a metal sheet canopy, between two small fires, since it is still sprinkling. Her gestures are sure and precise. Bent over, she pirouettes from one hearth to the other. On the left, scrambled eggs, on the right an enjera. Between the two, she forages for wood, turns the cake over, stirs here, cleans there, washing her hands in the process; a salivating morning choreography. With her lovely face she laughs at our wonderment before the spectacle of her domestic virtuosity; collects the eggshells, pivots again, returns to her fires, washes, rinses, scratches, while big clumsy youths draped in their *chama*, hands in their pockets, with a black gaze, skulk around her like vultures, idle and stooped; so goes the world...

This morning, the crowd is reconstituted. The night has not calmed them:

"*Youyouyouyou! Faranj, faranj, faranj! Birr, Birr, Birr!*"

Before being totally absorbed, we cast a last wave at Stephanos, who watches us go, his arms raised in a gesture of helplessness, his head inclined and a smile on his lips. On leaving Gudwa Ashekar, the uncoercible mob locks step with us, at first curious – we remain stoic – then noisy, then hysteric. Sonia, who holds up under the shock, exclaims: "It's the Forrest Gump syndrome!"

I burst out laughing. Woe to me for having done so! Little parrots seize the opportunity to mock loudly. Well, that's war. That will teach me. After a few minutes, all we can tell them in Amharic is exhausted. We walk. They want to understand why. Then they follow us. Want to stop us. Get us to climb into trucks. Insist. Hang onto our backpacks. Have fun. Keep busy. We have them in tow for five kilometers. An hour. Then they weary of it, the group thins out, disperses, whew! Finally we are going to be able to contemplate the greenery of this valley, barely believable after the aridity of the last few months. Pick our nose without triggering offensive laughter. The respite is short-lived; another group forms as if by disenchantment. The same aborted questions to make fun of the replies, pretexts for great fun at our expense. Not a second to look at the landscape, not a minute to talk to each other. So we put into practice the little polite sentences that Stephanos has taught us to make them understand that the comedy has lasted long enough: *"Atikata loun ibaki!"* (Please stop following us!)

It's like pissing in the wind.

"Zorbelou ibaki!" (Leave us alone, please!)

Or throwing oil on the fire.

"Hiddu wodébétachu!" (Go home!)

Worse and worse. That cuts them loose!

Bad idea, Stephanos! You can talk? Very nice: now, dance! No way to catch the leaders to try to reason with them. They slip between our fingers like trouts. All resistance turns against us, it becomes a game for them. We are beside ourselves. What to do? Lower our heads, grit our teeth and step up the pace. No other solution. After all, they're just children....Breathless, Sonia exclaims: *"Exit* Forrest Gump. Here is the Britney Spears syndrome. Advance pursued by yelping packs, with the flies to boot....It must really be hell to be a star!"

What resources she has! She remains calm and concentrated. Vents her stress with a wisecrack....How many would already have had a nervous breakdown with these little brats? That's all they want. We are moving right along. Trying to shake them. In vain. That is to forget that we are dealing with Ethiopians, famous marathoners. Nothing undeserved about that reputation, in the countryside as in the stadiums. We are wearing out. Sonia finally gets aggravated: "I'm not all the same going to get tendinitis because of these gluepots."...So we try the slow version, nonchalant, with a lame step, dragging our feet. No problem, they know how to do that too. When we stop, they stop, when I turn around, they pretend to flee, then come back to the charge. We resign ourselves. Have to live with it, have to walk with it. After all, we are in their land. We are less convinced when the *"Faranj, faranj! I kill you!"* resounds. Charming little urchins.

"Faranju belachou attitrou ibaki! Tekekel iedellem!" (Please stop calling us *faranj*! It's not nice!)

Then we just put up with it. We receive the insults, the parrots, the *"faranj,"* without reacting. If we are passive they turn it up a notch. When the beast is dead, you plant a stick where it hurts the most to see if it still moves...

And thus we receive our first stones. Oh, not paving stones, not even small rocks, more like gravel, but on the head, on the elbow or in the hollow of the knee, it doesn't leave you indifferent. It's particularly inside that it hurts. We are powerless. In a band of kids from eight to twelve, there are always older ones who play tough, shout louder, threaten us more theatrically. They take bigger and bigger pebbles that they amuse themselves throwing over our heads, like apprentice William Tells. We are off to a bad start. The people are nuts in this valley....It lasts all morning.

We arrive at Zaba done in. The same riot as this morning takes shape. I am beginning to be afraid for Sonia. A respectable man seems to be angry: we head straight for him, I ask him for help, he takes us by the hand and guides us to his house. He is the village nurse and his name is Serget. Woe to him for rescuing us, his house is surrounded on every side, he is forced to barricade us inside. The kids seem to be crying: "Don't think we're going to let the faranj get away like that! They are ours!" Here, they try to kick in the door, there a window is shattered by a stone. Sonia, terrorized, melts in tears. Outside, the children shout themselves hoarse: "*Faranj! faranj! faranj!*" Some adults come to help drive them away by swinging laths at them, but they return intermittently to watch us through the interstices of the disjointed planks. We are trapped like rats. Serget's wife, Emayou, is confounded; she whistles between her teeth, shaking her head. She can't believe her eyes. We are terribly sorry for this intrusion and for his broken window pane:

"*Yikerta enat! Yikerta cheggir! Yikerta messkot mesher!*" (We are terribly sorry, ma'am! Forgive us for the trouble, for the broken window pane...)

She comes over and takes Sonia's hands. "*Betam aznallo! Lidjotch akeberot yellem!*" (I am really confounded, the children have no respect!)

We have nothing to reproach ourselves for. I mention to Sonia, to console her, a book I had studied at Sciences-Po,[1] Gustave Lebon's *The Psychology of Crowds*, which explains the phenomena of allurement that make of a crowd much more than the sum of the individuals that compose it.

"They aren't responsible. These same children taken separately are all adorable little cherubs..."

"Yes, but when we leave, they won't be there separately, your cherubs..."

We put that off for later. To console us, Emayou brings us some melon and lemon: a little coolness in this world of brutes....Serget

---

[1] Nickname for the Institut d'Études Politiques in Paris.

tells us about his infirmary, shows us his walls covered with dia-grams and statistics: 47% of his diagnoses relate to malaria, which means 8200 persons affected per year in his communal zone, and close to 1000 deaths. But the figure is stationary despite the increase in the population, thanks to the distribution of mosquito netting. On the other hand, the number of victims of snakebite is rising, it has gone from 92 to 114....When I ask him where the head is, he answers: "Sorry, the hole has been full for two years, I haven't dug another, so we have no more toilets..."

What to do? The house is surrounded. On Serget's advice, I escape through a hidden door and reach a little wood of eucalyp-tus. I am quickly spotted. The kids come for a front-row seat: oh, yes! The faranj squat like anyone else....They stay there, watch-ing with laughter my uncomfortable gesticulations to try to make them leave. A GMS: a Great Moment of Solitude. When I leave, they rush in to observe my production...

When we awaken from our nap, our laundry is clean and dry. Sonia is amazed; she is ecstatic: "But why?"

The little lady replies: "Serget told me that you are going to Jerusalem, you must take my prayers there and my excuses for what you have been put through."

Sonia throws herself into her arms.

Serget has asked some companions to escort us out of the vil-lage. Everything goes all right. They have big sticks and seem to know how to wield them. We finally breathe in deeply the pure air. But the reprieve, once more, is short. Children appear from all over, and minute by minute the psychological trap is reconstituted, this morning's chain of causalities, that little by little, step by step, kilometer after kilometer, transforms a cute encounter with nice, turbulent children into a riot, with insults and throwing stones. No way to defuse the bomb, to interrupt the mounting violence.... We have tried everything, tears, pity, honor, silence, nothing has any effect.

"Ibaki! Betam dekemagny!" (Please, pity, we are very tired!)

"*Akeberot allé?*" (Don't you have a little respect?)

A salvo of gravel replies to our despair. Each time, Sonia warns me: "I've got a bad feeling. Pull your head in. It will be any time now!"

It never fails, unbelievable! Her outer ears are antennas. The woman has eyes in the back of her head! We pass through the village of Kencho on the run, not even stopping, walk late into the black of night to make up for lost time and reach Beto. We brush silently by people without seeing them, children by the dozens, but they don't see us either; never saw such a thick darkness; it's the phantasm of the invisible man finally realized, we just barely avoid collision with people coming in the other direction. Will we have to walk at night all the way to Addis?

In Beto, by miracle we find an English teacher who tells us about the last passage of Westerners, three years ago: rear-view mirrors torn off, windows blown out; they owed their salvation only to their flight. Welcome to Beto! Terrorized by the thought of a new incident, our gentle teacher takes us directly to...the police! We question him: "Why such behavior? Is there a particular poverty in the valley, a bad memory of Westerners?"

"Not at all! As you can see, the valley is rich, there are thousands of cows, abundant water and no misery – some poor, of course, but less than elsewhere. As for Westerners, we never see any; we have no historical sites, no picturesque tribes, therefore no tourists; during the war, the Italians never came this far. There is no reason for these outbursts, just excitement....They're just children."

We've had about enough of this argument. And not just Sonia. Especially since these "children" are looking more and more like adolescents. For two years we have lived all day with young Africans and we have never seen this. Mozambique and Malawi too were very poor. Even poorer in many ways. So poverty is not an argument. And besides, under the stones, no argument stands up. The days follow each other, as do the remote towns all the names of which remind us of problems, stress, tensions: Chala, Gofa, Genda, for it's always the same scenario. Have the fathers no authority over their children? Boys are kings as everywhere else but here they take advantage of it to play tyrants. And there is nowhere we can ask for help. Nowhere to take refuge. Nowhere you can drop your shorts in peace.

Here are some girls carrying sugar cane: no school for them, evidently. They are much nicer...and laden....We try to sympathize, but our heart isn't in it, we quickly find our old demons, we are hurt. Our trek grinds to a halt. What to do? Give up? Go to Addis for rest, then return? No. It's going to get better....It can only get better.

Ethiopia is not yet ready to welcome foreign hikers outside the circuits of organized treks with guides and porters, planned pauses and villages remunerated. From now on we know that this will remain the harshest memory of our trek. The exception that confirms the rule of the natural goodwill of which we have been the recipients for two years. Did there have to be an exception? Who could believe that we had walked the length of the African continent on a path strewn with roses? Here we step on their thorns.

Harsh from every point of view. No spontaneous hospitality. We are always invited in "by force" – for our safety – by representatives near or far from authority. Little aid. Much mockery. Distance. That we can't manage to close. Never felt that on earth! Even the indifference I experienced in China in the '90s is less hurtful. And China is opening herself to the world at grand speed, mutating everyday for the better. Here we are the permanent laughingstock. We are suffering. Thirty hostile persons on our heels is like ten kilos more in the backpack. Exhausting. The worst part is that because of it our trek is becoming absurd. Such behavior empties our trials of all their meaning. Africa Trek is turning against us. And yet, in this depression, exceptional, compassionate individuals, pearls, rare, as everywhere: to maintain hope.

One day, at noon, we take refuge under the road, in a concrete drainage pipe. Eager to escape people's gaze, we do not notice mud dauber wasps' nests on the ceiling; we are attacked right away on the head; they don't let us go until they have injected us with their avenging venom. Sonia curls up in a corner, whimpering, while I thrash about like the lion of the fable. Nervous crisis. I have five stings on the temples, she has two near the eyes and three on the right hand. Five all. A tie! God it's hard. Not to mention the heat. Coming back down to a thousand meters elevation, we are back in dry bush. It's even that which saves us provisionally. There are fewer people, fewer villages, the road is wider, straighter, we are moving right along.

This evening, we put our tent in a landscape of hills and valleys, uninhabited, finally alone under the stars. But without water. Trucks pass on the road. I go to meet them with our jerrycans. A trucker stops, fascinated at seeing a stranger come out of the night like this. He is from Addis. I tell him about our misadventures while he is filling my water bottle.

"You know," he replies, "they throw stones at us too, it's the national sport. Just because we come from somewhere else, because we are from Addis. We are Amharas in Oromo country! You mustn't take it ill…"

"Okay! But all the same, stones, insults.…It's not pleasant!"

"Stones aren't the only things we throw in this country…"

From his window he drops me some small loaves of bread and some oranges. As he leaves he promises to come back by tomorrow.

Sunday 8 December 2002, in the bush after Salamber Kucha, day 710, 36 km, 8682nd km

This morning, we are superpositive. What last night's trucker told us lifted a ton of guilt that was weighing on our shoulders: it's not our fault, it has nothing to do with us, they do that to everybody. Since yesterday morning, we have seen no one, not this morning either, this arid zone seems abandoned by men. Forty kilometers of respite. The road leads directly up a new massif. Other Ethiopians, we say to ourselves. It's finally going to change. And it changes. Except for the ever more numerous flies, we pass through villages without raising either riots or cries. Relief. The climb is pretty, the habitat is no longer the same at all: very high, wide huts with ribbed vaults and very fine thatch, with at their base, like a nose in the middle of a face: the entrance parapet. A young man invites us to accept a glass of milk. Sonia is beside herself with joy. These people are not Dorzés, even if they copy their famous huts, but Aris. The inner framework structure, black with soot, rises over ten meters high. The circular space is divided into two parts: the right, divided into cubicles for the livestock; the left, arranged around a small clay hearth, for men. After that glass of milk that gives the lie to our hasty conclusions, we resume our climb with a light foot. Tyranny of the circumstances, we tell ourselves, our experience is too subjective and too limited. We had bad luck, that's all. On our right, to the east, very far away in the clouds, rises Mount Gughé, the highest summit in the region. On the other side, on the Rift floor, we know the fabulous Lakes Chamo and Abaya extend, riddled with crocodiles, which we won't see because of our shortcut. In the terraced fields, around the houses, we see our first giant Abyssinian hornbills. I am ecstatic: "Wow! Look how huge they are! The color of their face is blue like that of the Somalian ostriches. What a strange mutation! You remember the hornbills we saw in the Serengeti had it red. Did you see that beak, that amazing protuberance on top?"

They waddle awkwardly in the thatch, but at my approach, they unfold broad, black wings and let themselves glide effortlessly into the slope. Superb. At the pass, the view takes our breath away, we have not yet had the leisure to express how magnificent the country is. The landscape and the foothills of Gughé are sculpted with terraces as far as you can see; around the houses, banana trees are growing in green tufts; the wild expanses are behind us. Here man has been master and possessor of nature for many centuries. From a house perched on the edge of the abyss, we are hailed: "*Faranju metachu!*" (Hey, you Whites! Come here!)

It is proposed so nicely that we do not hesitate. A family welcomes us into the shade of an immense toukoul. The rest is going to be ideal. In one corner, we hear a groan. A young boy gets up, grimacing, covered with flies and dirty bandages.

"*Lidjotch cheggir allé?*" (Does the child have a problem?)

His mother whistles between her teeth, dismayed....."*Deddeb Lidjotch! Dengaï méwerwer!*" (The children are crazy! They throw stones...)

"*Dengaï méwerwer*": we have already learned what that meant.... The kid was a victim of a vengeance. The flies make his life a hell; he no longer even has the strength to wave them away from his mouth and eyes. They pump away his humidity at its source. As if they had already sensed his death. For him we feel a surge of compassion. We have to help him. Before anything else, I slowly unroll the bandage on his tibia. The odor is pestilential, the linen foul. The flies go crazy. I discover the unthinkable: the flesh is exposed, the wound bulging, tumefied like a sausage slice. The wound is old but cannot manage to heal in such filth. I ask for hot water, soap and linen to clean with. A small crowd has assembled. Silent. But the flies have flocked in by the thousands. I ask for a little air. Sonia brings me the Betadine, I soak a sterile compress in it and apply it directly to the spot. The kid grits his teeth. His suffering is unspeakable. He scarcely flinches. We repeat the operation on the elbow and the knee. With clean linen, we remake his bandages. His face is badly scraped but less infected. I film the scene to preserve a testimony, since we will be suspected of exaggeration. You see there what we perhaps escaped....The mother doesn't know how to express her gratitude. We just ask to use her fire to prepare our noodle soup and a little quiet corner to rest two hours before leaving.

At the base of the slope is Salamber Kucha, a large village.

"We're going to try to find someplace decent or something where we can wash and rest..." I say to Sonia, at the risk of bending our rule of not going to a hotel. I think it is important to make a break.

We follow the road again on the way down, fantasizing on the prospect of a good bath. The minute we enter into the city, we run into a crowd of children getting out of school: the wrong time! On the pediment, a big red star above the three portraits of Marx, Engels and Lenin, souvenir of the still-recent influence of the Soviets around here. Our surprise and our smiles did not make the children smile. They place themselves across the road as if to bar our passage. We continue forward, paying them no notice. As we approach, they raise sticks, pick up pebbles, take karate postures, while laughing and singing the little air of the *"faranj."* I try to relax Sonia between my teeth: "No, children! Despite my ponytail, I am not Steven Seagal!"[2]

We try not to be disconcerted and keep going steadily and smilingly. The barrier opens, lets us pass and gaily follows close on our heels. The annoying part is that our Amharic has considerably improved recently and we understand better and better the insults that rain down during this apparent jubilation.

"Faranj! Faranj! Enat Lebda!" (son of a bitch!)

"Wusha faranj!" (white dog!)

We try to leverage older adolescents; they end their ping-pong game and join with the mocking swarm. I try to reason with the crowd: *"Zimebel ibaki!"* (Silence, please!)

I don't have time to finish my sentence before gravel flies at our backs...

"Hidt white face!" (Get out!)

Desperate, I look for adults, no one moves. The older ones?

---

[2] American actor, hero of karate films.

A helpless smile. And no uniform on the horizon. No nurse this time, no English teacher, no one who might incarnate an ounce of authority....We run to escape these maniacs. From the swarm rises a new cry: "Give me your money!"

Well! All the same, all the English lessons are not for nought.... This time, strangely enough, they don't follow us. They have won, they have driven us from Salamber Kucha. We see them from afar dancing and singing their victory, across the road. I am frightened; Sonia has shown remarkable self-control. But she is white as a sheet, her jaw clenched and lips blue.

"Sorry, my dear! It's not tonight that you will get your hot bath..."

"You know what, Alex? What we have just been through reminds me of the stupid game you played with your cousin on his Playstation, Tomb Raider or Resident Evil, something like that: you go from one board to another, you rack up points and clear obstacles, you get more and more numerous assailants out of your way, you avoid traps, you survive, you win lives, bonuses, you start over again, you think you're going to make it, but whatever you do, you always run into a bone and get busted. Game over. I have only one goal! To last as long as possible. We'll walk at night, I don't know what we'll do, but we will get to Addis on foot. Nothing will make us cheat."

It's true that every day trucks propose to take us to the capital, which is still over four hundred kilometers away. Again this morning our truckers of last night came by with some bread. They were very worried for us. They were right. What a crazy country where the worst is side-by-side with the best!

Once more, we bless a night alone. What a luxury! I have scruples about imposing this obstacle course on my love. Her right eye is a little black and her left hand is so swollen from the wasp stings that she has difficulty closing it on her walking stick. She ought to be on Christmas vacation, like everyone, in front of a nice fire, with a women's magazine in her hands, feet in cozy slippers. While I write in my notebook, lying on one elbow, I look at her lying all curled up and observe a long trail of tears dripping onto her camp mattress. Keep going. Get away from what is for us becoming a hell. This negation of Africa Trek. In two days Sodo, the regional capital of Woleyta! Sodo! Sodo! Long live Sodo!

At Gassouba, the next day, the inevitable swarm again gathers behind us. We pass through the village without a word, without answering the insults heard a hundred times. Nothing. Not a glance, not a word. In fact, we get used to anything. The stones begin to fly in all directions, which we cannot see coming, most of them in the legs; to that too we have become accustomed, we continue forward oblivious to all, but the mess kit that Sonia is carrying on her backpack explodes under a larger stone. She turns and stoops to pick it up stoically, but in so doing exposes herself to the stones....I hurry over to protect her when I see in the sky a half brick describing in slow motion a parabola toward her lowered neck....Horrific vision....I dive and intercept it with my right hand. Black curtain. A sharp pain makes me see stars; in my flight, I sprawl out completely and wake up in a nightmare. Never see people laugh so hard. Diabolical rictus. They are hilarious. Flee! We must flee! We run as fast as we can. They have won. They have driven us from their village. Again, that is what they wanted. A pastime like any other. My whole left side is bleeding, scraped by the fall. The knee, the thigh and the forearm. The flies are already at the feast. My right little finger is all blue and swollen. Broken. I am limping. Enraged. Humiliated. Wounded. Sonia is all right. God be praised!

After overcoming rhinoceros charges, elephants, lions, the killers of Alexandra township, the barbarity of the Zimbabwe war vets, cholera in Mozambique, famine in Malawi, the man-eating lions of Rungwa, the fevers of malaria, the vertigos of Kili, the heat of Natron, the tribal wars between Pokots and Turkanas, Dassanech and Hamers, thirst in the deserts of the Jade Sea, we succumb, powerless, to stones thrown by brats of nine acting under the vaguely collusive eyes of their parents...

What ought one to have done? Fire into the pile with my distress flares, use my tear gas? Surely not. We would instantly have been lynched. Our toys are just possibly operational against thieves and wild animals. Not against wild children. The only thing we ought to have done was not to go through Gassouba on foot. But we have no choice. Such is our fate. We had to go through Gassouba...

In the evening, in a hovel, with a consternated old woman, in tears of shame, I get some water to bind my wounds. I am out of order. This business does not trigger jaundice in me but a raging fever, with 42° C and chattering teeth. The grand slam! Sonia is shaken with tremors of terror. Still twenty-two kilometers to Sodo. I hallucinate.

"Sodo! Damned carrot after which we have been running since we entered Ethiopia! Hellish Sodo! Only twenty-two more kilometers! This time I swear you will have your hot bath....But we won't cheat."

We leave at five in the morning. The countryside is empty. We pass in front of an abandoned kolkhoz, with a caved-in silo, a toothless windmill, Soviet tractors in a row, rusted and lined up in front of barracks imported straight from Siberia. Do they take us for Russians? Or is it the opposite? For Americans? No, we are faranj, that's all. When our tormentors appear we put into practice a concept Sonia invented during the night in her insomnia: Christly Gandhism! She tried to explain to me in the dawn what she means by that, to keep me awake and encourage me despite my walking like a cripple and my fever: "You remember Gandhi's non-violence? You see him confront the English army alone, being caught in a frantic crowd in the massacres of the partition with Pakistan? Well, due allowance being made, this morning, we're going to do that, we're going to walk straight ahead without react-ing to anything, whatever happens....Can you see Jesus? His sta-tions of the cross? The people who spit in his face, deride him, his crown of thorns, the stones? Do you think he responded to the insults, that he ran after the rotten brats? No! He forgave them even before they harmed him. We are going to follow their example! We are going to be Zen autist monks!"

After *Forrest Gump* and Britney Spears, now the Jesus syndrome and *Rain Man*! Humility, suffering, love, peace, pity, forgiveness.... And guess what? It works! We reach Sodo without too much prob-lem; the little terrors are disarmed by our ataraxia, we stare at the ground or the sky, expressing unspeakable suffering, like an ambu-lant Pietà, and the laughter stops as well as the pursuits....I force the pathos a little, I exaggerate my limp, people silently make way as we pass. You don't shoot at an ambulance. We pass like sur-vivors of a catastrophe, and that disarms them. Sonia has saved us. It has to be said that looking the way we do we don't have to overdo it. We are scarcely within Sodo than we unfortunately pass in front of another school. (What do they teach them in these schools?): the pack again forms.

"*Faranj! Faranj! I fuck you bastard!*"

The whole repertory of De Niro and Al Pacino unwinds, amid the laughter of the crowd. But it slides off our mantle of suffering like water off the feathers of a...duck. We find refuge in the dispen-sary of the Kalé Hewot Protestant mission, where Vic and Cindy Anderson save us from the moral and physical abyss into which we are foundering.

When the door opens for us, Cindy exclaims: "Good Lord! What happened to you?"

"You won't believe us..."

Rest in Sodo, Wednesday 11 December 2002, day 713, 8747th km

We stay there for a few days healing our sores and hearts. First we have to figure out what is going on with this strange fever. Mary, the mission doctor, came right away to take a blood sample. She soon returns with the verdict: "*Plasmodium falciparum* malaria, a bad case. Given your state of shock and general weakness, if you hadn't stopped in here it could have finished you in three days…"

She has been in Ethiopia for twenty years and has specialized in malarial treatments. She is very pleased to learn that we have our di-hydro-artemisinine treatments with us, a medicine I had tested during my first episode of malaria, in Mitundu[3]:

"Do you know the history of di-hydro-artemisinine?"

"Yes. It's a Chinese medicine…"

"You know what it's taken from? You see my bed of orange flowers, there in the garden? The ones that look like gerberas? Well, that's it! That's what saves lives! It's that simple!"

"How?"

"This flower is called bitter artemisia. I make a simple infusion with the dried petals and I save hundreds of people…"

"And no Western laboratory has found it?"

"Ah, you're putting your finger on the problem! This molecule has been known by the Chinese since 1975. They discovered it by caring for the Vietcong wounded brought in from Vietnam. This medicine had the misfortune of being invented by Communists during the Cold War: for thirty years there has been an embargo on it.…The Chinese don't ask anybody for anything and treat all of Asia with it. The Indians copied it, and we are the only ones who hold out. To Africa's disadvantage.…The real problem, in fact, is that this medicine costs nothing whereas modern treatments painstakingly developed by our laboratories cost a fortune. Between one dollar and a hundred dollars, which treatment would you choose? Especially since the one-dollar one works much better, you've tested it yourself, right?"

---

[3] See vol. I, p. 390.

"But what of the WHO, the international organizations…?"

"That's the huge scandal, you shall see, this story will soon blow up in our faces. They took twenty years to get interested in this molecule! I would like to know why. I, for example, depend on international organizations to supply me with medicines. As you know, Ethiopia is under the sanitary control of many, many organizations. And since di-hydro-artemisinine is not officially recognized, I do not have the right to import it…so I grow it!"

"But what reasons do they give for rejecting it?"

"Oh! That the tests haven't proved anything, that they are still under way, that the protocols are very cumbersome and long to put in place, that it has to be synthesized, that it's a very complex molecule…"

We are incredulous. How can such important stakes be held up by such pettily commercial interests? But Mary takes the positive side: "Look, I manage all the same, with my flower beds. But you are going to have to drink a liter of my tisane every day, and it is really quite awful…"

I am over my malaria in forty-eight hours. As at Mitundu. It's akin to a miracle. This medicine is indeed really dangerous for Halfan, Lariam and our other marvels!…[4] Three thousand children die of malaria in Africa every day. How many in the last thirty years?

We are going to have dinner with Vic and Cindy. They have adopted two little Ethiopians. Jerusalem, a little girl of twelve and exceptionally mature, and Philip, nine, much more turbulent.…Vic very kindly asks us: "How long has it been since you have spoken with your parents?"

---

[4] Since our return, the powers-that-be seem to be accepting di-hydro-artemisinine. Its official recognition as complementary therapy by the WHO took place only a few months before our passage in Sodo, in April 2002. But the information had not yet reached Mary. Its production was turned over to two Western laboratories. The press did not begin to discuss it until 2004 with shattering declarations, giving credit for the discovery to those very same laboratories.…In China, the medicine has in fact been known for a thousand years. In France, Médecins Sans Frontières helped lead the battle for its recognition. Sanofi-Aventis is now producing it at cost-price for Africa.

"By telephone, about two and a half months, in Nairobi, but we were able to get news to them through Louise Leakey, at Koobi Fora. I am sure they would be happy to learn that we were able to cross this border and are now safe and sound..."

We call them; they confirm their visit for Christmas, in Addis. Some good news at last! Vic and Cindy are petrified by our tales. They travel only by car. They get a stone from time to time, but nothing like that. In their field work, they are always supervised by guides, translators, parishioners, and are always very well received everywhere. They really have a hard time believing us.

"But what did you do to deserve that?"

The question pierces our heart. We already know that it will be asked us hundreds of times. For such behavior must have a reason....Not unreason.

"Nothing, we do nothing, and whatever we do, it's worse."

"But why then do you insist on walking, on taking such risks; I would have taken a car or a truck at the first village! Might you be a bit masochistic...?"

Maso? Yes, maybe....But then it is our whole trek that is maso. Africa Trek is maso, we are masochating without knowing it..."

The Sodo revelation: we are masochists!

We try then to explain to them that we don't want to cheat with space, with time, with the sequence of our walk, with the meaning we have wished to give it, with all the promises and all the prayers that we carry with us, with the memory of our "saviors of the day" who have taken us in precisely because we were walking. All these people who cannot cheat with their living conditions, who cannot take the bus or expedients to spare themselves suffering. Taking on the African condition looks effete, in the mouth of a Westerner, but for us, for two years it has meant living on the same paths, in the same sunlight, sleeping on the same ground, scratching the same fleas, eating the same food, running the same risks, lions, diseases, it is to assume the same sufferings, hunger, thirst, filth, and...stones...knowing that all of them, in any case, suffer a hundredfold, and that our trek is a joke in the eyes of what they endure every day, all life long. Whereas we have a choice. And we have made that choice. And must assume it. These are elements of an answer to why we still prefer to take stones than a truck....Even if it hurts....For all of them, we cannot cheat, not even by ten meters. If they suffer, we must suffer. The reason for those stones? The proof of their suffering.

"Would you like to see a film on the VCR?"

Sonia exclaims: "Oh, yes! I miss so much seeing a good film!"

"I just got a new one. You want to see *Gandhi*, with Ben Kingsley?"

It's too much. The angels are having a good laugh at us! Sonia remains silent with her mouth open....Vic is concerned and looks at me: "What? What did I say...?"

Mourassa, Monday 16 December 2002, day 718, 45 km, 8832nd km

After Sodo, we have 354 kilometers to go in nine days to make our Christmas appointment in Addis. It's simple, we have to average 39 km a day....It's not over. In any event, we no longer have much desire to go slow. The path will be harsh, but the carrot is particularly attractive.

One day, in late afternoon, we are passing through a village. It is market day. Hundreds of men are assembled on our left, down below, seated among their livestock or sacks of produce, squatting before their onions or their eggs. It isn't very lively, it feels like day's end. We are fairly elevated, it is cold, they are all draped in green chamas. In keeping with our new habit, we go by taking care not to attract attention, heads down and turned so as not to catch anyone's glance. A few days ago, Sonia invented another trick: the animated conversation. We talk to each other eye to eye, very absorbed, and do not notice what is going on around us. That way we offer no foothold, we greet affably the rare persons who greet us to interrupt our conversation. It defuses them. It satisfies them. Mine clearance. Mind clearance...

Things seem to be going swimmingly when a cry rings out:

Faranj! Picked up and echoed by the crowd. All heads are raised and turn in our direction. We wave a greeting with a big smile and continue on as before. Too late, we will not escape them; on all sides appear children, adolescents, adults, we empty out the market: there are three hundred people on our heels, and the unhappy scenario so feared repeats itself. And at the end of the day they are less patient. Kids hang on our backpacks, shove us, have fun trying to throw us off balance. It could be amusing in other circumstances. Not there. When we turn around, we become frightened: the road more than a hundred meters back is black with this crowd that follows us, ever more threatening, ever more noisy; some want to stop us, others to drive us out – conflicts of interest; sticks are raised. Panicked, we start running, they start running; blows rain on our backpacks, the muted shock is terrifying, we bolt, it's a flight forward, desperate, the countryside goes by, the trees, houses, witnesses. Suddenly, in front of us appears an old woman in front of the door of a massive toukoul. She has seen it all. As we approach, and as the first stones are raining down, she motions to us to hurry with her little hand: "Quick! quick! Come in here and be safe!" We rush in like a tornado; she slams the door altogether with a heavy shutter. We are suffocating, out of breath, petrified, incredulous. Stones bounce off the door. The old woman shouts and hurls abuse at the assailants through the walls; the crowd answers her and screams: *"Faranj! faranj! white face! wusha faranj! You! You! Youyouyou!"* – a well-known refrain. My legs are trembling. Sonia is devastated. Rain starts to fall. "Hallelujah!" we think, it will disperse the crowd…

The pressure falls little by little. Calm seems to have returned. By a back door, the old woman's two big sons come to see what's going on, deferential and cautious. We try to explain calmly why we are there. Suddenly, a pike pierces the mud of the wall even with my head, throwing dirt in my eyes. Horror. I was within forty centimeters of being empaled. Another pike tries to take the toukoul down by serving as a lever. Sonia screams. The two sons utter cries of fury and exit the back way with long whips which their mother has handed them. In the meantime, a kid who has climbed onto the roof pulls out a panel of thatch and appears against the twilit sky: he is holding another stone, which I dodge by leaping toward a corner of the room. They want our skin. We're going to be lynched....The old woman throws a bowl of dirty water in the assailant's face; he lets go with a laugh like a gremlin. Already outside, the two sons crack their whips, triggering laughter. It's a game. Out of madness. Out of vice. I glance out through the hole that almost killed me to follow their operations. The two guys are effectual. They don't get any stones thrown at them. They threaten with their fingers. The swarm keeps a distance from the whips, then slowly disperses, derisive, rain doing the rest. The two sons return laughing. Really funny....We can't stay a minute more in this village. They want to hold us back, trying to reassure us by guaranteeing us that it is all over, that it is night outside, that it's dangerous at night because of the hyenas...

"*Bezu Jib!*" (Many hyenas!)

Indeed. Many hyenas....We put on our rain capes.

"*Enhid. Erdata Ibaki, sost kilo becha!*" (Let's go together. Please help us, just for three kilometers!)

They accept. We warmly thank the woman who saved us and are absorbed into the night. She will long remember us. What a terrible memory we leave her. Late in the evening of damp ink, framed by our two bodyguards, we comment on such behavior. For it is not hatred motivated by political or conjectural reasons linked to the news, it is not because we incarnate the disgraced West – it's all done in joy and good humor – it is because we are new and different. It's pure idiocy. The simplest expression of xenophobia, blind and deaf, bestial and sheeplike. As always, Sonia takes the bright side: "In fact, it is very formative and instructional to be a victim of racism. Whites so rarely experience that! It allows us to understand the pain of those who live it, in our own country, because of our peers..."

An angel. What luck to have her at my side! Whereas I, an impenitent male, dream of holding one of my aggressors in my hands, just one, and making him pay for all the others. Stupid. Finally, our two bodyguards leave us and head back with this traditionnal salutation: *"Exabir yerda!"* (May God protect you!)

"Amességuenallo lé hullu. Exabir yestellen." (Thank you for everything. God will reward you.)

We carry on alone, in the rain, in the dark. Walk, walk, to conjure the anguish, exorcise the nightmare. As long as we walk we live....Knock down one by one these kilometers that separate us from Addis. After a few minutes, I turn around. I thought I heard a noise; a man in his prime is following us. A policeman? We continue. Little by little, the distance grows smaller. He is lighter than we are. Fearing the worst, we keep our gas canisters at hand. The fellow catches up with us, passes us, smiles peaceably at us, with an air of contrition: *"Enider bété!"* (Welcome to my house!)

That is the Ethiopian *"Karibu." "Enider"*: welcome. The first time we have heard it in this country. The man watched the whole scene in the previous village. He knows about our anguish. We are soon at his house. He sends the curious away. He has understood that we need some calm. He extends clean mats in his large toukoul, sits us down on stools near a fire. Puts on water to heat. All in silence. He does not speak. We do not speak. We let him be, our eyes riveted on the flames, in his hands. All of a sudden he comes to me, kneels and begins to unlace my shoes. I try to stop him, but with a gesture full of love he disarms my modesty. I know the state of my socks and feet. He continues, pours warm water into a basin, removes my shoes, takes off my noxious socks and delicately takes my sticky feet, places them in the basin, then, one after the other, soaps them, massages them, rubs them, going up the calf black with dust, which makes me cry out with pain. With the filth and the cramps, the tensions and calluses, all the day's excretions are rinsed in the purifying water in the glow of the hearth, under the hand of this holy man. Ersumo Kabamo. That's his name. He is our savior this evening. His gesture puts into practice an old Ethiopian Coptic custom inspired by the scene of the washing of the feet. "Do you see this woman?" says Jesus to the Pharisee who is scandalized that his worthy host should allow a sinning woman to touch him, "I entered your house, you gave me no water for my feet, but she has wet my feet with her tears and wiped them with her hair. [...] Therefore I tell you, her sins, which are many, are forgiven, for she loved much; but he who is forgiven little, loves little."[5]

When he is finished, Ersumo takes my foot, lifts it to his mouth and reverentially kisses my big toe. He then turns to Sonia for the same treatment.

Ethiopia, Biblical land par excellence, where you get stoned and have your foot kissed the same day, among the demons and the saints, in fury and meditation.

The next day, we reach Hosaina, capital of Gouraghé country. Everything goes well; Ersumo has freed us from our fears. But our bodies bear the stigmata of our excesses. We hurt all over, with Sonia it's the hip and right knee, for me the little finger, the back, the arches and the anterior cruciate ligaments. I wish there was a bonesetter around....In front of a greasy spoon where we stop for a *chaï-dabo*,[6] Sonia slips on some gravel and sprawls on the ground. Three men rush to help her up. No laughter...compassion. Not a cry...normal behavior. What a shock, for us! We leave quite astounded. In the city, while we are walking in the effervescence of shops, a cry rings out behind us: "I love you!"

This time, no "*faranj! faranj!*" as if Ersumo had passed the word to the whole city, as if the saint had launched a legion of angels before us....We land with Cistercian Sisters who run the city's larg-

[5] Luke 7:44–47, Revised Standard Version.
[6] Tea and bread.

est school. In the infirmary, I finagle a cast for my finger with toothpicks and Elastoplast. Father Woldé Tensai receives us.

"There were many more of us before, but the Eritrean Fathers had to leave the country in 1994, just after the partition. It was a drama for the country since millions of displaced Eritreans had remade their lives here, and many Ethiopians were living in Eritrea. Today, the border between the two countries is closed and the tension is rising."

Leaving Hosaina, we immediately redescend into the Rift and enter the Silté region, peopled by Muslim Ethiopians who once came from Harar. Vic and Cindy, as good Americans, had predicted the worst if we ventured into these areas. We ask the Father what he thinks.

"You have nothing to fear! They are very gentle and hospitable people. And if, in addition, you tell them you are going to Jerusalem, you will have no problem. In our country, insecurity doesn't come from the minorities. We keep ourselves in line..."

Forced march. We sprint 41, 39, and 46 kilometers, the days follow on a Chinese road under construction, without hitches. The Father was right, the people of Silté whom we pass are affable, polite, hospitable, their boys well-bred and respectful. Fonko, Amberitchu Atchamo, Kibet, Butajira, Gogetti. We are driving hard, from the break of day to dusk, go straight to the schools that so recently we fled, ask the teachers for a classroom to put up our tent and a little water for our noodle soup which Sonia garnishes with tomatoes and onions purchased along the way. In the greasy spoons, bearded unknowns in white skullcaps and *saroual-kamiz*[7] secretly pay for our chaï-dabo after hearing us talk about our journey. We are now able to hold a half-hour's conversation in Amharic, control our effects before the public in cafés, the famous *bunna bet*,[8] tell the shamed adults about the untenable children of Woleyta and the stones

---

[7] The universal Muslim garb: wide, fine cotton trousers covered by a long shirt and a Mao collar.

[8] Literally, coffee houses.

thrown at us, who profit from it to drive off with great swings of the whip assembled children who are getting rowdy....None of that here! In Islam, children are disciplined. We are approached by a policeman in civvies who has been listening to the tale of our disillusionment; wary, he advises us not to tell our stories again. He concludes: "It was to show you their affection..."

I really wish I could show this hypocrite my affection. Nine kilometers before Haro, on a muddy incline that has been bulldozed, we pass our nine thousandth kilometer since the Cape of Good Hope. We celebrate the event by designing the number on the freshly rammed ground with some little white pebbles. It amuses us to imagine that in a few days they will be forever covered in asphalt. We film the scene. Each time, we try to vary the ritual. Just before Addis, again in an Orthodox zone, we reconnect with our good little devils and their throwing of stones. We are in Melka Kunturé, a capital of world paleoanthropology, one of the cradles of humanity....We do not even stop. Whether hewn a million six hundred thousand years ago or flying at us, to hell with stones! We are impervious to them. Despite the skirmish, some of the mechanisms of which we now master, a young polio victim is walking like us. As Sonia is limping because of her knee and her hips, as I am halting because of my inflamed arches, I first thought it was a mocker; my anger was coming on when I realized that his handicap was real. The two crippled faranj and the polio victim. We are the public laughing stock. Like bursts of machine-gun fire come from all sides the "*birr, birr, birr, money-money-money, youyouyou!*" It's like an itch triggered by our simple appearance. A brat pushes the humor to the point of launching the cry from atop a tree where he is trimming branches: the jabbering magpie!

Our courageous walker is a young Muslim. Hussein Rachid. He speaks admirable English. He understands everything. Our project, our trek, our bearing, he tells us about his country, his problems, reveals to us a deep sensitivity and unbelievable maturity. His brother is a contractor for the small works of art on this road.

He tells us about the mismanagement, the thickness of the asphalt, three times less than in the specifications and the contracts signed with the Chinese contractor. He shows us the places where the tarmac is already splitting even though the road isn't yet open. "Too much sand in the mixture," he asserts peremptorily, from his fourteen-year-old vantage point. The margin is shared by the different intermediaries and this little Hussein Rashid is informed about it all. Why not our people in charge? The European contractor's bid was much too high. But where does the money come from? From the European community, naturally. He adds: "Not to worry! You will pay again in three years to have it fixed…"

As we leave Jewé, forty-five kilometers from Addis, someone hails us. It happens a thousand times a day. We don't pay any attention. We continue on. He perseveres. In that case, we pretend not to hear. It is the best way to discourage pests. Unlucky for us to have done so. A big square-headed lump catches up with me, screaming, flings me to the ground and places a large caliber pistol against my temple. I saw nothing coming. He loads a bullet in the chamber. Sonia tries to stop him, he aims at her. He aims at my wife. A vision of horror. We're going to get shot at the gates of Addis in broad daylight. Fuck. The guy is furious and soused, drooling, spits with rage, his eyes reddened by alcohol.

"*Bolis! Méché malet kum! Kum no! Faranju temessasié!*" (Police! When I say stop, it's stop, even for Whites!)

A complete madman. Drunk to boot.

"*Yikerta, alawekum! Algebanyem! Aznallo.*" (Sorry, I didn't know I was doing something wrong. I didn't understand, terribly sorry.)

He calms down, picks me up, looks me over, puts his pistol away, begins his interrogation. I did not know the word *kum*. Big mistake. And he had not pronounced the word "police." How to die for a misunderstanding. He has the head of a butcher, close-cropped hair, a black leather jacket. A cop in civvies. He points at my Maasai sword: "*Mendé no?*" (What's that?)

We tell him about Africa.

"*Olalem Massaï no, ke Kenya, mekinyatoum African beggir akwaratellen, hulett amet beggir bicha, hullu beremidja, makina alfelegem, wodekat mesrat, Ethiopia sementenya agerachen no...*"[9]

He relaxes, gets hold of himself, and we of ourselves, we continue about the trek, the lions, the border, the kids, the stones, show him our official letter, our passports....He immediately changes face, like a mad Janus, shakes the dust off my shirt, bursts out laughing and grabs me by the shoulder to take me to have a beer with him. I start to decline, he all but lifts me from the ground. No desire to contrary him twice. In the bunna bet, the witnesses pretend nothing happened. This guy visibly reigns by terror hereabouts. He offers, with our money, a general round of *tedj*, the famous Ethiopian hydromel, for everybody, which we have not yet had the opportunity to taste. For this first time, it has a somewhat a bitter taste...

On Monday 23 December at three in the afternoon, after a sprint in a mental tunnel with light at the end, our lame feet touch down on the ring road. We have made it. We are in Addis. On time. Liberated.

A piece of advice, our experience leads us to think it is better not for the moment to come to Ethiopia as a backpacker, and especially not as an independent hiker, nor as a cyclist; it is better to pay the price, get yourself a good tour operator, there are some now for almost any price range: come as tourists! That is moreover what we are going to do, since my parents are coming to offer us some vacation in the historic north of the country, off our route – by car. Ah, the grandeurs of Ethiopian civilization! Finally!

---

[9] It's a Maasai olalem from Kenya, because we are crossing Africa on foot, we have been walking for two years, entirely, every step, we refuse automobiles, we are doing this to meet people, Ethiopia is our eighth country...

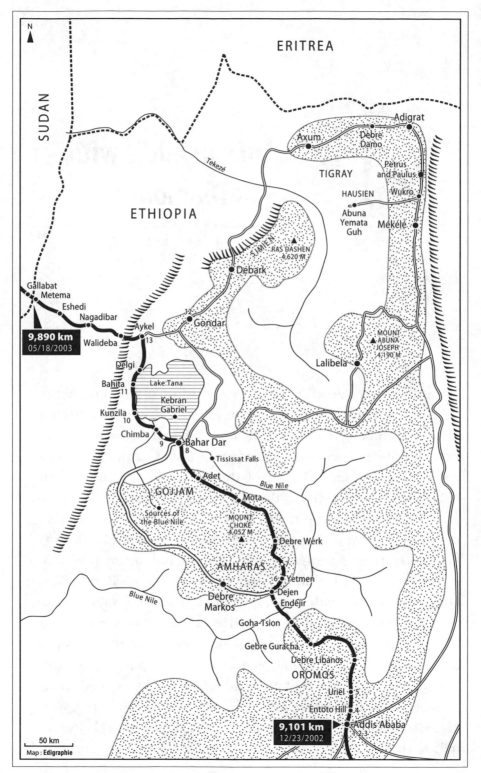

North Ethiopia

21

Lucy in Addis with Diamonds

ETHIOPIA

For two weeks, we visit the historic treasures of Ethiopia, beginning the anthology with a flight. *Ex abrupto*, we find ourselves in the quietude of Lake Tana, drifting toward the monastery of Kebran Gabriel perched on a mysterious island. On the way back we see the Tississat Falls, one of the mythic sources of the Blue Nile. Next there is Gondar, the impressive fortified city that radiated as far as Rome and traded with India. Its baths of Fasilades, its church with its ceiling decorated with legions of angels, little by little make us enter another world: the world of tourism. It is made up of visits to old buildings, comfortable nights, good meals and absence of contact with local populations. There is always a chauffeur, an admission ticket or a Cerberus to keep them at a distance. This comfort like our discomfort has its price. Tourism is cooler than hiking. The days follow on each other and pile up treasures: the Simien escarpment and its Geladas baboons, the splendid obelisks of Axum, a city whose past goes back to the loves of the Queen of Sheba and King Solomon, and which is supposed to shelter the Ark of the Covenant....Our car trip unfurls like music paper. To the east, Tigray and its dozens of rock-hewn churches perched on the summit of vertiginous peaks and decorated with ancient frescoes: Petrus and Paulus, Maryam Korkor, Abuna Yemata Guh: so many paradises for the anchorites. A few turns of the wheel farther, we come to Lalibela, the "Ethiopian Jerusalem," just in time for Orthodox Christmas. Thousands of pilgrims fill the holy city with prayers and sacred dances. Twelve monolithic churches, miracles of architecture, represent in stone the Christian faith, from Adam's tomb to Golgotha, passing by the house of the Savior of the world or the chapel of the Trinity....To visit Ethiopia as tourists makes us pass from one of these treasures to the next, in a wonderment constantly renewed, from hotel to hotel, site to site, pass without obstacle through crowds of beggars, taking their hand gestures for friendly greetings and the stone throwing for gravel kicked up by the wheels....It is an unforgettable trip. Something to reconcile you, if needed, with the country. Go there soon.[1]

Back in Addis after our touristico-cultural digressions, we plunge full time into writing the second part of our first book begun in Nairobi and retracing our steps from Cape Town to Kili. I have my lower back badly pinched: lumbago. Twelve days of automobile after two years of walking had the better of my lumbar vertebrae... a true little grandfather. Sitting in a car is exhausting.

Despite that, there is an appointment we cannot miss: with Lucy, our venerable ancestor or distant cousin, who since her discovery in 1974 by the team of Donald Johanson, including Yves Coppens, attracted the spotlight to Ethiopia as one of the numerous potential cradles of humanity.

To introduce her to us, we have the good fortune to run into a team of French scientists directed by Professor Henri de Lumley of the Musée de l'Homme. We had missed them in the Ethiopian south, just after we passed the Kenyan border into Dassanech territory: we passed unknowingly within five kilometers of their digs

---

[1] First you can find the details of these cultural marvels on our web site: www.africatrek.com.

at Fadjej, fifty kilometers before Omo Raté. They had passed us six days later on the northern road, just after Dimeka, and we had sputtered in the bush a few snatches of surprise and mutual admiration. Here they are again, this time in Addis, to study their discoveries. Professor Carbonnell, the famous Spanish specialist of Neanderthals at the Gran Dolina and Atapuerca sites, is among them. Vincenzo Celiberti, an Italian adopted by France and researcher at Tautavel, presents to us the object of their research: "We came to compare our findings in Fadjej with the tools from another site in the north of Ethiopia, the site of Cadagona, which turned up extraordinary tools, but a million years older. Maybe that will permit us to deduce the permanence of the techniques of the lithic industries as well as their transmission and their influence on our ancestors' alimentation."

In the basements of the Addis museum, we are lucky enough to be able to film a perfect replica of Lucy (the original being preserved in a highly inaccessible room). She lies there under the spotlights, on a case of black velvet, extraordinarily complete except for the cranial cap. Short, with arms a little too long to look really like us, but with an astonishingly modern hand, freed from quadrupedism, able to grasp objects, fruits, and take them to a safe place. Vincenzo, as a good Italian, talks about her as if she were a lover and mother.

"I have grown up with her, I have never ceased seeing her my whole life, lending her behavior consonant with her morphology and her capacities, to replace her in her faunal context, to make the fossils around her speak, it's a phantasmal relationship I have been maintaining with her for twenty years. There are so many enigmas that are not yet solved. We don't know, for example, whether she used tools; we think not, for no chopping tool has yet been found associated with the remains of *Australopithecus afarensis*. You need to know that Lucy is not the only specimen discovered of this species: an entire family has been found, it also, no doubt, drowned when it was trying to cross a river, or dead of a powerful epidemic.

But what is precious with Lucy is that she was immediately buried in the slime and spared by the teeth of carrion feeders, who are great destroyers of potential fossils. In two days, there is nothing left of an animal Lucy's size, everything is scattered, eaten, ground, dissipated by the vultures and hyenas. Now at that time, there was a species of hyena twice as large as today's, not to mention saber-tooth tigers…"

A moment of silence. A painting of smilodon, on the wall, makes us shudder with fright. The small, frail Lucy only becomes for that the more sympathetic and courageous in our eyes. Vincenzo picks up on his exposé: "What makes us fundamentally close to Lucy is her pelvis and the T-form of her femur head which betrays a well-assured bipedism even if, today, she appears to us a little awkward and swaying."

We respectfully salute our dear Lucy, in the footsteps of whom we have been walking so long, and think back to the footprints of Laetoli, which we crossed paths with over two thousand kilometers back….No doubt left by a member of her large family, and contemporary to her within two hundred thousand years.[2]

In Addis, our friends Jean-Claude and Amaretch Guilbert received us in their house and we are squatting not without scruples in the living room on their own mattress which they are doing without to sleep right on their box springs, and which their sons Matthias and Abel convert *ispo facto* into a trampoline. The appointment was made nearly three years ago. We are finally here, and at the Guilberts' a promise made is an eternal promise. Jean-Claude, a former journalist of renown, is presently plunged into the writing of his *Seven Doors*: a collection of memories and adventures shared with Hugo Pratt whose literary heir he also is since he is to take over the series of *Desert Scorpions* and continues to keep alive Captain Koïnski for whom he was the model. After that he will keep

---

[2] For those who wish to learn more about the work of Professor Lumley's team, you can find the rest of our paleoanthropological inquiry on www. africatrek.com.

going on a great Ethiopian historical saga in several volumes and on the Corto Maltese guide of Ethiopia....He has his work cut out for him!

Between my ergonomic chair lent by Jean-Baptiste Chauvin, cultural attaché of the embassy, and my therapeutic baths in the spa of the old Finfiné Hotel created by the Empress Taitou, my lumbar vertebrae are getting better. When they trouble me, I leave my little sky blue office set up in the calm of an annex and go plunge, lying down, into the full Corto, from *Ballad of the Salt Sea* to *Mu* by way of *Corto Maltese in Siberia*...My broken little finger is being re-educated on the keyboard of the computer, without great success. Dr. Gilles Landrivon, of the French embassy, directs me to Dr. de Dreux, of Doctors Without Borders, who is most appropriately receiving two French orthopedists. The verdict? Avulsion fracture of the palmar surface and wedging of the resulting bone fragment in the joint. Less serious than anticipated. The therapy? Above all do nothing. Wait for it to go away. My Elastoplast-toothpick bandage was not a bad idea, the doctor adds: "You ought to have immobilized the finger in a slightly bent position, as if you were holding a glass. The straight position is not that of a finger at rest, it is a little overextended. Therefore you will have a little trouble closing the finger....It will take a year to be healed."

Addis is not the most beautiful African city, not the ugliest either. Like all the cities where the colonial powers did not lay out wide avenues lined with trees, it is muddled and disordered, lacking distinct neighborhoods, where nice houses, offices, hotels or former imperial palaces list in the middle of shantytowns. A poverty composed of lepers, grime and misshapen people thus is side-by-side with the comfort of expatriates, the opulence of the representatives from the OAU (Organization for African Unity) or from the Gulf countries and the outlandish pomp of the Sheraton. You have to learn to desensitize yourself to go from one world to the other. The remark is unfortunate but it is the only way to live in Addis, unless you spend your time giving. Everyone finds a personal routine: never give, give once a day, support a leper family or two, give oneself rules to assuage one's conscience. Everyone has "his/her" poor. Thousands of black kites swirl in slow motion above the city uttering their lugubrious trills. They are the daytime trash men. The yellow dogs being the nighttime ones. They travel in packs, shriek, fight, copulate, groan, shattering the sleep of the city dwellers. The hirsute tufts of the eucalyptus imperfectly sponge up the acid odors of the open sewers into which garbage is poured. The blue smoke of out-of-tune motors mixes with the white smoke of the eucalyptus leaves or the incense that the inhabitants burn to drive away the miasmas. Two distinct axes drain traffic composed of enormous 4x4's tinted-glass-alloy-wheels-chrome-bumper and antique blue ramshackle Ladas inherited from commercial relations established with the Soviet big brother in the Derg[3] era: Churchill and Bole Roads, one leading to the old French Djibouti train station, the other to the brand new airport provided by the World Bank for the country's tourist expansion. Many Tigray beggars, a blue cross tattooed on their foreheads, have come down from their proud country in the hope, always disappointed, of harvesting crumbs of governmental manna which they have shared with the Oromos since the end of the Eritrean conflict and partition. Favoring Westerners, reputed to be more tender of heart, they make moving about in the city difficult. That's the way it is. It is done without aggressiveness, so you learn to live with it. Unlike some other African megalopolises, Addis is a safe city. The people we pass and meet are happy to see us here. A strange sensation. In other countries, it was in the countryside that we were safe, and in the city that we would be scared stiff.

In Addis we reconnect with social life. What fascinates us the most in the course of dinners and meetings with our fellow-countrymen is that no one ever asks us the slightest question about our journey, nor shows any interest in the countries we have visited.

---

[3] Literally "Committee," name of the Communist regime under Mengistu.

Conversations beat around the bush, airy, mundane, and willfully humorous. It's a contest to see who can make the best quip at the right time. The purpose is not to learn or to understand, but to amuse. Always at others' expense. We had forgotten how social life worked. No one wants to hear people who just hike. That's the way it is. If we had said we had swum here from Mars, they would not have made more of our odyssey. "Oh, really? Interesting! It's like me, last year I hiked across the Cevennes,[4] that took a lot out of me..." Dear Frenchmen! *Vanitas vanitatum et omnia vanitas*. A good lesson. Strange feeling also to reconnect with the banality of encounters among sedentary types whereas each of our nomadic encounters is a festival.

Day after day, the pages of our book are written as we walked the length of the continent step by step. Three chapters for Zimbabwe, one for Mozambique, five for Malawi and five for Tanzania, besides the twelve South African chapters written in Nairobi. But the sun of our days is really Loulith, "the pearl" in Amharic, a little girl three months old, abandoned one evening just before Christmas in a grubby hotel, and whom our friends have just adopted. Dying on delivery, she has gained weight, recovered life day by day and has enchanted us with her chatter. Never saw such an adorable baby! She is all smiles and goodness, funny faces and complete nights. A little round mug with light skin and large, black eyes, not a hair on her noggin, a tiny nose and a little split cherry instead of lips, she bobs her head and devours life and the chance that has been given to her. As if she knew. She is not an ingrate; Loulith gives as much love as she receives. We all adore her, Jean-Claude first of all, who is constantly exclaiming: "That girl is something, she is really a grace we have received!" They adopted her by telephone, sight unseen, the day they were leaving for a two-week trip to France, after drawing, in prayer and holding an Ethiopian cross, a little piece of paper that said "Yes" buried in the middle of

---

[4] A barren limestone plateau in southwest France, gouged with deep gorges.

seven "No" papers. Loulith or the ordeal. Amaretch, who worked for Mother Teresa's Sisters, whom she prayed every evening to find her a little girl after losing another little Loulith she was about to adopt to AIDS, knowing that, in her angelic purity, she would surely have some influence...

On Christmas Eve, just before going to midnight mass, Amaretch and Sonia go and embrace Loulith. While they are bent over the cradle like two fairies, Amaretch asks Sonia: "Would you be willing to be her godmother?"

Sonia replies after a moment of silence: "Thank you! That's the best Christmas present I ever received..."

In the same night, in our mail brought by our parents whom we just picked up at the airport, we receive from a French friend, who is unaware of Loulith's existence, an extract from Charles Péguy taken from *The Portal of the Mystery of Hope* that says: "Hope is a little bit of a girl who came on Christmas day..."

Gooseflesh all around. The angels are already having fun with Loulith!

Christmas 2002 is also a great day for Kenya, a renaissance, a revolution: a change of power has occurred without a bloodbath. The old Moi is leaving power with dignity, recognizing the defeat of his protégé Kenyatta – credited with only 24% of the vote against 70% for Kibaki, drafted by plebiscite. None of the Kenyans we met believed it would happen. They were all persuaded the election would be fixed, that the international observers would not be able to work, that their voices would not be counted. They were wrong. Political miracles are possible and the signal thus given by Kenya to all of Africa is historical. Peaceful and democratic political transfers are so rare on the continent – you can count them on one hand – that they deserve to be underscored. Not that the faces of Kenya and Africa are going to be changed, not the corruption of Moi's system eradicated from one day to the next, but it will just breathe a huge hope into all the people crushed under the boot of dictators. Not that Kibaki is a savior, he has already been vice-

president of the Kanu[5] for three years, eight times a minister of
Moi and he is quite used to the backrooms of power, but it proves
that the democratic game is possible, and that the people's voice
can be heard.

Just before we leave Addis, we learn of the death of my maternal grandfather, Antoine. This is the price of our long-term adventure: separation from one's loved ones. The sacrifice of not seeing
them grow, not being able to greet them before their great voyage,
no longer to bear their joys and sufferings. We had an intuition of
it in the elevator that had separated us from him two years and
three months ago. I had mysteriously wept with all the tears in my
body. As if by premonition, we succeeded in getting to him, two
days before his death, with the help of Philippe Pothon, a film-
maker passing through Addis, a letter and a little bronze Ethiopian
cross. Thanks to the rapidity of this last-minute messenger, it is
with him, held tightly in his hand, forever.

---

[5] Kenya African National Union.

CHAPTER
22

"Cheggir yellem!"

ETHIOPIA

The book completed, we resume our trek from the Guilberts' gate. For our first few kilometers, we have an exceptional companion: Haile Gebreselassie, Olympic champion in the ten thousand meters. The great sportsman, a small, humble, smiling man, accompanies us to the Entoto pass, which overlooks the city, where he trains every morning. Walking in his company gives us wings and places under good auspices our second start in Ethiopia. A train of friends follows us, in which figure Doron Grossman, Israeli ambassador to Ethiopia, sporting his favorite panama and closely followed by his big, winded bodyguard. He has been farsighted enough to provide us with maps and itineraries of the road from Eilat to the Sea of Galilee. He leads the hike with his broad strides. Jean-Claude, always game for walks, is naturally on board as well as a brochette of onlookers. Doron leaves us before the uphill portion with these words: *"Lashana Habaha b'Yerushaleim!"* (Next year in Jerusalem!)

A promise of arrival for all nomads and wanderers.

Haile leaves us at the pass, confessing that he would like to have

followed us farther, but he has the world track and field champion-
ship in Paris 2003 to prepare for. As he leaves with aerial stride, he
shouts: "I admire your endurance…"

The world upside down! We shout: *"Eizoch!"* (Keep it up!)

He replies with a laugh that we still seem to hear every time we
think of him. Haile or the smile of Ethiopia.

We remain alone, in the company of Amaretch Guilbert, who
is determined to get to the Debre Libanos monastery, a hundred
kilometers further north, and by Solene de Poix, a brilliant young
doctoral candidate in geography, in Ethiopia to study the commercial functioning of the Mercato, the Addis popular market, reputed
to be the largest in Africa. Our three months' pause in the capital
can be felt in the legs, but the pedometer is delighted to finally be
passing through its 9102nd kilometer; the sun shines in the fresh
air of the Sululta plateau and the kilometers go by: forty-one the
first day!

At the Entoto pass, we take a giant step: for the first time we
enter the hydrographic basin of the Nile. From now on, every drop
of water that falls from the sky is fated to flow towards the Mediterranean over more than four thousand kilometers, at the risk
of dying in the sands if it isn't evaporated by the sun.…The laws
of gravity draw us towards Egypt, to the north, this energizes our
morale since we have resumed the trek not without apprehension.
Nevertheless, the presence of Amaretch to whom we dedicate a
most deserved devotion reassures us. Humility, simplicity, goodness: she possesses all these qualities in a beauty as much exterior
as interior. A great lady. She has knotted her broad, curly head of
hair, covered herself with a white hat, coated with total screen since
she fears the sun of the high plateaus despite her lovely indigenous
skin. She walks courageously with her long, even steps while chat-
ting with Sonia. With her, everything goes fine: no stone-throwing,
no insults, no outlandish beggary or mocking arrogance. A Janus
country? What we do encounter again are the fleas that infest the

lodgings by legions, and the discomfort of the natural functions: our daily lot. An amazement for Amaretch.

We are invited to sleep by farmers, by the Orthodox priest of Uriel where a hive drips from a cornice of the roof on a cross covered with honey to which miraculous virtues are attributed. We often walk in open country by shortcuts and byroads. In the bright morning air resonate the cracking of whips and the eructations of laborers leading their pairs of oxen doggedly towing primitive plows. The songs and the promises of the earth on small plots of land as far as the eye can see.

Despite the apparent wealth of nature, fertile soil, cool air and good precipitation, the poverty equation produces merciless results: the usable territory is completely occupied, total deforestation, the population never stops growing, the father's hectare is divided with his elder son, who will do the same thing...the shagreen story again.[1]

In three and a half days, we reach the crossroad with the road to Debre Libanos monastery, and discover there the "Portuguese bridge," the three romanesque arches of which stride over a rocky river bed. Fifty meters below, the riverbed falls into the precipice of an immense canyon. Massive and yet aerial, this bridge has defied for four centuries the inclement weather, the vagaries of History, the hooves of donkeys and oxen. As slim as a footbridge, lacking a ledge, it is supported by its profiled piles on two large basalt blocks obstructing the flow of a dried-up river on the edge of the void. The view plunges into the canyon of one of the affluents of the Blue Nile, a thousand meters below.

A young guide explains to us the secret of its longevity.

"The Portuguese put ground ostrich eggs in their mortar, with the white, yellow and shell, which made it more resistant."

One thing is certain, they knew how to build at the most beautiful spot. We picture these small, sturdy Lusitanian masons. They

---

[1] See Chapter 8 of this volume.

doubtless arrived with the four hundred fifty musketeers of Christopher de Gama, son of the celebrated navigator, sent to save the Christian empire in Ethiopia at a time when it was bending under the assaults of the Muslim Ahmed Gragn, called "the lefty," who, aided by his Somali mercenaries, was trying to convert the countryside at swordpoint. The Jesuits, also part of the mix, by dint of infiltration and diplomacy, seduced Susneyous – the only Catholic emperor of Ethiopia since his son Fasilades was to establish his capital in Gondar and restore Orthodoxy.

This is where Amaretch leaves us: Jean-Claude, her husband, is coming by car to take her back to Addis. The poor princess has walked for three days without complaining of her huge blisters. In homage to the builders and in memory of my plunge into "God's jacuzzi" at Victoria Falls,[2] I allow myself a swan dive into a "sorcerer's cauldron" thirteen meters below the Portuguese Bridge, with the huge canyon in the backdrop. Eternal suspended seconds.

Without our Ethiopian guardian angel, things go sour quickly – which confirms that you mustn't move around alone in Ethiopia. We are back to our miseries. We won't tell you about them; their motives of incomprehension, ill-placed idleness and pride, we now know. Crass lethargy, excited raillery; the days succeed one another with each its lot of conflicts in a forced march to Bahar Dar, six hundred kilometers from Addis. On the way, we cross in a day and a half the gorges of the Blue Nile. For that, we have to descend a thousand meters to a bridge where the guards suspect we are spies because we are taking pictures of the valley. It is fifteen degrees hotter than higher up. Forty-five degrees! Overwhelming! Fortunately, that lasts only for a few kilometers before we climb again into Amhara country, in Gojjam. How are we going to survive in the Sudan?

At Dejen, back on the plateau, we decide to leave the main road

---

[2] See vol. I, p. 238.

that goes through Debre Markos, to walk up the course of the Nile along a less-used road all the way to Bahar Dar. In the villages, the hysteria resumes its course. "You will see," we had been proudly assured in Addis, "the noble Amharas are much more hospitable than those barbarous Oromos." We find the same packs of shameless children. We don't explain anymore such behavior to ourselves. We bear it. Full stop. We flee. All day, at every opportunity, witnesses repeat to us: "*Cheggir yellem!*" (There are no problems!)

Whereas everything is a problem. They are. We are. They and we. Not a day without its little drama. It begins in Yetmen, soon after Dejen, coming out of a little stand of eucalyptus. A little girl joins us and delights us with questions and laughter, Sonia's hand in hers. These moments are so rare that we are quite consoled by them. Suddenly, the kid lets out a scream and slumps onto the shoulder. We are terrified. What is going on? A stroke? A heart attack, epilepsy, a devastating migraine? Already people gather thinking we have beaten her, we help the girl up, she is holding her head. When she opens her hands they are covered in blood. She cries all the more. A stone. She was hit by a stone from behind that was surely intended for us. We saw nothing coming. Heard nothing. No witnesses. People come running, threatening, picking up stones, lifting their sticks, we are going to be lynched....*Cheggir yellem!* I proclaim, opening my arms to protest our innocence, while Sonia holds the girl up.

"*Ene iedellehu. Adega Nebber!*" (I have done nothing, it's an accident!)

In a sob, the girl exonerates us and points toward the little wood to which the avenging band now hurriedly repairs....Whew! *Cheggir yellem.* We enter a house to attend to the girl. In her tangle of hair, it is hard to find the wound. Black blood is running onto her neck. Under the thick head of hair, we finally, horrified, find the wound: the scalp has a deep gash over five centimeters long. *Cheggir yellem!* Nothing else to do than an emergency hemostatic bandage: she has to go get sewn up at the hospital. Sonia sprays the wound with Betadine while I make a compress with clean gauze. The child mews with pain. Sonya tries to distract her.

"*Semesh man no?*" (What's your name?)

"*Bizoualen!*"

"*Senté amet no?*" (How old are you?)

"*Sément amet!*" (Eight.)

The assembled witnesses watch us officiate, repeating in their consternation: "*Lidjotch, lidjotch, ah! lidjotch!*" (Children, children, children!)

I wrap her head in a scarf like a giant Easter egg, slipping a piece of gauze into the bandage to create some pressure on it. When it is done, Sonia gives this prescription to the witnesses present: "*Debre Markos Hospital téfélégallesh ahun!*" (She must go to Debre Markos hospital at once!)

Cheggir yellem! I go out to stop a truck to be quite sure they will go. A woman, we don't know whether she was a neighbor, an aunt or a friend, goes along with Bizoualen with some money we give her. When the truck has left, everyone moves back as if we had the plague: we bring bad luck. We pick up our backpacks and disappear. *Cheggir yellem!*

We are eager to get to the Sudan where the hospitality will be, according to what many transcontinental travelers have told us, proportional to the temperature! That evening, we keep going until well into the night, in silence, walking madly to exorcise our sorrow. Since the village of Yetmen, a solitary man has been following us at a distance, with a plastic bag in each hand. Eventually he is walking even with us; after a certain time, we greet each other mechanically. In a mixture of English and Amharic, he tells us his story. His name is Tekleye Asfaw, he is a lieutenant in the army and is going home on leave to Gondar. In the bus station of Addis, he was stripped of everything this morning by six bandits. He had two months' pay in his pockets....His income of 50 euros a month does not allow him to have a bank account. But *cheggir yellem*, by selling his shoes and jacket, he was able to buy a ticket as far as

Endejir, half-way there, and buy himself some old plastic shoes. He hasn't got a damned penny for food and is suffering from lack of solidarity with his peers. He saw us, in Yetmen, and heard what the people said about us...

"Not good people!" he regrets.

We soon make a gentlemen's agreement: we will take him under our arm and he will take us under his; he protects us and in exchange we will feed and lodge him with us in the only accommodation available: roadside brothels.

After five days in our company, spent heading off undesirables, driving off mockers, answering the suspicious, he is on edge; devoured by shame at the behaviors he is witnessing. He even comes to blows with a dumb-ass who, after seeing Sonia play with a little girl, addressed us in precise English that betrayed his habit of this sort of practice: "You like her? If you want, I can make an arrangement with her mother. Would two thousand dollars do? You are right to adopt little Ethiopians, we are the most handsome..."

We have tremendous sympathy for these little girls. We cannot forget that, in Gojjam, they are excised. Seven days after birth. Labia and clitoris. How do they manage to excise a seven-day-old clitoris? *Cheggir yellem!* In Addis, we met an Ethiopian woman doctor, a member of the NGO Save the Children, who has made of the campaign against mutilation her main preoccupation. She told us all the undersides of the question. Excision is practiced on a grand scale on millions of Ethiopan baby girls. The marriage of children is also common. After six or seven years, the girl can be married to an adult against a large dowry interminably negotiated by the parents. These marriages are doubtless the saddest on earth, the little wives go through the celebration in tears despite the gifts and glittering fabrics they are covered in. The men engage themselves by contract not to touch them before puberty. Unfortunately, because of men's alcoholism and idleness, many of them are deflowered before maturity, with terrible consequential gynecological problems,

perforations and fistulas,[3] which make them prematurely inconti-
nent or sterile, for which reasons they are repudiated and sent back
to their families....And for those who have not the money to purchase wives, there is the kidnaping of young girls. One means or
another to found a home. It is still a very common practice today.
Oromos, Amharas, same story. In the countryside, the better off
often send their daughters to the city, or to work in Saudi Arabia,
to protect them...

Another day, in Mota, in a coffeehouse, a group of Ethiopians
in suits and ties wearing nice square-toed shoes disembarks from
two Land Cruisers, visibly content with themselves. Culture shock.
Commotion in the village. They come proudly up to us to show
off their English. For us, it's an opportunity to ask questions and
learn a bit more about the region. They work for a Swedish NGO
that does microcredit. To cut short a possible sales pitch, we ask
them their interest rate. Our interlocutor is rather caught up short;
I repeat: "What rate do you give the poor peasants you save with
your loans?"

"Eighteen percent for six months."

Not bad. It's better than 26% at six months, 52% a year practiced by the Ministry of Agriculture in Malawi.[4] But it's still too
much. Imagine this rate for yourself! For your car! For your house!
Pray do have a banker explain to me one day why we can't provide the poor with the same borrowing rate as ours. I'm sure he's
got a good reason. Anyhow we would call 18% usury! And this is
done under the cover of a humanitarian organization. *Cheggir yellem!* And the poor get only poorer, again and always – what can you
invest and borrow when you have one hectare of land, no well, no
rain, and fifteen mouths to feed?

Vaguely puzzled, the guy keeps his chin up with a story

---

[3] Nine thousand cases a year, 1200 requiring surgery in the Fistula Hospital
   in Addis, directed by Dr. Hamlin, who with her husband has led an avant-
   garde battle on the subject. (See address at the end of this volume.)
[4] See vol. I, p. 299.

supposed to explain the deep bond between Amharas peasants and their highland plateaus.

"God made the first man out of clay. He put his first sketch into the fire, but not long enough: the man was white. God hurled him far into the north, and these were Europeans. On the second try, he left the figurine too long in the flames so that it became black. He hurled it to the south. The third attempt was just right. Satisfied with the baking and with his handiwork, God settled it on the land of the Amharas..."

In paradise, in short. Land bond or bank bondage? And to conclude his parable, our man asked a question to which he seemed already to know the answer: "Of all the peoples you have encountered in Africa, which is the most beautiful?"

"We encountered them very far south," replies Sonia. "They were short, pitch black, with flat noses and hearts of gold."

He has understood the message, *cheggir yellem*, rises and disappears, with his square-toed dress shoes and his super-salesman mouth. Tekleye dies laughing. We have an extraordinary complicity with him. He is up to everything. But he cannot all the same follow us everywhere...

"*Shent bet yet no?*" (Where are the toilets?)

The owner indicates I should go around. The head is foul. And full. Two fat beams thrown over a vague pit approximately hidden by a palisade of bent branches patched with pieces of torn metal sheet. *Cheggir yellem!* I am worked up by these inconvenient conveniences and concentrated on not sliding into the pit while a dozen adolescents amuse themselves throwing dried cowpies at me. There is no door, obviously. I'm not dreaming: I am getting sniped at with cowpies....I don't flinch. *Cheggir yellem!* It's one of two things: either they have followed me to trap me, or they spotted my white ass through the motheaten partitions. A Great Moment of Solitude in cinemascope! To each his humor! Their butts must still remember mine....*Cheggir yellem.*

Along the way, Tekleye manifests extraordinary energy. He

walks ahead when we enter a village, runs shouting in all directions and heaps insults on the insolent, hands out many blows with a stick to the brats that talk back to him; serves as rear guard when we leave villages, repelling any possible rowdy followers and stone-throwers. He can't get over the kids' brazenness. When the "*birr-birrs*" fly by the roadside, he teaches us new replies in Amarhic...

"*Faranj! Money-money-money!*"

"*Abatten teyek!*" (Go ask your father!)

Or again: "*Abatten Aydelahoum!*" (I am not your father!)

...Which provokes gales of laughter from the supefied bambinos. Another piece of advice: don't ever go to Ethiopia without "*Abatten teyek!*" and "*cheggir yellem!*" Tekleye walks without weakening all day on big blisters. Sonia, who is past doctor in blisters, tried to treat him with Compeed, but the dust makes the bandage come off. He doesn't flinch, continues to walk as if there were nothing wrong. Damned tough. *Cheggir yellem*. I ask him the secret of Ethiopians' stamina.

"It's simple, we spend our youth and sometimes our lives running after donkeys..."

It's our turn to laugh. It's true that we walk all day long with hundreds of saddled asses, overloaded with wood, hay or bags of combustible cowpies. They travel in twos one behind the other, and it is very difficult to pass them. When it is done, the leader invariably makes them pass you again, on the trot, running behind them, surely stung by the affront or piqued by curiosity, and you wear yourself out passing them again when they end up slowing down. This back-and-forth movement keeps us busy all day, gives us targets; we have the feeling of having covered a lot of ground when we have got rid of a herd. Many women, also, tread on the roads, bent under tremendous bundles of sticks, the strap encrusted in their forehead, or else buried under impressive stacks of enjera baskets on their heads, the large earthen disk of the enjera skillet slipped into a piece of linen carried on their back, and a baby swaddled in a stomach pouch – when they are not holding yet another by the hand. They wear a pleated dress in heavy green canvas, belted at the waist and always covered with their chama. Their hairdo is extraordinary. On the scalp, furrows separate the braided hair which is pulled together behind the neck and splayed in a thick corolla all around the neck, which gives them a strangely pharaonic look.

One morning, in an agricultural zone, while we are watching the operation of two plowmen who bark behind their oxen, waving the whip above their backs like a ventilator, a strange buzzing sound rises in the cool air: "Listen, Sonia! It sounds like a tractor....Now that's amazing! Our first Ethiopian tractor....That means they also plow with a machine!"

There it is coming into the road and passing us. It is towing a large trailer full of farmworkers equipped with...spades....Sonia makes fun of my vexation.

"No, no! It's hand workers transportation!"

The thirty guys are going to line up in the immense neighboring field. *Cheggir yellem.* Plowing with a plow might mean depriving them of their enjera. This surreal vision says a lot about peasants' distress. As the days go by, this activity on the road becomes another form of routine, between tension and admiration, exasperation and contemplation. To hike in Ethiopia is infuriating and astonishing a hundred times a day.

Our problems culminate in Adet, in a *bunna bet*[5], with a twenty-something young man who three times, with a provocative arrogance, tells us that *faranj* stink....No possible ambiguity, given the laughter he touches off by pinching his nose after pointing at us. We can feel our anger rising. According to the principle that the first time you let it go, the second time you tire of it and the third time you do something about it, he doesn't have time to say it a fourth time: Sonia bounds over to administer to him the correction he has doubtless never received from his father. And which I add to

---

5   Coffeehouse and greasy spoon.

when he is about to lay a hand on her as he may be used to doing with the women around him. *Cheggir yellem*. Provocateur in a group but not awfully courageous all alone, he rallies the troops. They all lay hold of bottles and chairs. Making a show of our tear gas calms the game down. Some pure anti–Africa Trek. We are touching bottom. It's really time for an end to this. To the police who burst into the room, our imbecile defends himself by saying that he doesn't like to eat his enjera in front of *"asama faranj,"* white pigs. Hey! We hadn't heard that one yet….We are really not walking for that. But okay, the policeman comes back to us with a smile: *cheggir yellem*…

The landscape of the high plateaus repeats itself: a lovely rich and fertile countryside that would make more than one African region green with envy. What a paradox! Such a poor country. Sometimes, it looks a lot like the Beauce or a Normandy grove or still yet small Tuscan valleys…and always these plowmen by the hundred leading their oxen and rudimentary plows like the ones in ancient Egypt, these ramparts of trees and eucalyptus tufts, these thousands of cattle in thalweg pastures, below the plowed fields. A land of milk and honey, an evocation of the Middle Ages, as much spiritual as material, as moral as behavioral.

I reflect out loud: "It's true that the backroads of Normandy groves in the Middle Ages must have been less secure, dotted with pitfalls and cutthroats, horrible children taunting the good-for-nothings and passing strangers…"

Ethiopia is really a world outside time. It has great charm from an automobile. It has a very high price on foot, when you walk in order to encounter populations which are not interested.

After five hundred kilometers of exertion that gives me tendinitis in the knee, we finally reach Bahar Dar and offer our friend Tekleye the last stretch of his bus ticket. In the effervescence of the bus station Sonia finds a little embroidered dress for his little girl so he won't come home from Gondar empty-handed. We split after a long fraternal embrace.

CHAPTER 23

Reconciliation with Ethiopia

ETHIOPIA

A t Bahar Dar, on the shores of Lake Tana, we indulge ourselves with a week to recover from my double knee tendinitis. I contracted it because of a rotational wearing of my shoes (towards the inside of the heel), a wear caused by walking exclusively on trails. Indeed, on unstable terrain, the ankle invariably twists toward the inside and the toes are raised toward the exterior by the concave form of trails left by livestock. As a result there is a type of wear on the shoe that strains the anterior cruciate ligaments of the knee. To re-establish a stable position, I had cut some rubber from the external side of the mid-sole, but whatever I tried, the only real therapy for a tendinitis is complete immobility and a high-dosage Voltaren treatment.

Our host, Franck Beernaert, a Belgian representative for Europe in the region, tells us his stories of the field. An agricultural engineer, he is responsible for putting in place programs of sustainable development. He has worked in Inner Mongolia, in Zaire, in Mozambique, in Burma….Each a picnic! He has therefore developed an amazing pragmatism. He vituperates against the Brussels technocrats who ask him *ad nauseam* for graphs, figures, reports, when he is trying to get ten olive trees to survive in a remote village.

"Last year, I had some money left to spend, so I had constructed, in four months, fifty kilometers of road by four thousand peasant volunteers with their bare hands to open up an isolated village. Well, you know, I had to fight for four more months for them to be paid 1.20 euros a day instead of the 75 centimes required by the government, and the 1.52 euros per day initially planned in the European budget..."

Always this principle according to which there must not be imbalances or inequalities created among workers in a given country, which leads local administrations to request that people in their district be paid less than planned...[1]

"Today, six months later, the workers still have not been paid, European money still being blocked in the account of the Amhara government of Bahar Dar. African syndrome. It may be that the regime is displeased to see the differential manna of construction contracts get away from it; since normal contracts are made with the Chinese and financed by these same European funds, the government doesn't get its cut this time. Might it also be that it is annoyed when we do its work in its stead?

"The government doesn't do anything out this way anyway. All its energy is concentrated in the south, to compensate for the injustices of a time when the Amhara region was more favored. The disastrous and criminal Italian adventure had left the country with an amazing highway network, with 3300 kilometers and 8354 bridges and viaducts constructed in two years by sixty thousand workers, but since, few new roads have been opened. The country remains utterly closed in, with remote and isolated regions, like the Himalayas. The Russians and Cubans, under the Derg, never succeeded in inculcating a real policy of large work projects." Franck, cranked up now, gets up and goes to get us three golden,

---

[1] See vol. I, p. 344.

cold Grimbergens from the refrigerator. Pschiit! Pschiit! Pschiit! My, does that do one good! Franck returns to his analysis.

"The real problem," he tells us, "is that the peasants don't own the land and that the two agrarian reforms have reduced the arable surface area to one hectare per family, a hectare that will have to be shared by the eight to ten children....The other problem is that *tef*, the cereal used for enjera, the basic diet of Ethiopians, is a sumptuary luxury: it's a primitive cereal that dates from the neolithic, from which the yields do not surpass two hundred kilos per hectare – whereas wheat produces a ton per hectare, corn three tons, and triticale, a new cereal, as much as eight tons."

According to Franck, the Ethiopians are starving themselves because of their obsession to eat nothing but enjera. Their diet is not compatible with their demographic growth. Tef is a variety of graminaceae scarcely taller than grass and its grains are lilliputian, even tinier than poppy seeds. But it's difficult to change a country's alimentary customs...

Franck continues: "There is something we are not taking into consideration: there are sixty-eight million Ethiopians living as in the Middle Ages. Now at that time, only one country was that numerous: China....But on a much vaster territory. Here, the pressure on the environment is extreme. Besides, above all, they are impoverishing the soil, taking out all its organic matter, putting nothing back. Cow dung is used as construction material and as fuel, hay and straw are used for fodder..."

"Isn't there a way to use fertilizer?"

"It serves no purpose because of what is called the 'plow layer.' It is a layer of soil compacted by the repeated passage of plowing oxen for centuries and which is found at thirty centimeters below the surface. It is impermeable and prevents nutriments from rising and the land from breathing. That means that this land that they are exhausting by scraping with their plows is dead land, sterile and unproductive."

"So what is to be done? It would take a plow and a tractor powerful enough to break up that compacted layer..."

"Can't be done, because of the stones. The Ethiopians willingly leave stones in their fields: that breaks plows but holds the soil, and especially the humidity. However, there is nevertheless a solution. In Debre Tabor, to the east of the lake, a South African who works for the Germans of GTZ[2] has perfected a longer, thinner and very hard knife for their plows that succeeds in breaking through the plowing level; the results are fantastic. It's as if the ground exploded and threw out an energy contained for centuries! Without the slightest addition of fertilizer, production was multiplied threefold....There are two of them who employ thirty Ethiopians. They have introduced two hundred vegetal species, strawberries, beans, cabbages, to broaden the alimentary habits of the region and supply Bahar Dar in fresh produce. They have the only irrigation system that is functioning in this area. That's what's called efficiency!"

He breathes in, takes a long swallow of beer and continues: "Oh, yes! It's like with water! People always think Ethiopia is a desert country, but it rains as much here as in many parts of France, much more than in South Africa in any case, but the problem is that the rains are concentrated in the four summer months. To fix that, you would just need to create some water reservoirs, some small village dams. You know, the Ethiopian plateau was an immense, wet forest – the Portuguese explorers who went to the court at Gondar spoke of impenetrable jungles riddled with brigands, of real foliage tunnels that hid the sunlight from them for days. It is that forest that made the earth of the high plateaus. Today, it has entirely disappeared. The trees you see in the country are reforestation eucalyptus that were introduced by Englishmen from Australia at the end of the nineteenth century, soon after the opening of the Suez Canal. The Ethiopians moreover baptized it *baharzaf*, which means

---

[2] Gesellschaft für Technische Zusammenarbeit, a German governmental organization for cooperation and development.

'tree of the sea.'…As for the soil, it rests on a hard volcanic base, between three and ten meters down, which retains water. If you just dig wells, water is at hand. But wells do not exist in Ethiopian culture, they prefer to send their daughters some distance away to get spring water. There are two hundred thousand wells to be dug in this country, and ten million dry toilets to be installed…"

That part is indeed true! Haven't seen any wells in this country. No more than cesspools. Why this reticence to dig in the ground? On the other hand, we have often walked for kilometers with cohorts of girls whose shoulders were cut by the straps of the heavy jars of water that they wedge into the small of their back. Franck dissipates our recollections by bringing up possible solutions.

"The totality of usable Ethiopian space being cultivated, there is no hope of finding new wealth. There are three things to do: first, privatize the land; second, create small industry with foreign investors to create jobs and thus draw to the cities the excess population that is strangling the countryside; and finally, third, develop draconian birth control. The land thus freed from its demographic pressure can be little by little mechanized. Unfortunately, none of these reforms is on the agenda. The government has maintained old communist reflexes, a Kafkaesque administration incapable of making the slightest decision and little disposed to give up the juicy revenue it gets from land leased to the destitute. The popes, for their part, don't want to lose their influence over the populations: all birth control is banned, they fear more than anything a demographic shift in favor of the Muslims of the east. To illustrate the state of mind of politics, here in Bahar Dar, the government has a bureau called the DPPC. You know what that means? Disaster Preparedness and Prevention Committee and in the NGO milieu it is called the Dependency Prolongation and Poverty Continuation or yet again the Disaster Preparation and Proposal Commission! This year, they invented a false famine. They announced two hundred thousand people affected in Ogaden and seventy thousand deaths on the horizon, the livestock wiped out. Fortunately we sent someone to see! There hadn't been so much rain in ten years. The grass was a meter high and the cows well fed. Pure bullshit, but this time we didn't fall into the trap! The problem is that by playing that game, when there will be a real famine, we'll always suspect them to have provoked it for some obscure political reasons, and we'll be slower to react."

After a few swallows of beer, he breathes again and continues.

"There is a competition among donor countries. The government pushes up the bidding. It's a battle to find out which will give the most, USAID, Europe, GTZ, the British Council, the Swedes, the Danes, the Japanese, the French, even the Israelis....When we balk at giving, they displace a population – the one that bothers them, of course – into a hot, dry spot where it will provoke a little humanitarian catastrophe that will prime the money pump once more....The American genetically engineeered wheat and corn, which nobody wants in Europe, comes here without restriction, brought by government trucks, which are paid to transport it. Consequently, they view askance the agricultural achievements of GTZ in Debre Tabor – they earn nothing from it....With such fallout, we are not out of the woods yet, I'm telling you! And I am constantly being visited by auditors and specialists from Brussels who write reports that nobody will read....Some of them call on me to organize the inspection of two of my projects in two days, as comfortably as possible....I answer these 'tourist consultants': 'Either you rent a helicopter, or you go to Disneyland. I for my part have work to do!' By car, it takes a day and a half of pitted roads to get to my first *wereda*[3]....In the reports they ask from me, sometimes I write in the middle of the text 'The laughing cow,' and a page further on, 'Have you seen the laughing cow?' I never received the slightest remark ..."

We have laughed enough. What therapy! Too bad there are only four technicians like him in the field, spread over the four

---

[3] District.

corners of the country – compared to thirty European functionaries in Addis.

Franck ends his speech with a wisecrack: "Would an inversion be more efficient for spending our European taxes? Thirty men in the field and four collaborators around the ambassador. That's an idea to submit in high places for saving money. With no chance!"

On my birthday, the third on African land, I receive the gift of Henriette Palavioux's arrival. She's marketing director at Terres d'Aventures, a French adventure tour operator, whom we had met at Lake Bogoria in Kenya. She had said: "One day I shall come walk with you..." And there she is, radiant and clever, maternal and fraternal at once, as if we had always known her. We had seen her only for half a day, but it had been love at first sight.

So we leave with her to skirt round Lake Tana on its west shore through isolated regions, with no roads and no visitors. We are apprehensive about our return to the countryside since we are no longer protected by Tekleye....However, from the first day, things go better: no more interminable swarms of unbearable urchins, no more unending conflicts; the fields are plowed, the countryside is empty, the men hole up in their *toukouls* as soon as the temperature starts rising. We do not set off mobs in the rare villages we pass through without incident, aggression, or automatic begging: Whites have never come here with their bad conscience, their complexes and bad reflexes, that can be seen right away: we are asked neither for money, nor T-shirts, nor pens....What bliss! There is only sympathetic and excited curiosity which our more and more able Amharic allows us to satisfy.

For the first time in Ethiopia, we manage to set up the tent without having to hide. We are in Chimba, below the sources of the Blue Nile, above Lake Tana. A red flower under a fig tree charms us, that is where we pitch our shelter, at the edge of those mythical waters that like us will travel as far as Cairo. I heat our noodle soup with Nile water on a little fire while on the other bank echo the cries and songs of a lively evening. We bless this calm of ours and go to sleep head to toe, with three of us in our minitent for two. The last guest to share our tent, before Amaretch, had been Helen Campbell, in Zimbabwe – same age as Henriette, same great form, same joy: real hardy women!

At noon, we are welcomed in superb traditional interiors, their furniture consisting of granaries, shelves, niches molded into the mud walls in round volumes, organic, tremendously feminine. In the door frame dozens of gazes check in, attentive to our every reaction, attuned to our every desire. Finally we encounter that famous tradition of Christian hospitality! And we can watch the making of the *enjera* crepes. The mistress of the house first heats on the fire a large, glazed terra cotta disk about eighty centimeters in diameter. With a scraped-out gourd, she then dips the batter from a jar where it has been fermenting for a minimum of three days. With a magnificent spiral motion starting with the center of the terra cotta disk, she pours a ribbon of batter that sizzles in contact with the hot surface, bursting thousands of microbubbles that make so many holes that run through the crepe. She smooths the crepe with the palm of her hand, and soon a large, flexible and homogenous cake goes to join the top of the pile she makes in a red basket, finely decorated, covered with a cone of the same kind. Over another fire she heats the *chourro*, the puree of chickpeas or split peas. During this time, a girl grinds peppers, herbs and a garlic clove in a stone mortar to prepare the *berbera*. The enjera is never solitary, it is shared in family around a platter of enameled iron. You are to tear off a bit of crepe and use it as a spoon to collect some of the puree garnish.

Mahadou, our host today, takes the first piece of the crepe and hands me the first bite as a mother would give a beakful to her baby.

"*Gursha!*"

Gursha is the way of honoring a guest, of showing one's respect. I open my mouth and swallow the whole mouthful at once, taking care not to bite his fingers. Sonia laughs it up when she sees me turn red to the ears. Mahadou went a little heavy on the berbera…

Chicks run in all directions in the house, where they can in complete safety pilfer grains and fleas. The latter are having a ball. We see them jumping all over. Their bites and our oaths trigger tornadoes of laughter.

"*Kebet kounitcha. Akeberot yellem!*" (The ornery fleas! Really they have no respect!)

The witnesses in the door frame repeat the comical formula to themselves while the chicks go after the parasites, leaping shamelessly onto our knees and as they go by grabbing crumbs of enjera. The women all wear around their necks one or two large silver crosses carved in Maria-Theresa thalers, an Austrian coin of the eighteenth and nineteenth centuries which then was used in the Horn of Africa, and reconverted today into religious jewels. Closer up, you can recognize the empress's arched nose on the branches of the cross, and on the reverse side the two-headed eagle. It gave later its name to a coin boasting a single-headed eagle and promised to a long posterity: the dollar. Women wear blue crosses tattooed on their foreheads, the cross potent or Jerusalem cross. Henriette is under the charm of human relations which she has difficulty finding on organized trips. No Westerner ever comes through here. The latter fact perhaps explains the former. The relations are not distorted or corrupt. Day after day, we become reconciled with Ethiopia and finally can say at every opportunity a sentence Tekleye taught us but which we had not been able to make our first use of in his company: "*Amésséguénallo sélé mesten guédo!*" (Thank you for your hospitality!)

In the daytime, we are sometimes accompanied while we walk, and it all goes very well. Once, it is with two girls, Emayou and Zinash, twelve and seventeen respectively. They are coming home from the Bahar Dar market, three days from here. One has a baby and is pregnant, the other has five. They have never been to school. They had never seen Westerners up close before us. They walk barefoot with a lively step, and emanate amazing strength and cheer. They are women. Women children. And we think again of

Dr. Hamlin,[4] of Franck Beernaert's analyses, of our twelve-year-old nieces....Giving life before one has lived. They are stupefied when we tell them that we have no children, that I was able to marry Sonia without paying a dowry....At thirty-one and thirty-three, we ought to be grandparents...

Everywhere we ask our way: *"Akwarat menged allé?"* (Is there a shortcut?)

We are shown shortcuts, the countryside echoes with *"enider!"* (welcome)! We are relieved not to have to impose that calvary on Henriette who hallucinates at the telling of our past misadventures. And yet the equilibrium is fragile. It takes little to go from tacit benevolence to explicit hostility. We must precipitously leave certain villages where we sense that the tension and excitement is rising. We want to be pretexts for fraternizing, not pretexts for venting rage. We are more and more in control of the workings of this psychological mechanism which tried our trek for nearly three months. Henriette is fascinated by this sixth sense that we have developed.

"You have become walking animals, my pets; you have an extra-sensory intuition. Normally, I am the one who guides people, and here I feel completely at sea. I don't capture anything."

One evening, by candlelight, our hostess, Fanta Degou, repeats the gesture of Ersumo Kabamo. She takes off our shoes and gently washes our sore feet before adding to the evangelical ritual an energetic massage that makes us cry out with suffering and pleasure. Henrietta exclaims: "It's the climax of a sensual experience. But the best part is really the little kiss on the big toe!"

Faith in action. Every walker is a pilgrim, *a fortiori* if he is heading to Jerusalem. In my travel notebook I have a photo of the Sea of Galilee, our destination, which I show to our hosts. It looks like the landscapes of Lake Tana. They know the story about Jesus calming the storm and walking on water. Laugh it up, give us to

---

[4] Founder of the Fistula Hospital of Addis Ababa.

understand that we must try to do the same, then take it back, vaguely ashamed of their little sacrilegious witticism. Here, you don't joke with the Holy Scriptures.

Next comes the *bunna* service, the traditional coffee, home-roasted. One of the finest domestic shows in the world. Fanta takes a slightly concave disk of sheet metal like what is used for panning gold, which she places on a terra cotta *goulditcha*, a sort of little brazier on three feet, which she has already filled with large embers. She pours water on the metal and wipes it with her palm to remove any trace of oxidation. Then she takes a good fistful of green coffee beans from a leather bag and pours them on the metal disk which pounds with joy, then she adds water. She rinses and washes the beans in warm water, rubbing them between her hands as if she were lathering up, then gets rid of the used water. She repeats the operation three times before placing the disk on the goulditcha. Then she lets the beans roast gently on the metal, stirring them with a metal bolt. As they heat, the beans release an aromatic oil that lubricates the disk and creates a heady smoke that soon fills the toukoul with its fragrance. It's a wonderful smell of coffee. The roasting must be uniform, above all the beans must not be burned, which would make the coffee bitter. So Fanta stirs constantly and the beans sing in a squeak on the metal. This lasts a good ten minutes. When it is done, she passes the hot disk under our noses. With the right hand, you are supposed to bring some of the smoke toward your face to appreciate the quality of the roast, in other words salivate a little and manifest your contentment. Her daughter presents us with a little *kolo* plate of roasted wheat grains which you munch on to pass the time. Fanta then pours the coffee beans into a wooden mortar and pounds them with a heavy metal bar. The sound of the mortar is muted by the toukoul's mud floor, which, becoming resonant like a drum, responds to the sharper note of the pestle against the wooden sides. Sweet music combined with the aromas of coffee and incense that make this ceremony into an occasion. You also hear the beans in the bottom of the mortar yielding with a promising crunch. During this operation, the girl of the house places fresh grass on the ground and small embers in a tiny censer. Then from her pocket she takes some drops of crystallized sap extracted by bleeding incense trees in the area. A thick white plume immediately emanates from it, conferring on the ceremony a pinch of religiosity. The coffee powder has been poured into a black earthen vial with a handle, a round bottom, a fine neck, and which is filled with water before setting it on the goulditcha. The pouring lip is fitted with a plug of a special dry grass that will serve as a filter – maybe that is the secret of the aroma of Ethiopian coffee? In the meantime, Fanta's daughter has placed on the fresh grass a rectangular footed platter on which are aligned little Chinese porcelain cups in the shape of a flared corolla. When the neck of the vial steams, Fanta takes it off the fire, pours into the little cups a little dense, black liquid, interrupting each jet with a brief movement of the wrist so not a drop will be lost. She finally declares solemnly: *"Andenya!"*

This is the first juice. The strongest and densest, which you sip slowly to take in all the power, all the edginess of this traditional coffee. A festival of aromas juggles in our heads, cinnamon, cardamom, clove: we have just absorbed a few drops of Oriental quintessence. A synesthetic explosion that juxtaposes souks and deserts, caravans and coffee tree forests, indigo skies and red soil, memories and anticipations, distant horizons and mud floors, this very real earth on which we are squatting, in the toukoul of Fanta Degu, contented and reassured, drunk with humanity and Ethiopia. It is here that coffee was invented, here that it is the most powerful. Espressos may jeer with jealousy, here you take your time. Next come the *hulettenya* and the *sostenya*, the second and third juice of the same coffee that prolong the pleasure while refining it, taming the full-bodied aromas to reveal more subtle ones yet, mentholated and peppered. Coffee has three dimensions. The fourth being time and the tradition shared in respect and meditation. To travel is to be in perpetual quest of these seconds of fourth dimension. To give sense to one's life and life to one's senses.

In this dry season, the level of Lake Tana is very low. Wide beaches of dried silt are exposed, and we tread on the cracks in it all day among a multitude of limicoline birds, Egyptian geese, unknown ducks, wading birds and splendid crowned cranes that take off by the hundreds as we approach them. We see child fishermen, stark naked, fiddling with their catfish of the day, a few hippopotamus prints, we are drunk with wind, freedom and space. Sometimes, in the evening, we pitch the tent in the electronic babble of weaver-birds suspended in their nests, and go to sleep lulled by the lapping of the lake under the protection of a giant fig tree. Kunzila, Isey Debir, Bahita, Delgi, poor burgs follow on each other, in a place that could be a produce paradise exporting to all of Africa...but that is another story...which remains to be written.

Always fields as far as you can see, punctuated by the green domes of fig trees. Vast pasture lands host cattle by the thousands, but there is still no way to put your hand on a bloody piece of meat: a constantly renewed African enigma. With seventy million head of livestock, Ethiopia has the largest herd in Africa. It must be said that we are still in a season of fast, the *tsom*. Ethiopians are maniacs for fasting: fifty days before Easter, forty days before Christmas, twelve days before Timkat, ten days before Meskal, the feast of the Cross, no meat, eggs, or milk products on Wednesday and Friday. In the rare greasy spoons where one could eat *tebs*, pieces of grilled kebab, we are always there the wrong day.

In any case, poor Henriette doesn't want anything, she is eaten by fleas, she had been emptying her guts for the last two hours and is walking by radar. Despite her lack of energy and the harassing of children, she keeps up her spirits: "My pets, no one will be able to imagine what you have experienced. After five days, I'm throwing in the towel and I promise you I'm tough. What you are doing is much too hard, you are completely crazy and you think that's normal! There was only one man who impressed me before you, and that was my pal Theodore Monod[5]..."

"But in his case it was for wisdom! Not for madness!"

After Delgi, we leave the lake and the waters of the Nile which we will rejoin in five hundred kilometers, at Wad Medani, in the Sudan. *Insha'Allah!* At Aykel, we come to the Yaho Maryam church, on the side of this road that descends, on the left, from the Ethiopian plateau to the Sahara. We make a side-trip to the right, to Gondar, whence Henriette, after five hundred kilometers in our company, is going to fly to Lalibela. Thank you Henriette for these shared sensations.

Gondar, Thursday 9 May 2003, day 861, 9747th km

In a restaurant of the imperial city where we had had lunch four months ago with my parents during our tourist jaunt in the historical north of the country, we hear about an English woman who, three years earlier, came from Addis on foot by way of Lalibela, accompanied by a donkey. She still lives here.

We meet her. Kate Fereday (Eshete) came to Ethiopia nine years ago after seeing, at the end of a television newscast, a short piece on the distress of street children.

"I sold everything, house and car, left my position as division chief in an electronics company in Plymouth, in England, to come work in humanitarian organizations based in Addis and in which I rapidly realized that the money I was collecting in charity sales was spent on wages, on administration and on 4x4's which were useless in the streets of the capital."

"And how did you come to Gondar?"

"First as a tourist! I had met Kindu, a little street orphan, covered with lice and starving, who decided my radical change of life.

---

[5] French naturalist, explorer, and humanist scholar, devoted to the Sahara (1902–2000).

I left Addis and founded Kindu Erdata, an association for rehabilitation of street children. *Erdata* means 'help' in Amharic. After a
while, I had opened seven hostels for eighty orphans in several of
the country's large cities, but I very soon abandoned this kind of
action which is not adapted to the children's real needs. Today, I
have changed focus to 'financial support at home' for almost two
hundred former street children, reinserted, thanks to godparents,
in their families of origin which didn't have the means of feeding
them."

"How does that work?"

"With twenty euros a month, given to the mother or the aunt
or the grandmother if the first has died, the whole family benefits
from an improvement in the living conditions. Most often, these
families have no fathers."

Kate has thus gone from hostels to reintegration into family units
because she realized the savings she could achieve in rent, cooks'
wages and operating costs. She calls this "family reunification."

"Thus, for the annual operating costs of a hostel for ten children, I realized I could now 'reunify' fifty children separated from
their families, and thus be even more effective! Moreover, these
children grow up in their own world and not in an artificial family
unit, in a group of desocialized children where violence and injus-
tice are reconstituted."

"How do you go about meeting these families?"

"First of all, we meet the children and interview them. We try
to find out where they come from, whether they have relatives, why
they are in the street. The reasons vary: they might have fled on
their free will because their father beat them, been sent to 'work' in
the city, been driven out for some misdeed, lost their family during
a population displacement....As part of that interview, we visit the
families and propose the 'family reunification' project to them. No
one ever refuses."

"And how do you manage to control whether the money you
give is used wisely by the mothers?"

We make monthly visits and a systematic control of the money spent by the mothers, or 'tutoresses,' which allow us to verify that this money has genuinely been used for food, clothing or tuition. It is evident that this manna benefits the brothers and sisters who are also in precarious situations – especially the little boys, less subject to home tasks than the girls, and who are consequently sent to try their luck in the streets. Another clue: I never give the money to the fathers..." Kate no longer believes in large orphanages; they have too many operating expenses and institutionalize poverty, whereas the families cast out their excess children most of the time for economic reasons that can easily be addressed.

"By doing here what in our countries is done by welfare and social protection, we break in the simplest way the vicious circle of poverty, misery and street children. It's a little like a family allocation system..."

Indeed, who can better raise a child than a mother, once she is given the means? But Kate has other resources. Radiant, with a part running through her hair which is pulled back into two pigtails, like Laura Ingalls in *The Little House on the Prairie*, with the same flowery dresses and the same freckles framing eyes full of kindness, she organizes hygiene workshops for mothers, information workshops on AIDS, visits to historical sites designed to make her protégés discover their country's culture; thus the children of Gondar go to Lalibela and vice versa; she has them perform plays, learn to ride on old mistreated nags which she recuperates and takes care of in her *Dinkenesh Fund* in memory of her donkey Dinkenesh, with which she crossed the high plateaus and which has since been stolen...

She invites us the next day to a "Gondar clean city" operation. Five weeks ago, she launched, with the city's social services, an operation of enticement and motivation of the street children, proposing that on Saturday morning they clean their city instead of begging, in exchange for which they receive, the first week, a pair of shoes, the second a T-shirt, the third a pair of pants and the fourth a jacket to get ready for the rainy season. The city for its part provides a shower[6] whereas Kindu Erdata covers the copious lunch that follows. At six in the morning, thirty-five street children show up.

"It's also a way for us to meet the newcomers in the city," Kate tells us. "They are constantly arriving from the countryside, sometimes even from great distances."

The joyous company, filthy and covered with mange, supplied with rubber gloves and stimulated by the martial slogans of Ato Mulugeta, a city representative, sets out with shovels and picks to take on the garbage in the neighborhood of the Debre Selassie church, the one that has a ceiling decorated with winged angels. On the way, the residents are open-mouthed: the *enfants terribles* are making themselves useful! Sonia dives in while I film; a child amputee is holding onto the back of his little comrades, another, a polio victim, limps among the piles of garbage wielding a shovel with virtuosity, they all are laughing, amusing themselves, and make a game of the chore. When there is a pause, Sonia picks up a little boy and affectionately caresses his shoulder, he then twists like a cat mewing around her hand. Love. How long ago was the last gesture of tenderness he received? Kate, simple and always radiant as the sun, works here, forages there, scrapes the ground, piles things up, points to a pile of detritus as a hen would for her covey of chicks among dead leaves. And what can we say about the joy inspired by the shoes, eagerly put on, the bliss of merited T-shirts, jackets won, the comforting shower, the restorative meal and the dignity recovered? Kate or the permanent miracle, Kate or our reconciliation with the children of Ethiopia, who have such need of love.

Kate has dozens on her waiting lists, waiting simply the opportunity to return to their families to receive like daily bread their ration of essential love, waiting for a sponsor. Others are HIV-

---

[6] We later learned that Kate even had to pay the city for the showers.

positive and have been rejected everywhere. Except by Kindu Erdata. Kate is an indefatigable worker.

"All sponsors receive twice a year a detailed account, photo included, of their protégé, drawings, school notebooks, and maybe one day, the first letters, the first fruits of recovered humanity, of a repaired childhood, a soul saved."

In two and a half years walking on this continent we have never seen an association so sober and effective, so lively. Small is beautiful! If there were only one to help, that would be the one. For it too is as humble as its founder (who lives in a mud hut without running water), for it is as simple as a reunited family, for it is as true as the happiness we have witnessed in those thirty-five lost children, one morning in the garbage of the Gondar streets. If you think you can help Kindu Erdata, find Kate's address at the end of the book. Twenty euros per month is a little restaurant meal, three movies, a CD....The salvation of an Ethiopian child.

Aykel, western escarpment of the Abyssinian plateau, Wednesday 14 May 2003, day 867, 9747th km

We are back at the Yaho Maryam church, the last in the country, or the first, it depends where you come from, at the very site where we ended our hike with Henriette, on the edge of the escarpment that leads to the Sudan. We are escorted this time by a young Québécois, Stéphane Brisebois, met in the overlanders' guest house in Gondar, the Beleguez boarding house. Walking with someone else apparently works for us. Amaretch, Tekleye, Henriette.... We're keeping the recipe. Stéphane is an atypical character. He is a mulatto, son of a Haitian father and an Algonquin mother. An employee in military robotics, he has perfected, with a heteroclite team of Gyro Gearloose and Wacko Kilowatt kind of guys such as the North American continent readily produces, a small unpiloted spy submarine. But he decided to change tracks.

"That stuff is not my thing! The military is not very amusing! I'm going back to my first love: the piano! In fact, I am a composer.

That's why I took a sabbatical year....To reflect! Meanwhile I would like the idea of walking a while with you!" We begin the vertiginous descent with him, to the west, the sun right in our eyes. In the distance, beyond the clouds inflamed by the white sun, we can imagine the infinite flat expanses, crushed by the sky. We pass a huge military base that defends the access to the country. The western gate of Ethiopia. Coming down from the Ethiopian plateau, we have the feeling of leaving an unassailable citadel raised over Africa, where live, isolated from the world, people entrenched behind their culture, their history and their misfortunes. The violent feeling of turning a page.

Stéphane tells us how he crossed the Sudan from Egypt, the incredible gentleness of the peoples of the Nile, their exceptional hospitality. And the heat, which forced him to hole up from ten in the morning to four in the afternoon. But he was traveling in an air-conditioned bus....Unfortunately, from the first evening, after the first village enjera, our courageous Québécois falls ill and empties his guts. The night doesn't help, which he spends bent double over a basin, at the home of a nice teacher from Walideba. The next day he is green, but valorously determined to try and walk. At the twenty-first kilometer, he is ready to faint. But he hangs on. We put him into a bus headed for the border, telling him to stop in the first village, Nagadibar. We will meet him there, in the evening, in an unnamed dump, livid. Rats are running across the beams above our heads. The heat is bestial. The village is made up of recently displaced populations. A certain tension prevails, hardly amenable to "cultural frenzy." The ballet of mosquitos and fleas resumes. Stéphane is eaten up. In a groan, he finds the means to be humorous.

"It's not glamorous walking with you guys! How many dudes like me have you killed to rip them off? And you've been living like this for two years? You got me! God, it's not possible."

At dawn, he can hardly stand up. We put him in a bus back to

Gondar. He leaves our lives as quickly as he entered, too bad, he was a super chum!

Remote ravine, 12 km after Eshedi, Saturday 17 May 2003, day 870, 37 km, 9864th km

Sonia is sleeping peacefully. A little bitty fire casts a glow on her harassed face and body curled up from fatigue. With the furnace of the day over, I brush my teeth in the moonlight, when on the distant edges of the ravine at the bottom of which we have pitched the tent, I see shadows moving, then stop.

Bandits! Without showing that I have seen them, I go back to the tent and return, in plain sight on a little butte, armed with my flares and my tear gas canister. In the night a cry rings out. Followed by a burst of sharp clacks, all around me, we are surrounded. I realize they have just, on orders, slammed the breech of their Kalash', inserting a bullet into the chamber. No doubt a military patrol. I slowly raise my hands to avoid a mistake and light up my face, shouting: *"Ene tourist! Cheggir yellem!"* (No problem!)

A shout back: *"Hezb sente no?"* (How many of you are there?)

"Hulett hezb becha. Ene ke Balebet." (Only two, me and my wife.)

They are indeed soldiers. From the dark appear some young recruits almost as panicked as I, only a finger away (the trigger one) from taking target practice on a *faranj* in his skivvies! When I return to the tent, Sonia murmurs: "Who was it?"

"Oh, nothing! I nearly got myself gunned down by eight rookies with Kalashnikovs..."

Gallabat, Sunday 18 May 2003, day 871, 26 km, 9890th km, entrance to the Sudan

And this morning, at a few cables' length from Metema, the Sudanese border, we are again in the hands of soldiers in a forward military post. The heat is devastating. We are tense, dripping. They are telling us about massacres perpetrated by bandits from over the border; just last week, two persons were killed on this trail that we are following...whence the night patrols.

Only a baby baboon, the mascot of these bored men, relaxes the atmosphere. He has taken refuge under Sonia's breast. She is very moved. The little guy is fascinated by her braid, snoops in her shirt, starts to open a button – to the great pleasure of the pimply guys in fatigues – rolls up, looks at her with large, desperate eyes. Caresses are all the same better than rangers' blows. Even for fun. We set out into dry, silent bush, deserted and burning.

Zimbabwean reminiscences. The silence is punctuated by the insistent cry of the yellow-billed hornbill that lulled us for thousands of kilometers. The bush is brutally deforested, cleared by slash-and-burn, the atmosphere full of smoke. It is full dry season, before the rains. We already miss the coolness of the Ethiopian high plateaus. We have lead feet. The anguish of the trek is no longer human, it is once more geographic. The road is deserted. Something is missing. We almost come to miss the hundreds of kids springing out of everywhere to pursue us. Everything is silent, dead and dry! The burnt trees extend their twisted arms toward the mercury heaven like ghosts. We walk in silence, frightened and demoralized by the heat and immensity that await us. Nevertheless, Metema arrives from afar. A much awaited event. Much feared. For two and a half years, we have been talking about it like the end of the world. Well here it is, the end of the world! Metema is here. Everything happens. We are incredulous. Deadened by heat and fatigue. Sonia whispers: "The Sea of Galilee will come in the same way. Maybe! Some day..."

This is where in 1997 three South African friends, Bruce Lawson, Carl Langdon and Christopher Joubert, were halted by the blow of a Kalashnikov stock on the back of Bruce's neck – which tore off his ear. It was their third attempt to cross the border post. This time forcibly. They had been rejected twice for no reason, although they were perfectly in order. The arbitrariness of a paranoid post captain who saw them as American spies, despite their

South African passports, had put an end to their long hike. We are frightened. Twice, they were sent back to Addis for additional authorizations and the intervention of higher-ups, but in vain. They had been refused twice by this stupid officer. It caused problems for the post captain, who did not forgive them for it. And the dream stopped there, in blood. Return to Go: Cape Town. God-damned game of the goose. Dismayed, broken, penniless and worn out by their ten thousand kilometers. They are nevertheless, to this day, holders of the world record for an unassisted hike in Africa. A record tryingly deserved. The three of them together had a broken ankle in Zimbabwe, a broken nose in Mozambique, twenty-four malaria bouts, El Niño floods in Tanzania, a full-fledged attack by Somali Shiftas who had emptied a magazine through their tent, in the desert just before Marsabit, in Kenya. They were the ones who warned us of the stones and the dangers of the Ethiopian country-side. I remember saying to myself then that being a couple would protect us, that we would be more in contact with the populations whose language we were learning, that our South African friends must not have been very diplomatic with their gigantic stature and their manner which they themselves described as "No brain, no pain!" In short, that we would be more clever than they...

It is true that, despite all, for now we are managing a bit better. And it is with a thought for them, far away to the south, that we stroll down the main street of Metema looking for a greasy spoon. We see our first white djellabas, which venture, delighted, onto this side of the border in search of a cold beer. First salaams. That relaxes the atmosphere. It is too hot to begin formalities. The Sudanese flag flies over there, on the other side of a little bridge, at Gallabat. First rest up to be in full possession of our faculties. We quickly find ourselves in front of what we hope will be our last enjera, this time – finally! – garnished with *tebs*, and two cold Cokes. Unfortunately, we come up against a band of noisy, mocking, exasperating youths. The last one, we say to ourselves. To the last drop, they will have exhausted us. We rush out of the dump and direct our steps toward Ethiopian immigration. Everything seems to be going well when a meticulous official vainly searches for our entry stamp at Moyale (on the Kenyan border). I have all the trouble in the world explaining to him that we did not go through Moyale and that for that we had a special authorization from the Ministry of Tourism. He asks for it. Oh-oh! We don't have it any more, since our visas were renewed in Addis. The plot thickens. An angel flies by....But the argument is good. We have already passed through the hands of his superiors in Addis for the renewal. So we are clear. In slow motion I see the exit stamp raising, going, going... stop! The owner of our greasy spoon shows up with a waitress to ask for the bill.

"But we already paid you!"

"No!"

"Yes! There were plenty of people around!"

"Nobody saw anything!"

The customs officer turns to us: "Well, you have only to pay!"

"But we're telling you we already paid the thirty birrs!"

The tone is rising. It's a trap. The customs man makes a pout.

"Have to settle that with the police."

Rather die than spend one more hour with them! I throw the thirty birrs of our freedom at the feet of the con man, who runs off like a laughing hyena. The stamp slams, amid derisive chortling. How to leave a country joyfully....We pass the bridge over a dry river bed as if we were getting out of prison, singing! The Sudanese flag flaps above our heads, a storm is brewing. Policemen black as ink in black uniforms, affable and calm, welcome us in English, nicely. They know.

"They tried to scam you?"

"How do you know?"

"Oh, you are not the first. Most foreigners get here very angry!"

We are not angry, we are happy and relieved, we are in the Sudan, in Gallabat, and world record holders! It's dumb, but that helps the pill go down.

SUDAN

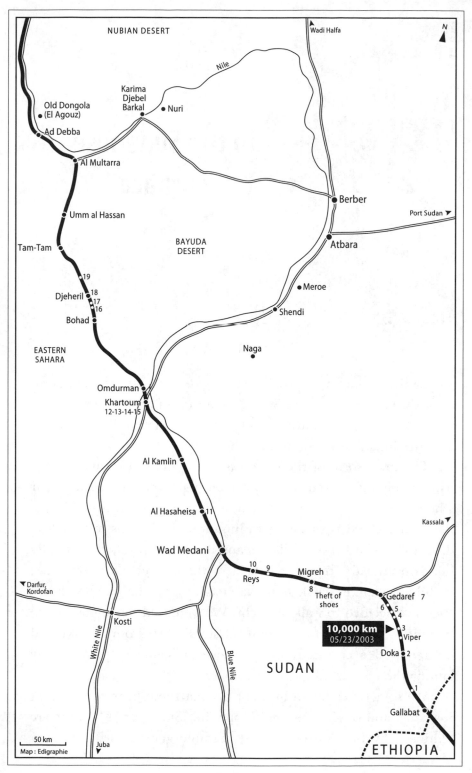

Sudan

CHAPTER 24

In the Sudanese Furnace

SUDAN

At five o'clock we leave Gallabat to enter without delay into the largest country in Africa. A country of wet jungles infested with marshes in the South, and of Saharan dunes in the North. We are entering in between, in the Sahel zone.

The first storm of the season is rolling its black anvil toward us, coming down from the Abyssinian high plateaus. Good augur when you step into the biggest desert of the world, isn't it? The impressive cloud is shaken with luminous explosions followed by drumrolls. The beast swells, moans, flees westward, then finally bursts overhead. Tried by the heat of the last few days, we stand joyfully under the buckets of water falling on the parched bush. We have decided to walk by night. We were told the region would be empty; yet small fires, like dead stars fallen from the sky and scattered all over, betray the presence of men. We pass silently among these horizontal constellations.

We sometimes brush up right against these hearths set up at roadside, and observe incognito our first Sudanese. The huts are reddened by fires surrounded by carmine ghosts. Little children

348

playing around the flames animate large shadows on the background. We pass like phantoms in the night. As always, we are intimidated the first days. It starts to rain again. Our shoes are drenched, our rain capes streaming. Very far away, straight ahead, a white light attracts us. Surely a police station where, we have been told, it will be possible to sleep. It becomes the objective, the bearing, like a star that never comes. The shower has passed spreading a veil of coolness on the sleeping bush. The insects are having a wonderful time. We walk mechanically. The light seems to be farther and farther away as we progress. We spend three hours and fifteen kilometers to unhook this bloody star: a neon light! Between two huts, we cross our first Sudanese doorway. It is ten o'clock.

Two black men wearing large djellabas rise as we enter, and calmly, in perfect English, whisper to us – because of the sleepers: "Welcome! Welcome! You must be tired, it is God who sends you, have a seat, have you eaten?"

An apparition. Not us. Them. Are we dreaming? Do they know us? We are speechless. Why so nice, so simple? It is not the police, but the camp of the managerial staff of Higleig, a company of public works whose task is to widen the road. Everything is clean, well organized. Moussa Ismael and Mohammed Tahir welcome us with no questions or suspicion. Immediately understand our project. Find it exciting. The nomad blood is never completely silent in their culture. They are themselves far from home. We float in the daze of our fatigue and this mental deliverance. In a restrained and calm conversation, they explain the reason for this operation and the trade agreement signed between Ethiopia and the Sudan: "In exchange for this remaking of the road that will facilitate the exportation of Ethiopian products, since they have to go around Eritrea which is closed to them, the Ethiopians have agreed to buy our oil."

We are being spoiled. Ice water, brochettes, rice and vegetables. The cook was awakened for us. We express our embarrassment to him. He gives us a big smile: "It's my duty!" We talk about Ethiopia, Kenya, Tanzania, Malawi, Zimbabwe. They listen to us calmly, no inquisition, no mockery, sensitively; for us the feeling is surreal. We share points of view with good understanding. We remake acquaintance with intellectual pleasure, with dialogue. Finally, in a little isolated corner of the camp, our hosts put up beds for us, with foam mattresses and clean sheets, after showing us the path to the toilets and bringing us a basin of warm water to wash with. We are stunned. Post Traumatic Syndrome. We had to leave Ethiopia to realize how much it had forced us to armor ourselves and how heavy this rejection-proof vest was. We are like two flagellants exclaiming: "Oh, how lovely!" once the whip is laid down.

Everything, around here, is placed under the sign of politeness and benevolence. The following days do not belie this first impression. If we had to contract it to a single word, which is a perilous thing to do, we would say that the Sudanese are wise. And you bet, that is not at all what we expected.

But if our relationship with the populations restores the spirit of our trek, the heat is more overwhelming than ever. The thermometer climbs every day to fifty degrees in the shade and the road is mortally boring, without trees or villages, straight as on a bleak, infinite steppe, which desperately awaits rain – we were told that in September green fields undulate here forever like the Beauce in the spring. We are four months too early. For us, the heat is such that at ten o'clock we must absolutely find shade. No shacks on the horizon. Most of the time, the head molten, on the verge of having our hoses blow, we hurriedly slip under the road into drainage pipes to wait like sick dogs, sticky and panting, for seven hours until the furnace passes.

Heat and light. Outside, everything shimmers and cooks in the sunlight. Everything is dead. We have been in one of those pipes for an hour. We stick to our camp mattresses, drink gulps of hot plastic water while reading to each other passages of Saint

Augustine's *Confessions* and Henry de Monfreid's *Adventures of a Red Sea Smuggler*. Two books that were given to us in Bahar Dar by a group of French tourists. The one repudiates his life of debauchery and the errors of his youth, the other vaunts the merits of his life of adventure, deals and freedom. One formulated surprisingly modern thoughts seventeen centuries ago; the other related ancestral stories fifty years ago. Nothing's new under the sun. Man gesticulates and time passes. Between the two books, between Augustine and Henry, an incredible dialogue is established, under the roadways of bridges, in pipes, in the Sudanese furnace.

A forge wind dives into our tube and dries us like two old pieces of beef jerky. Sonia is crimson. She looks desperately for coolness, fans herself with the aluminum cover of our mess kit. Ingenious, she finds something even better. With the help of a burning gust producing a venturi effect in the tube, she fills her skirt like a parachute.

"Look, Alex, I'm going to take off!"

"Sure! Well, be careful not to turn on your afterburner!"

She screams with laughter, her skirt suddenly folded down on her head. Wait. Wait. Wait. But waiting with her is not a problem. Every second is a second of laughter and happiness. Even here. And it has nothing to do with me. And there she is, exhausted, parched....What will we do in the Sahara, when there are no pipes? No shade? We will keel over. And she will find a way to laugh, to be happy, because we will be together....Marvel of a woman.

Hunger checks in. We still have to wait. Eat as late as possible to set out again kind of replenished around four or five. Today we open with emotion and delectation the first can given us by Henriette Palavioux in Gondar.

"It's a little hot. Give me your bread so I can pour the oil on it, on top of your Moroccan Vache-qui-rit!"

"'Yvon Ragobert.'...Doesn't sound French? Terrine of boar with green pepper....But really it's pig! It's contraband merchandise here! MMhhh! Delicious little taste of *haram*[1]..."

---

[1] Literally, "forbidden" or "sin." The opposite of *halal*.

Sonia now takes from her backpack two beautiful red delicious apples bought like caviar in Gallabat. They come from Washington state.

"The two apples have come a long way to meet us!"

She marvels, with an untranscribable accompaniment of gesture and onomatopoeia: "Can you imagine the path they have followed to reach us here? From an orchard in Washington they traveled by truck to a wholesaler, then to an exporter, who sent them to the airport; there they were loaded into an airplane on a belt, crossed the Atlantic. Then the Sahara, to land in Khartoum after several stops; there they were bought by wholesalers – '*Tuffah, djamil tuffah!*'[2] – who resold them to retailers, among them our grocer in Gallabat, who sent them across the steppes by truck, so we could buy them at the Ethiopian border – '*itnin tuffah minfadlak*'[3] and end up in our stomachs under this deathly road, in this tunnel! Do you realize the fate of these apples? The trip they have made? It's insane! By the way, when did we last have apples?"

"Remember? It was in the bus that took us to Uganda, when we went to see the gorillas in Bwindi. You remember, beside me there was a Pygmy from the Congo who was fascinated by this fruit. Beside him there was a giant Karamajong with whom he never ceased talking. Those two were fun to watch! The biggest and smallest that the human race has produced, they seemed to be as thick as thieves. They kept on squinting at my apple, they apparently had never seen one before. When I had finished it, the Karamajong turned to me: 'My little neighbor is asking me whether you could give him the seeds from your fruit?' And he hid them religiously in a handkerchief. Just think! He might have become the Congolese Johnny Appleseed!"

When we leave our den, the furnace has passed. Only the odors of terra cotta and dried herbs remain. The sky no longer burns but the ground radiates. Some Land Rovers pass us by, overflowing

---

[2] Apples! Beautiful apples!
[3] Two apples, please!

with tall Blacks gesticulating and astonished at our masochistic insistence on wanting to walk every step of this void. We initiate ourselves to Arabic: *"Al ardam fakhat! Bel arabiya la arid!"* (Only on foot! We don't want to go in a car!)

And the bouquet of black arms and white cotton drives off in front of its plume of dust chattering in the wind. To walk voluntarily in an ugly place, hot and deserted....A hard concept to explain in a country where people even for short distances prefer waiting a very long time for possible transportation rather than make the journey on foot. Sensible, the Sudanese! As the days go by, we slump. We can't manage any more to recover during the night, nor to sleep really in the daytime, during our forced siesta. Hard! Hard! Up at three or four every morning, we walk as much as possible at night.

Saboni, Friday 23 May 2003, day 876, 33 km, 10,008th km

That's what we do when we leave Doka, where Awad Gaddora took us in during the night. Since Doka is five kilometers from the main road, we cut on a diagonal in open fields to get back to it. The ground is dry as clay and cracked into millions of hexagons that crunch under our feet. Awad alerted us about the vipers that infest the region. We gallantly replied that in two and half years we have only seen two or three, and have our sticks to repel them. Behind us the sky pales. Indeed, all the way to Khartoum and the confluence of the two Niles, we are trekking west, the sun behind us in the morning, and in our faces in the evening. We advance, numb, carried away in our thoughts in the form of dreams. Today is a great day for us: we are going to pass our ten thousandth kilometer. The distance between Sonia and me has increased and I think to myself that it is foolish to multiply by two in this way the risk of encountering a viper. For economical reasons and in order not to frighten any possible shepherds lost in these steppes, we have turned off our headlamps. I think again of the viper on which I almost stepped in Sibiloi park and mechanically turn my lamp back on. Hell with savings! Suddenly, a little muffled cry stabs me in the heart. Sonia! A viper! She has been bitten, I am sure. I hurry to her rescue. Nightmare! It's all over. My love. My life. In a blink of an eye, the world has capsized. I find her haggard and stupefied, standing, her legs spread, shaking and trembling.

"It missed me…"

Halfway between her legs, two oily spots on the hem of her skirt betray the bite of the fangs. She melts into tears. I embrace her with all my soul. Shock state. Between two sobs, she describes what happened.

"I was going to step on its tail. It turned on me like a whip. I jumped by reflex, spreading my legs. It was an enormous cobra. Bououououh! It immediately disappeared in the crevasse, there!"

Death in half an hour.…I almost lost my wife out of negligence, worse, for economic reasons. Twenty-two kilometers before our ten thousandth. A reminder of the Damocles sword permanently suspended over our heads. Out of pure bad faith and consumed by guilt, I scold her: "But why the hell were you trailing behind like that?"

"It's you, the bastard who was forging ahead all alone. You could have waited! It wasn't my job to catch up with you! I wasn't feeling well, I don't know why but I was obsessed by the scenes from *The Devil's Advocate*, you know, the film with Keanu Reeves we saw in Addis, when he is struggling with female demons with death's heads.…Well I had that image in my head when I saw the cobra coiled up and my foot was going to crush it, it was as if time had stopped, I couldn't figure out if it was a vision or a scene from the movie."

The two spots are there to remind us that we are not in a film but in reality. We immediately establish a draconian walking procedure, one behind the other, headlamp lit, stick in hand and eyes peeled. As if to recompense our zeal, five minutes later a thick horned viper, gray and rough, appears in the beam of light. We go around it without troubling it, our two sticks pointed at it, and the pressure relaxes. When we turn around, ten meters further on, I utter a cry of rage and fear: ARGHHH! Another viper. My hair is on end. Is it the same one? No. Impossible. Are we surrounded? Panic. Have we fallen into a nest? The place is riddled with them. Our nerves are exposed frayed. The crevasses are full of vipers.

Sonia ventures: "You remember? We were told that vipers always travel in pairs..."

"Yeah, like us, a pair! But Chicks against snakes, we lose...[4] One day or another, we're going to get had....What foolishness, to take shortcuts in open fields..."

The cracked earth we tread provides endless refuges for these death reptiles. They are there for field mice and field rats that must teem during the harvests. We rejoin the road as one leaves a mined terrain.

In the dawning day, we walk for three hours before being passed by the first vehicle...the one that might have transported Sonia to a potential dispensary...or a morgue. Normal for there to be no one on the road today, it's Friday. The village muezzins, in the distance, are singing the call to prayer. The Grim Reaper brushed us by this morning. Alone on this desert road, we begin to pray like combine harvesters.

Four hours later, in full torpor, our pedometer approaches the day's twenty-fifth kilometer, in other words our ten thousandth kilometer on foot since the Cape of Good Hope, eight hundred seventy-six days ago. The road is straight and nothing in view marks the landscape, the steppe is vibrant and white, crushed with sunlight, the most anonymous spot imaginable. But it's there. It's only a figure, means nothing in itself, but so what, we must celebrate this moment with our little ritual, as when we crossed the equator. At 24.99 kilometers we make a pause and set up our video camera on its tripod. It takes only one step, one drop, to make the sea overflow. With our thirteen millionth step we pass ten thousand

---

[4] See vol. I, p. 15.

kilometers on foot. At the border, they gave us a little Sudanese flag which Sonia wears all day on the side of her backpack, and which flaps against her ear. We plant it in the ground, beside a leaf on which we have written 10,000. Then we set fire to our little paper milestone to illustrate symbolically the furnace which is the frame of this kilometric threshold. The wind which carries off the ashes into the desert makes our little flag applaud with joy. The witnesses of the scene who pass in cars think we are nuts. They are partly right.

Close to the sunstroke point, we go flop in the shade of a tipsy grass hut. An old peasant soon comes to join us, full of gentleness and attentiveness. His name is Haroun Kazali. He appeared as if by miracle in what looked like an abandoned village. He knows and understands our suffering. We lie down on broken-down twine beds which he brings us to let the time and heavenly fire pass. The shelter is exposed to the burning breeze. We must drink, sweat, evaporate, dry out, drink again, perspire again, dry out again to have an illusion of coolness. But drinking aggravates our hypoglycemia and as everyone knows, air conditioning takes juice, consumes energy; we can only pretend to be sleeping, anesthesize ourselves. We share this square of shade encumbered with detritus with four featherless hens, naked as miniature dinosaurs, who are doing the same thing as us, wetting themselves in water dirtied with excretions which Haroun poured into an old cut-up tire, then get up on their feet to take advantage of the evaporation, then get wet again. It's crazy how brilliant a hen can be....It's crazy how stupid and mean it is to be here. Sonia is done in. She speaks to me faintly with a Q-tip she forgot in her left ear. The sight is funny, I point at it, shaken with desperate and aphonic spasms. "What is it? What's wrong with me?" she rebels before putting her hand to her temple. We ache all over. The heat breaks your back. Life is suffering, space is suffering, time is suffering. Going on is suffering, staying is suffering. A desperate Buddhist affirmation. Have to go on, flee, be done with it, great fatigue. Space is sterile, time empty. The ideal would be to have no desire, but we have what I call for the occasion a "paroxystic orexis," a desire for everything, a frightening appetite for comfort, consumption, refined meals, big chow too, cleanliness, intimacy, sensuality, savings, investment, construction – no longer to exhaust ourselves, grill ourselves, kill ourselves. The Sudan has renewed our trip but it is already deadly monotonous. To get to Khartoum on foot. Is that beautiful? Is it good? Is there any sense to it? We no longer know. The desert and heat scorch your neurons, kill the senses. Hold out. Hold out. Hold out. We cling to this punctured buoy in an ocean of sun and thirst. We set out again exhausted. Late in the afternoon, a pickup stops beside us. It is Moussa Ismaël, our host of the first night, heading back to Khartoum. He knows it will do no good to propose that we get in, but he has a surprise for us: a coolbox! He hands us some super-cold water in a stainless steel goblet. Glug, glug, glug! It's enough to make your teeth explode and freeze your brain. God how that hurts! God how good it is! When we start walking again we go slosh, slosh with every step, the sun full in our faces. Moussa has indicated to us another camp of construction men where we can sleep tonight. When the sun goes down, we reconcile ourselves with our bodies, with life.

A little before a small burg, a handsome Black man in the prime of life joins us and opens a conversation in polished English. But he seems to be on his guard, uneasy, distant, talking without looking at us, between closed lips. "I was educated by the British, in Juba, in the Southern Sudan, in paradise. I am from the Nuer tribe. My whole family has been exterminated. I am a teacher in a government school for displaced Southerners. I was educated by the British…"

What we thought was a promising conversation turns into an incoherent, repetitive monologue: a clandestine, obsessive, confession.

"I withdrew from politics, I don't want to tell you about asinine doings, it's too risky, we are watched, I was educated by the British, when our country was at peace. My entire family has been exterminated. It was paradise. We were rich before. In fact, I was taken prisoner. They let me go on condition I come here and accept this position. So I keep quiet. But I don't forget..."

John Eustache has the hard, fixed gaze of people who have been tortured. We notice that he bears on the left side of his face, which up to then had been hidden from us, scars that give it odd angles. He tells us about that Sudan which we will not see. Of that hidden face. Forgotten by the world, genocided into silence since the decolonization which left this immense country made up of heteroclite peoples at the mercy of a merciless Arabization and Islamization policy practiced by the successive regimes in Khartoum. We approach a crossroads.

"I cannot invite you to my place, they would stir up difficulties for me, but I can offer you a red millet porridge which we eat in my home, in the South."

We sit down on twine beds in front of a huge black mama. They speak to each other in a Southern dialect. Suddenly John turns around: "You can't sit together on the same bed, I'm sorry, sharia [Islamic law] applies to everyone in this country. Where are you going to sleep tonight?"

"We were told about a camp of the Higleig company, a little farther..."

"Oh yes! Oil. The scourge of God. The misfortune of the poor. Higleig is one of the companies that hold the oil, in the South where we are from, and don't want to let it go. They will exterminate us and convert us to the very last one, and your governments are in collusion, especially you, the French: you know who owns the largest oil concession in the Sudanese South, still unexploited today? Total[5]! And the Canadians. That's why you don't say anything, you stay in line! For fear of scaring away the goose that lays the golden eggs..."

John swallows a big lump of porridge and resumes with a smile,

---

[5] French biggest oil multinational.

so as not to betray to people around us the gravity of what he's telling us.

"You have heard of the conflict that is setting Darfur ablaze? It's strange, the international community reacts strongly to that, it started scarcely two months ago and the entire world is already aware of it. Why such a difference with the conflict in the South? I am going to tell you! Because there is not a drop of oil in the Darfur mountains, and it is a Muslim population. An Islamist regime that kills Muslims is not normal, so everyone asks why, whereas killing us was normal. Anyway, for the South, this sad story is a blessing, it will put the spotlight on our country, displace armies to the western front and no doubt accelerate the peace process."[6]

John is inexhaustible, he manipulates the paradox with virtuosity. He reviews world geopolitics seen from the Sudanese window: "You, the French, who militate so much for the rights of peoples for self determination, who defend the Kosovars and the Palestinians, why does our cause find no echo with you? Because we don't kill enough innocent people? Blast ourselves? Because we don't make enough noise? I will tell you why! Because of oil! There are more than ten million of us Black Christians in the South and we don't want the Islamic regime that the Arabs in the North want to impose on us. Less than a century ago these same Arabs came to sell us into slavery. Nothing has changed. The Blacks in the South are employed in the North at ridiculous wages, a dollar or two a day! Our cause is legitimate. We are the forgotten of the world. It's the fault of the English, they ought to have divided the country in two when they left....Okay, I'll stop, I have already told you too much. Quiet! They're killing my people....You told me the Muslims were very nice to you, well don't ever forget that their regime is massacring us every day, tearing down our schools, burning our

---

[6] History seems to vindicate John. Nearly two years after we saw him, no doubt because of the degeneration of the situation in Darfur, a peace agreement between the North and South was signed in Naivasha, in Kenya, on 9 January 2005.

churches, bombarding our hospitals, with the silent complicity of your leaders…"

John gets up and disappears into the night. We are chilled. We meditate for a few kilometers over this dark shadow on the Sudanese picture and reach the campground of Higleig. The welcome is as warm, same beds, same politeness, same attentions, but tends in the direction of religion and politics. We listen, stupefied, to Mounir Abdelrazik: "Why can't you understand that the last prophet is Mohammed? That he abolishes and accomplishes all of what the others did before him? How can you believe that God had a son? And that the prophet Issa [Jesus] is God in person? Or a third of God, according to the Trinity doctrine? Your stories are too complicated. Mohammed came to simplify the message of God which the Christian sect worked over for seven centuries. In the Qu'ran, we recognize all of the twenty-six prophets from Ibrahim [Abraham] to Mohammed, including Moussa [Moses] and Yahya (John the Baptist): so they were all Muslims."

???

"Obviously! You think they are Jewish prophets, then two Christian prophets, but that doesn't meaning anything: they were all Muslims, which means 'submitted to God,' as are we all. In the Qu'ran, the prophet Issa even prophesizes that another prophet named Ahmed will come after him, it means that he was already a Muslim. And Ahmed is another name for Mu-Ahmed, Mohammed…"

We do the best we can by affirming that we believe in a single God shared by all men, a God of love: "*La-I-laha Illah-Allah…*"

"So you are Muslims without knowing it!"

"Maybe!"

And we have a good laugh. They think we are on the path to truth. Maybe they are right. We are all on the paths of Life and Truth…

"You are lucky to be able to go to Al Qods [Jerusalem]. For me, I will never get the five hundred divine credits for Al Qods…"

We are confused. He pursues: "I have my two thousand points

for Medina, and my ten thousand points for Mecca; I have done two *hadjs*, but I will never go to Al Qods as long as it is held by infidels..."

We are taken aback. In the twelve years I have been assiduously visiting Muslim countries, from Iraq to Pakistan by way of Niger or Syria, I have never heard about this spiritual accounting. Mounir explains that every gesture, every thought, every second of a Muslim's life is credited or debited with these points that will be marked in the ledger for the last judgment, points that God alone knows the value of; the Qu'ran, the sharia, the hadith[7] being there only to give advice and indications.

"To pray alone is one point, to pray with more than five in a mosque or in the street is five points for each, the Friday prayer ten points. This evening, for example, thanks to your presence, we are all going to earn ten points, for the Qu'ran commands us to receive well strangers passing by..."

Marvels and architectonic secrets of a culture. Biting my tongue, I dare to say: "So you ought to thank us."

Mounir and his companions burst out laughing. Whew! God too has a sense of humor.

---

[7] Commentaries of the Qu'ran and prescriptions dictated by the early caliphs who succeeded Mohammed, and complete the sharia. They have the statute of law in Islamic regimes.

CHAPTER
25

The Thieves and the Samaritans

SUDAN

Despite the mournful shadow floating far to the south, our first impressions of the Sudan are confirmed day by day. Wisdom and hospitality, both spontaneous and calculated, proportional to the heat, and landscapes infested with snakes. We kill our daily snake. With stones or sticks. Stupidly. But that's the way it is. Darwinian. Their life against ours. Not very ecological, but we all the same have, each time, the feeling of doing good, of saving a child, a woman gathering wood, a man in his field, of exorcising our demons of the other day. We do like everyone, we have become African: we try to kill as many snakes as we can.

Our first Sudanese villages look clean and orderly to us. The huts with impeccable thatch are all surrounded by palisades of woven straw assuring perfect privacy. The crowds and intrusiveness are past. Our hosts do not have to resist the invasion of the village. All the families have the benefit of functional septic tanks and a cemented, organized and thought-out place to wash. For us this is an immense comfort, which re-energizes us, resets our counters to zero. Everyone always has water despite the environment's hostility – which is to say that there is no such thing as determinism.

Ahmed Eissa, in charge of the municipal pump in Kadjira, declares to us: "The sea is forty meters under our feet, eternal!"

It is always good to know that water is only forty meters down, it's reassuring....We'll have to think about it when we are dying of thirst in the torridity of the day. In the countryside, the pump motors beat time, the tractors are working – a rare thing on the continent – and preparing the earth for its wedding with rain. But the real miracle is that freezers produce improbable Cokes cold even in the most isolated burgs. The great game, among the Sudanese, is to pay for our drinks surreptitiously and make tracks. With a little sign as discreet as in auction galleries, they have our Cokes, teas or cookies put on their tab. But we are not the sole beneficiaries of this generosity. They spend their time playing bad tricks on each other, earning spiritual points on each others' backs. When one of them is unmasked, there are great altercations of which the seller refuses to be the arbiter. It is the strongest one who wins. Thus the most generous. To us, it's just a show. It's only when it comes time to pay the bill that by proxy we discover our benefactor: "It was the old gentleman at the end of the room" or "the trucker who left when you were entering, he confirmed your crazy hike, for three days he has been passing you on the road..." Incontestably, we have reconnected with "civilities."

Everywhere jars of half-cooked terra cotta installed in metal structures on the roadsides, above the ground, just porous enough to cool the water by evaporation, are at the disposal of the passers-by for a drink or for ritual ablutions before prayer. That is the *sébil*. A marvel of delicacy and refinement, of altruism and wisdom. Which is to say that "civilization" is not necessarily technical.

Islam is omnipresent, in the life and heart of people, in their clothing and in their mouths. The women are all veiled with a *tobe*, the Sudanese version of the Islamic veil. It consists of a large sheet of diaphanous, colored tulle which they roll up in, a little like a sari that includes the head. It is the loveliest veil in the world, the most gracious, the most colorful, the most feminine. Fluorescent, modeled by the wind, they pop out two or three at a time from the corner of a house, like biped candies, like spinnakers filled by a gust of wind, leaving us speechless. If their intention was to pass unnoticed, it's a failure. What beauty, what elegance! The first is in flashy pink, the second in electric blue, the third in rainbow shades. They sneak off chortling with their charming faces, delighted with the little effect they have made. Unquestionably, the Sudanese woman is made sublime by her transparent veils…

In all the villages we can't manage to spend a single dinar! There are always groups of men draped in white who invite us to their homes or to greasy spoons.

"*Fadhal! fadhalu!*" (Come sit down! Welcome!)

It is the local version of "*Karibu*" and the rare "*Enider!*" Amiable curiosity and desire to show their benevolence. Some even say bluntly, with no hint of a smile: "We are doing our duty. To show you that we are good Muslims and not terrorists as you think."

"If we thought that we would not be here."

The conversation is often on the razor's edge, but in the Orient it is a studied exercise, of restraint and politeness, that knows how to respect the forms, save appearances, it must remain an agreeable pastime. Any break with its light and consensual character would be considered as vulgar and aggressive. Our point of view doesn't interest them at all, they seek above all to express theirs. Thus we listen more than we speak. If we had to accept all invitations, we would only walk five kilometers a day. In lieu of thanking our hosts, I often recite my favorite surates from the Qu'ran, *Ayat el Kursi*, the Traveler's surate, and *Kulwallah ahad*, the One God surate, and we set off in joy and laughter after answering "*Nousse, nousse!*" (half and half) to the obsessive question that torments them and invariably closes my recitation: "But…are you Muslims?"

In Gedaref, a medium-sized city on the road to Port Sudan, we get back to asphalt. We are greeted by Ahmed Gaddora, Awad's older brother, who had put us up at Doka. An engineer, he lives in an immense cubical three-story house where we hole up for two days, far from the furnace, in a filtered and air-conditioned atmosphere. Straight away we share passionate rapid-fire conversations. Ahmed is nostalgic for the Sudan of before the Islamic revolution. It was in 1990 that the Muslim Brothers took power, when General Omar al-Bashir, supported by the Islam ideologue Hassan al-Turabi, pulled off his coup d'état against the reigning government – one year later, Omar al-Bashir got rid of Turabi and threw him in prison. Ahmed tells us about the regime's economic failure, the closing of factories, the decline of the once-flourishing cotton market, of the largest sugar cane factory in the world, Kenana, also the most absurd, lost in the eastern desert in New Halfa, which uses fossil water[1] to produce sugar for Saudi Arabia. He laments his country's immense potential, spoiled by the interminable war with the South – he has lost to it one brother and several nephews. He misses the time when the Sudanese were free to be Muslims…

He pauses, observing our surprise, and continues: "Yes, of course! Before the Islamic regime and the imposition of sharia, I was a good Muslim; I did it by choice, by my own decision. Today, since it is obligatory, it revolts me. Everyone keeps an eye on everyone else. People are counted at the mosque, they go to be seen. I want nothing to do with this forced Islam, this totalitarian Islam."

"In fact it's a problem of freedom? If I understand you, it's because that takes away the merit of choosing the good willingly?"

"Of course! There is no love of God without freedom! That Islam attempts to impose the good on us: it acts like a dictatorship of the good. It's a society that is afraid of everything, afraid

---

[1] Water from prehistoric times, trapped in underground aquifer and pumped with very deep boreholes. Sometimes referred to as water mining because it is a nonrenewable ressource. Hence the waste and nonsense to grow cane, a water-guzzling plant, in the desert.

of freedom and of man's ill inclinations, it's a system that provides maximum security, it's absolutely risk averse. Thus, the best way of not cheating on your wife is not to love her, but to cloister her, the best way of not tempting others is to hide your wife, the best way of suppressing drunkenness is not to drink in moderation or to resist temptation, but to forbid drinking....Everything is forbidden, all behavior is codified, regulated, standardized, all thought must be Islamic thought, everything must be halal. You have no choice, society imposes it, and that, according to me, is the mistake, Islam ought to be a matter of free consent....How do Muslims live in France?"

"Free..."

"Ah, how fortunate they are! But be careful, the Islamists will try to influence them! Islam ought to be a religion of practice and not words, a personal relationship with God, not a mass and crowd religion..."

Next he tells us about the Islam of his heart, a religion of discretion and not ostentation, of humility and not extroversion, interiority and not appearance, peace and not violence. He suffers from seeing his religion ridiculed or misrepresented, in Iran, in Iraq, in Afghanistan, Malaysia, Algeria, you name it...

We leave Ahmed full of esteem and sympathy. Reassured also. He cannot be the only one to think this way. The days following, unfortunately, cause us to forget this example of an open mind. For our long midday pause we are often introduced into interiors where Sonia and I are split up; she goes into the women's quarter while I remain with the men. And I immediately regret being deprived of the women's company. While I am subjected to polite, demential propaganda, we hear them over the walls howl with laughter. I get the boring assignment. And so they nicely discuss with me subjects as light as "September 11: Mossad plot," "the inevitable Islamization of the world, inscribed in the Qu'ran and willed by God..." or yet "the massive suicides of young Europeans prove the decline of the West," "the alcoholism of Western women is the cause of their sterility..." Their hobbyhorse is "the massive conversion of Catholic priests to Islam" and "the increase by thousands in marriages between converted Frenchwomen and Muslim immigrants." I listen calmly, I opine, I never contradict. They read that every day in the newspapers. During this time, heavily scarified young Black women scurry about serving us dishes from the harem. I smilingly express surprise at the presence of women among us..."They are just Blacks...," they reply. I stiffen. And I almost choke when they explain that they have been in the service of the family for several generations without ever having been remunerated. I show my disapproval, and my hosts smile: "In any case, they do not know the South, they were born here, and besides, they are attached to us, they are free to flee! They stay here because here at least they are fed and have a safe place to stay."

"You can see why, in these conditions, the Sudan is reluctant to grant nationhood to the people of the South," Sonia points out when we rejoin after the stopover.

One thing is certain, our kind hosts lack objective information; the Friday rumor mill functions both as their business bulletin and as political forum. Once that is said, these enormities are allowable, insofar as our hosts remain calm and respectful. On her side, Sonia tells me stories of unguents and perfumes, recipes exchanged and clothes fittings carried out amidst the laughter of enormous women wrapped up like candies; she can't get over the questions constantly asked her about sexuality; and we comment interminably in the setting sun on that umpteenth way of being Muslim which the Sudanese incarnate, generous and kind, clean and upright, in a country where, even if it runs less well than before, by general consent, all the same, things function much better than in many places on this continent.

One night, we pitch the tent in open steppe, far from the main road where a noria of trucks hums in the wind. A little fire. A little soup. A little sleep. Around four in the morning, just before we wake, I dream I see a man running away with our shoes. I immediately awake; a white specter disappears, swallowed up in the dark. Our shoes have disappeared! In a second I am on foot, running like a madman, screaming in pursuit of our thief, furious that he should belie our first impressions. Ignoring crevasses and snakes, I wound my feet on sorghum stems cut on a bias. Without our shoes, we are done for. I must get them back. Suddenly, a whistle halts me; Sonia has fired a distress flare which explodes right over the head of my thief, whom I can see from a distance tangled up in his white djellaba. I alter my trajectory and resume my pursuit, my headlamp on. Soon I come across a shepherd walking tranquilly behind his cows, I catch him, question him, is he my thief? He is terrorized. That is understandable. A half-naked, screaming White cyclops! He swears solemnly, calls Allah to witness that he has done nothing and points into the dark to show me the direction the thief took.... His quick breathing and streaming sweat quickly betray the clumsy stratagem; I shake him a bit and he vanishes in the night like a rag blown in the wind, light and unreal. I am no closer to a solution and return empty-handed, feeling remorse. "What if he were telling the truth? If he wasn't the one?" No, he must either have been guilty or in collusion....At the tent, I find Sonia worried.

"You're crazy! He might have been armed!"

"Armed or not, his conscience wasn't easy. Let him steal the shoes of everybody in the world, but not ours! However, thanks for the flare! Let's wait for daylight, maybe we will find them; in the meantime I have to attend to my feet."

At dawn, we find our shoes and socks at flare range. At that point he had dropped them. Sonia has saved our soles. In total confidence, we had left our shoes beside our mosquito shelter. Our first theft in two years and a half. And in the country where it ought to be the rarest! Where it is most stifled, where there is a risk of having one's hand cut off for having tried to protect one's feet....Too much! Thus we travel for the exception that confirms the rule.

During the day a car stops and offers us a lift. It is a huge police general covered with stars. At first he interprets our refusal as fear, tries to reassure us. We explain that on the contrary he inspires confidence in us and we tell him about our last night's misadventure. He is dismayed. As proof of his compassion, he invites us to his house, in Wad Medani, where he is number one in all of Jazeera province. We could hardly have fallen into better hands.

The days in the desert steppe on this strip of hot asphalt follow one upon the other, very hard, counting the pylons, avoiding trucks, slaloming between the carcasses of their victims – camels, donkeys, goats, dogs or cows, same battle, same stink. There is carrion every two hundred meters. Frozen in a grotesque posture, ballooned and out of joint, or fallen into a glob of entrails spilled on the sand, and always skulls full of teeth, open mouth in a last cry like the cubist horses of *Guernica*. Grim milestones. We avoid walking downwind to eschew the bouquet. Little old men turbaned with a huge ball of white cotton, riding on the rumps of their jackasses, sometimes hobble at our sides, their dangling legs nearly scraping the ground. Old Morris trucks of the 1940s slowly pass, deploying towards us anemones of extended arms and hands. They all bear broad smiles. Obviously we are a curiosity. We sometimes walk in the desert, parallel to the road, but after an hour of sand or four kilometers of soft soil, we return to the asphalt: we have lost a kilometer. Then we walk a tightrope, we walk on the outer ten centimeters of the roadbed, taking care not to twist our ankles. Since the edge of the asphalt is irregular, we have to pay attention. I use our little mirror as a rearview, to watch for trucks coming from behind us. Especially the ones that are overtaking, because then there isn't room for everyone on the pavement and we have to bolt out of the way. Same thing for two trucks crossing each other where we are. This monotonous and noisy circus to escape the Grim Reaper keeps us busy all day. And ever these animal carcasses. When a mephitic wind takes us by surprise, we are seized with spasms that make us spit bile. It's pathetic and morbid. Everything stinks of death. Only the trucks to distract us. Many come from Germany or France; nineteen-eighties models, and we wonder by what miracle, by what strange path they have been resold in this area: a Norbert Dentressangle semitrailer thus passes an old Suzanne bus or a Domaine de l'Orme delivery truck. A little balm in the furnace and the stench. Who would have believed we could be moved by a truck tarpaulin?

A Philippine driver stops to give us a package of cookies. Another day, it is an Iraqi Kurd who hands us two cold Pepsis and a package of noodles. Yes, there is some sense in walking on this infernal road, no, it is not without purpose. It allows us to cross the destinies of a Philippine and a Kurd in the middle of the Sudanese desert. That reconciles us, were it needed, with all of humanity.

One day at midday, eyelids heavy and head numb, while we are despairing of finding shade or a pipe, we come providentially across an enormous late Scania model, broken down on the roadside. The driver gets out of the cabin when we approach. He has unmounted one wheel. Apparently a problem with the bearings.

"*Fadhal!*"

Even broken down, he finds a way to invite us! We who would have settled for the shade of his trailer, are delighted to enter his brand new cabin. Bahadi Mohammed is taking five huge steel pipes coated in black rubber from Port Soudan to Kosti, south of Khartoum.

"A cargo ship just delivered three thousand pipes from China for the Great South pipeline; all the technology is Chinese, they even imported huge machines to bury them with."

After divine oranges and cold water, Bahadi offers us his bunk beds.

"Take a little rest! You will set out again when it is less hot."

I climb into the upper bunk. The wind that rushes in at the windows refreshes us, the trucks going by make the cabin oscillate

and rock us. I fall into a sweet restorative sleep. I awaken at five
with a start: in my nightmare, Bahadi had fixed his wheel without
telling us and driven all the way to Khartoum...

On Sunday 1 June 2003, we celebrate our best shower on the
continent: it is at Reys, forty-eight kilometers before Wad Medani. You must know that there is a curse in Africa that makes all
showers lack something, something apparently insignificant but
which makes the operation difficult and acrobatic, sometimes even
dirty....A good shower is the result of a successful combination
of innumerable components. I am not talking about plumbing or
running water, that would be asking too much, no, a good African
shower is a smooth cement square in a place that closes, far from
the latrines. Because most of the times they are in the latrines,
above the same pit. The slope has to be calculated and the drain
not be plugged, that there be a light overhead, nails on the door
to hang your clothes on, a bucket of pure water with a cup to pour
water on your head, a plastic or twine stool to sit on, a bar of soap
and a soap dish to place it on when you've used it, a dry towel and
flip-flops for getting out, and finally, luxury of luxuries, a clean
change of clothes loaned by our hosts so we won't have to put on
our stinking clothes, which have been washed at the same time,
to take advantage of the opportunity. It doesn't look complicated,
but there is always one or more unavailable ingredients missing
in this recipe, that make the whole thing a wrestling battle, an
equilibrium ordeal, a painful pleasure. Tonight, our 885th night,
we combine them all for the first time at the home of Ajeb Abd el-
Rahman. *"Choukrane bezef, Ajeb!"*[2] Sated with pasta and tomatoes,
dressed in fine cotton djellabas, stretched out in the gentle evening
wind on beds set up under the stars with clean flowered sheets, we

---

[2] Many thanks, Ajeb!

sleep the sleep of the just. *Luxe, calme et volupté.*[3] Happiness is as simple as a shower.

It is with a strong sense of deliverance that we rejoin the Blue Nile at Wad Medani. On the bridge, we take out the movie camera to celebrate this reunion and our crossing of the desert. A bad idea. A soldier rushes at us, Kalashnikov first. Short. Narrow-minded.. Dumb. The sin of the world. We comply without flinching. He takes us to two national security guys, very black, Southerners, impeccable English, clever and funny, covered with war wounds, scars, bought by the regime, and placed. They are amused at us and let us go without further ado. Forty days of walking since Addis; one thousand two hundred kilometers. A good score. But we have paid a big price. The machine is worn down. Sonia has been limping courageously for several days and I have an acute pain between the metatarsals in my left foot. A pause is necessary. At the Central Police Station, we meet up with our three-star general. Jaffar Mohammed Youssif greets us like his children, lodges us in the room next to his own, in the hotel of one of his friends, takes us to the officers' mess where we are greeted by colossi proportionally huge to their number of stars, eagles or stripes on their epaulettes. Rank is apparently earned around here by virtue of girth. It's no doubt to avoid putsches; a replete can't be a rebel. Jafar is the highest-ranking, so he is the biggest, gentle as a lamb. They are very attentive to us. They are all appalled at this thief story.

"The Sudan is not like that! Besides, it must not be a Sudanese!" they claim. Of course. They shower us with presents, djellabas, sandals, saroual and hijab for Sonia, to repair their reputation. No need to try to deter them in doing so. We spend a few days' rest in their company. We find every morning the same *fatur*

---

[3] Luxury, calm, sensual delight: refrain of a poem of Baudelaire, *L'Invitation au voyage.*

banquet with our company of sumos in fatigues. The fatur is taken at ten in the morning and the *radha* at four, impossible times for the hikers we are since we must have fuel before ten, which is when we must stop, and we have no desire to gobble food in mid-afternoon. They stuff us with *foul*, a national dish of fava beans, oil and cheese, with *aceida*, or *kissera*, *kharouf*, *zabadi* and *taharniya*: so many sweets. One night, when we are returning with Jaffar from these feasts worthy of the Roman senators' orgies, minus the wine, we discover that our room has been visited; four hundred dollars are missing at roll call. Second theft in five days in sharia country. Everything has to start some time. Consternation among our potbellied cops. Consternation among the poor chicks. The Arsène Lupin[4] in djellaba nevertheless was tactful enough to leave us a hundred fifty euros and all our dinars. The next morning, to our great surprise, our benefactor, rather than launch an investigation among the hotel personnel, prefers to organize a collection. All the police services of the city are called upon: circulation, immigration, customs, public treasury, public streets, they scrape the drawers' bottoms, the service chiefs come one after another to bring envelopes. They ultimately pull together the sum of a hundred fifty dollars. We refuse, but Jaffar insists: "I will not let you leave until you have accepted! *Mektoub!*" (It is written.)

Elsewhere, they probably would have found the thief. Elsewhere, they would never have put us back in business like that. In Islam, the destinies of men are linked by a strange web woven under the eye of God. What must happen happens. That is fate. The guilty party is less the thief than Jaffar, who exposed us to the thief. Generous and responsible, he assumes his responsibility. For him, what happened to us is also a sign of the times. There is no chance in Islam.

Before leaving us, Jaffar confides: "In fact, it's a very delicate matter since I suspect it is the hotel owner. A poor person would

---

[4] A character invented by Maurice Leblanc, a sort of modern Robin Hood.

not have left you any money....Indeed I wanted to thank you. Owing to you, I began a diet three days ago. My goal is to lose thirty kilos..."

We leave toward Khartoum with a feeling of unease. Confidence is compromised. Sonia confesses to me along the way that the hotel owner, Mr. Salah, forced a kiss from her, feeling her up in a corner, pushing naïveté to the point of asking her: "Shall we go on?" One avowal calling for another, she tells me about Bahadi, the broken-down trucker. While I was sleeping on the upper bunk, he had begun to massage her aching feet, with a very extended concept of the ankle....She had to kick him when he made to go beyond the knee. She had been right to keep these affronts from me because I would have taken them badly....On the way to Khartoum, we meditate on this society in transition, on problematic and repressed sexuality, on material desires frustrated by the crisis, on the gentle, good Islam with its often demented diatribes, and try to figure out all these contradictions.

In Al-Hasaheisa, four days before Khartoum. We come to a stop before a singular vision. About twenty old canvas-covered biplanes are lined up on the right, under a Polish flag.

Stephan Gembalczyk, captain of the Sudana squadron, greets us warmly. He is in charge of spreading herbicide and pesticide on the governmental plantations in Jezeera. He comes from the south of Poland, near the Slovak border, and there they go, he and Sonia, on a "nostalgia" sequence for which Slavs own the patent. Stephan, Leszec, Krzysztof and Jeniec shower us with Malossol gherkins, Polish cheese, spinach meat pies and a homemade beer of which they are quite proud. Good timing this evening, the Poles have voted "yes" for Polish entrance into Europe. We have to celebrate that worthily. Stephan shows a still put together by the mechanic in a shed, that distills a rotgut that we inaugurate for the occasion.

"You aren't afraid of being caught?" Sonia wonders.

"No problem, I supply the local elites."

But the captain soon caps the evening, triumphal: "Tomorrow, we test the Antonov II we finished repairing today…"

At dawn, Leszec, the little mechanic, who looks just like Astérix[5], with his big nose and long yellow mustache, is busy about the airplane. There is no runway. I worry about it.

"With a headwind, it takes less than a hundred meters to take off. And fifty to land. This plane is one of the slowest in the world, it can fly at 160 km per hour for 1200 km: it never fails! Okay, it has one drawback, it isn't ecological: four liters of oil per hour and two hundred liters of fuel to feed the huge motor with nine radial cylinders.

Indeed. An enormous plume of blue smoke is emitted when the motor is started. On board, everything dates from before the plastic era: bakelite and laminates, aluminum and cloth: Soviet technology produced exclusively in Poland.

Stephan at the controls, one flick of the wings and we are airborne, as if catapulted: everything shakes and roars, we hear the whistle of the air on the drum of the wings. We can't believe it; is it that simple to fly? This enormous, ungainly, fat thing flits like a dragonfly in a racket of propellers. To fly! What bliss! There are neither seats nor belts for us, we are standing in the fuselage. The dull yellowish horizon limits visibility, under our wings the red Blue Nile winds between the desert to the east and the plantations to the west, bordered at a distance by the White Nile. In between the two rivers stretches the fertile horn of Jeezira, a huge checkerboard of irrigation canals, railway networks, railway yards and deserted warehouses.

"There remains only 30% of the colonial plantations of Jeezira," explains Stephan. "Everything is broken, abandoned. No reconversion was undertaken. This country is just an immense, fallow industrial and agricultural field that the Chinese and Saudis covet. And to think that the English had called the Sudan 'the

---

[5]   Comic hero from Uderzo's Asterix and Obelix starring an Gaul village resisting the Romans.

wheat basket of Africa'! Omar al-Bashir did nothing for his people, except maybe to send them to the slaughter with his stupid jihad against the Christians of the South. I knew this country before the sharia, under Nimeiri, it was paradise. We played billiards in the British clubs in Wad Medani, we held regattas on the Nile, all the communities frequented each other, there was a lifestyle unmatched anywhere. The Sudanese pound had the same value as the sterling pound. Since then, sorrow, sclerosis and sectarianism have fallen on the country..."

The motor misses some. Stephan manipulates a shaky lever and it's as good as 1940 again. We are blue, he is delighted, Sonia whispers: "It would upset our trek some if we crashed in an Antonov II..."

"Don't worry, this plane never crashes, even when it's fired at! It proved itself in the Vietnam and Korean Wars. The bullets passed right through the fabric and that's all! In fact, despite its appearance as a flying antique it is a formidable war machine: all the deadly bombardments carried out against the Southern populations in the South for decades and in the last few months in Darfur have been done at low altitude from Antonov II's."

Content with his little warm-up lap, Stephan returns and lands in a handkerchief, between two rows of planes. The overview helps us put into perspective what we are learning about this neglected country. In Khartoum, we know that we will have plenty of time to deepen our knowledge since it is impossible to cross the Sahara on foot in the summertime; we will have to wait...

In the endless outskirts of the capital, we pass an enormous factory strangely called GIAD. We quickly learn that it is an auto factory that also has weapons shops: a model of Nissan is assembled here under the name Giad. I wince. "Strange name for a car! It's as if Renault brought out a model called Holy War..."

As everywhere in Africa, you can tell you are near a capital city from the concentration of plastic bags hanging on the bushes and the branches of the scrubby trees, sinister foliage. Also from the effervescence, the concert of car horns and the shuttles dropping their loads of commuters. A few kilometers further on, we come to our first red light since South Africa. What a shock! Khartoum, here we are. On our knees. Sonia, with an eerie smile asks me: "Alex? Do you remember our phone number in Paris?"

"Uh....No!"

"Nor do I..."

CHAPTER
26

Khartoum, the Surprising Trunk

SUDAN

On the slimy banks of the Mougren, the confluence of the two Niles, we watch the thick waters roll that are the lifeblood of northeast Africa. They blend and interlace in a little tidal bore of fertility that made the Nile the artery of one of History's greatest civilizations. The Arabs baptized the spot *el-Khurtoum*, the elephant's trunk, because of the peninsula formed at the confluence, which changes shape with the floods and drops. Coming from the east, the Blue Nile is blood red. The torrential rains that are now falling on Ethiopia carry away its rich volcanic soil. From the south, the White Nile, milky and clayey, pours itself out lasciviously into the raging current of the Abyssinian waterway. It comes from farther away, it has wearied in the marshes of the Sudd.[1] Its water is less rich. We are in Khartoum, on the shores of the mythical river that we are going to follow as far as the Mediterranean

---

[1] A marshy region, natural border between the Arab Sudan and the Black Sudan, so feared by the numerous explorers who were searching for the sources of the Nile.

sea, Ariadne's thread and lifeline across the Sahara. And we enjoy in silence this moment so long awaited.

Serendipity: we are informed by an e-mail from my parents that a distant great-uncle, Etienne Renaud, of the White Fathers congregation, lives in Khartoum; he is expecting us at home at the CLIK (Catholic Language Institute of Khartoum), in the residential quarter of Amarat. What providence is this vast family! He is a short, smiling, ascetic man, with embers in his eyes. An alumnus of the Ecole Polytechnique, fascinated by the East and Africa, a specialist in inter-religious dialogue, he was for several years delegated to the Vatican. A great Islamologist and perfectly Arabophone, he spent eight years in Yemen, six in Tunisia. At the CLIK, he gives classes in Arabic to humanitarian collaborators, diplomats, religious and refugees of the Southern minorities. Khartoum is an organized city. The British plotted avenues here punctuated with roundabouts on the general design of the Union Jack, and planted now-enormous trees which make the walk on the shores of the Nile a must. Fine colonial buildings, palaces and columned ministries here and there line the avenues. Right in the center of this rational layout, an immense rectangle was cleared, where stands the city's most beautiful mosque, constructed in hewn stone. All around, the minibus station and the markets of the el-Arabi souk, the muddy lung of the city, its African heart and Oriental brain. The shivaree here is permanent, a noria of vehicles and a crowd of pedestrians. The informal at the service of African-style efficiency. Old arcades open onto butchers' displays, luscious fruits and vegetables but also on shops where golden bracelets are sold by the ton.

Women are very present in the crowds of Khartoum. The sharia has tacitly become more flexible these last few months, in the context of peace negotiations, agreements and cease-fires between the North and South. The veils of the Christian southerners often fall onto their shoulders with complicity of a free wind. Those of the "Northern" Muslim girls, no less eager for emancipation, seize the opportunity to hook onto the chignon or change to diaphanous tulle. Extreme burkas and impressive helmet-veils cleft with a visor also stroll by. All the women pass by as if no one was watching them but without being unaware that they drive the pupils crazy. The wealth, diversity and complexity of these adornments far surpass those of the Parisian uniforms of the fashion victims. Following a well-established exercise, the gaze is concentrated on the few bits of visible flesh: first of all, the feet, adorned with floral marvels painted with henna, then the hands if not covered in gloves and finally the very carefully made-up faces, angelically haloed by their hijabs – who do not fear the tight cuts or the flashy colors. The assortment of colors is very calculated. If the purely Islamic hijab prescribed by the Muslim Brothers must reduce the face to a perfect oval, it is often discreetly lined with a red or blue fabric that delicately fringes it. The girl therefore finds a way to let a sleeve or slip of the same color be seen to the same degree at the bottom of the chador which is generally of dull color, and will carry a little matching handbag. Everything is in the detail and the accessory, in phantasm and dissimulation. And in the gait....An Oriental catwalk. The head melancholically tilted, the little steps, the sad eyes, the right hand beating the air exaggeratedly, while the left raises the chador, revealing the lace slip. Here as elsewhere, the girls' skirts make the world go round, but with a devilishly sexy contained choreography and false reserve. The girls are always beautiful. Whatever you want to make of them. This confirms our Zanzibar impression; there is much intentional eroticism in this anything-but-modest dance of the veils. According to our encounters, glances reveal much of the effect my blue eyes have on them. They swoon theatrically as we pass. Sonia ironizes: "It's as if I didn't exist; they have eyes only for you, these turn-ons are beginning to annoy me..."

Never saw so much sexuality concentrated in a young girl's eyes. They rape me with their gaze. Hot! Hot! Hot sensation...

In this crowd pass old bedouins with creased faces and lordly bearing, ebony giants from the South, their foreheads with scarified bars, enormous mamas with senatorial demeanor, their wrists burdened with cuffs and gold rings and wearing on their cheeks the *shilloukh*, three deep vertical gashes that give them the gaze of dueñas. And men by the thousands in white djellabas, with a white turban or skull cap. All gracious and happy so see us among them.

Khartoum is the first African megalopolis that we extensively explore, of which we try to uncover the secrets. We comb behind the three banks, Khartoum, Omdurman and Bahari, in quest of souks, rituals, celebrations, prayers.

In the evening, the young assemble in "clubs" entirely surrounded by iron fences, sitting on the grass under floodlights that implicitly limit intimacy. They are allowed to mix and speak together, but not to touch in public. In private, it is authorized only after marriage. Much restraint and dignity emanate from these groups of youths, but marked by an undefinable sadness. Adults too have their clubs, each according to his social, religious or professional caste; there is the Coptic club, much in vogue since it is the only place in the capital where one can officially (but discreetly) drink alcohol, the Syrian club, the International Club and its pool, valued by the reasonably well-to-do expatriates, the officers' club, the diplomats' club, the Palace – a hotel for nabobs with a pool that has just been placed off limits to women – and of course the Hilton, the inescapable meeting place for all the country's deciders, intriguers, lobbyists, business men and expatriates at the top of the heap.

The heat is overpowering. It is over fifty degrees in the Bayuda desert we want to cross; we are therefore waiting for the first rains and profiting from this delay to obtain special authorizations from the Egyptian authorities since we have very pessimistic echoes coming from the North. In Egypt, it is forbidden to walk along the Nile and to move outside the police convoys that assure tourists' safety. We also give our first lecture at the French cultural center, before a public of a hundred or so francophone and francophile Sudanese. Florence Tran and Pascal Cardeilhac, our co-directress and our editor – who are also lovers in life – have sent us a first cut of an hour and a half of our footage, which is warmly applauded. We shall always remember this judgment of a spectator who came to thank us: "Thank you with all my heart for sacrificing three years of your lives, three years of comfort and safety, for our continent which is said to be hopeless, for one clearly sees through your images and your words that there is indeed hope: Africans are capable of such love. It's so good of you to express it to the French public."

This center, endowed with a fine air-conditioned media library, a terrace, and a director totally devoted to his mission, is the most active cultural institution in the city. Concerts, exhibits, workshops, classes, exchanges, lectures, trips, social assistance, humanitarian action, it participates in all causes and worthily represents our country's values. Bravo! The youth of Khartoum flock to it. For them it is also one of the rare places where girls and boys can talk together without fearing the control of the vice squad or their families: it is more or less the rendezvous point and meeting club of the city. A fine tool of French exception.

In the daytime, we snoop in the Omdurman souk, an unbelievable turntable between Africa, Asia and the Middle East; we track Sufi ceremonies in the four corners of the city, attend marriages, tribal spectacles and private rituals. We often visit the French Department of Sudanese Antiquities, active in the Sudan for over forty years, currently under the direction of Francis Geus, assisted by a young doctoral candidate, Raphaël Pourriel, who kindly open to us the doors of the laboratory where they work, among others, on the treasures exhumed from meroitic graves. Thus we discover the marvels left by the civilizations that have succeeded one another along the great river since the dawn of humanity and in the footsteps of which we are henceforth walking: iron arrowheads of Nubian archers, rings with engraved stones bearing griffins of forgotten gods, hellenistic cameos, perfume vases in blown glass, thick and heavy, the concretions of which await analysis, kohl compacts, neolithic make-up palettes in porphyry or graywacke, smooth as velvet, six thousand years old, antediluvian beads and jewels, terracotta big-bottomed statuettes strangely resembling our European neolithic Venuses. Raphaël is gluing together earthen pots that are finely decorated with amazingly modern animal motifs, full of humor and mastery. Here a croaking frog, there a leopard caught in mid-leap by the artist's eye...

At the Hilton, at UNICEF, at the United Nations, we encounter day after day a variety of consultants, peace makers, mediators, specialists in conflict resolution, businessmen, bankers, all nicer and full of good will than the others. They flood into Khartoum from the four winds to try at great expense to teach Northern Sudanese officials to make peace with the rebels in the South. This has been going on for thirty-nine years. And not succeeding. A game of dupes where the speakers always come away delighted with their richly remunerated presentations and which the recipients use in order to take in hand and delay the peace protocols, get around the journalists, diplomats and observers also implicated, blinded and instrumentalized by this ballet of lectures and lecturers. A smoke screen created by the government in order to pursue in complete freedom its policy of unification at all costs and its attacks on the human rights. And peace recedes. And the specter of war sticks its nose in again...[2]

Moreover, another front has just opened in Darfur, in the far west, near the Chad border. This time, it is Muslims who are revolting, tired of being the country's poor relatives. After the rebellion in Kassala, in the east, this one is being put down in blood. To serve as an example. Villages bombed, populations displaced, a

---

[2] On 9 January 2005, a peace treaty was finally signed between the North and South. A referendum on self-determination in the South is due for 2011. Unfortunately, John Garang, historical leader of the southerners SPLA was killed in a dubious helicopter crash seven months later, one month after having been invested as vice-president. The Darfur civil war, though it doubtless contributed to accelerating that signature, unfortunately was not included in that peace agreement. It has since then concentrated all international ire towards the Sudanese regime.

procession of horrors. The world is mobilizing, Khartoum is hopping, these thousands of Westerners confined to their hotels are in the starting blocks. They are finally going to be able to be useful, to go into action, and that is good, since that is their vocation, but it's strange, no one is interested in the cause of the evil, which is the regime. They treat it with kid gloves. It must be said that there are few people still on the terrain to confirm these informations. Ambassadors prudently raise the tone. It is a temporary crisis, they say to themselves, the revolt will soon be reduced and we will have offended for nothing this government that is "on the right track." Omar al-Bashir commits his little murders among friends, and the world comes and counts the bodies. So? Skirmishes or massacres?[3]

But what never ceases to surprise us is that in the course of the numerous encounters we have in the city, very rare are the expatriates of all nationalities who talk about the South, the war, the regime, the displaced populations, the closed universities, the newspapers shut down, the imprisoned journalists, the arbitrary arrests, the attacks on the fundamental rights of the "non-Arab" populations. As if all that didn't exist, as if everything was fine. Stockholm syndrome with a "Munich" tendency? In defense of those who say nothing, there is the fact that they are prisoners of the capital without any possibility of moving into those regions without special permits, and especially the fact that the Northern Sudanese are extraordinarily nice, exceptionally generous, which leads one to like their culture and "Sudanity" without restraint and sometimes without discernment. In the name of friendship, they neglect the flaws in the picture, the shadows of the South. Only from our Iranian friend Homayoun Alizadeh, Human Rights high commissioner, do we hear a dissonant bell, without ambiguity. In fact, peace is doing nothing but progress on paper, the

---

[3] At the time we were there, this fragmentary information already reported two thousand dead and villages bombarded; we know what has happened since then.

signatories have difficulty finding new cities in Kenya or elsewhere[4] to put down their signatures that are written in blood letters since, because in the field, the massacres and persecutions continue as if nothing had happened.

We are invited in the evenings to concerts, cocktails, dinners, to the 14 July, most appreciated throughout Khartoum for its famous bar; in the course of these worldly events, worlds apart from our trek, but to which our trek provides access, we meet people of such diverse horizons that in the long run it annoys some of the people in the French community.

"So when are you leaving?" we are constantly asked.

"We are waiting for a new pair of shoes and for the temperature to drop," we tell them. We don't have the same concerns. Notable are the great kindness and affability of the French Ambassador and Cultural Counselor, who receive, support and encourage us in our approaches to the Egyptian authorities. We are witnesses and observers without portfolio, with no label, attracting the friendship of the curious and the hostility of the ill-humored. Our second appearance in *Paris Match* causes certain teeth to gnash.

In the course of our strolls around Khartoum, in quest of interesting subjects to film, we find ourselves one Friday evening in the Hadj Youssif neighborhood, to the north of Bahari, a popular quarter of displaced Southerners, where Christians and Muslims live in harmony. The mud houses spread endlessly and innumerable Blacks stroll about on their long legs with or without djellabas. Here assemble, in an abandoned corner of the market, behind a round enclosure of extended tarps, the Sudan we will not see: the one of the Southern immensities, peopled with shy tribes whose names alone evoke beauty and Africanness: Dinkas, Nuers, Nubas, Shilluks. We are attending a gathering of Nuba wrestlers, one of

---

[4] N'Djamena, Abuja 1 and 2, Nairobi 1, 2 and 3, Pretoria, Addis Ababa, Akoret, Nakuru 1 and 2, Machakos 1, 2 and 3, Naivasha 1 and 2, the meetings follow each other with their shattering declarations, their steps forward and backward...

the country's one hundred fifty tribes, already long since Islamized, ethnically "Southern" (if that means something) but politically and religiously "Northern."

The arena is a hundred meters in diameter. All around the perimeter, four or five rows of spectators are seated on the ground. Two camps and two teams face each other. The reds and the blues, two localities in Hadj Youssif. Our arrival is noted. We are the only Westerners. The atmosphere at this end of the day is already hot, a circus clamor arises from the crowd. Two wrestlers face off, torsos bent over, arms extended and fingers spread. For the moment they are just doing the introductions. A whistle blows. It goes very fast. They rush at each other, grab each other by the back of the neck, forehead to forehead, and start turning like a two-bladed propeller, raising a cloud of dust. Suddenly blue takes a step backwards to try to unbalance red, who takes advantage of the move to move forward, grab blue under the armpits, trip him and drop him. He is down. It's over. Red has won and launches into a mad sprint, like a soccer player who has just scored, toward his joyful public who carry him in triumph, straight as an *I*, astraddle a bearer's shoulder.

Nuba wrestling was discovered in 1948 by an American war reporter, George Rodger, who, weary of the massacres of the Second World War, had come to Africa to renew himself amidst men who remained outside the contemporary world. From the Nuba mountains he brought back the famous photo of a wrestler covered in ashes, carried this way in triumph; his musculature, lordly nakedness, pure and savage beauty marked several generations of photographers and explorers. That very photo was to lead Leni Riefensthal, in quest of expiation, into these remote areas, where she was to take, in the 1960s and 1970s, splendid photos of a martial art that today is modernized and sanitized. Nostalgia for a lost tribalism? Myth of the "noble savage" restored by a *fin de siècle* in search of its identity? Her photos will remain, along with those of Carol Beckwith and Angela Fischer, irreplaceable ethnographic documentation on the beauty of men, their creativity, and the diversity of their practices. It would be impossible to reproduce these photos today. Our wrestlers are in designer fluorescent shorts and synthetic net T-shirts, the crowd is dressed in djellabas, and all would be hard pressed to reproduce their facial paintings, and most uneasy walking around naked...

The battle loses something in folklore and gains something in safety. Nuba wrestling today is very codified; it is no longer about splitting each other's skull open with bronze bracelets. The spectators are there for pleasure and relaxation. Instead of martial and initiatory, Nuba wrestling has become the Friday entertainment.

Resumption. After this appetizer, a giant rises from the red camp and takes a step into the arena. A huge clamor makes the public vibrate. He's the champion! Who immediately undertakes a comic dance, in the manner of a fighting cock, uttering with every step a sharp note that doesn't fit his stature. Hyper-arched, his behind in the air, he scrapes the ground with his foot like an enraged Minotaur, and with arms wide open and trembling hands, does a funny quickstep for intimidation and call to combat, turning his head from right to left, eyes bulging, to provoke the crowd. The blue camp is shaken with spasms. They don't know whom to send to the colossus. They have to save face. Two or three men get up, sit back down amidst invectives, get up again, there are tough negotiations going on. The referee punctuates them with whistle blows, and ratifies the choice of the new wrestler. He stimulates the crowd, wants it to participate. They're looking for a challenger! The referee is fair. Nuba wrestling is not a slaughter. He sends back several pretenders who, despite their bravery, would get themselves creamed. Don't have the caliber. The crowd judges with laughter and hurrahs these comings and goings, these recantations, these rejected pretenders. It's all part of the show. For the battles are very short and something must fill the endless interludes.

Finally a big, stocky guy advances. A hundred twenty solid kilos. A good head shorter than the other. More flesh than muscle, but dense flesh and the neck of a bull. Our athlete with narrow waist, broad shoulders and very long arms cracks a big smile; he must like rolling hippos in the dirt! The referee judges the match fair, he gives his approval and a loud whistle.

The colossal Apollo lowers himself and with his broadly spread palms caresses the sand in the arena to dry his hands. In his tribe, in South Kordofan, they used to cover themselves with ash during the ritual matches and there was no need of magnesia to assure a good hold. This gesture draws a salute and the beginning of the bout....The two titans look each other over, turn, and turn again, gauge and concentrate before any contact, then the hands begin with little slaps and dodges, with the heavyweights the battles don't last long, the violence of the shock is ten times as great; the one who has an advantage after the first hold has a good chance of winning, so they don't take risks, they wait for the other one to attack. And here, no one attacks, each waits for the other to make a mistake. They turn round and round, bent double, and wave their paws around as if they were two fans taking each other on. The tension rises in the crowd that calls for a fight, the referee threatens them with his whistle: the regulation time for the bout will soon expire. Many bouts end this way for want of combatants... but suddenly the bull springs forward and grasps one of Hercules's legs from underneath. He, surprised, goes over the bull's back and grabs him around his waist. He is raised off the ground; the reds, immediately on their feet, scream with terror, "no, not so fast, it can't happen!" With a strong thrust of the other leg and a hop, the Hercules unbalances the bull, who lets go so as not to fall on his ass, but counters by butting his lowered head into the giant's gut. The giant sees it coming, absorbs the charge, grabs the backbone of the mad ram and with a twist of the torso turns the muscles mass over, all fours up...

The whole crowd rises as one and runs in all directions. The victor helps the vanquished up, the first without pride, the second without rancor, a smile on his lips, as if he had just slipped on a banana peel. Carried in triumph like a god of the stadium, our giant bows from time to time so his admirers can with a big slap stick bills on the sweat of his brow. Everyone is happy, even the losers, you don't come to win but to see the champions. Two to nothing, the reds have the advantage. They keep it. At the end of the bouts, when the sun is flirting with the horizon, they win eight to one. Then, from a minaret that towers over the arena, comes the call to prayer *al-Maghreb*, the prayer of the setting sun, the crowd rises happy and quickly disperses. Control, restraint, sporting in spirit and good-natured, Nuba wrestling may have lost its traditional character, but it has retained its role in social and identity ferment. Far from the Nuba mountains, a granite-block chaos haunted by giant baobabs, the soul of a people continues on in joy, behind the tarps of a vacant lot.

On another vacant lot, another day, on the banks of Omdurman, we attend in late afternoon the Sufi ceremony of Hamad al-Nil. At the heart of a vast cemetery, a group of silver-domed mausoleums is the rallying point of a motley crowd of costumed dancers and spectators. Drums or cymbals give the rhythm, covered by reedy bombards[5]. The crowd opens into a wide circle. In this arena, men in line, dressed in white from head to toe, pass counterclockwise before the spectators with slow dragging steps. They are singing and clapping, followed by dervishes outfitted in extravagant gowns made up of thousands of little pieces of fabric sewn together, a patchwork decorated with amulets and pendants. Their eyes reddened by abuse of hashish and their step hesitating, their heads bristling with long interwoven braids, they size up their public, emaciated and ecstatic. They look like *sadhus* disguised as golliwogs: they are the whirling dervishes of Hamad an-Nil. Vaguely dragging about, in search of inspiration, our dancers make some simpering gestures, then, suddenly, at a mysterious call, begin to turn around in a gyrating procession. Their gowns spread into colored corollas, their braids come unfurled and beat

---

[5] Powerful blowing instrument, sounding a bit like the pipe chanter of a bagpipe.

the evening air, the public's excitement grows, spectators join in the round, elbow to elbow. Leopard skins and sticks stretched out, boubous and white djellabas, tambourines and the youyous of the women, nasal cornets and clapping, the ambiance is festive and baroque, chaotic and mystical. From this jumble rise fragments of prayers repeated until a trance is reached, but helter-skelter, in a moronic canon, in nascent sweat and setting sun. And the dervishes, who are still spinning, are intent on melting their individuality, their voices, souls, bodies, into this collective physical and spiritual debauchery. It has something of a rave, it's a moment from which all seem to derive joy and release, weekly safety valve for seven days of restraint, interdictions and gravity.

While I am filming, drowned in the heart of the mottled assembly, a young man in a white cap and thick beard accosts me to whisper in my ear: "What you are seeing there is not Islam. Understand that! It is forbidden! It is not halal. It is not pure. These are heretical practices! And we are going to put an end to them..."

Sensing he has been spotted, the young visionary immediately disappears, pursued by two clearly annoyed colossi. A brief skirmish follows of which I do not well perceive the outcome. An affable, mature man who has been watching the scene comes over to me.

"What did the young man say to you?"

"That these dances are heretical practices..."

"Don't believe him. It was surely a young man who has just been in Saudi Arabia. All our youths are obliged to go work there. They come back formatted by the Wahhabism of the emirs, prepared to reject the roots of Sudanese culture. It doesn't augur anything good for our country..."

In the evening, when we relate the scene to my uncle Etienne, he confirms the differences and rivalries that exist between the various Sufi brotherhoods and foreign Islamic influences. To him, Sudanese Sufism is one of the last examples of a cultural exception in the international convergence experienced by Sunni Islam thanks to the Internet, the satellite dishes, and the lowering of the transportation costs to Mecca.

"Sudanese Sufism is founded on the expectation of the Mahdi, the Messiah who will convert the entire world to Islam before the last judgment. The Mahdi has already returned several times in their history, the last time in 1880 during a revolt that was crushed in blood by Kitchener, after the sack of the city and the death of Gordon. Mahdi Mohammed Ahmed became a true warlord recognized everywhere in the Sudan, lived as an ascetic mendicant and sewed pieces of fabric taken from his victims on his djellaba. That is the origin of the traditional gowns worn by the dancers. Next week, I will show you a much more fascinating ceremony! You will really understand what the Sufi inspiration is...and its powerful spirituality."

The street is blocked. In front of the mosque, the roadway is entirely covered with plastic mats boasting camels. The setting sun casts a golden hue all over. Two minarets pointed heavenward indicate the straight way to Man. These are aligned along two walls on either side of the street, facing each other.

Close to a thousand men in long white cotton djellabas, fine and becoming. They have a diagonal leather cross-belt over their torso that lends a martial touch to their gathering. The sweet perfumes of all these close-shaved believers, washed and dolled up to please God, float in the syrupy evening air. At each end of the two-hundred-meter-long street, a row of men closes the white living rectangle. A black spot breaks this white string in the middle: the sheikh, draped in a thin jade cape with a magnificent turban. Minds are bent toward him. A general silence weighs on all these men standing at attention.

He suddenly raises his stick as a marshal would do, and lowers it right away, uttering a corporal's cry to begin the movement. Then slowly, with the inertia of a locomotive starting up, voices rise and torsos turn to the right, then to the left, punctuating their rotation with a slight movement of the head, which makes their sleeves beat like wings. The sheikh slowly accelerates the cadence with his stick, orchestra conductor of the great praying machine. In the mounting clamor, one can finally make out: *"La-Ilaha-Illa-Allah!"* (There is no God but God.)

Scanned in 4/4 time corresponding to right-face-left-face, but imperceptibly, the metronome picks up, adrenaline gets into it, throats are deployed, faces composed. Like a single man, like a single soul, joining gesture to word and dance to prayer, a thousand men enter little by little, fever in the temples and lungs swollen with God, into the collective intoxication of power and faith: this is a Sufi ceremony at the as-Sammaniyah mosque in Omdurman. One of the five hundred brotherhoods in the Sudan.

At a call, the twists are replaced with forward inflections, still in 4/4 time. The men become motion rods: *"La-Ilaha-Illa-Allah!"* with a syncope between each beat. Waltz with God, the eyes roll upward, breathing shortens and purrs in the throats like the air in forge pipes. The cadence again steps up, the warmup is over, the revving up is being prepared. They suffer, they pant, they sweat, curb little growls and sacrifice their effort to God, whom it pleases.

All at once the sheikh leaves the row, enters the dance, galvanizes his troops, alone in the middle of the great rectangle, and encourages the inflections like a sports club trainer, like the drum of a galley.

Seen from the roof where we have taken refuge, the rectangle of men, the mass of jumping links has become a single, flat body the white fringe of which palpitates in time like the lip of a jellyfish, like the foam of a human surf. At a cry, the inflection changes to a vertical leap; the men become pistons; then it seems that the rectangle, that the entire street takes flight at the name of God: *La* on the ground, *Ilaha* in flight, *Illa* on the ground, *Allah* in flight. The djellabas puffed up in the air current remain suspended a moment in space, halting time.

This is the paroxysm, the ecstasy, a thousand men fly and in their levitation chant the name of God like a throbbing heartbeat. The sheikh is in seventh heaven, he lowers his crank, the machine stops all at once, blissful and smoking. The mechanism is well broken in, well oiled. God is happy this evening.

Overhead, a network of misters linked by slender pipes spread perfumed coolness over the audience like the breath of the Almighty. Can't halt progress. Before the dances start again, the sheikh begins a sermon. His flock is all ears, together and united. Later, everyone will interrupt everything for the sundown prayer: *al-Maghreb*.

We are then very politely introduced into a room decorated with surates magnificently interlaced on a black velvet background, in which members of the brotherhood come to greet us, converse with us with authentic kindness in the eyes, most concerned about the bad image of Islam in the news in the last few years. We are with Father Etienne, jovial and luminous, and a great friend of the sheikh. Between translations, our hosts' explanations and the cups of tea we are served, he explains what we have just seen.

"Sudanese Sufism is a sort of collective ascesis, a quest of spiritual purity through physical purity, a sort of *mens sana in corpore sano*[6] applied to Islam. What we just saw is called a *zikr*, the physical exercise is not an end in itself but the means of putting in place a breath, a propitious breathing to praising God. The Russian Orthodox have something like it with the notion of perpetual prayer, the *Kyrie eleison*. They concentrate all their faith into a few syllables which are to express the ineffable."

He takes a swallow of burning tea and continues his explanation.

"Did you see the increase in power when they turn their heads from right to left, puffing HOU-HA-HI, as a runner catches his breath? The head slightly tilted toward the sky, they say HA, from

---

[6] A sound mind in a sound body.

left to right they say HOU and as they lean they say HI. Well, that
has a particular meaning: in the first HA, the believer must hold in
mind that God is everywhere, beyond and above all things; in the
HOU, the believer tries to be conscious that every movement or
every word comes from God, not from human will. It is to admit
an absolute divine determinism, God alone being the only free
entity, and the faithful being subject to divine law, the Qu'ran and
the sharia. The HI recalls essentially to men that they are mortal
and that we shall return to dust. Breath plays a determining role,
for hyperventilation and the release of endorphins confer a well-
being and a feeling of power immediately attributed to the virtues
of prayer and as a direct and personal response from God. You
might say that the Zikr is an existential experience of divine energy
at the end of which the faithful feel 'full' of God."

They bring us some more tea. Father Renaud continues: "These
Sufi brotherhoods appeared very early in the history of Islam, at
the beginning of the second millennium, in response to the limited
character of the *Shahada*, the Muslim declaration of belief, and the
application of the five daily prayers. They partake of a will to go
farther in the spiritual quest and to have a more complete religious
life....It is also an expression of devotion to the sheikh and total
submission to Islam."

Playing the devil's advocate, I query the Father: "Don't we
have there all the elements of extremism?"

He makes a pout. "As long as Sufism is content with the personal ascesis and does not get mixed up in politics, it will be spared
by the conflation of the spiritual and the temporal that Islam
experiences today, whether Sunni, Shiite, Wahhabite or Ismaelian.
Islam can only be total, conceived as a whole, a complete logic that
ill abides evolutions. Yet Sufism is one, so it isn't impossible, but
Wahhabism calls such practices heretic. Now it is gaining here. As
far as Sudanese Sufism is concerned, I believe that, despite appearances, it presents elements of ascesis and detachment that you can
find also in Hinduism, Buddhism and Christianity. For example,

the faithful of the Sammaniyah must respect four fundamental principles.

"The first is to reduce their food consumption, they say literally: 'The stomach is never full,' the second is silence and the purity of the word. Harmful, excessive, angry or impure words and thoughts are forbidden. They speak of 'silence of the heart to illicit thoughts.' The third principle is vigil, nighttime prayer, the struggle against sleep. They speak of 'divine insomnia for the awakening of the heart to illumination.' The fourth is solitude. You do not leave God when you leave the Sufi community: you find him again one on one.

"Therefore, with respect to all that, Sudanese Sufism offers a model of personal wisdom and not of extremism, but the Sudanese must remain vigilant in the face of external influences, crowd phenomena, the media. The Internet and the globalization of Islamic practices and beliefs unfortunately do not encourage these interesting particularisms."

One of the faithful takes me under his wing: Omar Sadiq. He is curious and wants to know everything about our odyssey, then we come to more personal questions. He admits, among other things, to being against polygamy, against excision and infibulation – practiced on 97% of women in the North, to being horrified by September 11, terrorism, resentful of Palestinian suicide bombers for besmirching the name of Islam, and of extremists for their violence and bloodletting.

"No suicide pleases God. Even if used to punish the guilty. *A fortiori* when it targets innocents! God alone is judge…"

He speaks of the debate over the Islamic veil in France in unexpected terms, but which we have already heard in Khartoum and Zanzibar: "It is not the veil that makes the purity of woman. It is the gaze of men. Have you seen the hypocrisy of our women? They take more time to veil themselves than yours do to do their makeup! With transparent veils! They do that to excite us! And woe to us if we look! They are teases! Here, the veil and what it hides have become modes of seduction and fantasizing, whereas its purpose ought to be to calm things down…"

When we leave, our Sufi ranks have resumed their gymnastic ballet under orangish spotlights and I cannot help seeing in the shadows projected on the walls, in the long gowns and leather belts, in the corporal unity of these soldiers of God, the atmosphere that must have prevailed in the Krak des Chevaliers, in Syria, where the crusading armies were mobilizing against Saladin. With a helmet and a big red cross on their backs, they would be perfect. All they need is a scimitar on their cross-belt. Happily, the charm evaporates and Omar Sadiq, who has chosen me, slips me as a token of friendship, with a broad smile and fraternal embrace, a package of Sudanese nougats.

CHAPTER

27

Meroe, the
Truncated Pyramids

SUDAN

A jawbone in the desert. That is how the mythical Meroe appears to us from a distance. A titanic fossil mandible with black stumps of teeth, sitting on the sand in desolation. Then we draw closer and recognize the slender but truncated pyramids, aligned at the summit of a rocky ridge smoothed by dunes which figure the gums of these historical fangs.

From a little closer still, you become aware of their dilapidation. A powerful melancholy emanates from the site. Of the forty or so pyramids still visible, a dozen, the largest, still bear the facings of tawny sandstone in quite vertical stairs. Decapitated, the pyramids have lost their equilibrium; advanced swellings from inside disjoint the blocks and threaten to cave in like the belly of a worm-eaten hulk. From the breaks in the masonry, the embankment that fills them pathetically pours itself out. The dunes that dance at the foot of these funereal monuments seem to be waiting until they can devour entirely these vestiges of the past that speak once more to us of the human grandeur, hopes and vanity.

Though fragile, these little pyramids hold up, brace themselves, maintain their rank! We review them; from some angles, they look almost intact, and the impeccable sides of one, the exposed edges of another, the symmetry of those two, or the singularity of this one, make of the site a homogeneous and powerful whole. They are united towards and against all, towards and against time. They have survived looters, explorers, treasure hunters, they survived annihilation, forgetfulness, and draw from that desperate survival against the elements something profoundly aristocratic.

From Khartoum we have taken a side-trip of two hundred kilometers down the Nile to pay homage to Meroe, the mysterious necropolis the civilization of which, from the third century B.C.E. to the third century C.E., never ceased to focus the attention of the Ancient world. Heliodorus, Herodotus, Strabo, Pliny and Seneca concocted fables of Upper Nubia, the realm of Cush, or that of Punt, which they collected under the term Ethiopia (from the Greek *aethiops*: burnt face, and by extension black face) – which more or less amalgamated, among phantasms of lost cities and extravagant tales of chimeras and cyclopses, all of interior Africa of which they saw only the treasures come out. Thus was little by little constructed the legend of Meroe, which would not be discovered until 1821 by a Frenchman, Frédéric Cailliaud.

However, since ancient Egypt, these regions and the civilizations that have succeeded one another have been known and feared: that of Kerma (from 2500 to 1500 B.C.E.) beyond the third falls of the Nile, much farther north, conquered by the Middle Empire, than that of Napata (this side of the fourth falls), which went to conquer Lower Egypt to found the XXVth dynasty, that of the Black pharaohs, which reigned as far as the Nile delta for more than a century.

Under other reigns, Nubia was a vassal; it was used as a footbridge between Black Africa and the Mediterranean world. They protected themselves from it, since it was too far away to be totally subjugated but they needed it for gold and ivory, to provide to the courts and circus games wild animals such as rhinoceroses, giraffes, lions, leopards, monkeys, and all the bestiary you see filing by on the frescoes of certain necropolises, relating in grand pomp the "Nubian tribute" brought to the pharaohs.

You also find there the fearsome "Nubian archers," mercenaries employed as far away as the Near East. But what best characterizes the Meroitic civilization and would mark its apogee is the role of the Kandakes (queens), whose renown would force the emperor Augustus to treat this distant empire on an equal footing. That is not insignificant!

We also discover our first Kandake on the pediment of a votive chapel placed beside a pyramid. Arithenyesbokhe is a warrior queen, huge and dreadful, who holds by the hair a cluster of bound enemies which she runs through with her spear. Under her feet, a lion is munching on the skull of a slave. Certain archeologists think prisoner sacrifices celebrated the victories of these regent matrons; others think these images are more like hyperboles and demonstration of power. The Kandake wears a tiara, with the attributes of power, the *uraei*: two serpents that incarnate the union of the two Egypts.

Sonia enters the chapel and utters an exclamation. On the walls of the small room are finely engraved in bas relief scenes of banquets, processions, devotions, where gods and the faithful, relatives and slaves parade bringing their offerings to the dead person's memory. There were also in these meroitic chapels statues of Ba about a meter tall, representing the head of the deceased with the body of a bird and long wings crossing in the back. They symbolized their soul. Finally a dominant stele vaunted the merits and power of the dead person, written in a language that has not yet been completely deciphered.

The pyramids are full, they are just memorials built on top of crypts dug in the rock, ten meters below, which you reach through a ramp that is now filled in, and that opened fifty meters from there. These chapels thus served only to perpetuate the memory of queens and kings, not to bury them. They were a place of worship and libations, rituals and offerings to Isis and Amon. Today, the altar has disappeared, as has the offering table, the votive stele and the Ba statues. All those treasures are dispersed in museums, to the four corners of the planet.

In the graves, on the other hand, Roman bronzes have been found, glasses from the Near East, Greek mirrors and many objects, which testify to exchanges that linked Meroe to the rest of the world. The city was celebrated for its foundries, which provided arrowheads and spearheads for their fearsome archers.

The sun is going down and a wind rises that combs the dunes, raising wisps of sand. At the corner of a chapel and between two lintels, we discover graffiti of Cailliaud, Letorzec and Linant de Bellefonds, hardy Frenchmen lost in these parts by the winds and the vagaries of History. A little farther it's an Italian knight or a Russian prince, the first European explorers who, at the sides of the Turkish colonists who had taken possession of Egypt, could penetrate these remote regions by joining up with immense armies decimated by the hardships of the journey. Here is how Frédéric Cailliaud described his discovery: "Never was my joy more extreme and intense than when I discovered the tops of these numerous pyramids shining in the sun's rays that seemed to gild the tops of these tombs that for so many centuries had been seen by no traveler. It seemed that never, for me, would there be a happier day than this one, I climbed the highest of these monuments to engrave there the name of d'Anville."

We too climb to the top of the intact pyramid of Tanyida-mani to enjoy the last rays of the sun and escape the gusts of a strong sandy wind. The ascension is vertiginous and vertical, but the small stone thrust faults form steps just wide enough for our feet. We watch out for scorpions and snakes which, by making us let go, could send us tumbling to the bottom. The summit peaks at twenty or thirty meters. It goes without saying that we do not engrave our names – *O tempora, o mores!*[1] Viewed from above, the pyramids are scraggly; we can understand clearly the depredations caused by looters who, as early as 1834, because of the Italian Ferlini, undertook to dismantle all the pyramid summits. He had just discovered the one hundred six golden objects of the fabulous treasure of Amanishaketo's crypt and thought he was protecting the site by pretending he had found it at the summit of the pyramid, of which there remains only the chapel and foundations. Today, half a dozen pyramids and chapels have been restored by German archeologists.

While the sun wallows in western gold, we evoke the arrival in this area of the Ethiopian king Ezana of Axum who, in 380, came and razed what was left of the city. The sun of Amon set forever over Meroe. From twenty meters up, two thousand years flow by at our feet in the red wind. Along the Nile that glimmers in the distance, civilizations have come and gone; how many tragedies have these deserts witnessed? Caravans, marching armies, Nubian archers, ferocious Kandakes, sacrifices, explorers, tomb raiders…

By following the Nile we are henceforth on a civilizational stairway, and to see what remains of these empires that made the earth tremble, that subjugated peoples, exploited untold riches, made the sound of their weapons resound to the ends of the known world, humbles our trek and puts each of our steps into perspective. *Vanitas vanitatum, et omnia vanitas.*[2]

---

[1] "Oh what times, oh what mores!" (Cicero)
[2] "Vanity of vanities, and all is vanity." (Ecclesiastes)

CHAPTER

28

The Doukhan and the Zar

SUDAN

E xceptionally, it is I, Sonia, who take up the pen, for my status as a woman has opened to me Sudanese doors to which Alexandre has no access.

The Sudan being placed under the rule of sharia, strict Islamic law, masculine and feminine societies are completely separate, at least in the private sphere, for in the public sphere women enjoy considerable freedom of movement, even a preponderant role. That is a Sudanese paradox. Women are present in public functions, omnipresent in the streets, where they have pride of place. The Sudanese woman has a sacred character. As for the mysteries of the gynaeceum, to which I have often been initiated, there is one which occupies a place of choice in the preoccupations of my amiable hostesses: the *doukhan*. It is a rite of seduction, an amorous preparation, and one can even without exaggeration speak of an apprenticeship in sexual devotion to the husband. A whole program!

Before entering into the quick of this juicy subject, rather unexpected in a society one mistakenly imagines as prudish, I must describe the extraordinary excitement which my presence provokes among these women of all ages. Their number often approaches a dozen; they pull me right and left, auscultate me in all directions, want to see how I am put together, fondle my hands, my hair, feel my skin, survey with a moue of disapproval my zones of blond fuzz and manipulate me laughingly like you discuss the weight of a chicken in the butcher's case.

They immediately adopt me. I am a woman, I am one of them. Their kindness is such that I lend myself willingly to their caprice, since in exchange that allows me to discover the hidden face of their lives. As a preamble, one remark: the expression that asserts that "you have to suffer to be pretty" takes on its full value in the Sudan. Are you ready, ladies? Let's go for the *doukhan....Yallah!*[1]

Samia opens the hostilities with the *halawa*, which literally, in Arabic, means "candy" or "sweet." In fact, it is the opposite, since it is a complete, violent rush that ends in a rash. One is not simply shaven, that would be too easy, no, it is a pursuit of the slightest hair, the slightest fuzz by plucking it. Everywhere! Arms, legs, shoulders, ears, cheeks, nose, mouth...*Alouette, je te plumerai!* And yes, evidently, the private parts, where you're the tenderest: everything must go. Ouch! ouch! ouch!

So why "candy," you may ask. Because the wax (which is not wax) is made of lemon juice and caramelized sugar. The objective, as you will have understood, is to be made soft to the touch. I have only partially respected the rules of this first set which made me squeal like a flayed pig, muffled by the screams of laughter of my joyous torturers.

Once I am totally plucked and washed, Samia moves on to the doukhan proper, which is a sort of artisanal sauna arranged in the women's quarters, in the corner of a courtyard. It is made up of a jar or amphora set into the ground up to the opening. In this cavity they burn an aromatic wood, *talaha*, from the South Sudanese jungles, which smokes terribly. Naked under a poncho made of a sheet and a mantle that covers me like a bell, I am seated over the fire. The goal

---

[1] Forward!

being a fumigation of the body, the pussy and the rest, but especially of the pussy. Ouch, ouch, ouch! The *prestou* can begin – which is to say, in the text, "the pressure cooker" (Sudanese women have great humor!). You are in for thirty minutes, an hour, even two hours of braising, the vapor coming not from the hearth but from perspiration. The neck of the poncho is transformed into a factory chimney that burns your nostrils and the love a woman has for her husband can be measured by the time she can keep simmering in the heat chamber; I must appear a very poor lover: I could not hold out for longer than twenty minutes! Let me recall that, in the daytime, the temperature varies between 40° C and 50° C. In these conditions, what you are dreaming of is a deep freeze, not a pressure cooker. The purpose of this operation is to make the skin soft, bright (yellow for me, golden for them), and to fix the perfumes that are to follow.

Samia takes off the poncho covering me, like a maître d'hôtel would do with his bell, to uncover a smoked salmon. Tinted in the body, I am now subjected to the *dilka*, complete exfoliation done with a sort of brown chestnut oily paste that vaguely resembles tar, but turns out to be deliciously perfumed (especially smoked). The dead skin softened by the smoker does not resist it, especially since the microspheres of apricot stone powder dear to our beauticians are replaced here by sand from the Nile....In short, the dilka is like trying to clean with glass paper a poor animal covered in fuel oil. Sexy and glam. As a balm to this series of epidermal traumas, I am now annointed with *dihin*, aromatic sesame oil that removes the tar.

I am finally ready, all pores alert, for the *khomra*, the "perfume ablutions." After the pressure cooker, now it's the precious hooker! I do not resist the temptation to give you the composition of this precious spikenard, worthy of the retort of a sensual alchemist: ambergris spit up by a sperm whale, concentrate of musk powder, sandalwood oil, adulterated French perfumes that answer to the sweet names of Fleur d'Amour, Rives d'Or, Soir de Paris, and especially, the fatal weapon, get ready: ground powder of crocodile claws, which transforms this poisonous perfume into a genuine love philter.

After being plucked, cooked, peeled and coated, red as a tomato, I am ready for the sanctification: the *bakhour*, purification by incense. Dressed again in a djellaba, I see Samia slide between my legs a censer from which the wisps of smoke rise to imbue my temple of love, scenting the great entertainment center...

After all these culinary operations, it remains only to get laid. It is formally forbidden to go outside. First of all, you would be noticed for kilometers around; second, it would be perceived as a call to rape. You go up to join your husband who is chafing at the bit. And let the fireworks begin!

The doukhan lasts on average three hours and must be carried out at least once a week, most often on Thursday evening (the eve of Friday, day of rest). Some of our hostesses, especially the young married ones, do it daily to be always ready for consummation.

This lovely erotic sacrifice hides less appetizing realities, knowing that 97% of the Sudanese women of Arabic culture are excised and infibulated and that they are not entitled to carnal pleasures. And we're not talking of the obscure tradition of remote villages, no, it concerns twenty million Sudanese women. The doukhan is to be sure an act of love, but also of submission to the man who is its principal beneficiary. See them all cheerful around me, delighted that I have made it through this initiatory passage, I can appreciate the extent of their present, and feel a great surge of tenderness and compassion for my Sudanese sisters.

The infibulation of women, called "pharaonic," is a sewing of the labia majora that tightens the vaginal orifice. It is in no way Islamic. It is a tradition that goes back to time immemorial, as its name suggests. Only the origin of excision is open to controversy, and its defenders attribute to Islam the authorization of a practice on which the texts remain evasive at best. The minor hadith 5271 related by Abu Daoud states that the prophet Mohammed responded to Umm Atiyya, an old exciser of Medina who asked him for advice: "Circumcise girls but not excessively, for a moderate excision is appreciated by the woman and loved by the husband. Leave a little extension, not cutting completely, that will make her face more radiant and will be more pleasing to the husband." Nevertheless the custom has remained current until now, justified by a faith according to which the clitoris and labia make women licentious. The British condemned it in 1946 and it has remained forbidden by two Sudanese laws, but the weight of traditions that govern society remains stronger. Certain Islamic ideologues have gone so far as to proclaim that the worldwide campaign against excision is a plot to spread promiscuity in Islam and corrupt the purity of its family model. The reality is that the operation in 95% of the cases results in chronic pelvic and vaginal, urinary and sometimes septicemic infections. My women friends have all confessed to me that they are affected by these problems. The doukhan thus assumes another dimension: its antiseptic virtues make it an intimate hygienic necessity. Infibulation, which makes any birthing impossible without a surgical intervention since a passageway has to be opened for the child, was supposed to prevent clandestine births, and thus allow the harem owner or caravanner with families in various cities to be assured of the legitimacy of his progeny. Today, modern life makes these notions all the more outdated that infibulation absolutely does not prevent adultery, but the practice has remained, often despite the wishes of husbands and wives, under the pressure of grandmothers and mothers-in-law. Young girls are excised and infibulated as early as the age of four. After each childbirth, the women are systematically sewn back up, since that is the best way to allow the labia to scar closed. According to tradition, these practices protect women from the perils of the flesh by suppressing their libido. The reality of their psychological consequences is much more complex. The less you feel, the more you seek...

During our sojourn in Khartoum, I get to know many Sudanese women and am privileged to attend, and even participate in Zar ceremonies, from which men are excluded – the vengeance of women!

The Zar cult is a ceremony of festive exorcism, practiced by groups of women who get together around a sheikha, the Zar priestess, who officiates, diagnoses, prescribes offerings and controls potential excesses.

Why "festive"? Because here, it is done in music, in costume, in dance and unwinding. It's not a matter of driving out "spirits," as in classic exorcism, but on the contrary of satisfying them, calming them and appeasing them with offerings and sacrifices.

The basic principle is the belief that everyone is inhabited and influenced by one or several Zars, good or bad spirits. Sufferings, illnesses; conjugal, familial, professional problems; obsessions, oppressions, anxieties, jealousies, are all attributed to Zars. There are ninety-nine of them, from all over. The most fearsome are the Sudanese ones, about fifteen of them, then come the Ethiopian Zars, again about fifteen, Nigerian, Egyptian, Saudi Zars and even a few Asian Zars, one of which is Ondura, king of China, or the *khawadja* Zars, the Western ones, such as Denadir: the pacha of Europe, Kafario the German, or Domayo the Britisher, represented with a colonial hat, shorts, long stockings, a cane and a pipe.

The Zar cult is forbidden by the present regime; it is therefore becoming rare, practiced in secret, more often in the old popular quarter of Omdurman. In Arabic, the Zar is also called *ar Rih al ahmar*, the red wind...

Will you take the risk of catching a Zar? Come on, I'll take you!

Nazik,[2] my lovely hostess, introduces me into a courtyard encumbered with *angarebs*, traditional plaited beds, and assorted pieces of furniture. A muffled rhythm of drums covers women's voices and makes the walls vibrate. Nazik disappears down a hidden passageway, and I find myself alone with a tied-up ram. We are in the Omdurman suburbs, in a residential neighborhood where large families gather into small, low, tangled houses. Nazik returns with her great-aunt, the sheikha, who has accepted my presence. Draped in green, her face puffy and ravaged by very impressive black scars

---

[2] All names have been changed for the protection of the participants.

that crease her cheeks, the *shilloukh*, she extends to me a hand black with henna. With eyes of embers, her mien benevolent and welcoming, she brings me in. Following her, we go through a maze of small corridors and nooks that make me think of a labyrinth, and the vibrations increase along with the beating of my heart.

All at once we come into a dark, crowded room which gives off sweltering heat, scented, smoky and damp. Along the walls, bedecked women of all ages are seated on the floor, smoking like chimneys, while four musicians beat drums, tambourines and cymbals, singing loudly. A censer comes toward us, Nazik waves the smoke at her face, her palms, the sole of her feet, and puts it under her tobe, her large pink veil. I do likewise. The purification of our "impure" parts. After us the ram comes in, outfitted with a small red mantle. The women rise and dance around the terrified animal, a candle in their hands, then a procession takes shape, the ram in front, and we proceed to the first courtyard through the labyrinth. When I reach it, the animal has already had his throat slit and his blood is caught in a soup bowl. Uneasy, I look away while the animal is dying and belching his last breath. This is the first propitiatory sacrifice.

We return to the room while Nazik lists for me the various offerings that can satisfy the Zars' whims: sugar, fruit, candles, candy, perfumes, gold, a cell phone or a couple of doves....Everyone returns to her place and the music strikes up again. Nazik explains: "For each rhythm there is a corresponding Zar and song; it is a call! If a woman in attendance believes herself tormented by the Zar which the music addresses, she rises and begins to dance to please it: there it's an Ethiopian Zar, sultan Kassa; you shall see, it has a particular exigency!"

Indeed two women who were dancing with their hair down suddenly stand back to a wall against which they violently bang their shoulders, causing the house to tremble. Blow after blow, one shoulder blade after the other, the eyes roll back, the hoarse cries which they utter change into the yapping of coyotes, the tension rises, the spectacle becomes painful – their faces are distorted by a rictus of pain. They are approaching a trance when the sheikha raises her arm. The drums immediately stop and the two winded women fall to all fours, crawling toward the sheikha, who takes them by the hair, whispering comforting words to them and pouring purificatory water on their faces. They rise tried but relieved, with serene faces: their Zar is satisfied, and will leave them alone, for a while.

Another rhythm, another call, other women rise. In turn we see the crocodile Zar (Tomsa), the buffalo Zar (Weldi Noura), the Saudi homosexual Zar (Ali Bey), the Zar of the Ethiopian prostitutes (Luliya, Kofé, Salma…), of the "old grandfather of the gold mountain" (Djebel Naado), of the "old woman at the bottom of the sea," the one who paralyzes and deadens limbs; all with their capricious and tyrannical needs to assuage. To satisfy them, they disguise themselves, they mime, crawl, gore, laugh, unwind, the veils fall to reveal sexy clothing, flattering necklines, they place cigarettes in their nostrils, they spray themselves with perfume, they whip themselves, they feign stabbing themselves in the stomach, they wiggle their rump as an offering, they muss their hair while uttering tigress cries, they put on a huge pectoral cross, all being Muslim, crossing themselves frantically. I watch a strange cathartic procession of all the hidden sufferings of Sudanese women. Here they find their outlet, their public confession, in theatre and faith, in sharing and compassion, in expiation and joy.

This jumble is orchestrated by the sheikha, who distributes advice to one and scolds another. The fact that the musical pieces are short allows each one time to recompose herself, not to totally lose her head. The ambiance remains warm. They feel good, they are happy to be together, that's their thing. Don't men have their Zikr? Well, the women have their Zar! Transgression of the forbidden, corporal expression, the feeling of unity, the need for comfort regularly call together these women who go home with a feeling of well-being. During this time, the husbands tremble, for certain facetious spirits covet gold jewelry or luxury perfumes…

And woe to them if they fail to comply!

The dance resumes, and all of them send me collusive glances, this is the call of one of the khawadja Zars, three women rise, one casts her tobe on the ground, revealing an English colonial costume that draws exclamations from the attendants. She walks like Michael Jackson in his Thriller clip, but with a cane in hand and a pipe in her mouth, boasting an arrogant mien. They suppress laughter, one must above all not make fun of a Zar! One after the other, the dancers disappear into an adjoining room and return, jovial and tipsy, wiping their mouths with the back of their hand. I ask Nasik: "Where are they going?"

"Sshh!" she says, with her finger on her lips.

Suddenly, I, who thought I was immune, am snatched by an unknown hand that draws me into the dance: stirs and protests from the assembly! Nasik comes to me: "Don't worry! Some women are saying that you don't have any Zar, that you are pure as a dove, and may catch one if you provoke it! They are saying that to protect you, but the sheikha wants you to dance…"

Persuaded by their priestess, my companions clap to a faster and faster, more and more jerky, rhythm, accompanied by shrill youyous. They make me turn like a top until I am breathless: no doubt the "dervish rock 'n' roll Zar"! Then the drums stop cold; panting, I fall at the feet of the sheikha, who, to reassure her flock, confirms to them that I have no Zar. I, however, know that I have one, which is the "crazy hiker" Zar, hungry for space and kilometers, horizons and ether. That is the hundredth Zar! Bizarre….Did you say bizarre? Yet I know it well! And it will soon be satisfied, for we have before us, at the gates of Omdurman, to pass through a trial of major proportions: we have to cross the Bayuda desert, three hundred eighty kilometers of dunes and *erg* to rejoin the loop in the Nile, near Ad Debba: probably two and a half weeks of sweat and thirst, exhaustion and "horizontal vertigo": with that, my Zar had better behave!

CHAPTER
29

The Bayuda Desert

L eaving the Nile behind is like letting go of a handrail, so it is with a certain apprehension that, after a last glance at it, we plunge into the alleys of Omdurman. The river makes a wide loop of nearly a thousand kilometers, a vast detour that we mean to skip by cutting across the Bayuda desert on a 400-km trajectory. It's that or twice the distance! But not so easy to do: there is the heat, the drudgery, and the emptiness of the Sahara over rectilinear asphalt, and scattered truck stops along this lethal trek where water will remain the key element. For water, we place our bets on the truckers.

The bedlam of Omdurman, its souks, traffic jams, saddled donkeys and its effervescence, keeps us from thinking too much about it, so by evening we are already outside the city in open desert. At dusk, the driver of a highway lorry parked on the shoulder for the *al-Maghreb* prayer fills our five-liter jerrycan and our two 1.5-liter bottles. Eight liters: enough for tonight's soup, overnight rehydration and tomorrow morning's porridge. An hour after sundown we take a right angle to move off of the road. Between two dunes, our first, we pitch the tent and go about our business in our under-things in order to dissipate the day's heat. It's been a long time since we camped alone and it is a really happy feeling. The ineffable caress of the night breeze on our naked torsos. Silently we watch our little fire of twigs gleaned in the desert and listen to the soup heating. We are absorbed by the fire. Everything has become so simple again with walking. We put our brains back on standby.

Suddenly, an enormous scorpion, attracted by the flames, bursts into our circle of light. My heel makes short work of him. In the sky, the constellation of the same name sends us an SOS…

The road is straight and hopelessly flat in a landscape devoid of the slightest feature, glum and monotonous, hot and white. Nothing upon which to fix your gaze. We could be anywhere, in the Iranian Dasht el-Lut or in Balutchistan, in the Mauritanian Adrar or the Niger's Aïr. But we are crossing the Bayuda! We have scarcely entered it, and have but one obsession: to get out. Deserts are only for passing through. You think you are getting away from people, and you can't wait to see them once you have set foot there. Our minds wander or endlessly repeat, time drags, we lose our bearings. Walking like machines, this is our daily lot, no stopping, no turning back. Endure. We have no choice but to endure. Every kilometer takes us farther from the Nile, farther from water. Keep going, nothing but heat and light, sand and desert. We are overcome by this horizontal vertigo, this inebriation of immensity, which turns vast spaces into abysses for the morale. We walk in silence, intimidated, so as not to betray our sinking spirits or waste saliva or energy. It is time to concentrate. In normal circumstances, it takes a four-hour walk and twenty kilometers to drain our stomachs, drain our batteries. In this desert, in this heat, in this sunlight, weakness overtakes us every fifteen kilometers. It is hard to walk more than three hours without stopping or getting some food.

And yet, this morning, a furious squall line hits us, pouring curtains of rain, buckets of life. The sky has turned to ink, the sand orange with fire. We put on our rain capes in open desert. The steppe dotted with dunes absorbs the first drops, but is rapidly saturated. Whereupon an extraordinary sight: dunes streaming with water; little lakes forming at their bases, running together to form a vast, shimmering expanse that reflects the torments of the sky. A vision of flood, and in all directions black draperies move their shadow theatres across the horizon, opening windows of light upon apocalyptic screens. This desert is allergic to water, it rejects and refuses to drink it. Only the road is not engulfed and we soon are walking, incredulous and ecstatic, between two infinite lakes. But all of a sudden the rain ceases, heaven's wrath passes and we find the landscape, itself incredulous and ecstatic, gurgling gently: what to do with all this water? What's the point in watering seeds that will die tomorrow? The seeds know why. One day is a whole lifetime for a flower. As many seconds in the sun as there are days in the life of the oldest man on earth: forty-four thousand. Life is short, ephemeral and fragile, be you man or flower. Tomorrow, the desert will have reclaimed its rights, and we will be gone.

Our hours are punctuated by the passing of buses and trucks; in time they get to know us. They are going to Dongola or Karima and back. Others, with heavier loads, are going as far as Wadi Halfa, on the Egyptian border, a thousand kilometers farther.... We get to know them by the sound. There are Nissan diesel buses daubed with gaudy Qu'ranic inscriptions, without windows, that pass at breakneck speed with the siren sound of a diving Stuka. It must be the fifth-gear cog that sings like that. We hear them coming from five kilometers away! There are the SAF-SAF express buses, 4×4 Mercedes trucks equipped with air-conditioned cabins, impervious to the dust of the desert, which have a deeper sound – because of their knobbed tires that hum on the asphalt. And then there are the Hino trucks painted orange, with a load piled so high they look like moving Pisa towers. Their motors almost idling, they do not go fast. They are the ones who stop to give us water. We fill up twice a day, morning and evening. You don't even need to ask them to stop; they do it spontaneously and each time invite us to climb aboard their tottering chateaus. There are always some large Blacks seated atop these piles of cotton bales or cases, their legs dangling above the driver. We are deaf to their calls with a polite obstinacy that cracks them up. "These *khawadjas*[1] are really crazy!" And they take off again with great, enthusiastic farewells after leaving us an orange or banana.

They all have horns with several notes which they modulate at will; some have acoustic signatures which we happen to recognize. They honk for no reason, with no obstacle or danger, just to call attention to themselves, to exist, to pass time. The desert road resounds with these anarchical tunes.

When the wind and sand plunge us into dirty yellow cotton, these vehicles appear only at the last second in a maelstrom of dust. Packed into our turbans and protected by our sunglasses, we amuse ourselves by trying to guess the nature of the missile and chauffeur we hear coming. We get passed often enough in this way to have an inkling of how crazy this undertaking is. It is as if, in the Pacific, a tugboat had offered a cable every ten minutes to d'Aboville[2]; as if, in the Arctic, a snowmobile had constantly come up to Mike Horn[3] and offered to let him sit down. We stick it out, we stick it out, we stick it out.

Djéhéril, Tuesday 19 August 2003, day 964, 33 km, 10,657th km

One day with the *rhaboub* blowing hard, that impressive sandy wind which plunges everything into an orangish darkness, we take shelter behind a locked shack, between oil cans and old tires. The wait begins. Sonia is curled up amidst the junk, her head hidden under her crimson Arab scarf wrapped like a shroud. Sinister vision. I

---

[1] White-skinned foreigners.
[2] Gérard d'Aboville, famous for rowing solo across both the Atlantic and the Pacific.
[3] He is known, among many exploits, for solo walking the Arctic Circle..

check whether she is sleeping: "Who said there was something glamorous about our trek?"

"A nerd…"

Okay, she's not asleep. The wind doesn't let up; in time it covers us with sand. After a couple of hours, I get up and look at my wife, a mummy half-dug in sand and debris; I am overcome by a violent emotion: she has been putting up with this for a thousand days. She commands my admiration and reveals to me once more the infinite limits of love. Hers, mine, ours.

A camel driver out of nowhere comes to see how we are doing. He is perched high on his beast and suffers less up there from the waves of sand that whip one's calves like a sandblaster. He fetches the key to the shack and soon returns. We take refuge in his shelter, piled high with curiously assorted objects. We are encrusted with sand and every move itches. I remember the Canadian blizzards of my childhood. It is devilishly similar. Except that here, it is not –40° C but +45° C. A family arrives in a small donkey cart to take shelter in what turns out to be a market stall. Little Suleiman, a smiling boy, takes his place in professional manner behind his counter, in front of the scale, between bags of onions and cookie packages. A pretty grandmother with a golden tooth hides a small child in the folds of her red dress. Sonia hurries over to shower him with kisses. He is fascinated. He was born in this furnace, he knows nothing else. Lord, how adaptable man is! A real little miracle. Resilient and persistent. How can anyone live here? It's inherited. The little Eskimo, born into a vast whiteness, also does not ask questions.

The august grandfather with a white mustache is amused by our movie camera. Violent gusts of wind spray sand into our shelter. We are fine with these gentle folk, waiting. The walls are decorated with clippings from Arabic military magazines and newspapers. My attention is attracted to a fighter jet which is unfamiliar to me: "The Mako HEAT? Guess what, Sonia, the photo was taken at the Le Bourget air show! And here, a French frigate? And there, look! A Sagem advertisement! Hey, there's the Leclerc tank, for goodness sake! Apparently Sagem doesn't sell only cell phones! There's even the address of GIAT Industries at the bottom of the page…'12, route de la Minière…Versailles…' Incredible! In this godforsaken shack in the middle of the Sahara! Makes you feel close to home!"

On the other wall, the face of Odai Saddam Hussein, before and after the attack of the American and Iraqi troops. I had met him in 1998 in Baghdad with a group of young Frenchmen sent unofficially by the parliamentary commission to study the embargo, toward the end of his convalescence following an assassination attempt that had miraculously left him alive with seventeen bullets in his body. This time, he didn't stomach them. The war rages on. The Sudanese too are under embargo. We read anxiety in their faces. The fate of the humble is always played out very far away and over their heads.

When we set out again, the wind sweeps ghostly drapes of sand across the pavement, which enchant us with their hypnotic motion. It's as if the whole sky had clamped down on us, as if we were wading in a soup of sand and stuff. There is nothing left but this walking that is walking in us, in elements deaf to our solitude. We lose all notion of time and distance, minutes stretch to hours, kilometers extend forever, with the mechanical pat, pat of our steps on this moving sidewalk of windswept tar. Fortunately, during these long hours of sandstorm, we can listen to our MP3 player. Against a background of the "Ride of the Valkyries," crazy trucks become mythological monsters; the *Carmina Burana* turns them into armored jousting knights and horses charging at full speed; the choirs of Mozart's *Requiem* conjure up hearses licked by tongues of sand like the caresses of an evil fire. By one of those weird ironies, the only music tempestuous enough to fit the *rhaboub* is "Winter" in Vivaldi's *Four Seasons*. In contrast, when the storm is over, it's amazing how well Alain Souchon[4] lends himself to walking! It's a question of rhythm and swing: *On avance, on*

---

[4] French pop singer.

avance, c'est une évidence…attirés par les étoiles, les voiles, que des choses pas commerciales…

A car stops alongside us. A bearded Westerner gets out.

"You need anything?"

"No thanks, everything is fine…"

"But what are you doing here?"

A worldly conversation on the side of the road. Josep Maldonado I Gili can't believe his ears. He is Catalan. Wants to know everything about our trek. No time, we have to get going.

"What about you, what are you doing on this road?"

"I'm fascinated with Africa. I spend all my vacations here, always far from the beaten path…and then I saw you. I am Sports Minister in the Catalan government…"

Our turn to think we're dreaming.

"Would you be interested in coming to give a lecture in Barcelona when you get back? I direct a lot of sporting associations; it would be great if you came to talk to our young kids…*Suerte! Viva Franca!*"

And he is off. Africa Trek! Even in this deathly boring desert, something is going on. As he is pulling out, he slips a package of cookies to us through the window. We stare at him to convince ourselves we have not been dreaming. These are really Spanish cookies…

"*Fibro natural…Sin azucar…*"

"Sugarless!"

"Too bad."

And we laugh, on this exhausting road, with our package of dietetic Catalan cookies…

In the desert our meals and our only pauses take place at truck stops. They are populated by lascivious men with hard glares who make all passers-by pay for their freedom, as if to avenge themselves on the fate that has stuck them there. We provoke incredulousness and snide laughter. They don't believe a word of our stories and endlessly repeat: *Khawadja majnoun*...[5] Happily, the drivers, who are beginning to know us pretty well, confirm our story in a cacophony of interjections and encouragements. We nomads understand each other. Our articles in Arabic, published in the Khartoum press, are our ambassadors; they are passed from hand to hand for at least an hour before they are returned to us, somewhat more wrinkled. Nobody any more knows a word of English, but our Arabic is by now serviceable. We can handle an hour's conversation and make our interlocutors laugh with our *doukhan* stories or tales about the Sufi ceremonies, our surates or how we chased down the shoe thief. They are charmed and impressed that we should put ourselves in the hands of fate. They were persuaded that this state of mind was peculiar to Muslims, and repeat all the time: *Allah Karim!* and *Souphan Allah!*[6]

At least, at these stops, we can swap our noodle soup for a nice dish of *foul medemmas*,[7] sponging up the oil with pita bread torn into thin strips and used as spoons. We take advantage of the subsequent wait to take a nap on an *angareb*. It lasts as much as seven hours. Seven hours of boredom and heat, tossing and turning on this twine that buries itself in your back. It is always a painful time for Sonia, who finds it more and more difficult to stand the lewd gaze of the men slouching in every corner. There is always one or several who stare nonchalantly at her behind wrapped in her long skirt or her sleeping bosom. You can't change men. Her very presence in the same room drives them nuts. When she turns over or tries to place something between their gaze and herself, they move over a little and reestablish a line of sight between their pupils and the object of their observation. Oh how they ogle. They can't help it and it makes her furious.

"Now I understand the chador! What a comfort it must be to become invisible. You know, you really can't say I am trying to

---

[5] These white guys are nuts.
[6] God will provide! Wonder of God!
[7] A national dish made from black fava beans.

provoke them with my nunnish garb, my braid filthy as a cow's tail and my fruitcake mug…"

We've got to get out of here. Getting started again at day's end always feels like a kind of liberation. It's the time when we can most easily talk together. The sun is no longer a threat, it is no longer a sledgehammer, it slowly turns white on a graying horizon, as pale as a Sudanese egg yolk, with as a bonus sunspots you can see with the naked eye – to think that that black spot on the sun is a hundred times larger than the earth! This is the time Sonia always chooses for her "quarter of craziness." A privileged moment for me, walking at her side. It is characterized by chatter that gains momentum, jokes, pointless laughter, she sings, skips…where does she find the energy to skip at this hour in the desert? Fifteen minutes hanging on my arm, taking a thought, a project off the deep end, to build castles in the air.…Fifteen minutes when I can't get a word in or do anything but watch her. She doesn't do it on purpose; it's not an application of the Coué method,[8] it is her way to conjure ambient desolation. A secret weapon that makes her the perfect hiker.

This evening, a surreal vision hits us in the middle of her "crazy quarter": a large mosque, fluorescent green all over, rises in the middle of the desert like an interplanetary vessel. It is the madrassa[9] of Djeheril. Eltayeb Isaak greets us right in the middle of the Qu'ran reading. He is one-armed; the other one he lost fighting alongside the Taliban, in Afghanistan. He has kept his shaggy black beard that hides his skeletal face, and the famous black turban of the "students" crazy with God. Fortunately, we are French. He is delighted. He had a French friend in the trenches. He is also delighted that we are married, but doesn't approve of my gold wedding band.

"The Prophet forbade the wearing of gold…"

"We bought the thinnest ones we could…"

---

[8] The healing method of pharmacist Émile Coué (1857–1926) was based on autosuggestion.

[9] Qu'ranic school.

"It's not about weight but the principle..."

An old man joins us. Our blood runs cold: he's the spitting image of Bin Laden. The same tall, ascetic stature, the same salt-and-pepper beard, the same white skullcap on his shaved head, the same gentle eyes, the same hooked nose and thick lips, the same broad gestures with his long, clean fingers, the same mottled camouflage vest over a Pakistani saroual-kamiz. We are so stupefied that I feel obliged to explain to him. They all burst out laughing, and he breaks out in a broad smile. I could not have paid him a finer compliment.

"He is the one who financed this madrassa, when he was living in the Sudan; he is the master of all of us. You must not believe the bad things people say about him. He is a holy man..."

The old sage continues: "You know, the worst enemies of Islam are not Bush and Blair, they are the presidents of the Arab or Muslim countries: dictators who persecute our Islamist brothers, and keep Islam from conquering the world. The worst of them is Moubarak, the next is King Abdullah of Jordan, Mohammed VI, Bouteflika, Ben Ali, Musharraf....Their prisons are full of our brothers."

This day of desert, sun, sandy wind and encounters has been a full one. It's amazing how many things are elicited by walking. We never cease wondering at it. It's unbelievable the things people confide in us, how freely they speak to us. We are only passing briefly through their lives and they confess their innermost thoughts with no reticence or afterthoughts. We receive as precious these witnesses to a real world, they do not constitute a significant academic or journalistic content, they speak of men and of their way of explaining their real world. The trek is our truth serum, our maieutics; we are the pretext of an exchange, we are discursive midwives for people who never have the opportunity of speaking to Westerners. Through us, they feel like they are speaking to the world. Each human being is an ambassador of his world, and we take our role as French ambassadors very seriously.

Tonight we sleep in Eltayeb's sandy bedroom after a sponge bath while teetering over clogged toilets.

Very few people live in this desert. A few bedouins all the same. We head to their tent in search of shade. We are always very well received. In such a harsh environment, all people can do is help each other.

One day, we find ourselves in the middle of an epidemic. Everyone is sick, burning with varying degrees of fever. A bad cold in this heat! Murphy's law. Four feverish girls are lying on a wide bed of slats held by little forks planted in the ground and assembled in a tent of camel hide stretched between mud walls. They are semi-nomads. A passel of cans, *guerbas*, utensils and ropes hangs from the tentposts. Tons of misery too. Tons of waiting. *Tristes tropiques*[10] right in the desert. The nomadic life depends on sparse rains and the price of lamb. It can be sinister. They wait for water as one waits for Godot. Well-fed sedentary people like us tend to idealize the nomads' existence. They on the contrary surely dream of settling down in some "valley of milk and honey": they are people without a country, cast into the void, along this road. Nothing, they have nothing. Except four daughters as lovely as you could want. But ill. The sickest of them all, Umm Balein, is a pure beauty. Her mother, Bakleid, asks us for medicine, but a pulse of 180 and a raging fever are symptoms too serious for an arbitrarily administered antibiotic. We advise her to get her to the dispensary in Djeheril where we slept the day before. The poor, weary woman replies that the trucks don't stop for them. I promise to take care of it. So I do. Indeed, the first one that comes along stops. I turn to call Sonia and see her emerging from her hiding place with the young woman in her arms. While I try to hold onto the driver, who has figured out what we're up to, Sonia staggers courageously across the sand. I rush

---

[10] *Tristes Tropiques* is the title of one of Claude Lévy-Strauss's most important books.

to her aid, take the lovely patient in my arms and start running toward the truck. She has dainty Yemeno-Ethiopian features ringed by fine black braids, and eyes enlarged by the fever that stare at me unbelievingly. The wind carries off her veil and reveals her astonishing beauty. Eternal seconds: enough to make you enlist in Doctors Without Borders. Too late; we are nothing but useless hikers. I set her down in the truck; her mother, tangled in her veil, finally catches up; I slip her some money to buy the needed medications, tell her about Eltayeb Isaak, and she disappears, carried off by the truck with a smile of gratitude. Really we haven't done anything. But that young desert princess has done something for us: she has allowed us to give back a hundredth part of the kindness we have been receiving every day for two years and nine months.

The days go by. Bohad, Gobolab, Tam-Tam, Umm al-Hassan, names of nowheres sown in nothingness. On both sides of this vital axis, the white furnace shimmers in the doldrums. Fortunately for us, there is this road, for us this is Ariadne's thread. We would be lost without it.

"Alex! Come look!"

Sonia startles me from my thoughts. She had stopped and is looking intently at the ground.

"A dead chick!"

A genuine dried-out chick on the roadside. How did this fragile yellow thing get here? We try to retrace its steps when we happen upon a second chick, then a third...

"It's a chick invasion! An Egyptian plague fallen from heaven. Remember the Hebrews' flights of quail."

"Moreover, they surely are coming from Egypt, but by truck. Piled into a box, they have died of thirst, and were tossed out the window..."

We are out of water. We have seen no one today, aside from one truck at dawn. Not surprising, it's Friday. We have stopped at noon in abandoned latrines, the sole vestige among some deserted roadworks shacks that still has a roof on it. Too small for us to be able to lie down. Have to wait hunched over for the sun to pass. And sweat and stick to our isotherm foam mattresses under this square meter of corrugated iron, drinking our five liters in five hours, in little hot swallows that taste of gas. How could we have made it without these surrealistic johns?

"Without others we are nothing. It is impossible to cross this desert."

"We absolutely must get a truck to stop before night or we are done for."

Thirst must have been a constant worry for our hominid ancestors who had no means of carrying containers and did not know the landscapes through which they traveled. They must never have gone very far from springs. They could only have crossed this part of the Sahara by following the Nile.

"Do you remember Xavier Le Pichon, the geophysicist from the Collège de France whom we saw before we left? He told us that the key to the origins of man is to be found in his fragility, his weakness and his capacity for transcending suffering. That the first man was perhaps the one who turned back to help someone back to his feet who was sick, old, wounded or dehydrated, who was falling behind, whereas he should have left him to the hyenas. By saving that useless mouth, that first man was mortgaging the future of the company....He committed an anti-ecological, anti-natural act..."

"Yes! And so?"

"Well, I think he was dead right....It's because he saw his weakness in the other that man survived, because he developed strategies of mutual aid, because he conceived society as based on a molecule of love. Man is a spark in the heart and the eye before he is a spark struck from a flint."

"I think a spark has blown one of your fuses!"

"All the same, if nobody comes to bring us water, we're going to drop like flies."

An hour later, at dusk, the hum of a truck in the distance delivers us from our anguish. It's a Hino. But the driver has no water. This never happens. We are beside ourselves. The man climbs down from his cab, muttering: *"Istanna, istanna! Telj fi…"*[11]

"What can that be? Telj?"

We follow him. He walks around the truck and opens a little case hanging under his trailer. He raises a hemp covering and appears a big and shiny ice block. Ice, out here in the desert! Why not give us the philosopher's stone? With a maul he breaks off half of it for us. We unpack our mess kit and leave the road heading straight into the desert with our *telj*, that strange stuff, that sublime luxury, improbable and ephemeral, and we suck it by turns with the eagerness of two divers sharing the same regulator at a depth of thirty meters. All evening, we religiously watch it melt, while flocks of satellites pursued by meteorites pass overhead. With frozen water, you no longer see the desert in the same way.

The next day, we halt in front of a petrified tree trunk standing in the emptiness. A meter of the past reaches toward the sky as if in defiance of the law of gravity. Here, a hundred fifty million years ago, stretched tropical jungles abuzz with insects. The bark, the strata, the fibers, time…are still visible. Time, that Gorgon. That vitrifies and mineralizes everything. Only what's living can resist that entropy. Temporarily. Eternally. Ephemeral and yet always there. Reproduced, re-begun, reborn, it too is fashioned by time. Led by natural selection. I pick up a piece of petrified wood with its warm colors, polished by the sandy winds, and hold it in the hollow of my left hand. We start walking again. In my right hand, our little MP3 player plucks off the first notes of Allegri's *Miserere*. Between my two hands, I contemplate the chasm of a hundred fifty million years that separates these two objects, this wood become stone, heavy and dense, these transient, immaterial, light notes produced by this tiny aluminum box, the fruit of a paroxysm of organized, organized, organized

---

[11] Wait, wait, I have some *telj*.

matter. So well organized, so complex that it can reproduce sounds produced by strings, woodwinds, vocal chords, and organized by an inspired brain. Between my two hands what a voyage, what breath, what inspiration! The path of the living.

An immense, dark, opaque scroll is heading silently toward us. A *rhaboub*. It catches us from behind and submerges us. God, how hostile this world is! We pick up our robotic rhythm, one behind the other, softly. This desert will ultimately get us. What's new is a blue panel that pops out of the blizzard every kilometer, covered with Qu'ranic inscriptions. To keep the drivers on the straight path, no doubt. "If you think you can exercise your power over others, do not forget the power that God has over you..." The spiritual highway code designed to remind men that God is great, that they are small and that they must go straight.

This evening a skinny tree stands in an endless plain. It has lost some branches and twigs that are scattered on the sand at its foot. We glean some of them for the fire. Sonia pitches the tent while I go looking for three stones to hold the cooking pot. It's no picnic. Buried in the ground I notice a small black globe; I dig it up: it's a perfect sphere of hard sandstone. That doesn't help me any for the fire. I find another one, then a third, then a whole collection of them. Strange spheres laid on the sand. Silver ants, shiny as quicksilver, swarm over my hands. This desert is really another planet. The next morning at dawn, after filling our bottles, we empty our jerrycan at the foot of the little lonesome tree. It gave us a little deadwood, we give it back a little life.

After thirteen days and three hundred fifty-nine kilometers of this regime out of this world and outside time, we spy behind a dune, at Al-Multarra, a rivulet of sap in the desert: the valley of the Nile. We have won our bet, we have crossed the Bayuda with no backup team, totally dependent, completely hopeful: we fall into each other's arms. It was one of those key passages in our long trek. From now on all we have to do is follow the lifeline all the way to Egypt: the Nile.

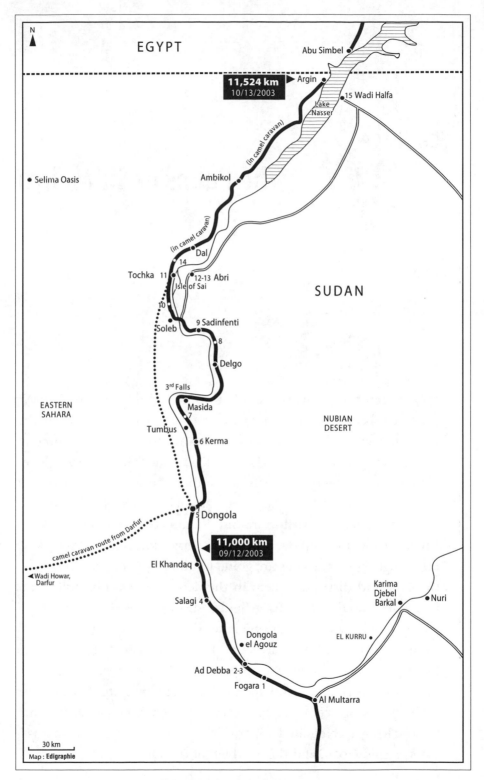

N

EGYPT

Abu Simbel

11,524 km
10/13/2003 → Argin

15 Wadi Halfa

Lake
Nasser

(in camel caravan)

• Selima Oasis

Ambikol

(in camel caravan)

Dal

Tochka 11 14

12-13 Abri
Isle of Sai

SUDAN

10

9 Sadinfenti

Soleb

8

Delgo

3rd Falls

Masida
7

EASTERN
SAHARA

Tumbus

6 Kerma

NUBIAN
DESERT

5 Dongola

11,000 km
09/12/2003 ◄

camel caravan route from Darfur

◄Wadi Howar,
Darfur

El Khandaq

Karima
Djebel
Barkal • Nuri

Salagi 4

EL KURRU

Dongola
el Agouz

Ad Debba 2-3

Fogara 1

Al Multarra

30 km

Map : **Edigraphie**

Shimaliya, North Sudan

CHAPTER 30

The Palms of Shimaliya

SUDAN

Between the palms the sun is turning red on the horizon. We have been walking for an hour. Last night we slept in the midst of Chinese workers on the banks of the Nile. Astonishment. Same straw hats as in the rice paddies, same white cotton gloves at the trucks' steering wheels, same dirty butts at the corners of the mouth, same flat espadrilles, same glass jars filled with cold tea with the leaves swirling around. Reminiscences of another continent. They are employed by a vast irrigation scheme work site. Four large diesel turbines are going to pump millions of liters from the Nile and distribute them in the desert. A noria of bulldozers is digging canals, smoothing fields, raising dikes. Great works of another time. Most of the Sudanese workers are big Black men from the South who speak much better English than their Arab foremen. Which annoy the latter badly. This motley assembly of men has greeted and pampered us all evening in a site that suggests a refugee camp, composed of jerry-built tents, effervescence and trash. Here we celebrated our triumph over the desert – a paradise: a cot, a cold Coke, and the goodwill of the Other.

This morning, the flat, hot asphalt is behind us. We are weaving our way among palm plantations, the Nile on the right, and are struggling in the sand. It isn't the same sport. The calf no longer skips, the sole no longer skims. The heel digs in, one must above all not push, all the power would be absorbed by the sand; we try to keep the foot flat, the leg half-extended – the stride shortens, and we focus on energy efficiency. The walking stick is compulsory; the tendons are severely tested, the muscles can no longer get by with purring along automatically, they are always under stress. Walking is thus more difficult but much less anguishing. No more problems with water, no more anxiety about men or not men. We just have to keep going.

Dawn is a blessed moment for us. The birds sing, the light gilds the fibrous trunks of the date trees, stretches shadows, the little donkeys bray, the noisy roosters re-establish their territory, the first Listers, those old single-cylinder colonial pumps, quietly begin to pulse, they are the heart of the palm plantations. Here, the palm plantation is not an isolated oasis: it is two thousand kilometers long and two hundred meters wide. On the edge of this green fringe bristling with palm trees, low houses spread out in the *fog*. The fog is an undefinable space between the desert and the edge of the plantations where people live. The vital space is so slim along the Nile that people don't live on the fertile land. Very wise. The houses thereby gain in size; they mushroom into large square courtyards a hundred meters on each side, protected from view by high walls and gates adorned with tympana and festoons, crenels and motifs. Scrap iron has long since replaced wood, but the function is the same. Over the walls, early in the morning, wisps of incense spread through the palm undergrowth. The women thus scent the slightest crannies of their dwellings to drive out the nighttime jinns. The angarebs are set up everywhere in the gardens and courtyards. Every evening, the Sudanese thus leave their beds outside to flee the interiors that endlessly release the stored-up heat; the starry nights are balm for the heat of the day.

We pass without awakening this serenity. But quite often an eye opens and even before allowing himself the time to be surprised in the haze of his awakening, the Sudanese begins to sing his leitmotiv: *"Fadhal! Fadhal!"*

It is the truest, most sincere, and most complete greeting on the planet. So far we have heard none so lovely. It means: "Sit down, rest yourself, what would you like to drink? And eat? Stay an hour, a day, a week, forever..." Our hosts sincerely mean it. But we are only passing through and a hundred times a day we renew the anguish of having to decline, excuse ourselves, thank, explain, all while walking in the soft sand. It keeps us busy full-time since these ambushes of hospitality are set for us every hundred meters.

Three or four times a day we yield and enter the lives of the Sudanese of Shimaliya. In the courtyards everything is tidy and plain. The compacted sand is swept like that of a Japanese garden, nothing is lying around, there is space and the center is dominated by the *sébil*, the water source, the fount; it does not flow, it is concealed under a mud and straw roof, between two walls ornamented with open work, in three porous jars that cool it to a refreshing 10° C on the hottest days. Just twice the temperature of a fridge! Without the help of Mr. Volt! Magical. Beside the sébil there is always a tree to take advantage of the dripping and ablutions and in return provides salutary shade. In a corner of the court, hens wait to be freed, in another the pigeons coo impatiently before clacking their wings in the cool morning air.

Up and gone without breakfast, at five in the morning, in the starting up of our Chinese friends' first bulldozers, our first stop is around eight for tea and biscuits: we have racked up no more than eight to ten kilometers instead of the planned fifteen because of the sand and the morning bliss. The family that awoke at our passage snorts and stretches gently, and they all welcome us with a smile; a bed is freed for us, the tea comes promptly. Time to exchange a few words and we must be off again. They are very sorry, would have

30

31

32

Photo legends begin on page 629

33

34

35

36

37

38

39

40

41

42

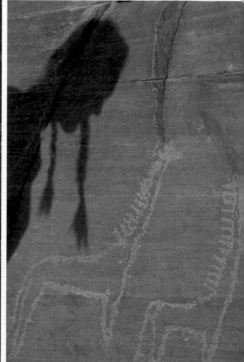
43

44

45

46

57

58

preferred we remain for the day. But to stay a minute longer is to risk never leaving.

We now leave the palm plantation to walk in the fog, on the desert side, parallel to it or in the road if it is not too far away. Why? To knock down some kilometers, to avoid succumbing to invitations, stopping for everyone who awaits us with a cup of steaming tea....The sun is climbing quickly into the sky and soon overwhelms us. Fortunately there are sébils of cool water every-where, even far from the dwellings, to slake the thirst of unknown passers-by. Toward ten-thirty or eleven, exhausted, with no more than fifteen or eighteen kilometers behind us, we head for the first house. It is always the right one. The rule is absolute. We need not even ask, we are welcomed with a naturalness that is as obvious and supernatural as the sky is blue. And the marvelous tirade of salamalecs, preamble to introductions, begins:

"Asalam aleykoum!"

"Maleykoum salam!"

"Kef?"

"Kullu tamam!"

"Insha'Allah koïsin!"

"Allah ibarik fi!"

"Barak Allah fi!"

"Alhamdoulillah!"

"Souphan Allah!"

(Peace be with you! And also with you! How are you? Very well. Thanks to God all is well! May God's luck protect you! There is divine grace! Praise be to God! God is wonderful!)

And the record repeats, two or three times according to the degree of surprise or joy, a degree augmented by our virtuosity at it. When it stops, everything becomes calm and serene. Placed under good auspices. God and men are content.

Above all, wash. A well-organized activity in Sudanese homes. Three times a day, despite the desert. Bliss. Never will we be so clean. We come out of these bucket-showers cool as cucumbers.

The *fatur* awaits us. A dish of *foul*, brown broad beans, *gibna*, a sort of feta, *eich*, good bread, and a thermos of tea. After the shared feasts, attended by curious and kindly neighbors, we fall with the sleep of the just for a long nap on angarebs set up in a draft, on clean sheets, in a tranquil part of the house. *Calme et volupté.*[1]

We are awakened with a *radha* around three thirty. Often chicken, tomato and cucumber salad, a light omelet and a sweet dessert. Never have we been treated like this. In Shimaliya, the traveling stranger is a king, the Sudanese are lords. We then overflow with gratitude, and our departure always follows in anguish. We draw tears from our hostesses, we sniffle. We do not understand how, so fast, we can feel so close to our hosts and vice versa. They think the same thing and thank us. "Thanks for stopping at our house!" we hear every time. How good is that! Roles reversed. With our fatigue and our hunger, our filth and our vulnerability, they treat us as French ambassadors. We would like to stay, they try everything. We resist against ourselves, yet we know that we will not go far, five or eight kilometers at most: the sun is quickly going down and we do not knock at a door at night. After ten days these little extras build up to fifty or eighty more kilometers up the Nile. That is not nil. So we must get going. And then, in the evening, the unending miracle of Sudanese hospitality repeats itself as if by a charm. In this way, every day we enter the life of three or four families who constitute gold beads on our necklace of encounters.

Fogara, Tuesday 26 August 2003, 971, 21 km, 10,870[th] km

Sometimes, some of them win and we do not manage to leave their house after radha. The first time that happens is at the home of Mostapha Abd el-Gadir. We are in Fogara, just before Ad Debba. We heard his pump. And there it is, in front of us, spitting out great quantities of pure fresh water into a collection basin where

---

[1] See note 3, p. 372.

originate small canals that irrigate the garden. Sonia has a pinched left sciatic nerve, no doubt because of walking in the sand. She is in considerable pain. The machine is thrown off, it needs a few days of adaptation. A big, Black farm worker comes timidly toward us. We explain that we would like to rest here for a few moments. He sets up two angarebs for us in the shade of the date palms and goes to report it to his "boss." He soon returns with Mostapha.

"Are you American?"

"No, French…"

"Al Hamdoullilah! Welcome, welcome! If you were American, I would have chased you out."

Though it isn't immediately evident, Mostapha is very gentle; the Iraqi conflict revolts him; he is short, stocky, a bald pate and vibrant eyes. He gives off formidable energy. This garden humming with birds and life was just a square in the desert ten years ago. We describe to him today's fantasy: to soak ourselves in his little basin to relax our aching muscles.

"*Aïwa!*[2] But separately. During that time, I will prepare you a *fatur*. Do you like *gourrassa*? And *weka*?"

One is a very filling flour crepe fried in oil, the other a gooey and slimy side-dish, translucent and hot, made from a sort of boiled spinach. The whole thing requires at least a three-hour nap to digest it. That suits us. In the fog, far from the Nile, the water is at a depth of twenty-five meters. Mostapha had to dig a very deep *babour*, a large masonry well ten meters in diameter by ten meters deep, at the bottom of which is found the pump connected by a belt to the famous Lister. You get to it by a winding stairway thick with smoke from the spluttering of the ancient beast. Gas against water. Thus does Africa run. He returns carrying a wide platter and accompanied by his frightfully bony son Aladdin.

"For five years he has had an acute form of malaria that takes away his appetite."

---

[2] Okay!

"How do you treat him?"

"With weekly chloroquine injections…"

It isn't malaria that's slowly killing him, it's the chemical…. We tell him about artemisinin. Hasn't heard of it. Naturally. Yet he is the nurse at the government dispensary in Fogara. And I recall how Dr. Mary, in Sodo, saved my life with her flowers, then think about all this water that Mostapha is ruining himself to pump from the sand to water the dates he cannot manage to sell, whereas he would save his son's life by growing those bitter artemisias that would cover his desert with orange petals. But the world economy is all wrong. They prefer to produce chloroquine and favor the con-sumer culture of petrol that subjugates twenty million Southern Sudanese, whereas these spaces are overwhelmed with solar energy and ancient Egypt used only gravity….Is this truly progress? Why do hikers constantly wish they could remake the world?

Once started on politics, Mostapha catches us off guard: "Whether Omar al-Bashir wants it or not, there will be a partition. Ninety percent of the people in Shimaliya want one. We are tired of sending our children to die in this absurd and interminable war. No one but the politicians talks about union, not the people. The North is for partition, the South is for partition, so there must be a separation. We will get along much better once that is done. There are five hundred tribes in this country, who speak a hundred thirty different languages: that is too many. Our country is too large. All this is because of the principle of "borders untouchability" inher-ited from the colonial period and behind which the African dicta-tors barricade themselves to protect their interests…"

He pauses. Never would we have expected such political matu-rity in a nurse–date planter. But Mostapha has not finished sur-prising us.

"Between us, we have nothing in common with those people. They have their own culture, they are Africans, we are Arabs. They pretend to convert, but we never know what they are really believ-ing in. Listen…my farm worker admits to having converted to

Islam so I would hire him, but I know perfectly well he doesn't give a damn. We can't have confidence in those people. They change their names all the time, we don't know anything about them, they live differently, they don't trust us. That's to be expected. We have always dominated them. Besides, they are going to bury us demographically. Here in Shimaliya we marry late, between thirty and thirty-five, and we have only two or three children because we know the soil is poor and the space limited. In the South, they marry at the age of twelve to twenty, they have between five and ten wives each of whom has at least ten children. Do the math. They are going to replace us faster than we can convert them."

His jovial pragmatism fascinates us. Ethnic, cultural and demographic peril as motivation for partition. He does not believe in marriage against nature. He has at least the merit of being honest.

After the siesta Mostapha forbids us to leave, he invites us to his house and enthusiastically introduces his wife Seida and his daughter Roumheissa. We decide to stay. A friendship trap has closed; we will stay three days. Mostapha gives me a Qu'ran in English. He is so surprised that I know so many surates by heart that he takes me for some kind of prophet. He has moreover dressed me in a fine white djellaba. My beard makes my case seem more persuasive. Sonia's skirt too, lengthened by the tobe that Rumheissa amused herself by putting on her. He senses that the terrain is promising.

"Issa is one of our prophets, you know? He is in the Qu'ran, his mother Myriam also, as well as the angel Gabriel; Islam does not contradict the Gospels, it accomplishes them…"

"Have you read them?"

"No need to, since they are abolished, renewed, replaced…"

I spend three days reading the holy book of Islam *in extenso*. For the third time. It talks mainly about the beauty of God, but also about the Jewish people, infidels, polytheists.…It codifies existence, it is normative, it tries to put a little order and rigor in the muddled life of desert cities. But the Jesus of the Qu'ran is

disappointing. He is silent. And a jokester: just before being cru-
cified, he disappears, goes to heaven and is replaced at the last
minute by a look-alike who is really the one who dies on the cross.
A true prophet of God cannot let himself be injustly murdered....
In this revelation made by the angel Gabriel to Mohammed, God
is everywhere, he is the greatest, above all description. He has
ninety-nine names and attributes, which we invariably find again
in all our hosts' houses, superbly calligraphed on a background of
black velvet in a handsome gilt frame, as in the home of our friend
Mostapha, who takes pleasure in reading them to us.

"*Ar rahman*, the Most Merciful, *ar rahim*, the All Merciful, *el
malik*, the Sovereign, *el djabbar*, the Dominator, *el wahhab*, the Generous, *el fatah*, the Conqueror, *el alim*, the Most Wise, *el khafiz*, He
who stoops, *el rafi*, He who dreams, *el hakam*, the Judge, *el latif*, the
Benevolent One, *el wahid*, the Only..."[3]

"And love?"

"That is men's duty."

And Mostapha well fulfills his duty. We are most satisfied but
exhausted. God is everywhere, in every clause, omnipresent, too
great. Our hosts name him more than a hundred times a day. We
need a pause, a little air, under other skies, under other gods. In
order not to be like Buridan's asses, starving between two buckets:
one filled with kilometers and sun, with a leaden cover, the other
filled with God and politics, with a cover of laws. So we decide to
take a side-trip to Djebel Barkal, one day's drive up the river, for a
history bath, outside the world, outside of time.

To travel in the Sudan is to discover the archeological sites as might
have done, in the nineteenth century, the great European travelers in Egypt like Vivant Denon, Giovanni Belzoni, Samuel Baker,
David Roberts and all the gentry. You are alone on half-buried sites,
and nothing recalls the twenty-first century. After Meroe, our trek

---

[3] For a link to an exhaustive list, see p. 624.

in time has us going back a few centuries with the civilization of Napata, in Karima, in the great loop of the Nile, at the foot of Djebel Barkal. A pickup we catch in the fog takes us there in a session of rodeo and vertebra puree. Each of our side-trips confirms that we could never have stood crossing this continent by car. The ordeal is unending. We bounce in the cargo bed against fat girls and tied-up sheep. Dust and contusions. Shame and confusion. Distance without effort also has a very high price.

The sacred mountain appears from afar like a black and golden lingot set on a plain, looking down from its height of a hundred meters on the course of the Nile. A spike extends from it, which has been represented in Egypt, in a tomb at Thebes, as an immense cobra. The Upper Egyptian one. No doubt it was decorated as a giant cobra at the time, since traces of gold leaf have been found on its summit. Today erosion has turned it into a sentinel. We immediately undertake to climb the mountain, going around to the back side. At the summit, the cliff over the river is vertiginous. An empire developed here, the foundations alone still to be seen: several temples dedicated to Amon or Hathor, the goddess of Arts and Music. In the distant setting sun rises a small group of more slender pyramids than those at Meroe. They have not been decapitated, but have lost their chapels. At the summit of this tutelary rock we celebrate our fourth wedding anniversary.

Moreover, on the way down we are invited to a wedding. A wink of fate. We promptly become distinguished guests. They lend me a djellaba, and Sonia a tobe. The *arroussa* and *arrousse*, bride and groom, are seated on two golden thrones before which the festivities take place. They aren't children: he is thirty-seven, she's two years less. The marriage was arranged between two families from Karima. There is first a dinner held separately, the women with the arroussa, the men with the arrousse. Then everyone is gathered together for the interminable gift ceremony. A karaoke system spits out the distorted voice of a master of ceremonies who is supposed to speak the praise of each generous donor. After each panegyric, he proclaims into the mike the number of golden bracelets or millions of dinars added to the dowry. Echoed by the "reverb" effect of the amplifier, the scene is comical, worthy of the rowdiest telethons. We are deafened by the millions-ions-ions-ions....To our great surprise, the two fiancés look like death. We are told that they are not supposed to show their joy in order to avoid attracting the evil eye. Then come the dances. Two ravishing young girls perform in the arena, with small, painful steps, their heads inclined to the side, one arm bent at a right angle, and the other with a mannered gesture constantly closing their tobes, which keep wanting to uncover them. Everyone applauds while a group of musicians begins traditional songs accompanied by a little one-stringed violin, and encouraged by the singer's nasal voice. Four dancers in a line twirl, brushing the ground, come and go around the two melancholic virgins whose shoulders jump slightly, but in rhythm, in what is supposed to represent sobs. The contrast between the male dancer's profligate energy and the languorous parsimony of the female dancers is fascinating. It is the metaphor of a courtship. The crowd is delighted and claps hard, crying *"Abschir! abschir!"*[4] When we slip out to go sleep, the fiancés still have not moved an eyelash under their garlands of red ribbons weighted down with gold bracelets and jewels.

A little downriver, the El-Kurru site reveals to us two magnificent crypts once buried under pyramids that have disappeared, at the bottom of very vertical stairs. Royal graves. Fine starred, night-blue vaults, skiffs bearing Amon suns, bevies of gods, stereotyped postures of offerings and the exquisite detail of polychrome faces make us feel eerily close to Egypt. On one side the princess is represented alive, on the other side, dead and mummified with a cross of life, the *ankh* key in her hand. It is moist and we take

---

[4] Super! super!

in, incredulous, the detail of this woman's hair, her beauty, the refinement of her clothing, the luxury of her living standard, the solemnity of her faith, here, two thousand six hundred years ago, in the heart of Africa, in the heart of the Sahara.

On the other bank, opposite Karima, the Nuri site includes dozens of pyramids, the country's largest and oldest, constructed by the famous XXVth dynasty, that of the Black pharaohs who reigned as far as the Nile delta during the ninth century B.C.E. In sandstone of lesser quality than at Meroe, they have been tortured by the wind; some are ogival, others flattened or worn down; none is intact, but their mass aligned between large dunes lends to the site great evocative power. From the top of the largest, that of the pharaoh Taharqa, you can divine other, smaller ones that have today disappeared. This pharaoh builder and restorer of temples reigned as far as to Jerusalem where he routed the Assyrian armies. The Nuri site has something virginal about it; one imagines hidden treasures, so forgotten and spared does it appear to have been. In archeology, everything remains to be done.

Back with Mostapha, we observe that Aladdin is much better. Our Chinese medicine has restored his appetite and he has had no new crisis. He has listened without interruption to our little MP3 and thus discovered classical music. A high-dosage transfusion of *Stabat Mater*, *Nisi Dominus* and of *Missa Solemnis*. Aladdin is converted.

"When the angels speak, it must sound like that. I did not know that in Europe you had invented anything so beautiful."

"You know, it is thanks to Aladdin and the genie from his magic oil lamp that the beauties of the East were revealed to us."

"Your lamp is the MP3."

We even have the integral "Mozart the Egyptian" that reconciles East and West in a cross-breeding orchestrated by Hughes de Courson – the muezzin's call answers to the *Turkish Rondo*, and the *Abduc-*

tion from the Seraglio resonates with the *oud*, that marvelous, deep eight-stringed zither. Beauty ought to have ninety-nine names.

The next day, after a short seventeen-kilometer day and moving farewells to Mostapha, Seïda, Rumheissa and Aladdin, we are invited to Ad Debba by the police captain Daniel Wani. He is a huge Black man with widely spaced eyes and teeth and a receding hairline. He comes from the deep South. He speaks gently in a deep voice, not calling on a single facial muscle, and raises his big arms with infinite slowness. He is welcoming us on the orders of his colonel, Imad Abd el-Gadir, whom we met by chance in the Bayuda desert. Imad is no relation of Mostapha's. Just the same name, which means "slave of God." Imad has a very strange resemblance to Jafar, our general of Wad Medani. With thirty kilos less. Just normal, he isn't a general yet. He has the same gentleness, the same niceness, the same pious devotion for Sonia. The captain and his colonel are in agreement on the partition of the Sudan, but for opposite reasons. They express themselves calmly, deliberately. A surreal conversation sets in which they seem to have had a hundred times already. I let myself be the fly on the wall.

"Yet you incarnate precisely the fact that, in the same uniform, under the same banner, you can defend the same justice, the same law, the same united state?"

Daniel corrects me: "I am like a foreign policeman in a country that is not his own; my whole family, my eighteen brothers and sisters and my three mothers are in the South and I do not want to become a Muslim; I am Catholic."

Imad opines, impotent and smiling: "There is a policeman who is supposed to apply the sharia and Islamic laws against his convictions. There is a contradiction between our Islamic regime and a multicultural ambition. Daniel does his job properly, but it's understandable he should feel like a foreigner here. I understand the demand of the people of the South; the problem is that they also feel Sudanese..."

Daniel relieves him: "That's true, but of the colonial Sudan, not of the Islamic Sudan. There are three regions in the South: Eastern, Central, and Western Equatoria. I feel like a Central Equatorian. But the name is already taken. If we obtain the creation of our country, we will call it Imatun from the name of the mountain that overlooks Juba. Then our problem will be to remain united, to struggle against tribalism."

Imad concludes, a bit nostalgically: "I took my honeymoon in the South. A real paradise, always green; a jungle full of fruits and animals. It is true that down there we are a colonial power. My dream is to return there as a tourist, to a country at peace, and not as a policeman..."

The muezzin calls to evening prayer. Imad rises to go and Daniel leads us to his little house beside the Nile, where Rose-Mary receives us.

TV news: the Israelis have once again missed Sheikh Yassine. Palestine is a war zone. Mahmoud Abbas is retiring. It is Arafat who is winning, for the moment. In Baghdad, the UN building has been blown up. Sergio de Mello, the envoy of Kofi Annan, has died. In Nadjaf, a bomb explodes in the Ali mosque, killing eminent spiritual leaders. Nothing is any longer respected. It is as if a bomb exploded at the Vatican or Mecca! Things are going badly. Sorcerer's apprentices. When the media feeding frenzy ends, it is followed by mental carnage: "Dynasty"! The Carrington family is invading Ad Debba! Quick! Turn off the television. And get going.

CHAPTER 31

History Earth Deep

SUDAN

"Sonia, rejoice! By leaving Ad Debba, we cross the latitude of Nouakchott, Timbuktu, and Agadez..."

"So?"

We pass a little saddled donkey with a cart of sugar cane. He has a jute sac for a hood over his head. Sonia exclaims: "It's so he can't recognize the address where they deliver the dope."

I break out laughing; the donkey brays in indignation.

We still have a short day ahead of us since we want to cross the Nile to go see on the other bank the ruins of Dongola el-Agouz, the capital of the ancient Christian realm of Makuria that prospered here for a thousand years. A little historical interval after our political glassful with Imad and Daniel.

We are only a hundred kilometers below Karima, but from Meroe times we are jumping forward twenty centuries in History, to the heart of the fourteenth century. The fort, a former royal palace of this city that was called the African Constantinople, is the sole intact vestige, saved from destruction for it was transformed into a mosque in 1367. We tread on shards of bones, fragments scattered for as far as the eye can see, ground skulls. The fort is a massive cube of land and brick built on an eminence and having very few openings. A *rhafir*[1] opens the door to us. We awaken the millions of bats that have taken possession of it and they take flight in an endless palpitating scarf of ruffled wings. Their rustling brings the desolate building alive, brushing against our ears. All the ceilings are little rounded brick vaults, squeezed together, which conferred on the whole its amazing longevity. The building is stocky like a Potala[2]. A wide stairway leads to the upper story. The mosque is installed in the former throne room, and the *mihrab*[3] opens in the eastern wall in the direction of Kaaba. In the mud and straw walls of cells open to the desert, thousands of nicks are slashed and gathered in desperate rectangles: so many days of incarceration. Days of waiting, days of slow death. Tartar steppe. The time is inscribed, boredom, despair, here, one day, someone. Far away, the pointed domes of *gubbas*, Muslim sepultures, seem the lost helmets of a defeated army. From this city of several tens of thousand inhabitants that extended its influence as far as Aswan, there is nothing else left. The Mamelukes came to raze its ruins at the beginning of the nineteenth century. Terrifying. Alone, at some distance from here, the great monolithic columns of the basilica, decorated with Byzantine crosses, still rise heavenward as exclamation points. Of the colossal ramparts that arrogantly protected the dominant city of the Nile, you see only sand, rockslide and ever these bone flakes by the million.

Salagi, Thursday 11 September 2003, day 987, 34 km, 10,996[th] km

Along the Nile, one bank always prevails over the other. At this latitude, the eastern bank is dead; the road and the villages are on the western bank. You don't really choose on which side you want

---

[1] Guardian.
[2] Castle of the Dalai Lamas in Lhasa, Tibet, stocky and resilient.
[3] Little empty and curved niche in every mosque that indicates Mecca's direction.

to walk, you walk where the life is. So we go back to the western bank. The fog, just behind the palm plantations, is now just an interminable chain of villages. All day, we follow in the soft sand the walls of private properties so as to remain as long as possible in their shade. We know that we have changed villages when we change mosques. We can use them as milestones as in Normandy the church spires, in a relay where each time we pass the gate with relief. One every hour, which is to say one every four kilometers. All identical and recent, as if they had been delivered in kits. They are financed by Dubai, Abu Dhabi and Saudi Arabia. Many are under construction. "Where did they used to pray before?" you wonder. Islam is young. Oil era. But with all these walls, we meet no one and walk stupidly and stubbornly, without stopping. Everyone is entrenched at home. A very hard day. We are exhausted and staggering, this evening, in Salagi, searching for our "savior of the day," that famous unknown who, for almost a thousand days, makes our trek possible, makes it human, makes it a constantly renewed miracle. Nose to the wind and with modest countenance, we call within for him, silently. Perhaps it is a prayer. Faith is this floating back and forth between doubt, miracle and reason. Who will it be tonight? A man? A woman? An old man? A young man? A rich man? A poor man? Suddenly, around the corner of a house, we are literally collared by an old man. Tonight, our savior has set up an ambush.

"It is heaven that sends you! On this sad anniversary of September 11, I am going to prove to you that we like Westerners! *Fadhal, fadhal!*"

Combat bustle. He cries over the walls, they bring us beds, mattresses, sheets, towels, glasses of cold water, cookies, there is a procession of children of all ages and sexes, who come to shake our hand, the one offering pillows, the other soap. Hassan Idriss hands out orders, sees to it that our slightest desires are accommodated, and in the right order. Sonia soon has her feet dipped in a cold water basin, while I munch on delicious doughnuts. When we are received, at noon or at night, Sonia always takes out a little scarf of blue-gray tulle with which she covers her head to scare off the evil eye and make herself discreet. Invariably, it is the opposite that occurs. It triggers a cascade of compliments on her beauty, which I receive with amusement and false modesty. Bareheaded, she was almost invisible; veiled, she elicits admiring exclamations and all the girls in the household come to comment on the event. And the men present, who did not dare look at her, can at leisure devour her with their eyes. Once more, we discover that veils reveal more than they hide.

Hassan takes advantage of this good humor to say: "Two years ago, a handful of terrorists disfigured the face of Islam. It can't be righteous to attack and kill innocents. *Malesh!* I am terribly sorry."

"Just as innocents die in Iraq. *Malesh!* I too am terribly sorry."

"Blessed be men of peace and goodwill. All that because of money! The Americans think they can buy the world and the Saudis think they can buy all the Muslims..."

"It is they, now, who are financing all these new mosques?"

Hassan flinches. "You have noticed?"

"Well, yes. It's a question of esthetics: we like your old mosques of mud and straw, whitewashed with low minarets that all have an original shape, with pretty little stairways. The ones we see everywhere under construction are in cement, and the long, multicolored minarets look like pastries or rockets..."

At this last word, he chuckles.

"You are putting your finger on a sensitive point. With these new mosques come young foreign imams. Our children go to study or work in Saudi Arabia and come back with new ideas about Islam. I fight with each of my sons over that. I am sixty-five, I have tried to be a good Muslim all my life and there are my sons, who have never done anything, pretending to teach me what true Islam is! Even our daughters are starting to do it! They spend years in Islamic universities under the influence of "Muslim sisters," but refuse to learn English. When they come home, they know the

Qu'ran by heart, split hairs over the slightest interpretation for hours, but don't know anything about the world and are useless about everything. They don't even know how to cook; they feel too superior to touch it. They criticize the wearing of the tobe, only want to wear veils that come from Malaysia – under the influence of the *djamaa islamiya*. Our children have lots of false notions in their heads, but especially, they have prepared for no profession!"

As the conversation proceeds, the conflict between generations is confirmed, added to the cultural conflicts internal to Sudanese Islam, which we witnessed at Hamad an Nil. Hassan hails one of his sons.

"Isaak, for example, lived six months in Paris, with a Saudi prince. Tell us again, what was the name of that street you lived on?"

The big lug with a Taliban beard, dressed all in white, since tomorrow is Friday, wriggles on his angareb, from which point he stares at Sonia, with that hard, straight stare that she hardly appreciates. He speaks not a word of English, but sputters, scratching his foot: "Lissan zélyzé…"

After a moment's reflection, Sonia exclaims: "The Champs-Élysées? Well, there are worse ways to spend six months in Paris! Did he like it?"

Hassan asks his son.

"He doesn't know, he never left the apartment…"

Less amiable than his father, the young man puts on the "Chirac-good-Bush-bad" record that summarizes most of our conversations with the young generation; a well-known song, with its couplets on the veil, American decadence, therefore ours, the war in Afghanistan, the aggression against Iraq, solely for oil…

To cut short the refrain, Sonia puts him on the ropes. "Is what the Americans are doing in Iraq not what you, the Sudanese, are doing in the South?"

Amused, Hassan translates for his son, who, highly annoyed at having his nose wiped by a woman, disappears without a word. His father turns toward us. *"Malesh!* You see? You can't discuss things with the young!"

Hassan too is nostalgic for the former Sudan and impatient for the Sudan of tomorrow. We tell him about our passionate and reassuring encounters, about the surreal kindness from which we have benefited. This comforts him and reconciles him with his own people, with himself.

"What you are telling me gives me infinite pleasure. I could die tomorrow. Please God it doesn't happen...! Tomorrow at the mosque, I shall pray for you, for your safety, that you will reach Al Qods."

"And along the way, we will pray for you...for your family. We will carry your name there if you wish, to the Dome of the Rock."

An angel flies by, and our old Hassan's eyes cloud, with dignity.

Before Dongola, the capital of Shimaliya, we pass at the foot of numerous fortress ruins, vestiges of the bastions that guarded the Christian realm of Makuria. They keep watch over the Nile from the rocky promontories where they melt slowly, like sugar cubes under the rain of the years. A thousand years of Christian history have flowed here. In 640, the Arab armies conquered Egypt but were not interested in Nubia nor in the *beled-es-sudan*, the "country of the Blacks." They signed a treaty of peace and mutual respect called the *Baqt*, according to which Nubia would each year deliver four hundred slaves to Egypt in exchange for wine and grain. The Sudanese of Shimaliya have not forgotten this page from their past, they tell us about it with affection, always concluding: "That is why we have nothing against the Christians!"

Under the stones of a fortress that we scaled in search of lost time, we discover shattered iron from the mouth of a cannon. We imagine the circumstances, the battle, right here, in this place, and the final assault, even if historians agree that isolation and slow assimilation were the causes of the disappearance of this civilization, of which the vestiges are the most numerous in the region, but the least documented. At the top, we receive the visit of a little red fox who stares at us for a moment, tries to tame us, then disappears in a trot behind the corner of an old wall. The guardian of passing time.

In Dongola, we are received by the police colonel Khalid Abd el-Rahman and his wife Salwa. He is the police chief for the whole district. He too complains about the regime.

"I have traveled, I have seen the world, I have even done a training stint with Interpol in Lyon, and I earn thirty-four dollars a month. It's true that I don't have a lot of work; there is essentially no criminality here, but I am ashamed of what we are doing everywhere, in the South, in Darfur. We have been at war for almost forty years. I have never known anything else. I fought in the South, I lost some friends for nothing. Two million dead for a status quo, that's absurd. I would like for my son to be able to study in England, travel like you, live in peace..."

I remember exactly the last sentence he said to us by way of farewell while we were walking together toward the ferry, to cross the Nile: "*Kullu nass fil alem ayiz salam. Siyasiyeen na Guish mafi, malesh.*" (Everyone on earth wants peace. Not the politicians and the military, unfortunately.)

Once more the goodwill of the civil population is confirmed. Dear Sudanese, if only you could manage to make yourselves heard!

Fareig, Saturday 20 September 2003, day 996, 32 km, 11,160th km

We have so far related mostly our masculine encounters, but in fact, most often, it is the women who take us in. The husbands are never home. They are in Saudi Arabia or in the Emirates, which explains the high standard of living of these families staying in this remote desert. At every pause, I am surrounded by creatures draped in magnificent colored tobes that glitter against the white lime on the walls of their houses. It's a funny feeling to be the rooster in the middle of a clucking farmyard, full of joy, being devoured voraciously by lascivious eyes. The presence of Sonia is the alibi for favors and attentions they would never allow themselves if she were not present. Or the contrary....I indulge in the comedy, beatific and stupidly submissive, while Sonia condescendingly watches the little game.

In every family there is an aroussa who pines for her husband. During their first year of marriage, young wives enjoy a privileged status; they have a nuptial room prepared for them, decorated with red ribbons, pink wall hangings, dominated by an immense bed covered with satin cushions, accompanied by its mirrored closet, night tables and dressing table. They are the queens of the house; everyone looks after them assiduously; they make themselves up, dress elegantly, they are spared all the household tasks. They have but one mission: to produce an heir. Unfortunately, the two or three visits by the sire are often insufficient and the young wife feels the pressure slowly rising. With the second year she falls from her pedestal; a third year of marriage without a child confirms the fall: she is moved out of the nuptial room; the fourth year, she becomes the house slave, the drudge of her sisters-in-law and nieces; the fifth year, she can be repudiated. We met representatives of each of these categories, but hopefully also of women fulfilled with adorable babies. Of them we retain a memory burning with love: Zeinab, Fatima, Leïla or Neimad, and their faces meld into a feminine person, gracious and jocular, funny and sensitive, the face of the Sudan that we want to remember.

Just to the north of Kerma, in Tumbus, we run into a children's ambush which reminds us of our bad memories: *"Pen! Pen! Pen! Khawadja! Money-money-money! Give me!"*

We are dismayed. This is the first time in this country. They don't want to let us go, become aggressive. We bawl them out in Arabic, they immediately shut up, stupefied that we could speak their language. Pitiless, Sonia whispers: "I bet you it's because Europeans come to see the Tumbus colossus that Francis Geus told us about. Blessed are the places where there is nothing to see."

An adult attracted by the noise comes and pummels a few of the scallywags to disperse them. He apologizes to us.

"*Malesh!* The tourists do not realize the bad habits they give to our children by giving them money which they have not earned by working. After that, they do nothing else: wait for the rare cars bringing *khawadjas*!"

Tumbus marks the ancient pharaonic border of Amenhotep III (1380 B.C.E.). This time, it is genuinely the Egypt of the New Empire and its splendors. On great granite blocks overlooking the Nile, an impressive collection of cartouches and hieroglyphics celebrates the grandeur of the Ancients. It was their end of the world: the third falls. The Nile rushes, tormented by rocks that scrape its belly. These falls were an important strategic point, feluccas and boats had to be hauled there by hundreds of men; it was also an ideal spot for the ambushes set for traders and to repel the armies of invaders coming up the river. Amid the rocks, on the other side of the road, an incomplete colossus lies on his back, barely extracted from his quarry. A culture from elsewhere. A sentinel cut down and abandoned. A pharaoh whose face was carried away. Enigmatic and improbable, almost extraterrestrial. The first of our trek, and we look at it with the same stupor that might have been felt by the walkers of tribal Africa who got here two or three thousand years ago.

The palm plantations and the fertile Kerma basin are behind us. The current of life on both sides of the Nile is now very spare and scarce, interrupted, uncertain. We have entered into the heart of the Sahara. The villages are becoming sporadic, grouped around oases or ruined fortresses, the course of the Nile begins to weave between the rocky massifs within which lie edenic landscapes, isolated fortified houses around lilliputian fields, worlds buttressed since the dawn of time against the environment's hostility.

At Masida, behind one of these stage set villages, there are in the desert, hidden between large blocks of basalt, the remains of an old Christian hermitage of which the remaining vaults are swallowed up by the rubble. One of them is only resting on a single crude brick. We admire this keystone, the metaphor of suspended time, suspended survival, fated for the universal fall. If some day we come back here, it will no longer be there. Suddenly, on the rock that served as end wall of the small nave, Sonia notices a finely engraved ram's head. We back up to get an overview of the whole pictogram and discover to our wonderment a huge Nilotic shepherd with his bannered spear and his flock. He is a two-meter giant, black, thick-lipped, with frizzy hair, wearing a loincloth that might be a Maasai *ol karasha*. Today, he is lost in the middle of lands long since conquered by populations from the north. One day the Christian chapel appropriated to itself this neolithic engraving ten thousand years old or more. It would be a good bet that it was called the chapel of the "good shepherd" or of the "lost sheep."... We depart fascinated by all this historical compression.

In Fareig, the next village, it is the mountains that are covered with pictograms: first boats, Egyptian skiffs with banana-shaped shells, hairy with oars and topped with the famous rectangular sail. The detail of the cabins, helmsmen or rigging is impressive. Next come the animals, as if they were to climb onto these postdiluvian arks: ostriches, giraffes, antelopes, zebus, that look like reindeer, so long and slim are their horns. This bestiary is galloping along the cliff's edge pursued by a lion or cheetah. A South African Therianthrope[4] even came this far. In person, by foot? Or in spirit, during a trance? Two notable absentees: the rhinoceros and the elephant. Two astonishing absentees: the hippopotamus and the crocodile. The ancient inhabitants of these shores must have turned their back on the Nile. More recent are bearded horsemen with heavy turbans galloping sabers drawn: surely Mamelukes who escaped the massacre orchestrated in 1811 by Mehemet Ali, an Albanian mercenary who became pasha of Egypt. They are caught up by an automobile and then by an airplane. You can't stop progress, nor

---

[4] A shaman transformed into an animal during a trance: see vol. I, p. 68.

the artistic drive of children. It is the whole history of men that is engraved there, in the yellow sandstone.

It is children moreover who this night take us by the hand to lead us to their home. Another wedding, but this time without the karaoke and the "millions-ions-ions." Under a scattering of stars, with a delirious family, we dance for a long time, sharing songs and revelry: "*Abschir! Abschir!*" God, how good men are!

The few days that follow introduce us into a world outside the world where the Nile is a lapis necklace adorned with ivory beads and diamonds. Men and villages here are pure jewels. Between Sadinfenti and Ageri, in the rocky curves of the lascivious river, lie hidden the loveliest villages in the country. The stocky houses back up to large rocks, the white lime contrasts with the colored gables, the contours of the windows or the friezes and crenels running along the tops of the walls. In certain villages these illuminations are dove gray, in others gold yellow or blood red, sometimes both in alternation. The doors are open onto courtyards splendid with serenity, lined with shaded ambulatories. Dovecotes let loose flights of immaculate doves against the raw sky. We could stop everywhere. All the women we pass hail us. Tantalus torment. We sometimes have to hide in the palm plantations to escape this frenetic hospitality. We have to stop everywhere. Eat everything. We are overwhelmed with kindness, exhausted by love. Remain forever. I mention this vision to Sonia.

"Just think! We throw everything overboard, we spend here sunny, immobile days, contemplative and sensual, surrounded by servile, attentive women…"

In lieu of a reply, she cuffs me overtly in front of my Areopagus of swooning women; my Oriental mirage immediately bursts amidst the laughter of the gynaeceum that I for a moment had taken for a siren chorus. How free and gay the women are far from the men! When one of them finally shows up, for inevitably a neighbor or cousin is alerted, pessimism falls on our little assembly;

this is the moment we choose to take our leave. In every language in the world, joy is feminine and tedium masculine.

Soleb, Wednesday 1 October 2003, day 1007, 24 km, 11,263rd km

It is at Wawa that we cross back over the Nile to go see the temple at Soleb, isolated on the western bank. Built by Amenhotep, son of Hapu, the architect of the first Luxor temple, to celebrate the greatness of Amenhotep III, it is our largest monument in over eleven thousand kilometers: gigantic columns extending enormous capitals into the sky like the affirmation of a superhuman will. We scale the pylon at the entrance to enjoy the view over the neighboring palm plantations, and are enchanted by this foretaste of Egypt: megalomaniac, solitary, delirious with ego, midwife of beauty and longevity. In our trek in the footsteps of Man, Soleb is the "gate of Prometheus": men's response to the mystery of their origin, a demonstration of their power in the face of the divinities and the elements, the weight of stone opposed to the anguish of emptiness and the fragility of life. Amenhotep III had insisted that the cult of Amon be celebrated here. So as to pacify the Nile and assure the return of the floods. So as to celebrate each year as well his birthday during the feast of Sed.

Today is Sonia's birthday, her third on African soil after Nairobi and Harare. She has Soleb for a cake, with its standing columns serving as candles. From the top of the north pylon we blow them all out. In the distance, over there, the Nile has been flowing silently at its foot for three thousand four hundred birthdays. Pitiless time has trampled this ambition for eternity. Everywhere, on the ground, hieroglyphs on stone blocks speak in rebuses and desperately search for the other words, the other symbols with which they formed sentences, meanings, the Verb that is lacking to make these stone enigmas speak. We seem to hear them whispering at our feet. We remain there a long time, in the setting sun, embracing, alone in the world at the top of our pylon.

The next day, we are invited to a radha with a very poor family.

How to say no? Why say no? Must one take away from the poor the only dignity that they have left? The power of giving, the power to receive guests? That is what we understand in sharing the plate of fish *gourrassa* of Fatima Eltayeb and Idriss Moussa. Fatima is fat and ugly. So what? Idriss is one-eyed and bedraggled. So what? She carries in her arms a little retarded baby, handicapped with a club foot. She hasn't got enough milk. They are frightfully destitute and dirty. Their interior is apocalyptic and yet we feel fine, and yet they are happy. They love each other and that can be seen in Idriss's eye, and it can be heard in the babble of the crippled child, and can be felt in this sharing of their ordinary meal. A neighbor comes to see what's happening. She is richly dressed, her hands painted with henna, fleshy and pretty, but she perspires with sadness. She has a little girl of fifteen months conceived on her wedding night. The next day her arrousse left for Saudi Arabia. She has not seen him since. She no longer mopes. She has switched to standby and each of her sighs whispers: "But what good does it do me to be rich, if I have no love?"

Two days later, we finally reach Sai, the island at the gates of the Batn-el-Hajar, literally "the stomach of the stone," the womb that gave birth to these petrified immensities, the impenetrable desert border that separates Egypt from Africa, which has always been its natural border, its fortified gate. In Tochka, a ferryman takes us to the island in his antediluvian felucca. The flat, flared shell is but an approximate patchwork of enormous wood beams. It is almost as wide as it is long, like an almond. The triangular sail is furled along a spar and is let out with one hand. The wind has always come from the north, against the current. It suffices to let the nose of the felucca go with the stream, the wind makes the craft rear up, the braces moan, the helm shake on which our buttressed ferryman sings. Without this northerly wind, there would be no navigation possible, there would be no Egypt. Mohammed Abdul, our felucca man, cracks us up.

"I have a seven-year-old son whose name is Clinton Mohammed, another of four whose name is Mandela Mohammed, and my wife is pregnant with a third whom I will call Chirac Mohammed!"

The isle of Sai has been excavated for more than thirty years by the team of Francis Geus[5], an archeologist from Lille who is based in Khartoum. Sai is his vocation. Francis is something of a cleric of the rock, of sober and deliberate speech, his pupil burning with a sacred fire. He unfortunately is not present and we try to remember the lecture he gave on his work at the Alliance Française in Khartoum. The richness of the island is immeasurable. The whole of world history is stratified in it. From deposits of the early paleolithic going back three hundred thousand years to Christian churches, by way of the pharaohs, the Cushites, the Ptolemies, the Greco-Romans, the modern Turks and the Egyptians. Everything here is mixed up in a pudding of matter and history where you find a stele covered in hieroglyphs transformed into a door lintel, where an overturned Corinthian capital serves as the base of an column decorated with cross pattées and itself serving as pillar of a Turkish mosque....Behind this chaos of ruins as far as the eye can see on the island plateau stretch necropolises and sepultures. Armies of the dead patiently awaiting the Second Coming, gutted tombs, whitened skulls still bearing shriveled ears, mummified skins that still have their fingerprints. The alluvial moraines have been cooked by a thousand million suns and resonate under our steps like metal stones. And the wind, the wind, the northerly wind, that whistles the oblivion of bodies and the wandering of souls.

We remain for a few days meditating on these history pile-ups and mix-ups and preparing for our passage of the Batn-el-Hajar, which separates us from Wadi-Halfa, the border post with Egypt. Overflown one evening at dusk by hundreds of bats brushing our faces, seated on Maltese crosses hewn on the rocks by primeval pilgrims, we write this poem in homage to so many bygone

---

[5] He died in August 2004.

centuries, so much blood shed and dried, to these dark waters that roll by before our eyes and where an orange moon dances under the horizon.

Le Nil

Chargé de limon rouge, il roule
    ses flots lourds
À travers les déserts.
Large comme une mer, il coule
    autant qu'il court
Sur la chair de la Terre.

Son sang irrigue cette grande
    assoiffée
De sable et de pierre.
Tout croît, tout suce et pompe
    la sève épanchée
De la géante artère.

Une frange de palme ourle ses
    berges lisses
Par l'ombre recouvertes:
Touk! Touk! Touk! Touk! Les
    Lister chantent et l'eau
    s'immisce
En une coulée verte,

Et des canaux d'argile
    distribuent la vie
Aux champs et aux fourrages
Que les chameaux, les ânes et
    les chèvres, ravis
Broutent en pâturages.

The Nile

Ferrying red slime, it rolls its
    heavy waters
Through the deserts.
Wide as the sea, it flows as
    much as it runs
On the flesh of the Earth.

Its blood irrigates this great
    parched land
Of sand and stone.
Everything grows, everything
    sucks and pumps the
    poured-out sap
Of the giant artery.

A fringe of palm hems its
    smooth banks
Covered in shade:
Touk! Touk! Touk! Touk! The
    Listers[6] sing and the water
    seeps
In a green flow,

And clay canals distribute life
To the fields and forages
On which delighted camels,
    donkeys and goats
Graze in pasture lands.

---

[6] Lister: an old monocylinder British
    pump with a characteristic sound.

À ce brun narghilé ourdi dans
le néant
Les hommes se raccrochent
Comme au sein d'une mère se
raccroche un enfant
Dans un enfer de roches.

Caravanes, empires et
civilisations
Ont trépassé par là,
Pyramides, colonnes et
fortifications
Se sont érigées là.

Kerma et Napata, archers
nubiens, Candaces,
Ont fait gronder le Nil
De tribulations, de coups
d'éclat, d'audace.
Carnage et goûts subtils:

Combien de prisonniers, de
colonnes d'esclaves,
De défenses d'ivoire,
De sang versé sur ces rivages
que l'eau lave?
Il nous semble tout voir:

Temples, châteaux, mosquées,
tombeaux, crânes blanchis
Fracassés par le temps,
Fantômes oubliés, mélangeant
leurs débris
Et leurs formes d'antan.

To this brown hookah stretched
in the void
Men cling
As a child clings to his
mother's breast
In a stony hell.

Caravans, empires and
civilizations
Have vanished here,
Pyramids, columns, and
fortifications
Have risen here.

Kerma and Napata, Nubian
archers, Kandakes,
Have made the Nile rumble
With tribulations, dazzle,
boldness.
Carnage and subtle tastes:

How many prisoners, slave
columns,
Or ivory tusks,
How much blood shed on these
banks rinsed by the waters?
We feel we can see it all:

Temples, chateaus, mosques,
tombs, whitened skulls
Shattered by time,
Forgotten phantoms, mixing
their debris
And the shapes of yesteryear.

Tout dort sous une pierre
    abrasée par le vent
Qui siffle entre les dunes,
Et le Nil éternel, sourd à tous
    ces tourments,
Miroite sous la lune

Everything sleeps under a stone
    abraded by the wind
That whistles between the
    dunes,
And the eternal Nile, deaf to
    all these torments,
Shimmers in the moonlight.

For Francis Geus and his team of archeologists, in memoriam.

CHAPTER
32

The Caravan of Batn-el-Hajar

SUDAN

"This is our main station. Like Heathrow Airport. Welcome to Tochka," says Anwar with a smile, squatting on his heels in the shade of a palm tree, facing the desert. We wait. They told us they would be here about noon. Time passes, we look at our watches, pinching ourselves, worried. In disbelief. It's been a week already that we have been wating in Abri, opposite Sai, on the other bank, at the home of Said Asafi. The sun rises high in the sky. Shadows are shrinking. We do not despair. In any case, we are trapped. Before us open the two hundred uncrossable kilometers of the Batn-el-Hajar, "the stomach of stone," ready to digest us. A totally empty desert, not a living soul and no water of any kind.

We are looking to the south, uneasy, our three years hanging on this hope, this dream, that might stop here, when suddenly a head appears far away, behind a dune, then another, then ten, then a hundred. Step by step, slowly, as if it were rising from the sand, our camel caravan extracts itself from the horizon. They come silently, in groups, look us over contemptuously. Only five men are driving them. Anwar engages the conversation with them and, while walking alongside the camel of the chief, communicates our request to him. The answer is no. Very simply *La!* It is laconic. We try now, dismayed but smiling, throwing into the battle, among the camels' legs, all our Arabic, all our trek, our eleven thousand kilometers: "*La taklak!* Don't worry! We will not be a burden, we have been walking for nearly three years, we sleep on the ground, we eat soup, we have to get to Al Qods…"

At this last word, he stops; the caravan goes by. I continue: "We will take your name to the Al-Aqsa mosque, on the Dome of the Rock, along with that of all our Muslim hosts!"

"*Anta Muslim?*" (Are you a Muslim?)

"*La, wallakin rabbuna wahid lana koullou no!*" (No, but we all have the same God!)

He cracks a broad smile. He accepts. He signals to two men at the back, who at once halt their mounts and leave us their saddles. So here we are perched in the train of life to the north and the exit gate from Sudan. It all went very quickly. We scarcely have time to salute Anwar, who returns, relieved, to squat under his palm tree.

Our caravanners come from the mountains of Darfur, one thousand two hundred kilometers to the southwest of here, near the border with Chad; they have crossed in a month the dry death of Wadi Howar, with just one water well per week. Hussein is driving three hundred fifty head, and two other identical groups follow, led by other teams, but it is he who is head of the caravan. He is the son of a sheikh. After the thousand bellies quickly fill up in a row on the bank of the Nile, we leave the life line with some emotion. Hussein Labd Mohammed Ahmed, our head caravanner, leads us due north into the desert, by rough estimate.

Sonia was uneasy about not knowing how to ride a dromedary; now she is reassured, seated high, slim waist and skirt billowing, the left fist on her hip or holding the rein, the right hand wielding the whip, straw hat on her head and nose in the air. She is sublime. You would think she has done this all her life! She turns toward me: "You remember that line of Paulo Coelho where he says that 'the whole world conspires to make your dreams come true'?"

Ours is advancing thanks to this little mysterious morning conspiracy which would have us on these dromedaries rather than moping in Abri.

Yesterday, while we were registering with the police who wondered what we were waiting for, we came across a group of travelers coming southward in over-equipped Land Rovers. Thanks to Padraig Murphy, an Irishman on his way to Cape Town, I managed to print secretly a birthday card for Sonia on his computer and color printer. Surreal! Padraig played the ventriloquist, waving a little stuffed dog belonging to his fiancée Mary, which he is taking with him just so it will have traveled, like Amélie Poulain's dwarf[1]: "When I'll be back home, I'll tell Mary that I met you and she won't believe me!" Two other travelers, the Frenchmen Loïc and Geoffroy de La Tullaye, who embarked on board an old Citroën Dyane for their "hydrotour,"[2] a trip around the world with a water theme, offered me a pair of pants. Given the rubbing of legs on the camel's neck, this present was providential.

There again it's a little Coehlian conspiracy. Do such conspiracies attach to the desert world alone? No, but in the virginal simplicity of survival, between sand and sun, they are more visible here. That's all. In the desert you can only be a believer or in despair. There is no room for the lukewarm. When we get home to noise, opulence and complexity, we will have to extend our ears and open our eyes to spot these silent, discreet conspiracies. They will be there, under tons of superfluous stuff. We will have to be vigilant. Not forget them.

The sun has set quickly on our first afternoon. It patiently stretched out red shadows to our right, a passel of outsize camels knitting in the sand on huge long legs. The full moon, to the east,

---

[1] In the film *Le Fabuleux Destin d'Amélie Poulain* (2001), distributed in the United States under the title *Amélie*.
[2] See address on p. 624.

sketches others to our left, this time blue. All is silence except for the breath of the animals and the soft swish of thousands of pads on the sand. We levitate with the swell of the humps that rock us with well-being. We feared the legendary seasickness of the desert ships. It does not happen. We walk straight ahead, carried on a wire. All of a sudden, an hour past midnight, the moon at its zenith, Hussein signals to his men to stop. We halt and here we are in the middle of nowhere, on compact sand, preparing to camp in the middle of these hobbled beasts. Noor Moussa, "Light of Moses," the young chef, prepares a fire for the *aceida*, a sort of sticky, acid paste, flavored with onion concentrate and spices: dinner.

The men assemble. This is the time for introductions. There is Abdallah Mohammed, the dean, fifty-eight years old, white beard and soft voice, the contemplative member of the band. Then comes Khamis Hussein, the fifth of the seven dwarfs, the one who laughs all the time with a little malicious chuckle and never leaves his turban, the black color of which clashes with his gray beard. There is Mohammed Rerebil Arabesh, who munches on an onion as you would munch on an apple, a feminine face, broad smile, and eyes so black they look made-up. There is also Adam Hussein, the largest, ascetic and athletic, beardless and with a Caucasian face, the group performer, who is always running to catch independent camels. Finally, Bindadur Tarbuch, impenitently loquacious, who also is endowed with the group's highest-pitched voice. No luck. When everyone has had enough of listening to him, he answers himself, debates, starts over, speaks for everyone with the speed of a machine gun. They have faces sculpted with a pruning knife, little black eyes like obsidian, prematurely wrinkled from too much squinting, the obligatory smile since their life is too hard to complain.

In five minutes the dinner is downed, nine right hands dipping into the platter; in five minutes we are lying on a wool rug which Hussein is lending us for the night, rolled in a blanket that Adam is sacrificing for our comfort. For the nights have become chilly in the last few days. Finally chilly! What bliss, this shivering of the skin to the cold caress of a little nighttime breeze; the gentle kiss of the stars on the temples, the energizing electricity of goose flesh! It is a sensation we had forgotten since Ethiopia and which I rediscover, unlike Sonia, with delight.

The camels have their left forelimb folded back by a hobble knotted under the knee. On three legs, they move around less easily and prefer lying down. In this extended bleakness under a lunar floodlight, they compose an island of shaggy rocks unfurling strange tentacles; a mass full of murmurs, sighs, crunching of feet on the fine sand and gurglings convoluted by dark ruminations. We fall into sleep like stones; the sandman is busy tonight.

Ambikol, Friday 10 October 2003, day 1017, 55 km, 11,405th km

At dawn, the sun springs on the horizon and we spring to our feet: the saddles of Adam and Hussein are waiting only for our backpacks. Action stations! The convoy gets under way like a train on time and we follow behind, walking clumsily with our stick in hand and rusty limbs, utterly seized up by the expected aches and pains. A brutal awakening. It starts off strong. Will we make it, on an empty stomach?

Walking behind our animals, we can observe at leisure their slow strides, long and mechanical. The padding of their wide feet embraces the sand and spreads out into a rubbery cushion. The humps bob and our camelids imperturbably advance, with pinched nostrils and gentle eyes, thick, flaccid lips but dignified bearing. Some of them limp, others have deformities, calluses, excrescences that bespeak their past sufferings, their destiny as pack animal. Not one is intact. We learn to our great surprise that in this immense herd there are only females. They remain unruffled. Perfectly adapted to walking in the desert. I named the one they loaned me Gédéon, the name of our producer. Not to entitle myself to whip him at will but for his soberness in confidence, his confidence despite the folly of our project, his folly in leaving the reins in our hands although we had no experience with camels....Thank you Stéphane. Would we be here without you? Yes, surely, but we would not have been filming confidently, freely, for so long.

The caravan neither waits nor drags, it is pitiless. The pace is sustained. The camel drivers perched in their saddles, sleeves puffed out and turban quivering, constantly whirl and crack their whips, shouting "hot-hot-hot!" It is a forced march. And yet the tranquil ships seem to be walking in slow motion. Or rather are we weakening? To walk thus in the soft sand drains the energy out of us. Every hour, we approach Hussein's saddle and Sonia's backpack from which hangs the hose of the camelback, a plastic wineskin used by cross-country runners, and rehydrate ourselves as we walk, to the great glee of our caravanners who come in turn to relish this little exercise in in-flight refueling, and leave repeating to any who would hear: "*Khawadja majnoun!*"[3] After three hours of duress, Hussein and Adam climb down and give us their mounts, which we reclaim as one passes a finish line. Whew, we withstood the shock! Our honor is saved. Later in the day, we will try to walk one hour out of two: that gets the rust out of our aching limbs and relieves our posteriors, much tested by the back-and-forth in the saddle. Each time I climb I entrust them with the pedometer to continue measuring the distance covered, and Adam or Hussein takes off cheerfully with the feeling of accomplishing a surveying mission.

We are following the tracks of preceding herds which the wind has not yet erased, and counting the morbid markers constituted by whitened camel skeletons that have fallen along the itinerary over fifty centuries. One hundred twenty-seven in one day. You keep busy how you can, don't you? The rib cages resemble claws attempting to rejoin themselves to life, but they no longer retain breath; the sand flows in between the ribs and the wind drums on their parchmented hides. Along the way we harvest two scapulae.

---

[3] These White folks are crazy!

The first medium of the first surates of the Qu'ran. I tell myself that some day we will find a calligrapher to copy two of them for us in classical Arabic. When I explain the reason for my gesture to our friends, they play their record again: "*Ya salam! Khawadjas majnoun! Laakin yumkin i rasul Allah!*"[4] And it's my turn to laugh....We sense that they like us. Our motivations are mysterious to them, but these desert people like mysteries, they don't seek to reveal them, they prefer to give them a halo of respectful silence. "*Souphan Allah!*" is their response to the incomprehensible. We offer them a little novelty in a walk where every day is a repetition of the day before. They understand that we are coming from far away, not for sport, nor for pride, and that we are going somewhere...

Between the sand and the sky, the shortest distance is prayer, so our camel drivers pray five times a day. Scrupulously, in turn, they recite the *Fatiha*[5] prostrate in Mecca's direction and run to catch up with the school of dromedaries. During this time, we get back in the saddle, act as shepherds, running here, trotting there, to keep the formation together. They keep an eye on us and we advance in rank when we bring an animal back to the fold. Sonia remains an enigma for them. They are fascinated and at the same time very respectful. The women never mount camels and in principle do not know how to drive them. She puts the lie to that belief and there she goes in a wild rodeo, in pursuit of a recalcitrant camel, yelling "hot-hot-hot!," cracking the whip and kicking up at the heel under torrents of laughter from Adam. She is adopted.

Physically, we pay dearly for every photo we take because then we must run in the sand to catch up with the herd, then get to the one carrying our backpacks, try to take our camera without being stepped over by the beast, go and take our picture and rush back to put the camera away, because carrying it on our chests is bruising

---

[4] Good Lord! These White folks are really crazy, but maybe they are prophets!

[5] First surate of the Qu'ran. Its seven verses are a prayer for God's guidance and stress the lordship and mercy of God.

us after a while. But that's not the toughest. We wear ourselves out trying to take both of us with camels in the background, using a timer. The two Maasai of Lake Natron[6] for their part were not gallivanting in all directions! This time, we first have to run very far ahead of the group; when that is done, winded, line up the camera on its tripod, anticipate the camels' position ten seconds later as well as their distance and our position within the frame, trip it at the right time, run to get in place at Sonia's side, panting, looking casual, staring at the blue line of dunes, pray I am in the frame, that a camel will not knock the tripod in the sand, pass anxiously, turn and run after the camera, and finally catch up, out of breath, with the caravan which is already three hundred meters ahead. Each time it takes me an hour to recover. All that just for a single photo that I am almost sure will not be any good....Even if I hope I can get a cover for the second volume out of it....Photography is an act of faith! Our drivers split a gut, repeating: "*Khawadja majnoun!*"

Right at noon, when the sun is high overhead, everyone stops. We are surrounded by rocky rises. Hussein points to one of them: "*Gebel Djamal*" – dromedary mountain. Sonia exclaims: "Look, Alex! Amazing! It's the drawing of Saint-Exupéry. You know, the boa-hat that swallows an elephant. Exactly the same shape, with the two humps!"

"And you are my sand rose. No thorns, no problems. It's time to get ourselves into the shade."

Bindadur comes to us with a large branch which he asks Sonia to hold vertical. He adjusts the four angles of four large blankets spread out as petals and attaches them to the top of the pike. He then uses the camel hobbles which he knots at the other angles, holding them down with a saddle. Sonia wants to make herself useful; Bindadur hands her the package of hobbles to keep her

---

[6] See Chapter 7.

busy; she hesitates a second and bursts out laughing: "In a word, if I understand correctly, he takes me for a hatrack!"

The current passes between them. Hussein is delighted. He took a heavy responsibility by accepting us in his group on a whim. The tent that will protect us from the sun has taken shape. Close to sunstroke, we squeeze in underneath for lunch. *Aceida* at every meal. That is hard. As early as day two, we are fed up and get out our noodle soup. But our friends only like *aceida* and grimace when they see our bowls. Bindadur questions me: "You think I could find a woman like yours in France who would be willing to follow me to the desert?"

"Bindadur, if you go as far as France on foot with your camel, I am sure you will have great success and will be able to seduce a woman with no problem!"

They all laugh out loud and slap each other on the back. Bindadur has a smile that is to die for. How beautiful they are, these men united against the elements, bent toward a single goal in this furnace! If one link broke the fragile equilibrium would be compromised.

Once sated, we are entitled to a little nap, comatose from sweat and heat. Outside, the beasts cook, they too overwhelmed. Overhead, on the made in China blankets, roar grotesque, leaping tigers while we steal a little sleep from our headlong rush. In fact, you have not a minute to yourself in a caravan, everything is commanded by the necessity of going onward, onward, onward...

In the afternoon, we traverse undefinable spaces, endlessly renewed, yellow, punctuated in the distance by rocky rises, so identical to those we saw just a little while ago, this morning, yesterday, that we have the disagreeable sensation of running in place. All the same we are advancing at a phenomenal pace. We go through passes, hundreds of rocky outcrops, and weave like an army in distress. Hussein, calm and composed, knows where he is going, we are all dependent on his knowledge, his wisdom; he is the chief. He holds our lives in his hands. Human tombs marked with a standing stone and animal carcasses strewn by a giant ogre playing Tom Thumb remind us of the simple dramas that have transpired here. Death, thirst, exhaustion. Dramas as evident as that the sand absorbs water. The desert or humility. When you get away from the caravan you are seized by an excruciating sensation of abandonment and loneliness. The sensation of the astronaut moving away from his capsule. Life hangs by a thread, the thread of walking. We get back in the saddle. That is a relief. As getting down from the saddle is a relief for our posterior, the only part of the body that is really suffering.

In the distance, the thousand heads strung out in the void but grouped in puddles of life walking in the same cadence, toward the same goal. Survival first. But also the butchery. Five hundred thousand enter every year afoot into Egypt to be converted into brochettes, *shawarmas* or leather items. Thinking about it, our trek suddenly takes on funereal overtones.

In the evening we quarter in a spot so like that of the day before that we are troubled by it. Have we been walking? Cold sweat. Hussein reassures us. This noplace has a name. Mysterious toponymy. It is called Ambikol. Yesterday, it was Dal. It is a proof that we have progressed. The pedometer acknowledges fifty-five kilometers. I cast a glance at my bit of photocopy of a British map of the 1950s. Dal is on it, and Ambikol as well, but on the Nile, fifteen or twenty kilometers to the east. By extension, the desert in the area takes the name of known places.

The days go by as do landscapes more and more disordered, innocent of thought, consequences, logic. It is a raw and brutal desert, a chaos of rocks draped with sand like sleeping sentinels and expanses blasted by the wind, which has spread forever little round, polished stones in a magic floor that sparkles in the sunlight. Elsewhere, we are crushed between titanium boulders and a leaden sky, we slide like a puddle of mercury, compact and heavy. Nothing that can fix itself in memory, everything flows, everything is wiped out, blurry, sand, nothing, anguish. Might we die of madness before we die of thirst?

As the days pass, the pain in my butt increases. My flesh is raw and I twist in all directions to change position. I was assigned the right flank of the herd. Whereas Sonia guards the left flank. When two lead camels take an eastern tangent, I spur with my two heels, arms spread and whip clacking, and bring back the whole herd on a gallop, shouting "hot-hot-hot!" – and sometimes "ouch, ouch, ouch!" – when I lean back on my abrasion, or else "oh, oh, oh" when I lean forward to protect my posterior, at the risk of my forward parts ground against the pommel of the saddle. In perhaps cowardly manner I calm my pain but administer a serious thrashing to the desperados. But it does no good, camels have no memory, and mine, weary, lets itself be slowly passed up by the herd; and at the head of the line the two rascals are acting up again. So I spend hours playing the suffering imp and the flogging father. Then I find a temporary solution by changing position: on one buttock, the opposite leg extended out and the other knee hooked around the famous pommel.

The fourth day, we rejoin the Nile. It is no longer the Nile, it is already Lake Nasser, immense and shimmering. Bliss: the tension relaxes, we can drink all we want, wash, come back to life. The camels seem to smile, seem to know. They fill up again in a great chorus of suction and stomach rumblings. These beasts are better when you get to know them: we now have the greatest respect for them, they are gentle, never complain, walk courageously, don't bite, in short they are much nicer than we had thought.

Grubby with salt and acid dust, I throw myself in the water, accompanied by the old Khamis Abdallah, contemptuous of crocodiles. It feels like coming to life again. We are made more of sea than of desert, our mass is three-quarters water. I have the impression of drinking through my pores.

This time, we pitch our little igloo tent and invite Hussein to come take shelter in it. The others are all busy washing their laundry or rounding up the camels that disperse to graze in the groves along the bank. Sonia takes the opportunity to do some sewing.

"Alex! This is serious. It's done for!"

"What's that?"

"My bra. This is the third time I have repaired it, but this time I think it's done for, and I can hardly see how I can get back in the saddle without something to hold me in place."

"Let me see it."

"Well, I hesitate a little to show it because it really has been through the war. I don't know whether you realize, but I've been wearing it every day for three years! That's a brand that would deserve some publicity. Here is the side that's most presentable. Look at it discreetly, there are eyes that might be impressed...by the size...of the cups."

"Stop 'bra-gging'!"

Sonia chortles at her swaggering. To unbend Hussein, who has missed none of the scene, I remark: *"Taban!"* (It's worn!)

To my technical appraisal, he politely replies, *"Taban!"*...

While we rest on the bank waiting for the aceida, a fisherman's skiff comes along. Encounter between two worlds.

"Salam Aleykoum!"

"Maleykoum salam!"

The world of the sea, the world of deserts. They don't know each other. They exchange peace. The one comes from the Red Sea, the other from the Chadian border; thousands of kilometers separate them, abolished by the same faith, the same desire for peace and sharing. They share a few words. They understand each other without speaking. They are of the same mettle, live by the same poverty, the same perils, the same sufferings, the same God. A fisherman hands some fish to Hussein. He awkwardly accepts. He has never eaten one and doesn't know how it is prepared. We reassure him: we will cook them for him. When the fishermen have left, everyone has a laugh.

"All the same, we aren't going to eat that thing!"

There is a tiger fish, a tilapia, a small Nile perch and a sort of prehistoric barbel. The old Abdallah, the dean of the caravan, holds his nose. "*Seuban! Cheitan!*[7] Never will I eat that! Ugh!"

Before their uneasy eyes, we clean and scale the fish, cut them into sections, sauté some onions in oil, prepare a court-bouillon with tomato concentrate, and the bland odor of fresh fish is soon replaced by the succulent odor of a simmering dish, to the great relief of our spectators. Three of the seven try it, love it, lick their chops and thank God with a rosary of "*Souphan Allah!*"[8] The others mock them and turn to their aceida.

On the evening of the next day, we abruptly run into the fence of Argin that runs directly west, in open desert: the Egyptian border. Our next to last border! After 1,020 days traveling and 11,524 kilometers traveled. The formalities begin. The camels pass. Not us. The border is not open to individuals. We knew this. Adam, Abdallah, Noor, Bindadur, Khamis and Mohammed descend from their saddles, get their things together and mix their mounts into the herd. Sonia is surprised: "How will you get home?"

"By truck! All the camels are going to Egypt."

We say goodbye to our company.

"Thank you for your blanket, it was great to ride your camel, dear Saddam Hussein."

Adam Hussein burst out laughing like a hand grenade. His companions repeat the word. With a name like that, he couldn't avoid it! In Iraq, the Americans are looking everywhere for him.

After long embraces, they leave. We remain there with Hussein and the custom officers. He has to pay some taxes. We have to cross to the other bank and take the boat in Wadi-Halfa for Aswan. To trespass the border clandestinely would be to expose ourselves to pure and simple arrest on the Egyptian side, to expulsion and the end of our odyssey, so near the end. We don't take that risk,

---

[7] It's a snake! A creature of the devil!

[8] What a marvel.

especially since crossing Egypt looks to be very problematic if not impossible.

In the evening, all the papers are in order. Hussein has to get back to his caravan. This is the moment when we must part, break an extremely strong bond, like a mooring that ties us to the port, who ties us to himself. It feels like we have only lived a day in their company, an endless day, punctuated with nights and suns, like we have unwound a film reduced to one image in a changeless landscape. One of the loveliest images in Africa Trek. We leave him moved to tears. He asks nothing of us. He thanks us for working at their sides and hopes for our visit to his home, in El-Genina, in the south of Darfur. Thereupon, he catapults into the saddle and takes off into the reddening horizon, his arms wide, and we long watch this little figurine perched on his proud mount, ambling along the fence that stretches infinitely to the west. And from this vision of a free man, alone in the glowing immensity, the intuition arises in us that here, with Hussein, lord of the desert, our African adventure, free, from village to village, under the blue sky, comes to an end. We weep all the more for that, all alone, in the setting sun.

EGYPT

1. Ayman Abd el-Kader
2. Magitt, Ayman, Mohammed and Aman
3. Imad and Aatif Baulus
4. Lieutenant Mahmoud, Nabil, Samir and Tariq
5. Yasser and Tafla Mohammed
6. Aziz, Sohad, Heba, Fifi, Asma and Maryam Baulus
7. General Samir Youssif
8. Hadj Delil
9. Yonan Adli
10. Guy-Hervé Perron
11. Nubions Ibrahim
12. Zina Aboukheïr
13. Badaoui el Adli
14. Francis Amin
15. François Larcher
16. Olga Gentil
17. Governor Adel Habib
18. Abuna Yonan and Iman
19. Abuna Abraham
20. Sister Sabah and Francis Nabil
21. Governor Ahmad Hammam Atia
22. Abuna Boutros
23. Salwa el-Sorughi
24. Eustaz Effat and Mrs. Ikhlas
25. Essam el-Moghraby
26. Jean-Pierre Corteggiani, Zahi Hawass, Dr. Sameh Sourour, Colonel Hicham Garib
27. Abuna Erinaos
28. Hassan el-Kureishi
29. Jean-Yves Empereur
30. Magdy Selim and Governor Fouad Gamal Eldin
31. Noura Sayed

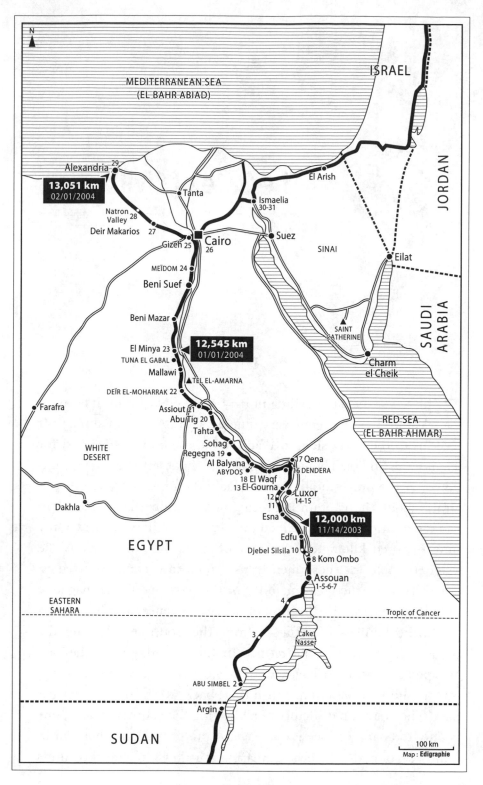

N

MEDITERRANEAN SEA
(EL BAHR ABIAD)

ISRAEL

JORDAN

SAUDI
ARABIA

RED SEA
(EL BAHR AHMAR)

Alexandria 29

13,051 km
02/01/2004

Tanta

El Arish

Ismaelia
30-31

Natron
Valley 28

Deir Makarios 27

Gizeh 25   Cairo
26

Suez

SINAI

Eilat

MEÏDOM 24

Beni Suef

Beni Mazar

El Minya 23

12,545 km
01/01/2004

TUNA EL GABAL

Mallawi

TEL EL-AMARNA

DEÏR EL-MOHARRAK 22

Farafra

Assiout 21
Abu Tig 20

Tahta

Sohag
Regegna 19

Al Balyana
ABYDOS

18 El Waqf
13 El-Gourna

12
11

Esna

17 Qena
16 DENDERA

Luxor
14-15

12,000 km
11/14/2003

Edfu

Djebel Silsila 10   9

8 Kom Ombo

Assouan
1-5-6-7

WHITE
DESERT

Dakhla

EGYPT

SAINT
CATHERINE

Charm
el Cheik

EASTERN
SAHARA

Tropic of Cancer

3

4

Lake
Nasser

ABU SIMBEL 2

Argin

SUDAN

100 km

Map : Edigraphie

Egypt

33 The Gate of Civilization

EGYPT

The *Saïd el-Naam* is sailing north on Lake Nasser on its way to Aswan. It all has gone very quickly. From Argin, a fishing skiff took us to the other side, to Wadi Halfa, the only border post for leaving the Sudan. There is no road. The boat left the port at sundown, at the prayer hour. On the deck, the prostrate men remonstrate about the captain's changes of direction that make them change position to remain lined up with Mecca. Funny mess. Only nine hundred kilometers due east of here, the Holy City is the magnetic pole for these men transformed into compass needles. For the others, the great majority of the passengers, the magnetic pole is the north, the direction of peace, opulence, and freedom.

Entire families of refugees from the South are leaving the Sudan on this river of no return. In their Sunday best, they are grouped around their baggage, their gaze vague or riveted on the setting sun, due west. They turn their backs to the others, to their past. They have no difficulty at all leaving the country. The regime is only too happy to see them leave. A pretty little girl, her hair in braids decorated with beads, wearing a little white smocked dress on which hangs a Miraculous Medal in blue enamel, comes and takes Sonia by the hand. They walk a while together on the deck. The tall blonde and the petite Black. She is a little girl you could meet in the chapel of the Rue du Bac[1], in Paris, praying for happy tomorrows, on this *bac*,[2] towards another life. Her family is going to land with political refugee status in a suburb of Cairo, antechamber for Australia, Canada or Europe. It will take the time it takes, but they will succeed. There is an extraordinary determination in their resigned attitude.

In seventeen hours we will be in Aswan. Night has fallen. We pass the lights of Argin, on the other shore, where we stopped walking, then, a little farther on, before the illuminated colossuses of Abu Simbel. They are only a luminous spot, very far to the west, but they are our lantern; that is where we hope to resume the trek, fragile hope, since the three hundred kilometers that separate Abu Simbel from Aswan are a military border zone, forbidden to foreigners, forbidden to hikers – and we do not want such a gap in the continuity of our itinerary. We will have to negotiate. When we left Khartoum, the Egyptian Interior Minister sent us a negative response; we have to comply with the legislation in force with respect to tourists' movements, which is police convoys. On this deck, rocked by the vibrations of the machines, there is much anguish and uncertainty; they, for their new life, we for the end of our trek.

The Aswan dam forms the northern end of Lake Nasser. End of the line. Everyone out. In the ruckus, an Egyptian officer comes to see us.

"Are you the two French people who are walking across Africa? Welcome to Egypt, follow me please!"

We are disconcerted. How do they know we are on board? They have us pass in front of everybody. We disembark onto the quay.

---

[1] Famous Parisian chapel among African pilgrims for apparitions of the Virgin Mary to St. Catherine Labouré in 1830.
[2] Ferry.

Two armed soldiers await us. What is going on? The unpleasant feeling of having done something wrong. The terminal gates open and reveal to us a reception line of braid-trimmed officers at attention. There must be some mistake....No, no mistake, it is really for us, a man in a black uniform, covered with stars and golden eagles, awaits us at the end of the row of policemen.

"Welcome to Egypt. Our government is very honored by your visit. Lieutenant-colonel Ayman Abd el-Kader here is at your service. Ask him what you will, your desires are orders."

??

"Do you want to begin walking right away? No problem! your escort is waiting for you! We know you do not cheat. There are fifteen kilometers to Aswan where a hotel room has been reserved for you: you should be there within three hours, if I am rightly informed..."

Still a bit stunned by the surprise, we attempt an all-or-nothing:

"Many thanks for your welcome. We are very honored, but we do not wish to go to Aswan at once, we would like to return to Abu Simbel to resume our walking there."

Our general, speechless, turns to the plain-clothes officer, they exchange a few words in Arabic and he turns back toward us.

"You will discuss the modalities of the project with the lieutenant-colonel. Bon voyage!"

Ayman motions to us to follow him.

"What about our passports?"

"They were stamped on board by the officer who came to get you, did you not notice?"

We are completely flummoxed. We leave the maritime station and two police cars, Ayman's pickup and a blue car full of policemen armed to the teeth are awaiting us along with two motorcycles. He turns to us: "Explain your project to me, I will have to make a few phone calls."

"You see, for us, arriving here on a ship was too easy, we want to deserve Aswan by getting there on foot, across the desert, from Abu

Simbel. We stopped walking just on the other side, in Argin, on the Sudanese side. But don't worry, we will follow the road and can be escorted by policemen, if volunteers are willing to walk with us."

He smiles.

"I doubt a single policeman in all Egypt will be willing to walk in that desert. But let me see what I can do…"

He stays glued to his mobile phone for a good fifteen minutes, pacing back and forth, argues, explains, persuades, smiles, hangs up and comes back over to us.

"I don't know who you are, but apparently the government is very interested in you, it is agreed that you can walk from Abu Simbel. This is the first time I have heard of such an exception. Okay, let's get going!"

He pauses.

"You don't want to go there on foot…?"

"No thanks! The return will be enough for us, I think."

And we head south, full speed ahead, between our escort of personal bodyguards and two motorcycle policemen with their sirens blaring. After the desert and solitude, Africa Trek is taking on a picaresque appearance.

If Man had been modest, we would still be in the trees. Abu Simbel or hyperbolic ego. The pride of Man made god. The gateway to an empire of the "ever more": ever richer, ever stronger, ever purer, ever more sacred. A colossal gateway to impress the barbarians. The sun rises and its first rays are for Pharaoh. A symbolic frontier that shouts to the world: "Here civilization begins." And as one colossus would not have been enough, here are four, twenty meters high. They are seated, but seem to be standing, so awesome are they. It is the same man, Rameses II, deified, but the faces express imperceptibly different emotions betraying progressive maturity. Only one head is missing. Decapitated by an earthquake. It's lying there at its feet. Four ages in the life of Pharaoh? On the left, he looks clumsy, almost babyish, under his crushing double crown, then he becomes more refined, more emaciated, hardens to become, in the colossus on the right, the uncontested master of the world, who made the earth shake from Nubia to Mesopotamia. Eternal, yet inscribed in time. Saved from the waters by UNESCO in 1968, as was Moses, his putative "half-brother," by Pharaoh's daughter. A mountain moved by the world's faith, love of the beautiful and respect for History. The whole was entirely cut up, dismantled and remounted into a reconstructed mountain. The temple proper, which burrows into the entrails of the cement mountain, is all to the glory of Pharaoh. Behind eight colossus-columns, which support the twelve-meter-high ceiling adorned with flying vultures; the victory at Qadesh faces clusters of enemies immolated to Amon; Rameses on his chariot impales an enemy or counts the severed hands and genitals. A little deeper in the mountain the space narrows, that is the room of offerings that precedes the sanctuary: a still smaller room, where Pharaoh, lifesize, is seated beside a triad of gods. Twice a year, on 21 October and 21 February,[3] the sun strikes Amun-Ra and Rameses at dawn, leaving Ptah, the god of Darkness, in the shadow. The 21st of October was just a few days ago, and this morning the sun still illuminates Pharaoh's muscular torso like a laser. The sixty meters of depth of the underground temple were dug in the proper axis, and what merely appeared megalomaniac becomes cosmic and initiatory.

But Abu Simbel is also a love story....Nefertari, Pharaoh's wife, is also entitled to her temple where she is deified as Hathor, goddess of Sweetness and Joy, of Arts and Heaven. The bas-reliefs here are superb and polychrome. Before one of them, a young woman is seated in meditation, with a little crystal pyramid set before her. We pass without troubling her but she exclaims: "Sonia? Alexandre? Unbelievable!"

She is a young Frenchwoman, Fabienne, who has been following

---

[3] These dates are symmetrical to the winter solstice, in December, and therefore at the same point on the ecliptic.

us in the media since the beginning of our trek. Incredible! How was she able to recognize us when we passed behind her? She has gifts. She frequently comes to Egypt to meditate before the frescoes and capture their "energy," in order to recharge her spiritual batteries....These Gauls are crazy! On our way out we are stupefied to discover the graffiti – small, discreet – of Ferdinand de Lesseps. But on Nefertari's pubis....Childishness or Gallic bawdiness?

At nine-thirty, an impressive crowd sweeps into the site that we had all to ourselves, with the exception of Fabienne, a Japanese photographer and a German watercolorist. It is the Aswan convoy. Eighty-one buses, two thousand six hundred Frenchmen....A tidal wave of fellow countrymen! We are in seventh heaven, all ears, we devour them with our eyes: three years since we have seen so many! There are the pushy ones who want to be first, camera in one hand and movie camera in the other; the complainers in white sunhats already bellyaching about the sun; the braggarts who compare the site to Petra so you'll know they've been there; the disappointed who find that "it looked bigger in the photo!"; the solemn ones exclaiming: "Now that, that's really something!"; the cynics: "Look at that, all these lemmings rushing in!"; the cultivated, their nose in their guidebooks; the asocial who go sulk on a bench. In the crowd, there is one, more interested in his fellow creatures than he is in the temple, who thinks we are Scandinavian: "Did you see the guy with the beard? Does he think he's Moses or what? And the girl with the skirt? They must be members of a sect.... Plenty of wackos come here." His companion punches him with her elbow: "No, keep quiet, they are French, I tell you, I'm sure it's the couple who are crossing Africa on foot..." We confirm this to them with an amiable glance. The man sneaks away, red with embarrassment.

Another lady, smiling, comes right up to us: "What are you doing here? Are you acting in a film?"

"No, we have come from Cape Town on foot."

Her smile falls flat, she hurries off, furious: "Sure! You take me for an idiot. It's not nice!"

The Oscar goes to an anxious guy who exclaims as he surveys the site: "It looks strong seen from here, it's endured so many centuries, but it's like the Buddhas of Bamiyan, it's at the mercy of a backward Taliban who has two balls, two neurons, and two rockets."

Those Gauls!

The next morning, a police car comes to get us at the governmental hotel where we were lodged. Our lieutenant-colonel had left to go back to Aswan the very night we arrived. We are ready. Lieutenant Magitt is going to escort us the whole way with three other policemen. No way to return to the fence at Argin, fifteen kilometers to the south. The zone is mined and highly militarized. There will therefore be a hiatus of fifteen kilometers in our trek. The first. But we can esteem ourselves fortunate. Let us leave megalomaniacal purism to the pharaohs.

We leave. Without our backpacks, we literally fly. They are carried by the car. We are willing to walk, not to suffer for free. There again, no stupid purism. We know how to be reasonable even if we don't look like it, hiking this way at foot speed in front of this automobile full of armed men, with a desert of three hundred kilometers to cross. From now on, we realize, there will be nothing but tar. An interminable ribbon of asphalt that is to take us from here to our destination: the Sea of Galilee, in over two thousand kilometers. From here to there, we will have to be followed by an automobile creeping along. It was that or nothing. So Africa Trek adapts. Like Man who hasn't ceased adapting in his slow evolution and long trek from Mrs. Ples[4] to Rameses.

In seven kilometers we have passed the airport and are already in the desert. We know in what sauce we will be eaten, for on the

---

[4] See vol. I, p. 142.

way here, with Ayman, we made ourselves a road plan, taking note of every piece of shade, refreshment stand, potential stop, with the help of the odometer. There are many fewer than in the Bayuda desert. The road is perfectly straight. On our left, a high-tension line with large pylons every three hundred thirty meters, so says my pedometer; fascinating....Not a tree, not a blade of grass. A desert as dead as the Batn-el-Hajar, except that it's flat and sandy, of undefinable color. The ugliest desert on earth. But we progress cheerily. The events of these last few days have trans-figured our trip and every novelty is entertaining. Our police-men have decided that it was too bothersome to follow us at our pace; so they pass us and stop where they can still see us, about a kilometer ahead. We take eleven to fifteen minutes to catch up with them. The automobile is a navy blue pick-up with a four-passenger cabin and a cargo bed behind covered with a metal roof and equipped with little lateral benches. Our backpacks are in the back with a cargo of bottles of mineral water. Often, a policeman comes and sits there to get some fresh air since it is miserably hot in the cockpit. When we reach them, three men are sleeping while the fourth keeps an eye on us. We go about a kilometer past them, they start up again, roar past us again with the siren on and stop again a kilometer ahead. That means we can drink twice an hour, and that between two furious sprints they can sleep for a half-hour. And in principle we will be playing this little overtake me game for a week...

Another difficulty is that our policemen don't speak a word of English. Not one. Not even *yes*, not even *no*. Not easy in these circumstances to understand each other. For Arabic has changed. It is no longer the same. We thought we were operational and here are unintelligible; there again we have to adapt. "*Izmak meno?*" becomes "*Ismak eh?*"; "*Min feyn?*" becomes "*Min when?*"; "*Djebel*" becomes "*Gabal*"[5] and so forth.

---

[5] What's your name? Where are you from? Mountain.

About eleven, we are passed by the bus convoy returning from Abu Simbel. The lead cars driven by policemen pass us in a scream of horns; the buses follow nose to tail, full speed ahead; we count ninety-three of them, twelve more than yesterday. It takes your breath away. An hour later, we come across a group of camels being loaded onto trucks with the help of much flogging. One of them falls off the ramp and gets back up a little dizzy. Sonia is horrified.

"Did you see how they treat them? Maybe they are ours?"

We go to see. Our cops turn up. For an instant the busy camel drivers are panicked by what they think a police raid. We reassure them.

"We are friends of the Sudanese sheikh Hussein Labd Mohammed Ahmed from El-Genina, are these his camels? Where are you taking them?"

"*Aïwa!* Yes, they are his. May God kill me if I lie! First to Daraw, near Kom Ombo, where there is a big market, then to Cairo."

They will be there before we will. Transformed....The trucks leave, taking with them tightly packed bouquets of necks and heads. Sonia, with a knot in her throat, waves to them; a charming gesture; the witnesses laugh it up.

"Poor Calimero![6] I am sure she alone could tell it was a voyage with no return: that's why she was objecting!"

The camel drivers have makeshift barracks. We go to pass the hot hours there, following a quick identity check. Already to remember, already to relate, and in Arabic besides; the guys are fascinated. They do not know the Sudan; everything comes out, from the doukhan to the zar, from the zikr to the delight of the palm plantations of Shimaliya....As soon as we left it, we realized

---

[6] This is the name Sonia had given to her mount that bleated from despair at every departure. Calimero is a hapless anthropomorphized cartoon chicken; the only black one in a family of yellow chickens. He wears half of his egg shell still on his head and is very unlucky.

how much we had loved the Sudan. We leave singing at the top of our lungs the Souchon hit song: "Soudan, mon Soudan soudain se soulève, c'est déjà ça...c'est déjà ça..."

Sahrab, Friday 31 October 2003, day 1038, 48 km, 11,660th km

One hundred twenty buses this morning. A convoy worthy of Operation Desert Storm! We have seen them pass in both directions, an hour earlier in the morning, an hour later in early afternoon, which proves we are making progress. Still, it's hard. Very hard. The most difficult and most absurd part in our three years. The most costly and most gratuitous. We wanted it. We got it. Our policemen must suffer all the more that Ramadan just began and we know that the first days are the hardest. Nevertheless, when we pass them, we see Magitt and Ayman eating a sandwich they went thirty kilometers from here in the car to get. This surprises me.

"But we are not Muslim! We are Christians, orthodox Copts."

We had noticed nothing. The two others, Aman and Mohammed, are sleeping in the back, comatose, mouth open in the midst of their scattered weapons. Our policemen are convinced we won't make it, do not understand our obstinacy in wanting to walk in this mortally boring emptiness. From time to time, they stop even with us, and Magitt, with a little collusive nod of the head, with his finger over his lips, indicates he will say nothing if we get in. A red-handed attempt to corrupt two hikers! We send him packing with a laugh, and it becomes a game between us...

Along the roadside, we glean pieces of wood for the fire. It's incredible how much wood you can find beside the road: shattered produce cases, stakes from work sites, fine blazes ahead. When the car passes us, we toss this harvest into the back. Magitt is disgusted by our noodle soup. He wonders how we manage to knock down so many kilometers with nothing in our stomachs but that bouillon. He is ill for us. Admiring and comic, he has christened us Mr. and Mrs. *Chorba*, Mr. and Mrs. Soup, and amuses himself singing our new name in the loudspeaker on the car. The desert must still echo with it. *"Chorba!* Toot-toot!" We also pass numerous piles of rotten fish, dried out, lost. Tons. Most of them are small tilapias. Magitt explains to us that they are poached in Lake Nasser by clandestine fishermen who move around at night, who get rid of them when they are afraid of a police action. They are unreal, these fish scattered in the desert, that died for nothing. Future fossils.

Suddenly, at kilometer 178, in the middle of nowhere, the truck-stop restaurant El-Sahrab, "the Mirage," appears. We are greeted there by Aatif and Imad Baulus, two enthusiastic Copts who immediately hand us some cold Cokes: "For three days everyone has been talking about you. I lost my bet, I thought it was a joke, and here you are! *Ya salam! Fadhal!"*[7]

Imad has been to Germany seven times and has visited Paris twice. A former masseur on big cruise ships on the Nile, he administers to each of us a "pommeling" with camphor oil, followed by a delicious plate of chicken and fries that we share with Magitt and Ayman. I exclaim: "Imad! This place isn't called El-Sahrab! But El-Djenna! Paradise!"

Meanwhile, our poor Aman and Mohammed throw downcast glances our way while drooling over the sex bombs in the video-clips broadcast by the Lebanese network Nagham. Hard work!

"Where are you going to sleep tonight? There is nothing from here to Aswan!"

"Anywhere at all in the desert!"

"No way. You will come back here to sleep, and tomorrow you will start again from the spot where you left off. You have the right to do that? I am sure that Lieutenant Magitt would rather sleep here than in the car, no?"

---

[7] "I can't believe my eyes! Welcome."

In open desert, Sunday 2 November 2003, day 1040, 49 km, 11,751st km

Team change. Yesterday we got the best of the automobile. Over-heating of motor and team. Too slow a regimen for the mechanism, too harsh a regimen for the stomachs. They have gone back to Aswan and been replaced by an entirely Muslim team, unfortunately already very weary when they got here. Mahmoud, the new lieutenant assigned to our escort, wanted to take us on board right away. He knew nothing of our trip, our authorizations, and refused to understand my Arabic. We almost came to blows. No question of having walked a hundred ninety kilometers for nothing. We learned at our expense that nothing was ever over, in this country, everything had to be worked out one day at a time. A phone call to Lieutenant-Colonel Abd el-Kader put things in order and Mahmoud on standby. It is true that we have no paper, no proof of our governmental support, no tangible authorization. We are dependent on the chain of information and command. If it is for an instant broken, the situation gets sticky. Besides handling ourselves, we learn to bear the humors of four other persons and an automobile. Africa Trek becomes the handling of human resources with multipolar managements and mechanical constraints: a real pain.

The bus convoy stops and we see passengers hop out to meet us. They are German or French, and know our whole story: "Since Abu Simbel, our tour operator has been talking about you on the microphone. We know all about you. What you are doing is marvelous! Here, this is for you."

They fill our hands with victuals, prepared meals and fruits, after the mandatory photo. Our everyday meal of noodle soup is getting distinctly better, to Mahmoud's rage. This desert is so boring that we have become a curiosity for the tour operators. It's too much! God knows through what grapevine they learned of our existence. But the state of grace does not last, Mahmoud is cooking up trouble for us. We have chanced across a bad number. For the lunch pause, he wants to take us to Aswan to sleep and come back tomorrow, citing the fact that we accepted to be driven to the restaurant in Magitt's car. We try to explain to him that we never go "forward" by car. He is furious. Above all he wants to break his fast at a good banquet in town and not with a bad sandwich downed on the roadside. We understand him. But that's the way it is. It's not our fault.

It's one already and we are bushed. No hint of shade anywhere. Mahmoud watches for us to flinch and is constantly coming back in the hope we will cave. Sonia takes pains to explain to him that in about three kilometers there is a concrete bus shelter under which we can take shelter from the sun. Not knowing where she got such information, he first treats her as a spy then a liar and moves on to psychological harassment. We hold out. He cannot understand that we scouted the road on our way down. I finally have to toss him, like a bone, that if in three kilometers we do not find the bus shelter, we would agree to return with him to Aswan. Three interminable kilometers, on the verge of sunstroke, scrutinizing the horizon for a bus shelter. After thirty-six minutes, an irreducible time for covering that distance, still nothing. Sonia is desperate, the other one gloats: *"Yalla! Arkab el arabiya!"*[8] I prepare to comply when a black square catches my eye in the distance: the shadow of our bus shelter. We forge on. Mahmoud, with an oath, gives his car a swift kick, the others laugh it up.

It is only once we are in the shade, exposed to the wind, that this question comes to mind: what is this bus shelter doing here in the desert? There is no crossroads, no trail here, nothing. It is here for us, on appointment. After a rich picnic enhanced by the marvels reserved to tourists, we find the sleep of the just in the company of the bawling Mahmoud and the others. We wait for the

---

[8] "Come on, get in!"

time we can start again, they wait for the time to break their fast. Life's always about waiting.

Late in the afternoon, we come upon twelve dead storks. White, immaculate, on the sand. What storm could have led them out here? They lost the way to South Africa. Sonia is moved: "Poor chicks from Alsace or the Carpathians! These birds will never know the happiness of Shimaliya oases, the splendors of the Rift, the riches of the Ngorongoro, they will never fly over Lake Malawi, Great Zimbabwe, will never surf on the Lesotho escarpments.... Alex! Some day, we'll have to make the trip in the opposite direction, but flying this time, like migratory chicks."

When we want to film these poor storks, Mahmoud rushes at us. "You are not allowed to film! This is a military zone. What do you want to do with these dead birds? Say we killed them? For propaganda? I knew you were spies. I'm going to report it to my superiors!"

A dangerous fool. Incapable of understanding the poetry of this still life. So dead.

This evening, he goes to dine in Aswan and leaves us with Nabil, a nice officer who apologizes in his own name for his irascibility. Around a little fire in the dunes, he comes and shares with us the remains of our prepared meals. When I want to film him to immortalize the scene, the autofocus of our movie camera can't manage to focus because of the dim light.

"Well, Nabil will remain anonymous, thanks to the autofocus!"

He soon goes to sleep curled up, in front of our tent, rolled up in a blanket, on his Kalashnikov.

Two days later, after hundreds of pylons and boredom, in the indentation of a cliff, we are stunned by a plunging view on the Nile. Finally something green after so much yellow! It's like an open sore in the arid bark of the Earth. A concentration of teeming life. We have succeeded in crossing the Sahara: one thousand eight hundred kilometers of heat, thirst and pain, doubts and anguish vanish at this view.

34 The Love of Philae

EGYPT

O ur first steps on the Aswan "Corniche" are an apotheosis: our transition-less reunion with opulence, comfort and the sweet and mild good life. It's perhaps not what you feel when you fly in from Paris. You may then have an Oriental thrill. For us, it is the opposite, we have a European thrill. Pretty girls in skimpy dresses go from their cruising ships to horse-drawn carriages. Men in bathing suits walk about at sidewalk level, around their pool, on the deck of these enormous vessels parked head to tail the whole length of the Promenade. A compression of worlds. We are both shocked and fascinated. Shocked because it has been so long since we have seen this, fascinated because it has been so long since we have seen this....Right away, our first priority, we go down two cold beers on the pontoon of a restaurant floating on the Nile. It's amazing how it has changed color! The water is translucent and black. It has lost all its silt, all its richness. The blood of the Nile is being slowly deposited at the bottom of Lake Nasser....Before our eyes, in the sensual foam of our golden tankards, the sails of silent feluccas dance in a ballet lit by the late afternoon gold. Aatif and

Imad Baulus, of the Sahrab restaurant, have notified their elder brother Aziz of our arrival. He comes to join us with his daughter Heba. He has but one leg. She is learning French at the university. They invite us to their house for dinner near the "charia el suq." As we leave the restaurant, we find our lieutenant-colonel Ayman Abd el-Kader. He was waiting for us to finish our glasses to see what we are up to.

"The governor wants to meet you, he wants you to know that you are his guests. Tomorrow, *insha'Allah*, we will make a program of visits. There is always a room for your use at the Nuba Nile Hotel..."

"Thank you, but we are invited to sleep at Aatif Baulus's whose elder brother here, Aziz, has invited us to dinner."

After a rapid checking of identities and an exchange of telephone numbers, Ayman says: "When you have finished dinner, call me, I will come get you and take you to Aatif's. Be aware that I am here for you and that you must inform me of all your plans and movements, this for your safety."

This is said with kindness and firmness. No question of taking off. We are the governor's guests and as such we enter a protocol grid that gives us at once a passkey and a leash. We discover another manner of experiencing our freedom.

Aziz Baulus is a tailor. He keeps a tiny shop with his wife Asma. Everywhere on the walls, in store windows, on the clock, an accumulation of pious images transforms this workplace into a genuine chapel. The Virgin appears calm and serene while her son is shedding rivers of blood on dolorous photo compositions full of thorns, nails and contortions. Asma is one-eyed, hunched up by a life of relentless labor; Chenouda, their employee, is dumb. Dumb but noisy. He expresses himself with many gestures and moans, opening wide his big cheerful eyes. This tiny room might resemble a *Cour des Miracles*,[1] but this family tried by fate radiates such joy

---

[1] A term which in pre-Revolutionary France referred to zones in large cities frequented by beggars with various infirmities.

that we are quite shaken by it. Heba explains the situation and the laughter that is unleashed around us.

"My father jumped onto a mine during the Six Day War. He miraculously survived thanks to a nurse whom he later married, my mother. Since then he has nursed a dream, which is to go on his crutches on a pilgrimage to the Holy Sepulchre in Jerusalem, to thank the Lord for keeping him alive. Your coming here encourages him and reinforces this idea. So we all tease him a bit!"

I immediately get psyched up about it. We conspire together. We estimate the distance, the number of kilometers he could do each day with his crutches; I reassure him about the hospitality granted to hikers.

"Your problem would still be to pass the Israeli border, but we know an ambassador well who could surely find a passage for you. Be sure that nothing stops a determined hiker. It ought to be feasible in six to eight months with an average of ten to fifteen kilometers a day. When you are ready to go, tell Heba to write to us and we will come walk for a stretch of it with you.

"I shall leave as soon as Heba has finished her studies and is married..."

The father tenderly takes his daughter, balancing on one leg, and kisses her forehead with infinite affection. In one corner of the room is a scale for weighing the rolls of fabric. I climb on it: seventy kilos! Ten less than when I left South Africa. The same weight as when I arrived in Addis. Six less than my normal weight. A variable geometry. The Sahara has tested us. During this time, Asma sews up the hem of Sonia's skirt on her machine. Nuns in Khartoum had added reinforcement at the buttock level – cut from what? Three guesses: from their veils. That zone had become transparent from wear: not too much, in sharia country....Don't forget that Sonia has only one skirt, the same one she has been wearing since the border between Zimbabwe and Mozambique; worn every day for over two years. This time, the zipper also has to be changed. When she learns the origin of these patches, Asma weeps with a contagious laughter that sets fire to an already overheated atmosphere....What mirth, among these folk, these statuettes and rococo chromos! A blessed family. But the space is too small for us to sleep here.

After a dinner of falafel eaten amidst pieces of leftover fabric and paper patterns, we call Ayman, who immediately appears. He must not have been far away. He comes into the shop; the ambiance instantly tanks. He emanates a natural authority that attracts every gaze and absorbs all the energy. He is shortish, with an arched nose and thick lips, a low, bare forehead over piercing eyes that constantly oscillate between carnivorous cruelty and restrained impishness; like a pulsation that sustains his lively gaze. The rest of his face is relatively inexpressive; he speaks in a low voice without moving his lips or raising his eyebrows, in short, clipped sentences that expect precise responses. When he has not rightly understood, or to give himself the time to reflect, he inclines his ear toward his interlocutor, giving his head a little threatening shake. He is a chief. He is always wearing on his belt the prominent pistol that makes him walk with his arms out to his sides. In fact, he seems straight out of a detective novel.

Ever escorted by four armed policemen, we reach Aatif's apartment, situated on the outskirts of the city, in a leprous Soviet apartment building inherited from the great Nasser era. His wife Fifi welcomes us in her houserobe. She was expecting us. The lodging is tidy. On the wall in our room stretches a fabulously kitsch Christ printed in Italy, blond with disproportionately large blue eyes, dripping with love, whom I, for Oriental eyes, have the misfortune (or fortune...) of resembling somewhat....Everyone has a hearty laugh about that.

At five-thirty two mornings later, the Isle of Philae is opened to us so we can film the sunrise before the arrival of the first visitors. Ayman has naturally come along with us. We get into a motorboat that takes us to the sanctuary situated above an old British dam from 1902 and below the great Nasser Dam, in the middle of a branch of the Nile that is framed by a jumble of red granite boulders. In the pale colors of dawn, the island appears an ark that has survived a flood, floating on the smooth surface of the water to save the last vestiges of pharaonic civilization. It is in fact here that it retrenched in the first five centuries of the present era during which it was reclaimed by the Greco-Romans before being definitively absorbed by rising Christianity.

Philae appears intact. All the temples, however, have been entirely dismantled, stone by stone, and reconstructed on the Isle of Agilka, near the original site, and reshaped by bulldozer so Isis would not be disoriented. We land. Wherever you look you detect no trace of displacement. This is archeological prestidigitation! A technical miracle to the credit of the international consensus brought about by UNESCO, right in the middle of the cold war.... We are greeted by a vast flagstone plaza lined by a long colonnade. The superb capitals capture our attention while we walk in silence, dumbfounded, toward the great pylon[2] which is animated by Pharaoh massacring enemies with an ax, and himself massacred with an ax by iconoclast avengers.

Sonia guides me with her commentaries drawn from various books: "Philae is the second Greek word proposed for the idea of love after *erôs*, physical love, and before *agapê*, spiritual and intellectual love. *Philia* designates the love of others."

Philae or the slow sedimentation of man's beliefs, deposited by the waves of time on an island saved from the waters.

We enter the first temple, the Mammisi temple, devoted to Isis the Ancient, mother of Horus, who dispenses eternal milk and the waters of the Nile – a rock close by was reputed to be the source of the Upper Nile. Isis, funerary goddess and thus the magician of rebirth, was its guardian. The prosperity of the entire Nile valley was dependent on the fervor expressed here, on this

---

[2] Monumental gate of a temple, open between two massive trapezoids decorated with scenes of massacres, offered by Pharaoh to the god to which the temple is devoted.

handful of square meters, and on the precision of the rituals performed....Three rooms introduce you into the holy of holies which has turned strangely, uniformly green by mold. A granite pedestal rises in the middle of the small, desperately empty room. It has lost its goddess: a statuette of pure gold that was brought outside every year in a procession to bring back the flood of the Nile. But Sonia reassures me.

"Despite appearances, Isis is still here, on this bas-relief on the right: look! She is nursing a little Horus, protector of the two Egypts. She is the *alma mater*, the 'mother of mothers,' the 'sovereign of the House of birth.' And for two thousand years, she has been officiating. Guess over what? Still today, women come here secretly to obtain fertility; they make three turns around the altar and caress the goddess's face."

By dint of much caressing, the face is now nothing but a hole, witness to the superstition that has come down through the centuries. For my amusement, Sonia performs the ritual....I make fun of her.

"I did not know that babies were made by putting a hand in a hole..."

Horus, gripping a pretty, round breast, seems to frown at this sacrilegious remark...[3]

We step back out into the light. In the Second Temple, the first room, the *pronaos*, has been converted into a chapel. The bas-reliefs on the walls have been methodically and uniformly erased up to a height of two meters by a thin and even poking. On the columns, the Egyptians converted to Christianity have engraved Byzantine crosses; on the right-hand wall a niche has been dug out before the altar to receive the tabernacle. Already this late temple, built by Greek pharaohs, the Ptolemies, was more or less conflating the gods of Olympus and those of Egypt, Roman emperors and pharaohs. Thus you find bas-reliefs about Osiris' resurrection,

---

[3] You can continue the Philae visit on our Internet site.

offerings dedicated to Tiberius or Domitian, a kiosk dedicated to Trajan, a temple built to the glory of Augustus, a gate in the form of an arch of triumph to celebrate Marcus Aurelius and Hadrian, built by Diocletian, whose cartouche in hieroglyphics is all over the place. It was nothing new that the zealots of the religion of Love should also appropriate Philae.

Among these time signatures, we find with the delight of collectors the graffiti of Holroyd, an obscure British traveler of 1836 whom we have been following since Naga, Meroe, Soleb and Abu Simbel, his name meticulously engraved in a frame, following the same calligraphy. A fanatic of the trace, obsessed with immortality, one of the first "tourists" of the Nile. The French are no exceptions to the rule but are not content with graffiti, they write a whole story beside pharaonic steles: some, like Balzac, Coquebert or Coraboeuf, who in year 7 of the Republic[4] measure the island's longitude at 30° 16' 22" relative to the Paris meridian and make it known in stone, or others, like Generals Desaix, Daoust and Belliard, who, on 13 Ventôse in the year 13,[5] boast of having hunted the defeated Mamelukes beyond the falls....But to have the last word, the British consul Henry Salt has the longitude of the temple engraved relative to the Greenwich meridian...

Early in the afternoon we are received by the governor of the region, General Samir Youssif. We hope in the course of the interview to learn more about what has earned us this favorable treatment by the authorities. Before we go in, Ahmed Kamal, a young representative of the Ministry of Tourism, whispers to us by way of preamble: "The governor is a military hero of the attack of 5 October 1973 when the Egyptian army was for twelve days able to break through the Israeli lines on the Suez Canal at Ismaïlia. This

---

[4] In 1799, in the Revolutionary calendar.
[5] 4 March 1805: Napoleon maintained the Revolutionary calendar until the end of 1805.

achievement washed away the affront of the Six Days' War and led to Tsahal's retreat from the Sinai…"

We are then given to understand that to meet a governor is almost the same thing as meeting President Moubarak in person, so great are the powers vested in him. We enter his office very intimidated, at the head of a zealous procession of translators, photographers, officials and obsequious underlings who slink along the walls trembling like leaves. The man comes up to us with a broad smile, his hand extended, and flatters us on our modest Arabic. He immediately puts us at ease. He has a square jaw, a virile voice and straight speech. A lordly head. Yet he is wearing nothing but a polo shirt over blue pants. The vast office is decorated with an incalculable number of medals, diplomas and photos with the president.

"I congratulate you on walking for peace to Palestine. It is a noble cause…"

We scarcely show our surprise. And rebound with a banality.

"The entire world needs peace. And as walkers, we are often received by peoples at war against each other; we see close up that they all possess goodwill, they share the same sufferings, the same hopes: Sometimes all that is missing is dialogue…"

Whew! We get through that all right. The rest just flows naturally, with its anecdotes and its kilometers, with his compliments and the assurance we may cross Egyptian territory, even Middle Egypt, under the protection of a police escort. We will never know anything more about the reasons that lie behind this exceptional treatment. The end of our trek "in the footsteps of Man" and the crossing of Egypt on foot are certainly worth a political takeover, for a good cause…

In late afternoon, the governor has invited us to tea on the terrace of the Old Cataract, the most city's prestigious hotel, camped on a granite protrusion over Elephantine Island. In a Victorian atmosphere, comfortably seated in armchairs in upholstered rattan, a front-row seat for the golden spectacle of the sun setting behind the Aga Khan's Mausoleum on the other bank, we sip with beatitude our Earl Grey in cups bearing the cipher of Howard Carter, enjoying fine pastries while the languid feluccas gravitate and silently cross paths around the Elephantine ruins. Behind us, three musicians sing a Nubian lament accompanied by *oud* and flute. At our right an old British lady in evening dress and pearl necklace, shaded by a broad flowered hat, fans herself with her menu and watches out of one eye the shadow of the palm trees projected on the screen of the sails, and reads with the other an Agatha Christie. Too real to be true...

The next day, we meet up with Yasser Mohammed, an Egyptian friend encountered for the first time in Zanzibar where we were resting after our Tanzanian trials, and a second time in Khartoum, where he had Kenyan artisanal objects convoyed to souks in touristic cities of the Red Sea. To our great surprise, he arrives accompanied by a woman veiled in black from head to toe, including her face and hands. Why are we surprised? Because in Zanzibar he was very relaxed around other men's wives, whether in swimsuits or skimpy outfits....Moreover, we had thought he had broken with his Egyptian wife, knowing that he had taken a second wife in Kenya. I awkwardly congratulate him on his reconciliation.

"Ah no, it's not that, *habibi*, this is my third wife, Tafla, she is from Dar es Salaam, I met her since we were together in Khartoum, I married her, and *al hamdoullilah*, she is two months pregnant..."

I step forward to greet her but he steps in: "*Malesh!* My wife does not greet men, but Sonia may shake her hand..."

So this is how Yasser, still sweating great drops and struggling with asthma, already swamped with his business deals, torn between three countries, tyrannized by his Egyptian in-laws with which three of his children live, ignored by his Kenyan in-laws with whom he has a son and a daughter, resolved his conjugal problems: by taking a third wife in a third country. We are the same age and he gives me vertigo.

"*Ya salam*, Yasser! What's your secret? I already have so much trouble with one wife who has no children..."

Sonia takes the opportunity to cuff me in front of everyone: a little act we are fond of particularly when we are surrounded with men, and which invariably provokes gales of laughter.

"You see how things work in Europe? Three wives? I dare not even think about it!"

In the evening, the four of us go to dine on a magnificent two-masted felucca, a *sandal*, that belongs to Guy-Hervé Perron, a friend of Henriette Palavioux, who came to walk with us in Ethiopia. The farther we walk, the smaller the world becomes....Africa Trek has become a catalyst for serendipitous coincidences that are no longer coincidences, a machine for meeting people, a machine to help our fate. Stretched out on benches embellished with Moroccan killims, we receive a call from the Dijon Adventure Screen Festival where a trailer of our coming films has just been presented by Florence Tran, our co-director. On the other end of the line, we hear, our heart leaping, the crowd applauding in the theatre, while Patrick Edel, president of the Guilde du Raid,[6] who has been waiting for us for three years, gives us an appointment for next year, in flesh and bone!

In any case it is time for us to hit the road again.

Kom Ombo, Tuesday 11 November 2003, day 1049, 45 km, 11,875th km

We leave Aswan at dawn from the Corniche where we arrived, escorted by Ayman and our bodyguards, and accompanied over six kilometers by Aziz, with his crutches, a foretaste of his own long trek. The resumption is harsh. If we stop for more than a week, it feels like starting from scratch again. At the city limits, Lieutenant-

---

[6] The Guilde Européenne du Raid is an NGO founded in 1967, and whose mission is to help young people to undertake adventures or humanitarian trips, and by providing them with grants and advice. Every year it gathers people for an international adventure film festival.

colonel Ayman puts us in the hands of Magitt and leaves us with an "I love you," unexpected from the lips of a superior officer.

The road along the Nile is crazy. The police car creeping along behind us is a fearsome obstacle to vehicles passing in both directions. Squeals of brakes, horns, avoidance swerves, we tremble for them. We would never forgive ourselves for being the cause of an accident. Our friend Magitt just laughs it off. We are still his "Mr. and Mrs. *Chorba*, a little *majnoun!*"[7] We are happy to be back with him, since he is full of goodwill and the unexpected amuses him. After a hellish day under the sign of roaring motors and exhaust gas plumes, we come to the outskirts of Kom Ombo in time for *iftar*[8], about five fifteen. We want to find a restaurant quickly for our two Muslim policemen, but they are all closed. We are hemming and hawing when we pass a banquet being given by the owner of what appears to be a garage. They are all turbaned and bearded. A loudspeaker near us screams the prayer for fast-breaking. They turn around, stupefied to see two tourists walking thus on this pestilential roadside, in an industrial zone, and at dusk. Someone hails us: "*Fadhal!*"

They have not seen the car following us. We cross the road to go see our astonished hosts. Our policemen suddenly go into action. The armed men jump out and spread out, slamming the doors; a moment of indecision during which we can sense hidden tensions between the uniforms and the turbans. But after brief introductions, Hadj Delil, our host, invites us with a broad sweep of the arm to sit down at the table. There are still many empty seats, being held for friends or the neighborhood poor. The rich and notables thus do their *zakat*[9] during Ramadan. And Hadj Delil, who tells us he has been to Mecca eighteen times, is surrounded by an Areopagus of faithful cut from the same pattern. He is rich, gen-

---

[7] Loony.
[8] Breaking of the fast.
[9] One of the five pillars of Islam: "legal alms" that allow you to purify yourself of reputedly impure material goods.

erous and loves to make it known. The table is adorned with all the delicacies Egypt has to offer: *hamam*, famous stuffed pigeons; *warag henap*, vine leaves; varied *kebabs*; *baba khanouj*, a puree of eggplant and garlic; *hummus* which we don't need to explain; and *kebda,* fried fowl liver cubes. The muezzin on the loudspeaker has finished, but Hadj Delil still delays slightly the moment to fall upon these marvels, as if the better to enjoy them, while discoursing with us on subjects far removed from the table. We soon understand that he belongs to the Muslim Brotherhood movement and has had clashes with the political police.

"You remember the stolen elections of 1991 in Algeria, when the people had massively voted for an Islamic regime? Well, that is what would happen in Egypt...if they let us vote. We do not believe in democracy, it is a false notion imported from the West, meant to deceive the people. We have only one constitution, which is the Qu'ran."

Magitt is tense. He is not familiar with the events of 1991 but understands that the conversation is spinning out of control. He tries to lower the pressure by letting it be known that we are walking "for peace in Palestine."

"Ah, yes, peace....That's the great passion of you Christians. But what peace? There will be no peace until the Jews have left Palestine and returned to Europe where you sent them away to wash your hands of the Shoah[10]."

OK. We're up against a tough nut. And uninhibited. An angel unseen passes, dressed in black, with a big scythe on his shoulder. Hadj Delil breaks the fast by drinking a big glass of guava juice. That's the signal for everybody. When I stretch out my hand to grab a kebab, he stops me with a raised finger and a black eye.

"No! You must start with the guava juice."

"*Aïwa. Malesh!*"

I comply. Despite the breaking of the fast and the beginning of

---

[10] Holocaust.

the meal, the tension doesn't drift away. On the contrary. According to custom, everyone eats in silence, unhurriedly and with no manifestation of relief; they all seem to vie for who can eat the slowest and most soberly, to show the others how he scorns hunger. Satiety and joy are supposed to be inside. Between two roaring trucks, only the sound of mastication and swallowing can be heard. *La chair est triste, hélas...*[11] Magitt is concerned about where we are going to sleep tonight, I tell him I don't know.

"*Allah Karim!*"[12]

The other guests laugh. Hadj smiles.

"How much do you know about Allah?"

"That He is most merciful..."

Magitt comes to my rescue: "And he knows *Ayat al Kursi!*"

At a sign from the hadj, I perform rapidly, reciting the long surate like a blaze of machine-gun fire. Finally he starts to smile. When I have finished, he concludes: "Now I know how you managed to cross Africa safe and sound: the Traveler's Surate protected you! But *yazoul al zalzala!*"

On this final word, which I have not understood, he stands and goes to pray in his garage, followed by his faithful. We don't even have the time to thank him. This first *iftar* leaves a rather bitter taste in our mouths. We resume our walk. Magitt theatrically accompanies us for a few hundred meters with his 9 mm Heckler *und* Koch short-barreled automatic pistol. I question him: "What did '*yazoul al zalzala*' mean?"

"It means: 'Beware of the last judgment...'"

In the heart of the city, a little farther on, a man comes straight up to us. This is always a moment of tension for the policemen whose job it is to protect us – they rush in with siren and motor

---

[11] "The flesh alas is sad," first line of *Brise marine*, a poem by Stéphane Mallarmé; *chair* ('flesh') here refers simultaneously to the flesh being consumed.

[12] God will provide!

roaring, all the more promptly since night has fallen and the out-door lighting is dim.

"I saw an article about your trip in the newspaper, I read that you sleep at people's houses, so allow me to invite you to mine."

We follow our man. He is feverish and excited. He leads us through a maze of narrow streets to a sort of barn with disjointed planks plugged with plastics. We are disillusioned.

Sonia laughs: "Now that's what's called a Kiss Cool[13] effect!"

A large poster of the Virgin tries to cheer up the more than modest interior, lined with benches that diffuse a strong smell of rat urine. Magitt looks somber. Yonan Adli is busily patting the cushions, raising clouds of dust, showing us unnamed latrines as if they were Cleopatra's baths. Behind our hosts's back, our lieuten-ant makes us little back-and-forth signs with his finger so we will go look for a more comfortable place. But we have a simple moral principle that is to never refuse the first hospitality.

Sonia reassures him: "We have slept in more Spartan places! Here, the benches have mattresses!"

We are so very weary that we fall into the sleep of the just, after drinking some warm Fantas which we cannot refuse offered by the poor Yonan, who must not often buy such things. There is one man who doesn't have to fear the "zalzala of the Valhalla"!

After a rapid visit to the Kom Ombo temple, devoted to the croco-dile Sobek, which raises its romantic ruins above the Nile, curved at its feet like an obeisance, we call our friend Guy-Hervé Perron, who ought to be in the area with his feluccas: "Greeting to the Poussins! Are you in Kom Ombo? We are just fifteen kilometers downstream, at the Silsila djebel. You have only to cross the Nile at the next ferry and find us…"

Already tired of the hellish traffic on the right bank, we see in

---

[13] A French brand of mentholated chewing gum whose advertisements are based on funny disillusions.

this the opportunity to go to the left bank, much less frequented. A quick call to Ayman Abd el-Kader frees Magitt from this responsibility: he agrees. Three hours later, after wandering through endless sugar cane plantations, we find the ferry and, further down, Guy-Hervé's *sandal*[14] and three *feluccas*, docked on the bank, at a palm plantation. The sailing boats are chartered by Terre d'Aventures[15]; they offer to visitors a true Egyptian *frisson*, outside of convoys and factory ships, going with the wind and the current, from site to site, following the passage of History. The French group warmly welcomes us. After a quick lunch aboard a small, early-twentieth-century steamboat arranged as a dining room, we take off across the palm plantation to find the djebel Silsila.

"You will see," says Guy-Hervé, "the site is fascinating, these are the ancient sandstone quarries for the whole Theban zone. On the contrary, in the north of Egypt, everything is built out of limestone from the Toura quarry."

At this point, the Nile is tightened into a rocky lock. The mountain has been dismantled by slices. From many nooks, speos[16] penetrate the cliffs on all sides.

"Silsila means 'chain' in Arabic. A great chain was extended across the Nile to prevent Nubian ships from going downriver toward Luxor."

We enter a maze of cavities, stairways, border steles or naos[17] covered with graffiti in which are seated divinities with eroded faces. Of the sepultures nothing remains. Everything has long since been stolen. Even the stone is soluble in time. Through the openings, you see the Nile flowing eternally. And constantly these very French names graffitied on the walls.

"Napoleon's old guard remained here for a very long time.

---

[14] A large felucca with a flat bottom and two sails, formerly used as a barge with a sail.

[15] A French travel agency specializing in walking tours.

[16] Rock hewn temple or memorial.

[17] Hidden cavity or Holy of Holies where the sacred statue of a divinity was stored.

That is why Champollion was able to study the site in depth. They camped in the tombs and the speos. Look at the vertical notches there! They were sharpening their bayonets on the sandstone…"

We resume our routine in front of our car; a routine made of interminable kilometers in sugar cane plantations, passing through very poor villages lined with fetid canals and dominated by impressive schools in red brick, all built on the same model, true buildings floating over the surrounding misery, the only tangible sign of the presence of the government and proof of a very clear intention of concentrating efforts on education. That might appear normal, but it is the first time we see it in three years. A government that governs. In the evening, in Edfou, we again meet up with our French group and visit the temple with them.[18]

The next day, between a canal and a sugar cane field, we celebrate our 12,000th kilometer. What do we have at our disposal for our little ritual? Policemen. What can we do? Sonia has a bright idea.

"We're going to try to get them so say something in French."

"You're playing high stakes!"

Indeed. After fifteen minutes of wild laughter and repetitions, we give up on getting anything intelligible out of the policemen. Nevertheless Sonia persists. The best pupil is Magitt. She plays the speech therapist, chides the policeman, even goes so far as to pull his ear when he misbehaves. Finally, like a lion trainer, she manages to make him pose armed with his henchmen and make him say: "Ici, c'est le douze millième kilomètre d'Alex et Sonia !" (This is Alex and Sonia's twelve thousandth kilometer!)

"YEEEES!"

We fall into their arms, taking care not to get the barrels of their submachine gun in the eye. They really have lent themselves in good faith to all our whims. Farewell dear Magitt! For he is

---

[18] If you would like to make this visit with us, you will find it on our web site.

leaving us. We are changing governorship to enter that of Luxor; we will be in the hands of new policemen. The exchange is made at a police station where we are deposited. Magitt is from Giza, near the pyramids. We promise each other to meet again.

The guys at the station are not very pleasant. They have not been forewarned and notified in advance and keep us waiting around while sizing us up haughtily. Magitt tries to explain that we have to walk, but he is outranked by the station commander, so his story doesn't carry much weight; he has to leave. We are stuck. The little chief wants to put us in a taxi for Esna. No way. I take out our newspaper article for him, illustrated with a photo with the governor; he asks for a license, a letter, a certificate, anything. We have none. And that is indeed the problem. And our Colonel Ayman is out of reach. We are "official" guests without "official" documents. The fellow waits for orders. We take our dilemma patiently; every hour that goes by we see five lost kilometers fly away. Evening comes. The commander now wants to send us to a hotel. *Niet!* We will sleep here. Our determination shakes him. He tries to convince us.

"*Mafish haga tinam aliha!*" (But there is no place here to sleep!)

"*Mafiche Mouchkilla, nenam ala al ard!*" (No problem, we will sleep on the floor!)

Torn between his policeman's will to make us comply and his natural insouciance that inclines him not to get involved in something that is no business of his, he lowers his guard, muttering in a strong Cairo accent a convenient "*khawaga magnoun.*"[19] The station is unspeakable. Flooded by stopped-up latrines. We prepare ourselves a little space on the ground in a grubby room full of junk but which has something precious: a door. We close it. The presence of a woman inside forbids anyone to open it inopportunely: Islam has very good sides, we are saved until tomorrow morning. But no way to find a basin to wash our feet; I am going to boil some water for

---

[19] These White people are crazy!

our soup. In a day, we have gone from the status of official guests to that of vagrants on house arrest. Long live contrasts! Before going to sleep I whisper to Sonia: "We all the same have to make sure there are no more breaks in the information chain..."

At ten the next morning, we decamp. The commander is not here. The underling throws his hands in the air. We assure him by saying we are going to Esna. That a three-hour wait, for us, is fifteen kilometers lost, and we would already be there if we had left at seven. To be sure, he tries to stop us, but a truck jam recalls him to his functions. He lets us go. Is the chain broken? Well, to hell with chains! Egypt, here we come! Without Cerberi and without interface. For six months we have been living in Islam, we are managing all right in Arabic, we are no longer afraid of anything...."*Yalla!*" We have three days to get to Luxor.

Very early we leave the main road to walk through sugar cane plantations along small, narrow railways used to carry harvests to the processing factories. Small plots are set apart in this tall greenery for truck farms. We are in full tomato harvest season. Piles of crates accumulate on the ballast and women harvesters stooping in the fields cheer up the landscape with their brightly colored clothing. On our right cruise ships go past with their cargo of Nordics as red as the tomatoes in the crates, unaware that their bare flesh is a sign of disrespect to the veiled women to whom they are exposing it. On board we wouldn't bother, from here we are shocked. Question of point of view. Two worlds brush shoulders in ignorance of each other, in unexpressed contempt of each other.

Freed of our bodyguards, we have punctured the protective bubble that prevented us from seeing Egypt as it really is. And now Egypt is as plain as the nose on our faces. Rural and poor, it gets little benefit from the tourist manna. It watches it pass before its eyes on big flashy ships. There's nothing there to facilitate understanding between these two worlds. The friction of cultures. Can't be a clash for there are no contacts. The stares cast at us are hard. They don't understand what tourists are doing wandering in the fields without policemen. Nevertheless, one man comes spontaneously up to us to bring us tomatoes, laughing and repeating: "Ramadan, Ramadan!" as if to specify that his present is dictated by the generosity rule that goes hand in hand with fasting. In the following field, while our backs are to the farm workers busy in their rows, a salvo of tomatoes breaks out all around us at the same time as the cry "Ramadan!" When, terrified, we look around at them, they are all at work as if nothing had happened. Sonia laughs.

"Thank you! Okay now, you're too kind, we have enough tomatoes!"

In fact, their gestures are a sign to us that we have insulted Ramadan because we were eating the tomatoes just offered to us. Funny payback. No doubt also a way of telling us that our place is on the boats, not in the fields. But were we to walk on the roads, we would immediately be stopped, because there are police roadblocks every five to ten kilometers. And we want, for just three days, to walk far from the exhaust gases, in this Egypt which we will not see, which no one sees, the Egypt where there is nothing to see...the real Egypt.

In the next village, dirt poor, laced with sewer-canals along which are aligned ill-constructed mud houses, swarming with filthy children running barefoot in refuse, our intrusion is traumatizing. People are uneasy. No smiles. No "*fadhal*"; instead children at our heels, more and more noisy and worked up. Reminiscenses of Ethiopia. But when they begin to come at us, with quips and goat turds, raging adults rush at them, angrily spitting on the ground between two *charmoute*'s or *Ibn kelb!'s*[20] meant for them. We call it progress. Nobody ever interfered in Ethiopia. It's always a comical scene. We make our exit. In almost every village this little skit is repeated. It's a game. That doesn't turn ugly. When we spin to talk to them, the kids ebb, they are afraid, then come back, then

---

[20] Son of a bitch! Son of a dog!

sing songs and escort us out of their village. Kind of cute. A bit stressful, but cute. We wanted contact, we got it. It is certain that with our policemen behind us, people would content themselves with responding to our greetings with an edgy, polite smile. In one of the villages, the old man who came to succor us is unable to disperse the scallywags. They then inveigh against us, laughing: "*Tahal! Tahal! Twin Towers!*"[21]

Did we rightly understand? They start dancing and chanting in place.

"*Twin Towers! Twin Towers! Twin Towers!*"

It's the War of the Buttons.[22] The children sadly ape adults. What can they be telling them to make them erupt so into violence at the mere sight of a Westerner? September 11 was two years ago and the children use it as a symbol of victory. Whose victory? What victory? Against whom? Against what? Victory of the goat turds over the *Nile Cruisers*.[23] It sends some shivers down our spines.

There's no way we can cook ourselves some noodle soup today. So we make do with cookies. A great famine! At the *iftar*, a peasant collars us. We don't let him repeat his invitation twice, we are exhausted. Sonia goes off with the women and I hear them laugh, laugh, and laugh some more. On my side, the guys parade in, but nobody's having fun. There is questioning. To find out why we are here where we should not be. The Egyptians know quite well that they have no right to speak to us, to pester us, that tourists are "sacred beings," super-protected by the government. And that rankles them. Attraction-repulsion. You can understand them. Their taxes maintain two million policemen throughout the country, a large share of whom are assigned to protection of the Westerners, and these villages are still without electricity. So here we are, vol-

---

[21] Come! Come on! Twin Towers! (Implicitly: we'll do to you what we did to the towers of the World Trade Center...)

[22] Name of a French film of 1962 about gangs of young boys.

[23] Large cruise ships on the Nile.

unteering to meet them halfway. And the ice melts little by little. I tell them about the Sudan; Nubions Ibrahim, our host, questions me: "It is said they are extremely poor, is that true?"

"Not the Sudan where we were traveling. On the contrary. They had a good standard of living, along the Nile…"

"Why?"

"I don't know, probably because there are not so many of them; the men go to work in Saudi Arabia and come back with dollars."

"Do you have dollars? I have never seen one! Could I see one?"

Nubions studies the green bill. He is disappointed. The Egyptian bills are much prettier. That is true. I translate for him: "In God we trust."

He objects: "No, Americans are infidels. Do you have any euros?"

"Sorry, we left Europe before there were any euros."

"*Ya salam!*"

Finally he laughs. A fat woman, still red from the bursts of laughter with Sonia, and molded into dark blue moiré velvet stretch material, brings us a wide platter of *iftar*. Before she disappears she says: "*Zaoudjatak koïs mabrouk!*" (Your wife is really super!)

What can she have done to them?

After the *iftar*, the men go to pray at the mosque; I remain alone setting down all my confused impressions of this "first" day in Egypt in my notebook.

La Moudira, Sunday 16 November, day 1054, 25 km, 12,062nd km

The next day I ask Sonia: "What were you telling those women to put them in such a state?"

"I did the *doukhan* and *zar* routine on them. They were stupefied that I should know about them. In fact, there was one of them who spoke a little English; she told me that these traditions originally came from Egypt. Their mothers all did it, then the old women began to relate and mime how they went about it…it was hilarious. There was one thing, on the other hand, which I did not expect here in Egypt: you know, they are also all excised, with exception of the little girls. But they are revolted by infibulation.... I had to make designs for them so that they could understand; imagine the outcry! They all asked me how I managed not to have any children; I showed them my pill; they had never heard of it. They didn't want to give that "miracle medicine" back to me. So I let them have it. It can't kill them, in any case, and I don't need it any more..."

"How's that? Oh, yes....In any case, there isn't any risk, since we are being separated all the time. Unless the Isis of Philae intervenes..."

Today it gets rough early. We leave the sugar cane and are walking through village after village clustered along the secondary roads. They come and challenge us. They inveigh against us, but with a smile. The feeling is ambiguous. We pass with an edgy smile, a cramp in the cheeks. Wave on all sides. We pull forced replies out of their mouths. They play sometimes the same game. In Armant, an adolescent whose hand is black with grease comes up to me, provocatively, determined to have me shake his hand; I refuse, saying to him in Arabic: "*Nazaf idak!*" (First go wash your hands...)

Howls of laughter from the witnesses. He acts offended so he can insult me.

Disagreeable childishness. Further on, a cookie vendor refuses to give me change. I finally get the best of him by invoking "*yazoul al zalzala!*"[24] but he throws back at me, running his thumb under his chin with a broad smile: "*Boukrah, Hatchepsout!*"[25]

Astonished, we leave amidst laughter, and tomatoes start to fly at our backs. This is really the season of flying tomatoes. Yet we know Egyptians aren't like that. But we would have to stop with all of them, talk to them for hours, become in spite of ourselves the

---

[24] Beware the last judgment!

[25] "Tomorrow, Hatchepsout!" Implying that tomorrow is the sinister anniversary of the mass killing of tourists at the Hatchepsout temple on 17 November 1997, in which 58 tourists, mostly Swiss, were methodically slaughtered, without any specific reason by unknown islamists. Scapegoats to destabilize the regime.

ambassadors of the world we embody, make the ice of ignorance melt, but we haven't got the time, we only want to pass through and take the temperature. And it is hot. The friction of the worlds is an exothermic reaction. And ever before our eyes the boats are passing by...

On the houses, painted by the hundreds, airplanes of unknown companies are flying with Arabic inscriptions that are translated by passers-by: *"yad Allah"* (the hand of Allah) or *"adalat Allah"* (the justice of Allah). But they are painted among boats, bicycles, mosques and towers, so we try to elude their real meaning, we don't dare take them seriously for what they are. There is just a little malaise amongst ambiguous smiles. Always this ambiguity that leads adolescent braggarts and clowns who see us pass to say "Good money" rather than "Good morning" and "Thank you! Fenk you! Fuck you!" There are also all the spitters who conspicuously aim just in front of our feet, innocently, knowing quite well how offensive that can be, but taking advantage of the doubt that is justified by the ban on swallowing one's saliva during Ramadan. When in doubt, we don't make an issue of it. It just annoys, forcibly. The whole thing is to play the dupes, to ignore it all, and it all goes all right, in that detestable and palpable ambiguity. But what notion is the western world sending them to deserve, through us, such contempt? All they know of the foreigners is the television and the passing boats, boasting lobsters in panties. That's all folks!

In the evening, on our way into Luxor, we pass in front of the impressive portico of a hotel on the edge of the desert: the Moudira. Sonia calls out to me: "Alex, might that be the hotel whose owner you met in a cybercafé in Aswan?"

"Indeed it is!" Zina Aboukheïr, a Franco-Lebanese woman, had told me to come and see her to offer us a drink. She wanted us to see her hotel of a new kind, far from the city, in the heart of a village, at the foot of the Theban mountain.

We had imagined a sort of boarding house. We were wrong: it is the latest thing in a grand hotel. We do not hold back. Adorable

Zina welcomes us into her reinvented Oriental paradise. The phantasm of the *Thousand and One Nights*: "I saw your article in the
newspaper. Super! I wondered when you would get here!"

So we meet again under a huge moucharabieh, before a mosaic
fountain filled with bougainvillea petals that quietly goes glug-glug
while we guzzle a cold Stella,[26] a cold Stella, a cold Stella....The
rest is but *luxe, calme*...and neatness[27]; canopy bed, suite, hammam[28], wall hangings and decor. The other Egypt. Thank you,
Zina! Tonight we were badly craving this particular Egypt.

The next day, before leaving Zina to go to Luxor, we tell her our
misadventures. "You went through a dangerous area. That's where
the police did massive raids after the massacre in the temple of
Hatchepsout. All those people have greatly suffered. Today is the
anniversary, to boot..."

I tell her about yesterday's gesture in very bad taste.

"He did that, the bastard! It has become a bad joke, to send the
tourists packing. You know, I am an Arab, so I hear such things...
not sad ones! As for 'Twin Towers,' that does not surprise me! You
should have seen the joy in the streets the day it happened. It
was like France winning the World Cup. But you mustn't hold it
against them, it's just words. They don't know anything about the
world. They are good people. And they suffered greatly from the
disaffection of tourism after the attack. Here, around Luxor, today
is a day of mourning."

We finally come to the small village of el-Gourna, opposite the
Luxor "Corniche," where Guy-Hervé[29] is putting us up with one
of his collaborators, Badaoui, in a three-story house built on the
Nile, directly opposite the temple. Here we will spend close to a

---

[26] An Egyptian beer served to tourists.
[27] Cf. chapter 25, note 2.
[28] Turkish bath.
[29] Since then he's had stolen all his belongings, houses and business, had his
life threatened and had to flee the country just for the simple fact of being
gay.

month receiving and rereading the manuscript sent back by Éditions Robert Laffont with minute corrections, lay out the photo pages following a selection worked out by Claude Chassin, Sonia's father, make the maps, choose the front cover, all the things that have to be decided before the first volume of our adventures can come out on our return. We take advantage of this work period to carry on our investigations, film subjects, link up again with the police who fortunately have not noticed that we have run off, meet the governor of the city, General el-Desouky el-Bana, visit the sites of the Valley of the Kings, Karnak and elsewhere among the cartloads of tourists, but incognito this time, without bodyguards, in postcard Egypt.

35

The Heart of Egypt

Olga Gentil, one of Sonia's super-pals, has joined us in our trek for a few days beginning in Luxor. Three years they haven't seen each other. It is hard for her to be deprived of her friends for so long. Filiform, Olga is all in white linen like an Egyptian princess. She cries in Sonia's arms, whispering to her in tender Russian words transmitted by her mamitchka. She arrived with a pharaonic picnic that we go enjoy on the bank of sacred Karnak Lake, in the shade of a palm tree. Lalande-de-Pomerol[1], Poilâne Camembert, Comté, garlic sausage: all of France on an offering stone for libations and sacrifices to Amon, above the "pure stores," a place where priests kept offerings for the temples. Karnak is a battlefield of overturned stones. The great upheaval of the centuries that telescopes nine pylons and packs ten temples inside each other, and in the midst of this jumble of Dynasties, this stone carnage, wander disfigured statues, broken obelisks, and lost rams.

---

[1] Lalande-de-Pomerol is a prominent Bordeaux vineyard, Poilâne a French traditional bakery brand and Comté a raw milk cooked cheese from Jura, semi-hard with flowery and nutty perfumes.

Here we meet two young French archeologists, Marie and Auré-lia, who are digging in the homes of priests under the direction of François Larcher. It's amazing what they can deduce about rituals in what until recently would have been considered a vulgar rubble embankment! This is the new school. They are less interested in the formal, hieratic character of temples than in the life that took place there; less in objects than in what is around the objects: sig-nature seals, papyrus fragments, the ashes of a hearth, the contents of a broken bowl, the position of a leaf, grains of wheat, every-thing is important to them. At the foot of old ramparts, they have found jewels, and show them to us feverishly. Imagine the joy of a young student discovering a necklace worn by a woman three thousand years ago! So far from us, and so close! A necklace that could be worn today. It's amazing the treasures that the ancient Egyptians left behind them, for the joy of future researchers.... Sonia concludes: "What beautiful things are we burying today? Nuclear waste, garbage! How many necklaces? Statues? Master-pieces? Gold coins? If we were to disappear, what thing of beauty would we leave behind? Who is attending to burying marvels for future civilizations?"

El Waqf, Sunday 14 December 2003, day 1082, 36 km, 12,171st km

Olga has left us. She walked with us to Denderah, the temple of Hathor, famous for its zodiacal ceiling, dismantled in 1820 by Jean-Baptiste Lelorrain and conserved in the Louvre.[2] We have resumed the trek on the main road. No more visits to temples in the Theban region: we have more than six hundred kilometers of Middle Egypt to go before reaching Cairo. This evening, the policemen who are escorting us again since Luxor are lodging us mandatorily in a Coptic parish protected by high walls, where we are welcomed by *Abuna*[3] Yonan. We have scarcely sat down to table

---

[2] You will find a detailed visit of it on our web site.
[3] "Christian priest" in Arab: Father.

under a pergola before glasses of carcadet[4] than a volley of stones from the street ricochets on the nearby metal sheet roof with a terrible din. Abuna Yonan, emaciated, his face swallowed up in a very black beard, makes a little pout: "Forgive the dilapidation of our church, it is crumbling a piece at a time…"

Seeing that we are not fooled, he confesses: "In Islam, we Copts have the status of *dhimmis*, 'protégés'. In fact, when we are in the minority, as we are here, we are just barely tolerated. The residents of this village dream of our leaving, but this is our home as much as theirs…"

The muezzin is calling to evening prayer. The loudspeaker screams so loud that it seems to be hung on the church tower. A second starts in, then a third, then others; the noise is such that we can no longer hear each other. The conversation is suspended…. When everything calms down, Abuna Yonan slowly starts over, as if he were drunk with fatigue…

"Where was I? Oh yes! We are dhimmis.[5] It was true in the past, and is still partly true in modern Egypt. There is a law that forbids us to restore, renovate or maintain our churches without making a request to the governorship, so they often fall into ruin…. For three years now we have been sending requests to repair our steeple, which is cracking, and repaint it white, and still no authorization in sight….The dossier gets lost each time in the meanders of the administration. During that time, a mosque was built right there" – he points in one direction – "and another is being built behind us. Five mosques encircle us. And if I put a nail in the wall, I go to prison. That's what happened the last time, when we wanted to clear up a lean-to behind the church. The initiative unleashed a riot in the village and I was arrested for 'undeclared works'…"

He looks emaciated. He notes our concern: "I am suffering

---

[4] A red tea of sepals from a variety of hibiscus, drunk hot or cold.
[5] The dhimmis did not have the right to own land or horses and had to pay a religious tax, the capitation.

from bilharziasis.[6] I spent my entire youth with my feet in the water in the sugar cane plantations....The disease leads to degeneration of the liver. So do not worry if I make faces when I am speaking, it is a shot of pain..."

Considering our baths in contaminated waters, in Malawi or elsewhere, he strongly advises us to begin a curative treatment in advance, in case we have been infected by parasites, since the incubation period is quite long.

I bring him back to the church.

"We have, however, met the governor of Qena, Adel Habib, who has reassured us with regard to the respect shown to the Christian minority....Moreover, everyone repeats insistently to us that there is no religious discrimination in this country...

"There is an official discourse, which is sincere, a genuine willingness on the side of the government to protect us, but there are the facts of our existence as second-class citizens. Unfortunately, the phenomenon has become more serious in the last fifteen years."

"But this is a state of law, with a police, a justice system..."

"In a legal or penal conflict, there is always an opportunity, in the process, to find a trifle against us. We know this. They know we know it, and do not abuse it. So we never complain, we just hunker down. Only prayer can save us..."

We enter his house where we'll spend the night. Everything is clean and cared for. He introduces us to his wife Iman, who takes Sonia under her wing. Our hostess is concerned that we have no children, is convinced, she too, that that is why we are doing this trek, and offers her by way of propitiation a little dress for a baby girl....Sonia is perplexed. The television announces the arrest of Saddam Hussein. Abuna Yonan remains impassive: "The news is our weather forecast. Every time an event affects the Arab or Muslim world, for us, the weather becomes stormy. The Americans

---

[6] A small parasite of the liver that perforates the walls of organs and can affect the whole abdomen.

don't realize the harm they do to Christians who live in Islamic lands....I am going to have to advise vigilance…"

The trek for the next few days is unpleasant. The traffic is intense, the countryside ugly; the disaffected industrial zones succeed to unhealthy commuting cities, isolated in open sugar cane fields. Yet another Egypt. The temperature chills. Sonia is obliged to put on wool tights under her skirt. We are walking in fleeces and gloves. The hardest part for us is to get the policemen to fetch us at eight in the morning, and not ten, else we lose ten kilometers' walking. Our relations with them oscillate between artistic blur and efficacity. We understand, with the passage of days and changes of teams, that everything is managed in the present, at the moment, on the spot, by word of mouth. We are passed from *merkaz*[7] to *merkaz*, with this sole order: "Follow them in a car to the limits of your *merkaz*." Unhappily, the relay never takes place at police stations; at each border, we must wait for a car to come from the headquarters to where we are to escort us through the territory for which it is responsible. We learn to anticipate: while walking, we get our policemen to order another car to make the relay without interruption. Thus they spend long hours with their ears glued to their walkie-talkie or their telephone shouting unintelligible sentences full of "*itnin françaouin*," "*Aïwa!*" and "*kullu beregli*," with "*la! Ma'arafsh leh?*" and "*Diouf el Mohafiz*" or even "*mashi a-basha,*[8]" which in the long run give our days a cadence between the "*turlu-tut*" of the phones and the horns of the trucks that brush past us. From time to time, the *molazim*, the *naqib* or the *raed*[9] who is responsible for us comes to limber up his legs at our sides. For them our trek is haloed in mysteries; they know we have come from a long way away, but Africa is still something very abstract to them:

---

[7] District.

[8] "Two Frenchmen," "yes!" "all on foot," "No! I don't know why," "guests of the governor," "Ok, chief!"

[9] The lieutenant, captain or commander.

they ask us if we have come by way of Nigeria or Senegal....Mostly people who were born in the delta, they are curious to know the true motives behind our trek. They have all studied for five or six years at the very serious Cairo Police Academy, but do not speak a word of English. So it's a little difficult to explain our quest "in the footsteps of Man," especially since they are completely closed to any notion of evolution or paleoanthropology. Both of these are areas contrary to the teachings of the Qu'ran. So we are walking for peace in Palestine. It's simpler. Although.

Thus we pass through Hiw, Nag Hamadi, Abu Shusha, Al Balyana, where we take advantage of a break in our police escort chain to go glance at the Abydos temple, built by Seti the first, father of Rameses.

"Do you remember? In the Sudan, the first cartouche we saw was of Seti I. At Tumbus. His territory extended that far!"

The temple consists of seven aligned chapels bearing exquisite polychrome engravings chiseled into limestone of unbelievable purity. An extraordinary piety emanates from every gesture, every ritual, every offering.

Such pomp, such deference, such decorum inspire me: "Do you realize? These pharaohs pushed power, religiosity, the splendor of their cult to the extreme, and today, all that remains of all those beliefs are these artistic frescoes..."

The proof of the vanity, fragility, and temporality of every cult. That faith so strong that it perhaps drove the power of religion to its paroxysm was dethroned and replaced by the words of barefoot, hirsute and poor men of the Levant, pacifists and few in number, extolling a new religion of equality and love. An ascendant faith – man creates the superhuman gods – replaced by a descending faith – God creates men and descends to become man.

Sonia plays the devil's advocate: "One day, maybe, when visiting the ruins of Notre Dame, worshipers of the navel, the divine cabbage, or the great golden phallus will have the same reflection..."

My ashamed laughter echoes through the colonnades of the hypostyle rooms.

In the evening once we have reached Girga, our new captain Walid looks for a Coptic oasis to lodge us in. We tell him that we wouldn't mind being hosted by a Muslim family. Negative. He looks concerned. We reassure him by saying that we have been living inside Islam for seven months, that we like Muslims and are not afraid to sleep in their homes....It has no effect. Even if Muslim himself, he sticks to orders. To each his own. Birds of the same feather must flock together. He fears for his three gold stars. After plugging into his walkie-talkie, he finally turns to us, looking worried: "There is a Coptic parish in Regegna, fifteen kilometers west of here; are you willing to go there by car?"

We are willing. He utters a sigh of relief. I explain to him that we want to begin again tomorrow at this crossroads, but he seems not to understand the word *"takatwa"* which I have just freshly drawn from my little dictionary. I postpone the problem for later. We get in and head west at full speed, sirens blaring as if the driver wanted vengeance for having had to drive at a walk speed all day...

When we pass through our first Coptic villages, Walid mutters prayers, *Bismillah I rarmen I rahim...* (By most powerful and most merciful God) as if he meant to conjure an evil spell. We can feel fear rising up in him. He is nervous and uneasy. Barks at the driver to go faster. The people come out of their houses, frightened, some topple over to avoid the car....We ask our reckless driver to slow down so we won't needlessly frighten the quietude of this country dusk, but it's no use, Walid replies: *"Rhatar katir, hinak..."* (It's very dangerous here...)

In Regegna, the same comedy, the motor roars, siren on full, we go around turns on two wheels, the children dive away in front of us, the goats are panicked....The men rise as we pass, bearded, turbaned, draped in long gallabiahs; nothing distinguishes them from Muslims. Really Walid is overdoing it, I insist he slow down:

"Bichewiche low samat, ana zaalan, Inta Rhatar!" (Please slow down, I'm very angry! It is you who are dangerous.)

The driver brakes hard, the soldiers deploy, we are here. Walid bangs unceremoniously on the large metal door of the presbytery. Had he come to arrest the village priest – knowing how traumatizing such an act would be for the community – he could not have made more noise; people gather worriedly, cries crackle, policemen violently push back the crowd, snap their cylinder heads; if they had wanted to incite a riot, they could not have done better. We get out of the car to try to calm things down a bit. It is total confusion, in the dust raised by the pounding of a hundred feet. The door finally opens, we dive in. Inside all is silence. A little man in black, calm and capped with a strange round toque, comes serenely up to us. Roundish, he is wearing a large, thick beard, a trifle comic, and a white braided leather pectoral cross. Walid is tense. Abuna Abraham introduces himself and asks us to follow him into a reception hall. For that, we have to go through the church. I signal the soldiers to stop on the threshold so as not to enter the nave with their weapons. It is a matter of respect. Abuna Abraham smiles, Walid apologizes. After brief explanations in a salon decorated with large posters of Coptic monks, Walid withdraws.

I again try to make him understand the famous word *takatwa*, the crossroads, in vain. I give up: *"Aïwa, chouffoun garib tani boukrah inch'allah, saa tamanya bezaht low samat..."* (Ok, we will see you tomorrow morning at eight sharp, please, God willing!)

"Insha'Allah!"

We hear the car leave and apologize in Arabic for all the racket. Abuna Abraham answers us in good English: "Don't worry, we're used to it, did you notice how he was trembling? This inexperienced young officer was afraid. Most Muslims in the delta do not know us and have wrong ideas about us. They almost think we're foreigners..."

After a brief presentation of our trek, we sit down in comfortable crimson velvet armchairs. An historian, Abuna Abraham has founded an historic library within his church. He requires little encouraging: "The young Egyptians don't know anything any more. Most of the time, for example, they don't even know that the word 'Egypt' derives from *Gyptos* which means 'Copt'. We are the first Egyptians, those of the pharaonic Egypt who converted to Christianity. We peacefully welcomed among us the Persians and then the Arabs. Many of us have converted to Islam to escape the status of dhimmi which was imposed on us little by little. Since then, the domination has never ceased since we have never revolted. There were twenty-four million of us Copts; only half of us are left now. When one of our daughters marries a Muslim, she becomes a Muslim, and our sons are not allowed to marry Muslim women, so we have never been mixed with the invaders."

"Yet you are all Egyptians?"

"Yes, but Egypt as an independent nation has only existed since 1956 and the arrival in power of Gamal abd el-Nasser, the first native Egyptian to rule Egypt since the pharaohs."

We pause for a moment; he rebounds on our confusion: "Oh, yes! For more than two thousand years we had lived under foreign domination, whence the extraordinary complexity of our history and origins. You will see. The Egypt of the Ptolemies was already Greco-Roman. Next, it was Byzantium that ruled over us, which led to many schisms and heresies, Nestorianism, Arianism, and the Monophysitism from which we derive. Under this fragile tutelage, the conquest of Cairo in 636 by Amr el-As, a lieutenant of Omar, second successor of Mohammed, was accomplished without difficulty. We all but welcomed him as a liberator! From then on, we were governed from Damascus by the Omeyyads, from Baghdad by the Abbassids, then we were conquered by the Fatamids who came from the Maghreb, then by Saladin and his ayyubid descendants from Lebanon, who were subsequently overturned by the Mamelukes from Baybars and finally by the Ottomans of Soliman the Magnificent, until Napoleon arrived and then the British. With all these comings and goings, we are the most mixed country of the

Ancient World; at Aswan you have doubtless seen Nubians black as ink; in the delta you will see descendants of the Berbers or the French crusaders, with red hair and blue eyes."

Overhead, very large posters of Coptic patriarchs gaze sternly down at us.

"That one is Baba Carolus, who died in 1971: everyone worshiped him, he performed miracles, he is a saint. And here is our current patriarch, Baba Chenouda, who unfortunately has just broken off the ecumenical dialogue with Pope John Paul II..."

We are interrupted by an upset loudspeaker that spits out a horrible scratchy voice. We are most taken aback since we had not noticed any mosque opposite the church. Abuna Abraham replies to our question: "They stretched a wire and put the loudspeaker on the roof of the house next door, until they get the minaret... The construction of the mosque will soon begin. The minaret will be two meters higher than our spire. It's so puerile!"

I become indignant: "Isn't there a law that spells out a perimeter to be respected for construction of a different place of worship?"

"Yes, but they get around it or ignore it and it is not reciprocal since we no longer have the right to build new churches. The rare exceptions are very costly. Here in Regegna, there are three thousand of us Christians against two thousand Muslims. No one wants to admit that it's a race for children. And we are slowly being overtaken. We have two churches, and they have three mosques, all of them built since Anwar el-Sadat. And a fourth one is planned. Their purpose is to have five in every village, to echo the symbolism of the five pillars of Islam and surround us with loudspeakers. My sense is that it is these loudspeakers that make them lose their heads. Before, we had no problems, we respected each other in silence. Now there is too much noise and too many foreign influences. The loudspeakers and satellite dishes have turned Islam crazy..."

The next morning, no police car in sight. Abuna Abraham has to leave; no one else speaks English. We are isolated. Furious.

Finally Captain Walid shows up....It is noon! And he insists on not understanding the word *takatwa*, the "crossroads" where we want to start walking today. I am fuming; I draw crossroads in the sand; he imagines I am making crosses, that we want to see another church....Everyone is laughing. One of the underlings in wool fatigues – a first-class illiterate soldier – then leans toward his ear: "*Ana fahim, el Khawaga kerem min el tâkâtwâ min embereh.*" (I think the stranger is speaking of yesterday's crossroad.)

Eureka! Something finally clicks between Walid's three stars and three neurons! The tâkâtwâ. Good gracious, but of course! Couldn't you have said it earlier: the tâkâtwâ!

"*Aïwa! Mafiche mouchkilla. Yalla fil tâkâtwâ.*" (Ok! No problem, let's go to the crossroad!)

Hence the nickname we spontaneously give our captain, to the great joy of the entire team: Walid el-Tâkâtwâ!

Year in and year out, day after day, we are descending the Nile while ascending to the north. At Sohag, the governor Mamdour Kidwani lodges us in a little cottage on an island in the heart of a large, decrepit industrial city where we arrive spent in the glacial cold. In the day, we walk amidst immense sugar cane plantations. Our policemen chew kilos of the stuff in the back of the car, spitting out the pulp noisily on the road after pressing out the juice which has nothing sugary about it but the name. That keeps them busy for a good part of the day. In the greenery flitter white egrets; reinforcement rods stick into the sky above unfinished hovels; horns mixed with the muezzin calls ring in the air. Along the canals we are following, live ducks and lifeless dogs go past in front of laundresses and girls busy doing dishes....The routine of our road. So many policemen follow one another at our sides, from *merkaz* to *merkaz*, that we no longer remember their names. Sometimes, we haven't even had time to speak to them before they are already relayed. We schlep our backpacks from car to car, greet, thank and go on. It's exhausting. Sonia, always resourceful, has put together a little bound dossier of all our articles that have come out in Arabic in Khartoum, Aswan and Luxor; articles complete with photos of us shaking hands with governors. She hands it to the new policemen by way of introduction, which keeps us from having to stop every time and repeat our stories. When they first arrive, they often have an expression of vague contempt for the pedestrians that we are, but they leave us enthusiastic and the mouths full of encouragements. What is so exalting in all these articles?

In the urban zones, the orders are that a policeman must walk at our sides as a bodyguard would do, with his Heckler *und* Koch automatic submachine gun in his hand or the Helwan pistol on his belt, an Egyptian copy of the fat Beretta 1951. In short, we do not pass unnoticed. This evening, before we enter Abu Tig, we are entitled to some large caliber stuff, to hell with the rusty old guns, we are escorted by an armored vehicle with a turret. Yes! A tank with wheels! With the barrel pointed between us and with a server in firing position. We are walking nonchalantly in front of a war machine.

The captain of the Abu Tig merkaz, completely flipped out, indeed tried to prevent us from entering his territory on foot under the pretext that there were "dangerous criminals, insane killers capable of anything" hereabouts, but Sonia has developed an excellent technique. While I am talking with the recalcitrant officer, she just walks off. When they notice that she is getting away, one or two policemen run after her though not daring to put a hand on her: you don't touch a young woman! Especially when her husband is nearby. Then I make the officer understand that I cannot leave my wife unprotected and run to join her with a guffaw. In this way we force many barriers or reluctances; in fact we save time and cut short the interminable and repetitive discussions. When they realize that our trek is serious and not just some cute idea of Western eccentrics, they give in and let us pass even in the zones where they themselves are *personae non gratae*.

So here we are at dusk, a little before Abu Tig, in front of our armored vehicle, accompanied by a policeman on foot. Suddenly, between two houses, children rush at us armed with bamboo sub-machine guns, wearing on their foreheads bands bearing Qu'ranic inscriptions. Our cop got a fright, starting a move to his holster. Stress for a short second. Once the surprise effect has passed, we say to ourselves that all these kids were just playing a kind of cow-boys and Indians. But they begin to jump from one foot to the other with their weapons raised high, yelling: "Hamas! Hamas! Hamas!"

The policeman yells at them: *"Khalas! Yekhreb beitkum!"*[10]

Couldn't care less, separated from us by the width of a small trench. Witnesses to the scene sneer. Ill at ease, our policeman returns while stones are bouncing off the armored vehicle.

"They're only children!" he says by way of excuse.

So? It's even more serious. Even more sad because they are only children. What are these children told? What future are they preparing for them? What do they know about Palestine? About Israel? About us? The mere sight of our westernism unleashes this irrational itch. We are stunned.

Once inside the city, the tension again rises. We do not press our little experiment further and climb into the armored vehicle which soon drops us off before a metal door that opens onto a lit-tle, frightened Catholic nun. Sister Sabah is Lebanese. She belongs to the Italian community of the Sisters of Caiani. Full-figured and generous as a smile, she takes in and educates a dozen orphaned girls of all faiths. She is worried about us: "It's a good thing you have the police. Otherwise, you would have many problems. These kids are the same as in Gaza or the Beirut of my childhood. You know, I grew up under the bombs and I will never forget. Poor kids! They have to be pitied. Except that they have not experienced the bombs; they are manipulated by ill-intentioned people."

It makes her lips and hands quake, this little courageous captain

---

[10] Enough of that! May your house fall upon you! (Understood: Woe to you!)

who is trying to bend the fate of twelve girls lost in this hostile, broken-down world where children sing calls to war. A door slams, she jumps and then laughs: "You see… I am traumatized…"

This evening *Notting Hill* is on the television, an American romance with Hugh Grant and Julia Roberts. The girls are glued to the screen. London, love, fun, freedom, opulence. We too are enthralled, but not for the same reason: the first kiss, on a public bench, was censored.…But not the one at the end, at the wedding. Morality is safe…

This morning, we manage to leave at dawn; our officer is too happy to get us to leave this city while it is still numb with cold and sleep. Francis, a neighbor of Sister Sabah with whom we had a long discussion the night before, went to buy me a sweater, since my fleece and Gore-Tex were no longer sufficient. Sonia found herself the recipient of a gray cardigan from the Caiani community. Once more, all of them have asked us to carry their names to Jerusalem. What a mission! All these names of Muslims and Christians united in our hearts and our heads, all these names of believers, all these hopes extended toward that city from which the best as well as the worst can come. We no longer know what to think. We carry. We are only passing passers.

Shitty day, shitty road, depression. Necessarily, walking on a motorway under construction, followed by an armored vehicle, between a railway and a putrid canal, makes you doubt.…The little solitary doubt of a lugubrious morning. Is there a f… point in this? My only sun is Sonia. She is there, in front of me, imperturbable. I see her little slender hands beating along the sides of her skirt. What grace in this grime! Her gaze goes back and forth over the refuse in the canals and the unwholesome huts. What levity in such gravity! With a single look, she transfigures ugliness, transforms toads into elves. She turns toward me and hums. "Well, now, Darling! What a face you make!"

What joy in all this grayness! She gives me wings.

At lunch, in a greasy spoon, everyone is nice to us, the people smiling, it makes me feel better; and the grilled chicken with lemon reconciles me with existence; a ray of sun shines through, they bring us some mezze,[11] some salad; I share my surprise with Sonia: "Today everything is first-rate…"

"Do you see very many clients who arrive escorted by an armed vehicle…?'"

I almost choke for laughing, to the general joy. Sonia is a miraculous antidote against moroseness.

We get to Assiout, the capital of Middle Egypt, where palaces inherited from the last splendors of the precolonial Egypt of Mehemet Ali are falling down. When Sonia worries about the perceived ruins, the affable *mohafiz*[12] Ahmad Hammam Atia takes out a large file concerning the restoration of a hundred or so of them. Here again the feeling of a plan. Governors govern. At each gubernatorial visit we receive official gifts, *tizkars*, which are piling up in a big sack which we had to buy for this purpose – often the emblem of the city, in metal, in a velvet frame. This time, we are gratified with a rug decorated with an Isis and an Osiris. Back on the road, I regret it is not a flying one.

Deïr el-Moharrak, Thursday 25 December 2003, day 1093, 12,456th km

Christmas in the heart of Egypt. Christmas without Christmas since the Copts celebrate it on 7 January. But more than Christmas, since it was here, precisely, that Joseph, Mary and Jesus came to take refuge during their flight into Egypt. We are received by Abuna Boutros, a giant of a priest, with very white skin, a very black beard, clearly designed eyes astride a large aquiline nose. A Christlike figure. He wears a traditional hat, black, ogival and close-fitting, embellished with a delicate embroidery – crosses in

---

[11] An assortment of tabouli, hummus, baba ghanouj, falafel, grape leaves, etc.
[12] Governor.

silver thread – which he made himself, according to the rule. Some ninth-century icons testify that the monks then used the same headdress. Abuna Boutros recalls for us a famous adventure.

"Just after the visit of the Three Kings to Bethlehem, the angel said to Joseph: 'Rise up, take the baby and his mother and flee into Egypt. Stay there until I tell you, for Herod is seeking the baby to put it to death.' And that was the Massacre of the Innocents. The first martyred saints of Christianity. Deïr el-Moharrak is the southernmost place which the Holy Family reached. We estimate they arrived here after two years of walking…"

"Two years for such a short distance?"

"They weren't going as fast as you are, and without a police escort! And besides they stopped for several months in many villages. Don't forget that they were traveling with a young baby. We have in this country nearly twenty-five sites that have preserved the memory of their passage. But it was here that they stayed the longest, about six months; six months after which Joseph received another visit from the angel, who told him: 'Rise up, take the child and his mother, and return to the land of Israel, for those who threatened his life are dead.' For the return, they descended the Nile for much of the trip."

Abuna Boutros leads us to the *husn*, the Roman dungeon, which since the fourth century has offered the monks a fall-back solution in case of attack. The tower, rectangular and massive, decorated with cross pattées and isolated by a drawbridge, seems unassailable.

"During periods of unrest, the monasteries are traditionally prey to looters, which is why they all have a dungeon like this one. But ours has never been used, for Deïr el-Moharrak has always enjoyed particular protection….The only death we have had to lament was five years ago, but outside the enclosure…"

"What happened?"

"It was the Father gardener; he had gone to demand that two Muslim peasants pay their rent on a piece of land that we had farmed out to them. It had been seven years since they had paid us anything. Our poor Father was paid with a submachine burst right in the stomach. The two brothers did three years in prison and then got out. They scoff at us now, over the walls…"

We reach the top of the dungeon by a series of winding stairways that conceal hiding places and secret passages.

Facing the crepuscular landscape which he scans with his eyes, the Father concludes: "Our only weapon is to love them more than they love us….And that is not hard!"

The countryside is rich and fertile around the monastery's high ramparts. Very far away rings through the air the call to prayer.

"Let us forget this sad story. Let me rather show you our treasury. We have on this site one of the oldest altars in Christendom, which is the stone on which the Holy Family slept! The first church was built as soon as Saint Mark came to Alexandria, in the year 38, and that stone became its altar."

We find it in a chapel unfortunately freshly painted shiny white, where authentically ancient icons mix with fluorescent posters of the worst kind. In fact, the whole monastery is under repair – whereas we would have liked to find its original state….He seems to notice our disappointment.

"You know, it's just a stone. When man was seeking God, he created temples, and you have seen that in Egypt we were capable of constructing immense temples out of stone, every more beautiful and powerful. What remains of them? Today, God is in us and we are the temple. The Church is not walls but men."

El Minya, Sunday 28 December 2003, day 1096, 48 km, 12,545th km

The little lady squeezed into her hijab has problems extricating herself from her car. She is the representative of the Ministry of Tourism who has come to meet us. Salwa el-Sorughi is short-winded but speaks impeccable French. Of her face rounded by a tight veil, you remember two vivid and cheerful eyes. Immediately she adopts us, but does not manage to conceal her worries.

"You are invited this evening by the governor to a concert given at the university; now the city center is ten kilometers from here.... We can't be late, especially if you want to go first to your hotel. We have reserved a room for you at the Cleopatra....Come on! Get in! I know you always refuse, but do this for me....Please!...It is dark..."

She is so nice that we accept. Everything goes very fast. Salwa is a formidable organizer. In a half-hour, we find ourselves seated in the first row of an immense modern theatre, in a velvet seat, among a bunch of officials and generals in dress uniform. Behind us, three thousand impeccably groomed students; the boys, short hair slicked back, a snug sweater, the girls all in the university hijab of the Muslim Sisters. Perfect silence. No need for campus police. The symphony orchestra take their places: dark suits and violins, long dresses and bow ties, real class. Exceptionally, we have an official English interpreter.

"This is the evening of the trimestrial closing and for the occasion the university has invited the very famous singer Iman el-Bahr Derviche. He is the grandson of our great revolutionary Saïd Derviche, liberation companion of Saad Zaghloul as early as 1919. He is something like our Frank Sinatra..."

Our guide is interrupted by the entrance of the star. All the girls have come to their feet in a single motion, shouting and applauding – true groupies.

The man is handsome, tall, slim, lithe: a mixture of Roch Voisine and Gary Cooper, a real actor's look. Slicked-down part, Ultrabrite smile, impeccable tux, mother-of-pearl cufflinks. He calms the crowd with a paternal gesture. After a brief formal speech, he turns toward the director who then lifts his baton and strikes up his orchestra. Despite the suits and the look, there is nothing western about the music that emanates from it. Much percussion and many plucked strings, Oriental wind instruments. The crooner's fine voice warms up; he grasps the foot of the microphone, realer than real. With one fell swoop, we have gone from the Egypt of the fellahs and endless construction sites to the prosperous Egypt of the megalopolises. With the succeeding song, the audience warms to him, the buck spins out his love songs full of *"habibi,"* *"bint,"* *"hadiya,"* and *"noor albi"*[13] which we can understand without the interpreter's help. The atmosphere moves up a notch with a song full of *"beledi,"* *"raïs,"* and *"horeya."*[14] Then, suddenly, on what is apparently a hit song, the crowd goes wild; the youth take up all together: *"Feyn! Feyn! Seyf Allah! Seyf an Nahr! Tahal! Philistin ihtag adala! Ma Zulfakar! Adini beled for el Aqsa! Tahal, Khalid ibn el Walid, tahal tani!"*

I turn to our ecstatic neighbor; he translates for us: "Where are you? Where are you? Sword of God! Sword of fire! Come! The Palestinians need justice! With Zulfakar![15] Give El-Aqsa[16] a country! Come, Khalid ibn el-Walid,[17] return!…"

Salwa, who from the end of her row has understood what was happening, casts an angry glance at our interpreter – who suddenly falls silent. We have heard enough. When he has finished his song, the temperature drops and the stage animal begins a speech. Our interpreter no longer translates for us, but it is not difficult to understand the sense of his words, full of "Israel," "America," "Iraq," "Muslimuna" – surely peaceful words….And what had begun as a nice little evening becomes more like a political rally which he closes by having the enraptured hall repeat a volley of *"Allah u Akbar!"* Happily, we are neither American nor Jewish, and even less enemies of Islam! In the vestibule, a television crew lies in wait for us.

"Well? Did you like it? We have read in all the newspapers

---

[13] My treasure, the girl, a present, light of my heart…

[14] My country, the president, freedom.

[15] The name of Mohammed's (Mahomet's) double-pointed sword.

[16] Mosque on the Jerusalem esplanade next to the Dome of the Rock; the El-Aqsa martyr brigade is a terrorist group that has claimed many attacks on Israelis.

[17] Companion in arms of the prophet Mohammed during the Hegira, Khalid ibn el-Walid was a glorious warrior who in vast battles successively defeated the insubmissive Bedouins, the Persians, the Byzantines, and the Syrians, and participated in the conquest of the Holy Land and Egypt. Mohammed christened him "the sword of God."

that you have been walking for three years for the liberation of Palestine..."

At least we now know why the articles were so successful....We leave this lovely evening disturbed from head to toe.

The following days are calm. Thanks to the attentions of our kind Salwa, we visit the historical sites of Tell el-Amarna, Beni Hassan and Tuna el-Gabal. Almost nothing remains of the first, so great was the care taken by the successors of Akhenaton to destroy all trace of his Amarnian revolution. Over the desolate pediment of the mountain glides the memory of the visionary pharaoh, promoter of a cult combining love, equality, God and the Sun, in one of the first of the monotheistic attempts of humanity. On the rare frescoes that are still intact, the sun god Aton extends to men dozens of little hands attached to ends of his beams: that's a good beginning. Beni Hassan is a revelation: painted on the stucco of the nobles' sepultures of the Middle Kingdom, dug into a limestone cliff, the Olympic games are already figured, wrestling, yoga, chess, juggling, acrobatics, corporal punishment....On the walls around us, the life of men in comic strips, more than four thousand years ago. Before Thebes, before Rameses! Here a cobbler is making sandals, there vintners are trampling the grapes, while over their heads glass blowers are protecting their works from the boomerangs of the bird trappers who are bringing down a flight of ducks in vast nets. All is jubilation. Who today could allow himself such an abode for eternity? At Tuna el-Gabal we fall into a swoon before the intact tomb of Petosiris, a pure Ptolemaic masterpiece the bas-reliefs of which retrace with extraordinary precision the gestures of Greco-Roman artisans, truer than the real thing. A lathe operator with his chisel, a gold-weigher with his scale, a linen spinner with her spool, a goldsmith with his jewels, a pharmacist with his flasks, stand opposite a laborer with his rudimentary plow, a reaper with his knife, a shepherd milking, a veterinarian attending a calving cow, an olive press....The faces have changed: Africans and Orientals are side-by-side with bearded Latins, fair-haired boys with mustaches, or athletes worthy of the Parthenon. Our favorite Egyptian monument. On the mountain side, there is the Ibistafion, a subterranean maze stuffed with six million ibis mummies. You can walk through it for three hundred meters filled of shivers, shadow and eternal silence. You, reader, really must come to El-Minya to see these marvels, far from the Luxor digs.

We spend New Year's Eve at the Cleopatra Hotel along with Sarwat, its owner, who also owns a pizzeria in Asnières in the Paris suburb, and three friends who came from France to join us: Agnès Niox-Château, as well as Laurence and Philippe de Grandmaison. They are quite determined to walk with us for a day or two. Having them here reminds us that we have fallen behind schedule. It makes us feel like horses hurrying on their way back to the stables. We had planned to finish our trek in three years. There are more than a thousand kilometers to go. This 31 December is also for us the opportunity to draw up a temporary balance sheet. We can tell from a glance at our logbook that year after year we are getting slower: 5000 kilometers the first year, 4100 the second, and 3440 the third....We are wearying. Have our interest in people and our research taken over the walk? It is also true that the trek has been harder and harder, more and more complex, richer and poorer at the same time. Three years ago, we were freezing in a bunker on the Cape of Good Hope; two years ago, we were sweating in the fairy-like dampness of the Mua mission in Malawi; last year we were singing opera arias in the Simien mountains, in Ethiopia, with a group of Italian tourists whom a local bubbly had made rather tipsy. This year, we are celebrating our entry into 2004 with a furious belly dance which we perform under the rhythmic tutelage of a voluptuous houri with a copious decolletage. Sonia whispers to me: "Watch out, Alex! There is a Slavic saying: 'As the year begins, so shall it end.' Go sit down, or you will be dancing all year."

Final sprint. The first days of the year come one upon another, as do the cities. We are tugging at the machine. Samalot, Beni Mazar, Maghagha, El-Fashn, Beni Suef, Bush, El-Wasitah…Bush? Did you say Bush? Poor village. Something funny happened to us there. Eustaz Effat, the mayor of El-Wasitah, doubtless eager for communication, finds us there with photographers and T-shirts: "Egypt, World Cup 2010." Indeed the country is a candidate to host the soccer World Cup, and this worthy representative of the people figures he can't let two sportsmen come through his merkaz without recruiting them for this noble cause. The cars in his retinue, the officers, orders and counter-orders barked into walkie-talkies create a monster traffic jam. Eustaz enjoys the mess. The end justifies the means. "If Egypt hosted the World Cup, all these problems would be resolved: poverty, development, terrorism…," our bouncy administrator summarizes for us. They're gone. Whew!

But it isn't over; they have prepared a little surprise for us: a little farther on, beside the road, a banquet has been set up for us, with a big cream cake, Pepsis and Fantas by the shovelful as well as a group of traditional dancers. No way to decline. Another lady from Tourism, Mrs. Ikhlas, greets us here all dolled up and perfumed, in a leopard hijab with matching handbag. Her assistant, not really spoiled by nature, is covered in gray and hidden behind heavy glasses for nearsightedness. She refuses my greeting – fine! – but is willing to shake Sonia's hand. When we are seated, a school bus unloads some little costumed dancers who are forced to gesticulate in the ambient clutter that was pathetic enough without these poor grimacing girls. Horrible Bush!

We finally leave, but Sonia remains silent. I try to relax her: "It was done with good intentions! And the cake was good!"

"It's not that. One thing I still can't swallow: Mrs. Ikhlas's assistant covered her hand with a flap of her hijab before she shook mine. In her eyes you could read that I was dirty and she was pure…"

She is interrupted by a spasm that makes her throw up on the roadside the excesses of sugar she has ingested. In the course of things, we learn of the death of thirty-eight French people in the unexplained crash at Sharm el-Sheikh; three days earlier, our Minister of the Interior went to the university al-Azhar to explain to the *ulemas*[18], with the support of the Egyptian government, his bill on the Islamic veil and secularism, and thus try to calm the debate raging in France and around the Mediterranean. At El-Wasitah, an associate of the mayor offers us in his manner his condolences for the loss of our compatriots: "If it is not the hand of a man, it is the hand of God." Always that ambiguity...

Two days later, as I am juggling with oranges while I walk, to entertain Commander Hani who is limbering up his limbs in our company, a taxi arrives in the wrong direction. He stops beside us; the doors open and out jump Florence Tran and Pascal Cardeilhac. This is the young couple who have been working patiently and passionately on our footage for two years. They took on our trek while it was in progress, at the request of Stéphane Millière, which is why we know them less well than they know us – they have reviewed more than three hundred hours of our reels. First and moving encounter. She is a loquacious petite Eurasian in whom one senses a perpetual questioning that is constantly simmering. He is an intelligent mixture of the Pyrenees and Great Britain, his feet solidly planted on the ground like a rugby prop and a view from on high that observes things with benevolent causticity. Together they form a most creative team. They have come to join us for our last two days before Cairo where we are to screen our first six twenty-six-minute episodes in a recording studio which they have reserved for us. We have a week in which to write the commentaries for these six films and synch them with the images....There's work to be done!

In the evening, we end up after much waffling from the police in the Malak Mikael church in el-Badrashayn. Florence has big blisters and aches. Pascal has suffered less, with his long legs. They

---

[18] The guardians of legal and religious tradition in Islam.

are going to discover that the difficulty of the trek is less in the walking itself than in its secondary aspects: no showers, a dinner of cold, greasy falafel, visits from the neighbors, policemen, priests. Having to talk about ourselves, forget ourselves, forget the pains of the day, strike out our intimacy....We could have gone to a hotel this evening; but they would have been missing what for three years has constituted half of our lives. The salt of Africa. Going to sleep drained from fatigue covered with sweat, hope and testimonials.

Cairo, Friday 9 January 2004, day 1108, 31 km, 12,810th km

It has broken through the horizon of the vague, grungy suburb. A pure diamond, it has risen a little higher with each step, pushing its tons of stone above the greasy spoons and scwer-canals: Cheops. A wave of emotion sweeps over us and washes away our recent trials. Yet Middle Egypt has been good to us; everyone has worked hard to make possible our crossing of the country: ministries, policemen, governors, Copt monks, but we are mentally and physically on our knees. Too much forced march, too much forced empathy. Having to understand why so many youths sing their hatred of Israel; having to put ourselves in the place of thousands of other people who suffer from petty, latent religious persecution, having to understand the resentment of a people without hope. The sudden vision of this pyramid that popped up around a corner takes it all away. This is the milestone, the pivot, the measure we are so awaiting, to which our hopes have been aspiring for so long. How many horizons, how many skies before the leaden sky notched by this monument built five thousand years ago for the love of eternity?

The notion of eternity must not have been very old at the time of Cheops; yet it was the Egyptian civilization that probably materialized it best. Since then, the faith of Man in eternity has never ceased to weaken. Today, it is nevertheless more than ever the greatest mystery, in its intimate marriage with the infinite.

Sonia seems to respond to my reflections: "It's incredible that five thousand years ago a man might have said to himself: Though my life be ephemeral, my tomb shall be eternal."

"Can you imagine how many men and bodies have disappeared ever since, swallowed up by the earth?"

"Cheops's also, moreover, which has still not been found!"

"Besides, I am curious to know what Jean-Pierre Corteggiani[19] is going to tell us on this topic…"

We slowly pick up the pace, lose our policemen in the bottlenecks, take off, find them again, climb the slope leading to the Giza plateau. There it is, immense, immutable, we keep going; Essam el-Moghraby,[20] the eminence grise who has been working for three months in the shadows so our footsteps would lead us here, is awaiting us with a armful of red roses for Sonia. He is our only welcoming committee. We embrace him and keep going; we have a rendezvous with a very old and noble lady, the only one of the seven wonders of the world still extant, the largest monument of gathered stones, and one of the oldest too; the monument of all the extremes; we step over the yellow rope that forbids access to it; fifteen meters, ten meters, five meters, contact.

---

[19] The Egyptologist responsible for scientific and technical relations of the IFAO (Institut français d'archéologie orientale).

[20] Director of Masr Studios where we are going to record the commentary for our films.

CHAPTER
36

The Pyramid and
the Butterfly

EGYPT

Cape to Cairo, it's done! It spins in our cleared-out heads. In silence, holding each other around the waist, we twice walk all the way around the pyramid. We have a thought for Ewart Grogan, the first man to achieve a crossing of the continent by land route, in 1900. The spirit of it was different. The purpose was to win the heart of a beautiful heiress whose father had refused him her hand. And also to open inner Africa to British colonizers – and to Cecil Rhodes, who dreamed of a railway from Cape Town to Cairo. Of the totality of the itinerary, Grogan only walked twelve hundred kilometers. The rest was done by sedan chair, by steamboat on the great lakes, and by train from Khartoum onwards. Another small difference: to survive, he had to kill a dozen people en route. Other times, other mores. Who said Africa was safer before?

We pass in front of a sign that says, as if to tempt us: *No climbing*. "That's not so certain!"

In the evening, at the Hotel Longchamps, Sonia empties her guts. Gastritis? Emotion? Florence goes to buy some medicine. A drop. Two drops. In doubt, she also bought a pregnancy test. The

541

blotter paper is impregnated with what it takes. In the little window on the plastic stick a little blue band appears: it takes two for a confirmation. Suspense! Our eyes, our lives, our future, are riveted on that little bit of moist paper.

"Sonia, I don't think any doubt is possible....Look, the second band is coming through."

"Not really....Oh!"

"Hee hee! We are all speechless....Here's a baby who begins its life with a simple bar code: two! 'Welcome to a world of brutes, little Chick!'" We are stunned, eyes wide open, facing this new reality invading our lives. Fleeting moment of fate.

Sonia, who has curled into my arms, suddenly has a worry: "Do we say it? Or keep it a secret for ourselves?"

"I don't think we can. But we will have to resist family pressures that will join forces to get us to end our trek."

The next day, we go see Dr. Sameh Sourour for a sonogram. The first shock is the heart. It's beating, it's racing, it's drumming like a madman in the loudspeaker. Next is the image. Seeing it with one's own eyes. It pulses, a tiny thing at the center of a little unformed bean....The miracle of life on the march. A formidable marcher, Sonia has all at once become a precious vessel. The doctor comments on our emotion.

"The little round thing is the vitelline sac, the pocket of food for the embryo, which is not yet a fetus. It will become one when it is connected to the feeding system of the placenta. I am going to take some measurements....Hold on now....It is...forty-one days old."

Third shock. Forty-one days already. That's six weeks! We fast-rewind the film; Sonia realizes: "That means I have been pregnant all the way across Egypt!"

"And that we might estimate the baby could say he is *made in Luxor*!"

Dr. Sourour laughs: "You'll have the choice between Rameses and Nefertiti for the first name..."

Sonia remembers: "Do you recall Iman, the wife of Abuna Yonan, who gave me a dress for a little girl?"

As if she had known.

"And the 'Bush' cake you didn't digest? Now you know why."

"I have walked eight hundred kilometers without knowing..."

"It's going to be harder, knowing this. We still have a thousand kilometers more to go....What do you think, doctor?"

"If the baby has stayed attached despite what you have been through, it's because he is a survivor. There is no reason for you to stop, except perhaps for comfort. Let's say that you should be very attentive to your body, ma'am, and not press too much, stop oftener, don't hesitate to take a nap. Sir, it is she who gives orders now!"

"Oh, doctor, that's not new. She has been giving orders since Cape Town!"

The doctor concludes with a big laugh: "Then there is no counter-indication."

A studious week spent writing and recording the commentary of our films, getting used to the idea of being parents, thinking already of our adventure with the past tense, resisting the siren songs that say to us: "Go home! You've done enough. Israel, Palestine, it's too dangerous, it's outside your subject, it's not in Africa any more, it's needless." Sonia asks: "Who was it who was already saying: 'It's all the more beautiful when it is useless?'"

"Wasn't it Cyranette de Ribérac?"[1]

Thanks again to Essam el-Moghraby, we have the privilege of being able to meet the inaccessible director of Egyptian Antiquities, Dr. Zahi Hawass, to communicate to him an exceptional request: we dream of climbing the great pyramid of Cheops, to ratify our "Cape Town to Cairo." He receives us in his socks, very

---

[1] Ribérac is the cradle of Sonia's paternal family, in Dordogne. Thus the analogy with Cyrano de Bergerac to whom belongs this famous tirade, among others.

busy ranting into the telephone, browbeating his secretaries, filing away dossiers. He motions to us to have a seat on a sofa at the end of his office. He is very energetic and very concentrated. I already sense our cause is lost. After a half-hour wait, watching him boil and wondering in what sauce we would be eaten, he finally joins us. After the usual civilities, we come to our request; his answer is unremitting: "No way!"

"But we have hiked thirteen hundred kilometers for that!"

"So? For a million kilometers I would say no."

"After the geographical summit of Africa, Kilimanjaro, we were hoping to conclude our trek with the continent's cultural summit."

He hesitates a second, but thinks better of it: "Impossible, it's too dangerous and it has been forbidden since 1974. No one has been there since, except for a few archeologists: one BBC journalist who paid dearly for it, and today I regret that permission given..."

I go for broke: "Look, *Paris Match* has already devoted two articles to us, the second begins with Kili, the third could begin with the top of the pyramids....You might even come with us!"

He doesn't fall for the vanity trap and begins to frown with scorn.

"What do you think? That I'm impressed? I have made the cover of the *Times*, the *Herald*, of *Stern*. I only have to pick up the phone to be on the cover of *Paris Match*!"

Okay, I have lost. I shut up. I am nothing but a clumsy turd. He sizes me up, gets up, victorious, and goes over to his desk. Essam tries to lower the tension with his deep, gentle voice: "Zahi, give them this present."

He turns around.

"If I do, I will have three hundred requests on my desk tomorrow..."

Sonia, who had been staying on the sidelines, makes herself heard.

"But no one will have come from so far on foot to ask you."

She makes a point. Essam drives the nail in: "And Zahi! She's bearing a little Egyptian! You can't refuse anything to a pregnant woman!"

Standing in front of his desk, he pretends to be reading a letter. Essam makes a face, we've got to go, we've been dismissed. As we're leaving, Zahi suddenly turns around: "OK, let's do it!"

We fall back on the sofa, overwhelmed by this reversal of the situation. Not daring to believe it. Essam is thrilled. Why this yes after so many no's? Who cares what the reason is! Cheops, here we come! Thank you, Zahi. Thank you also for the suspense. More relaxed, I dare to proffer: "So you're coming with us?"

"Do you think that's all I have to do?"

Right! Again I missed a chance to keep my big mouth shut! Quick! Let's get out before he changes his mind. Bows and abject thanks; we are outside, incredulous and thrilled. Tomorrow, Cheops! *Insh Zahi!*

"Ladies first!" say I to Sonia at the southwest corner of Cheops. With a pull-up she is already atop the first block. I join her. We go up quickly. Panic among the cops. Whistles all over. They are coming from all directions. We are already ten meters up. Fortunately, our personal squad of bodyguards assigned by Hicham Garib, the police colonel responsible for VIPs and more accustomed to American film stars than to French vagabonds, stops and reassures the guardians of the site. Once we have scaled the very large blocks of the base on which we seek crevices in which to wedge our feet, it becomes possible to climb the remaining ones in one big stride with the help of our hands. The sky is blue, the wind is cool, occasional clouds flow by overhead. After the nervous trepidations at the start, we get into a rhythm, an inner jubilation, that wants to savor every second, not letting a single one escape. The repetitive character of the motion lends itself to this delectation. Each stone whispers to us: "No, you aren't dreaming. Nothing can stop you now unless you fall. Be careful where you place your hands!" The stones are smooth and safe on the angles, but fragile, eroded and encumbered with debris on the sides of the pyramid. I risk it to take a picture of Sonia, who stands out magnificently on the edge against the sky-blue background. Zahi warned us: "If you fall, nothing will stop you until you hit bottom. Access to the pyramid was forbidden precisely following the fall of a German who reached the ground completely peeled like a potato." We climb respectfully, conscious of the fact that we are treading on a tomb. The direct view on the Kephren pyramid is breathtaking. We are oriented on the desert side, so we do not yet see Cairo. Silence falls with the wind and light. Step after step, the summit gets closer. We sense it more than we see it.

Under the summit we take a last pause before the final assault. We are hot despite the wind and take off our fleeces. A moment for gathering ourselves. We start up again. Religiously. A knot in the throat. I take Sonia by the hand, movie camera in the other; one block, we breathe out, two blocks, we breathe in, three blocks, the wooden pyramidion appears, four blocks, the terrace becomes visible, last step, emotion overtakes us, there it is, the summit, here we are! We sob with laughter and joy in a spinning embrace. Seconds, minutes of an intensity that is for us eternal. In our craziest dreams we pictured ourselves the two of us at the summit, and there are three of us....Life is ever more inventive than dreams.

A summit is always an apotheosis, the consecration of a long and hard effort. For us, no. Our ascension is an homage to all the folks who have made this waking dream possible. A walking reality. We turn in silence toward the south and meditate on the chain of solidarity each link of which has brought us here since Kilimanjaro: Habiba, Anastasia or Ersumo; Aladdin, Daniel or Fatima; Aziz, Iman or Abraham. A surge of gratitude overcomes us like a wind that tousles your hair. Each of them, despite his poverty or weakness, has brought us this far. If one link had been wanting, we would not be here. It is to them that we dedicate this summit.

Whereupon a butterfly comes and spins about us. Sonia grabs my arm.

"Alex! That butterflly!"

"Yes, so what? Looks like a Belle-Dame[2] butterfly. Suits you well! We have the same ones in France…"

"Yes, but this is the middle of winter, a hundred fifty meters above the desert. There isn't a flower to gather nectar from for kilometers around. How long has it been since we've seen a butterfly?"

She continues: Since I was very young, every time we see a *motilik*,[3] mum has said: 'Look, your grandfather is visiting us!'"

It is a Slovak tradition, a means of preserving the memory of dear persons.…I think of my maternal grandfather, whom I shall never see again. Maybe he has come to wink a wing at us. It would be like him, jokester that he was.

The frail insect spreads his wings in the sunlight of Amun. So fragile on this so-solid pyramid. The butterfly and the pyramid. The first as evanescent as the latter is stable and eternal. Yet miraculously, the butterfly wins over the pyramid. It has something the pyramid will never have. It's alive.

It is true that we have a personal history with butterflies. When I was still very young, living in Canada, I collected them. My favorite was the Monarch, coming all the way from Mexico. I was so impressed. Then they became the theme and decoration of our wedding. There were butterflies everywhere: on the walls, the clothing, the ladies' hats, in Sonia's hair.…What we like about them is their metamorphosis; that they can pass so quickly from worm to flight.

The Belle-Dame does not leave us as we do our photo session, pose in front of the self-timer, running all over the place, balancing on one foot, standing on our hands; it seems to want to play with us. I soon notice, at the center of the terrace of six or seven

---

[2] Scientific name: *Cynthia (Vanessa) Cardui.*
[3] "Butterfly" in Slovak.

meters on each side which constitutes the summit, a block painted in indigo blue.[4]

In the middle of the block is a heart engraved with the initials: A and S. Too much! I swear we didn't do it! Life seems to be like a dictation. Sonia has an inspiration: "Jenny! Her shell! You remember? The young handicapped Kenyan in Bogoria?[5] This is the perfect spot to leave the brooch she gave me."

And with a simple gesture she places the modest jewel carried for so long in her backpack at the center of the blue heart, under this sky so blue, in memory of our love for all those men and women of Africa.

"That way, every time she'll see the pyramid in a photo or on television, she'll say to herself that she came this far with us, and that her shell is up there…"

Our butterfly redoubles its energy, brushes us with its wing and disappears, carried off by a gust of wind.

The next day, we are again at the foot of the pyramid, but this time in the company of a knowledgeable man, Jean-Pierre Corteggiani, the Egyptologist famous for his dives and digs at the Alexandria lighthouse carried out in collaboration with Jean-Yves Empereur. He is a colossus with stiff beard and proud carriage. One senses formidable energy in him, restrained by his good nature, but which requires only a good cause to be unleashed. However, at the door of the immense sepulture, he becomes enigmatic: "You will see that the pyramid has not yet said its last word!"

We enter an irregular, serpentine passage.

"This is the ninth-century breach made by caliph Al-Mamoun – at least that's how tradition would have it. And which ends just behind the granite plugs wedged into the ascending." We come to them. I deduce out loud that the whole upper part was sealed

---

[4] Painted by Jean Verame, a Belgian artist famous for having painted blue some rocks of the Sinai.
[5] See Chapter 13.

off, and therefore that the pyramid was closed, then later violated. Jean-Pierre is amused.

"A hasty conclusion. Al-Mamoun didn't find anything. First let me tell you that everything I am going to relate is the result of nearly twenty years of very intense research by a driven French architect, Gilles Dormion, supported financially by a companion in thought and action, Jean-Yves Verd'hurt. They scrupulously repertoried, when they were still allowed to do so, the slightest details of this pyramid, with a minutia and precision that defy understanding. No one before them had done the work with such rigor. They are, moreover, soon going to publish a book on the subject.[6] They are not fanciful theoreticians, nor "pyramidiots" who appeal to extraterrestrials or telekinesis. They limited themselves to a rational, factual and architectural analysis that will not be unnoticed."

Our hearts racing, we enter the long ascending that takes us into the entrails of the mountain built by human hands.

"Don't forget that the granite plugs we just saw stop at the ceiling of a descending of seventy-two meters that leads to an uncompleted underground chamber."

"Why uncompleted?"

"We don't know. Probably simply because the architects or the pharaoh changed their mind. There is no trace of fracture or accident that would justify its abandonment. It is one of the quite numerous indications that lead one to think the pyramid was not constructed according to a pre-established plan, but an evolving one. It never stopped adapting empirically to what they found, and compensating for errors made. But there is no consensus among Egyptologists. There are two theories: one for the single plan, which holds, with Stadelmann, that all the pyramids have a single 'three chambers' system, and the other, put forward by Borchardt and taken up again by Jean-Yves Lauer or again by Dormion, for an evolving plan."

---

[6] Gilles Dormion and Jean-Yves Verd'hurt, *La Chambre de Chéops* (Paris: Fayard, 2004).

He pauses, catches his breath, and continues: "You see this ascending: it is partly hollowed out in already installed blocks and must originally have been sealed off by lateral portcullises. It is obvious that the architects changed their minds in the course of construction."

We come wide-eyed and short of breath into the "Grand Gallery," the floor of which slopes up to a platform, a true cathedral with corbels.

"This gallery is the only one of its kind in all of Egypt. No one understands its function in the framework of a perfect monument, but it can be explained in the framework of an evolving monument. In fact, it made it possible to leap over the so-called 'Queen's Chamber,' a second abandoned project – which, moreover, was never intended to house the sepulture of a royal spouse. All this in order to arrange what is called the 'King's Chamber,' the entrance of which you see up there at the top. It was indeed intended to become the 'eternal abode' of Cheops but you will see that it was never used. Let's go there!"

The climb into this grand gallery is an unforgettable moment; the low-angle lighting magnifies the perfect alignment of the corbeled ceiling. On the landing, before the entrance of the King's Chamber, Jean-Pierre points out to us, clear at the top on the left, above our heads, the orifice of a shaft.

"Just imagine for a second that you are tomb raiders: where will you start digging your shaft ?

"I would say, here on the left, or on the right, in the softer limestone, to go around the granite lintels…"

"Exactly. But you would do it here, at men's height, not up there seven meters high? Wouldn't you ? Come on, let's go in, you will understand why they did this."

Mesmerized, puzzled and marveling at the same time, we enter the King's Chamber. At the end, on the right, an empty sarcophagus has the pride of place in a slightly disappointing but very high-ceilinged room.

"You must know that each of the nine granite beams that make up the ceiling weighs about fifty tons. Why such masses, do you think?"

"To make a heavy-duty chamber, time-proof and crumble-proof..."

"Exactly. Whence an excess of precautions. Precautions that were the actual cause of a terrible accident. What you don't know is that above these beams there are five relieving chambers with about forty similar lintels; the whole thing weighs more than two thousand five hundred tons and was supposed to protect the pharaoh from any possible collapse. What happened was the opposite, and during the builders' lives, look here! All the granite lintels are fissured on the south side. Let's go back out. As I suggested a while ago, the fact that the shaft is so high and does not lead into the King's Chamber, but very precisely into the first discharge chamber is surely a proof that it is not a shaft made by thieves, but an inspection shaft of the architects themselves; they were the only ones who knew there was an empty space above the King's Chamber and they alone knew how to get to it."

"And what did they observe?"

"You'll never guess! That all the beams were fractured on their extrados on the north side, the opposite side. In fact, the entire southern bedrock of the chamber sagged, putting the beams under such a high pressure that they cracked. I remind you that we are off-center by eleven meters to the south here with respect to the pyramid axis, since it was necessary to pass over the Queen's Chamber, which is barely six meters below. With its fissures, the King's Chamber therefore ran the risk of collapsing at any time. They temporarily shored it up, as is shown by the black traces left by the wooden stays on each beam, but despite that, one can reasonably conjecture that the pharaoh's remains were hidden in a safer place."

We are aghast. What an immense fiasco such an event must have been, coming right at the end of the building process! We go back out to the upper landing and come back down to the lower landing of the Grand Gallery, the beginning of the passageway to the Queen's Chamber, mysteriously sealed off by a grill in recent days. Jean-Pierre summarizes.

"To recapitulate, we have an uncompleted subterranean chamber, a Queen's Chamber with no protection system and a defective King's Chamber. So where is Cheops?"

"Maybe he's not in the pyramid?"

"Why then did they prevent access to it with the granite plugs? In fact, he could still be there in an as-yet unknown chamber. And here we enter into the quick of the subject. Other Egyptologists are also searching for this chamber, but in the wrong place. It is very unlikely, for example, that it is to be found at the end of the so-called 'ventilation' shafts running out of the Queen's Chamber that weren't connected to it in the past. The only possible location, it seems to me, is at its immediate vicinity, in the core of the pyramid, and more precisely below it..."

"Why?"

"Because we find there a certain number of anomalies that impel us to that conclusion."

"But didn't the looters carry out digs in that chamber?"

"Yes, toward the east, during Antiquity, in the extension of a mysterious niche that leads nowhere, but which was no doubt, as Dormion has shown, a service chamber to operate the portcullises which might be below. The second dig was undertaken by Colonel Vyse, who, in 1837, dug vertically, but the poor fellow stopped a meter and a half too soon. By continuing a little farther, he might have discovered the passageway leading to an unknown chamber and, in all probability, to the intact Cheops' chamber."

"But how can one be so sure of its existence?"

"I will spare you the cluster of other convergent indications, notably on the flooring, but there is one that is hard to contradict: at three meters and a half beneath the chamber, a georadar has detected a horizontal rectilinear structure a little more than a meter wide, which is located exactly in the east-west axis of the pyramid. In plain language, that's called a passageway. And passageways are meant to go somewhere aren't they? It is already in itself a shattering breakthrough discovery – I remind you that since Al-Mamoun's break-in, nothing new has been found in this monument – apart maybe from the upper and empty relieving chambers, but when you look at the sections and ground plans of the pyramid, you realize that said passageway would lead, westwardly, to the absolute heart of the pyramid! What better spot could you dream of for a royal burial chamber?"

"And the georadar can't be wrong?"

"It's the same apparatus that is used to find the cavities and measure the risks of sagging under the planned route of the TGV.[7] It had better be reliable, don't you think?"

"Then why don't they dig?"

"Ah! Everything is there! Touching the Great Pyramid is a delicate issue. Gilles Dormion and Jean-Yves Verd'hurt are not Egyptologists, and they are going against the hypotheses of certain 'specialists' who have done everything they can to persuade the Egyptian authorities to refuse them the necessary authorizations for their work on the pretext that they are just 'amateurs.' As if that were a flaw! They are forgetting a little quickly that by their observations alone they discovered unknown relieving chambers in the Meidum pyramid, whereas no Egyptologist had suspected their existence. But maybe there are other interests in play that we don't see."

"What interests could be more important for tourism in Egypt and the entire world than the discovery of the chamber of Cheops?"

"I don't know, but let me tell you that if they found the burial furnishings of Cheops, little Tutankhamun, the child-pharaoh who hardly reigned at all, buried hastily in the tomb of the high priest

---

[7] French high-speed train (*train à grande vitesse*).

Ay, they can forget it and go play golden marbles! In any case, with Cheops, we get to absolute myth. I hope interested persons will soon understand the importance of the stakes or that their curiosity will ultimately carry the day. But, well, wait and see, the pyramid was there, is there and will still be…"

To test Sonia's strength, and before announcing the news of her pregnancy to our families, we decide to go see the sea at Alexandria, on foot naturally. This diverticulum of two hundred fifty kilometers is not on our itinerary, it is a luxury, but we think that a continent should be crossed from sea to sea!

Hicham Garib, our police colonel, asks us to go by way of the desert superhighway and not by the delta so he can more easily guarantee our protection. No more tanks and cars: policemen will relay each other on foot; Frenchmen are not the only ones who can walk! Delighted, we leave Cairo from the precise point where we stopped, which is the northeast corner of Cheops. Mohammed is today's policeman, in street shoes and black suit, ill concealing a prominent automatic pistol; kind and superprotective since he learned that Sonia is pregnant; he takes us by the hand to cross crowded roads, cocoons us, adorable. At every opportunity I repeat *"Zaoudjati Haamil!"*[8] That makes our interlocutors melt. I draw this formidable weapon with no hesitation: in Egypt it is an extraordinary passkey.

Leaving Cairo is hell. The highway has no shoulders or sidewalks, we walk a tightrope. After an hour of this balancing act, exhaust gas and horns, Mohammed begins to limp pathetically. He is done in and decides to hitchhike: he gets dropped off every kilometer at a shooting distance, and waits for us. The next day they send us Sayed, who informs us that poor Mohammed was hospitalized for synovial effusion. We have finally left the conurbation behind us. The highway plunges straight into the desert, lined with

---

[8] My wife is pregnant!

huge advertising billboards planted in the ground, every hundred meters as far as the eye can see. Never saw anything like it. Among them, a poster for the World Cup candidacy in 2010 is sadly coming unglued, revealing a poster for the 1997 candidacy....It reminds us of our clownish roadside dance at Bush. At the seventh kilometer, Sayed gives up, paralyzed with cramps. He climbs into trucks and meets us from time to time. We are more and more free. Every fifteen minutes we are passed by trucks carrying chicken manure, trailing behind them a terrifyingly pestilential pong. Each time, under the shock, Sonia doubles up, floored by nausea. It is cold. Everything is ugly in the extreme. We are voluntarily committed to a week in absurdia.

The third day, our third policeman is tougher. He escorts us in silence all day. In the evening at Deïr el-Makarios, in Wadi el-Natron, we discover that his feet are bleeding. He has not complained. He did not limp. Respect. Silence among the monks after the cacophony of the day! We are aghast. Here too, there is a *husn*, a dungeon, but this one has many times been used since the Deïr is situated on the route of the great Berber and Arabic invasions. Abuna Erinaos shows us, lifting a trapdoor in the fourth-century chapel, the skull of St. John the Baptist. How many heads are lent to the poor Anchorite? We had already seen him at the mosque of the Omeyyads in Damascus, who also claim it. John the Baptist is their prophet Yahya. There, it came "rolling," whereas here it arrived with the followers of St. Mark the Evangelist. Between the two versions, we opt for the most credible. Besides, we need a "leveler of roads" to hope to reach Israel without impediment. A suicide attack has once more killed dozens in Tel Aviv. The tension is rising dangerously, we are afraid of not being able to get through Rafah, the border post between Egypt and the Gaza Strip. Like Hamlet facing the historical skull, Abuna Erineos concludes: "We are but brief guests on this earth..."

Life is just a blink in an empty socket.

The fourth day, they don't send a policeman. They have let us go! We land, in the evening, in a house under construction where the bed is impregnated with a strong stench of cat urine.

"To bed in the cat litter tonight!"

"Come on! I can barely hold back the nausea."

"But look! It's still better than rat piss."

"Do you think I have to take my shoes off to sleep?"

"Of course. Have you seen the fresh tar smothering them?"

Like every evening in 1127 evenings, I record the day's impressions in my notebook. For me, there is no travel without writing and no writing without travel. Yet the harvest is meager today, except that Sonia compels my admiration and that I am living at her rhythm. Oh, yes, I almost forgot! Our fine host, Hassan el-Kureïshi, offered us a revelation.

"All that is pre-Islamic is of no interest to me. You who are believers, you know the Bible, the Qu'ran, what interest can you find in all these pagan gods with the heads of birds, cows or jackals? It's not serious. In Egypt, we are thoroughly annoyed by your fascination for these ruins of temples and scenes of offerings made to green or blue gods. We must not be turned toward the past but toward the future. Islam is the only Truth. You are not tourists like the others; you come to see us and not these pagan ruins, that is good. You are on the right path."

At dawn, Sonia admits she has slept poorly. I film her waking up.

"It was the mosquito ballet last night! I didn't get a wink of sleep! I had to cover my head with our mosquito net, but over my hood, because if there is contact with the skin, there is a bite, and there is necessarily a bite given the length of my nose!..."

She bursts out laughing. We are squatting in this sordid place, she hasn't slept, she didn't eat well the evening before, wasn't able to undress or wash, and she is jesting as she wakes up. This girl is an angel from the sky.

"I have to tell you that someone tried to enter during the night."

"I didn't hear anything."

"Well, sure, you big moron, with your ear plugs! I see how well you protect your little family…"

And then she tells me, laughing, how she wanted to pull out her tear gas canister to fend off anything that might happen, her tribulations, how she jabbed me repeatedly with her elbow, before being urgently called by morning sickness. My scruples paralyze me. Ought we continue? Anyone intelligent would stop in these conditions. I no longer know what to think. Each time I talk to her about it, she answers: "If I make it, it is for all those women we have met, who can never say 'stop.' I am not doing anything extraordinary, I go on, as they do, for them…"

The sixth day, at Amariya, thirty kilometers before Alexandria, before the end of this torture on the superhighway, we come to a halt in front of a McDonald's. Forgive us, but we rush in. For two vagabonds, it is a mirage come true. You cannot imagine what the view of a space full of shiny, empty surfaces can be like, with Céline Dion or Madonna in the background, toilets so clean that you could sleep in them better than in the bed where we spent the night. For the person who has not had one in three years, a Big Mac is gustatory fireworks: acid and sugar, soft and crunchy, sweet and smoky all at once.…Maybe you don't know this, but that is one masterpiece of a sandwich! Seeing ourselves in the mirror reveals the truth to us: three years of nomadism is about the limit. Hirsute and dirty, dressed in superposed layers, our backpacks covered with little plastic bags full of useless things that we have not been able to resign ourselves to throwing away for fear of needing them.…We have become bums. Oh, to stay somewhere! Never to leave again…as long as there is a view!

Today we have said goodbye to the lion. We passed him in flesh and bones in a tiny animal park beside the highway, lying on his rock, apparently in good health, but his gaze lost in the distance, to the south. Despite his despair, he found the strength, before the shameful eyes of the witnesses, to honor a submissive lioness. The reproduction instinct is the strongest. Even in prison. The king of Africa, one day before the end of our hike the length of the continent, gave us a bow, handsome, muscular and strong, in his pathetic cage. We have not forgotten that he has spared us.

The seventh day, we enter an Alexandria animated by the festivities of aït el-Kébir. From a suburban garage where they are mass-slaughtering sheep, a man covered with blood, his apron dripping, runs up to us drunk with joy to embrace us, to invite us to stay, have lunch, sleep. Reflexively we refuse this hospitable Jack the Ripper. He takes it badly. Of course. I immediately regret it. For you have to understand him. But you have to understand me. All day we watch cars go by covered with bloody handprints: on the bumpers, the hoods, the windows, everywhere. On the walls of houses too. In memory of God's first gesture toward men: the arms of Abraham restrained by the angel at the moment when the old man was going to sacrifice Isaac. The beginning of Judaism...and of Islam.

From a distance, across the lagoon of Lake Mareotis, Alexandria appears, bristling with buildings strung out along the coastline. We know there is a sea beyond that wall. Factories and smokestacks, industrial zones and superhighways are the decor of our last straight line. We forge ahead without drinking or eating. Eager to get it over with. We make a pause under the equestrian statue of Alexander the Great, the adventurer with no sepulture. From there, I suddenly catch, at the end of an avenue to the north, a small verdigris rectangle wedged between two apartment houses; euphoric, I point it out to Sonia.

"The sea!"

We come out soon after onto the corniche, wind in our faces, near the great library, in the embrace of Mediterranean spray. The sea is raging. A week of suffering for this fleeting second. We binge on iodine, relieved, sated. Before us, the fort of Qait Bay, the base of Alexandria's lighthouse. On the beach, with our feet in the water, we inscribe in the wet sand the kilometers on our pedometer: 13,051st kilometer. It is immediately swallowed up by a wave. Vanity. 1,131 days. Vanity. The continent this time is for good all behind us; immense; we can no longer go any farther. We have come on foot from the Cape of Good Hope. Because Good Hope is what it took. And because that's what we had.

In Cairo, we are lodged by the Samy's, French civil servants whom we met in Aswan, automatically assigned to the role of good Samaritans. From their home, we prepare our new departure towards the end of the Rift, our original objective. We receive a phone call from Ayman Abd el-Kader, our excellent colonel, who unrolled the Egyptian red carpet for us. He invites us to lunch to introduce to us his wife and children of whom he has so often spoken. We find him in a small apartment in a southern suburb of Cairo. A young veiled woman is looking after the children. I ask Ayman whether his wife will be there.

"But she is here. That's her..."

I realize my gaffe, ashamed and embarrassed. "*Malesh!* Excuse me. I did not recognize you, I had seen a photo of you and you look much younger in person..."

She blushes with pleasure. Ayman is flattered and replies: "Since I saw you two months ago she has decided to wear the veil and not wear makeup any more. I discovered this only a week ago, and it was a shock to me. I also had the impression that she looked younger....But it's her choice, so I respect it."

The young woman with angelic face feels called upon to justify herself. "I know that in France you are against the veil, but I decided to put it on because I have returned to my studies at the university since I was pining away without Ayman.[9]

Sonia doesn't see the connection.

"At the university everyone wears the veil, so that way I fit in better. At first, I went without a veil, and it was very hard, they

---

[9] Policemen can return home only every two months.

thought I was a Copt, they both tried to pick me up and insulted me. With the veil, they leave me alone…"

She begins to laugh.

"Besides, it saves me time in the morning: I no longer have to do my hair and my eyes.…All that is behind me now."

In Cairo we also meet journalists. One of them invites us to her place for an interview in front of a television camera. It all goes fine. Every time the operator pushes the button of his camera to begin a clip, he mutters: *"Bismillah I rarmen I rahim"* so everything will work right. And I imagine a cameraman on a Parisian set doing the same: "By the most powerful and merciful God!" Unfortunately, the camera's battery fails. While someone goes to get another one, we meet the owner of the place, who runs an upscale travel agency, in line with a concept of ecological tourism dear to the Anglo-Saxons. The man is appealing, tall, cosmopolitan, well dressed in expensive clothes. He is fascinated by our adventure because he has visited the great parks of Africa by car. But he is worried about the remainder of our itinerary: he wants to know why we want to end up in Israel. The geographical argument about the Rift does not satisfy him, he want us to end in Ramallah.… While we are replying to him – it is not in our plan to go through Palestine – a little boy comes through the room.

"Tahal Yassine!" our host calls out.

The child of about five carries a doll of a man in arms, a sort of Oriental "G.I. Joe" with a beard and white skullcap. Walid explains: "You should go see Yasser Arafat in the Moqata! Look at me, for example, I named my son in honor of Sheikh Yassine, the founder of Hamas. Every day I tell him he should take up the torch of the struggle against Israel."

Then he leans over the nice kid with big black eyes: "Yassine, show us your bin Laden doll."

Our blood freezes. The sequel is nauseating. Grenades and cartridge belts, sword and plastic Kalashnikov, violent antisemitism and persecution delirium.

"Every day I tell Yassine before he goes to sleep that he must hate the Jews and the Americans and that one day he must drive them out of Israel, until the last one, since I was unable to do so, nor was my father…"

We try to understand what is behind such hatred: "But aren't we about the same age? You haven't known the wars against Israel; why do you resent them so?"

"We are poor because of them! And because of colonization before them. Today we are the victims of American imperialism everywhere on earth, but fortunately there is Europe, and since you are representatives of Europe, you must end your trek in Palestine, not in Israel…"

We can't take this refrain any longer. We leave him with his little Yassine and Bin Laden doll. His wife is sorry about the way the conversation turned out. Not I. It is important to know that there are things that Ralph Lauren jeans and a Lacoste polo shirt can't hide…

During these preparatory days, we learn that the border post at Rafah will open exceptionally for us on the Israeli side. The Egyptian authorities comply. They couldn't do better. This saves us a detour of three hundred kilometers toward Taba and Eilat, the only border crossing open to Westerners. But it makes us miss the St. Catherine monastery, so we decide to make a quick side-trip before we resume our trek.[10]

Then it's the real departure. We definitively leave Cairo on foot, towards Ismailia, which we reach in three days. The governor wants to meet us there. Magdy Selim, director of the Mercure Hotel in that city, invites us there. Fouad Gamal Eldin is the eighth governor we have met. A Francophile and Anglophone, he has traveled everywhere, hunted in Zimbabwe, visited the Louvre. Of our affable conversation, we remember two things: Claude François

---

[10] Our discovery of St. Catherine's can be found on our website.

was born in Ismailia, and the governor is thinking of transforming the home where he was born into a museum. When we tell him about the poverty of the real Egypt through which we have come, he replies wistfully: "Our greatest problem is population growth. There are a million and a half more Egyptians every year. No economic growth can catch up with such a human wave. On every level: sanitation, education, construction, energy, hospitals, we are overtaken by the growing demand. We try to gain space on the desert, but the race is lost in advance, since it will take ever more water. Our religion forbids all birth control. It is a very sensitive subject between the government and Al-Azhar University."

The next day we visit the city with Noura Sayed, a representative of the governorate. She looks like a perfect Parisian of the 1980s: permanent and white jabot on a navy blue silk shirt, and loose trousers; careful makeup, gold jewelry. She takes us to visit the Suez Canal and the home of Ferdinand de Lesseps, then our conversation takes another turn.

"I am the only person in the entire governorate who does not yet wear the veil. Every day, my nine-year-old son comes home from school asking me to wear it, like his friends' mothers. It's a fashion phenomenon that came in with the new, light fabrics from Asia. When I was younger, only the fat, ugly or old women wore the veil willingly, still others were forced to by their husbands, but there was a choice. Today it has become the norm."

"Is it explained by a religious renewal?"

"Not just that. Above all a return to the look, the superficiality of appearance. It's very hypocritical! Like the mens' *zibiba*. That annoys me!"

"What's the *zibiba*?"

"It's the spot of hypocrites. Haven't you seen it, in the middle of the forehead? A brownish spot, or a sort of callus? The Egyptians do that to show they are good believers always prostrate on the ground. In reference to a surate in the Qu'ran[11] that says that one 'recognizes the Prophet's companions, for one sees on their forehead the evidence of their prostration on the ground.' They burn their flesh with garlic and needles, others use acid, but no one admits it. There again, it's an Egyptian fashion. Other Muslims in the Maghreb don't do that."

"Yet you are yourself a Muslim?"

"Of course. But my Islam is something inside me, not outside. To me the veil is a religious sign which one has no right to soil by bad thoughts or ugly words. And I do not feel good enough yet to wear the veil. I was raised by nuns. To them also the veil was the sign of their vows. If a sister acted badly, she sullied her veil. At my age, the girls are all veiled but make bitchy remarks behind each others' backs. I will not wear the veil until I have made my hadj,[12] in a few years....When I am retired."

"What do you think of the new law in France?"

"Your government is right. You ought not give in. All the Muslim women in the world are watching you. You are the only hope for a secularization of Islam. Here it is not possible, the religious have too much influence. Only in Europe can a modern Islam be born. Here they try to Islamize modernity, not modernize Islam. As long as you don't understand that, you will be the victims of a game of dupes."

The next day, we cross the Suez Canal on the impressive Japanese bridge at el-Kantara: six suspended kilometers. We are leaving African soil. The canal has been considerably widened since it was first dug. It measures four hundred meters across and the cargo ships go by in both directions, like trains. Back in the desert, we see them passing between the dunes, true mountains of metal making their way between two seas: fifteen thousand ships a year. Over a third of world maritime traffic comes through here, especially oil on its way to Europe and North America.

---

[11] Surate 48, verse 29.
[12] Pilgrimage to Mecca.

In a cafeteria, an interview we gave after our conversation with the governor of Ismailia is on the television. Everyone turns to look. People come to offer us Cokes and sandwiches. During the afternoon, truckers stop to shake our hand and congratulate us. We are happy to be leaving Egypt in such gay spirits. In the evening, our hosts fight over who gets to put us up. They gesticulate and shout, all pulling in opposite directions. Dear Egyptians! Attaching and exhausting at the same time. On the television they announce a new suicide attack in Tel Aviv: a massacre. Sonia despairs out loud: "How many innocent victims will it take? If the suicide volunteers blew themselves up without taking any victims, their acts would have much more impact. Look at Jan Palach,[13] they still talk about him as a universal myth of resistance more than thirty years later. What discredits the sacrifice of young Palestinians is that they try to kill as many people as possible. They would be more useful to their cause if they took no victims. And for them the result would be the same…"

I ironize: "You ought to be recycled as communications consultant to the martyr brigades…"

At El-Arich, we feel a sort of border effervescence. Much construction of villas and *Sam'suffit*'s[14] on the shore. Perpetual, uncompleted construction, ostentatious, verandas and patios, tiles and colonnades, stucco lions and showy porticos. A sarcastic functionary of the governorate freely comments while we in his company devour a grilled fish, in a grass hut on the Ananda beach.

"All that is diverted Palestinian money. The European funds which you give serve for the construction of these houses. Gaza is a leaky basket. Weapons are not the only thing that passes in the tunnels! With my wages I can't manage to save enough money to get married, so it disgusts me to see all this. Especially when you

---

[13] A young Czech student who set fire to himself on 2 January 1969 to protest the Soviet occupation.

[14] *Ça me suffit*: ironic term for a house that puts all its fancy appearances up front: decorations, ornaments, porticos, garden mills, kitsch fountains, lions, etc.; literally: "Enough for my content."

know that this money ought to have been used to build schools or dispensaries in Gaza..."

Sunday 29 February 2004, after thirty-four kilometers of walking, we reach the border post of Rafah, under construction. Red granite from Aswan and pylon gates, the building will be pharaonic. That proves that the Egyptian government believes in the imminent normalization of its relations with the Palestinian Authority and the opening of the Gaza Strip, which will then orient a significant share of its economy toward Egypt. The Egyptian formalities are rapid. We were expected. Then an officer makes us pass into a strange fallow zone, cut in two by a temporary wire fence. He indicates that we are to pass through a hole; I tease him: "Is that the border?"

He laughs. It's true Egyptians like laughing. It's the only way to handle them: make them laugh! Our last Egyptian. We leave him light-hearted. On the other side, a minibus takes us aboard to do two hundred meters that are forbidden to pedestrians on a stretch of collapsed road. Suddenly, around a wall heaves into view, above a small bunker, white and blue against the blue sky, the "Magen David," the Israeli flag.

ISRAEL–PALESTINE

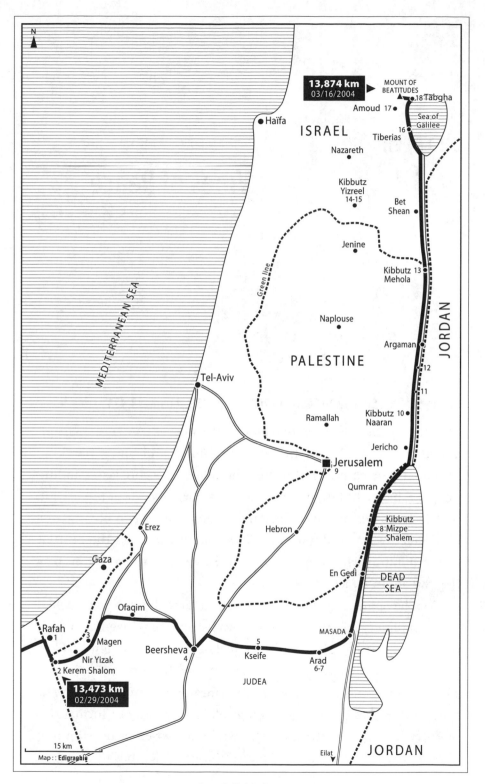

N

MEDITERRANEAN SEA

13,874 km
03/16/2004

MOUNT OF BEATITUDES
Amoud 17
18 Tabgha
Sea of Galilee
Tiberias 16

Haïfa

ISRAEL

Nazareth

Kibbutz Yizreel 14-15

Bet Shean

Jenine

Kibbutz 13 Mehola

JORDAN

Green line

Naplouse

PALESTINE

Argaman
12

Tel-Aviv

11

Ramallah

Kibbutz 10 Naaran

Jericho

Jerusalem
9

Qumran

Erez

Hebron

Kibbutz 8 Mizpe Shalem

Gaza

En Gedi

DEAD SEA

Ofaqim

Rafah 1

3

Magen

MASADA

Nir Yizak

Beersheva 4

Kseife 5

Arad 6-7

2 Kerem Shalom

13,473 km
02/29/2004

JUDEA

15 km

Eilat

JORDAN

Map : : **Edigraphie**

Israel–Palestine

CHAPTER
37

Vines of Peace

ISRAEL

Kerem Shalom, Sunday 29 February 2004, day 1155, 41 km, 13,473ʳᵈ km

She disappeared between two blocks of concrete. A fleeting vision. There she reappears in front of us. Blond and curly, her long unbound hair cascades onto her shoulders, her sunglasses hiding her gaze, her tight fatigues underscoring her athletic yet not ascetic body, she carries her M16 diagonally between her two breasts: our first Israeli woman. Bombshell. An assistant examines the bottom of the minibus with a mirror on wheels; we pass the anti-ram barrier; we are in Israel.

We have never crossed a border so quickly, nor felt such a contrast. Everything is clean and well-kept, organized and well thought-out. It has completely the feel of Europe. It might be Florida. It is Israel. Arriving by airplane would have been less stark. Miami palms and air-conditioned terminal; a calm and sanitized space, we are led by young, smiling soldiers toward our formalities of entry into the territory. A little bald man observes us, standing back a little. Surely that's our man. Indeed. He comes to us.

"Good day! I am Gelad Menashe, the post chief, I was expecting you, welcome to Israel. We unpack, under the amused glances of two chubby women customs officials, the repulsive contents of our backpacks, dirty socks with holes in them, used plastic bags, rags damaged by the sun, the salt and the trail. From my notebook, one of them takes our first article from *Paris Match*. She rounds up some of the other girls. It's a field day in the terminal! Everyone wants to see the magazine, they can't believe we have walked for so long. One of our photos was taken at Olduvai with an *Australopithecus boisei* skull which we are holding in our hands at eye level. One brunette, short hair and a big heater at her belt, remarks: "There were three of them at the outset...and that one gave up!"

We burst out laughing. Welcome home to humor. Sonia rubs her stomach, saying: "In fact, it's the opposite! There were two of us at the outset, and there are three of us now..."

They all melt and caress her tummy. Gelad restores a little order to the ranks and leads us to his office. He is a mountain bike fanatic. On the wall he has framed his favorite photo: a huge tree to the branches of which are attached a dozen bicycles like hanging fruits. Unexpected creativity in a border functionary.

"It was during a trip we made with friends in the Taurus mountains in Turkey." Beside it, in a smaller frame, an envelope bears three signatures. "Arafat, Clinton and Peres together on the same piece of paper. That is my own way of believing in peace. I was not able to meet Rabin before he was assassinated by an extremist Jew, so I replaced him with Peres. This is my own Camp David."

He takes us to the cafeteria. On the way, we exchange our Egyptian pounds into shekels. The cashier addresses us in perfect French: "I am a Tunisian Jew. I grew up in Paris."

Another thing we had forgotten. That 20% of the Jews living in Israel are Francophones or of French origin. Over a sandwich, a handsome bloke joins us. I recognize him. That amuses him. He was one of the Cerberi in black glasses who, finger on the trigger, framed our entry into the terminal, among a group of

Palestinians. Chestnut hair combed back, square chin, sexy nose and big hazelnut eyes flecked with gold, Ofer Buchnik has the profile of a ladykiller. Not even to mention the one meter ninety and the pectorals. In the course of the conversation, we learn that his job here is half-time, in fact he has a farm ten kilometers from here. For us that's just perfect. He quickly reaches the same conclusion. He invites us after a quick phone call to his wife. Gelad specifies: "You cannot begin walking precisely from here because we are surrounded by Palestinians and snipers shoot at us at every opportunity. This terminal is nonetheless a service we offer them: no Israeli or tourist comes through here, only Palestinians. And the Egyptians open their side only on the condition that we man the post; otherwise they would close the border. But that's the way it is. Every time we get shot at, we close the post for a few days; it harms only the Palestinians. I am sorry for them, they are the victims of their extremists."

We climb into an armored truck. In fact, we were not yet really in Israel but in an isolated no man's land between Egypt and the Gaza Strip, which is, however, the international border of Israel. While we are on the road, Gelad explains: "On the right, Egypt, on the left, Palestinian villages. Beneath us pass the tunnels of arms smugglers. We find one every week. In general, they come out in private houses. That's why we flatten them down. Here we are; we have only three kilometers to go between these two fences..."

"That means you make us cheat by three kilometers!"

"Yes, that's true! But that's better than your getting shot at. You see the twisted post there? Three years ago, one of my female employees, Noah Dahan, was killed here. We left it as it was so we wouldn't forget. That is also the reason why we come to the terminal with an armored vehicle, after parking in Kerem Shalom. When we go by, they practice shooting at us, but they know they can't hurt us."

Kerem Shalom. The vines of peace. Two large iron gates open onto green fields as far as you can see. Our second vision of Israel.

An empty space, flat and green. On the other side of the border, just two hundred meters to our right, is desert.

We thank Gelad. On the hood of his car, Ofer draws us a little map to guide us to his farm, in the *moshav* of Yated. We are loosed into an empty countryside, onto a road of perfect asphalt decorated with white paint and reflectors. We have had the police on our tail for so long that we are completely disoriented. Not a man in sight. The space is freed from any demographic pressure. The land is there to produce. It is inhabited elsewhere. In organized places made for that purpose. The cities. This difference in the manner of occupying the territory is a physical shock for us. We walk in silence in a fertile immensity where every square meter has been the object of particular care. In an hour we are in Yated. Ofer and Daniella welcome us here in a pretty, simple house decorated with African sculptures. Daniella is curvy and smiling, easy-going and frank.

"Here this is not a kibbutz. Thirty-two small farms have been grouped into a sort of cooperative without any living in common. We call that a moshav."

A boy comes in with a superb macaw on his shoulder, followed by a little girl with a squirrelish face.

"Here are our children, Hor and Youval. They are just back from Paris, where they went to spend their vacation with an uncle. Come on, let's show you my farm while it's still light out. Don't worry, it isn't big!"

We head toward some huge greenhouses. Ofer is a tomato planter.

"Until last year, I had twenty Palestinian farm workers with whom I had no problem. I paid them three thousand shekels a month, which was good pay for Gaza. I had gone to school with some of them. I had to let them go because of the constant border closings following multiple terrorist attacks – once I almost lost my harvest for that reason. I often have them on the telephone; they have no income now, they are desperate. They live in hell in Gaza.

Hamas forcibly enrolls them and if they refuse they are persecuted. I try to help two families, I get free crates of tomatoes to them, and they sell them to survive..."

We have passed through an airlock and a footbath. The greenhouse is protected by screens. Everything operates by drip irrigation.

"I have four thousand square meters hydroponic and eight thousand square meters in the ground. Now I have only four Thai workers for the same job. I am sad for the Palestinians. They lose everything in this crisis."

At dinner, Daniella tells us that she was supposed to be in the car with Noah Dahan who was shot at. "Noah came by to pick me up. I too work at the terminal. I was pressed for time, my hair was wet. I told her I would get there a little later in my car. She was my office mate. She had founded an association for Israeli-Palestinian friendship that organized picnics of Jewish families on the Palestinian beach at Khan Yunis. Pairings of schools and a fund of school support for the children of Gaza. They adored her. They really chose the wrong target! It was I who found her body and her Renault Express riddled with bullets."

Moved, she unfolds some newspaper clippings. We see Noah, a stout woman, red hair, dressed in black, with a wool hat, shoes with platform heels and an energetic face. The energy of peace.

"Two days later was my birthday, 10 November 2002. I was in complete mourning when there was a knock at the door. A delivery man was bringing me a gift from Noah. I passed out. She had bought it for me by mail. It was the aquarium you see there. It is my most precious possession..."

She pauses while this burning memory surges over her anew. The aquarium purrs behind us. The multicolored fish dance with bubbles to keep the memory of Noah alive.

"A month later, when the border post reopened, I cleaned up her office. Her calendar was open to the page for 7 November, the day before she died, where she had written: *"Berega, Néhémélet, Bli milim!"*[1] That's a song of the Shoah[2]..."

Ofer has a friend who was blown up in a bus. And who survived, quadriplegic. Steve Aberbuch. A former member of the special forces.

"He had found the suicide bomber. He had the time to load his pistol. But not to shoot....Everyone, in this country, has a relative or knows someone who has been hit by a terrorist act. We have to get out of Gaza and the territories. Sharon is going to do it. You shall see! No one believes it, but he is going to do it.[3]"

As in South Africa, our Buchnik friends come to get us on the road the next evening so we can spend another night with them. The walk has been sublime. A green Beauce[4] without the Chartres spires; then the aromas of the Costa Brava in an orange plantation. Wheat! Wheat! And an ostrich farm! And our first poppies! Not a single car horn, not a stop, we have spoken to no one today. Even in the heart of the Sahara that never happened. Nobody here has time to hawk, gawk and stroll. The guys we saw were cellphone-wielding comets. Busy. Ofer has come back to get us in Ofaqim.

Daniella's parents, who speak French, welcome us for dinner in the moshav Magen. Rachel and Baruch came from Morocco in 1948; they met in a kibbutz. He has a furrowed mug and the knotted hands of old peasants; she has all the qualities of homemaker. She takes Sonia to the kitchen to give her the recipe for *harira*, while Daniella shows us her production of gilt cherubs and gouaches. For Rachel is an artist. Youval has a cold. She has spent the day with the scouts, who made her swim across a river. Daniella now shows us the DVD from Youval's recent bat mitzvah. The girl curls into her grandfather's arms. The little film is love condensed: her birth, her diapers, her first patties on the beach, her dolls, her costumes,

---

[1] "In the blink of an eye, one disappears, without a word..."
[2] Holocaust.
[3] Quite prophetic! It was completed a year and a half later on September 12, 2005.
[4] Historical breadbasket plains south of Paris.

her birthdays, her animals, her pals….We watch the progress of a normal little girl's life realizing how much these little moments of joy are "abnormal," exceptional; how many, among the children met over these last years, have had Youval's luck? How many know what childhood is?

And we can't help thinking of these images of Palestinian children wandering by the thousands in the streets of Gaza, a stone in their hands and the follies of adults in their minds. Stolen childhoods.

Ofer and Daniella do not understand our emotion. They expected to bore us with the "cutie pie film." On the contrary, it reveals to us what love and the gift of life imply in the way of eternal investment. To make a child is to accompany it for a long time, take care of it, comfort it with all that love built day by day, which we see happening before our eyes. Youval or our rediscovery of childhood. Sonia now says, touching her stomach: "I cannot manage to believe that he will always be here, he will grow up, he too will experience all those things, he will…"

"Why *he*?"

"You're right, in fact! Why? From the beginning we have been talking about the baby in the masculine, we have even found a boy's name for him."

Youval is embarrassed because we saw her naked as a baby on the beach. To put her at ease I ask her the meaning of what is printed on her T-shirt in the middle of a big heart. She answers me in Hebrew: "*Mashou lé mishou, shéhou mamash mashou mashou.*"

We burst out laughing. Ofer translates for us: "Something for someone who is really exceptional!"

So I follow on by reciting to them a little sentence in Arabic we learnt from our dear friend Francis Amin in Luxor: "*Mashi bé oul lé mashi tégui namshi, alo mashi!*"

It's their turn to have a good laugh. The "Peter Piper picked a peck of pickled peppers" in Hebrew and Arabic, for once united! I translate for Youval since her parents speak Palestinian very well: "One hiker says to another, 'You want to hike? Okay, let's go!'"

The twelve-year-old catches me at my own game: "Can I come hike with you tomorrow?"

At dawn, we learn from the newscast that a Kassam missile fired from the Gaza Strip fell seven kilometers from the house. Ofer takes the news philosophically: "These are homemade devices without any guidance system, that always fall into the fields. But the ugly thing is that they are aiming at the chemical insecticide plant in Nir-Yizak in front of which you passed yesterday....There are already six craters around it and each time they get closer..."

As bad news never comes unaccompanied, we learn that a young Russian Jewish couple, Eitan Kukoi and Rima Novikov, were brutally murdered the day before yesterday on the road between Beersheva and Arad: the road we will be walking on in two or three days...

I worry: "Yet I saw on the map that that road passes very far from Palestine and the occupied territories."

"Yes. But there is no border, no wall or fence there, just pasture lands, so young fanatics easily come down from Hebron through the mountain and fire on cars at night. Usually they withdraw immediately, but there they went to finish the job at point blank range. The miracle is that there was a little girl in the back; she survived....You don't run any risk, since you are passing there in daylight and on foot..."

"Yeah, sure....That's exactly what the Tanzanians told us about the lions in Rungwa!"

There is a sort of fatalistic sorrow in his eyes. He knows that his happiness is fragile. Youval is getting ready. She has laced her walking shoes and put on a little Mickey Mouse backpack full of suckers and Chipsters. Today the objective is to get to Beersheva. After a big bowl of cereal, Ofer drives us back to Ofaqim. Warm embraces with Daniella. She re-opens the car door which she has just closed: "By the way, I forgot to tell you. It's going to be a girl!"

We walk all day in the country with little Youval. She speaks only Hebrew but we are not bored; she is as lively as a brook whose name she bears. We pass bedouins leading their herds of sheep between fields to graze on the wild grass and flowers of the fallow land. Their black wool tents stretched over the roadsides remind us that before being fertile fields, these lands were pastoral and semi-arid, caught between the Negev desert and that of Judea. A phone call informs us that in Canada my younger brother just had a little Jeanne. Two journalists from the *Jerusalem Post* catch up with us for an improvised interview in the buttercups and poppies, since we are giving a lecture at the university in Beersheva tomorrow evening. It is our contact with the Israel Academic Center in Cairo, Dr. Sariel Chalev, who put us in touch with some scientists and anthropologists at the university. They organized it at short notice when they learned that we have some film shorts with us.

In the evening, just before entering the city, Ofer joins us for the final kilometers. Daniella has dropped him off with a load of sandwiches. Long live logistical support! When he learns that his little Youval has knocked down her thirty-eight kilometers without flinching, a father's pride lights up his face.

We have an appointment in a café with Youval Yékutihéli,[5] the historian who has organized the lecture. He recognizes us right away. He hides little myopic eyes behind heavy glasses, over a lovely, calm smile. The handing over of the Poussins takes place in the parking lot. We embrace Ofer, Youval and Daniella, promising to see each other again some day. Our good Samaritan tells us: "This evening I am taking you to the home of Patrice Kaminski, the draftsman for the archeology department, he is French like you. For my part, I will receive you when you reach Arad, in two or three days."

The evening with Patrice is very emotional. It seems moreover that here all the evenings have to be very emotional. Calm with a soft voice, blue wrinkled eyes, straw hair and laughter in the corner of his eye, Patrice is affable. But he doesn't have many funny stories to tell us.

---

[5] Youval can be a man's name as well.

"When they told me you were French, at first I refused to receive you. Finally, I changed my mind. My whole family was deported. Drancy, Auschwitz. By miracle my parents survived, but they were in bad shape. They both died when I was two. I was placed at the Paris DASS.[6] I was a little boy like you see in Dois-neau's photos. You won't believe me, but I was persecuted during my entire childhood…"

We are transfixed.

"They only talk about antisemitism before or during the war, but the reflexes did not just fly out of people's minds at the Liberation. I lived a real martyrdom, after the war. We were persecuted on the pretext that the sufferings endured in Europe were 'our fault.' Bullying, vexations, I was roughed up, kept apart, isolated by my comrades; it was awful. I fled the orphanage and found refuge with prostitutes in Pigalle; I was a messenger for them, I did errands for them.…I came to Israel as soon as I could, in 1979, when I was thirty. So forgive my skepticism. When I see the return of disguised antisemitism in France, it stirs bad memories in me.… There is only one country in Europe where I return every year and really feel at home…"

My throat knotted with shame, I seize the opportunity to change the subject: "Oh? Where's that?"

"Oh, you surely aren't familiar with it. It's a very small country…"

"Malta? Liechtenstein?"

"No, Slovakia."

Sonia almost falls over backwards. Patrice is a fan. He has thrown his lot in with that people. His only friends are Slovaks, he drinks only Slovak, speaks Slovak, listens only to Slovak folk music, dreams in Slovak.…He runs to his computer to show us the site of the webcam that continuously records Narodny Dom square, in Banska Bystrica.

---

[6] *Direction des Affaires Sanitaires et Sociales*, which provides various health and social services. Notably, the care of orphaned children.

"I can't begin the day without spending five minutes on this site. Just watching people go by....But...why are you crying?"

"My mother is from Banska..."

Patrice takes Sonia paternally by her lean shoulder. The evening relaxes; both of them wax emotional with memories of the "Slovak paradise," a famous place in the Tratras, near the Polish border; he shows us dozens of plates of designs on which he inventories pottery and objects from digs of all periods, then we go sleep after a little *malinovitsa*[7] from his secret stash.

The next day's lecture brings together specialists of all extractions. There are Russians, Yemenites, Americans, Moroccans, Poles, Ethiopians, Jews from the four cardinal points. An extraordinary laboratory of cosmopolitanism. Our lecture is very well received. No problem here with evolution. The campus is full of girls basking in the grass under the first sunbeams of spring. Beauties with bare midriffs, shapely butts, startling necklines and exposed thongs; so relaxed, legs wide open, bending forward humongous breasts. Coming from where we are, we are made uncomfortable. Especially me. I can't help ogling and slavering. Need some unshocking. Between repression and hypersexuality, there could be some reasonable middle ground, couldn't there?

We leave Beersheva on the road to Hebron, but turn right towards Arad. We have an appointment with Professor Aref Abu Rabia, an ethno-botanist who came to our lecture, who lives with his own kind in a valley inhabited by Arab Israelis, along our route. The landscape has changed completely. We are walking along the southern foothills of Palestine, dry and rolling like a scrubland. Flattened dogs reappear with their stench. Poor inhabitants surrounded by trash. Idle children. Aref built his house on top of a small hill. He greets us with his wife and four children, who

---

[7] A raspberry liqueur, a Slovak specialty.

are trilingual – Arabic, Hebrew, English. We share with him our impressions of the day, which do not surprise him.

"Arab Israelis represent more than 25% of the Israeli population. We are not Palestinian. Here we're called bedouins. Our ancestors came from the Arabian peninsula three hundred years ago. We have Israeli passports, we vote, we have representatives in the Knesset."

"But then why is there such social and economic inequality?"

"Many of us refuse to be brought together in villages and remain dispersed in the mountains. The government cannot bring water and electricity to each and every encampment. This comes from our nomadic origins. We play ourselves off-side by attachment to our way of life because by staying here we are far from schools or hospitals, garbage collection routes, and so forth. Those who accept coming together in villages built by the government see the social disparities rapidly reduced. But in a certain way, it is to renounce our patriarchal traditions. In an encampment, there is a family head. In a village that brings several families together, there is a mayor....And problems among the families."

We are taken aback by the discovery of this other side of Israel. Aref continues: "Here our approach was reversed. First we got the property of this valley officially recognized for my tribe, then we created the village. It has just been recognized as such and not as an encampment since we have over five hundred inhabitants, so the state will release funds to bring us water and electricity, build a primary school and a dispensary. It wasn't easy, but we got it."

"You did not wish to ask to be connected to Palestine? For your valley abuts the green line,[8] does it not?"

---

[8] The theoretical border between Israel and Palestine, established by the U.N. back in 1949, but broken through in 1967 by Tsahal, who occupied all of Palestine to avenge the Six Day War and the coalition of Arab nations. Since then, Arafat twice refused to return to this border before he was forced to accept it. In exchange, the Israelis must withdraw completely from Palestine, which will take time...

"Out of the question. We are very content to be Israelis. The Palestinians consider us as traitors and collaborators; besides, it will be some time before they work things out. No. We have been at home here for three hundred years and Israel provides us with law and order as well as social services. Many of us live only off of our meager herds and family subsidies."

"We saw many bedouins grazing their livestock near Ofaqim..."

"That's a good example of an arrangement between our nomadic traditions and the sedentary laws. The lands are not ours, but we are allowed to move to summer pastures on precise dates and in free locations, on condition we submit to sanitary and veterinary controls provided by the Agriculture Ministry. All the shepherds you saw have a license. Israel is a state of law. If you respect the law you can lead the kind of life you wish. In exchange, we pay our taxes and must perform our military service like the others."

"We weren't expecting 'pro-Israeli' talk on your part..."

He smiles.

"Look at my children. What's to complain about? As Muslims we are perfectly respected. The media have a tendency to make the Palestinian problem into a religious problem because of the Hamas extremists on the one hand, and the ultra-orthodox Jews on the other, but both are minorities. Seventy-five percent of the Jews are atheists today; as for the Palestinians, they live under the terror of the Islamists; among them there are Christians, and the others aspire only to peace. It is a problem of power and a land issue. I tell you, I would not be a Palestinian for anything in the world, it's the law of the jungle over there. I pity them."

On his hill he has planted rare essences of Judea and the desert. Alimentary plants and plants used in the bedouin pharmacopoeia. He is in the process of making a definitive inventory for the benefit of science, dietetics, and the pharmaceutical industry. He takes Jewish and Muslim children who grow up together in the same schools to see his botanical hill. Before our eyes, in silence, his children are doing their homework.

Purim. We are in Arad, a city in celebration. Costumed children converge on the schools. Porit Yékutihéli, Youval's wife, is a school teacher. She takes us in.

"The Purim festival dates from the Persian exile, after Babylon. Ahasuerus, king of the Persians, had a favorite servant who was Jewish, Mordechai. He refused to worship the god Baal. Haman, the king's prime minister, wanted to have him killed, him and all the Jews in the country. The king, at a ball, fell hopelessly in love with Esther, Mordechai's niece, and married her. She then suggested to the king that it was easier to do away with one man than an entire people. Haman was executed and Mordechai became the prime minister."

"But why the celebration and why the costumes?"

"Because we consider it as a victory over adversity won by ruse. That Providence can make something good from something evil. And that one must not rely on appearances, hence the masks and disguises. Since the Shoah, Purim has had a particular resonance, for we compare Haman to Hitler."

Around the school, security has been reinforced. These pink butterflies, blue imps and fairies followed by soldiers in heavy helmets and bullet-proof vests are an awesome paradox. We are astonished.

"Ten years ago, Baruch Goldstein, an extremist Jew, slaughtered twenty-six Muslims in a mosque the day of Purim. Since then, every year, terrorists try to avenge themselves by targeting children. That is the reason for this deployment of security. But don't worry, I have informed the headmistress of your visit."

Inside all is happiness. Superman and Bozo the clown, green caterpillar and Zorro, lion king and gray mouse. This is the children's celebration. They sing while dancing in a circle in the courtyard. The world of children needs to be protected.

Porit is writing a thesis in ethnology on a small Israeli community: the Ivrim or "Black Hebrews."

"These are Black Americans who came in 1966 with, at their head the guru Ben Carter, a former Chicago foundry worker who was said to have been visited by the angel Gabriel, who had revealed to him that he descended from one of the lost tribes of Israel, by way of Africa and slavery, and that he had to return to Eretz Yisrael."[9]

"Are they recognized as Jews?"

"No. The grand council of rabbis says no, but they are in the process of obtaining a somewhat particular status as Israelis. They have been here for almost forty years. There are only two thousand of them but we quite admire them. Their integration has worked well because they are hard workers and not troublesome, and their children are sometimes better behaved than ours....Their integration is an example. By the way, did you not tell me you needed to sew up a shirt? That's good because I have an Ivrim seamstress who needs some work."

We soon arrive at Netanya's. She is a beautiful Black woman with short, finely braided cornrows. Dressed in a long, psychedelic tunic, she greets us very calmly: "It is my divine pleasure to welcome you." Next she serves us some fruit juice. Her house is impeccable. Right away she tells us of her journey.

"The United States was a hell for us. We were enslaved by alcohol, drugs, prostitution, violence, racism. Ben Carter liberated us from those evils. Here we are in peace. Israel is our salvation."

Once more, we had not expected to hear Israel spoken of in such terms, especially in the present intifada climate. She pursues: "We have reason to hope we will soon be recognized. We could then have a more active share in the life of the nation by paying the price in blood. We have a famous gospel singer who was just killed during a bar-mitzvah. And that attracts a lot of attention."

---

[9] The Land of Israel.

"Porit told us you are polygamous?"

"That is what, for the moment, is preventing our legal integration, but we are evolving toward monogamy. Life is too hard. I, for example, am my husband's only wife. The real problem is that we reject all religion. Religions are too divisive among men..."

"But you have your own religion!"

"No, we follow life rules, that is all. We are complete vegetarians, we fast on Sabbath, practice male circumcision, speak Hebrew, study the Torah; alcohol and cigarettes are forbidden as well as sex before marriage and homosexuality. We are strict on all those points."

When she unfolds Sonia's shirt, she covers her mouth with her hand from stupor: "What happened to you?"

She is very attuned to what we tell her about Africa. Her movement was part of the Black Power wave, the purpose of which was to restore dignity to Afro-American victims of segregation. That this shirt is a patchwork created by the work of African seamstresses from all over moves her greatly. Sonia takes the inventory.

"In fact, it is the uniform shirt of a Kenyan schoolgirl. Here is an Ethiopian repair, there it was done by a Sudanese Muslim, there by a Catholic Sister in Khartoum, there by an old Copt woman in Egypt. The épaulettes were cut from an old djellaba by a Muslim in Alexandria; it only wants you, a repair signed Black Hebrew..."

"And the heart there in the middle of the back?"

"That was me. I needed a double thickness to protect my backpack from the friction of my brassiere fasteners."

"No, it is a heart of support and unity to all the peoples of Africa, a mosaic of love."

Leaving Arad, we begin a sublime descent into the biblical landscape of the Judean desert. The escarpment again! We rejoin the Rift, the void and the Dead Sea. There it is, way down on the floor, at the bottom of the world, green and flat. Before us, a suspended plateau extends from the escarpment, like an aircraft carrier heading out to sea, Masada.

Masada, Saturday 6 March 2004, day 1161, 26 km, 13,621ˢᵗ km

A hot wind coming up from the Dead Sea tousles our hair. Masada is one of the founding myths of Israel, but its history is quite real. It is one of the most important symbols of the Jewish people's heroism and their struggle for freedom through millennia of persecution. Everything is still in place in the frame of the drama: the fortified citadel, the access ramp patiently built by the Roman assailants, the retrenched camps of their overwhelming army.

We are soon at the foot of the ramp. The slope is steep. Made of backfill brought on men's backs by the soldiers of Flavius Silva, who came to pursue this far the last zealots of the great Jewish revolt against Rome, an insurrection that led to the destruction of the Temple of Jerusalem in the year 70. The siege of Masada lasted seven months, during which the nine hundred sixty zealots and Essenes of the plateau, under the rule of Eléazar Ben Yaïr, held a hundred fifteen thousand Romans at bay. At the top of the ramp, we pass the Byzantine gate. It was here that the fate of Masada was engaged. The Romans mounted up to here an assault tower on the ramp, sheltered from the Jews' projectiles. The attack did not last long, but the victory was bitter for the Romans. The plateau was deserted. They called. No reply. Behind a house, they found the carnage. The Jews had all killed themselves so as not to fall into their hands. Rather dead than slaves, rather free than their honor flouted.

We walk this suspended and preserved battlefield as one would tread the altar stone of a bloody holocaust. Nine hundred sixty people mutually slaughtered one another. A shudder goes down our spine. The historian Flavius Josephus, a Jew who had defected to Rome, is very precise: "They designated by lot ten among them to kill the others, then one of the ten to kill the nine others, and who then fell on his sword. Two women and five children hidden in a cistern survived and told the story."

The ruins of the plateau recount the comfort and the pomp that Herod the Great had wanted: dovecotes and cisterns, polychromic synagogue and rooms, hammam and ritual pools, mosaics and a royal palace – hanging gardens in the desert.

At the local youth hostel, a real brand-new five star, a group of American Jews haughtily ignores a group of young Israeli Arabs who have come here with their school in the framework of a volitional integration politicy. The tension is palpable. A cultural Atlantic separates them which Masada tries to bridge. "In my father's house are many mansions," once said a famous Jew.[10] That is more than ever the great challenge for this nation: unity despite extreme diversity. May Masada remain a symbol of pacific resistance and common sacrifice and not that of conquering nationalism, for that would be to betray the memory of the zealots.

---

[10] Jesus Christ.

CHAPTER 38

On the Mount of Beatitudes

We are traveling straight north along the banks of the Dead Sea. On the Rift floor, four hundred meters below sea level. Since Cairo we have been walking due east. This time, it is really the last straight line. All we have left to do is to go up the Jordan valley to its source. On pebble beaches, large concretions of salt shine in the sun. A strong wind whips up a fringe of foam and tears from it patriarchal beards carried into the sky. We are intoxicated with joy and wind. On our left, the cliffs of the escarpment form an impressive wall. At their foot, we arrive in the evening at a kibbutz lost in the heart of grandiosity: Mizpe Shalem. This is where Ahava beauty products are made, mud masks from the Dead Sea, exfoliating creams and cleansing soaps. Sonia is fully enticed by them. We cool our heels before the bunker of the young orderlies who guard the kibbutz when a good-looking guy arrives in a Kangoo.[1]

"You just crossed Africa on foot? Telling me you were coming from Masada was enough, you know! Come on, get in!"

Oren and Hannat Cleydermann welcome us for dinner in a

---

[1] A utility vehicle made by Renault.

tiny apartment which they share with a Great Dane and two little girls who turn it into a permanent junk room. Everything ends up on the ground. A complete shambles. They don't care. They are super easy-going. He is a tall filiform, athletic blond; she a petite, sexy brunette.

"Guess what! In 1994, after our military service, we drove for eight months, from the Cape of Good Hope to Cape MacLear, in Malawi..."

We remake Africa all evening while Tamara and Alma, still disguised in Purim lion costumes watch, fascinated, a DVD of *The Lion King*. The Cleydermanns run the Mezoke Deragot guest house for the kibbutz, perched way up high on the summit of the escarpment overlooking the Dead Sea. They take us there for the night.

"Do not go out tonight. One of the last leopards in Judea is prowling around us these days. He ate three dogs in En-Gedi, and I found myself nose to nose with him ten days ago...

On the Dead Sea a lunar bridge unites with its roadway Israel and Jordan – the lights of which twinkle on the other shore.

Jerusalem, Monday 8 March 2004, day 1163, 13,683rd km

Sunrise at Qumran. This is where in 1947 a young bedouin found the famous Dead Sea Scrolls. He had tossed a stone into a cave to dislodge an errant goat, but instead of the anticipated "baa," he heard a "clink" from one of the seven jars that had been protecting some old papyrus scrolls for almost two thousand years. The discovery was shattering; it confirmed the miraculous intangibility of the texts that have come down through the centuries thanks to the "digital" reliability of copyists. We must not forget that for certain sacred texts, one relied until then on ninth-century copies. Qumran put the world back in direct contact with the actors and witnesses of the Scriptures.

The Essene sect lived here. A community that no doubt prefigured monastic life and was particularly attached to ritual purity since seven pools and basins have been found on the site. The sect was driven off in the year 68 and reverted to Masada where it disappeared.

We are on our way to Jerusalem. A necessary side-trip, to fulfill our mission: to deposit in the Holy City the prayers of our Christian and Muslim hosts. We reach it on an awful road on a very steep incline. In all times, reaching Jerusalem has been hard work. You arrive humbly and weary, from below. And it is a shock! The apparition of its ramparts surmounted by the Golden Dome of Abraham's Rock. For us it is a rediscovery. We came here for Christmas 2000, a year before our great departure. We enjoy rediscovering the Damascus Gate and the Arab quarter. Going down the *Cardo Maximus* on immense monoliths rounded off and polished by people's soles since the destruction of the Temple is one of the most delicious pedestrian sensations in the world. Every toe marries and embraces the ground. Stalls and shops have been attracting customers here for millennia. A Franciscan passes a bedouin who avoids a hassid[2] walking with his head bent down under his black felt cap. Children run, porters carry, vendors gape at the crows. Jerusalem, we are back! It is our favorite city. Below on the left, after the fork, we turn into the Via Dolorosa toward the Notre Dame de Sion convent. The sisters there have rooms and balconies looking onto the Esplanade of the Mosques; and above all, they hide in their basement the fabulous *lithostrotos*, the pavement of the Antonia fortress where Jesus was flogged by the Roman soldiers, after Pontius Pilate had washed his hands of him. That is where he uttered the words that determined his Passion: "Behold the man."

The Holy Sepulchre[3] at opening time. The bearer of the keys is a Muslim. His family has been devoted to guarding this holy place since Saladin. Immediately on the right as you enter the basilica: Golgotha. You get to it by an inconspicuous stairway. Three chapels share this space. One Catholic, on the right, with a muted blue

---

[2] Member of a Jewish orthodox sect.
[3] Basilica containing the tomb of Jesus and the last stations of his Passion.

mosaic; one Orthodox, at the foot of the cross, richly adorned in censers and icons; one Armenian, on the left. In the blue one, an African nun embodies a presence. Her eyes are turned toward the sky that comes in through a small window, and heavy tears run down her cheeks. This is the eleventh station of the Jesus' Passion. That of his crucifixion. Sonia and I sit down on the ground, our backs to a pillar, and begin reading our very long list of names, trying each time to remember the faces and stories of these men and women of Africa, to keep our promise, to sustain their memory, to entrust them to God. We go through these names as one says a rosary, and our sweet sister continues to weep, without apparent pain, like a never-ending spring. She seems to bear the sufferings and hopes of our hosts as well as those of all of Africa. A Mater Dolorosa dressed in blue in a blue chapel. When we have finished, Sonia rises and goes to embrace her. She shows no surprise; smiles at her silently and gratifies her in return with a caress on the cheek. We withdraw. We will never know her name. Our unknown sister. Valiant soldier of the heart, who incarnates so well all the affection we have received from the continent.

Dome of the Rock. After showing our credentials, we can enter the Esplanade of the Mosques. If Jerusalem is an inextricable tangle of little streets and communities, here the space is open to the sky. First because it is here that the angel came to restrain Abraham's arm, and also because it is here that the prophet Mohammed, for a billion men, ascended to heaven in the arms of the angel Gabriel. The whole esplanade was the Jewish temple of Jerusalem. It is also where Christ will return in the Parousy, the end of time, on a cloud of glory. And here the three religions are in agreement. Too bad it is for the last page of History! The hexagon of Iranian mosaic supporting the Golden Dome is a marvel: blue ceramic of Kashan decorated with floral and geometrical motifs. A feeling of entering the shrine of a treasury, stepping in a reliquary. This is the third holy place of Islam. Pilgrimage here is an obligation that very few pious Muslims will be able to realize. We do it for them. Sitting against a pillar in the ambulatory, we recite, after our travelers' surate, the names of all our Muslim hosts, beginning with Naeem Omar, the South African friend who gave us our shoes, to our Egyptian friend Essam el-Moghraby, who opened us the summit of the pyramids, by way of our camel driver, Sheikh Hussein Mohammed Ahmed, and all the other Sudanese. Some curious individuals are surprised to hear us reciting so many names that are familiar to them. A young Mohammed who has been our official clerk for the visit explains to them the reason behind this litany. Our eyes are besotted by the richness of the decoration of the dome and this empty space. The naked rock bearing the so-called last footprint of the Prophet reminds us of the rock of Laetoli: that of the first man.

Yad Vashem. The "hand of God." The memorial to the victims of the Shoah. My great-uncle, abbé René de Naurois,[4] older brother of my deceased grandfather, has a "Tree of the Righteous" there. To pay tribute to his courage, we make a pilgrimage to his Tree. Lucien Lazare, one of his dearest friends, awaits us in the lobby of the memorial.

"It is a great honor for us to welcome you. René is very important for Yad Vashem; he is very dear to our hearts. In Hebrew we say that he is *"Rhassid oumot ha olam,"* in other words "Righteous among the Nations."

We walk through the site under construction. A long building cuts it in two.

"That is the axis of memory that also represents the fracture of the Holocaust in our history. A scar with which all humanity must learn to live. Inside, you can retrace the path of the Shoah." Everywhere this path, on terraces, in the heart of little gardens, guides us to sculptures expressing the loss, the anguish, the torture, the horror of the death camps. Here a red bronze tree of which the

---

[4] See *Aumônier de la France libre: mémoires de René de Naurois* (Paris: Perrin, 2004).

leaves are men; there a candelabra with six branches, one for each million victims; elsewhere, steles of white marble dedicated to the purity of soul of the lost children. We soon go down avenues of trees at the foot of which small plaques are placed, each bearing a name and number.

"These names are those of persons who riskcd their lives to save Jews during the war. In our scriptures, we read that 'saving a man is like saving all of humanity.' By saving a Jew from extermination, these men and women saved the dignity of all our humanity. Your great-uncle is one of these heroes of whom we should be proud....Here is his tree."

Facing the valley, at the edge of a steep slope, above a place bearing the number 2066, a young pine with a trunk like a thigh stands among its peers, except that it is unique in my eyes. It is his. It becomes mine in a way. It behooves me to be forever worthy of it. Never to betray this tree, from its roots to its needles. We kiss it. Then we lean with our backs to its trunk for a moment's meditation. Lucien is moved by our emotion.

"Your uncle's trajectory is exemplary in more than one way, from the warnings he was already giving when he spent some time in Germany before the war, to his disembarkment on D-Day, June the 6th, 1944, as chaplain of the Free French Forces, by way of his acts of resistance and his saving of many Jews[5]..."

We religiously collect some thorns and bark from this tree, not to make laurel wreaths of them, but to share these tokens with my very numerous cousins in memory of what he did. Without the hand of men, there is no hand of God. That is what this forest seems to say.

Return to Qumran. We must go around Jericho. The entire city is under Palestinian authority. Surrounded like a ghetto. It must not

---

[5] He died on January the 12th, 2006, aged 99, six months after the publication of this book in France.

be pleasant living there. So hot, so hot, so hot behind the barbed wire. The wind has died down. We sweat great drops on this detour road with radiant asphalt. A pause in the shade of a eucalyptus tree beside the Jordan. But we cannot go near the water. Too many grates and barbed wire fences. When we start again, we decide not to continue our way on the burning roadway but to follow the wire fence on what looks like a recently cleared patrol pathway. The soil is soft under our feet, restful. The road runs a hundred meters to our left. Many cars wave and honk, the sun is shining, a good feeling of summer. A half-hour later, an Israeli army Humvee comes at us in a cloud of dust.

"Uh-oh! I have the strange feeling we've done something stupid…"

The car stops at a good distance and soldiers deploy cautiously behind armed shields, pointing their weapons at us. An officer calls out to us with a megaphone: "Stop! Stay where you are! Raise your hands!"

At your beck and call. You bet!. They come closer. The officer quickly realizes the situation, lowers his guard and comes to us.

"Are you tourists?"

"Yes!"

"Did you not see the *schwilkeeshtoosh*?"

"The what?"

"The *schwilkeeshtoosh*, this finely raked strip of land along the fencing. Strictly forbidden…"

"Oops! So sorry! We didn't know. We thought it was a sort of customs road…"

He can't repress a laugh under his heavy helmet. And shares the joke on his radio with some snipers overlooking the scene.

"When we find a footprint on the *schwilkeeshtoosh*, that means a terrorist from Jordan has infiltrated, and we unleash a manhunt throughout the sector…"

He looks over our shoulders at the *schwilkeeshtoosh* behind us.

"Today, the harvest is good. I think we have a few hundred footprints!"

We are dismayed. He offers us a lift. We prefer to get back on the pavement. They leave with guffaws. They are not about to forget the two Frenchmen of the *schwilkeeshtoosh*...

In the evening, we knock at the door of the Naaran kibbutz. Oren told us we would be welcome here since the average age of the kibbutzim here is twenty-three....Shiran ben Yakov is our "good Samaritan" of the evening. He invites us to his little house which he shares with an enormous cat and a one-eyed, lame dog. The cat is apparently the stronger. He has a real library. It is the first we have seen in over three years. Africa is poor in books. On the shelves, Brassaï and Doisneau side by side with Sartre, Heidegger and Baudelaire. Shiran's passions are history, photography and jazz. He writes poems and songs. After a shower, he takes us along to the refectory for dinner in common. There, thirty youths are seated at table around large platters. Friendly, but without stress or special effort. Natural. They are rather disparate. Many freaks and grungies with pierced ears, dreadlocks and earrings, Rastafarian hats or purple hair. Others look like U.S. Marines, crew cut and square chin. The girls have low-riding jeans, big breasts and Lolita hair; yet others wear overalls. The young, you know! Except that their M16's and Uzis are placed negligently there on the ground behind them.

On the menu are tomato soup and large potatoes with tarragon. After dinner, they assemble in the parlor around a cup of coffee to debrief for the day. They want to hear from us. The conversation is engaged. Passionate. Everything comes into play: the perception of Israel in the world, Sudanese Sufism, John Paul II, the hospitality of Africans, paleoanthropology....We find them asking lots of existential and metaphysical questions. They debate them collectively with a rarely encountered respect for what the other has to say. Soul-searching and self-criticism are very present on their lips. Humor and hilarious frenzy when they learn about our goof on the *Schwilkeeshtoosh*. There are nineteen houses in this kibbutz; everybody has his role to play, a precise function. There are the

treasurer, the farmers in charge of the banana plantation, the technicians who manage the plastic packaging factory, the guards, the
gardeners, the cooks, the mechanic and Shiran, who is responsible
for the water and power supply. A true Smurf village. But lacking a
Papa Smurf. To close the evening they sing for us in vibrant voice,
with guitar accompaniment, a ballad: *"Hatishma koli, Rekhoki sheli,
Hatishma koli, Béasher hinsha. Tevel zo raba, Udrakhim barrar, Nif-
gashot ledak, Nifradot daad..."*[6]

The next day, Adam Israeli, Lyor Yahav, Youval Shapiro and
Michal Braun come with us. They are thirsty for freedom. We find
out as we go that they carry a huge burden on their shoulders.
Unquenchable thirst to talk. The day passes very quickly. They get
everything off their chests.

"What we're doing in the territories is not right. We are all
against it. The colonists and the religious are only a very small
minority of our population. We ought not to be here. We were all
born after 1967 and the Six Day War. All we have known is the
Intifada, this 'dirty war.' We want two states. Let the Palestinians
finally have their own home. I personally am for dismantling."

"I've had enough of risking my skin for young religious who,
besides being conscientious objectors, refuse to work; enough of
having to feed them with our taxes. All to occupy these god-for-
saken pebbles in Palestinian territory and provoke all this chaos!"

On the other hand, they come to terms with responsibilities
that young Westerners no longer have. They are the builders of
their nation. They love it and are ready to die to defend it. Not in
some vague, distant future. Today, tomorrow. But they no longer
want to carry the burden of the harm they do to the Palestinians in
the spiral of violence; between perpetual vengeance and reprisals.

"In Hebron I had a dirty job, I had to empty out houses that

---

[6] Will you hear my voice? My distant love! Will you hear my voice? Wherever you are! This earth is large, one can take many paths in it, which fur-
tively cross, and separate forever...

had sheltered presumed terrorists. It is atrocious to have to blame old women and children. I had nightmares…"

I underscore their contradiction.

"You tell us that you are against the colonies and settlements; yet isn't Naaran a colony, precisely? Are you not in Palestinian territory?"

"That is true. But the whole Jordan valley poses a problem: it constitutes an international border and we cannot abandon it. It's not like these embedded settlements on inland Palestine hills that are stuck like a wart on a nose. Here, the Jordan provides water for agriculture, and moreover the first Palestinians you reach are much higher up, in the mountains, ten kilometers away from here…"

"Yes, but they could come to Naaran! Instead of you…"

"I don't think so. The valley floor will remain Israeli."

All the complexity of a youth torn between generous principles and harsh realities. In the evening, despite our escort team, we are refused lodging in the Argaman kibbutz. The man in charge replied: "It's not my business." He is right, it's not his business. Shiran and Lyor are baffled. "They know us. They know we are leftists…" We return to sleep at Naaran. At the entry post, a young soldier of Spanish origin, visibly upset, announces to us: "A terrorist attack hit the heart of Madrid. In the metro, at rush hour, this morning. There are two hundred dead and a thousand injured…"

We are overwhelmed. Michal Braun, a girl who has walked all day with us without saying much, turns to us: "Tomorrow, it will be London, Berlin or Paris, and maybe then you will understand better what it's like to live here…"

Mehola, Friday 12 March 2004, day 1167, 35 km, 13,786[th] km

The road is wild and hemmed in by the steep banks of the grand valley of the Jordan. No more kibbutzes, no more Palestinians. The mountain is desert on the left, the border is nearby, on the right. Many greenhouses and crops on the Jordanian side. As far as you can see. Covering thousands of hectares. Our elevation has risen;

the Rift has narrowed; we walk free-spirited and happy, knowing that our stop for the night is assured. Shiran has organized something to compensate for the mean trick at Argaman. Suddenly a bus stops in front of us, in open countryside; an African jumps out, shouting with joy. Sonia exclaims: "Franck!"

Franck Bonneveau was one of our wedding best men. It is he who introduced us. I grew up with him in Passy-Buzenval[7]. He is a Frenchman of Benin and Ivory Coast origins. We fall into each other's arms. Franck is someone who is extroverted and generous. He knows only how to give; he militates for peace in Palestine, but rather on the Palestinian side. He wanted us to go see him in Bethlehem or Ramallah, he wanted us to walk in Palestine. To feel the sufferings of the entrapped populations. But Sonia's pregnancy requires us not to prolong the walk. Franck has been calling us for several days, playing the melody of *"j'arrive, j'arrive pas"*[8] and here he is, vibrant and noisy as a tornado.

We yak and yak across pasture lands. A phone call from Shiran informs us a little later that we are invited to the traditionalist kibbutz in Mehola. One of his friends, Rénana Hakarmi, will wait for us at the gate at four o'clock. We speed up. If we arrive late, the Sabbath will have begun and she will no longer be able to press the button on the electric iron gate to let us in. Franck flips out: "I'd better not tell them I just came from Ramallah!"

Rénana is a beautiful, radiant girl. No fuss and no makeup. Simple and healthy. Mehola is an oasis of greenery in empty pasture lands. The Hakarmi family welcomes us as if we were their children. There were supposed to be two of us, there are three, but no matter....In a nice, arboreous garden we enjoy fruit juices with some neighbors. At Mehola they make greenhouse herbs: mint, cilantro, flat and curly parsley, basil, dill...which are exported to every corner of the globe. I share my observation of the day with our hosts.

---

[7] Catholic Boarding School in Rueil-Malmaison.
[8] I'm coming, I'm not coming...

"On the other bank, the Jordanians also grow in greenhouses.... I don't remember having seen so many during our previous trip in 2000..."

"You are quite right. That is an aspect of the exchanges that resulted from the peace agreements. Israeli engineers have been sent there to develop micro-dripping. The technology is Israeli: the greenhouses, pumps, plastic films, pipes, spray heads....This was vital for Israel, since they were wasting the water of the Jordan for ridiculous yields....With better management, there is more for everybody."

The neighbors, who take Franck for a Falacha,[9] address him in Hebrew. With each new arrival, he politely responds: "Sorry, I am French!" Those who made the mistake join with those who laugh to set a trap for the next one. Repetition humor. Franck excels at it. Seated on garden furniture, we could be in a suburb of Boston, London, or Auckland in the summertime. In the large park children are playing and laughing. We had not expected this relaxed atmosphere.

"You must not confuse traditionalist Jews with Orthodox Jews. We honor the Sabbath and religious holidays, that's all; otherwise, we live a normal life. By the way, it will soon be the hour of prayer. You are welcome to come."

All the families in the kibbutz converge on the synagogue in "Sunday" style. The women in long skirts and hair tied, the men with their *tallit*, their prayer shawl, around their shoulders. Some wear a pistol in their belt. Franck and I proudly wear a *kippa,* a Jewish skullcap – Sonia did not need to be loaned clothing to conform to traditional decency. She fits in perfectly in her Africa Trek attire! In the assembly, while the rabbi chants or reads sacred texts, the faithful talk or move about, stand up, sit down, or greet one another. We expected something more formal. No. The beginning of Sabbath is a rejoicing. We are gratified by benevolent gazes, we

---

[9] Ethiopian Jew.

are all ears, this is the first time that we have attended a Jewish celebration, and yet we feel like we are on familiar ground. The return home is full of friendly rituals. You kiss the *mezuzah* placed on one of the gate posts.[10] All the lights have been regulated by a timer and the food is ready. Moshé, the paterfamilias, begins singing the *Shabbat Shalom*, reads a psalm, sings *Shabbat Aléheïm*, blesses the bread, blesses the wine, recites a blessing, asks God for peace for his family, for his country, for the world. Next comes the *Shalom el-malak*, the salute to the angels. Between the chants and the prayers, the meal has begun. Moshé's vibrant accents resonate with the Coptic Egyptian litanies we heard at Deïr el-Moharrak and in the Wadi el-Natron. Echoes of the Orient. Beauty of a moment devoted to family life and conviviality after a week of hard work. We are enchanted.

We go to sleep in the little prefabricated house of Moshé's parents. They have recently died. Both had returned from death camps. They were among the founders of Mehola. Their photo on the wall, showing them close together, with round tortoise-shell glasses and little faces tested by life, makes us suddenly feel like orphans.

Sixty-four thousand hectares, thirty-eight villages, forty-six kilometers of electrified fences: Beni Segall manages all this. Here there will be no wall.

"The media make it a 'wall of shame': that's absurd! The concrete slabs have been put where people were shooting at each other, to spare victims on both sides. But I agree with the fact that it is foolish to cut a village in two. You ought to go around it and make concessions. For by far the greater part of its trajectory, there will only be an apparatus lighter than the Jordanian border. Come along, I will show you."

---

[10] A small sacred roll containing a parchment with a prayer written by hand by a rabbi for the protection of the house.

At the gate of the Newe Ur kibbutz, after a day's walk in the greenery and prosperity of Betshean, we have encountered Beni, who at once invited us to his house, in the Yizreel kibbutz, in the Armaggedon valley. It is a kibbutz of founders of Israel, formerly very communist, and today one of the rare kibbutzes to have preserved a communal way of life, but with some modifications. We soon come to a track running along a new fence; I show off: "Are you going to make a *schwilkeeshtoosh* here?"

Beni looks askance at me: "How do you know about that?"

When he learns of our gaffe, his laughter comes within an inch of crashing us into a pole.

"The government cannot worry about the totality of this border. It contracts with local collectivities, which in turn contract with private companies that must respect a certain bill of specifications. For the trajectory, I was subjected to pressure from the orthodox religious. They wanted me to collect a maximum of empty hills and virgin slopes from the Palestinians. I refused them cold. Over the forty-six kilometers that fall under my jurisdiction, I stuck strictly to the green line. I have several Arab Israeli villages in my territory; our relations are excellent because they are based on confidence and mutual respect."

We tell him about Mehola.

"That kibbutz is going to pose a problem because it is just inside the green line on the Palestinian side. I am sure it will be subject to arbitration, be exchanged for another parcel of land somewhere else; you mentioned Naaran to me, well, that is a kibbutz that might be yielded more easily, it has less of a history than Mehola."

He pauses a moment, wistful, and continues, weighing his words: "The drama of this border is not its principle – after all, it is not we who wanted this Palestinian state – but its application, constantly torn between two imperatives: going fast, to prevent the infiltration of terrorists, and the length of case-by-case arbitrations, to circumvent such-and-such a Palestinian olive tree, our giving up such-and-such an Israeli spring...and into this hesitation gets mixed mendacity on both sides, against a background of massacres. It is difficult to see clearly through all that. One thing is certain: there will have to be sacrifices on both sides. I would be rather in favor of an international commission to help us; in that way we would not look like mean land thieves, at the very time when we have accepted to yield a territory back to the Palestinians. It is in our interests for the situation to be normalized as soon as possible. We need the Palestinians as much as they need us. In my development, there is a border post for the road to Jenine, a switching station for merchandise with a great hall, and a military post. We collaborate moreover with the city council in Jenine. We have modernized their everything-to-the-sewer system because it was overflowing and trickling in here..."

Beni is unstoppable. Back in Yizreel we continue the visit. They have milk cows. Fine. They raise Arabian purebreds. Okay. A factory to make metal frames for electronic equipment. Good. They raise giant Japanese koi goldfish at six hundred dollars apiece. What then? An incubator and its aviary for the reproduction of a hundred kinds of parrots and rare birds. Enough! Oh yes, I forgot...they are the inventors and makers of an automaton for cleaning swimming pools that is sold worldwide: the Dolphin, fourteen thousand of them exported to the United States every year, six thousand to Europe. Stop! No mas! These people are exhausting. Even the most enterprising South Africans are surpassed. When I say that, Beni cracks up: he is South African; he was born near Aliwal North, in Jamestown, a little village we passed through, coming down from Liliekloof....We go to get over our emotions in front of a glass of the house limoncello, of which Philippa gives Sonia the recipe while Beni is showing Franck and me the panorama of the valley of Armaggedon.

"Here, at least, I will have a front-row seat for the end of the world, comfortably seated and with a glass in hand!"

Tiberias, Sunday 14 March 2004, day 1169, 33 km, 13,852nd km

At breakfast we meet the gardener-landscapist of Yizreel, Johanna. She is a young French student. She has made her *aliyah*.[11]

"I could no longer take the atmosphere in France, the delinquency, antisemitism disguised as defense of the Palestinian cause, the lack of perspectives, the disenchantment of youth, the anxious materialism. I wanted to be involved, to participate in a collective, constructive adventure, so I came here and am very happy."

Beloved France! In what state are we going to find thee? Already the anxiousness of the return, despite the joy of the approaching conclusion of our trek, is arising in us. You end up forgetting where you have come from when you are so busy worrying about where you are going. While walking towards our destination today, we talk about this with Franck. Seen from the East, it looks to us as if the entire West is ducking its head between its shoulders. The internet bubble. 11 September and its aftermath. The euro. The Franco-American spat. Inflation. The emergence of China which seems to be wanting to absorb all the world's work and resources with no regard yet to the human rights. The challenge to our republican secularism. The regression of women's rights in the cities. The ghetto cities. The *"tournantes"*[12] phenomenon among the young. The birth of alter-globalization. The increase in unemployment. Big Brother and "reality" shows. It looks like the world has greatly changed in three years, while we were hiking under a blue sky, on red soil, at ground level, in the heart of Africa. Will we recognize it?

A fine row of century-old olive trees. A bicycle path. Broad expanses of fresh green grass recently mown. The lake is getting closer. We can feel it. From over there, at the turn, I am sure we will see it. Tick-tock, tick-tock, in the legs; boom-boom, boom-boom in the rib cage. We go around the turn, hand in hand, and way

---

[11] Name of the voyage that Jews of the diaspora make when they decide to settle in Israel. Literally "the climb."

[12] Gang rape.

down there, at the end of the road, where it joins the vanishing point, between two trees, what do you think? A blue square: the lake. Water. The source. The end. The beginning. The biblical Sea of Galilee, now called Lake Tiberias. The end of the Great Rift. Franck is again our best man for this great moment of happiness.

In a few minutes we find ourselves at the table of a restaurant around a grilled St. Peter's fish and a bottle of white wine from the Golan plateau. Sun. Palms and satiety. Is it really over? It is really real? We are after an end, our end. It cannot be a meal. So we set out again. How far? To where? Are we going to spend our whole lives gravitating around this lake? Late in the afternoon, we enter Tiberias. Roman baths, still functional, are steaming on our left. The permanence of history and geography. The Rift is still alive around here. Franck has to leave us. He has a date in Jerusalem. We have one tomorrow with a paleoanthropologist at the University of Tel Aviv, who will come join us here. We go down to the port.

In the declining day, fishermen's skiffs drop their nets for the night harvest. One is standing in the bow, the other rows. The first seems to be sowing, the other reaping. They have long beards and wool caps. Noisy gulls ricochet on the smooth surface of the waters which echo and amplify the banging of the oars against the shell. Some Russian *olim*,[13] recognizable by their caps, are lined up on the quay in dirty cotton tank tops, with fishing poles, their eyes riveted on the neck of their vodka bottle wanting for a cork, and on the cork on their line wanting for a strike. The sun is going down; we join a fast food queue. Yes indeed! Everything comes to an end. While we are waiting, someone comes and caresses me gently on the shoulder from behind. I turn around and the owner of this kindly hand immediately withdraws it, ashamed and embarrassed; he had thought I was someone else.

"Sorry! I'm very sorry! I thought you were a Russian friend! You look the same from the back with your long blond hair!"

---

[13] Immigrants.

His accent is unmistakable; I put him at ease: "Vous êtes Français?"

"Oui! vous aussi?"

Henri Samuel made his aliyah in 1983. Over a hamburger, he tells us his life story. He was born in 1941. Just before being deported, his parents were able to entrust the nursling he was to a neighbor on the landing.

"I never knew her name. I remember she was called 'mademoiselle' and was very pious. I even have a picture of her. After the war, I was a pupil of the nation. When I was twelve, an association of deported persons found my true mother. She had survived, but she was ill. Something was broken between us. I felt a stranger to her suffering. There was no love under our roof. I loved only 'mademoiselle.' I had some half-brothers and a stepfather whom people called 'the old man.' I became an electrician."

Samuel trembles a little, he hasn't spoken French for twenty years.

"Why did you come to Israel?"

He seems to hesitate. Not to want to offend us.

"You know, in the building trades, Jews are not very popular. I had had enough of 'dirty Jews' here and 'dirty Jews' there....People don't necessarily think it, but we can't help it, we are more sensitive than others, also more fragile..."

We are silent with shame. The hamburger won't go down. Henri is sorry he said that and, as if to compensate, adds: "And so, I took early retirement after a painful divorce. It's a very small pension, but I am living better here than in La Courneuve[14]. Life there was no longer tolerable. I receive two reparation pensions of four hundred euros a month, one from France and one from Germany. With that I can pay for my daughter's studies in Tel Aviv....She wants to be a pediatrician."

"Your children followed you?"

---

[14] Paris suburban city, with a majority of uprooted and idle immigrants from Africa.

"No, I remarried here, I had two children, and I divorced again…"

He starts to laugh. To laugh about his life. About his trials. About our meeting.

"I've done nothing but talk about myself, whereas you have just done the length of the continent on foot, I am ashamed. Where are you sleeping tonight?"

"We don't know yet, but we have a youth hostel in mind."

"If you can be satisfied by a small couch, you are welcome at my place. It's only a modest studio in Ezor Tahasia, the industrial zone, but it is very neat."

The next morning, Erella Hovers, a specialist in the Neanderthals of Israel, comes by to pick us up. We wanted to meet her to cap our "trek in the footsteps of Man" in a symbolic place: the Amud cave, which figures among the most ancient intentional sepultures on the planet. Belief in life after death, respect brought to the carnal envelope – which implies consciousness of self and the recognition of an immaterial aspect of being – is in the scientific world the widely recognized boundary between what is assuredly human and what perhaps is not yet quite.

Brown-skinned with long curly hair, Erella is dressed all in black, with leather pants and broad black glasses. Liberated woman. She drives us north of Lake Tiberias in her black Golf through a lovely Mediterranean countryside and parks near a small stream. We walk up the brook for a few hundred meters in steep-sided gorges, heading for a rocky needle that stands out from the cliff like a lingam. Erella begins her presentation: "Here we are possibly on the territory of the first men. Fire and tools were not sufficient to make our ancestors fully human. It took art, speech, exchange, social life, a form of belief, of religion. This level was attained a hundred thousand years ago in surely many places on the planet, but the oldest sepultures have been found between Mesopotamia, at Shanidar, and here, in Galilee. In both instances we are in the presence of

Neanderthals. So they were human. What is incredible is that they coexisted for a very long time with *Homo sapiens sapiens*."

When we reach the rocky needle, we climb the limestone cliff on the left toward a sort of terrace. Erella continues: "As you know, the Neanderthal man is European. He descends from the first waves of *Homo erectus* that conquered the entire world between 1.8 and 1 million years ago, and underwent a specific adaptation during the ice age that affected the northern hemisphere. During that time, *sapiens sapiens* was developing in Africa. These two populations shifted and finally came into contact. And the logical meeting point is here."

We get to the open terrace above a sublime landscape limited in the distance by Lake Tiberias. I ask the fateful question: "So did they make love or war?"

She chuckles. "Probably neither one. We have found no battle-fields and genetics has just shown that they were probably two distinct human races. However, they cohabited for more than ten thousand years. What we see on the sites is that there were exchanges among them. *Sapiens* as a result improved his lithic industry and created jewelry that the Neanderthal had already possessed for a long time, as well as a form of religiosity. As early as 90,000, at Shanidar, in Iraq, Neanderthal ritualized sepulture with heaps of flowers and 'provisions' for the voyage to the life beyond. We find the same thing here, at 55,000 years. Between these two periods, the ancestors of Cro-Magnon, already entirely modern, arrived from Africa and learned all that. And from that encounter came a cultural and artistic explosion which was to develop the world over in decorated caves, but without the Neanderthals. That's more positive than war, isn't it?"

"Thus, to sum up, we all descend from these latter African conquerors who supplanted more archaic humans, produced by local evolutions in geographical dead-ends such as Neanderthal in Europe or Java in Asia?"

"That is what the digs and the dates seem to prove, and genetics to confirm since none of these 'primitive' characters persists today in the global population."

"So are we all Africans?"

Again she smiles.

"Probably. Skin colors and morphotypes are in any case very recent phenomena which could diversify rapidly with isolated demographic explosions, and which can disappear even faster with the hybridization of an open world."

She kneels and points to the place where the remains of a Neanderthal baby were found buried between the haunches of a buck. We have a thought for it, hoping it had a good voyage afterward...

When we are about to head back, Sonia exclaims:

"It's unbelievable! I can't buckle the belt of my backpack."

Our baby seems to have decided that the trip was over. Almost!

We find Henri in his little apartment. He has a little caged mouse. Sonia loves it. Henri worries: "For two months now it hasn't drunk a drop of water! I don't understand how it manages to stay alive..."

She fills a small dish. The mouse lunges avidly at it, sucks it all up and springs into its wheel for a sprint of madness. We all laugh.

"How would you like a little pastis? I make it myself! I put sticks of licorice in vodka. It costs me nine shekels instead of sixty."

His little slanty eyes fizz with joy in his wrinkled face. Mice and men are thirsty.

"It's been a long time since I have had visitors. Occasionally a youth comes to see me. I pick them up in the port, delinquents, alcoholics, scrappers, many are Russian. I help them find work. I train some in electricity. And I try to get them existing again. To prove to them that they are not good for nothing; that they can be useful. I go with them to homes that have emergencies: a circuit-board that blew, a defective electric radiator....When the customers are too poor, I don't ask for anything..."

And this timid man, to whom one would almost give a coin in

the street, saves mice, supports his daughter, takes in two hikers, recaptures lost lambs. Despite his age, his past, his modest income, he has not lost the power of giving. Like so many of our hosts. Dear Henri Samuel! Our last host.

The Mount of the Beatitudes, Tuesday 16 March 2004, day 1171 and last, 22 km, 13,874th and last kilometer

The hills are covered with yellow flowers. Goldfinches pour forth in the blue sky with swallows. It's the avant-garde returning already. In less than two months, these two hundred grams of feather and courage have covered a distance that took us nearly thirty-nine months. In the branches of the lake shore a cuckoo sings. We laugh inwardly at it. Cuckoo! Here I am! It's me! You are almost home! The water is like oil. Squadrons of kingfishers execute in the sky the flight of the Holy Spirit, hieratic and immobile, before diving like darts onto little silvery fish. After a few hills, we reach Tabgha, the presumed site of Jesus' miracle of the loaves and fishes. We meander through ancient olive trees in the direction of the eminence that reigns over the site: the Mount of Beatitudes. All is calm and silent. Something attracts us up there. The anguish of the last step. Of an unknown finish line where no one awaits us. We wish to end our trek as it began: incognito. Coming out of the olive trees, we enter fields of rye and green wheat. A little path seems to invite us to keep going higher. It passes between two fields. It climbs toward the basilica of Beatitudes. It is lined with two hedges of flowers yellow like suns; a luminous guard of honor. The shafts are straight and extended skyward like a nutritional army. The long rye beards hiss vaguely under the very soft caress of the crystalline air. No need to shout, nor to exult, we have done no more than to walk and meet. We have been blessed. The harvest has been more than generous. It is a serene and silent joy. Beatitude, perhaps. But not at all the feeling of having achieved something. Of beginning, rather. As if it wasn't over yet. As if we would be walking forever…

We are in the middle of a field, among the shafts. It is here. We will go no farther. We turn to face the Sea of Galilee. Toward the south, toward Africa. To which we owe this beatitude. At this very place, two thousand years ago, in a field of men, Jesus spoke in public for the first time, he was thirty years old:

> Blessed are the poor in spirit, for theirs is the kingdom of heaven.
>
> Blessed are they that mourn, for they shall be comforted.
>
> Blessed are the meek, for they shall inherit the earth.
>
> Blessed are they which do hunger and thirst after righteousness, for they shall be filled.
>
> Blessed are the merciful, for they shall obtain mercy.
>
> Blessed are the pure in heart, for they shall see God.
>
> Blessed are the peacemakers, for they shall be called the children of God.
>
> Blessed are they which are persecuted for righteousness' sake, for theirs is the kingdom of heaven.
>
> Blessed are ye, when men shall revile you, and persecute you, and shall say all manner of evil against you falsely, for my sake.
>
> Rejoice, and be exceeding glad…[15]

What a lovely spot to stop, to begin! On words that suit so many of our African hosts so well: poor, mournful, meek, thirsty, merciful, pure, just, persecuted, but blessed! Sometimes joyless, for life is hard, but never desperate. What a lesson! We remember the words of a friend before our departure: "You are going to walk

---

[15] Matthew 5:3–12, King James version.

from the Cape of Good Hope to the Mount of Beatitudes, and you will realize, once you are there, that the first beatitude is perhaps to have hope." His name is Father Olivier Human. He was right. We are very little, and we are blessed. *Ecce Homo.*

Begun 4 September 2004 in Paris

Completed 10 April 2005 at the home of Franck Viénot.[16]

Last review of the last page of this English version
on 24 September 2008, in the morning,
mourning my father who reached his beatitude summit during the night,
surrounded by his four loving children and wife.
Almost exceeding glad. Showing us the way. Blessed Man.

Alexandre Poussin

---

[16] Franck is our neighbor across the landing, who became our friend, who seeing us laboring over the writing of this book, in our hard return to the complexity of Parisian life, exclaimed: "But come and write in peace in my place during the daytime, while I'm not here!" The adventure lasted for five months. Hospitality exists also in France, as elsewhere.

Epilogue

Busy, busy, busy. Since we've been back. Blessed by the coming of a little girl, Philae. Both Iman Yonan and Daniella Buchnik were right! Welcoming life helped us to be put back on track; even if a fifty-square-meter flat in Paris with a wall for a view was a bit harsh, we had so much sun in our memories and so much love in our hearts that sedentarity was not painful. One cannot really enjoy the pleasure of walking barefoot on a soft carpet, the thrill of intimacy, the orgasm of the clean Q-tip, the ecstasy of a ribbon of pure water forever or the miracle of the switch, when one has not been deprived of all these amenities for three years. And then, so much to share, so much to give back. Fulfill our witness duty, praise our hosts' generosity: deliver a different message out of Africa. No time for baby blues, not for Sonia, nor for myself. Media whirlpool, the minute we landed, the second six episodes of our series to write and record while the first six were aired, our second volume to start writing, between baby bottles and interviews, festivals, bookfairs and book signings for volume 1. Philae was carried along anywhere and everywhere in her baby cot. Call it training! She got her name from the Nubian temple, whereabout she was conceived, and which for us symbolizes universal brotherhood of cultures that were united by UNESCO in a time of cold war to rescue a treasure of a lost culture. It's also a place where all kinds of worship have been chanted. The ultimate one being the love of all human beings. That's also what it means. Philae, the second love of the Ancient Greek, after *Eros*, and before *Agape,* the *Philia* is the fraternity and brotherhood among humans. *Agape* is more spiritual, but a funny first name to give!

In these last four years we've been lecturing with our long feature movie all around France, in more than 500 theatres, spreading better words and news of the continent as a whole and from the individuals we've met. We've also been to hundreds of schools, communities and companies to give motivational speeches. Produced a photo album to sort out our 15,000 slides, and supported a good number of NGOs working in Africa, by events or fundraising. But my dream, which soon became an obsession, was to be translated in English. Not for pride or ego, but because I felt I owed it to our hosts. A nonmaterialistic payback. So that they could read one day how good they are. Because the only mirror-image the First World is sending back to them is a sinister one. You know the story. But time was short and we had to get going for another trip, before this dream was achieved. Everything was planned. And no publisher in sight. A couple of months before our departure we found out that another French couple was busy doing the same trip, and a week later that Sonia was pregnant. (Three days in Rome to celebrate our seventh wedding anniversary proved fatal!) Everything was canceled. We had to find a bigger place for the four of us, and complete that oath: find an English-speaking publisher. Both miracles happened. Just to give us time to welcome properly Ulysse in our frantic lives.

To make two long stories short: being depressed by real estate brochures boasting boring Parisian flats at peak prices we had lunch at a friend's on a sunny Saturday just outside Paris. At the end of the meal, he told us: "There's a house for sale in the village, it's very rare, we should go and have a look, let's call the agent!" At the gate she stated: "This house belonged to Gaston Maspero at the end of the 19th century." We had a strike. Maspero, famous French Egyptologist, was known among other things to be the savior of the Philae temple. Without him it would have been dismantled by the British and brought back to London. We never visited a second house. Thank you Ulysse! You postponed our trip, because surely you wanted to be part of it, and you granted us a magic old house and a home.

Now the second little miracle: the story of the English version you've been reading: my French publisher and I had 127 rejections in the last four years of professional attempts to convince an English-speaking publisher to translate *Africa Trek*. They all must have had good reasons but I became a joke in the business. "Why is he trying again? Why is he dreaming? Why isn't he giving up? It'll never happen…" Couldn't help it.

But I must confess that I finally did, when eventually Sterling, the last publisher interested, said no: the 127th no. I gave up. I remember perfectly where I was : shoveling a pile of garden manure. It was 11 o'clock in the morning on Wednesday 14 May. The same day, in the afternoon, I received a phone call from an Ethiopian friend we were hosting in our little Paris bachelor flat: "Somebody called concerning your book in English; here are the details." I called, and here's what a young lady told me: "You don't know me, I'm a French expatriate in Portland, Oregon, and when I've read on your website the refusal of Sterling, being a reader and a great lover of your story, I told myself it was not fair and I felt empowered and entitled to contact a publisher, which I did, I just came out of his office and he really wants to talk to you; here are his details…" I was stunned. All was cleared for me while I was in despair. She managed with her pure enthusiasm, without the numbers, without even a copy, to succeed where we all failed officially and stubbornly for more than three years. The following day, after

I had talked to this enthusiastic publisher while pinching myself, he sent a contract to mine. It was signed back over the weekend.

All it took was the flutter of an angel's wing. It became true the day I gave up. You don't achieve something by pride, will or ego, but because angels help you or allow it to you.

When you stop running after an idea, it turns back and smiles at you.

Our angel had succeeded where all attempts had failed, against all conventions, systems and editing procedures, where 14,000 km on foot and 1200 African families hadn't been enough, because she had put in motion hope and candor, innocence and joy, selflessness and faith.

My deeper joy is that this story looks so much like Africa Trek.

We must all be angels for one another.

It's a duty to be everyday someone else's angel.

Nothing happens by chance, thanks to ourselves, but all through others, thanks to others.

Gabrielle Esbeck

Paradise – it's the Others.
Pray do be this Other sometimes,
Here was ours one day: Gabrielle.
Our angel Gabrielle.

But then my new publisher had a problem to solve, how and where could he find a good translator available for a fast-track publication? A week later he came back to me unsatisfied by the samples he had received. I suddenly remembered that two months before I had received via our website a translated chapter sent by Philip Stewart, a pre-retired professor of French Literature from Duke University. He had done it for the pleasure of it, and the love of our story he had discovered during a trip in France the previous summer. I truly recognised my style within his. I found his number on the white pages, which was not that easy considering that there are a couple of P. Stewarts in the US, and after having found the right one, asked him if he could help us find a solution. Here was his answer: "There was no secret agenda in my gift! I've only translated Voltaire, Rousseau, and Montesquieu in my career, and I don't know any official translator..." He didn't see my point. I replied him I wished he would do the whole job because again, his generous move looked like Africa Trek so much. But it needed to be done within two months. "Impossible," the academic replied. I begged him to sleep on it and give me his final call the following day. On the phone after a night fanned by angel wings, he acknowledged: "When you were at the Cape of Good Hope, everybody told you that your endeavor was impossible, and you tried....So I can't do anything but try!"

Here he is: Philip Stewart, our benefactor, the man who has translated the 64 chapters of our two books, one chapter a day during two summer months.

Philip Stewart

Now that this dream of you reading *Africa Trek* is completed, we've got another one to fulfill. There's always another one. Dreams breed dreams. We want to go back to three places we've been in Africa with an eye surgeon, probably American, because we have noticed in all the villages we've been through a high prevalence of early cataract likely caused by diabetes among men with 45 to 50 years of age. By giving them back their eyesight we can give them back their life, their dignity, their work, and their ability to feed their family. With a simple surgical gesture. Maybe a way for us to give back some bits of all the love and care we've been granted. It will be called Africa Vision and you can follow and help its development on our website, www.africatrek.com

Concerning trips, of course there will be some others, but we can't tell you where in advance because we want to remain free to go somewhere else! One thing we can tell you is that our two children will be part of it and that we hope they'll be good ambassadors. (So far taking pictures with them looks like hell! Rings a bell with you?)

We dearly hope reading *Africa Trek* has changed or deepened your perception of the African continent, and inspired in you the love of its cultures and people. They deserve it badly, the world and history having been terribly unfair to its natural, human and spiritual resources. Now, you have to go there yourself, they need you. But try to favor community lodging instead of luxurious hotels and try at one stage to climb down from the coaches or cars, and walk...

Alexandre and Sonia Poussin, Paris, 8 September 2008

Hosts and Benefactors

Without these 646 hosts encountered in 639 days, the writing of this second volume would not have been possible. Africa Trek is the meeting and testimonial of 1147 persons in 1171 days and 13,874 km on foot.

Tanzania:

Habiba Amiri Shoko, Rehema and Augustino Jovita, Christopher Elibariki, Victor, Bernard Murunya, Tonya Siebert, Frédéric Mendonca, Kadogo Lerimba, Ozias Kileo, John Pareso, Dr. Fidelios Masao, Charles Saanane, Peggy Hawkins, Michael Skutar, Father Bill Blum, Mohammed, Abbi Matthew, the Maasais of Irkong, Jorg Keller, Mtui, Ross Withey, Raphael Romani, Paulo, Maya, Maria, Maciar.

Kenya:

Anthony Russell, Elisabeth Warner, Anthony Turner, Arnaud and Laure Thépenier, Patrick and Claire Cellier, Cyril Baise, David and Liz Hopkins, Daphne Sheldrick, Jill Woodley, Brigit Syombua, Nigel Pavitt, Kevin Ward, Patrick Arnaud, Harald Bohn, Sabine Pruss, Anthony White, John Masikonté Niiti, Anne and Paul Suntaï, Joyce Kojay, Margaret Nkoile, Anne and Hoceah Sankalé, Daniel Njenga, Nahason and Evelyne Naïja, James and Elisabeth Saneth, Simon, Anastasia Djioki, Nancy Rose, Peter Likomo, Pius

Mulwa and Husna Abdallah, Spencer Gelthorpe, Anna Waedimou, Joël Limo, Daniel Momani, Sisters Helen, Maria Goretti and Irmina Nungari, Father Bernard Cullingham, Benjamin Salbé, Desmond Rotitch, Emmanuel Toroititch, Henriette Palavioux, William Kimosop, Brooks Childress, Susie Mills, Jenny Rollings, Wim van den Bossche, Velia Carn, Héléne Momoï, Nelson and Christine Lekichep, Alexandra and Mark Archer, Ross Withey and Carol Robert, Protestant Pastor Thomas and Jane Nanok, Joseph, Clarkson Ekouleou, Robert Ignolan, Padre Rico, Sister Louise, Bernard Katoï, Akim Lorotwakan, Kip and Ketty Lines, Philip Evi, Robert and Tina Jaynes, Bill and Leah Westfall, Theophilus Loburo, Isaac Kinyango, Moses Lowoya, Jesus Longori, Peter Lokichar, Halwign Scheuermann, Daniel Akales, David Erot, Peter Losinien, Simon Namuya, Paul Moru, Mr. Njorogwe, Louise Leakey, Ahmed Bakari.

Ethiopia:

Théodoros, Michaela and Michal Buranska, Richard Brackett, Duk, Samson Teferi, Donna Clawson and Thabata Cox, Oita and Noho, Claude Leterrier, Kasayé Makonen, Samuel Dredgir, Andenet and Stephanos Astakté, Emayou and Serget, Cindy and Vic Anderson, Dr. Mary, Mullu, Ersumo Kabamo, Fathers Woldé Tensaï and Adeno Monat, Sisters Martha, Walété and Medina, Nuredin Nasir, Mifta Reshid, Zam-Zam, Abayn, Tofik, Belacho, Chetu Gebreselassie, Osman Ahmed, Maru Mendera, Azalech, Hussein Rachid, Jean-Claude and Amaretch Guilbert, Claude and Djedda Villain, Abuna Gabremariam Amante, Maurizio Malvestiti, Mgr Silvano Tomasi, Roland and Marie André de Sorbier, Jean-Baptiste and Marianne Chauvin, Doron Grossman, Meseret Gebre, Semret Abate, Senait Egziagher, Solène de Poix, Guillaume and Geneviève Capois, Gilles Landrivon, Olivier Evreux, Aboubacar Traoré, Marie-Claude and Sheikh Malikite, Thérèse and William Amelewonou, Menkir Bitew, Vincenzo Celiberti, Haïlé Gébrésélassié, Ato Tullu Kebede, Abbat Melakhaïl Telahun Mekonnen, Tamirat Fikadou, Sentayo

Aspalehou, Demmelash Aysheshim Birilie, Winchet Abebe, Bizoualen, Tekleye Asfaw, Demelé Bezab, Sentayo Ayalehou, Winchet Ayil, Getenet Tamer, Abiyou Bassi, Zelalem Kassa, Téhé Badma, Santayo Fataloum, Milguleta Kendé, Beokatou Bélété, Abrahet Mehachou, Nezanet Ayenow, Mavet Tchané, Temalen, Seraten, Mummina, Franck Beernaert and Almaz Kiflé, Henriette Palavioux, Abiyé Azéné, Gebru Améra, John Abébé, Fanta Degou, Mahadou Dérédjé, Tigabu Bizu, Ato Naga Alem, Tarafu Nendu and Amaretch Getu, Djamila Ababer, Asfaw Mellié, Kate Fereday Eshete, Tsahaïnesh Tsahaï and Gashaw Turuna, Kassaw Tamen and Genet Gashaw.

Sudan:

Ahmed Ali, Mohammed Agir, Tom Mustapha, Yarenebi, Omar Mohammed Ahmed, Moussa Ismael, Mohammed Tahir, John Eustache, Zaïre Mohammed Tahir, Haroun Kazali, Awad Gaddora, Hadi Adem, Awad Abdallah, Mounir Abd el-Razik, Mohammed Noor, Ahmed Eissa, Mohammed el-Tayeb, Abdallah Muhadjir, Ahmed and Wida Gaddora, Ali Abd el-Rahman, Abdallah Manofalli, Bahadi Mohammed, Ibrahim Abd el-Kedir, Almajid Syed Ahmed, Ajeb and Youssouf Abd el-Rahman, Tayeb Mohammed Ali, Amina and Oumoïma, Abu Bakr Mohammed el Amin el Rhabshaoui, Yassal Enazir, Ali Mohammed, Salah Saad, General Jaffar Mohammed Youssif, Hassan Bachir, Sarah Atamanan, Bellal Jaffar Bellal, Stephan Gembalczyk, Leszec Mycka, Rawinij Krzysztof, Jeneiec Tadeuzs, Robert Kniecik, Abu Baker Rodwan, Mustapha Abd el Mounen, Sarah Michael, Peter Daniel, Father Étienne Renaud, Sisters Patricia Hogan and Theresa Byrne, Gabriel Wei, Rianne Tamis, Suzy Candido, Brother Michel Fleury and Brother Yves Lecoq, Raphaël Pouriel, Yves Lecointe, Francis Geus, Mgr Dominique Mamberti, Sister Angèle and Sister Sana, Sisters Mary, Paule Germaine, Caroline and Renata, Dominique Renaux, Robert Piva Crehange, Philippe Garcia de la Rosa, Thierry and Agnès Quinqueton, Homayoun and Mahvash Alizadeh,

Janet Mc Elligott, Johanna Van der Gerte, Pieter Stapel, Sheikh Garibullah, Omar Sadiq, Samia, Samia Hussein, Nazik abd el-Karim, Mohammed Bindary, Adil Mileik, Mohammed Ghoneim, Mohammed Hammam, Josep Maldonado I Gili, Suleiman, Eltayeb Isaak, Ali Mohammed, Bakleid and Djimal, Umm Balein, Mariam and How, Salah, Abdu Bakri, Gourachi Sheriff, Mostapha, Seïda, Rumheïssa and Aladin Abd el-Gadir, Daniel, Rose-Mary and Katy Wani, Abdelazim, Colonel Imad Abd el-Gadir, Zeinab Hassan and Ibrahim Agid, Samson, Hassan Idriss, Isaac Hassan, Hawa Idriss, Ahmed Youssif, Sabir Ismaël, Fadir Awat, Ali Mohammed, Amir, Amin Ahmed, Abd el-Gadir Mohammed Saïd, Colonel Khalid Abd el-Rahman and Salwa, Oussam Chetti, Mohammed Idriss Othman, Anouar Delil, Mohammed Kamal, Mohammed Hassan, Farah Ahmed, Ibrahim Ali, Awad Mahmoud Mohammed el-Kheïr, Sabrinha, Neimad, Nedjoud, Hilla and Menahil Mohammed, Zeinab Abd el-Karim, Sabri Mohammed Idriss, Saabri, Eltayeb and Mamdour, Fatima and Maha, Mohammed Saïd, Issam Abd el-Rahim and Nadia, Bakhit, Adri Ibrahim, Mergani Idriss and Fawaz Fahd, Adri Abd el-Rahim and Nadia, Leïla Bashir Shamed, Holub, Rifat Mahmood Ali, Soussan Abbas, Abdu Rabu, Mohammed Ahmed, Moubarak Ali, Fatima Eltayeb and Idriss Moussa, Mohammed Abdul, Mohammed Ali Kursi, Saïd Othman, Loïc and Geoffroy de La Tullaye, Peter and Sarah Greenway, Padraig Murphy, Jasper Day and Emma Wallaker, Renata Volkmann and Harald Radtke, Saïd Asafi and Wafa, Riri Rahiya, Eïmad Chorbadji, Anouar Hadi, Sheikh Husseïn Labd Mohammed Ahmed, Nour Moussa, Abdallah Mohammed, Adam Husseïn, Khamis Abdallah, Mohammed Rerebil Arabesh, Bindadur Tarbouch, Sabri and Mahmoud, Mimi Sherif, Midhat Mahir, Ivan Bulik, Lubos Suitek.

Egypt:

Lieutenant-Colonel Ayman Abd el-Kader, Raed Rosas, Lieutenants Magitt and Ayman, Policemen Mohammed and Aman, Tinus du Preez, Imad and Aatif Baulus, Nasri Adir, Policemen Mahmoud,

Nabil, Samir and Tariq, Brahim Suleiman Mahmoud, Aaziz, Sohad and Heba Baulus, Fifi and Myriam Baulus, Magda Makarios, Yasser Mohammed and Tafla, Béatrice and Chenouda, Hamed Kamal, Véronique from Club Méd, Eric and Nathalie Samy, Governor Samir Youssif, Hadj Delil, Yonan Adli, Ahmed Mohammed, Hussein Nurbi and Shahada, Assad Thaba, Ibrahim el-Baya, Zina Aboukheïr, Badaoui el-Adli, Guy-Hervé Perron, Cyril and Claudine Le Tourneur d'Ison, Francis Amin, Governor el-Desouky el-Banna, Nubions Ibrahim, Sisters Angèle and Julienne, Domitille Roze, Hélène de Becdelièvre, Julie Guitton and Chiara Bertoya, Mohammed Taya, Olga Gentil, François Larcher, Marie and Aurélia, Amba Beïman, Policeman Mahmoud, Morgos and Asma, Romani Fauzi and Folla Wannis, Governor Adel Habib, Abuna Yonan and Iman, Sister Marie Bernard, Lieutenant Hazim, Adil Gad Choukri and Anna William, Kombos Paula Fouad, Nesmah Wagih, Nama Sale, Abuna Abraham and Sana Selim, Captain Walid el-Masri, Governor of Sohag Mamdour Kidwani, Lieutenant Mahmoud, Sister Isis, Father Petrus, Father Moussa, Father Francis Faez, Ayman Faez, Sisters Sabah, Francesca, Bianca, Soad, Néhid and Rita, Francis and Carolus Nabil, Fathers Johanna, Lucas and Milad, Nagua and Thérésa, Sisters Nada, Soad 1 and Soad 2, and Marcelle Quéméner, Governor of Assyout Ahmad Hammam Atia, Mostapha Ramadan, Mohammed Hussein, Abuna Boutros, Sister Marie Joseph Pavageau, Sister Roger Attala, Sister Hortense Dossoumon, Salwa el-Sorughi, Sarwat, M. Sobkhi, Governor Hassan Hamida, Atta Makramallah, Agnès Niox Château, Laurence and Philippe de Grandmaison, Naama, Justina and Carolus Baulus, Michel Mahfouz, Abuna Stephanos, Abuna Youssif, Eustaz Effat, Abuna Serabamon, Mrs. Ikhlas, Raed Hani Shakir, General Tarek el-Nadi, Abuna Hannah Maken, Marie, Gabriel and Mikael, Kamil Fauzi, Florence Tran, Pascal Cardeilhac, Raed Gamal, Essam el-Moghraby, Colonel Hicham Garib, Hebba Bakri, Martine Gambard Trébucien, Jean-Claude Cousseran, Thierry Sansonnetti, Jean-Pierre Corteggiani, Zahi Hawass, Sheriff Omar, Dr. Sariel

Chalev, Oren Azoulay, Dr. Sameh Sourour, May Shehab, Dounia Abourachid, General Fathy Tayel, Ozlem and Larry Fife, Camilla and Bernard Platel, Philippe Barbiéri, Salwa Mourad, Leïla Habib, Mohammed abd el-Bahri, Molazim Mohammed, Molazim Sayed, Molazim Ashraf, Abuna Erinaos, Hassan el Kureïshi, Ahmed Metwaly, Jean-Yves Empereur, Thierry Gonon, Essam Eldin, Governor Fouad Saad Eldin, Magdy Selim, Noura Sayed, Mohammed Hadj, Salam Jahroudy Souleiman, General Mahmoud, Governor Ahmed Hamid.

Israel:

Gelad Menashe, Ofer, Daniella, Hor and Youval Buchnik, Rachel and Baruch Acedou, Yitzheim Orenstein, Ronen Tal, Youval and Porit Yékutihéli, Patrice Kaminski, Professor Isaac Gilead, Dr. Aref Abu Rabia and Adiba, Akram, Amir, Ibrahim, Ari, Netanya Ivrim, Avi and Orli El Khayani, Oren and Hannat Cleydermann, Youval and Shira Berman, Lucien Lazare, Mordechaï Paldiel, Simon Hamedian, Hagaï Ram, Tamir Yaar, Shiran ben Yakov, Adam Israeli, Lyor Yahav, Youval Shapiro, Michal Braun, Franck Bonneveau, Hannah, Moshe and Renana Hakarmi, Beni, Philippa, Yoav and Sivan Segall, Johanna Neisha, Henri Samuel, Erella Hovers, Harel Stanton, Mounir Sbeït, Fathers Jonas and Samuel, Rose-Mary, Walter and Hildegard Greinert, Simon Hamedian, Dr. Yoel Rak, Alexandre Sorrentino.

Special acknowledgments:

Dagmar, Alexandra and Claude Chassin, Béatrice and Jean-François Poussin, Stéphane Millière, Florence Tran and Pascal Cardeilhac, Hervé Postic and Vanille Attié, Christophe Mouton, François Fèvre, Jean Réveillon, Fabrice Puchault, Patricia Bouttinard-Ruelle, Janusz Bosacki, Jean-Marc Viotte, Aurélie Tonani, Xavier Péron, Christel Mouchard, Catherine Bourgey, Franck Viénot, Adrien and Caroline de Naurois, Philippe and Tina de Naurois, Eugénie de Naurois, Janet Mc Elligot, Andrew Bergman, Richard Tuggle, Dalton Delan, Robert Sebbag, Leslie Hare, Ann Isom, Nicholas George Hayek, Frank and Caroline van Wezel, Bob Kaiser, Gabrielle Esbeck, Jeremy Solomon, Philip and Joanne Stewart, Linda Franklin, Masha Shubin, Colleen Welch, Jennifer Bassuk, Victor Bevine....

If you wish to find certain of our friends or continue our trip on the Internet:

From Kilimanjaro to the Serengeti, *http://www.tanganyika.com*

A night in paradise: *http://www.ngorongorocrater.com*

When sustainable tourism meets the African dream: *http://www.shompole.com*

The elephant orphanage of Nairobi: *http://www.sheldrickwildlifetrust.org*

For current information on the ivory trade: *http://www.cites.org*

To see the gorillas of Bwindi: *http://www.uwa.or.ug*

To devote yourself to a cause and "drop the holiday on the beach" unless it's for turtle rescue: *http://www.earthwatch.org/expedition*

By Nigel Pavitt, two essential photographic books: *Turkana* and *Africa's Great Rift Valley*

Protection of rhinos in Kenya: *http://rhinorescue.org/lakenakuru.htm*

Lobolo Camp (Lodge), the haven of the world: *http://www.yellowpageskenya.com/travel/?pkg=2&isCurr=1&art=22*

Find Louise Leakey and participate in her digs: *http://www.kfrp.com*

Graham Hancock, *The Sign and the Seal*, Touchstone, July 1993

For documentation on Dr. Hamlin: *www.fistulahospital.org*

To support Kate Fereday Eshete and her street children:
http://www.kateferedayeshete.net/

The calligraphed 99 names of God:
http://www.sufism.org/society/asma/

Find the trip of Loïc and Geoffroy de La Tullaye:
http://www.hydrotour.org

To find the treasure before everybody: G. Dormion, *La Chambre de Chéops*, Fayard.

So as not to forget: *http://www.yadvashem.org*

To find us: *http://www.africatrek.com*

Legends for the Photo Inserts

Cover:

From the Mount of Beatitudes, we look to the south, contemplating the 13,874 kilometers that separate us from the Cape of Good Hope. A serene joy in homage to our 1,147 hosts.

First group:

1. Valley of Debre Libanos in Ethiopia, 100 km to the north of Addis Ababa, the natural border between the Oromos and Amharas regions. Once framed, this picture was taken by a little shepherd. The agreed signal was my raised arm. Below flows an affluent of the Blue Nile. Out of our 15,000 slides, this is the only one that wasn't taken by ourselves or the self-timer. I couldn't run the 200 meters in 15 seconds...

2. 7,177[th] km. The shores of Lake Natron in Tanzania, in the company of Paulo and Maya, two morans we met along the way. We are following the trail of a herd of zebra. Paulo explains to Sonia that at this precise spot, last year, he and his brothers killed a lion.

3. A Turkana girl of the Kerio valley in Kenya. She is amazed to find the place of her country amidst other African countries

and the world. This umbrella served as a parasol and occasional shelter during sandstorms that strike suddenly on these empty spaces.

4. In a little museum of the Olduvai Gorge, we put our feet in the oldest known footprints of hominids. They were cast in Laetoli, at 35 km from here, at a site now covered over. Three million six hundred thousand years separate our feet from those of that couple.

5. 7,252nd km. At night we reach Sesaï, our first Kenyan village, clandestine, exhausted and lacking visas. We pitch our tent against the *enkaji* of a Maasai family of which the youngest member appreciates our morning porridge. (TST)[1]

6. For the seventh time we are walking in the footsteps of lions, on the banks of Lake Natron. All told, we will have seen them thrice in flesh and blood and walked in their territory thirteen times. This one is from a huge male that – we were told afterwards – was sleeping in the grass not far away with his pride.

7. John Masikonté Ntiiti, who escorted us in the Magadi valley in the south of Kenya, on the floor of the Rift, in lion territory. Straddling his Maasai culture and a Catholic education received in a large boarding school, he was for us a marvelous ambassador of his people's cause and an inexhaustible source of information.

8. A Turkana habitation on piles in the Kerio valley, in the shade of large acacias. Two meters above the ground, they are protected from sudden floods that threaten when the river is high. It is also cooler off the ground, and these raised huts allow one not to sleep in the dust.

9. At the Sheldrick Wildlife Trust in Nairobi, Sonia watches over Wendy, an orphan elephant calf about a dozen days old, which

---

[1] TST refers to pictures taken on tripod with self-timer.

has just undergone a transfusion of blood plasma to reinforce her immune system and fight severe dysentery. She recovered.

10. From the 2878-meter summit of the active volcano Ol Doinyo Lengai, the sacred mountain of the Maasai, we enjoy a fabulous view over the Gregory Rift of which the escarpment is visible in the upper left, and on Lake Natron, the banks of which can be dimly seen to the north. The small cones in the crater spit carbonatite, a lava unlike any other in the world, which turns white as it cools. The ascension is a nocturnal marathon requiring six hours of intense effort. (TST)

11. 7,658th km. Lake Bogoria, in the north of Kenya. Hot water springs make it proliferate in spirulina, the phytoplankton which is the sole food of the pink flamingos that come here by the million. Note one of the numerous geysers lining the lake above my right arm. (TST)

12. In the deserts that surround Lake Turkana ferocious sandstorms come quickly. We take (relative) refuge behind small, thorny bushes. Note the Maasai olalem which I wear on my belt and which saved us from a terrible trap set for us by thorny acacias from the luggas, these dry river beds that spread in the steppe.

13. Our first encounter with the Dassanech on the border between Kenya and Ethiopia. We were the first Westerners they had ever seen. They received us very well.

14. Scarified torso of a Dassanech. This motif indicates that the warrior has already killed enemies. Among pastoral tribes, the body becomes an artistic medium and men spend hours decorating themselves, working on their hair, their ritual paintings or their scarifications.

15. As a symbol both of fertility and of chastity, Dassanech girls wear on their goat hide dresses a bell and metal chimes that must strike their pubis. Their movements are thus signalled in the bush.

16. 7,826th km. In the Suguta valley, in the north of Kenya, we cross a no man's land between two rival tribes, the Pokots and the Turkanas, which maintain a pitiless ancestral war. Armed by the governments, Clarkson and Robert are two Turkana Askaris who escort us outside the dangerous zone. (TST)

17. 8,188th km. In the Sibiloi National Park, on the eastern shore of Lake Turkana, we experience the endless savannah. In these cases, we walk due north by the compass. (TST)

18. A meeting in the Sibiloi with three Dassanech warriors: "That way to Jerusalem?" (TST)

19. A lake at the heart of a lake. The volcanic cone of Central Island contains alkaline water very rich in spirulina, which gives it this apple green tint. (TST)

20. A border marker lost in open steppe between Kenya and Ethiopia. Three young Dassanech witness the passage of our 8,241st km. Note the propulsion weapon in the form of a boomerang on the shoulder of the young man on the right. (TST)

21. A Turkana baby. Our long midday naps, waiting for the sun to let us start walking again, were conducive to these intimate moments.

22. Passing through our first Dassanech village to the north of Lake Turkana. Between skimpy huts tilapias slit lengthwise are drying in the sun.

23. Midday pause at the Kachila spring, under a wild olive tree. Robert, one of our Askaris, spontaneously reaches out to Sonia's blonde hair, such as he had never touched. He exclaims: "*Mzuri kabissa!*"(It's really pretty!)

24. During an *ukuli*, the adult passage of a young Hamer in the extreme south of Ethiopia, women in the family undergo the trial of the whip to prove the valor of their bloodline. They come out of it with their backs bleeding and striped with wounds from which they will proudly bear the swollen scars.

25. One of the Hamer tormenters, whose mission is to test the valor of the women of Urgo's family; as a young initiate Urgo must leap over his father's finest bulls to become a man.

26. 8,389th km. Young Hamer women of Turmi.

27. A young Hamer warrior. When we cross their territory, the Hamers are at war with the Dassanech, whom we had just visited, and for whom they set ambushes. A few days earlier, forty-one persons were killed in one day. Here Kalashnikovs have replaced spears.

28. Duk, the young woman on the right, invites us to drink chorro, a drink made of coffee bark, in her hut. Her mother holds a little unexpected visitor in her arms. It has been more than a year since we last saw a cat…

29. The Hamer "women's drum." In order to affront the whips without flinching, they give themselves courage by dancing, chanting and drinking a traditional beer. The ground vibrates with the beating of their feet, their ankles heavily encircled with steel.

Second group:

30. Young carriers of sugar cane in the valley of Gudwa Ashekar, in the south of Ethiopia. To take this picture, Sonia had to sprint forward while taking the camera from her bag and setting it.

31. Overwhelmed by dysentery between Omo Raté and Turmi, in the no man's land between the Dassanech and Hamers, I have to stop every three kilometers. In three days, I will lose six kilos.

32. 8,832th km. Ersumo Kabamo repeats for Sonia the gesture of the sinning woman at the Pharisee's house: the washing of feet. It is an old tradition of Ethiopian hospitality.

33. Gondar, 9,747th km, the street children of Kindu Erdata, Kate Fereday Eshete's association, escort us from the city.

34. A jovial delousing session. 9800th km. Our last days in Ethiopia.

Portrait gallery: (from top to bottom and from left to right)
Left page:

> **Row 1:** 1. A young Maasai initiate met at the foot of Kerimasi volcano in Tanzania. 2. Noho, a young Bena woman in South Ethiopia. 3. A Hamer tormenter, South Ethiopia. 4. Duk, a Hamer woman. **Row 2:** 5. A Dassanech warrior, North Kenya. 6. A Turkana girl, North Kenya. 7. A Turkana grandmother. 8. Zinash, a young Ethiopian woman from Laka Tana. **Row 3:** 9. A Turkana youngster. 10. An Amhara woman in Gojjam. 11. A little Tigrean girl. 12. A Sudanese sheikha. **Row 4:** 13. Gabriel Weï, a Nuer in exile in Khartoum. 14. Umm Balein, a Bayuda nomad. 15. Belal Jaffar Billal, a Sudanese Arab. 16. Sarah Michael, a Juba Catholic exiled in Khartoum.

Right page:

> **Row 1:** 1. Felucca boatman, in Luxor. 2. Nazik abd el-Karim, Khartoum. 3. Abuna Youssif, an Egyptian Coptic priest. 4. Haroun Kazali, at our 10,000th km. **Row 2:** 5. Seïda Mostapha Abd el-Gadir, from Fogara, Shimaliya. 6. Nadia abd el-Rahim. 7. Sheikh Hussein Labd Mohammed Ahmed, our caravan leader from Darfur. 8. Rhafir, from Naga. **Row 3:** 9. Zeïnab abd el-Karim, from Fareig, Sudanese Nubia. 10. Little boy at the Qu'ranic school in Djeheril, in the Bayuda. 11. Aroussa from Argin, Sudanese Nubia. 12. Abuna Boutros, Deïr el-Moharrak, Middle Egypt. **Row 4:** 13. Egyptian policeman in Deir el-Adara. 14. Henri Samuel, a Franco-Israeli in Tiberias. 15. A young Palestinian refugee in Rafah. 16. A young Israeli schoolgirl in Arad, during the Purim celebration.

35. Last ledge in the climb toward the rock-hewn church of Abuna Yematah Guh, in Tigray.

36. The large obelisk in Axum.

37. Swan dive at the "Portuguese Bridge" built in the 15th century

at Debré Libanos. At the bottom flows an affluent of the Blue Nile.

38. At the monastery of Kebran Gabriel, on an island in Lake Tana, an Orthodox monk shows us a 15th-century Bible, richly illuminated with St. George killing the dragon.

39. Two ephemeral shadows on Biéta Giorghis, the monolithic masterpiece of Lalibela. (TST)

40. Daniel, Rose-Mary and Katy Wani, a Catholic family on duty in Ad Debba, on the shores of the Nile, in Sudanese Shimaliya. (TST)

41. Nave of the rock-hewn church of Abuna Yemata Guh, in Tigray. On the ceiling, the intact frescos of nine apostles painted in the 16th century. In Ethiopia every church preserves a *Tabot*, a copy of the Tablets of the Law.

42. Abiyé Azéné. Lake Tana. Disturbing resemblance between the face of her baby and that of the angels painted on the ceiling of the Debré Birhan Sélassié church in Gondar. In Gojjam, many men and women wear a cross tattooed on their foreheads.

43. 11,166th km. At Fareig, in Sudanese Nubia, in the heart of the Sahara, cliffs covered with petroglyphs, proof that human and animal life prospered there in the Neolithic.

44. Pyramids of Meroe, in the Sudan. (TST)

45. Crossing of the Batn el-Hagar desert, the Womb of the Stone, with a caravan of a thousand camels that had come from Darfur. For the first time in three years, we are not carrying our backpacks.

46. Sandstorm in the Bayuda desert. Thirteen days and 359 km of asphalt lost in the middle of nowhere. We were supplied in water by truckers whose offers of a ride we obviously declined.

47. The hand of Abuna Boutros, of Deir el-Moharrak. The Copts

have the tradition of tattooing a small cross on the back of the hand or on the inside of the wrist.

48. Bas-relief of a tribute in slaves offered to Rameses II, at the entrance to Abu Simbel.

49. Sudanese women will leave us an imperishable memory.

50. Samia initiates Sonia into the secrets of the *doukhan*, the traditional Sudanese sauna, while smoking a hookah. Might as well be smoked on both ends! (TST)

51. Three hundred six kilometers of asphalt separate Abu Simbel from Aswan. For the first time we are walking with a police motor escort. The advantage is that we are not carrying our backpacks. The Abu Simbel convoys pass us in the morning in the other direction, and overtake us in midday in a tornado of screeching metal, sometimes numbering close to a hundred buses. (TST)

52. 12,810[th] km. Atop the Cheops pyramid we find, on a stone painted blue, a heart engraved with an *A* and an *S*. We promise it isn't us! A fortunate coincidence to accomplish our mission of leaving a shell given us by Jenny, a young handicapped Kenyan, and which Sonia carried for 5,115 km in her backpack.

53. In the most fundamentalist regions of Middle Egypt we were escorted for several days by armored vehicles.

54. Dear villages of Shimaliya, curled into the loops of the Nile! Leaving them was always hard.

55. A makeshift tent put up to shelter us from the exhausting sun of the Batn el-Hajar. We share our caravaners' meal: aceida, a brown dough of sorghum flour and onions browned in oil with a bouillon cube and spices. Hard, hard!

56. In little Suleiman's shop, where we took shelter during a sandstorm, Sonia shows a clip we made to a family which is also taking refuge. Sudanese women allow themselves to be filmed without objection.

57. Love is a question of balance. (TST)

58. From the Mount of Beatitudes, we look to the south, contemplating the 13,874 kilometers that separate us from the Cape of Good Hope. A serene joy in homage to our 1147 hosts. (TST)

About Alexandre
and Sonia

Alexandre graduated in Political Sciences and mastered in Geo-politics. Between these two cycles, he cycled with his best friend around the world and brought back a best seller *On a roulé sur la Terre* (Laffont '96) – 25,000 km through 35 countries in a year. Sonia joined them to cross the Andes between Argentina and Chile. In '98, still with the same friend, he walked the longest trek ever in the Himalayas, from Bhutan to Tajikistan, 5000 km in one sweep, sneaking in and out of nine countries with a mad clandestine crossing of Tibet for 500 km. A breathtaking and unequaled undertaking. A book and TV documentary came out: *La Marche dans le Ciel* (Laffont '98). Sonia also took part in that trek by circling with the mavericks the Manaslu peak. Between these two big trips, Alexandre was a TV presenter of a mountaineering magazine on national channel France 3. But Africa Trek was the project he was waiting to devote himself to with his newlywed wife Sonia.

Sonia graduated in Social Studies at the Sorbonne, and mastered in Educational Practices of Developing Countries. She led for six months an orphanage in Kathmandu, where she was in charge of 36 little pariah girls. She backpacked alone in India when Alexandre walked the Himalayas then went on a schooling mission in Vietnam and worked at UNESCO for a while before presenting a show on television on the French channel Voyage. She joined Alexandre in his two big journeys, got engaged between the two, married after the second, and embarked on the third. Big time. A three-year long honeymoon in Africa. When she signed on, she missed the word: "walking..."

Since their return, they have devoted their time to sharing the human treasures they brought back from Africa, and also to lecturing a lot for the benefit of numerous associations that work in Africa. Reporting about the world in a deeper and slower way is their way of practicing journalism. They raise their two children just outside Paris, surrounded by fields, forests and horses, and are preparing another journey with them.

You can catch up with them on their website **www.africatrek. com**.

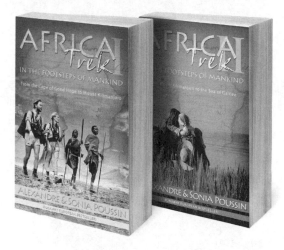
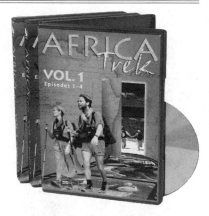